Grade 7

Addison-Wesley Mathematics

Robert E. Eicholz   *Phares G. O'Daffer*   *Randall I. Charles*
Sharon L. Young   *Carne S. Barnett*   *Charles R. Fleenor*

Stanley R. Clemens   *Carol A. Thornton*
Andy Reeves   *Joan E. Westley*

▲▼ Addison-Wesley Publishing Company

Menlo Park, California ■ *Reading, Massachusetts* ■ *New York*
Don Mills, Ontario ■ *Wokingham, England* ■ *Amsterdam* ■ *Bonn*
Sydney ■ *Singapore* ■ *Tokyo* ■ *Madrid* ■ *San Juan*

PROGRAM ADVISORS

John A. Dossey
Professor of Mathematics
Illinois State University
Normal, Illinois

David C. Brummett
Educational Consultant
Palo Alto, California

Irene Medina
Mathematics Coordinator
Tom Browne Middle School
Corpus Christi, Texas

Freddie Renfro
K-12 Mathematics
    Coordinator
La Porte Independent
    School District
La Porte, Texas

William J. Driscoll
Chairman
Department of
    Mathematical Sciences
Central Connecticut State
    University
Burlington, Connecticut

Bonnie Armbruster
Associate Professor
Center for the Study of
    Reading
University of Illinois
Champaign, Illinois

Betty C. Lee
Assistant Principal
Ferry Elementary School
Detroit, Michigan

Rosalie C. Whitlock
Educational Consultant
Stanford, California

CONTRIBUTING WRITERS

Betsy Franco
Marilyn Jacobson
Marny Sorgen
Judith K. Wells

Mary Heinrich
Ann Muench
Connie Thorpe

Penny Holland
Gini Shimabukuro
Sandra Ward

EXECUTIVE EDITOR

Diane H. Fernández

Cover Photo credit: *Steven Hunt/The Image Bank*

TI-12 Math Explorer™ is a trademark of Texas Instruments.

ISBN: 0-201-27700-X

8 9 10 11 12 - VH - 95

Contents

3

DATA ANALYSIS AND STATISTICS

4

GEOMETRY

5

NUMBER THEORY AND FRACTIONS

10

APPLICATIONS OF PERCENT

11

INTEGERS

12 PROBABILITY

13 AREA AND VOLUME

14

MOTION GEOMETRY

RESOURCE BANK AND APPENDIX

Dear Student:

Welcome to an exciting year of mathematics. This year, you will discover many new useful and exciting ways to solve problems, as well as build on the concepts you have already learned.

You will see how to measure various shapes in different ways, including area and volume. You will explore exponents, statistics, and scientific notation so that you can use your mathematics skills in science, money matters, and many other areas. You will be introduced to the fascinating worlds of number theory and motion geometry.

The lessons are designed to be interesting, and to be applied to real-life situations. They will show you how mathematics is useful to you. You will use your new skills to take a fresh look at music, food, clothes, sports, racing, art and other things of interest to you.

When you apply problem-solving skills to your daily life and interests, they become meaningful and exciting. You will have opportunities to work in groups and with partners for fun with problem-solving.

Be sure to look through our Resource Bank at the back of the book. You will find a Data Bank, a Skills Review Bank, a Calculator Bank, a Computer Bank, a Table of Measures, Mathematical Symbols, and much more. These resources were prepared to increase your math power.

Good luck this year!

From your friends at Addison-Wesley.

1

OPERATIONS, PROPERTIES, AND PROBLEM SOLVING

MATH AND SCIENCE

DATA BANK

Use the Science Data Bank on page 494 to answer the questions.

1 Which two groups watched the least amount of television each week? Which group watched the most?

2 How many times as much television did teens watch on weekday afternoons as they watched on Saturday mornings?

3 How much more daytime television did preschoolers watch than children 6 to 11 years old watched?

4 **Using Critical Thinking** Compare the percentages of households with telephones, radios, televisions, and VCR's during the years 1950 through 1987. Predict what the percentages will be in 1999.

Number and Place Value

A great part of the study of mathematics involves numbers.

EXPLORE **Study the Article**

Here are three ways numbers are used.

- **Cardinal**–tells how many or how much.
  A program ran 90 minutes.
- **Ordinal**–gives order or rank.
  The 4th ranked show was 2nd last year.
- **Nominal**–names something.
  Channel 12 carries educational programs.

Teens Vote TV Viewing #1

CHICAGO-A survey of 1350 teenagers shows that TV viewing is still a favorite pastime. In a similar survey last year, 629 teens chose viewing first compared to this year.

SURVEY RESULTS		
1st	TV	506
2nd	Radio	419
3rd	Sports	272
4th	Other	153

TALK ABOUT IT

1. Which numbers in the newspaper story are cardinal numbers? Which numbers are ordinal? Which are nominal?

2. Does it make sense to add nominal numbers? Explain.

Standard numerals such as 2,746,389,501 can be read in words: "two billion, seven hundred forty-six million, three hundred eighty-nine thousand, five hundred one."

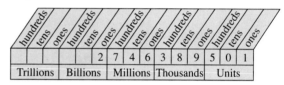

Trillions			Billions			Millions			Thousands			Units		
					2	7	4	6	3	8	9	5	0	1

A whole number 3,289 can be written in **expanded notation**. That way the **place value** of each digit can be shown.

$$3,289 = (3 \times 1,000) + (2 \times 100) + (8 \times 10) + (9 \times 1)$$

In this example, the place value of the 3 is 1,000; it is in the thousands place. So the 3 stands for three thousand.

Write each number in words.

1. 781   **2.** 9,002   **3.** 34,005,010

Write each number using expanded notation.

4. 154   **5.** 1,837   **6.** 69,009

Write each number in words.

1. 2,351   **2.** 508   **3.** 12,647   **4.** $1,085   **5.** $3,200

Write each number using expanded notation.

6. 2,159   **7.** 20,084   **8.** 7,000,001

Write the standard numeral for each number.

9. three thousand, two hundred forty-seven

10. eleven thousand eleven

11. eighteen million, five hundred thousand, one hundred twenty

APPLY

MATH REASONING Suppose a calculator is designed to display an eight-digit number.

12. What is the largest whole number that can be shown on this calculator?

13. How many different whole numbers can this calculator show?

Each time one dial goes around ten times, the dial to its left goes around once.

PROBLEM SOLVING

14. Science Data Bank The Data Banks on pages 490–504 contain information used throughout this book. Find three examples of cardinal and nominal numbers in the Science Data Bank. Then find three examples of ordinal numbers in other Data Banks.

DATA BANK

MIXED REVIEW

Find the answers.

15. 42
−33

16. 82
−17

17. 67
+ 3

18. 18
×22

19. 7)4,915

20. 35
× 3

21. 63
× 7

22. 99
×99

23. 654
− 99

24. 20)8,652

More Practice, page 522, set A

5

Relating the Operations

EXPLORE Look for Relationships

Work in groups. Reason carefully to find the missing number.
You should not have to calculate.

A. $84 + 84 + 84 + 84 = 336$ so   ▦ $\times\ 84 = 336$

B. $678 + 229 = 907$ so $907 -$ ▦ $= 678$

C. $56 \times 73 = 4{,}088$ so $4{,}088 \div 73 =$ ▦

D. $1{,}047 - 349 - 349 - 349 = 0$ so $1{,}047 \div 349 =$ ▦

TALK ABOUT IT

1. Which pair of equations relates multiplication and repeated addition?

2. Which pair of equations relates division and repeated subtraction?

3. Which pair of equations relates division and multiplication?

The **numerical expression** 7×4 stands for the number 28.
Numerical expressions usually include operations and other
symbols. When two expressions name the same number, we can
show this in an **equation.**

$$7 + 7 + 7 + 7 = 4 \times 7$$

Evaluating a numerical expression means finding the number
it represents.

$$120 + 240 + 150 = 510$$

1. Write an addition problem that would help you solve
   $15 - 8 =$ ▦

2. Write a multiplication expression related to $32 \div 4 =$ ▦

3. How many times can you subtract 5 from 30? What is $30 \div 5$?

1. Write an addition problem that would help you solve
   $16 - 7$.

2. Write a multiplication problem that would help you solve
   $48 \div 6$.

3. Write an addition expression using only 8s that is the same
   as 5×8.

4. How many times can you subtract 12 from 60?
   What is $60 \div 12$?

5. Write one division problem you can solve
   if you know $7 \times 23 = 161$.

APPLY

MATH REASONING

6. Use the relationship between addition and
   subtraction to give four problems, one of
   which is $24 - 7 = 17$.

PROBLEM SOLVING

7. Dan collects money from his paper route three nights
   a week. Each night he collects from 23 families.
   How many families does he collect from each week?

8. A newspaper costs $7 a week. What does it cost for a
   year?

▶ **USING CRITICAL THINKING   Discover a Relationship**

9. How many different values are possible for a? for b?

   - $12 \div 3 = a$, so $3 \times a = 12$. Then $a = \underline{\ ?\ }$.
   - $24 \div 4 = b$, so $4 \times b = 24$. Then $b = \underline{\ ?\ }$.

10. **a.** Suppose you saw $18 \div 0 = a$, so $0 \times a = 18$.
    How many values of a make the second equation true?

    b. Suppose you saw $0 \div 0 = b$, so $0 \times b = 0$.
    How many values of b make the second equation true?

    c. Why do we say, "You cannot divide by 0"?

More Practice, page 522, set B

7

Order of Operations

When you have to find the value of a numerical expression with several operations such as $22 + 8 \times 2$, the order in which you compute may affect the result.

EXPLORE **Search for Patterns**

Evaluate each expression. Do the operation marked in red first. Show your work. As you work, compare the values you get, and look for patterns.

Set A	Set B
23 + 42 − 15 = ?	12 × 8 + 5 = ?
23 + 42 − 15 = ?	12 × 8 + 5 = ?

Set C	Set D
24 − 12 ÷ 6 = ?	8 × 20 ÷ 4 = ?
24 − 12 ÷ 6 = ?	8 × 20 ÷ 4 = ?

TALK ABOUT IT

1. In which set(s) do the expressions have the same value? What pairs of operations are in those sets?

2. In which set(s) do the expressions have different values? What pairs of operations are in those sets?

3. Make up a numerical expression with both addition and division to help you decide if it matters whether you add or divide first.

The **order** in which operations are done is important. To make sure that we get one value for an expression, we agree to use this set of rules:

Here is the way to evaluate the expression $15 \times (9 + 1) - 25$.

Order of Operations
1. Compute inside parentheses first.
2. Do all multiplications and divisions next, left to right.
3. Do all additions and subtractions last, left to right.

$$15 \times (9 + 1) - 25 = 15 \times 10 - 25 \quad \text{Compute inside parentheses first.}$$
$$= 150 - 25 \quad \text{Multiply before subtracting.}$$
$$= 125 \quad \text{Finally, subtract.}$$

Evaluate each expression. Follow the order of operations.

1. $15 + 8 \times 2$
2. $7 \times 6 + 24$
3. $20 \div 2 - 5 \times 2$

4. $4 \times (11 - 6)$
5. $(12 + 8) \times 10$
6. $(14 - 3) + (24 \times 2)$

Evaluate each numerical expression. Follow the order of operations.

1. $17 - 5 \times 2$ **2.** $1 \times 10 + 10$ **3.** $9 \div 3 + 12 \div 3$

4. $11 \times (9 - 8)$ **5.** $(11 \times 9) - 8$ **6.** $(14 - 3) + (24 \times 2)$

7. $3 - 2 - 1$ **8.** $3 - (2 - 1)$ **9.** $3 + 2 + 1$

10. $3 + (2 + 1)$ **11.** $8 \times 4 \times 2$ **12.** $8 \div (4 \div 2)$

13. $(8 \div 4) \div 2$ **14.** $(8 \times 4) \times 2$ **15.** $44 - (9 + 7) \times 2$

16. $5 \times (16 - 7) - 18$ **17.** $12 \times 3 + (8 - 2) \times 6$ **18.** $54 \div (10 - 5 + 4)$

APPLY

MATH REASONING   Write each operation sign $(+, -, \times, \div)$ one time to get the indicated value.

19. $4 \text{ ||| } 5 \text{ ||| } 3 \text{ ||| } 3 \text{ ||| } 8 = 1$ **20.** $9 \text{ ||| } 3 \text{ ||| } 4 \text{ ||| } 1 \text{ ||| } 8 = 31$

PROBLEM SOLVING

21. Maria bought 4 tickets to the school dance. Each ticket cost $5. How much did she pay in all?

22. The dance started at 7:30 p.m. and ended at 12:15 a.m. How long did the dance last?

▶ **CALCULATOR**

Some calculators are programmed to follow the order of operations. With others you must apply the rules of order of operations, and enter numbers and operations in the order in which they must be performed. Test your calculator by entering:

$6 \boxed{\times} 2 \boxed{+} 8 \boxed{\div} 4 \boxed{=}$

Now do it by hand. Does your calculator follow the order of operations? If it does, it is said to use algebraic logic.

Use your calculator to evaluate each expression.

23. $56 + 9 \times 12$ **24.** $2 \times 2 + 2 \times 3$

25. $76 \times 2 + 54 \times 10$ **26.** $350 + 350 \div 14$

27. $456 - (223 + 177)$ **28.** $21,045 \div 345 + 38$

More Practice, page 522, set C   **9**

Introduction to Problem Solving

LEARN ABOUT IT

This checklist is a guide to problem solving. Multiple step problems can be solved by using one or more operations and the strategy **Choose the Operations**. Read the following problem carefully.

Find the total cost for band concert tickets for the 14 girls and 15 boys in Ms. Kirsch's class, Ms. Kirsch, and an adult helper.

PROBLEM-SOLVING CHECKLIST
■ **Understand** the situation.
■ **Analyze** the data.
■ **Plan** the solution.
■ **Estimate** the answer.
■ **Solve** the problem.
■ **Examine** the answer.

TICKET PRICES

ADULTS	$10.50
STUDENTS (7-16 years)	$8.00
SENIOR CITIZENS	$6.00

Understand the Situation

We want the total cost for all of the tickets.

Analyze the Data

students: 14 girls and 15 boys   tickets: $8.00 each

adults: 2   tickets: $10.50

Plan the Solution

We can first find the total cost for students and the total cost for the adults, then add.

Estimate the Answer

14 + 15 is about 30. 30 × 8 is 240.
2 × 10.50 is about 20. 240 + 20 = 260

Solve the Problem

14 + 15 = 29 students, so 29 × 8 = $232 for student tickets

2 × 10.50 = $21 for adult tickets $232 + $21 = $253 total

It will cost $253 for tickets for the 29 students and 2 adults.

Examine the Answer

$253 is close to $260. The answer seems reasonable.

TRY IT OUT

1. Find another way to choose the operations to solve the problem above.

2. The price of a T-shirt is $12.00 and the tax is $0.72. What would 6 T-shirts cost?

Pick the statement that shows how you could solve the problem.

1. What could concert tickets cost for 2 adults and a student?
   A. multiply 10.50 by 2; then add 8
   B. add 10.50 and 8; then multiply by 2

2. The band plays 12 pieces in 2 hours. What is the average time in minutes of each piece?
   A. multiply 2 by 60; then divide by 12
   B. multiply 12 by 60; then divide by 2

3. What would tickets cost for 1 adult and 2 senior citizens?
   A. multiply 8 by 2; then add 10.50
   B. multiply 6 by 2; then add 10.50

4. A concert poster cost $4.00 and $0.24 tax. What would 3 posters cost?
   A. add 4 and 0.24; then multiply by 3
   B. multiply 4 and 3; then add 0.24

Solve. Use data from page 10 as needed.

5. A 16-ounce lemonade costs $1.85. In one night 895 were sold. About how much money was taken in for lemonade?

6. A series ticket is $25 for students. How much would you save with a series ticket if you went to 3 concerts?

7. How much change should you get from a $50 bill for 6 tickets for senior citizens?

8. **Data Hunt.** Find the total ticket cost for your class to visit a special place in your town.

▶ UNDERSTANDING THE OPERATIONS

Read the chart at the right. Name the operation you could use to solve each problem. Replace variables with numbers that make sense and solve the problem.

9. How much money do you need for a program that costs x if you have only y?

10. Discount tickets for p students cost a total of q. What is the cost of each ticket?

11. Rock concert tickets cost w each. How many tickets can you buy if you have z dollars?

Some Key Actions for Operations

Addition
- put together

Subtraction
- take away ■ compare
- find the missing part

Multiplication
- put together same-size groups
- find combinations

Division
- separate into equal groups of a given size (repeated subtraction)
- separate into equal number of groups (sharing)

Using Critical Thinking

"Flowcharts are handy," said Lin Li, as she looked at the shapes used to make the charts. "You can use them to give directions for doing anything."

"Yes," said Jong. "My mom uses them to design computer programs."

Lin Li said, "Look at the flowchart I made. It makes a list of even numbers and a list of odd numbers."

Jong studied Lin Li's chart for a few minutes and smiled. He said, "The person who follows your directions is going to get pretty tired!"

TALK ABOUT IT

1. What is the purpose of a flowchart?

2. Why do you think there are different shapes for flowchart boxes?

3. What did Lin Li want the flowchart to do?

4. Explain what the flowchart does. Then explain Jong's last remark.

5. How could you improve the flowchart?

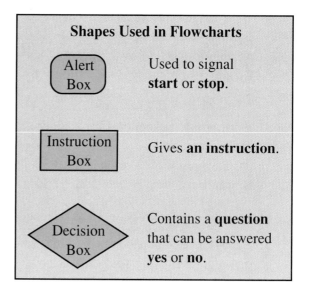

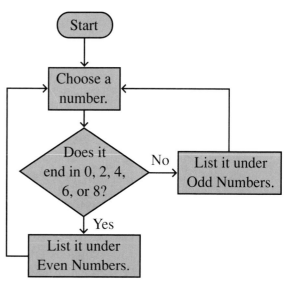

TRY IT OUT

1. Make a flowchart for calling a friend from these instructions; make sure to use the correct box shape for each instruction.

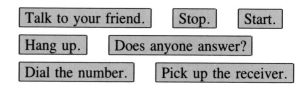

2. Make a flowchart that uses guess and check methods to find that number which when multiplied by itself gives 1024, and then writes "You Got It!" after it finds the number.

MIDCHAPTER REVIEW/QUIZ

Match each numerical expression with the letter of the appropriate phrase.

1. 24 × 3

2. 3 + 24

3. 24 ÷ 3

4. 24 − 3

A. the sum of 3 and 24

B. 3 less than 24

C. 24 divided by 3

D. the product of 24 and 3

Evaluate each numerical expression. Use the order of operations.

5. 10 × (2 × 6)

6. (10 × 2) × 6

7. (12 − 8) − 4

8. (12 ÷ 2) × 6

9. 12 ÷ (2 × 6)

10. (42 − 12) ÷ 3

11. 42 − 12 ÷ 3

12. 16 + 4 × 2

13. 15 − 3 + 4

14. 16 − 12 ÷ (4 + 2)

15. 15 × 4 + 3 × 8

16. 46 − (8 + 2) × 3

Use the relationships between the operations to help you answer the following.

17. 35 + 35 + 35 + 35 + 35 = 175, so 35 × 5 = ▥

18. 63 − 21 − 21 − 21 = 0, so 63 ÷ 21 = ▥

19. 3 × 6 = 18, so 18 ÷ 3 = ▥ and 18 ÷ 6 = ▥

20. How many times can you subtract 6 from 42? What is 42 ÷ 6?

21. What multiplication problem would help you solve 54 ÷ 9?

22. Write a division problem you can solve using 81 ÷ 3 = 27.

23. Write two subtraction problems you can solve using 37 + 16 = 53.

PROBLEM SOLVING

24. How many of the 35 households surveyed had more than 1 television set?

25. How many of the 35 households surveyed did not have a television set?

26. Estimate the total number of television sets in all 35 households.

Survey of Number of Television Sets in 35 Households	
1 television set	15
2 television sets	16
3 television sets	3
more than 3 sets	0

13

Basic Properties

EXPLORE **Study the Information**

Match each equation with one of the generalizations in the boxes.

■ **Commutative Property**–The sum (product) of two numbers is the same in either order.
■ **Associative Property**–You can group addends (factors) in any way and the sum (product) remains the same.
■ **Identity for Multiplication**–Any number times one is equal to the number.
■ **Identity for Addition**–Any number plus zero is equal to the number.
■ **Distributive Property**–Multiplying a sum by a number is the same as multiplying each addend by the number, then adding the products.

A. $\frac{1}{2} \times 1 = 1 \times \frac{1}{2} = \frac{1}{2}$

B. $9 \times 5 = 5 \times 9$

C. $12.6 + 107.7 = 107.7 + 12.6$

D. $45 + 0 = 0 + 45$

E. $5 \times (10 + 2) = (5 \times 10) + (5 \times 2)$

F. $(9 \times 10) \times 11 = 9 \times (10 \times 11)$

G. $\left(\frac{1}{3} + \frac{1}{4}\right) + \frac{1}{5} = \frac{1}{3} + \left(\frac{1}{4} + \frac{1}{5}\right)$

TALK ABOUT IT

1. The distributive property is sometimes called the distributive property of multiplication over addition. Why?

Basic properties let us rearrange numbers to make computations easier.

$$
\begin{aligned}
(24 + 38) + 16 &= (38 + 24) + 16 \quad \text{commutative property for addition} \\
&= 38 + (24 + 16) \quad \text{associative property for addition} \\
&= 38 + 40 = 78
\end{aligned}
$$

Name the property used.

1. $35 \times 1 = 35$

2. $(16 + 5) + 32 = 16 + (5 + 32)$

Name the property used.

1. $3.1416 + 0 = 3.1416$

2. $(13 \times 7) + (13 \times 20) = 13 \times (7 + 20)$

3. $1,288 \times 1 = 1,288$

4. $(0 \times 45) \times 107 = 0 \times (45 \times 107)$

5. $34.5 \times 781 = 781 \times 34.5$

6. $(12.98 + 1.2) + 0.5 = 12.98 + (1.2 + 0.5)$

Find the missing numbers. Use the basic properties to help.

7. $27 \times 26 = n \times 27$

8. $9 + (8 + 2) = 9 + (n + 8)$

9. $43 \times n = 43$

10. $20 \times (n + 5) = (20 \times 30) + (20 \times 5)$

11. $n \times 6 = 6 \times 19$

12. $n \times 1 = 124$

APPLY

MATH REASONING   Name the property that justifies each step.

13.
$$
\begin{aligned}
14 + 23 &= [(1 \times 10) + 4] + [(2 \times 10) + 3] &&\text{\textit{expanded form}} \\
&= (1 \times 10) + [4 + (2 \times 10)] + 3 &&\underline{\quad ? \quad} \\
&= (1 \times 10) + [(2 \times 10) + 4] + 3 &&\underline{\quad ? \quad} \\
&= [(1 \times 10) + (2 \times 10)] + (4 + 3) &&\underline{\quad ? \quad} \\
&= (1 + 2) \times 10 + (4 + 3) &&\underline{\quad ? \quad} \\
&= (3 \times 10) + 7 &&\text{\textit{adding}} \\
&= 37 &&\text{\textit{place value}}
\end{aligned}
$$

PROBLEM SOLVING

14. Helena took a bus to the mall and home. One-way fare is 50¢. She spent $8 at the mall. What was the total cost of the trip?

▶ **USING CRITICAL THINKING: Find a Counterexample**

Do you think the basic properties apply to all operations? Write yes or no for each of the following. If you write no, show a **counterexample**—an example showing that the statement is not true.

15. Is there a commutative property for subtraction? an associative property for subtraction?

16. Is there a distributive property of addition over multiplication: $a + (b \times c) = (a + b) \times (a + c)$?

More Practice, page 522, set D

Mental Math Techniques

EXPLORE **Solve the Problem**

The *Video Visions* store rents video tapes and equipment. What is the total rental fee for a VCR and one tape? How many tapes were rented on the weekend?

■ To find the total rental fee for a VCR and one video tape, add.

Find $28 + $3

If an addend or subtrahend is 1, 2, or 3 (or 10, 20, or 30) **count on** *or* **back.**

THINK: One addend is a 3. Start with 28 and count on.
28 . . . 29, 30, 31 so 28 + 3 = 31
The total rental fee is $31.

■ How many tapes were rented on Friday, Saturday, and Sunday?

Find 25 + 37 + 75

Look for **compatible numbers** *which you can add or multiply easily.*

THINK: 25 and 75 are easy to add mentally. Add them.
Then add 37.
25 + 75 = 100 and 100 + 37 = 137, so
25 + 37 + 75 = 137
A total of 137 tapes were rented.

WEEKEND RENTAL FEES
•VCR.................$28
•VIDEO TAPES......$3

Tapes Rented
Friday   25
Saturday   37
Sunday   75

TALK ABOUT IT

1. Name some numbers that are compatible for addition; for multiplication.

Evaluate using mental math.

1. 46 − 2

2. 3 + 129

3. $1.50 + $0.69 + $0.50

4. 6 × 12 × 10

5. 77 + 10 + 3

6. 263 − 20

Evaluate using mental math. Count on or back.

1. 21 − 3   **2.** 496 + 30   **3.** 943 − 10   **4.** 694.3 + 2

Evaluate using mental math. Use compatible numbers.

5. 208 + 52 + 9   **6.** 1.9 + 8.6 + 3.1   **7.** 7 × 10 × 4   **8.** 92 + 8 + 86

Evaluate using mental math. Choose a mental math technique.

9. 2 × 50 × 110   **10.** 81 + 9 − 30   **11.** 89 − 3 + 30   **12.** 6,112 − 20

13. 215 + 20   **14.** 87 + 24 − 27   **15.** 135 + 2 + 10   **16.** 4 × 77 × 25

APPLY

MATH REASONING   Name the basic property applied at each step.

17. (28 + 17) + 12 = 28 + (17 + 12) _____?_____

                   = 28 + (12 + 17) _____?_____

                   = (28 + 12) + 17 _____?_____

                   = 40 + 17 = 57

Basic Properties
■ commutative
■ associative
■ identity
■ distributive

PROBLEM SOLVING

18. Sundays through Thursdays, *Video Visions* rents tapes for $2. How much less did the store make on Sunday than on Friday and Saturday combined?

DATA BANK

19. Science Data Bank   Sam and Lori's TV viewing is about average for teens. How many hours of TV would you expect them to watch in two weeks?

MIXED REVIEW

Find the answers.

20.   257   **21.**   14,901   **22.** 41)‾4,387   **23.**   4,007   **24.**   8,090
       × 892   + 27,854   × 186   − 1,982

Find the value of each expression.

25. 38 − 3 × 8   **26.** (38 − 3) × 8   **27.** 14 + 72 ÷ 9   **28.** 6 × (9 ÷ 3)

29. 38 − 3 × 8   **30.** (38 − 3) × 8   **31.** 14 + 72 ÷ 9   **32.** 6 × (18 ÷ 6) − 10

More Practice, page 522, set E

Choosing Estimation Techniques

LEARN ABOUT IT

EXPLORE Study the Situation

Have you ever read a sign in an elevator that tells how many people can ride in it or the total amount of weight it can hold?

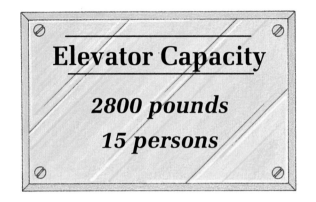

- *Estimate the largest acceptable average weight in pounds of the 15 people.*

  PLAN: This problem can be solved by estimating 2800 ÷ 15. You can estimate by **substituting compatible numbers**.

  THINK: 15 is close to 14, and 14 divides evenly into 28. 2800 ÷ 14 = 200, so 2800 ÷ 15 is about 200.

- *23 children, weighing about 95 pounds each, want to squeeze in this elevator for a school contest. Can the elevator hold their total weight?*

  PLAN: This problem can be solved by estimating 23 × 95. You can estimate this product by **rounding.**

  THINK: 23 rounds to 20, and 95 rounds to 100. 20 × 100 = 2,000, so 23 × 95 is about 2,000.

TALK ABOUT IT

1. Do you think the estimates above would be less than or greater than the exact answers? Why?

2. Write answers to the two problems above. Use complete sentences.

TRY IT OUT

Estimate.

1. 24 + 76	**2.** 331 ÷ 8	**3.** 198 × 4	**4.** 318 ÷ 78
5. 41 + 61	**6.** 98 − 19	**7.** 69 ÷ 11	**8.** 69 × 11

Estimate. Use rounding.

1. 275 × 12   **2.** 83 × 83   **3.** 4,499 + 4,480   **4.** 3,501 + 3,507

5. 551 − 549   **6.** 596 − 509   **7.** 2,716 ÷ 87   **8.** 6,335 × 49

Estimate. Substitute compatible numbers.

9. 49 ÷ 8   **10.** 91 + 89   **11.** 21 + 780   **12.** 281 − 102

13. 663 − 64   **14.** 290 + 111   **15.** 1,616 ÷ 7   **16.** 1,616 × 9

Estimate. Choose an estimation technique.

17. 2,828 ÷ 28   **18.** 149 ÷ 7   **19.** 425 − 124   **20.** 78 × 53

21. 880 − 221   **22.** 17 × 101   **23.** 4,018 ÷ 2,085   **24.** 113 ÷ 11

25. 391 − 295   **26.** 8,655 − 7,201   **27.** 3,839 + 4,837   **28.** 29.99 + 14.99

APPLY

MATH REASONING

29. Write three different digits in the boxes so that the sum is about 525.

276 + ☐ ☐ ☐

30. Write two different digits in the boxes so that the product is about 2,400.

62 × ☐ ☐

PROBLEM SOLVING

31. Suppose the 189 people on a jet plane each have 2 bags weighing an average of 125 pounds for both. About how much do all of these bags weigh?

32. A sign on an old bridge reads, "Do not exceed 10,000 pounds." About how many cars each weighing about 2,200 pounds could be on the bridge at the same time?

▶ COMMUNICATION   **Writing to Learn**

33. List the steps you must follow to round whole numbers. Give examples to show that your steps work.

Problem Solving
Developing a Plan

UNDERSTAND
ANALYZE DATA
PLAN
ESTIMATE
SOLVE
EXAMINE

LEARN ABOUT IT

As you develop a plan to solve a problem, ask two questions.

- Do I need an exact answer or an estimate?
- Which calculation method should I use?

Deciding When to Estimate

Suppose you babysit for $4 an hour. You work for 2 hours and 30 minutes, and afterwards the parents ask, "How much do we owe you?" The parents want an exact amount.

Suppose you mow lawns for $5 an hour. A client asks, "About how long would it take to mow my yard?" The client wants an idea of the cost, and probably expects an estimate.

Choosing a Calculation Method

When you need to compute, decide which calculation method would be best.

Calculation Methods
■ mental math
■ paper and pencil
■ calculator

- *Try mental math first.* $125 + 264 + 275$ may seem difficult, but look carefully. 125 and 275 are easy to add. $125 + 275 = 400$, and $400 + 264 = 664$.

- *Decide between paper and pencil, and a calculator.* $424.75 - $68.98 has many steps: it would require regrouping several times using paper and pencil, so a calculator may be better. However, $462 - 56$ does not require much regrouping, so you might use paper and pencil.

TRY IT OUT

1. You and your brother are going to the movies. Your mother asks, "How much money do you need for two tickets?" Do you need an exact answer or an estimate? Tell why.

Choose a calculation method and evaluate each expression. Tell which method you used for each.

2. $73 + 180 - 53$ 3. $427 - 18$ 4. $4,295 \times 817$ 5. $1,548 \div 12$

Decide if you need an exact answer or an estimate. Tell why.

1. You have saved $35 for a sweater and a blouse. You ask your mother, ''Do I have enough money for the sweater and blouse I saw?''

2. Cassette tapes cost 3 for $10. You ask the clerk, ''What would it cost to buy 5 tapes?''

3. You bought some groceries for your parents with a $5 bill. You want to check whether the amount of change you were given is correct.

4. You have 20 more pages to read in an exciting book. It's your turn to walk the dog. Your father asks, ''How soon will you be ready to walk the dog?''

5. You have developed plans for a dog house. You need to decide how much lumber and paint, and how many nails you need to build it.

Choose a calculation method and evaluate each expression. Tell which method you used for each expression.

6. $29 + 807 - 9$ 7. $751 + 1,396$ 8. $28,028 \div 14$ 9. 958×286

10. $717 - 39$ 11. $1,717 + 309$ 12. $45 + 46 + 53$ 13. $549 \div 9$

14. $9,295 \div 715$ 15. $41 - 12 + 2$ 16. $40,149 \div 1,487$ 17. 22×24

18. $636 + 29$ 19. $147 + 391 - 292$ 20. 19.99×10 21. $4,712 - 108$

▶ BE A PROBLEM FINDER

22. Give two questions that can be answered using data in the chart. One should call for an estimate; the other an exact answer.

Wake Up ! Wake Up !

Time we usually get out of bed on a typical weekday morning. (A survey of 100 men and 100 women.)

	Men	Women
Before 6 a.m.	40	26
Between 6 and 7	27	40
Between 7 and 8	19	21
After 8	10	11
Not sure	4	2

Exploring Algebra
Variables and Algebraic Expressions

LEARN ABOUT IT

EXPLORE **Study the Problem**

In the equations below, each letter (a, b, c, d, and e) stands for one number. Use reasoning to decide what numbers each letter can stand for.

$$a + b = 20 \qquad c \times d = c \qquad e \times e = 64 \qquad e \times b = 24 \qquad d + c = 12$$

TALK ABOUT IT

1. What basic properties can help you to determine the value of d?

2. Could $e \times e = 64$ stand for $4 \times 16 = 64$? Why?

A **variable** is a letter, such as n, that reserves a place for a number. An expression containing a variable is an **algebraic expression**.

To evaluate an algebraic expression for a number, replace the variable with the number and evaluate the numerical expression that results.

Examples

A Evaluate $n + 12$ for $n = 38$.

$$n + 12 = 38 + 12 \qquad \text{Replace the variable } n \text{ with the number 38.}$$
$$= 50$$

B Evaluate $a \times b - 9$ for $a = 15$ and $b = 3$.

$$a \times b - 9 = 15 \times 3 - 9$$
$$= 45 - 9 = 36$$

TRY IT OUT

Evaluate each algebraic expression for the give number.

1. $45 - x$ for $x = 17$

2. $y \div 7$ for $y = 35$

3. $m + 64$ for $m = 17$

4. $(3 \times j) + 4$ for $j = 5$

5. $(p + q) - 6$ for $p = 12$ and $q = 15$

6. $(t - 3) \times s$ for $t = 23$ and $s = 5$

Evaluate each algebraic expression.

1. $x + 56$ for $x = 35$ **2.** $n - 18$ for $n = 65$ **3.** $k \times 33$ for $k = 5$

4. $z \div 12$ for $z = 96$ **5.** $3 \times x - 7$ for $x = 7$ **6.** $(u + 5) \times 8$ for $u = 8$

7. $n + 18$ for $n = 12$, for $n = 123$

Evaluate each algebraic expression for $p = 3$, $q = 7$, and $r = 5$

8. $q \times r$ **9.** $p + q$ **10.** $q - p$

11. $(p \times q) + 5$ **12.** $2 \times (q - r)$ **13.** $12 - (p + r)$

Copy and complete each table by evaluating each expression for the numbers given.

	m	$(4 \times m) - 2$
	6	$(4 \times 6) - 2 = 22$
14.	1	
15.	8	
16.	10	

	a	b	$(a \times b) + a$
	2	4	$(2 \times 4) + 2 = 10$
17.	10	5	
18.	20	30	
19.	15	0	

MATH REASONING

20. Find number replacements for x and y so $x + y = 12$ and $x - y = 2$.

21. Find number replacements for m and n so $m \div n = 2$ and $m - n = n$.

PROBLEM SOLVING

22. Ian charges $2 an hour plus $3 to babysit. The expression $(2 \times H) + 3$ gives the amount he will make in H hours. How much would Ian make in 5 hours?

▶ **USING CRITICAL THINKING**   **Discover a Rule**

23. Suppose variables m and n are replaced by odd or even numbers. Try several values for m and n. Copy and complete the table to tell whether the product is odd or even.

24. Which values of w will make $3w$ even? odd?

m	n	$m \times n$
even	even	odd or even
odd	odd	odd or even
even	odd	odd or even
odd	even	odd or even

Group Decision Making

UNDERSTAND
ANALYZE DATA
PLAN
ESTIMATE
SOLVE
EXAMINE

Group Skills
Listen to Others
Encourage and Respect Others
Explain and Summarize
Check for Understanding
Disagree in an Agreeable Way

Many lessons in this book ask you to work as a group and make decisions cooperatively. In order to do this, each group member must help other group members. Some of the ways you can do this are shown in the group skills list.

You can help other members of your group by explaining something that is unclear or by summarizing important points. One way to explain is to give examples. Work with your group to think of ways you could explain to a younger child what a circle is.

Cooperative Activity

Choose a direction-giver for your group. This person will pick one of the figures below without telling the rest of the group which one. Then the direction-giver will tell the rest of the group how to draw a picture similar to the chosen one. The picture drawn by the group does not have to be the same size as the one in the book but should have similar proportions. The rules are as follows:

1. The direction-giver can talk but cannot point or gesture.

2. The other group members can talk with each other but may not talk to, or ask questions of the direction-giver.

3. All books except the direction-giver's must be closed.

Choose another direction-giver and try the activity again.

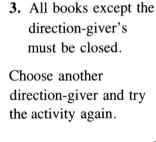

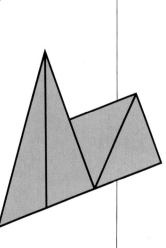

Some Questions to Answer

1. How were the figures you drew similar to the ones described by the other members of your group? How were they different?

2. Work together to make a list of some of the mathematical terms that were used to describe the figures.

3. What kinds of descriptions or explanations were most helpful to you?

Check Your Group Skills

4. In what ways did your group work well together? What group skills could you improve?

25

WRAP UP

Identify the Idea

Study this problem.

> On the first 10 stops of a bus run, an average of 4 persons get on and 1 gets off. On each of the remaining 5 stops, about 3 persons get off and 1 gets on. The fare is $1.00. How much money can the bus company expect to collect on an average bus run?

Discuss the problem solving idea(s) each quotation represents.

1. "It only matters how many riders get on."

2. "The calculations should be easy. I don't need a calculator."

3. "I have to multiply the total number of riders by the fare."

4. "There are fewer than 50 riders, and the fare is $1, so the answer should be less than $50."

5. "I got $55. That's too big. I'll have to check my work."

- Solve the problem
- Estimate the answer
- Understand the situation
- Examine the answer
- Plan the solution
- Analyze the data

Sometimes, Always, Never

Which word should go in the blank, *sometimes*, *always*, or *never*? Explain your choice.

6. An expression in which you would add before dividing must __?__ have parentheses.

7. A numerical expression __?__ contains variables.

8. Addition, subtraction, multiplication, and division are __?__ related.

Project

Collect newspaper stories and headlines that use numbers or number ideas. Sort them as:

- numbers that are exact or estimates
- numbers that are cardinal, ordinal, or nominal
- standard numbers or numerical expressions

Make a bulletin board display from the better examples.

CHAPTER REVIEW/TEST

Part 1 Understanding

1. In the number 743,685, the value of 4 is

   A 4,000   B 400   C 40,000

2. Fill in the missing number.
   1,104 − 368 − 368 − 368 = 0, so
   1,104 ÷ ▓ = 3

Name the properties used.

3. (22 + 16) + 5 = 22 + (5 + 16)

4. (4 × 20) + (4 × 7) = 4(20 + 7)

5. To evaluate 77 + 50 + 3, you could count on or use compatible numbers. Which numbers are compatible?

6. Is 30 a good estimate for 2,376 ÷ 83 using rounding? Explain.

Part 2 Skills

7. Write 3,605,450 in words.

8. Write the standard numeral for five billion, twenty-six million, four hundred fifty-five thousand, seventy.

Evaluate the expressions. Use order of operations.

9. 12 × (9 − 5)   10. 50 − (13 − 9) × 6   11. 10 × 3 + 5

Evaluate each algebraic expression.

12. $m \div 8$ for $m = 104$ 13. $(n − 5) × 7$ for $n = 8$ 14. $4 × p − 3$ for $p = 12$

Part 3 Applications

15. The price of a baseball cap is $8 plus $0.32 tax. What would 9 caps cost?

16. Guido bought 4 tickets to a concert. He gave the cashier $95. He received $3 in change. What did each ticket cost?

17. Make a flow chart for frying an egg from these instructions:
    Crack egg into skillet.
    Put butter in skillet.
    Start.
    Get skillet hot.
    Stop.
    Is egg done to liking?
    Fry.

18. **Challenge** Decide if you need an exact answer or an estimate. You are buying shoes for $34.95 and socks for $3.25. You have two $20 bills. Do you have enough money? Will you get back change?

ENRICHMENT
Spreadsheets

A favorite tool of people who use computers is a program called a *spreadsheet*. It is a grid of rows and columns in which you can put numbers or words. The spreadsheet user defines what each row and column means.

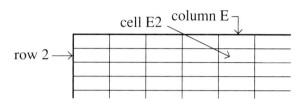

Suppose you want to keep track of your paper route money. Start by deciding what you know and what you need to find out. The spreadsheet below is based on the idea that you—

know:
- how many papers you sell each month.
- how much one paper costs.
- how much profit you make on one paper.
- how much you collect each month.

want to find:
- your monthly and total cost.
- your monthly and total profit.
- your total collections.
- what you still have to collect.

	A	B	C	D	E	F
1	**Month**	**No. of Papers**	**Cost**	**Profit**	**Collected**	**Still Due**
2	Jan	611	91.65	122.20	206.00	7.85
3	Feb					
4	March					

Suppose you—
- sell 611 papers in January
- pay 15¢ for each one
- make 20¢ for each one
- collect $206.00 in January

To complete Row 2 for January, you—
- put 611 in cell B2
- multiply B2 by 0.15 to find C2
- multiply B2 by 0.20 to find D2
- put 206 in E2
- add C2 and D2, and subtract E2, to find F2.

Use a calculator. Copy the spreadsheet and continue it, assuming—

- in February you sold 520 papers, collected $7.85 more for January, and $171.50 for February.
- in March you sold 560 papers, collected $10.50 more for February, and $185.50 for March.

On a computer, you define by formula what each cell means. You don't have to calculate. For this job, you would only enter numbers in columns B and E—the computer would do the rest!

CUMULATIVE REVIEW

1. Add.

14,331
+ 62,284

A 76,515
B 77,515
C 47,953
D not given

2. Subtract.

9.02
− 5.34

A 3.68
B 4.78
C 4.36
D not given

3. Multiply.

322 × 265

A 85,930
B 85,330
C 8,533
D not given

4. Divide.

23)4,762

A 207R1
B 206R22
C 207R9
D 207

5. Name the space figure.

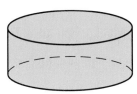

A cone
B sphere
C cylinder
D not given

6. Give the number of faces.

A 3
B 4
C 5
D 6

7. What kind of triangle is this?

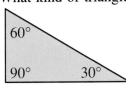

A acute
B right
C obtuse
D not given

8. Name the property used.
14 × (3 + 70) = (14 × 3) + (14 × 70)

A distributive   B associative
C commutative   D identity for addition

9. What is the place value of the 3 in 632,089,450?

A 100,000,000   B 10,000,000
C 1,000,000   D 100,000

10. Evaluate the numerical expression:
24 ÷ (3 − 1) + 6

A 3   B 18
C 13   D 6

11. Evaluate using mental math.
73 + 68 + 27

A 170   B 168
C 178   D 158

12. Evaluate the algebraic expression
$(n - 5) \times 7$ for $n = 35$.

A 49   B 240
C 0   D 210

13. The average weight of baggage for each of the 119 people on a jet is 63 lb. Which is a good estimate of the total weight of baggage?

A 7,200 lb   B 66,000 lb
C 5,000 lb   D not given

14. Olivia sold 144 magazine subscriptions for her club. She did this over a 9-day period. Which statement shows how you could find her average number of sales each day?

A multiply 144 by 9   B divide 144 by 9
C subtract 9 from 144   D not given

2

DECIMALS AND MEASUREMENT

MATH AND SOCIAL STUDIES

DATA BANK

Use the Social Studies Data Bank on page 498 to answer the questions.

1 How is the Canadian monetary system like the one used in the United States? How is it different?

2 What are some differences between the monetary systems of Mexico and Japan? What are some similarities?

3 Which was worth the most in United States dollars in 1970: the Japanese yen, the British pound, the Canadian dollar, or the Mexican peso?

4 **Using Critical Thinking** Look at exchange rates for the Japanese yen for the years from 1970 through 1985. Is there a trend? Can you safely predict the 1995 exchange rate based on previous years' rates?

31

Understanding Decimals

EXPLORE Study the Information

Numbers are represented in the decimal system using the digits 0 through 9 and grouping by tens. The way we record money is based on the decimal system.

Sporting Goods Sale

- skis $323.79   **Door Prize!**
- poles $54.95 **One LUCKY Winner!**
- boots $79.95 **Rocky Mountain Ski Trip!**

TALK ABOUT IT

1. How do you know what each 3 represents in the price of the skis?

2. How are dimes related to pennies? How are dimes related to dollars?

3. How is each place in a number related to the place on the right? To the place on the left?

Decimals can express numbers that fall between whole numbers.

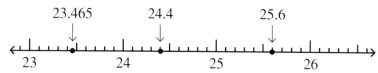

The place value chart shows how to read and write decimals.

thousands	hundreds	tens	ones	tenths	hundredths	thousandths	ten-thousandths	
1,000	100	10	1	$\frac{1}{10}$	$\frac{1}{100}$	$\frac{1}{1000}$	$\frac{1}{10,000}$	place values
		2	3 •	4	6	5		standard form

We read this as, "twenty three **and** four hundred sixty-five thousandths."

A number written in **expanded notation** shows the value of each place.

$$23.465 = (2 \times 10) + (3 \times 1) + (4 \times 0.1) + (6 \times 0.01) + (5 \times 0.001)$$

TRY IT OUT

Write each number in standard form.

1. forty-five ten-thousandths

2. twenty and seven hundredths

Give the value of the red digit in each decimal.

1. 6.087   **2.** 0.0875   **3.** 5.692   **4.** 32.091

5. 284.7   **6.** 0.0579   **7.** 1.906   **8.** 3.4008

Write each number in standard form.

9. two and seventy-three thousandths

10. two hundred and seventy-three thousandths

11. $(1 \times 0.01) + (2 \times 0.001) + (1 \times 0.0001)$

12. $(1 \times 1) + (2 \times 0.01) + (1 \times 0.001)$

Write >, <, or = for each ▥.

13. 2.72 ▥ 2.716   **14.** 0.660 ▥ 0.0693

15. 0.007 ▥ 0.070   **16.** 24.95 ▥ 23.95

17. 0.2678 ▥ 0.2695   **18.** 0.5 ▥ 0.55

> **To Compare Decimals**
>
> 1. Start at the left. Find the first place where the digits are different.
> 2. The numbers compare the same way these digits compare.

Write each set of numbers in order from least to greatest.

19. 5.143, 5.185, 5.147   **20.** 0.043, 0.34, 0.24

MATH REASONING Find two decimal values for x that make the sentence true.

21. $0.9 < x < 1$ **22.** $3.2 < x < 3.3$ **23.** $2.3 > x > 2.03$

PROBLEM SOLVING

24. The same style ski jacket was on sale at four different stores for $44.99, $45.69, $44.75, and $44.89. What was the lowest price for the jacket?

25. A ski rack for a car costs 10 times as much as a carrying case for skis. The carrying case costs $35.50. What is the cost of the ski rack?

▶ **USING CRITICAL THINKING** **Find a Counterexample**

Write true or false. If a statement is false, give a counterexample.

26. Every decimal is a whole number.   **27.** Every whole number is a decimal.

28. Since the billions place is three places to the left of the millions place, the billionths place must be three places to the left of the millionths place.

More Practice, page 523, set B

Reviewing Decimal Operations
Addition, Subtraction, and Multiplication

You can use what you know about adding, subtracting, and multiplying whole numbers to do the same operations with decimals.

To **add** or **subtract** decimals:

- Arrange the numbers in columns with the decimal points lined up.
- Annex zeros if they are needed.
- Add or subtract as with whole numbers.
- Place the decimal point in the sum or difference in line with the other decimals.

$$
\begin{array}{r}
0.652 \\
22.410 \\
+ \ 3.800 \\
\hline
26.862
\end{array}
$$

$$
\begin{array}{r}
16.040 \\
- \ 1.397 \\
\hline
14.643
\end{array}
$$

To **multiply** decimals:

- Multiply as with whole numbers.
- Place the decimal point in the product so that the product has the same number of decimal places as the total number of decimal places in the factors.

$$
\begin{array}{rl}
14.6 & \text{[1 decimal place]} \\
\times 3.05 & \text{[2 decimal places]} \\
\hline
730 & \\
4380 & \\
\hline
44.530 & \text{[3 decimal places]}
\end{array}
$$

Find each sum.

1. $1.385 + 2.776$ **2.** $9.27 + 5.969$ **3.** $\$78.02 + \$35.43$

4. $3.04 + 1.99$ **5.** $\$18.00 + \$3.96$ **6.** $0.42 + 0.817$

Find each difference.

7. $3.04 - 0.74$ **8.** $165.9 - 57.51$ **9.** $8.04 - 0.7854$

10. $37 - 3.78$ **11.** $25.9 - 7.52$ **12.** $\$0.73 - \$0.08$

Place the decimal point in each product.

13. $25.4 \times 3.7 = 9398$ **14.** $38.7 \times 0.26 = 10062$ **15.** $125 \times 0.008 = 10000$

Find each sum or difference.

1. 3.04 + 1.62   **2.** 18.05 + 3.96   **3.** $35.00 − $29.13   **4.** 62 − 9.31

5. 34.81 + 27.4   **6.** 9.14 − 4.715   **7.** 56.13 − 17.59   **8.** 3.06 + 19.17

Place the decimal point in each product.

9. 25.3 × 0.43 = 10879   **10.** 3.45 × 1.04 = 35880   **11.** 23.1 × 0.157 = 36267

Find the product.

12. 4.9 × 1.4   **13.** 91 × 3.1   **14.** 9.06 × 0.061   **15.** 0.45 × 1.6

16. 9.26 × 0.08   **17.** $6.09 × 6   **18.** 24 × 0.09   **19.** 3.3 × 0.0008

MATH REASONING You may want to use your calculator.

20. Copy the boxes at the right. Place the digits 1, 2, 3, and 4 in the boxes to make a problem with the largest possible product.

21. Write a multiplication problem with a product between 24.5 and 25.0.

PROBLEM SOLVING

22. Write Your Own Problem Use the data to the right to write a word problem that can be solved using subtraction.

23. Thai's odometer read 106.4 km at the beginning of a trip. When she returned home the odometer reading was three times as great as the original reading. What was the final odometer reading?

Adults take about 20 breaths per minute

Activity	Amount of air with each breath
Resting	0.75 L
Light work	1.62 L
Heavy work	2.14 L

24. Thai's car uses 6 L of gasoline to go 57 km. How far can she drive on 1 L of gasoline?

▶ **ESTIMATION**

Estimate the answer to each problem.

25. 12.4 × 18.9   **26.** 0.313 + 0.398   **27.** 29.124 − 18.88

28. 0.74 − 0.198   **29.** 8.73 × 114.5   **30.** 24.8 + 73.6

More Practice, page 523, set C

Choosing Estimation Techniques

LEARN ABOUT IT

<u>EXPLORE</u> **Examine the Table**

The results of a fundraiser for after-school sports are shown in the chart at the right.

Team	Pizzas Sold	Amount
Football	262	$655.00
Field Hockey	237	$602.50
Basketball	251	$637.50
Soccer	274	$672.50
Baseball	248	$620.00

TALK ABOUT IT

1. Which team sold the most pizzas?

2. About how many pizzas did each team sell?

One technique for estimating sums is called **clustering.** This method is useful when several addends are near the same number.

Example About how many pizzas were sold altogether?

Each addend is near 250. There are 5 addends.
$5 \times 250 = 1{,}250$ so $262 + 237 + 251 + 274 + 248$ is about 1,250. About 1,250 pizzas were sold.

Front-end estimation is another technique for estimating sums.

Example About how much money was raised?

Add the front-end digits.
$6 + 6 + 6 + 6 + 6 = 30$ 30 represents $3,000.

Adjust the total using the remaining digits.
55.50 + 2.50 + 37.50 is about 100.
        72.50 + 20.50 is about 100.

The total amount raised was about $3,000 + $200 or $3,200.00.

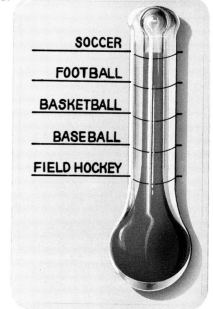

SOCCER
FOOTBALL
BASKETBALL
BASEBALL
FIELD HOCKEY

TRY IT OUT

Estimate. Use clustering or front-end estimation.

1. 13.2 + 12.9 + 13.08 + 12.87

2. 2.23 + 2.01 + 1.99

3. 45.2 + 32.2 + 18.4 + 64.7

4. 645 + 231.56 + 345 + 128 + 189

Estimate. Use clustering.

1. 205 + 197 + 196 + 204

2. 18 + 19 + 21

3. 24.7 + 23.9 + 25.57 + 26.41

4. 12.0 + 11.95 + 12.12 + 11.8

Estimate. Use front-end estimation.

5. 128 + 374 + 298

6. 19 + 32 + 59 + 47

7. 3.48 + 5.14 + 8.53

8. 27.6 + 81.8 + 43.1

Estimate. Choose your own method.

9. 8.719 + 7.299 + 8.9

10. 27.44 + 40.09 + 33.77

11. 2.93 + 2.87 + 3.21 + 3.19

12. 54.4 + 25.1 + 45.3 + 36.23

APPLY

MATH REASONING

13. Give four numbers whose sum when estimated using clustering is 120.

14. Give three numbers whose sum when estimated using front-end estimation is 150.

PROBLEM SOLVING

15. Cross-country ski team members recorded how far they skied in a week. They skied 54.67 km, 63.29 km and 72.8 km. Estimate the total distance skied.

16. Last year Natalie swam the 500-meter freestyle in 6:52.43 min. This year her time was 6:49.05. About how much faster is she this year? **3.5 sec**

MIXED REVIEW

Evaluate each numerical expression.

17. 23 + (36 − 18)   **18.** 82 − (10 + 3)   **19.** 22 + 4 × 5   **20.** 24 ÷ 2 − 18 ÷ 3

Evaluate each algebraic expression.

21. x − 32 for x = 40   **22.** 80 − n for n = 25   **23.** 200 ÷ q for q = 20

More Practice, page 523, set D

Dividing Decimals

Division with decimals is similar to division with whole numbers.

EXPLORE **Solve to Understand**

If one United States dollar is worth 0.56 British pounds (£), how many United States dollars would you need to buy an original Beatles record that sells for £ 14?

Multiply the divisor by a power of 10 to make it a whole number.	Multiply the dividend by the same power of 10.	Divide.

$0.56\overline{)14}$

Multiply by 100.

$56\overline{)14.00.}$ **Annex zeros as needed.**

Multiply by 100.

$$\begin{array}{r} 25 \\ 56\overline{)1400} \\ \underline{112} \\ 280 \\ \underline{280} \\ 0 \end{array}$$

You need 25 United States dollars ($25.00).

TALK ABOUT IT

1. Why is division the operation needed to solve this problem?

2. Why do you multiply both the divisor and the dividend by 100?

3. How can you use multiplication to check the reasonableness of the quotient?

Examples Find the quotient.

A

Record all zeros to the right of the decimal point.

$$\begin{array}{r} 0.03 \\ 400\overline{)12.00} \\ \underline{12\ 00} \\ 0 \end{array}$$

B

Round to the nearest tenth.

Multiply the divisor and dividend by 100.

$$\begin{array}{r} 0.37 \rightarrow 0.4 \\ 0.48\overline{)0.17.8} \\ \underline{14\ 4} \\ 3\ 40 \\ \underline{3\ 36} \\ 4 \end{array}$$

Find each quotient to the nearest tenth.

1. $3.8\overline{)53.7}$ 2. $0.42\overline{)1.848}$ 3. $0.082\overline{)0.1487}$

Give the number you would multiply the divisor by to make it a whole number.

1. $2.8\overline{)130}$ **2.** $0.75\overline{)3.882}$ **3.** $1.23\overline{)0.1}$

4. $2.001\overline{)1,725.4}$ **5.** $0.7\overline{)0.0028}$ **6.** $0.054\overline{)0.05}$

Find each quotient to the nearest tenth.

7. $0.25\overline{)6}$ **8.** $15\overline{)4.05}$ **9.** $7.3\overline{)38.42}$ **10.** $3.6\overline{)23.74}$

11. $0.052\overline{)0.159}$ **12.** $0.5\overline{)8.925}$ **13.** $0.11\overline{)0.4184}$ **14.** $1.6\overline{)0.9284}$

Estimate each quotient.

15. $6.2\overline{)35.6}$ **16.** $1.8\overline{)0.204}$ **17.** $0.53\overline{)1.966}$ **18.** $0.9\overline{)6.17}$

19. $2.1\overline{)10.31}$ **20.** $0.78\overline{)3.192}$ **21.** $0.86\overline{)2.702}$ **22.** $6.9\overline{)34.9}$

MATH REASONING Evaluate each expression. Round to the nearest hundredth.

23. $n \div 2.5$ for $n = 8.25$ **24.** $m \div 0.65$ for $m = 1.44$

25. $(x + y) \div 4$ for $x = 23.4$ and $y = 6.7$ **26.** $(m - n) \div 3.1$ for $m = 43.2$ and $n = 19.5$

PROBLEM SOLVING

27. In 1987 a Canadian dollar was worth about $0.82 in United States money. How much was one United States dollar worth in Canadian money?

28. Social Studies Data Bank What was the value of 500 British pounds in United States currency in 1985?

▶ **ALGEBRA**

The expression, "3 times n," can be shown in four ways:

$$3 \times n \qquad 3 \cdot n \qquad 3(n) \qquad 3n$$

The expression, "n divided by 8," can be shown in two ways:

$$n \div 8 \qquad \frac{n}{8}$$

Evaluate each expression. Round to the nearest tenth.

29. $5n$ for $n = 31.5$ **30.** $\dfrac{m}{3.5}$ for $m = 6.8$ **31.** $5.2m$ for $m = 15.4$

More Practice, page 523, set E

Problem Solving
Understanding the Question

UNDERSTAND
ANALYZE DATA
PLAN
ESTIMATE
SOLVE
EXAMINE

Lechuguilla Cave in southern New Mexico is the second deepest cave in the United States. In 1988, its depth reached 1,501 ft. Only Columbine Crawl in Wyoming with a depth of 1,550 ft is deeper. How much deeper is Columbine Crawl?

One of the first steps in solving a problem is to understand the question. Sometimes it helps to ask the question in a different way.

First, I'll read the question.

How much deeper is Columbine Crawl?

Then, I'll ask the question in a different way.

What is the difference between the depth of Columbine Crawl and the depth of Lechuguilla Cave?

TRY IT OUT

Read each problem. State which question is a different way of asking the question in the problem.

1. In August 1987, Lechuguilla Cave was 1,058 ft deep. Later that year the depth was extended by 149 ft. During a one-week period in the spring of 1988, the depth was extended another 208 ft. How many feet was the depth extended?
   a. How deep is the cave now?
   b. How many feet were added to the depth of the cave?

2. At 5,036 ft, Reseau Jean Bernard in France is the world's deepest cave. A mile is 5,280 ft. How many feet less than a mile is the depth of Reseau Jean Bernard?
   a. How many feet more than a mile is the depth of the cave?
   b. How many more feet are there in a mile than in the depth of the cave?

Now write a question to complete each problem.

3. The first level of Carlsbad Caverns in New Mexico is 754 ft below the surface. The second level is 900 ft below the surface and the third level is 420 feet below the second level.

4. The Sarawak Chamber in Malaysia is one of the world's largest one-room caves. It is 2,302 ft long. It has an average width of 980 ft and it is over 230 ft high.

Solve. Use any problem solving strategy.

1. Mr. Jimenez took his class on a field trip to some caves. Use the chart to find how much 23 students and 2 adults paid for admission.

2. Joel had $10.00. He paid for student admission and for 6 postcards. Use the chart to find how much Joel has left.

3. The Grand Canyon is 217 miles long and over 1 mile deep. Its width varies from 4 miles to 18 miles. By how many miles does the width vary?

4. Use the table to find the length of the Pacific coastline between Canada and Mexico.

5. Use the table to find how much longer the coastline of California is than the combined coastlines of Oregon and Washington.

6. The largest single-chamber cave is in Borneo. The volume of the cave is 350,000,000 cubic feet which is about 50 times the volume of the Washington Cathedral. About what is the volume of the Washington Cathedral?

7. The National Park system has 49 parks which cover 47,242,673.78 acres. Estimate the average number of acres in each park.

Coastlines of the United States	
State	Length (mi)
Washington	157
Oregon	296
California	840

8. **Suppose . . .**
   Solve. Jesse spent $19.25 on posters of Carlsbad Caverns. Each poster cost $2.75. How many posters did Jesse buy?

   State which of the following information would change the solution to the problem above.

   a. Jesse paid for the posters with a $20 bill.
   b. One of the posters was on sale for $1.95.
   c. Jesse also bought a book about the Caverns.

Exponents and Scientific Notation

Scientists have devised a way to write large numbers so they are easier to read and use.

> **Pluto is about 5,900,000,000 km from the sun**
> **That's 5.9 × 10 × 10 × 10 × 10 × 10**
> **× 10 × 10 × 10 × 10 km.**

EXPLORE Find a Pattern

Complete the chart.

Repeated Factors	Short Form
5 × 5 × 5 × 5	5^4
3 × 3	3^2
2 × 2 × 2 × 2 × 2	2^5
4 × 4 × 4	?
?	6^2
?	10^6

TALK ABOUT IT

1. What does the **superscript** (small raised number) in 5^4 mean?

2. Do you see an advantage to writing 2^5 instead of 2 × 2 × 2 × 2 × 2?

An **exponent** tells how many times a number is used as a factor. For example, 7 × 7 × 7 is written as 7^3 in **exponential notation.** The **base** is 7; the **exponent** is 3.

6^3 is ''six cubed'' or ''six to the third power''
5^2 is ''five squared'' or ''five to the second power''
10^1 is ''ten to the first power''
b^4 is $b \cdot b \cdot b \cdot b$ or ''b to the fourth power''

Scientific notation is a method for writing numbers using **powers of ten.**

$$7,420,000 \qquad = \qquad 7.42 \qquad \times \qquad 10^6$$

Standard numeral   **A number greater than**   **A power of 10**
                            or equal to 1,
                            but less than 10

Examples

$1,460 = 1.460 \times 10^3$ **Move the decimal point 3 places to the left. The exponent is a 3.**

$2.3 \times 10^4 = 23,000$ **Multiplying by 10^4 moves the decimal point 4 places to the right.**

Give the missing exponent.

1. $6,000 = 6.0 \times 10^{\parallel}$

2. $24,500 = 2.45 \times 10^{\parallel}$

3. $1,700,000 = 1.7 \times 10^{\parallel}$

Write each in exponential notation.

1. $4 \times 4 \times 4 \times 4 \times 4$ **2.** $87 \times 87 \times 87$ **3.** $r \cdot r$

Write as a product of like factors and, if possible, as a standard numeral.

4. 7^3 **5.** 2^{10} **6.** 100^2 **7.** m^3

Give the missing exponent.

8. $3,200 = 3.2 \times 10^{\parallel\parallel}$ **9.** $34,500 = 3.45 \times 10^{\parallel\parallel}$ **10.** $87,430 = 8.743 \times 10^{\parallel\parallel}$

Give the missing factor.

11. $23,400 = \parallel\parallel\parallel \times 10^4$ **12.** $487,000 = \parallel\parallel\parallel \times 10^5$ **13.** $9,764 = \parallel\parallel\parallel \times 10^3$

Write each number in standard notation.

14. 2.75198×10^3 **15.** 0.019×10^6 **16.** 100×1^{12} **17.** 570×10^1

Write each number in scientific notation.

18. $157,983,000$ **19.** $200,000$ **20.** 12.459 **21.** $23,500,000,000$

APPLY

MATH REASONING Find the value of each expression.

22. $4^2 \times 3^2$ **23.** $2^3 \times 5^2$ **24.** $3^2 \times 6^1$ **25.** $4^2 \times 10^3$

PROBLEM SOLVING

26. The distance from the sun to the earth is about 150 million kilometers. Express this distance in scientific notation.

27. A 70 year old man earned as many dollars as he was seconds old. How does that compare to his friend's lifetime earnings of $1,700,000,000?

▶ **CALCULATOR**

Some calculators can express numbers in scientific notation. Try this if your calculator has an EE key.

ON/AC   43,196   EE   =

The display reads 4.3196 04 .

Express the following numbers in scientific notation.

1. $4,701,864$ **2.** $987,765$ **3.** 12.587

4. $3,761$ **5.** $17,928$ **6.** $9,961,032$

More Practice, page 524, set A

Exploring Algebra
Understanding Variables

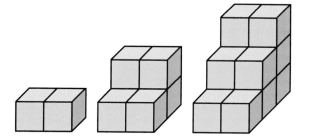

EXPLORE **Use Blocks. Work in Groups.**

The picture at the right shows a pattern for building stairs using blocks. One step uses 2 blocks, 2 steps use 6 blocks, and so on. Use blocks to build stairs 4 steps high.

TALK ABOUT IT

1. How many blocks are needed to build stairs 4 steps high?

2. Without building the stairs, can you tell how many blocks are needed to build stairs 5 steps high?

3. What is the relationship between the number of steps and the number of blocks?

In this situation, the number of blocks **varies** with the number of steps. The **number of steps** and the **number of blocks** are variables. Making a table helps organize information so that relationships can be seen more easily.

Example Complete the table to show how the stairs and blocks are related in the situation above.

Let s = number of steps

Let b = number of blocks

s	1	2	3	4	5	10
b	2	6	12	20	30	110

$1 \times 2 = 2$

$2 \times 3 = 6$

$3 \times 4 = 12$

$10 \times 11 = 110$

TRY IT OUT

1. Use blocks to help you complete the table to show how the variables are related.

Let a = area

p = perimeter

a	1	3	5	7	9	11	33
p	4	8	12	16	?	?	?

44

Use blocks to help you complete the table to show how the variables are related.

1.

area (a)	1	2	3	4	5	10
perimeter (p)	4	6	8	10	?	?

2.

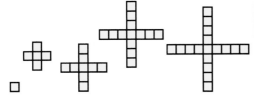

area (a)	1	5	9	13	17	25
perimeter (p)	4	12	20	?	?	?

Complete the tables to show how the variables are related.

3.

people (p)	1	2	3	4	5	9
beverages (b)	2	4	6	?	?	?

4.

adults (a)	2	4	6	8	10	20
kids (k)	1	2	3	?	?	?

5.

people (p)	10	15	20	25	50	100
cost (c)	30	45	60	?	?	?

6.

people (p)	4	8	12	16	20	100
bikes (b)	1	2	3	?	?	?

7.

cars (c)	12	28	40	50	100	500
trucks (t)	6	14	20	?	?	?

8.

people (p)	4	8	12	16	20	100
chairs (c)	3	6	9	12	?	?

MATH REASONING

9. Make a table like the ones above. Exchange with a classmate. Complete each other's table.

PROBLEM SOLVING

10. A cab ride costs $1.50 plus $3.00 per mile. Copy and complete the table. How much would a 10-mile ride cost?

miles traveled (m)	1	2	3	4	5	6
cost (c)	$4.50	?	?	?	?	?

▶ **MENTAL MATH**

Use mental math to evaluate each expression.

11. $m + 35 + n$ for $m = 25$ and $n = 75$

12. $a + 3 + b$ for $a = 28$ and $b = 30$

13. $2gh$ for $g = 28$ and $h = 10$

14. $18de$ for $d = 4$ and $e = 50$.

45

Using Critical Thinking
Analyzing Decimal Patterns

LEARN ABOUT IT

Darlene discovered an interesting decimal pattern while she was dividing numbers on her calculator. When she divided 4 by 9 the calculator showed 0.4444444. When she divided 3 by 9 the calculator showed 0.3333333.

"Look at this pattern," she said. "I can get my calculator to show a decimal point followed by a repeating digit by dividing that digit by 9."

Julian wondered if a similar pattern could be found in order to get the calculator to show two repeating digits, like 0.34343434.

Darlene thought a minute. "We could try dividing a 2-digit number by 99."

TALK ABOUT IT

1. What decimal pattern did Darlene get when she divided a single digit by 9?

2. Do you think Darlene's idea for getting a decimal answer with two repeating digits will work? Why?

3. What would Darlene's rule be if the repeating part of the decimal had been a 3-digit number? a 4-digit number? a 5-digit number?

TRY IT OUT

Use the patterns to decide what two numbers you could divide to obtain the given decimal.

1. 0.2222222... 2. 0.7777777... 3. 0.86868686... 4. 0.3131313...

5. 0.412412412... 6. 0.37823782... 7. 0.0101010... 8. 0.113113113...

Use the patterns to decide what decimal will result when you divide.

9. 5 ÷ 9 10. 87 ÷ 99 11. 752 ÷ 999 12. 2715 ÷ 9999

MIDCHAPTER REVIEW/QUIZ

1. Write in order from greatest to least: 0.5   0.55   0.505   0.055

Find each sum or difference.

2. $0.423 + 2.453 + 6.124$

3. $5.0104 - 2.324$

4. $\$6.25 + \$8.96 + \$17.77$

5. $\$20 - \$15.37$

6. $3.807 - 1.9176$

7. $0.013 + 0.2005$

Estimate the sums.

8. $68 + 68 + 71 + 72 + 69 + 76$

9. $\$13.22 + \$1.87 + \$29.44 + \$16.60 + \$2.05$

10. $236.5 + 392.8 + 512.6$

11. $0.060 + 0.058 + 0.063 + 0.06 + 0.059$

Find each product or quotient.

12. 0.25×1.2

13. $\$3.57 \times 107$

14. $0.032\overline{)1.664}$

15. $5.5\overline{)74.8}$

Write each in standard form.

16. $(2 \times 10) + (3 \times 0.001)$

17. $6 \times 6 \times 6$

18. 23.309188×10^5

19. 0.03×1

20. $10^6 \times 10^3$

21. $2^3 \times 5^2$

Write each using exponential notation.

22. 4×4

23. $23 \times 23 \times 23 \times 23$

24. $n \cdot n \cdot n \cdot n \cdot n \cdot n \cdot n$

Write each using scientific notation.

25. $23{,}045$

26. $100{,}000{,}000{,}000$

27. 973.088

28. Complete the table.

dots in bottom row	1	2	3	4	5
dots in triangle	1	3	6	?	?

PROBLEM SOLVING

29. Decide whether **a** or **b** asks the same question. In 1985, the value of the US dollar was about ¥238 (yen). In 1986, the value dropped to ¥168 and then to ¥148 in 1987. How much more had the value dropped during 1986 than during 1987?

    a. How does the 1987 drop compare to the 1986 drop?

    b. How much had the value dropped in two years?

30. Write a question to complete the problem. Then answer the question. During recent years the value of the Canadian dollar dropped $0.0125 and then increased $0.0304 to reach a value of $0.75 in US dollars.

Metric Units of Length

LEARN ABOUT IT

EXPLORE **Discover a Pattern**

Use the meterstick to find each missing length in the chart.

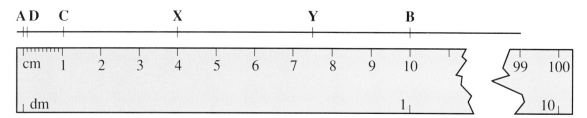

TALK ABOUT IT

1. How are centimeters related to decimeters? to millimeters?

2. If point *A* is at 0, and point *B* is at 0.1 m, what decimals would be associated with the points *C*, *D*, *X*, and *Y*?

	Unit of Measure		
length	mm	cm	dm
AB	?	?	1
AC	?	1	?
AD	1	?	?
AX	?	?	?
AY	?	?	?

The **meter** is the standard unit of length.

kilometer (km)	hectometer (hm)	dekameter (dam)	meter (m)	decimeter (dm)	centimeter (cm)	millimeter (mm)
thousands 1,000 m	hundreds 100 m	tens 10 m	ones 1 m	tenths 0.1 m	hundredths 0.01 m	thousandths 0.001 m

Each unit is 10 times greater than the unit to the right, we can change from one unit to another by shifting the decimal point.

Examples

A 1.43 m = 143 cm
Shift 2 places to the right

B 3245 mm = 3.245 m
Shift 3 places to the left

C 3.7 cm = 37 mm
Shift 1 place to the right

TRY IT OUT

Find the missing lengths.

1. 1 m = ▦ km

2. 1,500 m = ▦ mm

3. 29.4 mm = ▦ cm

Find the missing lengths.

1. 62 cm = ▥ m

2. 3 m = ▥ km

3. 17 mm = ▥ km

4. 276 dm = ▥ cm

5. 0.09 cm = ▥ mm

6. 19.7 km = ▥ m

7. 25.4 dm = ▥ m

8. 176 m = ▥ km

9. 1.83 m = ▥ cm

10. 5.87 mm = ▥ cm

11. 3,509 m = ▥ mm

12. 42 mm = ▥ dm

13. 78 cm = ▥ dm

14. 359 m = ▥ dm

15. 0.56 cm = ▥ mm

Choose the best estimate.

16. The width of a door is about 1 __?__.   **A** dm   **B** m   **C** km

17. The thickness of a dime is about 1 __?__.   **A** mm   **B** dm   **C** dam

18. The height of the seat of a chair is about 50 __?__.   **A** hm   **B** cm   **C** dm

19. The flying altitude of a jet might be 100 __?__.   **A** hm   **B** m   **C** km

20. The length of a small car might be 500 __?__.   **A** m   **B** dm   **C** cm

MATH REASONING Complete the statement.

21. 3.48 m = 348 __?__

22. 26 km = 26,000 __?__

23. 7.5 m = 750 __?__

24. 654 mm = 6.54 __?__

25. 0.09 km, = 90 __?__

26. 67 cm = 0.67 __?__

PROBLEM SOLVING

27. An Olympic-sized swimming pool is 50 m long. If Keisha swims 1 km, how many laps does she swim.

28. The water in a diving well is 0.5 dekameters deep. How many meters deep is the diving well?

▶ **CALCULATOR**

Use a calculator to evaluate each expression.

29. $8^2 + 3^4$

30. $9^3 + 2^6$

31. $8^2 - 2^3$

32. $1^{10} + 10^1$

33. $7^3 - 2^4$

34. $5^3 - 5^2$

35. $3^4 \times 2^3$

36. $4^2 \times 8^3$

37. $6^3 \times 3^2$

Precision in Measurement

EXPLORE **Study the Chart**

The chart shows the measurements of coins from five different countries. The coins were first measured using centimeters (A). They were measured again using millimeters (B). Place the coins in order from largest to smallest using each set of measurements.

Coin	A	B
	Diameter (nearest cm)	Diameter (nearest mm)
Haiti 10 centimes	2 cm	2.1 cm
Panama $\frac{1}{4}$ balboa	2 cm	2.4 cm
Peru 10 centavos	2 cm	2.1 cm
Greenland kroner	3 cm	3.3 cm
Liberia 50 cent	3 cm	2.9 cm

TALK ABOUT IT

1. Which coin has the largest diameter?

2. Why do you think the Panamanian and the Peruvian coins have the same A measurements, but different B measurements?

3. How could you make an even more precise measurement of the Haitian coin?

The **greatest possible error (GPE)** of a measurement is half (0.5) the measurement unit used. For example, if the diameter of a coin is measured at 3 cm to the nearest cm, the actual length of the diameter must be between 2.5 cm and 3.5 cm. In this case the GPE is 0.5 cm.

Example Which measurement is more precise, 23 m to the nearest meter or 23.40 m to the nearest centimeter?

The GPE of the first measurement is 0.5 m. The GPE of the second is 0.5 cm. This means 23.40 m to the nearest centimeter is a more precise measurement than 23 m to the nearest meter.

Which measurement is more precise? Give the GPE of each.

1. 34 m to the nearest m or 34.34 m to the nearest cm

2. 5,000 m to the nearest m or 1.56 km to the nearest dam

3. 55 cm to the nearest mm or 3 m to the nearest m

Give the greatest possible error (GPE) of each measurement.

1. 12 cm   **2.** 31 km   **3.** 9 mm   **4.** 4 dm   **5.** 643 m

State which measurement is more precise.

6. 65 m to the nearest m of 65.0 m to the nearest cm

7. 71.0 cm to the nearest mm or 3 m to the nearest m

8. 3,901 m to the nearest m or 3.79 km to the nearest km

9. 12 dm to the nearest dm or 18,765 mm to the nearest mm

10. Copy and complete the chart. Record the shortest and longest possible lengths in meters.

Measurement	GPE	Shortest	Longest
4 km to the nearest km			
670 m to the nearest m			
20 dm to the nearest dm			

MATH REASONING

11. Distances from a watermelon spitting contest were measured in meters (A), then in centimeters (B). List the contestants in order from 1st to 4th place using both sets of measurements.

Contestant	Tim	Art	Pete	Jose
Distance A	8 m	7 m	8 m	7 m
Distance B	762 cm	742 cm	759 cm	749 cm

PROBLEM SOLVING

12. Social Studies Data Bank   What is the difference between the high and the low prices of a share of ToysRU stock?

DATA BANK

13. The diameter of the 1956 Haitian 20 centimes coin is 26.20 mm to the nearest mm. What is the GPE of this measurement?

State which basic operation is associated with each phrase.

14. the sum of 2 and 10   **15.** 18 times 100   **16.** the quotient of 80 and 40

Find the value of each expression.

17. $30 - 5 \times 4$ **18.** $9 \times 3 - 1$ **19.** $9 \times (3 - 1)$ **20.** $25 - 5 - 5 \div 5$

More Practice, page 524, set C

Mass and Capacity

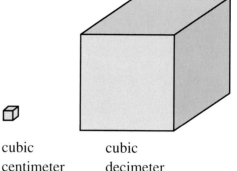

cubic centimeter   cubic decimeter

EXPLORE **Use Centimeter Graph Paper**
Make a cube with each edge 10 cm or 1 dm long. This is a decimeter cube (dm-cube) or a **cubic decimeter** (dm^3). A cube with edges of 1 cm is called a centimeter cube or a **cubic centimeter** (cm^3).

TALK ABOUT IT

1. How many centimeter cubes would you need to cover the bottom of the cubic decimeter with a single layer of cubes?

2. How many centimeter cubes would you need to fill the decimeter cube completely?

A dm-cube filled with water has a **capacity** of 1 **liter** (**L**). The **mass** of 1 L of water is 1 **kilogram** (**kg**).

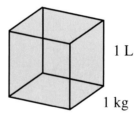

1 L

1 kg

A cm-cube filled with water has a **capacity** of 1 **milliliter** (**mL**). The mass of 1 mL of water is 1 **gram** (**g**).

1 mL

1 g

You can change from one unit of mass or capacity to another by multiplying or dividing by powers of 10.

Examples

A 27 L = ___?___ mL
    1L = 1,000 mL
    27 L = 27,000 mL

B 457 g = ___?___ kg
    1 g = 0.001 kg
    457 g = 0.457 kg

Complete the following statements.

1. 2 L = ▦ mL

2. 567 mL = ▦ L

3. 35 g = ▦ kg

4. 1.4 kg = ▦ g

5. 3.2 L = ▦ mL

6. 2 mL = ▦ L

7. 5 g = ▦ kg

8. 7.98 kg = ▦ g

Complete the "?" sections in the charts.

1. CAPACITY

kL	hL	dkL	L	dL	cL	mL
?			5L			?
?			?			125
0.04			?			?

2. MASS

kg	hg	dkg	g	dg	cg	mg
5			?			?
			125			?
?			?			40

Complete the following statements.

3. 108 g = ▦ kg   **4.** 19 g = ▦ kg   **5.** 8 g = ▦ kg

6. 16 mL = ▦ L   **7.** 4.09 kg = ▦ g   **8.** 6.7 L = ▦ mL

Name the larger measurement in each pair.

9. 250 mL; 2 L   **10.** 0.3 L; 2.346 mL

11. 4 kL; 5,256 mL   **12.** 0.01 kL; 0.6 L

MATH REASONING

13. How many liters of water are needed to fill a cubic meter container?

14. If a dm-cube is half-filled with water, what is the mass of the water?

PROBLEM SOLVING

15. **Data Hunt** Each of the prefixes, **giga-,** **mega-, micro-, nano-,** and **pico-,** represents a power of 10. Find the meaning of each prefix.

16. One metric ton is equivalent to 1,000 kg. The mass of a 747 jet is 700,000 kg. Express the mass of the jet in metric tons.

▶ **ESTIMATION**

Choose the best estimate.

17. The capacity of a large serving spoon is __?__.   **A** 0.5 L   **B** 5 L   **C** 50 mL

18. The capacity of a water balloon is __?__.   **A** 1,400 mL   **B** 5 L   **C** 0.01 L

19. The mass of a 6-pack of pencils is __?__.   **A** 1,200 mg   **B** 8 g   **C** 75 g

20. The mass of a paper clip is __?__.   **A** 0.02 kg   **B** 20 mg   **C** 2 g

More Practice, page 524, set D

Problem Solving
Using the Strategies

| UNDERSTAND |
| ANALYZE DATA |
| PLAN |
| ESTIMATE |
| SOLVE |
| EXAMINE |

You can often use more than one strategy to solve a problem. Frank **Used Objects** to solve the problem at the right. Lori used the strategy **Draw a Picture.**

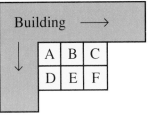

Building ⟶

| A | B | C |
| D | E | F |

The Espinoza ranch has a rectangular corral which is divided into 6 individual pens. Two sides of the corral are buildings so there are only 12 sections of fence. Which 6 sections of fence could be removed to convert the corral to 2 square pens?

The corral could be converted to 2 square pens by removing the outside fences of F and the sections of fence which separate A, B, C, D and E.

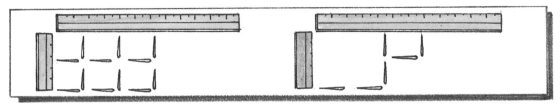

Frank's solution

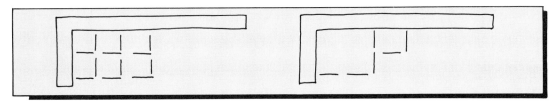

Lori's solution

TRY IT OUT

Solve. Use the strategies Draw a Picture or Use Objects.

1. The corral below has 17 sections of fence. Nancy made 4 square pens of the same size by removing only 3 sections of fence. Which sections did she remove?

2. Tony built a rectangular corral 60 ft long and 42 ft wide. He put one post at each corner and one every 6 ft in between. How many posts did Tony use?

Solve. Use any problem solving strategy.

Some Strategies	
Act Out	Solve a Simpler Problem
Use Objects	Make an Organized List
Choose an Operation	Work Backward
Draw a Picture	Look for a Pattern
Guess and Check	Use Logical Reasoning
Make a Table	Write an Equation

1. In 1988 Winning Colors won the Kentucky Derby. The winner's purse was $611,200. The winner's purse at the first Kentucky Derby in 1875 was $2,850. About how many times greater was the purse in 1988 than in 1875?

2. Ricardo cut a long board into 10 equal segments. How many cuts did he make?

3. There are 4 horses in stalls along one wall of the stable: Champ, Titan, White Star, and Ebony. White Star is to the left of Ebony. Ebony is between Champ and White Star. Titan is at one end. Which horses are in the middle stalls?

4. Brad wants to stack 36 bales of hay as shown in the picture. How many bales should he put in the bottom row?

5. Gia has a 1.5 L bottle of juice. She drank 375 mL of the juice with her lunch. How many mL does Gia have left?

6. Danielle built a water trough for a corral. Use the diagram to find how much greater the length of the trough is than the width.

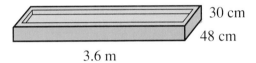

30 cm
48 cm
3.6 m

7. Ray has one piece of pipe 1.3 m long and another piece 30 cm long. How can he use these 2 pieces of pipe to measure 2 m on a third piece of pipe?

8. Kayla bought 5 sacks of feed for $5.69 each. She gave the clerk 2 $20 bills. How much change did Kayla get?

Data Collection and Analysis
Group Decision Making

UNDERSTAND
ANALYZE DATA
PLAN
ESTIMATE
SOLVE
EXAMINE

Doing a Survey
Group Skill:
Check for Understanding

Your principal is interested in starting an after-school sports program. Your group will conduct a survey to find out what sports most students would participate in, and whether they would participate on Wednesday, Thursday, or either day.

Collecting Data

1. The people you select for your survey are called your **sample.** The sports program will include both boys and girls. What are some of the things you should consider when you select your sample?

2. Work with your group to make a list of at least four sports in which students might want to participate.

3. Make a table to record the information you get from your survey.

Example

4. Ask the students in your sample whether or not they would participate in each sport on the list. For each sport make a tally on one or both days to show which days, if any, each student would participate in the program.

Sport	Wednesday	Thursday
Soccer |卌 ||	卌 卌 卌
Volleyball		

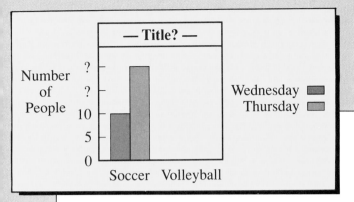

— Title? —

Number of People

Wednesday ▇
Thursday ▇

Soccer Volleyball

6. Prepare a brief group report for the principal to accompany your graph. Which sports and which day do you recommend for after-school sports?

Organizing Data

5. Combine the data your group collected with the data collected by another group. Make a double bar graph using the combined data.

   Check to be sure you have titled and labeled your graph.

57

WRAP UP

Three for All

The digit 3 is used in each of the expressions below. Describe what the 3 represents in each of them.

1. 937

2. 3.1×10^6

3. 2^3

4. $\frac{3}{7}$

5. 8.03

6. $3\frac{1}{5}$

Find the correct metric unit for each measurement.

7. The length of Mike's shoe: 29 __?__

8. The milk in a carton: 186 __?__

9. The length of the school building: 90 __?__

10. The water in a bathtub: 120 __?__

Sometimes, Always, Never

Which word should go in the blank, *sometimes*, *always*, or *never*? Explain your choice.

11. A decimal number with two digits is __?__ equal to a decimal number with three digits.

12. Scientific notation __?__ makes numbers with exponents easier to read.

13. Careful measurements __?__ give exact answers.

Project

Be an aware consumer. Examine supermarket products for metric quantities. Find several sizes of the same item, either at home or in the supermarket. Do the metric quantities make it easier to compare the unit prices? Write the unit prices for several items such as cereal or detergent that come in a variety of sizes. Also investigate packaging. Does the packaging make smaller quantities seem larger? What other questions should consumers consider as they make purchasing decisions?

Chapter Review/Test

Part 1 Understanding

1. The value of the 2 in 4.028 is

   A 200   B $\frac{2}{10}$ C $\frac{2}{100}$

2. Place the decimal point in the product.

   $23.4 \times 0.57 = 13338$

3. Match each decimal to the instruction that will make it a whole number.

   A 3.4   X. multiply by 10
   B 0.034   Y. multiply by 100
   C 3.04   Z. multiply by 1,000

4. Find the missing exponent by matching.

   A $10{,}000 = 10^{\text{IIIII}}$ X. 3
   B $4{,}836 = 4.836 \times 10^{\text{IIIII}}$ Y. 4
   C $y \cdot y \cdot y \cdot y \cdot y = y^{\text{IIIII}}$ Z. 5

5. Which method, clustering or front-end, would you use to estimate the sum $14.8 + 15.3 + 14.07 + 15.98$?

6. Which measurement is more precise?

   A 3.3 cm to the nearest mm
   B 3 cm to the nearest cm

Part 2 Skills

7. $3.06 + 2.895$

8. $1.078 - 0.904$

9. 8.03×0.47

10. $0.039\overline{)0.814}$

11. $4\overline{)29.12}$

12. $0.64\overline{)85}$

13. 275 cm = __?__ m

14. 8 g = __?__ kg

15. 3 L = __?__ mL

Write in standard notation.

16. thirty and seventy-five thousandths

17. 6.4×10^5

18. Complete the table.

hours (h)	1	2	3	4	5	9
earnings (e)	3	6	9			

Part 3 Applications

19. A plane flying at 4,000 ft dropped a thousand feet. How far above the ground was it? Which is a different way of asking the question in the problem?

    A What is the distance between the ground and the plane?
    B How much closer to the ground was it?

20. **Challenge** Draw a picture to solve.

    The combined height of Jack and Bob is 3.4 m. This is 158 cm more than Al's height. Al is 8 cm taller than Jack. How tall is Bob?

ENRICHMENT
The Invention of Decimals

Simon Stevin (1548–1620), a Flemish engineer, invented a method of writing decimals instead of fractions. His book, *La Thiende (The Tenth),* published in 1585, showed how to write and compute with decimals instead of fractions.

Stevin did not actually use a decimal point. Instead small circled numerals were used between digits of the numeral to show the place value, 10ths, 100ths, 1,000ths, and so on, for each digit.

THIENDE. 13
HET ANDER DEEL
DER THIENDE VANDE
WERCKINCHE.

I. VOORSTEL VANDE
VERGADERINGHE.

Wefende ghegeven Thiendetalen te vergaderen: hare Somme te vinden.

T'GHEGHEVEN. Het fijn drie oirdens van Thiendetalen, welcker eerfte 27 ③ 8 ① 4 ② 7 ③ , de tweede, 37 ⓪ 6 ① 7 ② 5 ③ , de derde, 875 ⓪ 7 ① 8 ② 2 ③ , T'BEGHEERDE. Wy moeten haer Somme vinden . WERCKING. Men fal de ghegheven ghetalen in oirden ftellen als hier neven, die vergaderende naer de ghemeene maniere der vergaderinghe van heelegetalen aldus:

⓪	①	②	③
2 7	8	4	7
3 7	6	7	5
8 7 5	7	8	2
9 4 1	3	0	4

Fraction	Decimal	Stevin's notation
$9 + \frac{7}{10} + \frac{3}{100}$	9.73	9 ⓪ 7 ① 3 ②
$12 + \frac{5}{10} + \frac{1}{100} + \frac{4}{1000}$	12.514	12 ⓪ 5 ① 1 ② 4 ③

When doing computation with decimals the circled digits were written above the corresponding places in the decimal.

The importance of Stevin's invention is that it allowed computation to be performed as if working with whole numbers instead of difficult fractions.

Write each numeral using Stevin's decimal notation.

1. 3.925

2. 82.127

3. 10.025

4. $3 + \frac{7}{10} + \frac{8}{100}$

5. $16 + \frac{5}{10}$

6. $1 + \frac{2}{10} + \frac{3}{100} + \frac{4}{1000}$

Write a decimal for each of these symbols.

7. 7 ⓪ 8 ① 4 ②

8. 23 ⓪ 9 ① 4 ②

9. 1 ⓪ 8 ① 6 ② 6 ③ 2 ④

10. What is 4 ⓪ 3 ① 9 ② plus 7 ⓪ 9 ① 6 ②

11. Multiply 8 ⓪ 4 ① 6 ② by 3 ⓪ 8 ①

1. Subtract.

2,308 − 194

A 2,214

B 2,114

C 1,402

D not given

2. Add.

56.935 + 47.09

A 104.025

B 61.644

C 103.944

D not given

3. Name the polygon.

A parallelogram

B trapezoid

C rhombus

D not given

4. What is m ∠C?

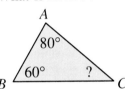

A 90°

B 50°

C 40°

D 45°

5. What is the standard numeral for seven million, forty-six thousand, eight hundred seven?

A 7,460,807   B 7,460,870

C 7,046,807   D 7,406,870

6. Choose the best estimate.

276

× 54

A 15,000

B 1,500

C 10,000

D 18,000

7. Evaluate using mental math.

59¢ + 83¢ + 41¢ + 42¢

A $2.00   B $2.25

C $2.20   D $1.85

8. Which equation is not related to the other three equations?

A 60 ÷ 5 = 12   B 12 × 5 = 60

C 5 × 12 = 60   D 60 − 12 = 48

9. Evaluate: $4 \times (15 - 6) - 18$

A 18   B 8

C 36   D not given

10. Evaluate the algebraic expression $3 \times (a - b)$ for $a = 9$ and $b = 2$.

A 10   B 25

C 21   D 33

11. Joel used a calculator to find 6,565 ÷ 65. Which answer should he have gotten?

A 1.01   B 101

C 1,010   D 6,500

12. What is the decimal for ninety and forty-eight thousandths?

A 90,048   B 90.48

C 90.0048   D 90.048

13. A baseball was pitched at a speed of 88.5 mph. A tennis ball was hit at a speed 1.5 times faster. What was the speed of the tennis ball?

A 25,66 mph   B 40 mph

C 53.55 mph   D not given

14. A container of milk holds 1.9 L. Marco used 280 mL to make bread. How many mL of milk are left?

A 162 mL   B 1,620 mL

C 0.9 mL   D 90 mL

3

DATA
ANALYSIS
AND
STATISTICS

MATH AND SCIENCE

DATA BANK

Use the Science Data Bank on page 490 to answer the questions.

1 In what type of African environment do the majority of primate species live? In what type of environment do the fewest species live?

2 Name the region that has three times as many woodland primate species as the continent of Asia.

3 What is the total number of primate species living in the rain forests of Africa and Madagascar? in the woodlands of Africa and Asia? in the savannas of Africa and the Neotropics?

4 **Using Critical Thinking** How many times longer is the lifespan of each primate than its infant phase? Is there a pattern? Do you think there is a relationship between the lengths of a primate's lifespan and its infant phase?

Multiple Line Graphs

LEARN ABOUT IT

A multiple line graph lets you compare several sets of data.

EXPLORE Look for a Trend

When do you think more compact discs will be sold than albums and cassettes? Use the graph at the right to help you decide.

TALK ABOUT IT

1. What do each of the three lines on the graph stand for?

2. Describe the three trends in sales from 1978 to 1986.

3. In about what year did cassettes begin selling more than albums?

You can make **predictions** on a multiple line graph by mentally extending the lines. You might predict from the graph that album sales should have been down to about 400 or 500 million dollars by 1990.

To make multiple line graphs:

- Choose a color for each line.
- Select an appropriate scale for each axis.
- Plot the points for each data set and connect the points.
- Label and title the graph.

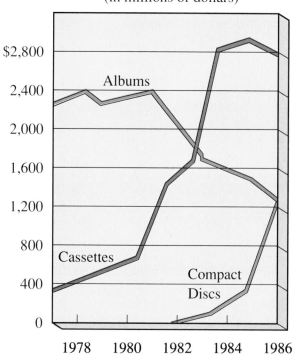

Recorded-Music Sales in U.S.
(in millions of dollars)

TRY IT OUT

Use the graph above to answer these questions.

1. Were compact disc sales more or less than cassette sales in 1984?

2. In about what year were album sales equal to cassette sales?

3. When was the difference between cassette and album sales the greatest?

4. Predict the year that cassettes and compact disc sales should be equal.

1. The multiple line graph at the right compares electricity usage for one family for a five-month period. Use the data in the table to copy and complete the graph.

Kilowatt-Hours Used		
	This Year	Last Year
Jan	20.4	20.1
Feb	20.2	18.9
Mar	17.1	18.1
Apr	18.7	17.2
May	14.9	16.3
Jun	14.0	14.3

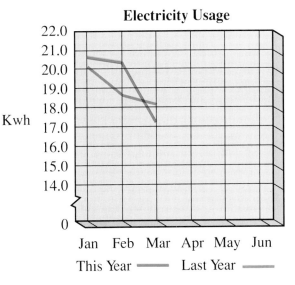

Electricity Usage

Kwh

This Year ——— Last Year ———

APPLY

MATH REASONING

2. Make a multiple line graph showing the following data.

Amount of Time on the Phone Per Day (in minutes)												
Age	10		11		12		13		14		15	
	Girls	Boys	Girls	Boys	Girls	Boys	Girls	Boys	Girls	Boys	Girls	Boys
Time	4.5	3.8	9.8	5.2	13.0	9.3	20.7	15.3	22.4	21.7	23.8	24.3

PROBLEM SOLVING

Use the graph on page 64.

3. Suppose each album in 1978 cost $10 and each cassette cost $5. Were more albums or cassettes sold in 1978? About how many more?

4. Suppose a compact disc cost $15 in 1985. About how many compact discs were sold that year?

▶ USING CRITICAL THINKING   Analyze the Data

5. Examine the graph in exercise 1. Barry said, "Extending the lines suggests that 0 kilowatt-hours were used both last year and this year in December." Does Barry's argument make sense? Explain.

More Practice, page 525, set A

Circle Graphs

Willie's Diet
11 pounds daily

13% peanuts
5% fruit
19% protein and chow
63% vegetables

Cleo's Diet
16 pounds daily

56% fruit
13% milk
25% vegetables
6% protein and chow

LEARN ABOUT IT

A circle graph shows how parts are related to a whole.

EXPLORE Examine the graph

These circle graphs show the proportion of foods in the diets of an orangutan and a gorilla.

TALK ABOUT IT

Willie, an Orangutan, and Cleo, a gorilla, live at the Los Angeles Zoo.

1. How much food does Willie eat daily?

2. Is more or less than half of Cleo's diet fruit?

3. What is the sum of the percentages in each circle?

You can use these as benchmarks to estimate the size of a section of a circle graph, or the number each part represents.

$$50\% = \frac{1}{2} \quad 25\% = \frac{1}{4} \quad 33\% \approx \frac{1}{3} \quad 10\% = \frac{1}{10}$$

About how many pounds of fruit does Cleo eat daily?
56% is a little more than $\frac{1}{2}$, and $\frac{1}{2}$ of 16 is 8.
So Cleo eats about 8 pounds of fruit each day.

TRY IT OUT

Use the circle graph above to answer these questions.

1. Does Willie eat more peanuts or more protein and chow?

2. Does the milk in Cleo's diet include more or less than $\frac{1}{10}$ of her entire diet? How do you know?

3. About how many pounds of vegetables does Cleo eat each day?

4. About how much of Willie's diet is peanuts?

In 1960 George Schaller studied a group of mountain gorillas in Kabara, Africa. This graph compares adult male, adult female, juvenile, and infant gorillas. Use the circle graph to answer these questions.

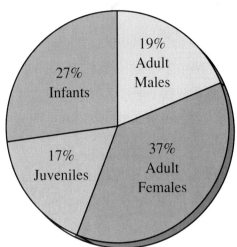

1. By how much did adult females outnumber adult males?

2. Were more or less than half of the gorillas adult females?

3. Out of 1,000 gorillas, about how many would you expect to be juvenile?

4. Are more or less than a third of the gorillas studied adult females?

5. About one fourth of the gorillas are what age?

6. Out of 50 gorillas, about how many would you expect to be infants?

APPLY

MATH REASONING Tell what is wrong with each circle graph.

7.
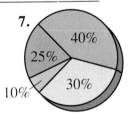

8.
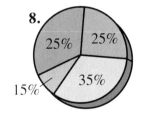

9.
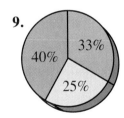

PROBLEM SOLVING

10. **Science Data Bank** Make a list of regions of the world in which there are native primates, in order from most to fewest species. Include the number of species.

DATA BANK

▶ **ALGEBRA**

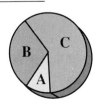

Part C is six times part A. Part B is half of part C. Find the percent for each part.

More Practice, page 525, set B

Scattergrams

Consumer Ratings: Windsurfer Boards

<u>EXPLORE</u> **Examine the graph**

Ordered pairs of data called **data points** can be shown in a **scattergram.** Here, each data point stands for the cost and rating of one brand of windsurfer board.

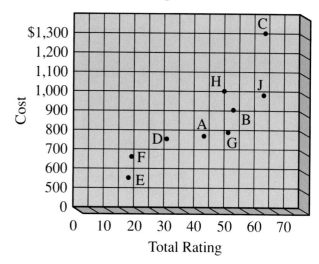

Brands	
A Freestyle Surfer	E Wild Board
B Tahiti Board	F Shark Board
C Caribbi 270	G XJ300 Wind
D Surfer Mate	H Sleek Surf
	J Breeze Board

TALK ABOUT IT

1. Which board is the most expensive? the least expensive?

2. Which board has the highest rating? the lowest rating?

3. Which boards would you consider to be good buys? Why?

One relationship between measured quantities is the **correlation.**

Positive Correlation
Both sets of data increase together.

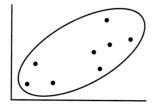

Negative Correlation
One set of data increases as the other decreases.

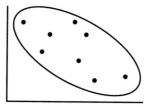

If data points are scattered over the graph, we say there is **no correlation.**

Use the Windsurfer Boards scattergram above to answer these questions.

1. What is the approximate cost and rating of the Breeze Board?

2. Does the scattergram show positive, negative, or no correlation?

Use these scattergrams for problems 1–3.

Tell whether there appears to be a positive correlation, a negative correlation, or no correlation for each of the following.

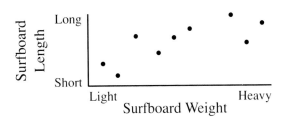

1. surfboard handling and weight

2. surfboard length and weight

3. True or false: The heavier a surfboard, the easier it is to handle.

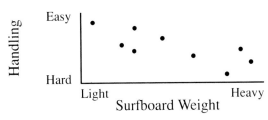

APPLY

MATH REASONING

4. Make a scattergram from the data below. Describe the relationship between test scores and studying time using the idea of correlation.

Minutes of study	75	30	0	15	60	45	120	90	90	15
Test score	85	68	43	94	87	68	98	89	93	65

PROBLEM SOLVING

Use the scattergram on page 68 where necessary.

5. Suppose a surfboard had a rating of 65. How much might you expect to pay for it?

6. Suppose a surfboard costs $950. What might you expect its rating to be?

7. Kikki bought 3 surfboards. They were three different lengths and each cost $50 more than the one that was next shortest. In all, she paid $375. How much was each board?

MIXED REVIEW

Write $>$, $<$, or $=$ for each ▥.

8. 3.145 ▥ 3.045   9. 0.66 ▥ 0.066   10. 0.2 ▥ 0.20   11. 213.02 ▥ 211.03

Evaluate.

12. $3.6 + 1.28 + 9$ 13. $1.8 - 0.635$ 14. $16 - 2.75$ 15. $0.04\overline{)2.008}$

More Practice, page 525, set C

Choosing Mental Math Techniques

EXPLORE Use the Graph

Have you ever made a New Year's resolution? The graph at the right shows the results of a survey of 635 adults about New Year's resolutions.

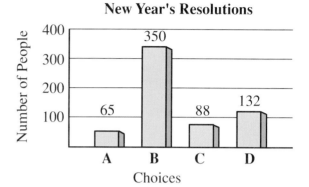

New Year's Resolutions

TALK ABOUT IT

1. Estimate how many people said either "save more money" or "lose weight."

2. 350 + 90 = 440, so is 350 + 88 less than or greater than 440? Why?

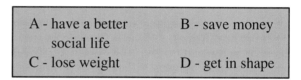

A - have a better social life   B - save money

C - lose weight   D - get in shape

To find how many people said, "save more money" or "lose weight" find:

350 + 88   THINK: 350 + 90 = 440, and 88 is 2 less than 90, so the exact sum is 2 less than 440.

350 + 88 = 438

When you replace one number with another to make computation easy and then adjust to the exact answer, you are using **compensation.**

To find the total number of people who said, "have a better social life" or "get in shape," find:

132 + 65   THINK: Break apart 132 as 100 + 30 + 2 and break apart 65 as 60 + 5, so the sum 132 + 65 is 100 + 90 + 7.

132 + 65 = 197

Sometimes you can use place value ideas to **break apart** *a number to make smaller, easier calculations.*

Solve using mental math. Use compensation or break apart.

1. 215 + 60   2. 4 × 31   3. 359 − 98

4. 9 × 45   5. 210 × 5   6. 7 × 42

70

Solve using mental math. Use compensation.

1. 7×21 **2.** 9×38 **3.** $151 - 43$ **4.** $216 + 39$ **5.** 29×4

6. $150 + 576$ **7.** $406 - 98$ **8.** $\$9.98 \times 5$ **9.** $631 - 133$ **10.** $438 + 297$

Solve using mental math. Use the break apart technique.

11. $63 + 25$ **12.** $52 + 46$ **13.** 42×4 **14.** 53×3 **15.** $52 + 130$

16. 35×4 **17.** 210×5 **18.** $425 + 30$ **19.** 4×506 **20.** $170 + 38$

Solve using mental math. Use compensation or the break apart technique.

21. $220 - 7$ **22.** 23×5 **23.** 9×62 **24.** $748 + 198$ **25.** $163 - 65$

26. 305×8 **27.** 17×30 **28.** $\$5.98 \times 3$ **29.** 99×18 **30.** $617 + 68$

APPLY

MATH REASONING

31. Name the basic property for the second step.

$$43 \times 2 = (40 + 3) \times 2$$
$$= (40 \times 2) + (3 \times 2) \ \underline{\ ?\ }$$
$$= 80 + 6 = 86$$

Basic Properties
■ commutative
■ associative
■ distributive
■ identity

PROBLEM SOLVING

32. How many more people said "get in shape" than said "lose weight"?

33. Fifty-four students were given a choice of "more clothes" or "more records" for a New Year's "wish." Twice as many people picked "more clothes" than "more records." How many picked each?

▶ **MENTAL MATH**

Solve using mental math.

34. $152 + 20$ **35.** $496 - 98$

36. $124 + 35 + 26$ **37.** $67 + 404$

38. $1,008 - 30$ **39.** $50 \times 13 \times 2$

Mental Math Techniques
■ compatible numbers
■ count on or back
■ compensation
■ break apart

More Practice, page 525, set D

Using Critical Thinking

Because their great-grandparents survived the San Francisco earthquake in 1906, Li and Tim decided to report on major earthquakes for social studies.

Earthquakes are measured in units on the "Richter Scale": the higher the number, the stronger the earthquake. They collected data and separately made graphs to show what they had found.

"I think a line graph is best for this data," said Li. "No, a bar graph is better," said Tim. They had to decide which graph to put in their report.

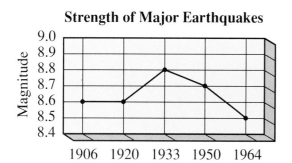

Strength of Major Earthquakes

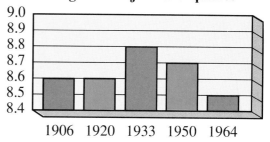

Strength of Major Earthquakes

1. What did Tim and Li have to decide?

2. Do both graphs show the same data?

3. Do you agree with Li or Tim?

4. What are line graphs most useful for?

5. When should you consider using a bar graph?

TRY IT OUT

Tell whether you would use a bar graph or a line graph for each of these sets of data. Tell why.

1. TV Top Ratings		**2.** Puppy Growth		**3.** Number of Students	
Comedy	60.2	March	12.5 pounds	1960	32,468
Drama	53.3	April	15.3 pounds	1970	38,573
News	47.7	May	18.8 pounds	1980	45,281
Movie	47.2	June	24.1 pounds	1990	52,482

MIDCHAPTER REVIEW/QUIZ

Two plants were grown naturally. Then, one plant was put in a darkened room while the other received normal light.

1. Make a multiple line graph to show the plants' growth.

2. Which plant grew faster?

3. When did each plant show the most growth?

4. Write a short statement describing your graph.

Height of Plants (in centimeters)		
	normal	dark
Monday	4.0	4.0
Friday	5.3	4.5
Monday	6.4	4.9
Friday	7.3	5.0
Monday	7.8	5.1
Friday	8.1	5.2

The circle graph to the right shows approximate 1980 census results for the U.S. population in the different age groups.

5. Write a statement comparing the population under age 20 to the population 65 and over.

6. What fraction of the population is over age 19?

Population of U.S. by Age

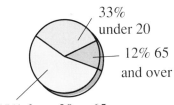

33% under 20

12% 65 and over

55% from 20 to 65

The scattergram compares daily temperatures of two cities.

7. As the normal temperature in Seattle increases, what usually happens to the temperature in Spokane?

8. Is this a positive or a negative correlation?

9. When Seattle's normal temperature is 50°, what could you expect the temperature to be in Spokane?

Normal Daily Temperatures for 12 Months

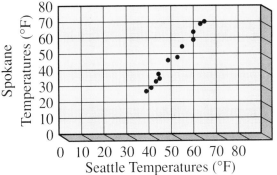

Solve using mental math.

10. 202 × 8   **11.** 5.2 + 384.5   **12.** 275 − 198   **13.** 25 × 19   **14.** 1,000 − 405

PROBLEM SOLVING

15. How much more does an average gorilla weigh than an average chimpanzee?

16. About how many chimpanzees would balance 1 gorilla?

17. If the combined weight of a gorilla and chimpanzee is about the same as 7 seventh graders, about how much does a seventh grader weigh?

Average Weights	
Gorilla	204.2 kg
Chimpanzee	68.1 kg

Problem Solving
Using the Strategies

UNDERSTAND
ANALYZE DATA
PLAN
ESTIMATE
SOLVE
EXAMINE

You can solve many problems in more than one way. To solve this problem, Amy used the strategy **Guess and Check.** Ken used the strategy **Draw a Picture.**

Darrin's class is decorating the gym for a dance. Lin bought gold streamers with glitter and black streamers. They have 26 rolls in 9 packages. How many rolls of each kind did they get?

STREAMERS
Gold Glitter - Package of 2
Black - Package of 4

Amy's solution:

Try 3 pkg of gold $3 \times 2 + 6 \times 4 = 30$ too big
Try 6 pkg of gold $6 \times 2 + 3 \times 4 = 24$ too small
Try 5 pkg of gold $5 \times 2 + 4 \times 4 = 26$ correct

Ken's solution:

- Draw nine boxes.
- Draw 2 rolls in each box.
- Draw 2 more rolls in enough boxes to make 26.

Solution: They got 5 rolls of gold streamers and 4 rolls of black streamers.

TRY IT OUT

Solve. Use Guess and Check or Draw a Picture.

1. The first 8 groups to arrive at the dance had either 2 or 3 students in them. There were 21 students in all. How many groups of 3 were there?

2. Ann made a display with 45 juice cans for the refreshment table. She put 1 less can in each row than was in the row below. How many cans were in the bottom row?

74

Solve. Use any problem solving strategy.

Some Strategies	
Act Out	Solve a Simpler Problem
Use Objects	Make an Organized List
Choose an Operation	Work Backward
Draw a Picture	Look for a Pattern
Guess and Check	Use Logical Reasoning
Make a Table	Write an Equation

1. Erica bought a new skirt and sweater for the dance. The skirt cost $24.95 and the sweater cost $19.50. She gave the clerk $50.00. How much did Erica spend?

2. The students had $145 to spend on refreshments. They bought 45 6-packs of juice and 15 packages of oatmeal bars. How much money did they have left?

3. Lee is putting balloons around 3 sides of the refreshment table. The table is 10 ft long and 4 ft wide. She wants to put the balloons 1 ft apart with a balloon at each corner. How many balloons will she need?

4. There were 280 students at a dance. Use the graph to find out how many were seventh grade boys.

5. Amber can't decide what to wear to the dance. She is considering 4 skirts— plaid, red, black, and blue denim—and 3 sweaters—white, yellow and pink. From how many outfits can Amber choose?

6. There were 12 more seventh graders at the dance than eighth graders. Edie counted 178 students. How many seventh graders came to the dance?

7. Mr. McDowell bought 4 rolls of film for $13.78. He took 96 pictures at the dance. How many pictures did he get from each roll?

8. Dang put 8 balloons around the entrance, 5 in the center of the room, and 1 in each of the 4 corners. He had 6 left. How many did he have when he started?

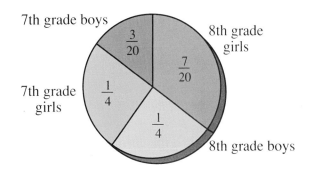

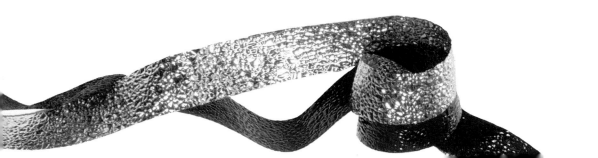

Mean, Median, and Mode

EXPLORE **Analyze the Data**

A zoologist studying a band of 6 chimpanzees found that their weights were 66.0 kg, 64.5 kg, 62.3 kg, 67.4 kg, 76.7 kg, and 64.5 kg. The zoologist wanted to determine a typical chimpanzee's weight.

TALK ABOUT IT

1. What are the largest and smallest weights?

2. What weight is found for more than one chimpanzee?

3. What would you estimate a typical weight to be? Why?

To find the **mean** of a set of numbers, add all the values and divide the sum by the total number of values.

The **median** is the middle number of a set of numbers arranged in order. If there is no single middle number, the median is the mean of the two middle numbers.

The **mode** of a set of numbers is the value that occurs most frequently. If each value occurs the same number of times, there is no mode.

The mean is the most commonly used typical value. If there are a few values much higher or lower than most of the data, the median may be a better typical value. The mode is useful in smaller data sets where several values are the same.

TRY IT OUT

Give the mean, median, and mode for each set of data.

1. Event	Score
Floor Exercise	8.7
Vault	8.3
Rings	8.5
Parallel Bars	8.9
Side Horse	8.9

2. Year	Water Used
1985	365,303 gallons
1986	345,298 gallons
1987	365,444 gallons
1988	249,220 gallons
1989	359,356 gallons

1. Copy and complete this chart using data from the survey below. Use a calculator.

		All workers	Females	Males	Years of School	
					12 or less	13 or more
Salary	Mean					
	Median					

Survey Results From 20 Workers							
Worker	Salary	Gender	Years of School	Worker	Salary	Gender	Years of School
1	$23,900	F	14	11	$19,000	F	16
2	$36,700	M	16	12	$43,200	M	16
3	$24,000	F	12	13	$29,200	F	12
4	$15,600	F	12	14	$25,600	F	12
5	$18,400	M	13	15	$32,400	M	13
6	$47,500	M	10	16	$34,600	F	16
7	$20,400	F	10	17	$56,000	M	14
8	$32,000	F	14	18	$17,500	M	10
9	$33,600	M	12	19	$15,800	F	16
10	$83,500	M	18	20	$20,400	F	12

MATH REASONING

2. Make a scattergram of the years of school and yearly salaries. Describe the relationship using the idea of correlation.

PROBLEM SOLVING

3. What are the mean, median, and mode weights of the chimpanzees on page 76?

4. **Science Data Bank** What is the mean length of the infant phase of the listed primates?
DATA BANK

▶ **CALCULATOR**

Find the missing numbers so that the mean of each diagonal is 87.

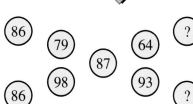

Stem and Leaf Plots

Data can often be organized in ways to make easy comparisons. One way to organize data is with a **stem and leaf plot.**

EXPLORE **Analyze the Data**

Twenty students with summer jobs were surveyed concerning how much they earned per hour. The data are: $3.75, $4.25, $3.90, $4.50, $4.50, $5.25, $4.75, $5.75, $6.10, $4.60, $4.85, $5.10, $5.15, $4.80, $4.70, $4.80, $5.10, $6.04, $4.25, $4.90

TALK ABOUT IT

1. Did any student earn less than $3 an hour?

2. What is the greatest salary?

3. Were most salaries in the $3, $4, $5, or $6 range?

Here's how to organize the data above using a stem and leaf plot.

Step 1: Set up the table.	*stem*	*leaf*
Step 2: Choose the stems.	3	75, 90
Enter them in the table.	4	25, 50, 50, 75, 60, 85, 80, 70, 80, 25, 90
	5	25, 75, 10, 15, 10
Step 3: Enter the leaves.	6	10, 5

TRY IT OUT

Use the stem and leaf plot above to answer these questions.

1. Were most salaries in the $3, $4, $5, or $6 range? Why does the stem and leaf plot make this easy to determine?

2. Name a salary that was earned by more than one student.

3. Make a stem and leaf plot for the following data. Number of hours worked per week: 12, 22, 25, 18, 15, 30, 24, 25, 16, 34, 25, 28, 17, 20, 15, 15, 24, 32, 40, 35

Use the stem and leaf plot at the right.

1. Was the $3, $4, $5, or $6 price range most common?

2. Which price range was least common?

3. What was the greatest price? least price?

4. Name a price that was given by three theaters.

5. Make a stem and leaf plot using the data below.

Movie Theater Prices
(dollars and cents)

Stem	Leaf
3	25, 25, 50, 50
4	00, 50, 25, 25, 00
5	00, 00, 50, 75, 00
6	00, 25

Takeoffs and Landings in One Year		
(rounded to the nearest thousand, data given in thousands)		
Chicago O'Hare—604	Las Vegas—296	Philadelphia—330
Los Angeles—479	St. Louis—291	Honolulu—309
Miami—350	Dallas—441	Pittsburgh—307
Houston Intercontinental—337	Atlanta—572	New York-La Guardia—292
San Francisco—324	Denver—467	New York-Kennedy—290
Washington National—307	Phoenix—349	

APPLY

MATH REASONING

6. Use the data above for movie ticket prices to make a bar graph. List two advantages of showing data with a stem and leaf plot and two advantages of showing data with a bar graph.

PROBLEM SOLVING

7. Use the stem and leaf plot at the right to find the mean, median, and mode of the data.

100-Meter Finishing Times
(seconds and hundredths of seconds)

Stem	Leaf
10	02, 35
11	40, 25, 50, 61, 50, 20
12	00, 02, 50

▶ **ESTIMATION**

8. Use this stem and leaf plot to estimate the mean cost of renting a videotape.

Video Rental Fees (dollars and cents)

Stem	Leaf
1	00, 25, 50, 25, 75
2	00, 25, 25, 00, 50, 50, 75
3	00, 00, 25, 75
4	00, 25

More Practice, page 526, set A

79

Frequency Tables and Histograms

You can organize data using a **frequency table.** Data from a frequency table can be shown in a graph called a **histogram.**

EXPLORE **Compare the Data**

A survey was taken about people's knowledge of the Alamo. A frequency table was made to organize the responses, and a histogram was made to show the results. The survey question was: In what year was the battle of the Alamo? (answer 1836)

Survey

Response	Tally	Frequency
1800–1820	ⱵⱵ	5
1821–1840	ⱵⱵ |||	8
1841–1860	ⱵⱵ ⱵⱵ |||	13
1861–1880	|||	3

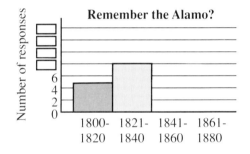

TALK ABOUT IT

1. What response was chosen by the most people?

2. How many people does ⱵⱵ represent?

3. What do you notice about the bars in the histogram?

To make a frequency table

- Select an interval for grouping the data.
- Make equal-size intervals.
- Make tallies to show the number in each interval. Count the tallies; this is the frequency.

To make a histogram

- Make a frequency table.
- Draw and label the graph.
- Draw the bars. The bars should touch to show that the data is continuous.

1. Copy and complete the histogram at the top of the page.

2. Make a histogram to show the responses to this question. When was the Golden Gate Bridge completed? (answer 1937)

Response	Tally	Frequency
1900–1910	ⱵⱵ |||	8
1911–1920	ⱵⱵ ⱵⱵ |||	13
1921–1930	ⱵⱵ ⱵⱵ ⱵⱵ	15
1931–1940	ⱵⱵ ⱵⱵ ⱵⱵ |||	18
1941–1950	|||	3

1. Use the data below. Copy and complete the frequency table.

2. Make another frequency table using the same data, but with an interval of 10 years.

3. Make a histogram using the frequency table from either exercise 1 or 2.

Age Interval	Tally	Frequency
41-45		
46-50		
51-55		

American Presidents' Age at Inauguration							
Washington	57	Taylor	64	Cleveland	47	Roosevelt	51
Adams	61	Fillmore	50	Harrison	55	Truman	60
Jefferson	57	Pierce	48	Cleveland	55	Eisenhower	62
Madison	57	Buchanan	65	McKinley	54	Kennedy	43
Monroe	58	Lincoln	52	Roosevelt	42	Johnson	55
Adams	57	Johnson	56	Taft	51	Nixon	56
Jackson	61	Grant	46	Wilson	56	Ford	61
Van Buren	54	Hayes	54	Harding	55	Carter	52
Harrison	68	Garfield	49	Coolidge	51	Reagan	69
Tyler	51	Arthur	50	Hoover	54	Bush	64
Polk	49						

APPLY

MATH REASONING

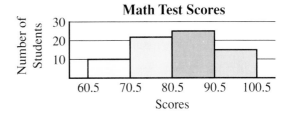

Math Test Scores

4. Make a frequency table using the histogram shown at the right.

PROBLEM SOLVING

5. Most college test scores fell between what two numbers?

6. What is the middle score of each interval?

7. How many people scored below the national average of 500?

College Test Scores	
Score Interval	Frequency
299.5 – 399.5	3
399.5 – 499.5	15
499.5 – 599.5	41
599.5 – 699.5	30
699.5 – 799.5	11
total	100

MIXED REVIEW

Find each product.

8. 2.9×6.4 **9.** 3.9×0.8 **10.** 0.89×1.2 **11.** 2.81×40.6

Estimate.

12. $31 + 33 + 28 + 29 + 27 + 34$ **13.** $51.2 + 49.8 + 48.9 + 50.4 + 51.5$

More Practice, page 526, set B

Exploring Algebra
More About Variables

Babysitting Rates
$ 3.00 ... start up
$ 2.00 ... each hour
Call Cora at
555-1234
References available.

LEARN ABOUT IT

A variable can represent one number or a range of numbers.

EXPLORE Explain the Pattern

Do you baby-sit to earn money? Did you ever wonder how much to charge? Cora charges the rates shown when she baby-sits.

TALK ABOUT IT

1. How much would she make for a 2-hour job? A 3-hour job? A 12-hour job? A 30-minute job?

2. Why do you think she charges a start-up fee?

Charge or cost **varies** with the number of hours of baby-sitting. You can make a table to show the cost for a specific number of hours. Also, you can give a **rule** for the relationship between the number of hours and the cost. Cora's table might look like this:

hours	1	2	3	4	5	6	7	8
cost ($)	5	7	9	11	13	15	17	19

The rule is: *The cost is 3 more than twice the number of hours.*

TRY IT OUT

Cora raised her rates to $4, plus $2.50 per hour.

1. Copy and complete the table below:

hours	1	2	3	4	5	6	7	8
cost ($)	6.50							

2. In words, write a rule to find the cost for a given number of hours.

Copy and complete these tables. Give a rule in words that relates the top variable in the table to the bottom variable in the table.

1.

students	1	2	3	4	5	15
cost ($)	4	8	12			

2.

squares	1	2	3	4	5	10
triangles	3	7	11			

3.

gerbils	20	30	40	100	200
birds	9	14	19		

4.

people	6	10	20	50	100	500
prizes	2	4	9	24		

5.

teams	2	3	4	5	10	20
games	1	3	6	10		

6.

bass	100	200	500	1,000	5,000
bream	450	950	2,450		

$(3 \times 4) \div 2$

$200 \times 5 - ?$

MATH REASONING

7. The library charges $0.10 per day when a book is overdue, plus $0.35 for sending an "overdue notice" on the sixth day. Use mental math to complete the table below.

days late	1	2	3	4	5	6	7	30	365
cost ($)	0.10								

PROBLEM SOLVING

Use the data on page 82.

8. If Cora baby-sat after school from 3:00 till 5:00, how much could she earn a week?

9. **Talk about your solution** Compare your solution to exercise 8 with a classmate. Did you solve it the same way? Could you have solved it a different way?

▶ **CALCULATOR**

10. The recommended pulse rate for a person who exercises is given by the expression "$176 - 0.8A$" for a person of age "A". Make a table that gives the pulse for ages 10, 20, 30, 40, 50, 60, 70, and 80.

Problem Solving
Extra Data

UNDERSTAND
ANALYZE DATA
PLAN
ESTIMATE
SOLVE
EXAMINE

Sometimes a problem has **extra data.** Extra data are not needed to solve the problem.

> Siberian tigers are the world's largest tigers. The largest one ever measured was 10 ft 11 in. long and weighed 932 lb. An average adult male is about 10 ft long and 585 lb. How much more did the largest tiger weigh than the average male?

> First I'll find the data I need to solve the problem.

> The other data are extra.

> Now, I'll solve the problem using only the needed data.

The largest tiger weighed 932 lb.

The average adult male weighs 585 lb.

The length of the average male and the length of the largest tiger are not needed.

$$932 - 585 = 347$$

The largest tiger weighed 347 lb more than an average adult male.

TRY IT OUT

1. A 400 lb tiger can leap 30 ft over level ground or 15 feet into the air. It can creep to within 20 ft of another animal without being heard. How much farther can it jump over level ground than in the air?

2. A tiger has 4 canine teeth. Each one is about 10 times as long as the longest tooth in your mouth. If your longest tooth is 0.5 cm, about how long is the tiger's canine tooth?

3. At birth, a tiger cub is about 12 in. long and weighs about 2 lb. During its first 6 months it gains an average of about 33 lb each month. How much would a typical tiger weigh at six months?

4. A 585 lb tiger can drag an animal that weighs 4 times more. It would take 13 men to move the same weight. How many pounds can a tiger move?

1. In one year a tiger must eat about 70 deer or other large animals. A tiger may live 20 years. About how many large animals does it eat in its lifetime?

2. For a 12-year-old person weighing 100 lb to eat like a tiger, he or she would have to eat about 20 lb in one meal. If a hamburger and bun weighs about 0.4 lb, how many hamburgers would that be?

3. The Park is fencing a rectangular area for the monkeys. The area is 42 ft wide and 78 ft long. There is a post at each corner and every 6 ft in between. How many posts are there?

4. The Wild Animal Park made a graph showing the number of tickets sold. Use the graph to estimate the number of tickets sold each day.

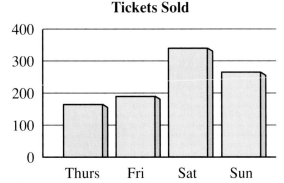

Tickets Sold

5. A large, hungry tiger can eat about 0.2 of its own weight at one meal. How many pounds of meat can a 585 lb tiger eat?

6. Keiko's class went to the Wild Animal Park. They bought 27 student tickets and 2 adult tickets. How much did they spend?

Adults $3.50 Students $1.75

7. Megan had $19.00 to spend. She bought a student ticket and 3 posters for $2.50 each. How much did Megan spend?

8. **Talk About Your Solution**

   The park sells small picture postcards in packages of 3 and large picture postcards in packages of 2. Sam bought 19 postcards. How many of each size did he get?

   Explain your solution to a classmate. Compare your solutions and decide which is better.

Applied Problem Solving
Group Decision Making

UNDERSTAND
ANALYZE DATA
PLAN
ESTIMATE
SOLVE
EXAMINE

Doing an Investigation

Group Skill:
Listen to Others

Your friend's dog is lost. She needs your group's help writing an ad and placing it in two newspapers. What should the ad say and how many days should your friend advertise in each newspaper?

Facts to Consider

- She has a total of $40 to spend from her savings.
- Ad fees are as follows for the two newspapers in town:

- Ads in the newspapers have 24 characters per line. Spaces and punctuation are counted as characters. There is a 2-line minimum.
- Here are some facts about the dog:

The dog is a springer spaniel. He is 2 years old. He is white with a black circle around his left eye. His tag says "Tiny." His front paws are white and his back paws are black. He was last seen at the Midtown Shopping Center on January 12 at 2 p.m. He loves chicken livers. The reward is $50. The contact telephone number is 555-7865. No one is home to answer the phone until 5 p.m. on weekdays.

**Sunny Times
(Circulation:
65,000 customers)**

	Per line per day
1 day	$3.78
2–3 days	$2.83
4 days	$2.20
5 days	$1.94
6 days	$1.84
7 days	$1.73
8–10 days	$1.68
11 days	$1.31

**Town Crier
(Circulation:
112,000 customers)**

	Per line per day
1 day	$7.75
2 days	$6.48
3 days	$5.11
4–6 days	$3.91
7 days	$3.27
8–11 days	$3.21
12–29 days	$3.06

Some Questions to Answer

1. Suppose the ad is 3 lines long. If your friend advertised only in the Sunny Times, what is the maximum number of days she could advertise?

2. If your friend advertised only in the Town Crier, what is the maximum number of days she could afford for a 3-line ad?

3. Do you think your friend should place the ad for the same number of days in both papers? Why or why not?

4. What are the most important facts to include in the ad? How many lines would they take up?

What Is Your Decision?

Present your group's ad to the class. Write it in 24-character lines. Explain your advertising plan and show how much it will cost. Defend your group's choice.

WRAP UP

I Auto-Graph

Often, one type of graph is best for a particular purpose. Choose the appropriate graph or graphs from the box for each situation.

bar graph	circle graph	histogram	scattergram
multiple line graph	stem and leaf table		line graph

1. Compare sales of two record albums for six months.

2. Show how a family's budget is spent for food, rent, clothing, and other expenses.

3. Decide if there is a connection between the heights and weights of thirteen-year-old boys.

4. Show the high and low temperatures in your city for a month.

5. Show the price of a loaf of bread for each year, 1970 to the present.

6. Show the price of five brands of shampoo.

7. Show whether more people in their twenties, thirties, or forties attended a certain movie.

Sometimes, Always, Never

Which word should go in the blank, *sometimes*, *always*, or *never*? Explain your choice.

8. The median of a set of data is __?__ less than the mean.

9. All the numbers in a set of data are __?__ greater than the mean.

10. The mean and the median of a set of data are __?__ equal.

Project

News articles often use graphs to present data in an interesting and easy-to-understand format. Find a graph in a newspaper or magazine. Evaluate the effectiveness of the graph. Why do you think the writer used this type of graph?

CHAPTER REVIEW/TEST

Part 1   Understanding

Match.

1. Stem-and-leaf table

2. Multiple line graph

3. Scattergram

4. Circle graph

A helps to predict a trend

B shows if two sets of data are related

C helps to group data according to size

D shows how parts make up a whole

Part 2   Skills

Solve using mental math.

5. $170 + 58 + 130$

6. $\$9.95 \times 5$

Pearl made this circle graph to show how she uses her time each day.

7. Does she spend more or less than $\frac{1}{3}$ of her time in school?

8. What percent of her time is spent for recreation?

9. About how many hours a day are spent for study and meals?

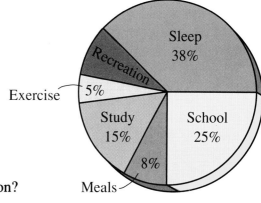

10. Complete the table. Write a rule.

Students	5	10	15	20	25
Cost	17	32	47		

Use the line graph for questions 11 to 14. Find each.

11. mode   12. median   13. mean

Part 3   Applications

14. Make a histogram to show the data in the line graph.

Darrin set up a refreshment display. There were 3 cases of juice boxes. He made a display with 28 juice boxes by stacking one less box on each level than was in the level below.

15. There was one box on the top row. How many boxes were in the bottom row?

16. **Challenge** A case holds 12 juice boxes. Can he add another level of boxes? How many boxes?

ENRICHMENT
Box and Whiskers Graphs

Which player is the best scorer? One way to compare the scores is to make a box and whisker graph for each player. Let's start with Amos.

Amos	Brooks	Carpenter
19	16	22
17	19	23
21	27	22
24	25	20
25	22	21
27	25	22
19	16	23
20	15	19

- Arrange the 8 scores in order and find the median (20.5).

- Divide the scores into fourths or quartiles.

17 19   19 20 21 24   25 27

bottom fourth   middle two   top fourth or
or quartile   fourths or   quartile
                   quartiles

- Find the median of the upper half of the scores (24.5). This is the upper quartile (Q_U).
- Find the median of the lower half of the scores (19). This is the lower quartile (Q_L).
- On a number line, mark the highest score, the lowest score, Q_U, Q_L, and the median.

```
lowest                          highest
 score   Q_L median    Q_U      score
└─┴─┬─┴─┬─┴─┬┴─┬─┴─┬─┴─┬┴─┴─┬─┴─┬─┴─┘
14    16    18    20    22    24    26    28
```

- Draw a box from Q_U to Q_L and mark the median. Draw lines or whiskers from the box to the highest and lowest scores.

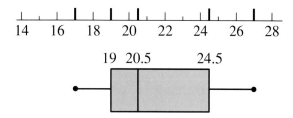

```
└─┴─┬─┴─┬─┴─┬┴─┬─┴─┬─┴─┬┴─┴─┬─┴─┬─┴─┘
14    16    18    20    22    24    26    28
        19  20.5      24.5
```

1. Copy the scale and graph for Amos.

2. Using the same scale, make a box and whisker graph for Brooks and one for Carpenter.

3. Which player do you think was the best scorer? Why?

CUMULATIVE REVIEW

1. Divide.

$21\overline{)4{,}347}$
  A 206R22   **B** 207R9

  C 207   **D** not given

2. Multiply.

    5.7   **A** 0.0399   **B** 0.399
  $\times 0.07$ **C** 3.99   **D** 399

3. Divide. $27.84 \div 2.9$

  A 9.6   **B** 0.96

  C 96   **D** 960

4. Evaluate $16 \times (l - 7)$ for $l = 10$.

  A 1   **B** 90

  C 153   **D** 48

5. Name the property used.
$33 + 70 = 70 + 33$

  A associative   **B** commutative

  C distributive   **D** identity

6. Find the missing length.
$850 \text{ mm} = \underline{\quad ? \quad} \text{ m}$

  A 0.085   **B** 8.5

  C 0.85   **D** 85

7. Which does a multiple line graph show?

  A total   **B** trend

  C rating   **D** summary

8. In a scattergram what is the correlation when both sets of data increase?

  A positive   **B** negative

  C equal   **D** none

Use the circle graph to answer 9 and 10

9. Which type of movie was shown the most?

  A science fiction

  B drama

  C adventure

  D comedy

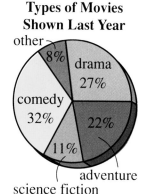

Types of Movies Shown Last Year

other 8% · drama 27% · comedy 32% · 22% · 11% · adventure · science fiction

10. Which type was shown about $\frac{1}{10}$ of the time?

  A comedy   **B** adventure

  C other   **D** science fiction

11. The first 8 rows of an airplane have either 4 or 6 seats in them. There are 38 seats in these rows. How many rows have only 4 seats?

  A 5   **B** 3   **C** 4   **D** 6

Use this table for problems 12 and 13.

airport vans (v)	1	2	3	4	5	6
passengers (g)	9	18	27	?	?	?

12. Select the set of numbers to complete the table.

  A 35, 42, 49   **B** 32, 36, 42

  C 36, 45, 54   **D** 35, 45, 56

13. Each passenger pays $27 for the trip to the airport. How much money is collected for one full van?

  A $246   **B** $270

  C $243   **D** $315

4

GEOMETRY

MATH AND SCIENCE

DATA BANK

Use the Science Data Bank on page 493 to answer the questions.

1 How many sides does a heavy hexagon bolthead have? Why do you think most boltheads are made with this number of sides?

2 If the diameter (D) of a heavy hexagon bolthead is 2 inches, how wide (W) is the top of the bolt?

3 A truss is a rigid framework that can be used to support a bridge or a roof. Which trusses are built entirely of straight edges? Which truss has a curved edge?

4 **Using Critical Thinking** Compare the Pratt, Warren, and Bowstring trusses. Why is each truss is made up of triangles instead of rectangles? Do you think the number of triangles in a truss affects its strength?

Exploring Solid Figures

EXPLORE Find a Pattern

Three-dimensional figures are called solid or space figures.
Follow these steps to make a **tetrahedron** from an envelope.

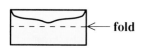

← fold

Seal the envelope and fold it in half.

Fold a corner down as shown and label the point P. Cut along $\overline{AB}$.

Fold along $\overline{CP}$ and $\overline{DP}$. Spread the open end of the envelope until points A and B meet. Tape this edge closed.

TALK ABOUT IT

1. How many faces does this space figure have?

2. How many vertices? How many edges?

A **pyramid** has one face called the **base.** The other faces are triangular.

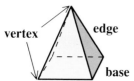

vertex   edge

base

Rectangular Pyramid   **Pentagonal Pyramid**   **Hexagonal Pyramid**

A **prism** has two identical bases in parallel planes. Its other faces are parallelograms.

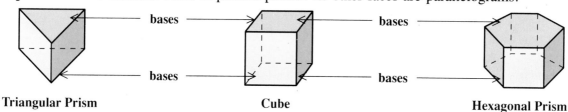

bases   bases

bases   bases

Triangular Prism   **Cube**   **Hexagonal Prism**

TRY IT OUT

Give the number of vertices (V), faces (F), and edges (E) of each
figure. State whether the figure is a pyramid, a prism, or neither.

1.   **2.**   **3.**   **4.**

Make a table showing the number of vertices (V), faces (F), and edges (E) of each figure. State whether the figure is a pyramid, a prism, or neither.

1.   **2.** 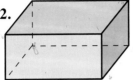 **3.**   **4.**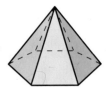

5.   **6.** 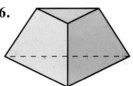 **7.**   **8.**

Draw the following figures.

9. a pyramid with a triangular base.

10. a prism with a triangular base.

11. a pyramid with a square base

12. a prism with a square base

MATH REASONING

13. Use your answers from exercises 1–8 to show that $V + F - E = 2$.

14. Is $V + F$ greater than, equal to, or less than E?

15. A dodecahedron has 12 faces. How many edges and vertices does it have?

PROBLEM SOLVING

16. Assume that $V + F - E = 2$ is true for this space figure. There are 7 vertices, 9 edges, and 3 faces visible. But 3 vertices and 6 edges are hidden. How many faces does the figure have? How many hidden faces does it have?

▶ **USING CRITICAL THINKING   Take a Look**

17. State which of these patterns will fold into a cube.

a. 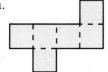 b.  c. 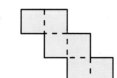 d.

More Practice, page 526, set C

Visualizing Cross Sections

LEARN ABOUT IT

The face of a solid or space figure is a polygonal region that lies in a plane. You can think of a **plane** as a flat surface like a desktop that continues in all directions.

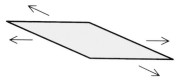

EXPLORE Imagine

You work for an engineering company that designs bridges and other large structures. One skill you will use is visualizing the **cross section** of a solid cut with a plane.

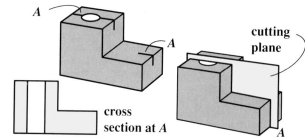

cross section at A

cutting plane

TALK ABOUT IT

1. The cross section at *A* shows that a hole has been drilled through the block. How can you tell?

2. Can you tell by looking at the original picture of the block that there is a hole in it? How?

3. Suppose the cross section looked like this. What would it tell you about the block?

The shape of a cross section depends on the position of the cutting plane. Here are cross sections for cutting planes at *B*, *C*, and *D*.

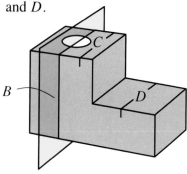

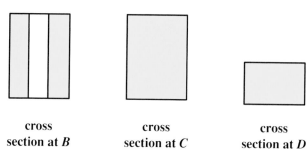

cross section at *B*   cross section at *C*   cross section at *D*

TRY IT OUT

1. Which is the cross section at *A*?

2. Which is the cross section at *B*?

3. Which is the cross section at *C*?

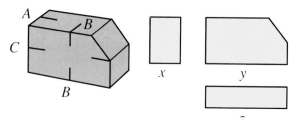

96

PRACTICE

1. Which is the cross section at *A*?

2. Which is the cross section at *B*?

3. Which is the cross section at *C*?

4. Which is the cross section at *A*?

5. Which is the cross section at *B*?

6. Which is the cross section at *C*?

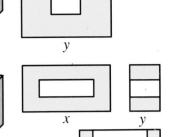

Draw a picture of each cross section.

7.

Triangular Prism

8.

Cube

9.

Triangular Pyramid

10.

Cube

APPLY

MATH REASONING True or false. If false, explain with a diagram.

11. Only a cube has a square cross section.

12. All cross sections of a triangular prism are triangles.

PROBLEM SOLVING

13. **Math and Science Data Bank**
    Imagine removing the nut from the hexagonal bolt.
    Draw the cross sections of the nut:
    a. when cut by a horizontal plane.
    b. when cut by a vertical plane.

    DATA BANK

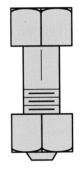

MIXED REVIEW

Name the property used.

14. $18 \times 10 = 10 \times 18$

15. $3 + (2 + 8) = (3 + 2) + 8$

Evaluate each algebraic expression for $a = 10$, $b = 2$, $c = 6$.

16. $a \times (b + c)$

17. $(a \times b) + (a \times c)$

18. $a \times (c + b)$

Find the answers to the nearest tenth.

19. $71 - 1.25$

20. $14 + (25 - 8)$

21. $100 + 2.4 \times 5$

22. 2.8×0.06

More Practice, page 526, set D

Drawing Plane Figures

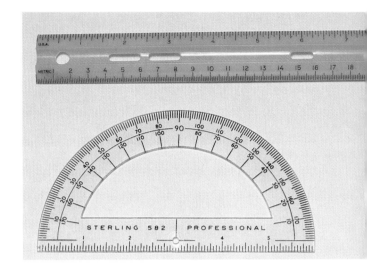

LEARN ABOUT IT

EXPLORE Think About the Process

Use a centimeter ruler and a protractor.

- Draw and label a segment $\overline{AB}$ 3 cm long.
- Draw and label ray $\overrightarrow{CD}$.
- Draw and label two rays with the same endpoint E to form a 40° angle.
- Draw $\overline{FG}$ 6 cm long. Draw a 45° angle at F and a 60° angle at G to form a triangle.

TALK ABOUT IT

1. How many endpoints does a segment have? a ray?

2. How do the drawings of $\overline{AB}$ and $\overrightarrow{CD}$ differ?

3. How can you use the points on the rays that form the 40° angle to name it?

Angles are classified according to their measures.

Acute angle	Right angle	Obtuse angle	Straight angle
$m\angle ABC < 90°$	$m\angle DEF = 90°$	$m\angle GHI > 90°$	$m\angle D = 180°$

Two angles are complementary if their measures have a sum of 90°.

$\angle A$ and $\angle B$ are complementary

Two angles are supplementary if their measures have a sum of 180°.

$\angle C$ and $\angle D$ are supplementary

TRY IT OUT

Draw and label each geometric figure.

1. 40° angle ABC
2. 120° angle POQ
3. 70° angle XYZ
4. a right angle RST
5. a triangle with an obtuse angle
6. a quadrilateral with a right angle and an obtuse angle

Give the measure of each angle. State if the angle is **right, acute, obtuse,** or **straight.**

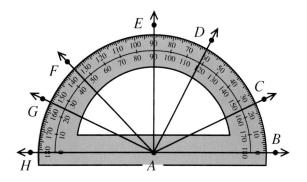

1. ∠BAC
2. ∠BAD
3. ∠BAE
4. ∠BAF
5. ∠BAG
6. ∠BAH
7. ∠EAF
8. ∠GAH

9. Draw a 50° angle.   10. Draw a 120° angle.   11. Draw a 25° angle.

Give the measure of each angle's complementary angle.

12. 40°   13. 12°   14. 67°   15. 86°

Give the measure of each angle's supplementary angle.

16. 50°   17. 107°   18. 135°   19. 30°

MATH REASONING

20. Draw a triangle with a right angle.

21. Draw a triangle whose angles include a 30° and a 50° angle.

22. Draw a quadrilateral whose angles include two right angles.

23. Draw a quadrilateral whose angles include an 80° and a 110° angle.

PROBLEM SOLVING

Use a protractor and a straightedge to draw what each figure might look like.

24. Fran's garden is the shape of a right triangle. One of the angles is 35°.

25. Geoff's patio is a quadrilateral with no right angles. Two of the angles are acute and two are obtuse.

MENTAL MATH

Find the measure of the complementary angle.

26. 35°   27. 48°   28. 22°

Find the measure of the supplementary angle.

29. 70°   30. 110°   31. 50°

> To find the complement of 25°, first find 100 − 25 and get 75°. Since 100 is more than 90, subtract 10 and get 65°.

More Practice, page 526, set E

Using Critical Thinking

Tom's class made these bulletin boards to show how triangles and quadrilaterals can be classified by sides and angles.

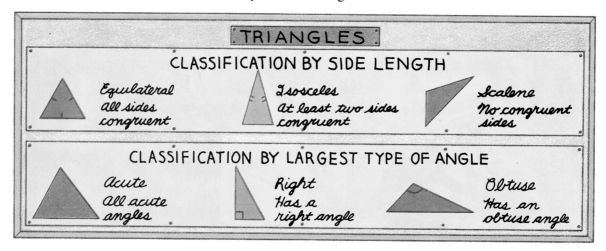

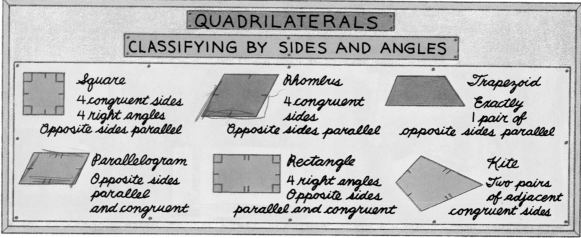

"The bulletin boards are nice," said Tom's teacher, "but they raise a lot of questions." "Maybe diagrams like these can help us answer them!"

He drew what Tom thought were strange looking loops on the chalkboard. Tom wondered how the diagrams could help.

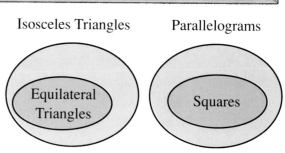

Isosceles Triangles   Parallelograms

Equilateral Triangles

Squares

1. Mr. MacLean's diagrams show that equilateral triangles are also isosceles triangles and that squares are also parallelograms. Do you agree? Explain.

2. Are all isosceles triangles also equilateral triangles? Are all parallelograms also squares?

3. Is every square a rectangle? Explain. How would you draw a diagram to show that every square is a rectangle?

4. Look at the bulletin boards and create a diagram that tells something about the figures described.

TRY IT OUT

Write a statement for each diagram. Tell whether the statement is true or false. Explain why.

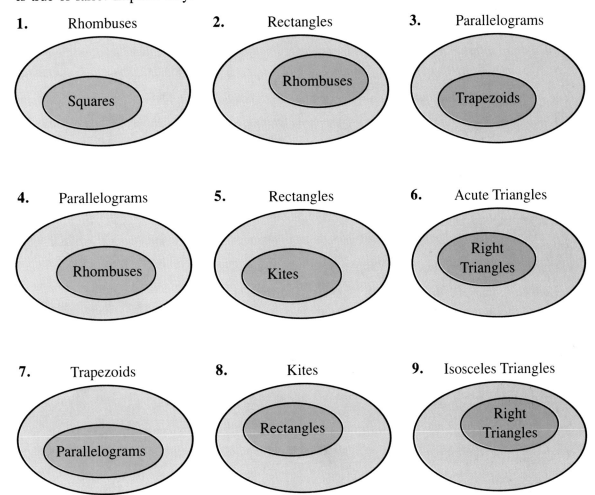

1. Rhombuses — Squares

2. Rectangles — Rhombuses

3. Parallelograms — Trapezoids

4. Parallelograms — Rhombuses

5. Rectangles — Kites

6. Acute Triangles — Right Triangles

7. Trapezoids — Parallelograms

8. Kites — Rectangles

9. Isosceles Triangles — Right Triangles

101

Angle Sum Relationships

EXPLORE **Discover a Relationship** Work in groups.

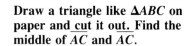

Draw a triangle like △ABC on paper and cut it out. Find the middle of $\overline{AC}$ and $\overline{AC}$.

Fold the triangular region at the middle points so that vertex A just touches $\overline{BC}$.

Fold B and C over as shown.

TALK ABOUT IT

1. Do angles A, B, and C fit together along the bottom edge of the paper? What is the sum of the measures of $\angle A$, $\angle B$, and $\angle C$?

2. Fold a right triangle as shown in the diagram. What is the sum of the measures of the acute angles of a right triangle?

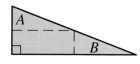

The sum of the measures of the angles of any triangle is 180°.

> **Example** $m\angle A = 50°$ and $m\angle B = 60°$. What is $m\angle C$?
> $m\angle A + m\angle B = 50° + 60° = 110°$.
> $m\angle C = 180° - 110° = 70°$.

The acute angles of a right triangle are complementary.

> **Example** $m\angle D = 58°$
> $m\angle E = 90° - 58° = 32°$.

The sum of the measures of the angles of a quadrilateral is 360°.

To see this, tear off the vertices of a paper quadrilateral. Arrange them around one vertex as shown.

$$m\angle A + m\angle B + m\angle C + m\angle D \doteq 360°.$$

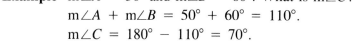

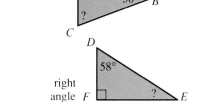

TRY IT OUT

Find the measure of $\angle A$ in each figure.

1.
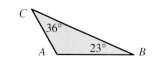

2.
3.
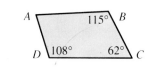

102

PRACTICE

Find the missing measure in each triangle.

1.

2.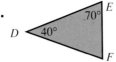

3.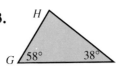

4.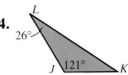

Find the missing measure in each quadrilateral.

5.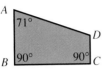

6.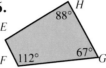

7.

APPLY

MATH REASONING

8. The measures of two angles of a triangle are 23° and 88°. Find the measure of the third angle.

9. The measures of three angles of a quadrilateral are 88°, 112°, and 47°. Find the measure of the fourth angle.

10. One angle of a triangle has a measure of 48°. The other two angles have equal measures. Find the measure of the other two angles.

11. The measures of two angles of a triangle are 37° and 36°. Estimate the measure of the third angle. Is the triangle acute or obtuse?

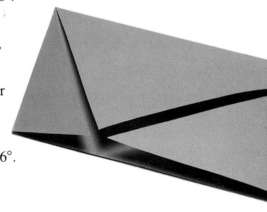

PROBLEM SOLVING

12. **Develop a Plan** The corners A, B, and C of a property have been located by a surveyor. A string stretched from A to E forms a 90° angle with the street. Which of these plans do you recommend to locate point D? Why?
   a. Stand at C facing B and turn 72° to the right and measure about 150 ft.
   b. Stretch a string to form a 72° angle at C. Extend the string until it crosses the string AE.

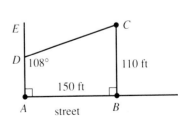

USING CRITICAL THINKING Support Your Conclusion

13. Can a triangle have two obtuse angles? Explain your answer.

14. How many obtuse angles can a quadrilateral have? Explain.

Exploring Algebra
Understanding Equations

A. $3.1 \times 2.4 = 10.7 - 3.26$

B. $(6 + 14) \times 7 = 6 + (14 \times 7)$

C. $78 \times 37 = (78 \times 7) + (78 \times 30)$

D. $587 \times 0 \times 963 = 2874 + 5 - 2879$

EXPLORE **Examine the Equations**

Work in groups. Decide which of the statements on the chalkboard are true. Use any calculation method.

TALK ABOUT IT

1. Which of the statements can you decide about without actually doing the computation? Why?

2. What affect do parentheses have in a problem?

3. Which symbol, $>$ or $<$, should replace $=$ to make **B** a true statement?

An **equation** is a mathematical sentence that uses the equality sign ($=$) to state that two expressions represent the same value.

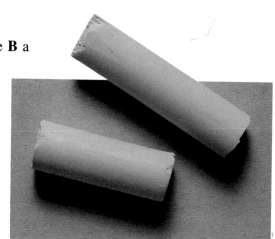

$14.8 + 7.3 = 22.1$	**is** an equation.
$3 + 5 = 2 \times 4$	**is** an equation.
$5.3 + 17 + 84.3$	**is not** an equation.
$3 < 17$	**is not** an equation.

TRY IT OUT

Decide if each example is an equation. Write yes or no.

1. $3.4 + 6.8 = 5 + 5.2$ 2. $14 = 4 \times 3.5$ 3. $6 + 4.3 > 6.3 + 4$

Make a true equation by supplying the missing number.

4. $3 \times 5.1 = 20.4 - x$ 5. $a + 3.2 = 17.4 - 3$ 6. $14.8 - 7.2 = 2 \times x$

7. $4.8 + 17.9 = 25 - n$ 8. $88 \div 4 = b \times 2$ 9. $39 - 21.9 + y = 30$

Use Mental Math. Use $<$, $>$, or $=$ to make the statement true.

10. 199×4 ▥ $799 + 1$ 11. $51 + 49$ ▥ $200 \div 2$ 12. 0.5×1000 ▥ $498 + 3$

13. Make up 2 statements like those in problems 10 through 12, one that uses $=$ and one that uses $<$ or $>$.
    Ask the others in your group which statements are equations.

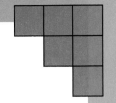

A hole is drilled through this wooden block as shown.

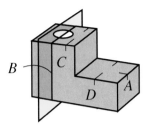   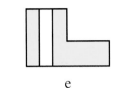

a   b   c   d   e

1. Which is the cross section at A?

2. Which is the cross section at B?

3. Which is the cross section at C?

Draw and label a large triangle ABC so that $\angle B$ is an obtuse angle.

4. Draw $\angle E$ so that it is supplementary to $\angle B$.

Find the measure of the missing angle.

5.

6.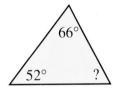

7.

In quadrilateral $WXYZ$, $m\angle W = 47°$, $m\angle X = 108°$ and $m\angle Y = 90°$.

8. What is $m\angle Z$?

9. Which of the angles are right angles? Obtuse angles?

10. What is the measure of an angle complementary to $\angle W$?

11. What is the measure of an angle supplementary to $\angle W$?

12. Use the words parallelogram, square, rhombus, and rectangle to make as many true statements as you can: Every ___?___ is a ___?___ .

PROBLEM SOLVING

A wedge of cheese and a piece of cake are sliced into parts A, B, C, and D as shown.

13. Draw the cross sections.

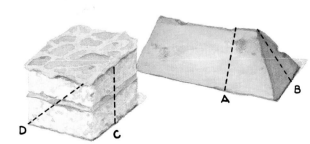

Problem Solving
Using the Strategies

| UNDERSTAND |
| ANALYZE DATA |
| PLAN |
| ESTIMATE |
| SOLVE |
| EXAMINE |

LEARN ABOUT IT

This problem can be solved in more than one way. Andrea first tried **Guess and Check.** Then she solved the problem again by using the strategy **Make an Organized List.**

> This year the county Science Fair is featuring a contest. Teams of students compete by answering questions about science. Each question is worth either 3 points or 5 points. Bert's team scored 42 points with 12 answers. How many 5-point questions did the team answer?

Andrea's first solution:

> Try 2 5-pt and 10 3-pt
> 10 + 30 = 40   not enough!
> Try 3 5 pt and 9 3-pt
> 15 + 27 = 42   Correct!

Andrea's second solution:

Number of 5-pt	Number of 3-pt	Total Points
0	12	36
1	11	38
2	10	40
3	9	42
4	8	44

Bert's team answered three 5-point questions.

TRY IT OUT

Solve. Use Guess and Check or Make an Organized List.

1. Experiments at the Science Fair are set up for groups of 2 or 4 students. At the fair a class of 32 students was divided into 9 groups. How many groups of each size were there?

2. Joel had some dimes and quarters in his pocket. He used 12 coins to buy a poster of the solar system for $1.80. How many coins of each kind did he use?

Solve. Use any problem solving strategy.

Some Strategies	
Act Out	Solve a Simpler Problem
Use Objects	Make an Organized List
Choose an Operation	Work Backward
Draw a Picture	Look for a Pattern
Guess and Check	Use Logical Reasoning
Make a Table	Write an Equation

1. Five teams competed in the science contest. The Wizards scored more points than the Newtons. The Mad Scientists beat the Superstars, but were 2 points behind the Newtons. The Einsteins won first place. In what order did the teams finish?

2. Forty-seven students from Deer Park Junior High are going to the Science Fair. Thirty-two students will ride in a bus. The rest will go on in cars. Each car can take 5 students. How many cars are needed?

3. The Science Fair lasted 3 days. Use the graph below to find how many students attended the fair.

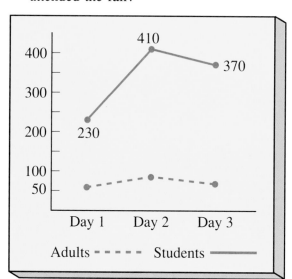

4. Admission to the Science Fair is $3.00 for students and $4.00 for adults. Mr. Simmons bought 15 tickets for $49. How many adult tickets did he buy?

5. Franklin has $0.63 in change. He has fewer than 10 coins. What coins could he have?

6. A small park is in the shape of a triangle. One side is 26 ft long. Two of the angles measure 70 each. What is the measure of the third angle?

7. One angle of a triangle is twice as large as another. The third angle measures 4° more than the smallest angle. Find the measure of each angle.

8. The Golden Gate Bridge is suspended from 2 cables that are $36\frac{3}{8}$ inches in diameter. Each cable contains 27,572 wires that have been bunched into 61 strands. How many wires are in each strand?

Parallel and Perpendicular Lines

LEARN ABOUT IT

Parallel and perpendicular lines lead to angle relationships which engineers and others who use applied mathematics often use in their work.

EXPLORE Discover a Relationship

- Draw 2 lines, 1 on either side of a ruler.
- Draw a line that intersects both of these lines.
- Measure $\angle 1$ through $\angle 8$ using a protractor. Record the measures in a table.

TALK ABOUT IT

1. How does m$\angle 2$ compare to m$\angle 6$?

2. How does m$\angle 4$ compare to m$\angle 8$?

3. How does m$\angle 1$ compare to m$\angle 2$? to m$\angle 3$?

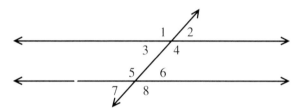

Two lines that intersect to form four right angles are called **perpendicular** lines.

Two lines in the same plane that do not intersect are **parallel** lines.

Lines a and b are perpendicular.
We write: $a \perp b$

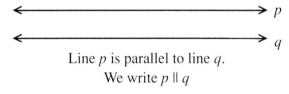

Line p is parallel to line q.
We write $p \parallel q$

A line that intersects two other lines is called a **transversal.** The angles formed by parallel lines and a transversal are related in the following ways.

$$m\angle 1 = m\angle 4 = m\angle 5 = m\angle 8$$
$$m\angle 2 = m\angle 3 = m\angle 6 = m\angle 7$$
$$m\angle 1 + m\angle 2 = 180°$$

TRY IT OUT

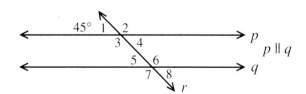

$p \parallel q$

1. Which angles measure 45°?

2. What is the measure of $\angle 2$? of $\angle 7$?

Lines p and q are parallel lines.

1. Name two right angles.

2. Name a pair of perpendicular lines.

3. Name a transversal.

4. Which angles measure 130°?

5. What is the measure of ∠9? of ∠7?

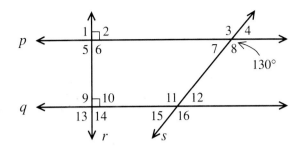

Lines p and q are parallel, and r and s are parallel.

6. Find m∠1.　　　7. Find m∠2.

8. Find m∠3.　　　9. Find m∠4.

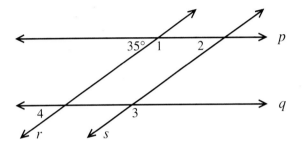

MATH REASONING

10. Fold paper to form lines a, b, and c as shown. Which of these generalizations are always true? Use paperfolding to defend your decision.
    a. A line perpendicular to one of two parallel lines is perpendicular to the other line.
    b. Two lines that intersect to form one right angle are perpendicular lines.
    c. Two lines perpendicular to the same line are parallel to each other.

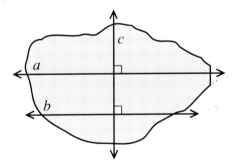

PROBLEM SOLVING

11. An engineer is designing a section of bridge. The measure of $D = 38°$ and $AB \parallel CD$. What is m∠2?

12. **Math and Science Data Bank** Choose one bridge-truss diagram. Copy the diagram and locate the truss's parallel lines and its transversals.

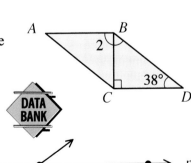

DATA BANK

▶ **EXPLORING ALGEBRA**

13. Lines p and q are parallel. Find m∠a in terms of x.

14. Find m∠b in terms of x.

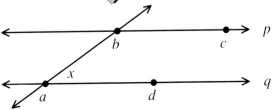

More Practice, page 527, set B

Constructing Parallel and Perpendicular Lines

EXPLORE **Think About the Process**

A Construct a line perpendicular to a line through a point on the line.

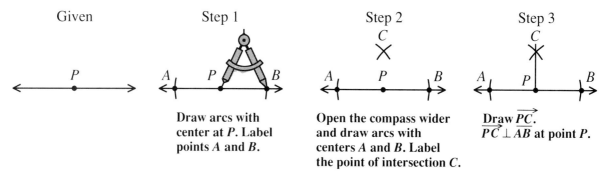

Given	Step 1	Step 2	Step 3

Draw arcs with center at *P*. Label points *A* and *B*.

Open the compass wider and draw arcs with centers *A* and *B*. Label the point of intersection *C*.

Draw $\overrightarrow{PC}$. $\overrightarrow{PC} \perp \overleftrightarrow{AB}$ at point *P*.

B Construct a line parallel to a given line.

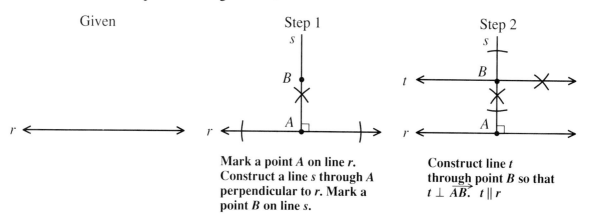

Mark a point *A* on line *r*. Construct a line *s* through *A* perpendicular to *r*. Mark a point *B* on line *s*.

Construct line *t* through point *B* so that $t \perp \overrightarrow{AB}$. $t \parallel r$

TALK ABOUT IT

1. Explain why the steps in **A** give a line perpendicular to the given line.

2. Explain why the steps in **B** give a line parallel to the given line.

TRY IT OUT

1. Draw a line *t* and mark a point *R* on the line. Construct a line *m* through *R* perpendicular to *t*.

2. Draw any line *m*. Construct a line *n* parallel to *m*.

Use a compass and straightedge to complete these exercises.

1. Draw a line *p* and mark a point *S* on the line. Construct a line *q* through *S* perpendicular to *t*.

2. Draw a line *q* and construct a line parallel to *q*.

3. Draw any line *t*. Construct two lines each parallel to *t* and on opposite sides of *t*.

4. Construct a rectangle.

5. Construct a trapezoid that has two obtuse angles.

MATH REASONING

6. Draw $\overline{AB}$. Construct two lines, each perpendicular to $\overline{AB}$, one through *A* and the other through *B*. How are the two constructed lines related?

PROBLEM SOLVING

7. Trace this drawing of the foundation of a house. Suppose the owner wants to build a rectangular screened porch with corners at *A* and *B*. Use a compass and a straightedge to construct the location of the corner *P* of the porch.

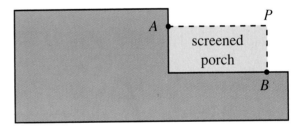

8. A goat is tied to the corner of a building at *A* and can reach as far as point *D* on his chain. Trace the figure and use a compass to construct the boundary of the region that the goat can reach.

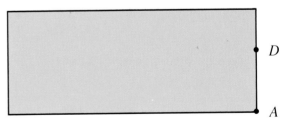

CALCULATOR

9. Sarah was doing an experiment in her science class. She recorded the length of a shadow from a 10-meter pole each half hour beginning at 7:00 A.M. and ending at 11:00 A.M. The data she recorded was: 37.32 m, 24.14 m, 17.32 m, 13.03 m, 10 m, 7.67 m, 5.77 m, 4.14 m, and 2.67 m. What was the mean of these shadow lengths?

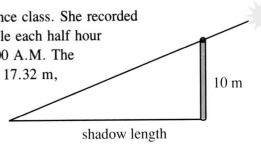

More Practice, page 527, set C

Constructing Angle and Segment Bisectors

EXPLORE Think About the Process

A geometric figure is **bisected** if it is divided into two parts of equal measure.

A Construct the perpendicular bisector of a segment.

Given:

Step 1 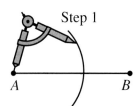 Step 2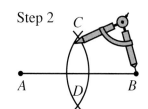

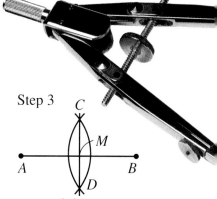

Step 3

Open the compass to more than one half the length of $\overline{AB}$ and draw an arc with center at A.

With the same opening, draw an arc with center B. Label the intersections of the arcs C and D.

Draw $\overleftrightarrow{CD}$. Label point M. M bisects $\overline{AB}$. $\overleftrightarrow{CD} \perp$ bis $\overline{AB}$.

B Construct the bisector of an angle.

Given:

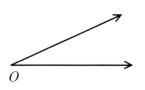

Step 1 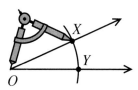 Step 2 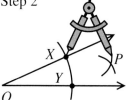 Step 3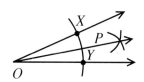

Draw any arc with center O. Label points X and Y.

Draw arcs from points X and Y. Label the intersection P.

Draw $\overrightarrow{OP}$. $\overrightarrow{OP}$ bisects $\angle XOY$.

TALK ABOUT IT

1. How do you know $\overline{CD}$ is a perpendicular to $\overline{AB}$?

2. Explain why $\overrightarrow{OP}$ bisects $\angle XOY$.

1. Draw $\overline{AB}$. Then construct the perpendicular bisector of $\overline{AB}$.

2. Draw $\angle C$. Then bisect $\angle C$ with a compass and ruler.

Use a compass and a straightedge to complete these exercises.

1. Draw an obtuse angle. Construct its angle bisector.

2. Construct a right angle. Bisect it to construct a 45° angle.

3. Copy $\overline{AB}$. Use a compass and a straightedge to divide $\overline{AB}$ into 4 equal segments.

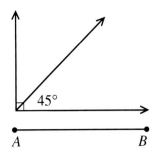

APPLY

MATH REASONING

4. Without using a protractor construct an angle that measures $22\frac{1}{2}°$.

PROBLEM SOLVING

5. A housing plot was in the shape of an acute triangle. The architects wanted the center of the house to be the same distance from each of the vertices of the triangle. One architect said, "Construct the perpendicular bisectors of each side to find the center." Another said, "Construct the angle bisectors of each angle." Who do you think is correct? Why?

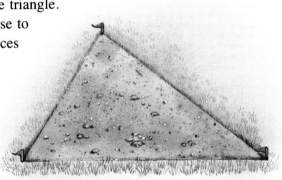

▶ ESTIMATION

6. Which one of these angles comes the closest to being bisected

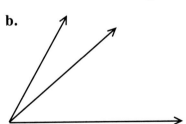
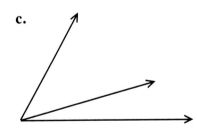

   a.   b.   c.

7. Which one of these angles is closest to being a 45° angle? Think of a right angle being bisected.

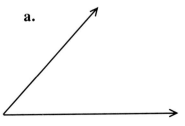

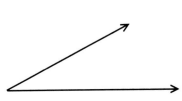

   a.   b.   c.

More Practice, page 528, set A   **113**

Constructing Triangles

EXPLORE **Think About the Process**

You can use a compass and straightedge to construct a triangle when you are given the lengths of the triangle's sides.

Use $\overline{AB}$, $\overline{BC}$, and $\overline{AC}$ to construct a triangle.

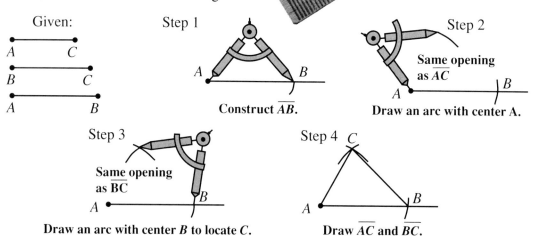

Given:

Step 1
Construct $\overline{AB}$.

Step 2
Same opening as $\overline{AC}$
Draw an arc with center A.

Step 3
Same opening as $\overline{BC}$
Draw an arc with center B to locate C.

Step 4
Draw $\overline{AC}$ and $\overline{BC}$.

TALK ABOUT IT

1. Why is it necessary to draw $\overline{AC}$ in Step 4 instead of in Step 2?

2. Try the construction again, this time beginning with $\overline{AC}$. How does this triangle compare with the first one you constructed?

TRY IT OUT

Use a compass and straightedge to do the constructions.

1. Given $\overline{PR}$, $\overline{PQ}$, and $\overline{QR}$, construct $\triangle PQR$.

2. Given $\overline{XZ}$, $\overline{XY}$, and $\overline{YZ}$, construct $\triangle XYZ$.

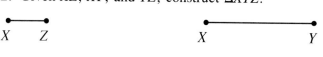

PRACTICE

Use a compass and straightedge to do the constructions.

1. Given $\overline{RT}$, $\overline{RS}$, and $\overline{ST}$, construct $\triangle RST$.

2. Given $\overline{DF}$, $\overline{DE}$, and $\overline{EF}$, construct $\triangle DEF$.

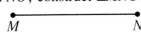

3. Given $\overline{MO}$, $\overline{MN}$, and $\overline{NO}$, construct $\triangle MNO$.

4. Construct a right triangle with one side $\overline{AB}$ and another $\overline{AC}$.

5. Construct an equilateral triangle with sides x.

6. Construct an isosceles triangle with two sides of the length of $\overline{AB}$.

MATH REASONING

7. Can you construct a triangle with sides $\overline{AB}$, $\overline{AC}$, and $\overline{BC}$? Explain.

PROBLEM SOLVING

8. The 30-ft long Francisquito Creek Bridge is built of a series of equilateral triangles with sides 2.5 ft long. How many triangles are on one side of the bridge?

MIXED REVIEW

Solve using mental math.

9. 2000 − 4   **10.** 175 + 82 + 25   **11.** 5 × 32   **12.** 8 × 230

Write each expression using exponential notation.

13. 4 × 4 × 4 × 4   **14.** $s \cdot s \cdot s$ **15.** 10 × 10 × 10 × 10

Write each number using scientific notation.

16. 189477   **17.** 8765542765   **18.** 567

Problem Solving
Data from a Chart

UNDERSTAND
ANALYZE DATA
PLAN
ESTIMATE
SOLVE
EXAMINE

To solve some problems you need data from a table, a graph, or some other source outside the problem. To solve this problem, you need data from a mileage chart.

Paula's family went to Mexico for a vacation. They drove from Mexico City to Guadalajara and then to Acapulco. How much farther was the drive from Guadalajara to Acapulco than the drive from Mexico City to Guadalajara?

Mileage Between Principal Cities	Acapulco	Ciudad Juarez	Guadalajara	Leon	Mazatlan	Merida	Mexico City	Monterrey	Nogales	Nuevo Laredo	Tampico	Tijuana	Veracruz
Ciudad Juarez	1379	●	943	913	871	2085	1130	743	385	721	1120	750	1390
Guadalajara	611	943	●	144	321	1317	362	472	1062	615	469	1438	622
Merida	1204	2085	1317	1221	1638	●	955	1371	2379	1514	1012	2255	695
Mexico City	249	1130	362	266	683	955	●	591	1424	734	326	1800	254
Monterrey	840	743	472	442	582	1371	591	●	1323	143	359	1699	676
Tijuana	2049	750	1438	1582	1117	2755	1800	1699	510	1842	1860	●	2060

I'll find Mexico City on the left and then look across that row until I find the column with Guadalajara at the top.

Then, I'll do the same thing for Guadalajara and Acapulco.

Now I'll subtract to find the difference.

362

611

611 − 362 = 249

The drive from Guadalajara to Acapulco was 249 miles farther than the drive from Mexico City to Guadalajara.

TRY IT OUT

Solve. Use the data from the mileage chart when necessary.

1. Maria drove from Tijuana to Nogales and from Nogales to Ciudad Juarez. How many miles did she drive?

2. Carl drove from Monterrey to Merida and from Veracruz to Guadalajara. How much shorter than the first trip was his second trip?

116

Solve. Use any problem solving strategy.

1. Rachell is driving from Tijuana to Acapulco. She drove 387 miles the first day. How many miles does she have left to drive?

2. Last year Lee drove between Tampico and Mexico City six times. How many miles did he drive?

3. Jay's family drove a total of 46 hours on their trip to Mexico. They drove 8 hours fewer the second week than the first week. How many hours did they drive each week?

4. Eight friends went out to dinner. Some of them ordered the enchilada special. The others ordered shrimp fajitas. The bill was $66.00. How many people ordered each dinner?

Menu

Specials | **Fajitas**
Tacos $6.50 | Chicken $7.95
Enchiladas $7.00 | Beef $8.25
Combination | Shrimp $9.00
Plate $7.25

5. Juanita bought a blue skirt for $12.95, a white blouse for $7.50, and a pair of sandals for $9.00. She paid for her purchases out of her first paycheck which was for $63.75. How much did Juanita spend?

6. Tara has been working at a restaurant for six weeks. She earns $3.75 per hour and works 18 hours per week. How much does she earn each week?

7. Melanie lives in Monterrey. Last month she drove 1802 miles. She made one round trip to Guadalajara. The rest of her trips were to Nuevo Laredo. How many trips did she make between Monterrey and Nuevo Laredo?

8. **Understanding the Operations** Name the operations you would use to solve this problem. Replace the variables with numbers that make sense and solve the problem.

   Reiko wants to buy a basket for each of her friends. She has already purchased x baskets, but she still has y baskets to buy. For how many friends does Reiko want to buy baskets?

Data Collection and Analysis
Group Decision Making

UNDERSTAND
ANALYZE DATA
PLAN
ESTIMATE
SOLVE
EXAMINE

Doing a Questionnaire

Group Skill:
Explain and Summarize

Work in groups. Adults and teenagers are sometimes believed to have different opinions about appropriate rules and guidelines for teens. Is it possible that they agree more than most people think? Develop a group **questionnaire** (a written set of questions) to find out what adults and teenagers think. People are often more open when they answer questionnaires because a questionnaire offers privacy.

Collecting Data

1. Use the question format given below for your questionnaire. The questions ask students to rate their answers.

2. Test your group's questionnaire on a few classmates. Revise questions that are confusing or difficult to answer.

3. Give copies of the questionnaire to 15 adults and 15 teenagers. Keep the identities of the persons who fill out the questionnaires confidential.

Check one: _____ adult _____ teenager

Rate how much freedom teenager should have to make their own decisions about each of the following

	no freedom				unlimited freedom
1. When to begin dating	1	2	3	4	5
2. What friends to see	1	2	3	4	5
3. What clothes to wear	1	2	3	4	5
4. _____	1	2	3	4	5
5. _____	1	2	3	4	5

4. Separate adults' questionnaires from teenagers' questionnaires. Organize the data from each question into a table. You may want to combine the data from your group with that of another group.

5. Use the data you collected from one of the questions to make a double bar graph comparing adult and teen responses.

6. Compare the average ratings given by adults to the average ratings given by teenagers for each question. What do you notice?

7. Do you think adults and teenagers mostly agree or disagree? What evidence do you have to support your opinion?

WRAP UP

Two Out of Three

In each group decide which figure does not belong with the other two. Be ready to explain your reasoning. (Some questions may have more than one correct answer.)

1. tetrahedron   cube   rectangular prism

2. trapezoid   pentagon   rhombus

3. kite   parallelogram   square

4. square pyramid   cube   triangular prism

5. ray   segment   line

6. trapezoid   kite   parallelogram

Sometimes, Always, Never

Which word should go in the blank, *sometimes*, *always*, or *never*? Explain your choice.

7. The acute angles of a right triangle are __?__ supplementary angles.

8. The cross section of a cylinder is __?__ a circle.

9. You can __?__ construct a triangle if you know the lengths of its 3 sides.

10. Complementary angles are __?__ equal.

Project

Be creative! Design a sculpture using different geometric solids and plane figures. You can make the solids yourself or use containers in various shapes. Cut the plane figures out of cardboard. Try to combine shapes to create new ones.

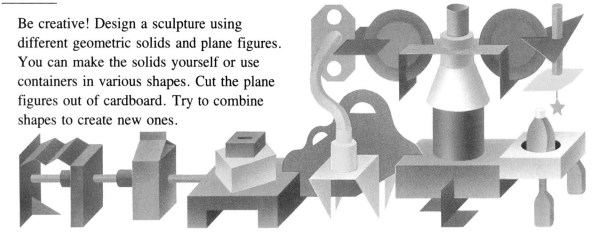

CHAPTER REVIEW/TEST

Part 1 Understanding

Use the figure to complete this chart.

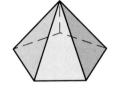

		Number
1.	faces	?
2.	edges	?
3.	vertices	?

5. Draw a cross section of the pyramid above.

4. An isosceles triangle has

    A no congruent sides

    B a 90° angle

    C two congruent sides

    D all of the above

Part 2 Skills

6. Find the measure of $\angle BCA$.

7. $\triangle ABC$ is

    A isoscles triangle   **C** an acute triangle

    B a right triangle   **D** an obtuse triangle

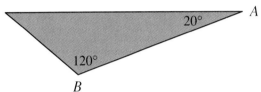

Solve each equation for n.

8. $15 + 27 = n \times 6$ **9.** $45 - 38.3 + n = 30$ **10.** $3 \times n = 20 - 6.2$

11. What is the measure of $\angle 3$?

12. What is the measure of $\angle 14$?

13. Name a transversal.

14. Which angles measure 125°?

15. Draw a 70° angle. Construct its angle bisector.

16. Construct a right triangle with sides $\overline{AB}$ and $\overline{AC}$.

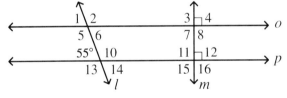

Part 3 Applications

17. A solid figure has 5 faces and 5 vertices. How many edges must it have? Remember $V + F - E = 2$.

18. How many 4-digit numbers can you make from the digits 3, 5, 2, and 4. Use each digit only once.

19. Together Naomi and Paul spent $26.80. Naomi spent $2.50 more than Paul. How much did Paul spend?

20. Challenge A quadrilateral has 2 65°-angles and 2 angles supplementary to them. What shapes could the figure be?

ENRICHMENT
Views of Space Figures

Architects, builders, machine operators, and others often work from blueprints, drawings, or plans that show different views of space figures.

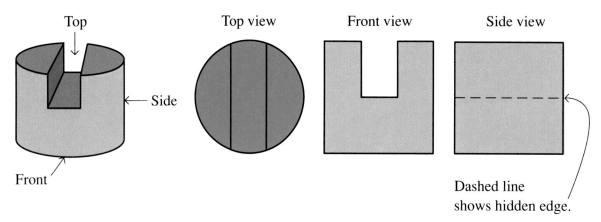

Top

Side

Front

Top view

Front view

Side view

Dashed line shows hidden edge.

Draw front, top, and side views of each space figure.

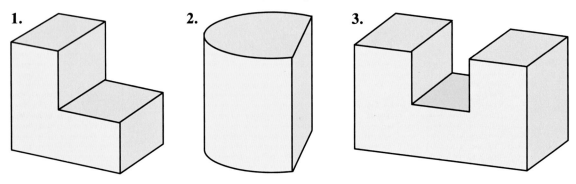

1.

2.

3.

Make a paper model or draw a picture of a space figure with these views.

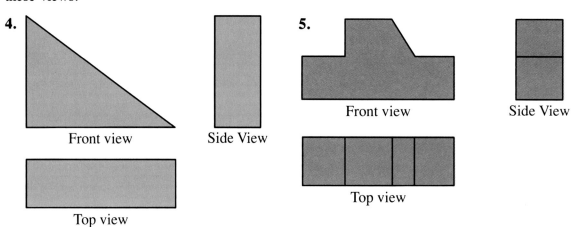

4.

Front view

Side View

Top view

5.

Front view

Side View

Top view

CUMULATIVE REVIEW

1. Which digit in 35,246,789 is in the ten thousands place?

   A 3   B 4

   C 2   D 6

2. Which problem helps you solve
   $48 \div 3 =$ ____?

   A $24 + 24 = 48$ B $48 \div 6 = 8$

   C $3 \times 16 = 48$ D $8 \times 6 = 48$

3. Evaluate the algebraic expression
   $(k + 7) \times 9$ for $k = 5$.

   A 108   B 52

   C 68   D 21

4. What is the missing number?
   $0.967 \text{ kg} = \underline{} \text{ g}$

   A 9,670   B 967

   C 96.7   D 9.67

5. Estimate the sum.
   $2.37 + 6.58 + 9.94$

   A 1.5   B 14

   C 19   D 22

6. Which is correct?

   A $3.072 < 3.017$ B $3.072 > 3.72$

   C $3.072 = 3.07$ D $3.072 < 3.7$

7. Multiply 2.76×9.3.

   A 25.668   B 286.68

   C 28.668   C 256.68

8. Divide. $24\overline{)4.212}$

   A 0.1755   B 0.175

   C 0.176   D 0.1756

9. Which measurement is the most precise?

   A 5 dm   B 5 m

   C 5 mm   D 5 cm

10. What is the standard notation for 3.9×10^5?

    A 39,000   B 3,900,000

    C 390,000   D 0.00039

11. What is the greatest number in the stem and leaf table?

    A 91   B 98

    C 47   D 48

Stem	Leaf
1	0, 9, 2
2	6
3	5, 1, 4
4	7, 8, 7

12. What is the median of 2, 4, 5, 7, 9, 12, 13, and 14?

    A 7.5   B 8

    C 8.25   D 8.5

13. A 7-minute telephone call costs $0.54 for the first minute and $0.38 for each additional minute. What is the total cost of the call?

    A $2.82   B $0.92

    C $3.78   D $3.20

14. Mara caught three catfish and one trout. Two of the catfish were 34 cm long. The other was 55 cm long and the trout was 30 cm long. What was the average length of the catfish?

    A 51 cm   B 41 cm

    C 40 cm   D 62 cm

5

NUMBER THEORY AND FRACTIONS

MATH AND FINE ARTS

DATA BANK

Use the Fine Arts Data Bank on page 505 to answer the questions.

1 A musician can tell how long to play a note by the note's value. How long is a half note compared to a quarter note? compared to a sixteenth note?

2 How many sixteenth notes are needed to equal 1 dotted eighth note? How many thirty-second notes are needed to equal 1 dotted eighth note?

3 How does the frequency of C_1 (middle C) compare with the frequency of C_2 (the C an octave higher)? How does the frequency of C_2 compare with the frequency of C_3?

4 Using Critical Thinking Compare the frequencies of the Diatonic Scale with the corresponding notes on the keyboard. What pattern do you see? How does the frequency of a note affect its pitch?

Divisibility

EXPLORE **Solve to Understand**

At camp, Taryn was in charge of organizing a giant water balloon fight. She had to divide 387 campers into 11 or fewer equal teams. How many teams could there be?

TALK ABOUT IT

1. What data do you need to solve the problem?

2. What is the problem asking you to do?

If one number can be divided by another with a zero remainder, the first number is **divisible** by the second.

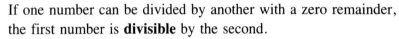

Factor	Test for Divisibility
3	Is the sum of the digits divisible by 3?
4	Is the number formed by the last two digits divisible by 4?
6	Is the number divisible by both 2 and 3?
8	Is the number formed by the last 3 digits divisible by 8?
9	Is the sum of the digits divisible by 9?

Example Is 387 divisible by . . .?

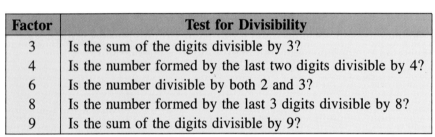

3	**yes**	3 + 8 + 7 = 18, and 18 is divisible by 3.
4	no	87 is not divisible by 4.
6	no	387 is not divisible by 2.
8	no	387 is not divisible by 8.
9	**yes**	3 + 8 + 7 = 18, and 18 is divisible by 9.

Taryn can divide the campers into 3 or 9 equal teams.

Decide if the first number is divisible by the second. Explain.

1. 912 by 6   **2.** 88,948 by 4   **3.** 8,577 by 9   **4.** 9,995 by 4

5. 5,960 by 8   **6.** 4,158 by 9   **7.** 1,264 by 3   **8.** 168 by 8

Decide if each number is divisible by 3.

1. 723   **2.** 5,918   **3.** 4,608   **4.** 89,571

5. 6,085   **6.** 111,112   **7.** 39,603   **8.** 14,987

Decide if each number is divisible by 4.

9. 1,752   **10.** 930   **11.** 27,004   **12.** 31,728

13. 441   **14.** 975,162   **15.** 179,340   **16.** 90,706

Decide if each number is divisible by 3, 4, 6, 8, 9, or none of these.

17. 4,095   **18.** 6,018   **19.** 30,400   **20.** 9,036

21. 17,084   **22.** 48,131   **23.** 929,205   **24.** 544,128

APPLY

MATH REASONING True or false? If false, give a counterexample.

25. Any number divisible by 9 is divisible by 3.

26. Any number divisible by 6 is divisible by 12.

27. Any number divisible by 2 and 4 is divisible by 8.

PROBLEM SOLVING

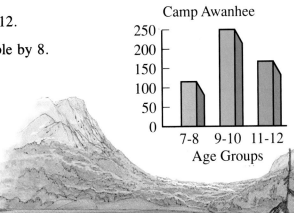

28. Tony, a counselor-in-training, was asked to divide 114 campers into groups of 6 for a canoeing trip. Without dividing he said it was impossible. Do you agree? Why?

29. The camp director said there were at least twice as many campers in the 9–10 age group as there were in the 7–8 and 11–12 age groups combined. Do you agree? Why?

▶ **USING CRITICAL THINKING**

30. Use the digits 4, 5 and 6 to make as many different three-digit numbers as you can. Use all three digits in each number. All of the numbers you created are divisible by what number?

More Practice, page 528, set B

Factors, Primes, and Composites

<u>EXPLORE</u> **Complete the Table**

Work in groups. Find how many factors each of the numbers 1 through 25 has.

TALK ABOUT IT

1. Which number has the most factors? The fewest factors?

2. Which numbers have exactly 2 factors?

3. What do you notice about the numbers with an odd number of factors?

A **prime** number is a number with **exactly** 2 factors.

A **composite** number is a number with **more** than 2 factors.

0 and 1 are neither prime nor composite. The number 1 has only one factor ($1 \times 1 = 1$). Every number is a factor of zero ($0 \times 5 = 0$).

Use division to find out if one number is a factor of another.

Number	How Many Factors
1	1
2	2
.	.
.	.
.	.
10	4
.	.
.	.
.	.
25	3

Example Find the factors of 18. Use divisibility rules to help you.

$1 \times 18 = 18$
$2 \times 9 \ = 18$
$3 \times 6 \ = 18$ 4 and 5 are not factors of 18.
$6 \times 3 \ = 18$ The factors start repeating here so you can stop.

The factors of 18 are 1, 2, 3, 6, 9 and 18.

TRY IT OUT

Decide if the first number is a factor of the second.

1. 18, 684 **2.** 16, 500 **3.** 23, 529 **4.** 54, 324

List all the factors of each number.

5. 10 **6.** 16 **7.** 33 **8.** 36

Write prime or composite for each number.

1. 29   **2.** 57   **3.** 108   **4.** 61

Is the first number a factor of the second?

5. 16, 432   **6.** 24, 830   **7.** 12, 8,732   **8.** 36, 5,688

9. 26, 4,981   **10.** 37, 3,774   **11.** 112, 1,232   **12.** 54, 6,480

List all the factors of each number.

13. 28   **14.** 51   **15.** 54   **16.** 20

APPLY

MATH REASONING

17. The number 6 and the number 28 are called perfect numbers.

Factors of 6: 1, 2, 3, 6 $1 + 2 + 3 = 6$

Factors of 28: 1, 2, 4, 7, 14, 28 $1 + 2 + 4 + 7 + 14 = 28$

Write a sentence that tells what a perfect number is.

PROBLEM SOLVING

18. Juan is laying out 117 yearbook photos. Can there be the same number of photos on each page? How many?

19. Judy has 126 yearbooks stacked in equal piles. Name all the ways the books could be stacked.

20. Understanding the Operations What operation is needed to solve this problem? Replace the variables with numbers that make sense and solve the problem.

Juanita delivered x yearbooks on Tuesday. By Friday she had delivered all y of the yearbooks she had sold. How many yearbooks did she deliver Wednesday through Friday?

▶ MENTAL MATH

The Russian mathematician Christian Goldbach predicted that every odd number greater than 7 can be expressed as the sum of 3 prime numbers. List the first 15 prime numbers. Use mental math to test Goldbach's theory on these numbers.

21. 43   **22.** 31   **23.** 27   **24.** 49

Prime Factorization

LEARN ABOUT IT

EXPLORE **Complete the Table**

Find the prime factors of the numbers 2 through 20.

TALK ABOUT IT

1. How can you express 20 as the product of different factors?

2. How can you express 20 as the product of only prime numbers?

3. Is there more than one way to write 20 as the product of prime numbers?

A composite number can be written as the product of prime numbers.

$3 \cdot 2 \cdot 2$ or $3 \cdot 2^2$ is the **prime factorization** of 12.

Example Give the prime factorization of 48. Use a factor tree to help.

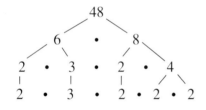

Find any two factors.

Find factors of those two factors.

Keep factoring until all the factors at the bottom of the tree are prime.

You can write the prime factorization of a number using exponents.

$48 = 2 \cdot 3 \cdot 2 \cdot 2 \cdot 2 = 2^4 \cdot 3$

Other Examples Give the prime factorization of each number.

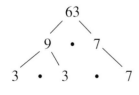

$63 = 3 \cdot 3 \cdot 7 = 3^2 \cdot 7$

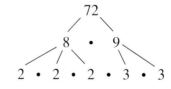

$72 = 2 \cdot 2 \cdot 2 \cdot 3 \cdot 3 = 2^3 \cdot 3^2$

TRY IT OUT

Make a factor tree. Give the prime factorization of each number.

1. 36　　　　　**2.** 45　　　　　**3.** 35　　　　　**4.** 18

Complete each factor tree. Give the prime factorization of each number.

1.
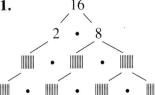

2.
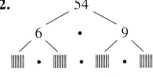

3.
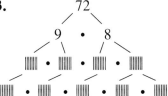

4.
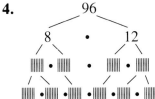

5.
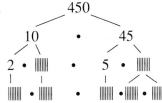

6.
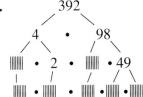

Make a factor tree for each number. Write the prime factorization of the number using exponents.

7. $968 = 2 \cdot 2 \cdot 2 \cdot 11 \cdot 11 = \underline{\;?\;}$

8. $1,125 = 3 \cdot 3 \cdot 5 \cdot 5 \cdot 5 = \underline{\;?\;}$

9. $432 = 2 \cdot 2 \cdot 2 \cdot 2 \cdot 3 \cdot 3 \cdot 3 = \underline{\;?\;}$

10. $980 = 2 \cdot 2 \cdot 5 \cdot 7 \cdot 7 = \underline{\;?\;}$

11. 125   **12.** 642   **13.** 2,008   **14.** 869

MATH REASONING Find the missing prime factor. You may want to use a calculator.

15. $4,116 = 2^2 \cdot 7^3 \cdot n$

16. $6,776 = 2^3 \cdot 11^2 \cdot n$

17. $396 = 2^2 \cdot 3^2 \cdot n$

18. $162 = 3^4 \cdot n$

19. $207,515 = 7^3 \cdot 11^2 \cdot n$

20. $300 = 2^2 \cdot 5^2 \cdot n$

PROBLEM SOLVING

21. A child made a pattern of cubes. There was 1 cube on the top, 3 cubes on the second row from the top, 5 cubes on the third row from the top, and so on for 10 rows. How many cubes were used all together?

▶ **EXPLORING ALGEBRA**

22. A quarter and dime balance with 3 dimes. How many dimes would it take to balance four quarters?

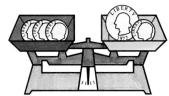

More Practice, page 528, set D

Greatest Common Factor

EXPLORE **Analyze the Situation**

The 7th graders are going to divide a 36 ft by 44 ft field into equal squares. The sides of the squares will be whole number lengths. Each square will be sold for $5. A goat will wander in the field for 30 minutes. The last square the goat eats from will be the winning square. What sizes could the squares be? What is the largest size the squares could be?

TALK ABOUT IT

1. What picture could you draw to help solve the problem?

2. How do you know that the squares cannot be 5 ft by 5 ft?

3. Can the field be divided into 6 ft by 6 ft squares? Explain.

The largest factor that two or more numbers have in common is called their **greatest common factor (GCF).** If the GCF of two numbers is 1, the numbers are **relatively prime.**

Here are two methods for finding the GCF of 36 and 44.

Method 1 List the Factors	**Method 2 Prime Factorization**
Factors of 36: 1, 2, 3, 4, 6, 9, 12, 18, 36 Factors of 44: 1, 2, 4, 11, 22, 44 Common factors: 1, 2, 4 GCF = 4	$36 = 2 \cdot 2 \cdot 3 \cdot 3$ $44 = 2 \cdot 2 \cdot 11$ $GCF = 2 \cdot 2 = 4$ The GCF is the product of all the prime factors 36 and 44 have in common.

Examples   Find the GCF of each pair of numbers.

A 4, 5

    Factors of 4: 4, 2, 1
    Factors of 5: 5, 1
    GCF is 1; 4 and 5 are relatively prime.

B 45, 90

    $45 = 3 \cdot 3 \cdot 5$
    $90 = 2 \cdot 3 \cdot 3 \cdot 5$
    $GCF = 3 \cdot 3 \cdot 5 = 45$

TRY IT OUT

Use two methods to find the GCF of each pair of numbers.

1. 4, 10   **2.** 22, 33   **3.** 24, 30   **4.** 45, 75

List the common factors and give the GCF.

1. 3, 18   **2.** 12, 24   **3.** 60, 45   **4.** 24, 56

Use the prime factorizations to find the GCF.

5. $9 = 3 \cdot 3$ **6.** $18 = 2 \cdot 3 \cdot 3$ **7.** $75 = 3 \cdot 5 \cdot 5$ **8.** $40 = 2 \cdot 2 \cdot 2 \cdot 5$
   $45 = 3 \cdot 3 \cdot 5$ $30 = 2 \cdot 3 \cdot 5$ $90 = 2 \cdot 3 \cdot 3 \cdot 5$ $100 = 2 \cdot 2 \cdot 5 \cdot 5$

Use prime factorization to find the GCF.

9. 42, 28   **10.** 63, 18   **11.** 96, 64   **12.** 50, 125

13. 110, 99   **14.** 48, 36   **15.** 70, 20   **16.** 63, 882

Find the GCF of each pair of numbers.

17. 18, 24   **18.** 12, 72   **19.** 80, 48   **20.** 34, 51

21. 15, 27   **22.** 32, 48   **23.** 24, 66   **24.** 16, 33

APPLY

MATH REASONING

25. m is between 50 and 60. The GCF of m and 21 is 7. What is m?

26. s is between 62 and 70. The GCF of s and 24 is 1. What is s?

PROBLEM SOLVING

27. Lopez School is holding a dance-a-thon. The students, 78 seventh graders and 72 eighth graders, will be divided into equal teams with students from only one grade on each team. How many students can be on each team?

28. At the school carwash, students made $51 during the first shift, but only $24 during the rainy second shift. What whole dollar amounts could the students have charged per car?

MIXED REVIEW

Write each number in scientific notation.

29. 234,000   **30.** 140.0178   **31.** 12.196   **32.** 23,000,000

Find the value of each expression.

33. $8 + 3.1 \times 10$ **34.** $(16 \div 0.1) + (12 \times 0.1)$ **35.** $3 \times 40 - 72 \div 9$

More Practice, page 529, set A

Least Common Multiple

EXPLORE **Solve to Understand**

Ralph picked two numbers, 6 and 8, out of a hat. Today every 6th customer will get a free sandwich and every 8th customer will get a free drink. Suppose 64 customers come into the store. Which ones will win both a free drink and a free sandwich?

TALK ABOUT IT

1. Which three customers were first to get free sandwiches? Free drinks?

2. Which customer was first to get both a free drink and a free sandwich?

To find the multiples of a number, multiply that number by 0, 1, 2, 3 and so on. The multiples of 12 are 0, 12, 24, 36, . . . The **least common multiple (LCM)** of two numbers is the smallest nonzero multiple which the numbers have in common.

Example Find the LCM of 12 and 18.

Method 1 List the nonzero multiples of each number until you reach a common multiple:

multiples of 12: 12, 24, 36, . . .
multiples of 18: 18, 36, . . .

The LCM of 12 and 18 is 36.

Method 2 List the prime factors of each number. Multiply the highest powers of each factor.

$12 = 2 \cdot 2 \cdot 3 = 2^2 \cdot 3$
$18 = 2 \cdot 3 \cdot 3 = 2 \cdot 3^2$

The LCM of 12 and 18 is $2^2 \cdot 3^2$ or 36.

TRY IT OUT

oth methods to find the LCM of each pair of numbers.

6 **2.** 10, 25 **3.** 6, 18 **4.** 8, 24

You may want to use a calculator. List multiples to find the
LCM of each pair of numbers.

1. 30, 12   **2.** 10, 14   **3.** 9, 24   **4.** 10, 6

5. 16, 12   **6.** 18, 30   **7.** 24, 18   **8.** 35, 28

Use prime factorizations to find the LCM of each pair of numbers.

9. $14 = 2 \cdot 7$ **10.** $12 = 2 \cdot 2 \cdot 3$ **11.** $18 = 2 \cdot 3 \cdot 3$ **12.** $14 = 2 \cdot 7$

    $35 = 5 \cdot 7$ $20 = 2 \cdot 2 \cdot 5$ $45 = 3 \cdot 3 \cdot 5$ $26 = 2 \cdot 13$

Find the LCM of each pair of numbers.

13. 9, 15   **14.** 21, 28   **15.** 8, 12   **16.** 16, 48

17. 20, 14   **18.** 15, 25   **19.** 100, 6   **20.** 32, 80

21. 54, 36   **22.** 40, 18   **23.** 17, 22   **24.** 24, 15

25. Find the LCM of 10 and 12.   **26.** Find the LCM of 6 and 21.

APPLY

MATH REASONING Find the LCM of each pair of numbers. Use
mental math. Write a sentence describing how you found the
LCM for the pairs of numbers in each group.

27. Group 1: 4, 8   6, 18   7, 28   9, 27   12, 60

28. Group 2: 6, 5   3, 2   9, 7   4, 5   4, 7

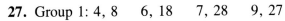

PROBLEM SOLVING

29. As a promotion, a T-shirt factory gave
every 7th and 8th student a discount
coupon. Every 20th student received a
free T-shirt. Which student was first to
get both?

30. The person to guess closest to the actual
wingspan of the largest known butterfly
won free admission to the zoo for a
year. Josh guessed 15 inches. The
wingspan is 11.02 inches. How far off
was Josh?

▶ **USING CRITICAL THINKING**   Discover a Relationship

31. Joan said that she could find the LCM of two numbers by
performing one operation if she knew the product of the
two numbers and the GCF. Try a few pairs of numbers,
such as 6 and 9, to discover what operation Joan used to
get the LCM.

More Practice, page 529, set B

Using Critical Thinking

Jill asked Robert to help her make a table of the first twenty-five prime numbers. As Robert wrote the list, with five numbers in each row, he noticed a pattern. "Look Jill, every row has a pair of numbers that are two apart!"

"I see," said Jill. "But I don't think the pattern will continue."

"I think it will," said Robert. "If we continue the table, it will probably follow this pattern forever."

First Twenty-Five Primes

2	3	5	7	11
13	17	19	23	29
31	37	41	43	

TALK ABOUT IT

1. Prime numbers that differ by 2 are called **twin primes.** Does each row of the table have a pair of twin primes?

2. Do you agree with Robert that the pattern probably continues forever? What could you do to test your idea?

3. Do you notice any other patterns in the table? Explain.

TRY IT OUT

First Fifty Prime Numbers

2	3	5	7	11	13	17	19	23	29
31	37	41	43	47	53	59	61	67	71
73	79	83	89	97	101	103	107	109	113
127	131	137	139	149	151	157	163	167	173
179	181	191	193	197	199	211	223	227	229

1. How many pairs of twin primes are in the first 25 prime numbers? How many do you predict are in the first 50?

2. Based on the twin primes in this table, what do you think the last digits of the numbers in a twin prime are most likely to be?

3. List all the pairs of twin primes by rows. How many are there?

4. Can you find 3 consecutive prime numbers that differ by 2 in the table?

List the numbers from the box that are divisible by each of the following.

726	52,167
94	1,404
5,280	23,400
93,512	61,335

1. by 3

2. by 4

3. by 6

4. by 8

5. What is the only even prime number?

Find the factors of the composite number in each list.

6. 23, 36, 59, 89

7. 77, 67, 47, 37

8. 0, 1, 100, 101

Make a factor tree for each number.

9. 48

10. 360

List the common factors and give the GCF.

11. 12, 30

12. 14, 98

13. 56, 13

Use prime factorization to find the GCF.

14. 21, 66

15. 72, 90

16. 48. 120

List common multiples to find the LCM.

17. 7, 8

18. 9, 12

19. 17, 34

Use prime factorization to find the LCM.

20. 8, 20

21. 12, 30

22. 36, 54

PROBLEM SOLVING

23. Chris is knitting a 42-inch scarf. If she knits 3 inches each day, will she finish in two weeks?

24. Ricardo has 36 photos for his scrapbook. List all the ways he can use fewer than 15 pages to put the same number of photos on each page.

25. Last week, Tom earned $24 babysitting. This week he earned $15. What whole dollar amounts could he have charged per hour?

Equivalent Fractions

EXPLORE **Analyze the Situation**

Work in groups. Have you ever seen a card section at a football game? Use a 10 by 10 grid to design a card section that says "GO." Each square of the grid represents one card. Use $\frac{1}{4}$ of the cards for the letter "G."

TALK ABOUT IT

1. Can you divide the grid into fourths in more than one way? How?

2. How many cards out of 100 make up $\frac{1}{4}$ of the cards?

Equivalent fractions are fractions that name the same amount. You can form an equivalent fraction by multiplying or dividing the numerator and denominator of a fraction by the same nonzero number.

$$\begin{array}{l} \text{Numerator} \rightarrow \\ \text{Denominator} \rightarrow \end{array} \frac{1 \times 25}{4 \times 25} = \frac{25}{100} \qquad \frac{1}{4} \text{ is equivalent to } \frac{25}{100}.$$

$$\begin{array}{l} \text{Numerator} \rightarrow \\ \text{Denominator} \rightarrow \end{array} \frac{25 \div 5}{30 \div 5} = \frac{5}{6} \qquad \frac{25}{30} \text{ is equivalent to } \frac{5}{6}.$$

To make a set of equivalent fractions, multiply or divide the numerator and denominator of a fraction by 2, 3, 4, and so on.

$$\frac{3 \times 2}{4 \times 2} = \frac{6}{8} \qquad \frac{3 \times 3}{4 \times 3} = \frac{9}{12} \qquad \frac{3 \times 4}{4 \times 4} = \frac{12}{16}$$

TRY IT OUT

Give the value for n.

1. $\frac{5 \times 3}{8 \times 3} = \frac{n}{24}$

2. $\frac{2 \times 4}{3 \times 4} = \frac{8}{n}$

3. $\frac{3 \times 10}{5 \times 10} = \frac{n}{50}$

Give the next 2 equivalent fractions.

4. $\frac{1}{2}, \frac{2}{4}, \text{---}, \text{---}$

5. $\frac{3}{4}, \frac{6}{8}, \text{---}, \text{---}$

6. $\frac{1}{3}, \frac{2}{6}, \text{---}, \text{---}$

Give the value for n.

1. $\dfrac{2 \times 4}{3 \times 4} = \dfrac{n}{12}$

2. $\dfrac{4}{7} = \dfrac{12}{n}$

3. $\dfrac{5}{6} = \dfrac{n}{30}$

4. $\dfrac{8}{12} = \dfrac{n}{6}$

5. $\dfrac{3}{5} = \dfrac{n}{35}$

6. $\dfrac{3}{4} = \dfrac{9}{n}$

7. $\dfrac{20}{36} = \dfrac{5}{n}$

8. $\dfrac{16}{20} = \dfrac{n}{5}$

9. $\dfrac{24}{56} = \dfrac{3}{n}$

10. $\dfrac{7}{15} = \dfrac{28}{n}$

11. $\dfrac{11}{12} = \dfrac{n}{72}$

12. $\dfrac{36}{54} = \dfrac{n}{9}$

Give the next three equivalent fractions.

13. $\dfrac{3}{8}, \dfrac{6}{16}, \dfrac{9}{24}$, ▓, ▓, ▓

14. $\dfrac{2}{5}, \dfrac{4}{10}, \dfrac{6}{15}$, ▓, ▓, ▓

15. $\dfrac{3}{7}, \dfrac{6}{14}, \dfrac{9}{21}$, ▓, ▓, ▓

16. Write a fraction equivalent to $\dfrac{5}{12}$ with a denominator of 60.

17. Is $\dfrac{3}{8}$ equivalent to $\dfrac{9}{24}$?

MATH REASONING

18. Find the product of the red numbers and the product of the black numbers in each pair of equivalent fractions. These products are called **cross products.** Complete the sentence below.

$$\dfrac{3}{4} = \dfrac{15}{20} \qquad \dfrac{5}{8} = \dfrac{25}{40} \qquad \dfrac{28}{63} = \dfrac{4}{9}$$

"If two fractions are equivalent then their cross products are ___?___."

PROBLEM SOLVING

19. A design of a muskrat, the school mascot, took up 64 out of 100 squares of a card section. Did the design take up $\dfrac{1}{4}$, $\dfrac{6}{10}$, $\dfrac{16}{25}$, or $\dfrac{16}{20}$ of the squares?

20. For the first football game, 132 students sat together in the stands. The same number sat in each row. Without dividing, decide if there were 5, 6, or 9 students in each row.

▶ **COMMUNICATION   Writing to Learn**

21. Suppose you are tutoring a fifth grade student who is having trouble finding equivalent fractions. Write an explanation the student can take home showing how to find equivalent fractions. Use examples and diagrams.

More Practice, page 529, set C

Lowest Terms

LEARN ABOUT IT

EXPLORE Analyze the Situation

Students from the All-City School Brass Band met for a practice session. Kennis told a reporter that $\frac{6}{18}$ of the students in the band played the trombone.

TALK ABOUT IT

1. What fractions with smaller denominators could Kennis have used?

2. Group the names in the lists to show how the different fractions you found in question 1 describe the same situation.

3. Which fraction do you think the reporter used in his article? Why?

To write a fraction in **lowest terms,** divide the numerator and denominator by the same number. A fraction is in lowest terms when the GCF of the numerator and denominator is 1.

Method 1	Method 2
$$\frac{12 \div 2}{30 \div 2} = \frac{6}{15}$$ $$\frac{6 \div 3}{15 \div 3} = \frac{2}{5}$$ Divide until the GCF of the numerator and denominator is 1.	$$\frac{12 \div 6}{30 \div 6} = \frac{2}{5}$$ Divide the numerator and denominator by their GCF.

TRY IT OUT

Give the GCF of the numerator and denominator.

1. $\frac{20}{24}$ 2. $\frac{12}{45}$ 3. $\frac{21}{28}$ 4. $\frac{11}{13}$

Write each fraction in lowest terms.

5. $\frac{6}{8}$ 6. $\frac{12}{18}$ 7. $\frac{35}{50}$ 8. $\frac{24}{28}$

Give the GCF of the numerator and the denominator.

1. $\frac{16}{30}$ **2.** $\frac{25}{30}$ **3.** $\frac{36}{48}$ **4.** $\frac{36}{60}$

Write each fraction in lowest terms.

5. $\frac{8}{12}$ **6.** $\frac{14}{35}$ **7.** $\frac{9}{30}$ **8.** $\frac{12}{25}$

9. $\frac{20}{36}$ **10.** $\frac{28}{42}$ **11.** $\frac{40}{48}$ **12.** $\frac{24}{56}$

13. $\frac{66}{99}$ **14.** $\frac{28}{35}$ **15.** $\frac{22}{110}$ **16.** $\frac{42}{49}$

APPLY

MATH REASONING

17. Find all the ways the numbers 2, 4, 8, and 16 can be written in the squares to make a true statement.

$$\frac{\square}{\square} = \frac{\square}{\square}$$

PROBLEM SOLVING

18. Of the students in the All-City Band, $\frac{12}{18}$ came from North High School. What fraction could be used in a newspaper article reporting this fact?

19. The band director passed out 156 copies of Sousa's *Stars and Stripes*. Five out of every twelve copies had printing errors. How many copies had no errors?

20. Fine Arts Data Bank Make a fraction using the frequencies of C1 and G1. Use divisibility rules to find common factors for the numerator and denominator. Write the fraction in lowest terms.

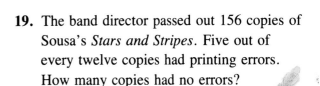

▶ **ESTIMATION**

You can estimate fractional parts by substituting compatible numbers for the numerator and/or denominator and then writing the fraction in lowest terms.

$\frac{7}{18}$ is about $\frac{6}{18} = \frac{1}{3}$ $\frac{29}{61}$ is about $\frac{30}{60} = \frac{1}{2}$

Substitute compatible numbers and write in lowest terms.

21. $\frac{22}{40}$ **22.** $\frac{31}{69}$ **23.** $\frac{26}{101}$

Improper Fractions and Mixed Numbers

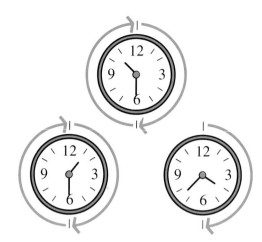

LEARN ABOUT IT

EXPLORE **Examine the Situation**

To David's surprise, his social life actually improved after he got braces. But he did spend a lot of time at the orthodontist's office. In two months he had 5 half-hour appointments.

TALK ABOUT IT

1. Explain why 5 half-hours can be written as $\frac{5}{2}$ hours.

2. Four hours equals how many half hours? Express this as a fraction.

An **improper fraction** is a fraction with a numerator greater than or equal to its denominator. A **mixed number** is the sum of a whole number and a fraction.

Improper Fraction → Mixed Number	**Mixed Number → Improper Fraction**
Write $\frac{7}{2}$ as a mixed number.	Write $2\frac{3}{4}$ as an improper fraction.
$\frac{7}{2}$ means 7 divided by 2.	$2 \times 4 = 8$ Multiply the whole number by the denominator of the fraction.
$\frac{7}{2} \rightarrow 2\overline{)7} \begin{array}{c} 3 \\ \end{array}$, so $\frac{7}{2} = 3\frac{1}{2}$ $\begin{array}{c} \underline{6} \\ 1 \end{array}$	$8 + 3 = 11$ Add this product to the numerator of the fraction.
	$2\frac{3}{4} = \frac{11}{4}$ Write the sum over the denominator.

TRY IT OUT

Write each improper fraction as a mixed number or a whole number.

1. $\frac{11}{3}$ **2.** $\frac{16}{4}$ **3.** $\frac{23}{5}$ **4.** $\frac{22}{8}$

Write each mixed number as an improper fraction.

5. $3\frac{5}{6}$ **6.** $2\frac{1}{4}$ **7.** $5\frac{2}{3}$ **8.** $7\frac{5}{8}$

Write each improper fraction as a mixed number or a whole number.

1. $\frac{9}{8}$ **2.** $\frac{17}{7}$ **3.** $\frac{20}{8}$ **4.** $\frac{14}{3}$

5. $\frac{36}{6}$ **6.** $\frac{34}{10}$ **7.** $\frac{38}{4}$ **8.** $\frac{29}{9}$

Write each mixed number as an improper fraction.

9. $7\frac{1}{3}$ **10.** $7\frac{5}{7}$ **11.** $1\frac{7}{12}$ **12.** $3\frac{3}{13}$

13. $8\frac{1}{6}$ **14.** $12\frac{5}{6}$ **15.** $9\frac{7}{20}$ **16.** $11\frac{10}{11}$

MATH REASONING Copy and complete. Use the skills you learned in this lesson to find the pattern.

17. $1\frac{2}{7}$, $2\frac{4}{7}$, $3\frac{6}{7}$, $5\frac{1}{7}$, ——, ——

18. $5\frac{4}{5}$, $5\frac{2}{5}$, 5, $4\frac{3}{5}$, ——, ——

PROBLEM SOLVING

19. Ted spent about $\frac{1}{3}$ of an hour before his orthodontist appointments playing videogames in the waiting room. In 11 appointments, how many hours did he spend on videogames?

▶ **MENTAL MATH**

20. Jerry kept a chart showing how long he wore his head gear every night. He recorded the times in a strange way to keep his parents' nagging to a minimum. He was supposed to wear the gear 14 or more hours per day. Use mental math to decide which days he fell short.

M	T	W	Th	F	S	S
$13\frac{5}{5}$	$1\frac{150}{10}$	$13\frac{11}{12}$	$\frac{140}{14}$	$12\frac{7}{3}$	$10\frac{70}{20}$	$11\frac{11}{4}$

Exploring Algebra
More About Equations

LEARN ABOUT IT

EXPLORE **Analyze the Situation**

The scales at the right are balanced. Similar
objects in both pictures weigh the same.

TALK ABOUT IT

1. How many blocks would it take to balance 2 buckets?

2. How many paper bags would it take to balance 10 blocks?

3. A bucket and a bag on the left pan would balance how many blocks?

You can add objects of the same weight to both sides of a scale
or remove objects of the same weight from both sides and the
scale will remain balanced.

Examples Decide whether each scale is balanced. Use the
scales above to help you decide.

Yes, it is balanced.
The paper bag weighs the same as 2 blocks.

Yes, it is balanced. A bucket and 1 block weigh
the same as 4 blocks, which is the same as 2 bags.
One baseball has been added to each side.

TRY IT OUT

The scales to the right are
balanced. Which of the scales
below are also balanced?

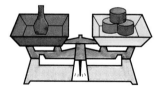

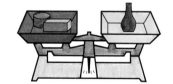

1.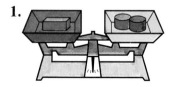

2.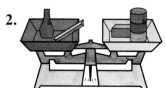

3.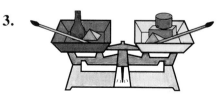

These 3 scales are balanced. Are the scales below also balanced?

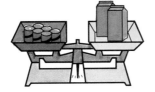

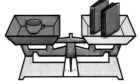

1.

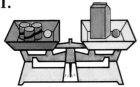

2.

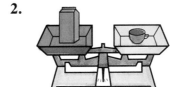

3.

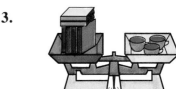

4.

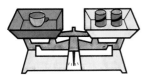

5.

6.

APPLY

MATH REASONING

7. An equation for problem 1 is $3J + m = Q + m$. J, m, and Q are the weights of a can of juice, a marble, and a quart of milk. Write an equation for each of the balanced scales in problems 2–6. Use c and b for the weight of a cup and a book, respectively.

PROBLEM SOLVING

8. The Lee twins and Ma triplets balance on a see-saw. Each twin weighs 123 lbs. What is the average weight of the triplets?

9. If each Lee twin and each Ma triplet gains 2 lb, will they still balance?

▶ **USING CRITICAL THINKING   Use Logical Reasoning**

10. These scales are balanced. If the mass of the baseball is 50 g. What is the mass of the bucket?

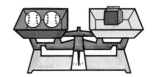

Fractions and Decimals

LEARN ABOUT IT

EXPLORE **Examine the Table**

At one recording center for the blind, $\frac{3}{10}$ of the books recorded were for 9th–12th graders. What decimal part of the total books recorded were for these students? Use the grid to help you decide.

TALK ABOUT IT

1. How do you know the decimal for $\frac{3}{10}$ must be less than 0.50?

2. What fraction with a denominator of 100 is equivalent to $\frac{3}{10}$?

To find a decimal for a fraction, first write an equivalent fraction with a denominator of 10, 100, 1000, . . . Then write the fraction as a decimal.

$$\frac{9}{20} = \frac{9 \times 5}{20 \times 5} = \frac{45}{100} = 0.45$$

You can also write a decimal as a fraction or mixed number.

$$0.36 = \frac{36}{100} = \frac{36}{100} = \frac{9}{25}$$

Fraction of Books
at Each Grade Level

■ 5th-8th grade $\frac{1}{4}$

■ 9th-12th grade $\frac{3}{10}$

□ College $\frac{9}{20}$

Examples

A Write a decimal for $\frac{201}{500}$.

$$\frac{201}{500} = \frac{201 \times 2}{500 \times 2} = \frac{402}{1000}$$

$$\frac{402}{1000} = 0.402$$

B Write a fraction for 5.4.

$$5.4 = 5\frac{4}{10} = 5\frac{2}{5}$$

TRY IT OUT

Write each fraction or mixed number as a decimal.

1. $\frac{4}{5}$
2. $\frac{32}{50}$
3. $2\frac{3}{5}$
4. $\frac{117}{250}$

Write each decimal as a lowest-terms fraction or mixed number.

5. 0.28
6. 0.2
7. 3.06
8. 2.25

Write each decimal as a lowest-terms fraction or a mixed number.

1. 0.14
2. 0.76
3. 1.8
4. 3.08

5. 0.106
6. 5.375
7. 0.96
8. 7.9

Write each fraction or mixed number as a decimal.

9. $\frac{8}{10}$
10. $1\frac{3}{5}$
11. $2\frac{8}{25}$
12. $4\frac{11}{20}$

13. $7\frac{21}{100}$
14. $8\frac{21}{40}$
15. $6\frac{7}{1000}$
16. $\frac{7}{8}$

APPLY

MATH REASONING

17. Copy the number line below. Use mental math to estimate the position of each fraction on the number line by changing it to a decimal.

$$\frac{1}{4}, \frac{4}{25}, \frac{1}{2}, \frac{9}{10}, \frac{7}{20},$$

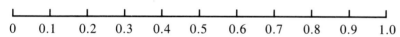

PROBLEM SOLVING

18. Of the books at the Center for the Blind, $\frac{1}{4}$ are for 5th–8th graders. What decimal names this fractional part?

19. Jolene has recorded 0.4 of *Moby Dick* onto cassette tape. What fraction of the book has she recorded?

MIXED REVIEW

Find the measure of the third angle in each triangle.

20.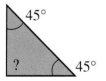

21.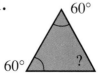

22.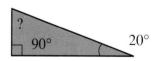

Solve. Use mental math.

23. 302×7
24. $445 + 98$
25. $30 + 32 + 70$
26. $999 + 999 + 999$

Find each quotient to the nearest hundredth.

27. $0.08\overline{)1.025}$
28. $19\overline{)124.01}$
29. $61\overline{)1.78}$

More Practice, page 530, set B

147

Terminating and Repeating Decimals

EXPLORE Use a Calculator

To change a fraction to a decimal, you can divide the numerator by the denominator. Use this fact to help you discover a pattern.

$\frac{1}{5}$, 0.2, $\frac{2}{5}$, 0.4, ____, ____, ____, ____   The bar means the 1 repeats without end.

$\frac{1}{9}$, $0.\overline{1}$, $\frac{2}{9}$, ____, ____, ____, ____, ____

$\frac{1}{8}$, 0.125, $\frac{2}{8}$, ____, ____, ____, ____, ____

$\frac{1}{11}$, $0.\overline{09}$, $\frac{2}{11}$, ____, ____, ____, ____, ____

TALK ABOUT IT

1. Describe the pattern you found in each row.

2. What would you expect the decimal equivalent of $\frac{7}{9}$ to be?

If there is a zero remainder you get a **terminating decimal.** Sometimes you get a **repeating decimal,** which means that one or more digits repeat without end.

Examples

The frequency of the musical note *middle C* is 264. *F above middle C* has the frequency 352. And *G below middle C* has the frequency 396. We can compare these notes as follows.

Terminating Decimals
Compare middle C to F

$$\frac{264}{352} = \frac{3}{4} \rightarrow 4\overline{)3.00}$$
$$\begin{array}{r} 0.75 \\ \underline{2\ 8} \\ 20 \\ \underline{20} \\ 0 \end{array} \text{ (remainder is zero)}$$

Repeating Decimals
Compare middle C to G

$$\frac{264}{396} = \frac{2}{3} \rightarrow 3\overline{)2.000}\ldots \qquad \frac{2}{3} = 0.\overline{6}$$
$$\begin{array}{r} 0.666\ldots \\ \underline{1\ 8} \\ 20 \\ \underline{18} \\ 20 \text{ (this keeps repeating)} \\ \underline{18} \end{array}$$

Change each fraction to a decimal. Use bar notation for repeating decimals.

1. $\frac{7}{12}$ 2. $\frac{2}{3}$ 3. $\frac{4}{27}$ 4. $\frac{1}{6}$

Write each repeating decimal using bar notation.

1. 0.434343 . . .   **2.** 0.231231231 . . .   **3.** 0.0575757 . . .   **4.** 0.27276666 . . .

Change each fraction to a decimal. Use bar notation to show repeating decimals.

5. $\frac{3}{18}$ **6.** $\frac{7}{15}$ **7.** $\frac{3}{10}$ **8.** $\frac{28}{32}$ **9.** $\frac{4}{18}$

10. $\frac{20}{32}$ **11.** $\frac{30}{111}$ **12.** $\frac{18}{54}$ **13.** $\frac{5}{3}$ **14.** $\frac{5}{30}$

APPLY

MATH REASONING

15. Some of the fractions below can be changed to decimals by dividing mentally. Identify those fractions and change them to decimals.

$\frac{3}{5}$ $\quad$ $\frac{4}{8}$ $\quad$ $\frac{2}{10}$ $\quad$ $\frac{2}{9}$ $\quad$ $\frac{1}{12}$ $\quad$ $\frac{2}{5}$

$\frac{4}{5}$ $\quad$ $\frac{6}{20}$ $\quad$ $\frac{2}{15}$ $\quad$ $\frac{1}{5}$ $\quad$ $\frac{12}{10}$ $\quad$ $\frac{3}{1}$

PROBLEM SOLVING

16. On the chromatic scale in music, the interval between any note and its sharp (♯) or flat (♭) is about $\frac{24}{25}$. Change this value to a decimal.

17. The interval from B♭ to B is $\frac{475}{495}$. Write this in lowest terms, and change the result to a decimal.

18. Write the fraction for the interval from A♭ to A. Then write it in lowest terms and change the result to a decimal.

♪ ♫ Chromatic Scale ♫ ♪	
Note	**Frequency**
B♯	516
B	495
B♭	475
A♯	458
A	440
A♭	422
G♯	412
G	396
G♭	380

19. Math and Fine Arts Data Bank To create music on a computer you need to express note values as decimals. If a whole note plays for one second, what decimal expresses the length of time the ♩ note would play? the ♪ note? the ♪. note?

► USING CRITICAL THINKING   Make a Prediction

20. Find the decimal for $\frac{2}{7}$ on the calculator. Predict the decimals for $\frac{3}{7}$ and $\frac{4}{7}$ without dividing. Then check your predictions on the calculator.

Comparing and Ordering Fractions

EXPLORE **Examine the Data**

Jackson Junior High held a donkey basketball game. The scorekeeper kept track of baskets made (b) and attempts (a). Did Bob play better on a donkey or on his feet?

TALK ABOUT IT

1. What 2 numbers did you use from the table?

2. How did you decide which way Bob did better?

To compare two or more fractions use the steps below.

If denominators are unlike, write equivalent fractions with like denominators.	Then compare the numerators.	The fractions compare the same way the numerators compare.

$$\frac{4}{9} = \frac{20}{45}, \frac{8}{15} = \frac{24}{45} \qquad 20 < 24 \qquad \frac{20}{45} < \frac{24}{45}, \text{ so } \frac{4}{9} < \frac{8}{15}$$

To compare mixed numbers, first compare the whole numbers. Then compare the fractions if necessary.

Examples

A Compare $6\frac{9}{10}$ and $6\frac{3}{4}$

The whole numbers are the same, so compare the fractions.

$$\frac{9}{10} = \frac{18}{20}, \frac{3}{4} = \frac{15}{20}$$

So, $6\frac{9}{10} > 6\frac{3}{4}$

B Compare $3\frac{1}{2}$ and $2\frac{3}{4}$

The whole numbers differ.

$3 > 2$

So, $3\frac{1}{2} > 2\frac{3}{4}$

Write $<$, $>$, or $=$ for each ▥.

1. $\frac{3}{4}$ ▥ $\frac{9}{16}$

2. $\frac{3}{5}$ ▥ $\frac{7}{12}$

3. $\frac{7}{10}$ ▥ $\frac{11}{15}$

4. $2\frac{1}{3}$ ▥ $2\frac{1}{4}$

PRACTICE

Write <, >, or = for each .

1. $\dfrac{5}{6}$ ⦙ $\dfrac{4}{7}$ **2.** $\dfrac{5}{8}$ ⦙ $\dfrac{13}{15}$ **3.** $\dfrac{2}{7}$ ⦙ $\dfrac{1}{3}$ **4.** $\dfrac{4}{9}$ ⦙ $\dfrac{2}{3}$

5. $\dfrac{7}{8}$ ⦙ $\dfrac{13}{16}$ **6.** $\dfrac{5}{8}$ ⦙ $\dfrac{9}{19}$ **7.** $\dfrac{19}{28}$ ⦙ $\dfrac{15}{26}$ **8.** $\dfrac{73}{150}$ ⦙ $\dfrac{49}{100}$

Write <, >, or = for each ○.

9. $1\dfrac{4}{5}$ ⦙ $1\dfrac{1}{2}$ **10.** $2\dfrac{1}{2}$ ⦙ $3\dfrac{1}{8}$ **11.** $9\dfrac{7}{8}$ ⦙ $9\dfrac{16}{27}$ **12.** $6\dfrac{9}{10}$ ⦙ $6\dfrac{3}{4}$

13. $1\dfrac{1}{6}$ ⦙ $1\dfrac{2}{13}$ **14.** $5\dfrac{3}{10}$ ⦙ $5\dfrac{27}{100}$ **15.** $11\dfrac{9}{11}$ ⦙ $11\dfrac{27}{33}$ **16.** $7\dfrac{11}{25}$ ⦙ $7\dfrac{13}{27}$

Arrange the fractions in order from smallest to largest.

17. $\dfrac{1}{2}, \dfrac{3}{8}, \dfrac{5}{8}, \dfrac{1}{4}$ **18.** $\dfrac{2}{3}, \dfrac{9}{10}, \dfrac{7}{8}, \dfrac{3}{4}$ **19.** $\dfrac{2}{7}, \dfrac{9}{11}, \dfrac{3}{5}, \dfrac{1}{3}$

APPLY

MATH REASONING Write <, >, or = for each ⦙.

20. $\dfrac{1}{2}$ ⦙ 0.5   **21.** $\dfrac{5}{7}$ ⦙ 0.71   **22.** $\dfrac{3}{5}$ ⦙ 0.57   **23.** $\dfrac{7}{10}$ ⦙ 0.71

24. $\dfrac{2}{3}$ ⦙ 0.67   **25.** $\dfrac{7}{8}$ ⦙ 0.78   **26.** $\dfrac{11}{15}$ ⦙ 0.73   **27.** $\dfrac{5}{9}$ ⦙ 0.491

PROBLEM SOLVING

28. In the last regular game, was Jan or Flores more accurate?

29. Order the players from most accurate to least accurate on donkey day.

▶ **CALCULATOR**

30. Here is how to enter a mixed number on some calculators. $4\dfrac{7}{8} \rightarrow 4 + 7 \div 8$

Use your calculator to compare fractions, mixed numbers, and decimals. List from smallest to largest.

$\dfrac{5}{6}, 2\dfrac{4}{5}, 4.729, 0.6, \dfrac{9}{11}, \dfrac{19}{4}$

More Practice, page 530, set D

Problem Solving
Using the Strategies

UNDERSTAND
FIND DATA
PLAN
ESTIMATE
SOLVE
CHECK

This problem asks you to find how many different combinations of classes are possible. You can solve the problem in more than one way.

> Jennie was able to choose two of her classes this year, math class and fine arts class. How many different combinations of classes could she take?
>
> | Math Classes | Fine Arts Classes |
> |---|---|
> | Math 7 | Chorus |
> | Pre-Algebra | Band |
> | | Orchestra |
> | | Art |

One way to solve this problem is to **Draw a Picture.**

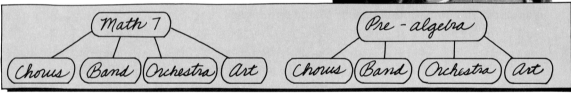

Another way to solve this problem is to **Make an Organized List.**

$$m - c \qquad p - c$$
$$m - B \qquad p - B$$
$$m - o \qquad p - o$$
$$m - a \qquad p - a$$

There are 8 different combinations of math and fine arts classes possible.

TRY IT OUT

1. Linda wants to wear a skirt and sweater to school. She has 4 skirts—green, red, navy, and tan. She also has 3 sweaters—white, blue, and gray. How many different outfits can Linda choose?

2. Ted makes a sandwich to take to school each day. This morning he could choose from 3 kinds of bread—french, rye, and whole wheat, and 3 fillings—cheese, ham and tuna. How many different kinds of sandwiches could Ted make?

Solve. Use any problem solving strategy.

Some Strategies	
Act Out	Solve a Simpler Problem
Use Objects	Make an Organized List
Choose an Operation	Work Backward
Draw a Picture	Look for a Pattern
Guess and Check	Use Logical Reasoning
Make a Table	Write an Equation

1. Martin Luther King Junior High School has 836 students. Half of them take art. 133 of them take chorus and 89 take band. How many of the students take art?

2. Jonas has this ballot for the class election. How many different election outcomes are possible?

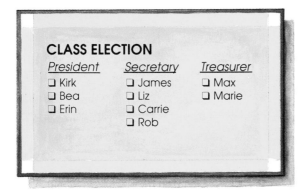

CLASS ELECTION

President	Secretary	Treasurer
❑ Kirk	❑ James	❑ Max
❑ Bea	❑ Liz	❑ Marie
❑ Erin	❑ Carrie	
	❑ Rob	

3. Katie's mother paid $285 for season tickets to the symphony. Her tickets included 12 performances. The single ticket price is $28. How much did Katie's mother save by buying season tickets?

4. Kayla ordered a beef taco. She wants to add 2 different toppings. How many combinations of 2 toppings are possible?

5. There are 79 students taking art or music, but not both. There are 9 more students taking art than music. How many students take art? How many take music?

6. Phil has 5 classes before lunch—PE, math, English, social studies, and shop. PE comes after social studies, but before math. He goes directly to lunch from shop class. He is sometimes late to English from PE. What is Phil's schedule before lunch?

7. Last year 32 students were in the band. Some changed to chorus. Now there are 27 band students. How many changed to chorus?

8. Ms. Chung spent $238.50 on concert tickets. Each ticket cost $26.50. How many tickets did she buy?

Applied Problem Solving
Group Decision Making

UNDERSTAND
FIND DATA
PLAN
ESTIMATE
SOLVE
CHECK

Group Skill:
Disagree in an agreeable way

The 7th grade is planning a fundraising picnic. Your group is in charge of making 3-foot long sandwiches to sell. You need to write out instructions for the students who will be making the sandwiches so that each work shift makes the sandwiches with the same amounts of ingredients. You are also responsible for deciding the prices for the four sizes of sandwiches.

Facts to Consider

- Sandwich ingredients:

Ingredient	Cost
Salami (about 64 slices per pound)	$1.22 per $\frac{1}{4}$ lb
Lettuce (about 15 leaves per head)	59¢ per head
Tomato (about 4 tomatoes per pound)	64¢ per lb
Bread (in 3-foot lengths)	$1.29 per foot
Cheese (15 slices per pound)	$1.53 per $\frac{1}{2}$ lb

- Sandwich sizes:

  small (for one person)
  1-foot long
  2-foot long
  3-foot long

- Each 3-foot long sandwich can be cut into 6 small sandwiches.

- For every $\frac{1}{4}$ foot of sandwich, you will need:

  3 slices of meat
  3 slices of cheese
  2 slices of tomato
  1 leaf lettuce

1. About how much does one pound of salami cost? About how much does one slice cost?

2. About how much does one whole tomato cost? one slice?

3. How could drawing a picture help you figure out how much of each ingredient to use in a small sandwich?

4. What is the profit on a small sandwich? Will you encourage people to buy larger sandwiches by making them a "better buy?"

Make a table to show the amount of each ingredient in a 3-foot sandwich. Explain how you decided the price of each size sandwich.

WRAP UP

Multiple Choice

Choose the correct answer for each question.

1. Which number is *not* divisible by 2, by 3, and by 4?

    A 16   **B** 36   **C** 13,044

2. Which number is *not* composite?

    A 57   **B** 2   **C** 33

Sometimes, Always, Never

Which word should go in the blank, sometimes, always, or never? Explain your choice.

3. A prime number is __?__ divisible by 2.

4. Once you know that a number is prime, there is __?__ a need to test for divisibility.

5. Composite numbers are __?__ relatively prime.

6. Multiples of 5 are __?__ multiples of 6.

7. Twin primes are __?__ separated by a multiple of 6.

8. A proper fraction is __?__ larger than a mixed number.

Project

Play this game with a partner. Write the numbers from 1 to 50 across the top of a piece of paper. Divide the rest of the paper in half. Choose a number and write it on your side. Then your partner chooses all the factors of that number and writes them on his or her side. As soon as a number or factor is chosen, it is circled and may not be used again. If a number is chosen and all the factors have been used, the next person's turn begins. Play until all the numbers have been chosen. Add the numbers on each side. You may want to use a calculator. The player with the highest total wins.

<table>
<tr><td colspan="2">① ② ③ ④ 5 ⑥ ⑦ 8 ⑨ 10</td></tr>
<tr><td colspan="2">11 ⑫ 13 ⑭ 15 16 17 ⑱ 19 20</td></tr>
<tr><td colspan="2">㉑ 22 23 24 25 26 27 28 29 30</td></tr>
<tr><td colspan="2">31 32 33 34 35 ㊱ 37 38 39 40</td></tr>
<tr><td colspan="2">41 42 43 44 45 46 47 48 49 50</td></tr>
<tr><td>Chuck</td><td>Sue</td></tr>
<tr><td>1.   36</td><td>1,2,18,3,
12,4,9,6</td></tr>
<tr><td>   7</td><td>2. 21</td></tr>
<tr><td>3. 14</td><td>no factors left</td></tr>
<tr><td></td><td>4. 33</td></tr>
</table>

CHAPTER REVIEW/TEST

Part 1   Understanding

1. Into what size groups can 12 students be equally divided?

2. Which numbers are multiples of 18?

   A 18   B 35   C 54   D 78

3. Which numbers are prime?

   A 71   B 105   C 672   D 89

4. What is the GCF of 12 and 18?

Part 2   Skills

Find the lowest common multiple of each pair of numbers

5. 7, 15

6. 6, 21

Write the prime factorization of each number using exponents.

7. 64

8. 108

Find the greatest common factor of each pair of numbers.

9. 44, 36

10. 30, 105

11. 18, 36

Give the value for n.

12. $\frac{2}{5} = \frac{n}{20}$

13. $\frac{8}{12} = \frac{n}{3}$

14. $\frac{7}{3} = \frac{n}{6}$

15. Write $\frac{44}{6}$ as a mixed number.

16. Write $3\frac{5}{8}$ as an improper fraction.

17. Write 5.24 as a lowest-terms mixed number.

18. Write $\frac{17}{25}$ as a decimal.

Write $<, >,$ or $=$ for each ▥ .

19. $\frac{7}{12}$ ▥ $\frac{3}{4}$

20. $2\frac{3}{8}$ ▥ $2\frac{15}{40}$

21. $\frac{9}{8}$ ▥ $\frac{8}{9}$

Part 3   Applications

22. At a class picnic, there were 2 kinds of juice, 3 kinds of salads, and 2 kinds of sandwiches. How many 3-item combinations of lunch were possible?

23. There are 36 black keys and 52 white keys on a piano. Compare the black keys to the total number of keys. Write the result as a decimal.

24. **Challenge.** Of the first fifty prime numbers, all except two end with the digit 1, 3, 7, or 9. What two primes do not end with these digits?

ENRICHMENT
Pythagorean Theorem

Enrico, Monica, and Chad were making right triangles with a 1-m piece of string. Chad said, "This reminds me of the Pythagorean Theorem!" Using the triangle at the right, they each stated what they thought was the Pythagorean Theorem.

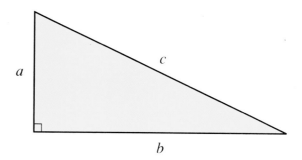

Enrico: $a^2 + b^2 = c$

Monica: $a^2 + b^2 = c^2$

Chad: $a + b = c$

Work in groups. Use a 1-m string to make five right triangles. Measure the sides to the nearest cm. Use a calculator and complete a table like the one shown. Which student made the correct statement?

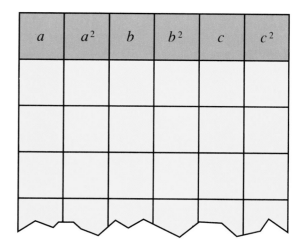

a	a^2	b	b^2	c	c^2

The picture at the right is one way to show why the Pythagorean Theorem holds for certain kinds of right triangles.

1. Write a paragraph that would convince others why this picture shows the Pythagorean Theorem.

2. Draw a right triangle with the lengths of the legs not equal. Draw a square on each of the sides. Does this method for showing the Pythagorean Theorem work for your triangle?

3. Does the Pythagorean Theorem hold only for right triangles? Try the method used above for a triangle without a right angle. What do you discover?

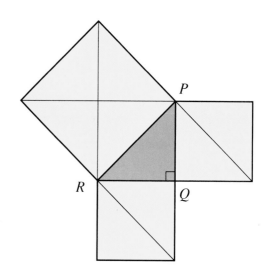

158

CUMULATIVE REVIEW

1. Find the quotient for $0.18\overline{)4,212}$.

   A 234   **B** 2.34   **C** 23.4   **D** 23,400

2. Find the value for $3^2 \times 4^3$.

   A 72   **B** 576   **C** 60   **D** 648

3. Complete. 2.7 L = _____ mL

   A 0.027   **B** 2,700

   C 270   **D** 27

4. On which type of graph would you find data points?

   A circle graph   **B** bar graph

   C scattergram   **D** histogram

5. What is the mode of the earnings?

   A $3.87

   B $3.93

   C $4.00

   D $3.92

Hourly Wage	Number of People
$3.35	3
3.30	5
3.75	8
4.00	11
4.10	4
4.50	2

6. What is the name of a bar graph that shows frequencies?

   A pictograph   **B** histogram

   C scattergram   **D** line segment graph

7. Which set of numbers correctly completes the table?

tables (t)	1	2	3	4	5
chairs (c)	4	8	?	?	?

   A 10, 12, 14   **B** 12, 16, 20

   C 16, 32, 64   **D** 9, 10, 11

8. Identify the space figure.

   A pyramid

   B prism

   C parallelogram

   D pentagon

9. The measures of two angles of a triangle are 37° and 90°. What is the measure of the third angle?

   A 90°   **B** 180°

   C 53°   **D** 63°

10. Which angle is complementary to an angle of 35°?

   A 50°   **B** 55°

   C 145°   **D** 155°

11. Which is the cross section?

   A   **B**   **C**   **D**

12. What is the missing number in the equation $5.7 + 18.3 = \text{▦} \times 3$?

   A 8   **B** 72

   C 6   **D** 24

13. One angle of a triangle is 104° and another is half that. What is the measure of the third angle?

   A 204°   **B** 76°

   C 24°   **D** 156°

6

FRACTION OPERATIONS

MATH AND
HEALTH AND FITNESS

DATA BANK

Use the Health and Fitness
Data Bank on page 500 to
answer the questions.

1 About how many cups of
cheese will you get if you
grate 1 pound of cheese?
2 pounds?

2 How many sticks of margarine are needed to triple the Pizza Snackers recipe? How many cups of margarine?

3 How many green onions will be needed if the Pizza Snackers recipe is increased to use a full pound of cheese?

4 Using Critical Thinking
Explain the saying, "A pint's a pound, the world around." When might the saying be correct? When might it be inaccurate? How do you think sayings like this originate?

Adding and Subtracting Fractions

What you know about least common multiples can help you add and subtract fractions with unlike denominators. The **least common denominator (LCD)** of two fractions is the least common multiple of the denominators.

"The only things certain in life are birth, death, and taxes!" The graph at the right shows some responses to the statement: "My tax refund this year was ____." What fraction of the respondents received a refund about the same size or larger than the previous year?

"My tax refund this year was ____"

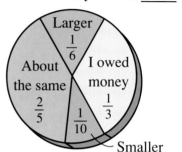

Are the denominators the same? If not, find the LCD.	Write equivalent fractions using the LCD.	Add (subtract) the numerators. Write the sum (difference) over the LCD.

$$\begin{array}{r} \frac{1}{6} \\ + \frac{2}{5} \\ \hline \end{array}$$ **Denominators are not the same. LCD is 30.**

$$\begin{array}{r} \frac{1}{6} = \frac{5}{30} \\ + \frac{2}{5} = \frac{12}{30} \\ \hline \end{array}$$

$$\begin{array}{r} \frac{5}{30} \\ + \frac{12}{30} \\ \hline \frac{17}{30} \end{array}$$

TALK ABOUT IT

1. How do you find the LCD for the two fractions above?

2. How could you estimate the answer to the problem?

3. Use a complete sentence to answer the problem above.

Other Examples

A $\frac{5}{12} - \frac{1}{3} = \frac{5}{12} - \frac{4}{12} = \frac{1}{12}$

B $\frac{5}{8} + \frac{5}{6} = \frac{15}{24} + \frac{20}{24} = \frac{35}{24} = 1\frac{11}{24}$

Add or subtract. Express each sum or difference in lowest terms.

1. $\frac{7}{8} - \frac{3}{8}$ **2.** $\frac{8}{10} + \frac{5}{10}$ **3.** $\frac{5}{6} - \frac{5}{8}$ **4.** $\frac{3}{4} + \frac{5}{6}$

Add or subtract. Express each sum or difference lowest terms.

1. $\dfrac{5}{6}$
$-\dfrac{1}{6}$

2. $\dfrac{7}{12}$
$+\dfrac{11}{12}$

3. $\dfrac{5}{16}$
$-\dfrac{2}{9}$

4. $\dfrac{2}{5}$
$+\dfrac{1}{6}$

5. $\dfrac{11}{12} + \dfrac{3}{7}$

6. $\dfrac{3}{4} - \dfrac{5}{8}$

7. $\dfrac{4}{5} + \dfrac{1}{2}$

8. $\dfrac{3}{4} - \dfrac{5}{12}$

9. $\dfrac{7}{9} + \dfrac{13}{18}$

10. $\dfrac{11}{16} + \dfrac{1}{4}$

11. $\dfrac{3}{5} - \dfrac{2}{7}$

12. $\dfrac{9}{11} + \dfrac{2}{3}$

Simplify the expressions. Compute inside parentheses first.

13. $\left(\dfrac{5}{8} + \dfrac{1}{4}\right) - \dfrac{1}{2}$

14. $\left(\dfrac{2}{5} - \dfrac{3}{10}\right) + \dfrac{3}{4}$

15. $\dfrac{7}{12} + \left(\dfrac{1}{3} + \dfrac{1}{6}\right)$

APPLY

MATH REASONING Place the digits 2, 4, 6, and 8 in the boxes at the right to make:

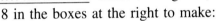

16. the smallest possible sum

17. the largest possible sum

18. the smallest possible difference

19. the largest possible difference

PROBLEM SOLVING

20. What fraction of the people shown by the graph did their own taxes this year?

21. **Write Your Own Problem.** Make up a problem that can be solved using data from the circle graph and subtraction.

▶ **USING CRITICAL THINKING**   Discover a Pattern

22. Copy and complete the fraction magic square. The sum in each row, column, and diagonal must be 1.

Who prepares your tax return?

Last year I did it. This year I hired someone.

$\dfrac{1}{50}$

Last year someone else, this year I did it.

$\dfrac{3}{50}$

$\dfrac{2}{5}$

$\dfrac{13}{25}$

I did them last year and this year.

I never do my own taxes.

	$\dfrac{1}{15}$	
$\dfrac{1}{5}$	$\dfrac{1}{3}$	
		$\dfrac{2}{15}$

Estimating Sums and Differences

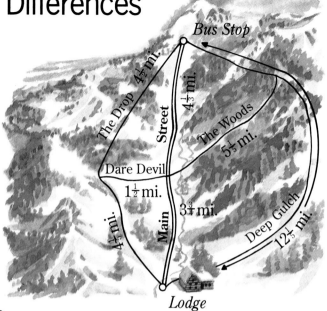

LEARN ABOUT IT

EXPLORE Analyze the Process

A cross country ski resort has several trails from which skiers can choose. About how far can a skier go on the Main Street trail?

Why is addition the operation needed to solve this problem?

Since the question asks "About how far . . . .," all that is needed is an estimate. Here's one way to find an estimate.

Write the needed expression.	Round mixed numbers to the nearest whole number.	Compute.
$3\frac{3}{4} + 4\frac{1}{3}$	$3\frac{3}{4} \rightarrow 4$ $4\frac{1}{3} \rightarrow 4$	$4 + 4 = 8$

TALK ABOUT IT

1. What is $6\frac{1}{2}$ rounded to the nearest whole number? Explain.

2. Can you always round a mixed number to a whole number?

3. Use a complete sentence to answer the problem above.

Other Examples Estimate each sum or difference.

A $12\frac{1}{8} - 5\frac{1}{4}$

$12\frac{1}{8} \rightarrow 12$

$5\frac{1}{4} \rightarrow 5$

$12\frac{1}{8} - 5\frac{1}{4} \rightarrow 7$

B $23 - 11\frac{5}{8}$

$11\frac{5}{8} \rightarrow 12$

$23 - 11\frac{5}{8} \rightarrow 11$

C $7\frac{1}{2} + 15\frac{1}{2}$

$7\frac{1}{2} \rightarrow 8$

$15\frac{1}{2} \rightarrow 16$

$7\frac{1}{2} + 15\frac{1}{2} \rightarrow 24$

TRY IT OUT

Estimate each sum or difference. Use rounding.

1. $10\frac{1}{4} - 6\frac{2}{3}$

2. $3\frac{7}{8} + 5\frac{3}{4}$

3. $9\frac{1}{2} + 4\frac{1}{16}$

4. $16\frac{7}{9} - 9\frac{1}{3}$

Estimate each sum or difference. Use rounding.

1. $3\frac{6}{7} + 4\frac{1}{8}$

2. $6\frac{1}{2} + 3\frac{8}{9}$

3. $4\frac{3}{5} - 2\frac{2}{3}$

4. $9\frac{3}{8} - 7\frac{7}{8}$

5. $1\frac{1}{12} + 3\frac{4}{5}$

6. $5\frac{5}{6} - 4\frac{9}{10}$

7. $10\frac{1}{8} - 5\frac{1}{3}$

8. $8\frac{1}{2} + 2\frac{4}{5}$

9. $3\frac{1}{5} - 2\frac{4}{5}$

10. $7 - 1\frac{7}{8}$

11. $12\frac{7}{12} + 3\frac{2}{3}$

12. $\frac{9}{10} + 8\frac{3}{4}$

13. $\frac{3}{4} + 5\frac{1}{2} + 2\frac{5}{8}$

14. $\left(18\frac{1}{2} - 5\frac{3}{4}\right) + 1\frac{9}{10}$

15. $25 - \left(16\frac{1}{5} + 2\frac{4}{5}\right)$

MATH REASONING Estimate which number should replace the variable in each equation.

16. $24\frac{2}{5} + n = 75\frac{1}{2}$

A. $29\frac{1}{10}$

B. $99\frac{1}{2}$

C. $51\frac{1}{10}$

17. $38\frac{2}{3} - x = 13\frac{1}{6}$

A. $25\frac{1}{2}$

B. $21\frac{5}{6}$

C. $19\frac{1}{3}$

PROBLEM SOLVING

18. How much longer is Deep Gulch than The Drop?

19. Determining Reasonable Answers. Daryl used a calculator to solve the problem below. Is the calculator answer reasonable? If not, tell why and give a reasonable answer.

A group skied from the Lodge to The Bus Stop on Main Street and skied back on The Drop. How far did they ski?

Give the prime factorization for each number.

20. 32

21. 60

22. 105

23. 36

Write each decimal as a lowest-terms fraction or mixed number.

24. 0.4

25. 0.32

26. 3.14

27. 14.02

Evaluate each expression for $a = 18$, $b = 0.98$, $c = 0.02$.

28. $a(b + c)$

29. $ab + ac$

30. $(a + b) + c$

31. $a + (b + c)$

Adding Mixed Numbers

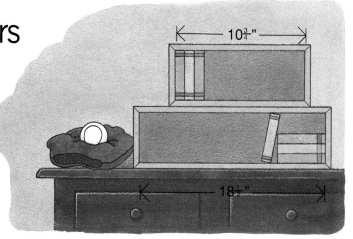

$10\frac{3}{4}"$

$18\frac{1}{2}"$

LEARN ABOUT IT

EXPLORE **Analyze the Process**

Raveena wants to cover the shelves of her CD and cassette tape holders. What is the combined length of the shelves?

Do the fractions have the same denominators?	If not, rename with a common denominator.	Add the fractions. Then add the whole numbers.

$$18\frac{1}{2}$$
$$+\ 10\frac{3}{4}$$

$$18\frac{1}{2} = 18\frac{2}{4}$$
$$+\ 10\frac{3}{4} = 10\frac{3}{4}$$

$$18\frac{2}{4}$$
$$+\ 10\frac{3}{4}$$
$$\overline{28\frac{5}{4}} = 29\frac{1}{4}$$

TALK ABOUT IT

1. How does renaming $18\frac{1}{2}$ help you find the sum?

2. How would you have estimated this sum?

3. Use a complete sentence to answer the problem above.

Sometimes it helps to change mixed numbers to improper fractions.

Examples

A $3\frac{3}{5} + 2\frac{1}{2} = \frac{18}{5} + \frac{5}{2}$

$\qquad = \frac{36}{10} + \frac{25}{10}$

$\qquad = \frac{36 + 25}{10}$

$\qquad = \frac{61}{10} = 6\frac{1}{10}$

B $5\frac{2}{3} + 2\frac{5}{6} = \frac{17}{3} + \frac{17}{6}$

$\qquad = \frac{34}{6} + \frac{17}{6}$

$\qquad = \frac{34 + 17}{6}$

$\qquad = \frac{51}{6} = 8\frac{3}{6} = 8\frac{1}{2}$

TRY IT OUT

Add. Express in lowest terms.

1. $4 + 5\frac{4}{5}$

2. $3\frac{2}{3} + \frac{1}{9}$

3. $7\frac{1}{8} + 1\frac{3}{8}$

4. $15\frac{1}{2} + 8\frac{5}{8}$

Add. Express in lowest terms.

1. $2\frac{5}{6}$
$+ 3\frac{1}{2}$

2. $4\frac{2}{3}$
$+ 1\frac{7}{9}$

3. 5
$+ 4\frac{6}{7}$

4. $12\frac{3}{4}$
$+ 2\frac{2}{3}$

5. $7\frac{5}{8}$
$+ 8\frac{3}{16}$

6. $8\frac{1}{4}$
$+ 1\frac{5}{6}$

7. $13\frac{2}{5}$
$+ 5\frac{3}{4}$

8. $11\frac{2}{3}$
$+ 10\frac{4}{5}$

9. $4\frac{3}{8} + 19\frac{3}{5}$

10. $15\frac{2}{3} + 4\frac{3}{8}$

11. $2\frac{1}{2} + \frac{11}{16}$

12. $12\frac{7}{10} + 9\frac{5}{6}$

13. $4\frac{1}{2} + 3\frac{3}{4} + 6\frac{1}{4}$

14. $6\frac{5}{12} + 3\frac{1}{4} + \frac{1}{3}$

15. $7\frac{5}{6} + 2\frac{1}{8} + 1\frac{1}{2}$

16. $5\frac{2}{3} + 1\frac{5}{6} + 2\frac{1}{2}$

Estimate the sum.

17. $4\frac{7}{8} + 3\frac{2}{3}$

18. $16 + 8\frac{5}{7}$

19. $29\frac{4}{5} + 50\frac{1}{3}$

20. $46\frac{11}{25} + 11\frac{1}{8}$

MATH REASONING Replace the variables with whole numbers to make a true equation.

21. $7\frac{x}{5} + 2\frac{2}{y} = 9\frac{3}{5}$

22. $12\frac{1}{3} + x\frac{y}{z} = 19$

PROBLEM SOLVING

23. What is the total height of the bicycle shown at the right?

24. What is the total length of the bicycle?

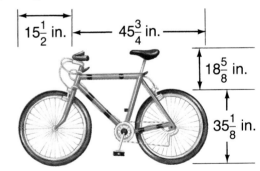

$15\frac{1}{2}$ in. ← $45\frac{3}{4}$ in. →

$18\frac{5}{8}$ in.

$35\frac{1}{8}$ in.

▶ **MENTAL MATH**

Some mixed numbers can be added easily using mental math.
Look for **compatible** fractions whose sum is 1.

25. $3\frac{1}{8} + 2\frac{7}{8} + 5\frac{1}{4}$

26. $3\frac{1}{6} + 4\frac{4}{5} + 1\frac{5}{6}$

27. $\frac{1}{4} + 2\frac{1}{2} + 9\frac{1}{4}$

28. $6\frac{7}{9} + 8\frac{1}{3} + 6\frac{2}{9}$

29. $4\frac{2}{3} + 3\frac{1}{3} + 1\frac{2}{3}$

30. $6\frac{3}{10} + 4\frac{3}{5} + 7\frac{7}{10}$

Subtracting Mixed Numbers

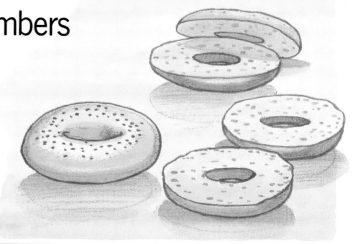

EXPLORE Analyze the Process

Work in groups. Sari's bagel recipe calls for $5\frac{1}{4}$ cups of flour. She has $1\frac{1}{2}$ cups. How much more flour does she need?

Do the fractions have the same denominators? If not, rename with a common denominator.	Rename the mixed number if necessary.	Subtract the fractions, then the whole numbers

$$5\frac{1}{4} = 5\frac{1}{4}$$
$$-1\frac{1}{2} = 1\frac{2}{4}$$

$$5\frac{1}{4} = 4\frac{5}{4}$$
$$-1\frac{2}{4} = 1\frac{2}{4}$$

$$4\frac{5}{4}$$
$$-1\frac{2}{4}$$
$$\overline{3\frac{3}{4}}$$

TALK ABOUT IT

1. $1\frac{1}{2}$ was renamed $1\frac{2}{4}$. Why?

2. $5\frac{1}{4}$ was renamed $4\frac{5}{4}$. Why?

3. How would you have estimated the difference?

4. Use a complete sentence to give the answer to the problem.

Sometimes changing fractions to mixed numbers may help.

Other Examples

A $6\frac{1}{8} - 2\frac{3}{4} = \frac{49}{8} - \frac{11}{4}$

$\qquad = \frac{49}{8} - \frac{22}{8}$

$\qquad = \frac{27}{8} = 3\frac{3}{8}$

B $5 - 1\frac{1}{5} = 5 - \frac{6}{5}$

$\qquad = \frac{50}{10} - \frac{12}{10}$

$\qquad = \frac{38}{10} = 3\frac{8}{10} = 3\frac{4}{5}$

Subtract. Express in lowest terms.

1. $3\frac{1}{4} - 1\frac{3}{4}$
2. $5\frac{3}{16} - 2\frac{3}{4}$
3. $6 - 3\frac{7}{10}$
4. $15\frac{1}{2} - 3\frac{5}{6}$

Subtract. Express in lowest terms.

1. $6\frac{2}{5}$
$-\ 3\frac{4}{5}$

2. $4\frac{5}{8}$
$-\ 2\frac{1}{2}$

3. $7\frac{5}{6}$
$-\ 3\frac{2}{3}$

4. $9\frac{1}{10}$
$-\ 3\frac{3}{10}$

5. $10\frac{1}{2}$
$-\ 4\frac{2}{3}$

6. $8\frac{3}{8}$
$-\ 7\frac{3}{4}$

7. 7
$-\ 5\frac{4}{7}$

Estimate each difference.

8. $14\frac{7}{8} - 5\frac{1}{3}$

9. $10\frac{1}{4} - 5\frac{2}{3}$

10. $22\frac{1}{16} - 9\frac{1}{8}$

11. $20\frac{5}{8} - 10\frac{1}{2}$

12. $37\frac{7}{10} - 19\frac{1}{5}$

13. $47\frac{2}{9} - 41\frac{1}{6}$

14. $72\frac{3}{4} - 39\frac{7}{8}$

15. $79\frac{1}{10} - 28\frac{13}{16}$

MATH REASONING

16. Write the mixed numbers $1\frac{1}{2}$, $4\frac{1}{2}$, $5\frac{1}{4}$, $6\frac{3}{4}$, $2\frac{1}{4}$, and $3\frac{3}{4}$ in the circles so that the sum along each side is $10\frac{1}{2}$.

PROBLEM SOLVING

17. Health and Fitness Data Bank Find the difference between $\frac{1}{2}$ quart and $\frac{3}{8}$ quart. How many tablespoons is that?

DATA BANK

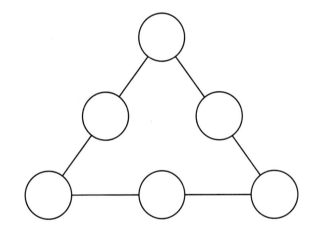

18. Sari needs $1\frac{1}{2}$ cups of honey for the bagels. The jar she bought contains $3\frac{1}{4}$ cups. How much honey will be left over?

▶ **MENTAL MATH**

You can find some differences using compensation.

$5 - 2\frac{3}{4} = n$ **Think: 5 − 3 = 2** **Too much was subtracted. Add back $\frac{1}{4}$.** $2 + \frac{1}{4} = 2\frac{1}{4}$

Find each difference. Use mental math.

19. $12 - 4\frac{1}{2}$

20. $8 - 6\frac{3}{8}$

21. $100 - 23\frac{1}{3}$

22. $18 - 10\frac{9}{10}$

23. $11 - 10\frac{1}{6}$

24. $30 - 19\frac{7}{8}$

More Practice, page 531, set B

Problem Solving
Using the Strategies

UNDERSTAND
ANALYZE DATA
PLAN
ESTIMATE
SOLVE
EXAMINE

LEARN ABOUT IT

On Friday afternoon, 8 friends agreed to call each other over the weekend. Each friend talked to every other friend once. How many phone calls were made?

To solve some problems, you may want to use more than one strategy. To solve this problem, you can use the strategies **Draw a Picture, Make a Table,** and **Look for a Pattern.**

You can begin by **drawing a picture** to represent friends and phone calls.

2 friends 1 call   3 friends 3 calls   4 friends 6 calls

Then you can **make a table** showing the number of friends and the number of phone calls and **look for a pattern.**

Number of friends	Number of calls
2	1 > up 2
3	3 > up 3
4	6 > up 4
5	10 > up 5
6	15 > up 6
7	21 > up 7
8	28

Twenty-eight phone calls were made.

TRY IT OUT

Solve. Use Draw a Picture, Make a Table or Look for a Pattern.

1. The Chess Club has 10 members. Each member wants to play one game with every other member. How many games need to be played?

2. Mimi is planting gazanias in a triangular plot. She put 1 gazania in the first row, 3 in the second row, 5 in the third, and so on. She planted 9 rows. How many gazanias did she plant?

170

Solve. Use any problem solving strategy.

1. One week Vanessa spent $2\frac{3}{4}$ hours on the telephone talking to 2 friends. The next week she talked to 3 friends for $4\frac{1}{3}$ hours. About how much longer did Vanessa spend on the phone the second week than the first week?

2. The Back Roads Bike Club which has 81 members set up a telephone tree. Art called 2 club members on Monday. On Tuesday each of the 2 called 2 other members and so on. At this rate, how many days will it take to reach all of the members?

3. Bernardo practices his trumpet for 5 hours each week. So far, he has practiced $3\frac{1}{4}$ hours. How many hours does he still need to practice?

4. Gina talked to 5 friends one evening. Each telephone call was 3 minutes longer than the call before. If she spent a total of 55 minutes on the phone, how long was her last call?

5. Damont lives in Fairfax. Friday afternoon he called his uncle in Connecticut and talked for 6 minutes. Use the table to find how much Damont's call cost.

Long Distance Rates

Time	1st min	Each additional min
8:00 am - 5:00 pm	$.32	$.27
5:00 pm - 11:00 pm	.20	.18
11:00 pm - 8:00 am	.16	.14

Some Strategies

Act Out	Solve a Simpler Problem
Use Objects	Make an Organized List
Choose an Operation	Work Backward
Draw a Picture	Look for a Pattern
Guess and Check	Use Logical Reasoning
Make a Table	Write an Equation

6. Ann can't remember the area code for her grandparents' telephone number. But she does remember that it has the digits 2, 5, and 8. What area codes are possible?

7. A survey of 1500 households found that $\frac{2}{5}$ of the homes have 2 telephones and $\frac{1}{8}$ have 3 or more telephones. What fraction of the households surveyed have more than one telephone?

8. Aki is cutting a rectangular piece of paper into smaller rectangles. When she makes 1 cut, she gets 2 pieces. When she makes 2 cuts, she gets 4 pieces. With 3 cuts, she gets 8 pieces, and so on. How many pieces would she get from 9 cuts?

Using Critical Thinking
Discovering Methods of Computing

Dr. Shortcutt programmed his robot, ICON, to do computations very quickly.

Felix watched as Diane gave ICON the sum $\frac{2}{3} + \frac{4}{5}$ to test his skill.

"Wow!" said Felix. "That's not the way I learned to add fractions! What is ICON doing?"

"I think I've figured it out," said Diane. "He is multiplying and adding to find the two numbers for his answer!"

$$\frac{2}{3} + \frac{4}{5}$$
$$10, 12, 22, 15$$
$$\text{The sum is } \frac{22}{15} \dots$$

TALK ABOUT IT

1. What is this situation about? How do you think ICON found the fraction sum?

2. Do you think ICON's method works? Could the method be used to add any pair of fractions?

3. Could you use this method to subtract two fractions?

Use ICON's method. Write numbers to show your thinking.

1. $\frac{3}{4} + \frac{2}{5}$

2. $\frac{1}{5} + \frac{3}{7}$

3. $\frac{4}{5} + \frac{5}{6}$

4. $\frac{1}{2} + \frac{1}{3}$

5. $\frac{3}{8} + \frac{3}{8}$

6. $\frac{2}{9} + \frac{2}{3}$

What do you think ICON would write for these subtraction problems?

7. $\frac{3}{4} - \frac{1}{3}$

8. $\frac{7}{8} - \frac{2}{3}$

9. $\frac{14}{3} - \frac{1}{2}$

10. $\frac{2}{3} - \frac{2}{5}$

11. $\frac{7}{8} - \frac{1}{3}$

12. $\frac{11}{15} - \frac{1}{10}$

Estimate each sum or difference.

1. $2\frac{1}{4} + 1\frac{1}{5}$

2. $11\frac{5}{6} - 10\frac{3}{8}$

3. $4\frac{5}{9} + 7\frac{3}{7}$

4. $\frac{11}{21} + 3\frac{5}{7} + 1\frac{7}{9}$

5. $6\frac{7}{8} + 1\frac{1}{9}$

6. $21\frac{2}{5} - 14\frac{6}{7}$

7. $6\frac{7}{10} - 4\frac{3}{4}$

8. $9\frac{2}{3} - \left(2\frac{5}{8} - 1\frac{4}{15}\right)$

Add or subtract. Write answers in lowest terms. Estimate if answers are reasonable.

9. $\frac{3}{8} - \frac{1}{4}$

10. $\frac{1}{9} + \frac{1}{5}$

11. $\frac{5}{6} + \frac{3}{4}$

12. $\frac{2}{3} - \frac{5}{8}$

13. $\frac{7}{12} + \frac{9}{16}$

14. $\frac{9}{8} - \frac{1}{2}$

15. $1\frac{1}{2} + \frac{1}{6}$

16. $8\frac{3}{8} + 2\frac{1}{3}$

17. $12 - 11\frac{5}{9}$

18. $5\frac{5}{6} - 1\frac{1}{3}$

19. $7\frac{5}{12} + 1\frac{5}{9}$

20. $7\frac{3}{8} - 2\frac{2}{3}$

21. $6\frac{2}{7} - 5\frac{2}{5}$

22. $4\frac{2}{3} + 9\frac{3}{4}$

23. $13\frac{7}{12} - 2\frac{5}{8}$

24. $\left(\frac{3}{5} - \frac{1}{2}\right) + \frac{1}{10}$

25. $\left(\frac{11}{12} + \frac{1}{2}\right) - \frac{2}{3}$

26. $2\frac{2}{3} + \left(1\frac{1}{4} + 1\frac{1}{6}\right)$

27. $\left(3\frac{5}{9} - 1\frac{1}{3}\right) + 2\frac{5}{6}$

28. $\left(\frac{1}{3} + \frac{1}{2}\right) - \frac{1}{6}$

PROBLEM SOLVING

32. The recycling plant wants to collect 500 pounds of aluminum cans. Each week they plan to collect 5 pounds more than they collect the previous week. If they collect 5 pounds the first week, when will they reach their goal?

33. Geddy began his pattern in tiles with one blue square tile. He continued to make a larger square by adding a row and a column, alternately using red tiles and then blue tiles, until he used 100 tiles.

a. How many rows of tiles did Geddy use?

b. How many of the 100 tiles were red and how many were blue?

c. Can he continue this pattern and use exactly 500 tiles?

173

Exploring Algebra
Thinking About Functions

EXPLORE **Conduct a Survey**

Ask the question, "What sports do you like?" Make a table like the one below to show your results.

Name				
Sport				
Sport				
Sport				

TALK ABOUT IT

1. How many students named only one sport?

2. Is it possible for a student to name more than one sport?

Here are the results of two similar surveys.

A
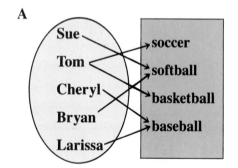

B
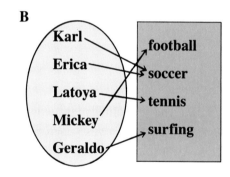

In survey A, everyone except Tom is matched with one sport. He is matched with two. In survey B, each student is matched with only one sport. A relation between two sets is called a **function** if each element of the first set is matched to exactly one element of another set. The relation in A is not a function; the relation in B is a function.

TRY IT OUT

Tell whether the relation shown is a function. Explain.

1.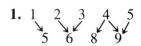

2.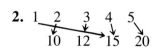

174

Tell whether the relation shown is a function.

1.

2.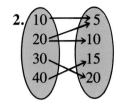

3.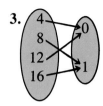

Tell whether the relation which matches each number in the top row to a number in the bottom row is a function.

4.

x	1	2	3	4	5	6
y	3	5	7	9	11	13

5.

x	1	1	2	2	3	3
y	0	1	0	1	0	1

Tell whether the relation which matches each first member of the ordered pair to the second member of the order pair is a function.

6. (2, 4) (3, 5) (4, 6) (5, 7)

7. (1, 1) (2, 3) (1, 5) (3, 5) (4, 6)

8. (5, 0) (6, 0) (8, 0) (3, 0)

9. (6, 2) (6, 3) (6, 1) (6, 0) (6, 4)

MATH REASONING

10. Copy the diagram two times. First show a relation which is a function and then show a relation which is not a function.

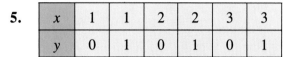

PROBLEM SOLVING

11. **Data Hunt** Find an example of a functional relation in the newspaper.

▶ **CALCULATOR**

Use a calculator to explore the patterns. Complete each pattern.

12. $2^2 =$ ___, $2^3 =$ ___, $2^4 =$ ___, $2^5 =$ ___, $2^6 =$ ___, $2^7 =$ ___, $2^8 =$ ___

What would you predict is the digit in the ones place for 2^{15}?

13. $8^1 =$ ___, $8^2 =$ ___, $8^3 =$ ___, $8^4 =$ ___, $8^5 =$ ___, $8^6 =$ ___

What digit would you predict is in the ones place for 8^{16}?

Multiplying Fractions and Whole Numbers

LEARN ABOUT IT

The picture at the right shows that 1 out of 3 groups or $\frac{1}{3}$ of the surfboards have stripes.

EXPLORE **Solve to Understand**

Use objects or draw pictures to solve this problem:

One-third of the 12 members of a surf club own both a regular surfboard and a windsurfing board. One third own just a regular surfboard, and one third own just a windsurfing board. How many members own both kinds of boards?

TALK ABOUT IT

1. How can drawing a picture help you complete this activity?

2. The expression "one third" means the club is divided into how many groups?

3. Suppose $\frac{2}{3}$ of the members own wetsuits. How can you find what number this represents?

To find $\frac{1}{3}$ of a number, divide the number by 3.	To find $\frac{2}{3}$ of a number, find $\frac{1}{3}$ of the number. Then multiply by 2.

We think: $\frac{1}{3}$ of 12 is 4.

We write: $\frac{1}{3} \times 12 = 4$.

We think: $\frac{1}{3}$ of 12 is 4. $2 \times 4 = 8$.

$\frac{2}{3}$ of 12 is 8.

We write: $\frac{2}{3} \times 12 = 8$.

TRY IT OUT

Find the fraction of the number.

1. $\frac{1}{3}$ of 9

2. $\frac{1}{4}$ of 24

3. $\frac{1}{5}$ of 30

4. $\frac{1}{8}$ of 40

5. $\frac{1}{4} \times 32$

6. $\frac{2}{3} \times 15$

7. $\frac{3}{5} \times 40$

8. $\frac{1}{2}$ of 100

Find the fraction of the number.

1. $\frac{1}{4} \times 16$ **2.** $\frac{1}{6}$ of 18 **3.** $\frac{1}{5}$ of 50 **4.** $\frac{1}{7} \times 28$

5. $\frac{1}{10} \times 100$ **6.** $\frac{1}{2} \times 34$ **7.** $\frac{1}{9}$ of 45 **8.** $\frac{3}{4} \times 12$

APPLY

MATH REASONING Give the whole-number value for each variable.

9. $\frac{1}{n} \cdot 24 = 3$ **10.** $\frac{1}{m} \cdot 56 = 8$ **11.** $\frac{1}{k} \cdot 100 = 5$

12. $\frac{a}{5} \cdot 20 = 12$ **13.** $\frac{b}{6} \cdot 42 = 35$ **14.** $\frac{m}{n} \times 20 = 16$

PROBLEM SOLVING

Use the circle graph at the right.

15. How many customers bought surfboards?

16. How many customers bought windsurfing boards?

17. How many fewer customers bought rafts than belly boards?

18. What is the total number of people who bought rafts and belly boards? [Hint: The sum of all the numbers is 120.]

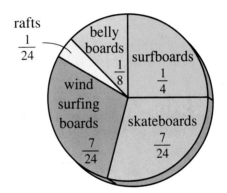

**Beach Shop
Weekend Sales
(120 customers)**

▷ **ESTIMATION**

You can substitute compatible numbers to estimate the product of a fraction and a whole number.

Example: $\frac{1}{5} \cdot 34$ **Think: 34 is close to 35 which is divisible by 5.**

$\frac{1}{5} \cdot 34$ is about $\frac{1}{5} \times 35$ or 7.

Substitute compatible numbers to estimate each product.

19. $\frac{2}{3} \times 22$ **20.** $\frac{3}{4}$ of 15 **21.** $\frac{2}{5}$ of 26 **22.** $\frac{5}{7} \times 205$

23. $\frac{1}{8} \times 409$ **24.** $\frac{5}{6}$ of 1181 **25.** $\frac{2}{9} \times 643$ **26.** $\frac{2}{3} \times 352$

More Practice, page 531, set C

Multiplying Fractions

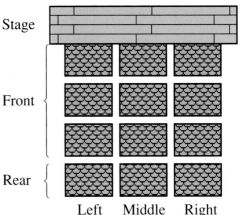

Stage

Front

Rear

Left   Middle   Right

EXPLORE **Examine the Diagram**

Seats at an outdoor theatre are divided into same-size sections. A diagram of the seating arrangement is shown at the right.

TALK ABOUT IT

1. What fraction of the seats are in the front section?

2. What fraction of the seats are in the middle section?

3. What fraction of the seats are in the front-middle section?

You can find what part one fraction is of another by using multiplication.

Multiply the numerators.	Multiply the denominators.	Express in lowest terms.
$\dfrac{3}{4} \times \dfrac{1}{3} = \dfrac{3}{-}$	$\dfrac{3}{4} \times \dfrac{1}{3} = \dfrac{3}{12}$	$\dfrac{3}{12} = \dfrac{1}{4}$

Here is a shortcut for multiplying two fractions.

$$\dfrac{\overset{1}{\cancel{3}}}{4} \times \dfrac{1}{\underset{1}{\cancel{3}}} = \dfrac{1}{4}$$

The numerator and denominator were divided by the common factor 2.

Other Examples

A $\dfrac{2}{5} \times \dfrac{3}{8} = \dfrac{6}{40} = \dfrac{3}{20}$

B $\dfrac{5}{6} \times \dfrac{3}{10} = \dfrac{15}{60} = \dfrac{1}{4}$

C $\dfrac{3}{4} \times 8 = \dfrac{3}{4} \times \dfrac{8}{1} = \dfrac{24}{4} = 6$

D $\dfrac{\overset{1}{\cancel{5}}}{\underset{2}{\cancel{8}}} \times \dfrac{\overset{1}{\cancel{4}}}{\underset{5}{\cancel{25}}} = \dfrac{1}{10}$

E $\dfrac{\overset{1}{\cancel{3}}}{\underset{5}{\cancel{10}}} \times \dfrac{\overset{1}{\cancel{2}}}{\underset{3}{\cancel{9}}} = \dfrac{1}{15}$

F $\dfrac{\overset{1}{\cancel{4}}}{\underset{1}{\cancel{8}}} \times \dfrac{\overset{4}{\cancel{20}}}{\underset{16}{\cancel{64}}} = \dfrac{4}{16} = \dfrac{1}{4}$

Multiply. Do not use the shortcut.

1. $\dfrac{2}{3} \times \dfrac{1}{4}$

2. $\dfrac{9}{10} \times \dfrac{1}{3}$

3. $\dfrac{4}{5} \times \dfrac{3}{5}$

4. $\dfrac{5}{6} \times \dfrac{3}{10}$

Multiply. Use the shortcut.

5. $\dfrac{6}{10} \times \dfrac{5}{6}$

6. $\dfrac{4}{5} \times \dfrac{5}{4}$

7. $\dfrac{3}{8} \times \dfrac{4}{9}$

8. $\dfrac{1}{8} \times \dfrac{6}{7}$

Multiply. Do not use the shortcut.

1. $\frac{1}{3} \times \frac{1}{3}$ **2.** $\frac{2}{9} \times \frac{3}{8}$ **3.** $\frac{2}{3} \times \frac{3}{10}$ **4.** $\frac{8}{9} \times \frac{3}{2}$

Multiply. Use the shortcut.

5. $\frac{1}{6} \times \frac{9}{10}$ **6.** $\frac{3}{8} \times \frac{8}{9}$ **7.** $\frac{2}{5} \times \frac{5}{2}$ **8.** $\frac{10}{8} \times \frac{3}{5}$

9. $\frac{5}{8} \times \frac{4}{5} \times \frac{1}{2}$ **10.** $\frac{7}{8} \times \frac{2}{7} \times \frac{4}{9}$ **11.** $\frac{1}{2} \times \frac{4}{5} \times \frac{3}{8}$

12. $\frac{4}{5} \times \frac{1}{3} \times \frac{5}{12}$ **13.** $\frac{5}{8} \times 2 \times \frac{4}{5}$ **14.** $\frac{2}{3} \times \frac{3}{4} \times \frac{4}{5}$

APPLY

MATH REASONING

15. Draw a picture that shows that $\frac{1}{2}$ of $\frac{3}{4}$ is $\frac{3}{8}$.

16. Draw a picture that shows that $\frac{1}{3}$ of $\frac{2}{5}$ is $\frac{2}{15}$.

PROBLEM SOLVING

17. Three-fourths of the tickets to a play at an outdoor theater were sold the first day they went on sale. Of these tickets, $\frac{1}{2}$ were sold to senior citizens. What fraction of all the tickets were sold to senior citizens the first day?

18. Leslie wanted to read half of her library book over the weekend. On Monday, she told her mother she had read only $\frac{1}{4}$ of what she had wanted to read. What fraction of the book did she read on the weekend?

▶ USING CRITICAL THINKING   Discover a Rule

Fractions such as $\frac{3}{3}$, $\frac{5}{5}$, and $\frac{24}{24}$ are different names for 1. Use this idea to find replacements for the variables.

19. $\frac{2}{3} \cdot \frac{x}{y} = 1$ **20.** $\frac{1}{5} \cdot \frac{n}{m} = 1$ **21.** $\frac{3}{4} \cdot \frac{p}{q} = 1$

22. Write a sentence that for any given fraction tells what you should multiply by to get 1.

Multiplying Mixed Numbers

LEARN ABOUT IT

You can use what you know about multiplying whole numbers and fractions to multiply mixed numbers.

EXPLORE **Analyze the Process**

The recipe at the right serves 4–6 people. Suppose Perry needs $3\frac{1}{2}$ times as much stew as this recipe makes. How many cups of oysters should he use?

Why is multiplication needed to solve this problem?

Write mixed numbers as fractions.	Multiply the fractions.	Express in lowest terms.

$$3\frac{1}{2} \times 2\frac{1}{2} = \frac{7}{2} \times \frac{5}{2} \qquad \frac{7}{2} \times \frac{5}{2} = \frac{7 \times 5}{2 \times 2} = \frac{35}{4} \qquad \frac{35}{4} = 8\frac{3}{4}$$

TALK ABOUT IT

1. Explain how each mixed number was changed to an improper fraction.

2. Using rounding, what would you have estimated the answer to be?

3. Use a complete sentence to give a reasonable answer to the problem above.

Other Examples

A $5\frac{3}{4} \times \frac{8}{9} = \frac{23}{4} \times \frac{8}{9}$

$$= \frac{46}{9}$$

$$= 5\frac{1}{9}$$

B $2\frac{1}{2} \times 3\frac{2}{5} = \frac{5}{2} \times \frac{17}{5}$

$$= \frac{17}{2}$$

$$= 8\frac{1}{2}$$

TRY IT OUT

Multiply. Express the product in lowest terms.

1. $1\frac{4}{5} \times 1\frac{1}{3}$

2. $2\frac{1}{3} \times 1\frac{7}{8}$

3. $4 \times 3\frac{1}{6}$

4. $4\frac{1}{2} \times 1\frac{1}{3}$

5. $2\frac{4}{5} \times \frac{3}{7}$

6. $5\frac{3}{5} \times 10$

7. $3\frac{1}{2} \times 3\frac{1}{5}$

8. $2\frac{4}{9} \times 3\frac{3}{4}$

Multiply. Express the product in lowest terms.

1. $2\frac{1}{2} \times 2\frac{2}{3}$ 　　**2.** $4\frac{4}{5} \times \frac{2}{3}$ 　　**3.** $3\frac{1}{3} \times 4\frac{1}{8}$ 　　**4.** $1\frac{7}{8} \times 3\frac{2}{3}$

5. $2\frac{5}{8} \times 1\frac{3}{7}$ 　　**6.** $7\frac{1}{2} \times 4\frac{2}{5}$ 　　**7.** $9 \times \frac{1}{9}$ 　　**8.** $1\frac{5}{6} \times 4\frac{2}{7}$

9. $2\frac{2}{3} \times \frac{3}{10} \times 5$ 　　**10.** $1\frac{1}{2} \times 2\frac{1}{4} \times 3\frac{1}{3}$ 　　**11.** $6 \times 7\frac{1}{3} \times \frac{3}{4}$

Estimate each product.

12. $3\frac{5}{6} \times 4\frac{1}{8}$ 　　**13.** $7\frac{2}{5} \times 5\frac{2}{3}$ 　　**14.** $10\frac{1}{16} \times 4\frac{3}{8}$ 　　**15.** $8\frac{1}{2} \times 7\frac{7}{9}$

16. $\frac{4}{5} \times 7\frac{2}{3} \times 5\frac{1}{7}$ 　　**17.** $6\frac{2}{3} \times 4\frac{1}{8} \times 4\frac{1}{2}$ 　　**18.** $5\frac{3}{4} \times \frac{7}{8} \times 9\frac{5}{6}$

MATH REASONING

19. Give a number that you can multiply by $5\frac{1}{4}$ and have a product less than $5\frac{1}{4}$.

20. Give two mixed numbers whose product is between 5 and 6.

PROBLEM SOLVING

21. How much butter would Perry need to make 6 batches of stew?

22. Health and Fitness Data Bank Perry wants to make Pizza Snackers but he wants to use an entire 6-oz can of tomato paste. Write the new amounts for the increased recipe.

DATA BANK

MIXED REVIEW

Find the fourth angle of a quadrilateral with the given angles.

23. 128°, 32°, 81° 　　**24.** 90°, 90°, 90° 　　**25.** 90°, 79°, 88° 　　**26.** 98°, 105°, 37°

Find the decimal for each fraction. Use a bar to show repeating decimals.

27. $\frac{1}{6}$ 　　**28.** $\frac{7}{20}$ 　　**29.** $\frac{5}{6}$ 　　**30.** $\frac{3}{8}$

Score 1	5
Score 2	9
Score 3	8
Score 4	9
Score 5	10
Score 6	9

31. Find the mean for the scores.

32. Find the median for the scores.

33. Find the mode for the scores.

More Practice, page 531, set E

Dividing Fractions

LEARN ABOUT IT

One way to think about $12 \div 4$ is, "How many 4's are in 12?" Thinking about division this way can help you understand dividing fractions.

EXPLORE **Analyze the Process**

Draw a diagram to show the answer to each of the following division problems. Use a circle to represent 1 whole unit.

- $2 \div \frac{1}{4} = x$;   How many $\frac{1}{4}$'s are in 2?

- $\frac{2}{3} \div \frac{1}{6} = m$;   How many $\frac{1}{6}$'s are in $\frac{2}{3}$?

To divide fractions, we use **reciprocals.** Two numbers are reciprocals of each other if their product is 1.

$$\frac{1}{6} \times \frac{6}{1} = \frac{6}{6} = 1 \qquad\qquad \frac{1}{6} \text{ and } \frac{6}{1} \text{ are reciprocals of each other.}$$

Look at the divisor.	Find the reciprocal of the divisor.	Multiply the dividend by the reciprocal of the divisor.
$\frac{2}{3} \div \frac{1}{6}$	$\frac{6}{1}$	$\frac{2}{3} \times \frac{6}{1} = \frac{12}{3} = 4$

TALK ABOUT IT

1. How can you be sure that 6 is the reciprocal of $\frac{1}{6}$?

2. Use a complete sentence to answer to the problem above.

Other Examples

A $\frac{4}{5} \div \frac{5}{8} = \frac{4}{5} \times \frac{8}{5} = \frac{32}{25} = 1\frac{7}{25}$

B $12 \div \frac{3}{8} = 12 \times \frac{8}{3} = \frac{96}{3} = 32$

TRY IT OUT

Divide.

1. $\frac{3}{8} \div \frac{2}{3}$
2. $\frac{5}{6} \div \frac{3}{4}$
3. $\frac{4}{7} \div 8$
4. $\frac{3}{5} \div \frac{9}{10}$

Divide.

1. $\frac{1}{3} \div \frac{1}{6}$ **2.** $\frac{3}{4} \div \frac{1}{2}$ **3.** $\frac{5}{8} \div \frac{1}{16}$ **4.** $\frac{1}{12} \div \frac{2}{3}$

5. $\frac{6}{7} \div 12$ **6.** $\frac{3}{5} \div \frac{3}{10}$ **7.** $\frac{7}{10} \div \frac{1}{2}$ **8.** $\frac{4}{9} \div \frac{2}{5}$

9. $\frac{4}{15} \div \frac{4}{5}$ **10.** $\frac{15}{16} \div \frac{5}{8}$ **11.** $\frac{7}{16} \div \frac{1}{4}$ **12.** $\frac{5}{12} \div \frac{3}{16}$

13. Find the quotient when $\frac{8}{10}$ is divided by $\frac{4}{6}$.

APPLY

MATH REASONING Write a description of what was done in each step of this proof to show why you multiply by the reciprocal when dividing by a fraction.

14. $\frac{2}{3} \div \frac{1}{6} = \left(\frac{2}{3} \times \frac{6}{1} \right) \div \left(\frac{1}{6} \times \frac{6}{1} \right)$

$= \left(\frac{2}{3} \times \frac{6}{1} \right) \div 1$

$= \frac{2}{3} \times \frac{6}{1}$

PROBLEM SOLVING

15. An aquarium is to be filled $\frac{2}{3}$ full of water. It takes 1 minute to fill it $\frac{1}{4}$ full. How long will it take to fill the aquarium?

16. It takes a certain lumberjack $\frac{1}{2}$ minute to cut a certain size log into 3 pieces. How long would it take this person to cut the same size log into 6 pieces?

▶ **USING CRITICAL THINKING   Test Your Conjecture**

17. Decide whether the following conjecture is always true. Use examples to convince a classmate you are correct.

Conjecture: When you divide two fractions, the quotient is always greater than the dividend.

18. Make another conjecture about division of fractions and test your conjecture.

More Practice, page 531, set F

Dividing Mixed Numbers

You can use what you know about dividing fractions to divide mixed numbers.

EXPLORE **Analyze the Process**

A road crew can repair about $\frac{3}{8}$ mile of road each day. How many days will it take the crew to repair a stretch of road $4\frac{1}{2}$ miles long?

- Tell why division is the operation needed to solve this problem.

Here is how to find the exact answer.

Write mixed numbers or whole number as improper fractions.	Divide the fractions.

$$4\frac{1}{2} \div \frac{3}{8} = \frac{9}{2} \div \frac{3}{8}$$

$$\frac{9}{2} \div \frac{3}{8} = \frac{9}{2} \times \frac{8}{3} = \frac{72}{6} = 12$$

TALK ABOUT IT

1. Does it matter if the fractions do not have the same denominator?

2. How could you have estimated the answer?

3. Use a complete sentence to answer the problem above.

Other Examples

A $6\frac{2}{3} \div 5\frac{1}{3} = \frac{20}{3} \div \frac{16}{3}$

$$= \frac{\overset{5}{\cancel{20}}}{\underset{1}{\cancel{3}}} \times \frac{\overset{1}{\cancel{3}}}{\underset{4}{\cancel{16}}} = \frac{5}{4}$$

$$= 1\frac{1}{4}$$

B $3\frac{1}{4} \div 2 = \frac{13}{4} \div \frac{2}{1}$

$$= \frac{13}{4} \times \frac{1}{2} = \frac{13}{8}$$

$$= 1\frac{5}{8}$$

Find the quotient.

1. $1\frac{3}{4} \div \frac{7}{8}$

2. $1\frac{2}{3} \div 1\frac{1}{9}$

3. $4 \div 2\frac{2}{9}$

4. $3\frac{1}{2} \div 2\frac{4}{5}$

Find the quotient.

1. $2\frac{4}{5} \div \frac{7}{10}$ **2.** $1\frac{5}{8} \div \frac{1}{2}$ **3.** $4 \div 1\frac{1}{7}$ **4.** $2\frac{3}{8} \div 4\frac{3}{4}$

5. $4\frac{1}{6} \div 3\frac{3}{4}$ **6.** $2\frac{1}{2} \div 3\frac{3}{4}$ **7.** $1\frac{1}{3} \div 2\frac{5}{6}$ **8.** $6\frac{1}{4} \div 5$

9. $6\frac{2}{3} \div 3\frac{1}{9}$ **10.** $3\frac{7}{8} \div \frac{3}{16}$ **11.** $4\frac{4}{5} \div 3\frac{1}{5}$ **13.** $1\frac{3}{4} \div \frac{7}{8}$

Estimate each quotient.

13. $2\frac{1}{2} \div \frac{3}{4}$ **14.** $11\frac{7}{8} \div 2\frac{5}{6}$ **15.** $11\frac{3}{4} \div 5\frac{3}{4}$ **16.** $\frac{11}{16} \div \frac{3}{16}$

17. $20\frac{1}{8} \div 4\frac{3}{8}$ **18.** $26\frac{8}{9} \div 6\frac{1}{2}$ **19.** $1\frac{5}{6} \div \frac{1}{2}$ **20.** $33\frac{7}{12} \div 5$

APPLY

MATH REASONING Find the value of the variable.

21. $n \div 2\frac{1}{3} = 1\frac{2}{3}$ **22.** $m \div \frac{7}{8} = 2\frac{1}{3}$ **23.** $5\frac{1}{4} \div p = 2\frac{1}{2}$

PROBLEM SOLVING

24. A certain road crew can lay $2\frac{1}{4}$ miles of divider sections each day. At this rate, how many days would it take the crew to complete 20 miles of highway?

25. Missing Data This problem has missing data. Make up reasonable data. Then solve the problem using your data.

The distance from home plate to first base on a softball field is 60 ft. About how many strides would a typical 7th grade student use to run from home plate to first base?

▶ **EXPLORING ALGEBRA**

You can simplify fractional expressions involving variables using the same processes as for fractions.

Example Simplify $\dfrac{2xy}{4x}$

$$\frac{2xy}{4x} = \frac{\overset{11}{\cancel{2}x y}}{\underset{21}{\cancel{4x}}} = \frac{1 \cdot 1 \cdot y}{2 \cdot 1} = \frac{y}{2}$$

26. $\dfrac{9ab}{3bc}$ **27.** $\dfrac{4mn}{10m}$ **28.** $\dfrac{9x}{21xz}$

More Practice, page 532, set A

Problem Solving
Determining Reasonable Answers

UNDERSTAND
ANALYZE DATA
PLAN
ESTIMATE
SOLVE
EXAMINE

LEARN ABOUT IT

An important part of evaluating your thinking and work when you solve problems is checking your work. The chart shows some ways to do this.

Check Your Work
- Is the answer reasonable?
- Is the arithmetic correct?
- Did you use the strategies correctly?

Examples Do not solve the problem.

Decide if the answer given is reasonable. If it is not reasonable, explain why.

Problem: Jon is 13 years old and weighs 108 pounds. According to the chart, how many calories does he need to consume for each pound of body weight?

Answer: Jon needs to consume 250 calories for each pound.

Daily Calories			
Boys		**Girls**	
Age	**Calories**	**Age**	**Calories**
1–14	2700	11–14	2200
15–18	2800	15–18	2100

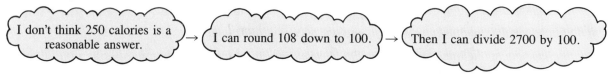

I don't think 250 calories is a reasonable answer. → I can round 108 down to 100. → Then I can divide 2700 by 100.

$$108 \, lb \longrightarrow 100 \, lb \qquad 2700 \div 100 = 27$$

But the correct answer must be less than 27 since I rounded down.

250 calories per pound is not a reasonable answer.

TRY IT OUT

Do not solve the problem. Decide if the answer given is reasonable. If it is not reasonable, explain why.

1. Valerie is 12 years old. For breakfast and lunch she ate a total of 1350 calories. How many calories should she eat for dinner?

   Answer: Valerie should eat 950 calories.

2. A glass of milk has 140 calories. Juan drank 6 glasses of milk. How many calories did the milk have?

   Answer: The milk had 940 calories.

186

1. Greg wants to bake 3 loaves of buttermilk bread. He decided to make $1\frac{1}{2}$ recipes. How much flour does he need?

2. Darla bought a quart of buttermilk for $1.39 to make buttermilk bread. How many times will she be able to make the recipe?

3. Dylan has a 12-ounce jar of honey and 4 packages of yeast. He used $\frac{1}{3}$ of the honey to make bread. How many ounces does he have left?

4. Mrs. Meyers wants to eat 2,150 calories each day. So far today, she has eaten 320 calories for breakfast and 550 calories for lunch. How many more calories should she eat today?

5. For lunch Joel ate an apple, a turkey sandwich made with 2 slices of bread, 4 oz of turkey, and 1 tablespoon of mayonnaise, and an 8-ounce glass of chocolate milk. Use the table to find how many calories Joel ate.

Food	Calories
Apple	96
Whole Wheat Bread	85/slice
Turkey (8 oz)	416
Mayonnaise 1 T.	103
Chocolate Milk	212

Buttermilk Bread

makes 2 loaves

Ingredients:
- 2 tsp. yeast
- $1\frac{1}{4}$ cups warm water
- $1\frac{1}{3}$ cups buttermilk
- $\frac{1}{4}$ cup honey
- $5\frac{2}{3}$ cups whole wheat flour
- 2 tsp. salt

6. The school cafeteria started selling granola bars on Monday. One was sold the first day, 4 the second day, and 7 the third day. At this rate, how many granola bars will be sold on the 12th day?

7. Rachelle should eat at least 46 grams of protein each day. She has eaten $\frac{3}{5}$ of her daily requirement. About how many grams of protein has she eaten?

8. **Think About Your Solution**
   Solve. Doug ate 36 peanuts and cashews. The nuts had 10 grams of protein. If 8 peanuts have 2 grams of protein and 3 cashews have 1 gram of protein, how many nuts of each kind did Doug eat?

   a. Write your answer in a complete sentence.

   b. Write a description of how you solved the problem.

   c. Name the strategy or strategies you used.

187

Data Collection and Analysis
Group Decision Making

UNDERSTAND
ANALYZE DATA
PLAN
ESTIMATE
SOLVE
EXAMINE

Doing a Simulation

Group Skill:
Encourage and Respect Others

On a teen quiz you can win a surfboard, a trip to Hawaii with your family, or a $500 gift certificate in a clothing store. The contestant spins two wheels, and a prize is won if the spins match. Predict how often there is a winner. One out of two contestants? One out of three contestants? Work in groups to find out what is likely to happen. Conduct a **simulation** to gather data by acting out the situation.

Collecting Data

1. You will need two wheels with the names of the prizes on each.

2. Pretend the members of your group are contestants and take turns spinning the **pair** of wheels. Record how many contestants must spin before a match is made and a prize is won. Keep a record of 25 trials.

Trial	Number of contestants before a prize is won
Trial 1	3
Trial 2	7
Trial 3	5
Trial 4	5
Trial 5	. . . .
. . . . . .	. . . . .
. . . . . .	. . . . . .

3. Use the data your group collects to make a bar graph. Select the scales on the graph to suit the group's data.

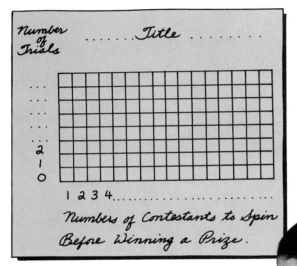

4. Check! Did you title and label the graph?

5. Were you surprised by how many contestants had to spin the wheels in order to win a prize? Did you think prizes would be given more often or less often? Explain the results of your simulation.

6. Were your results similar to the results of other groups?

189

WRAP UP

Fractured Fractions

Match the fraction parts to the descriptions. You should have no parts left over when you are finished.

1. A fraction equal to $\frac{2}{7}$.

2. The reciprocal of $\frac{2}{3}$.

3. The sum of $\frac{3}{5}$ and $\frac{2}{6}$.

4. The difference between $\frac{7}{8}$ and $\frac{1}{4}$.

5. A mixed number that rounds to 3.

6. The product of $\frac{4}{5}$ and $\frac{2}{3}$.

7. One half of two and three fourths.

8. The number of halves in two and three fourths.

1	3	5	$\overline{14}$
$1\underline{}$	$3\underline{}$	$\underline{}6$	$\overline{15}$
$1\underline{}$	$3\underline{}$	$\underline{}8$	$\underline{28}$
$\underline{}2$	$4\underline{}$	$8\underline{}$	$\overline{30}$
$\underline{}2$	$5\underline{}$	$\underline{}8$	$\overline{}$

Sometimes, Always, Never

Which word should go in the blank, *sometimes*, *always*, or *never*? Explain your choice.

9. The product of two mixed numbers is __?__ greater than either of the factors.

10. The sum of a fraction and its reciprocal is __?__ equal to 1.

11. The product of a fraction and its reciprocal is __?__ 1.

12. The difference between a fraction and its reciprocal is __?__ zero.

13. The quotient of two whole numbers is __?__ a fraction that is less than 1.

Project

Make a model. Use construction paper, a newspaper, or strips of paper to model these situations.

- Fold rectangles to show halves, thirds, fourths, sixths, eighths, ninths, and sixteenths.
- Fold equilateral triangles to illustrate thirds and sixths.

CHAPTER REVIEW/TEST

Part 1   Understanding

1. Estimate the difference using rounding.

$$33\frac{2}{5} - 13\frac{5}{8}$$

2. In the problem $9\frac{2}{5} - 1\frac{2}{10}$, the number $9\frac{2}{5}$ should be renamed as ____?____.

  A $9\frac{20}{50}$ **B** $9\frac{4}{10}$

  C $1\frac{14}{20}$ **D** $1\frac{3}{5}$

3. Is the relation shown in the table a function?

1	2	3	4	5	6
5	7	9	11	13	15

Part 2   Skills

Compute. Write the answer in lowest terms.

4. $\frac{3}{4} + \frac{7}{12}$ **5.** $\frac{4}{5} - \frac{3}{10}$ **6.** $6\frac{1}{4} \times \frac{1}{2}$ **7.** $3\frac{1}{4} \div 2\frac{1}{2}$

Find the fraction of the number.

8. $\frac{2}{3}$ of 12   **9.** $\frac{3}{4} \times 16$

Part 3   Applications

10. In 1987 Stella and Bob each started a job that paid $20,000. Each year Stella got a raise of $5,000 and Bob got a raise of $1,500. In what year will Stella be earning twice as much as Bob?

11. Which set of numbers can help you find the sum?

$$\frac{5}{8} + \frac{3}{4}$$

A	8	12	20	32
B	20	24	44	32
C	15	32	47	32

Give the value for each variable.

12. $\frac{5}{m} \cdot 36 = 20$ **13.** $\frac{n}{7} \cdot 28 = 24$

14. **Challenge** An aquarium tide pool will be filled $\frac{7}{8}$ full of water. The pool now contains 520 gallons and is $\frac{1}{4}$ full. How many gallons will be in the pool when it is $\frac{7}{8}$ full? Is the answer, 9,100 gallons reasonable or unreasonable? Explain why.

Imagine a drawing of an island made by following these instructions.

- The first stage is an equilateral triangle.
- The second stage is formed by constructing equilateral triangles outwardly on the middle third of each side of the triangle.
- The third stage is formed by constructing equilateral triangles outwardly on each middle third of each segment of the figure in the previous stage.
- Repeat the process described in step 3 as many times as you wish or can.

The resulting figure is called a **Koch Island,** named after Helge Von Koch (1870–1924). Koch islands are part of a branch of geometry called **fractal geometry.** Fractal geometry deals with complex shapes such as coastlines, snowflakes, and other irregular shapes. The word fractal was coined by Benoit B. Mandelbrot in 1975 when he published the first book on this subject.

1. Draw a large equilateral triangle on a sheet of newsprint. Construct as many stages of Koch Island as you can.

2. Estimate the area of the Koch Island you have made. Does the area increase with each stage? Do you think the area will increase without limit?

3. Find the perimeter of each stage of the Koch Island you have made. If you continued the stages would the perimeter become larger and larger? Do you think there is any limit to the perimeter?

4. Suppose a Koch Island were made starting with an equilateral triangle 120 cm on each side. What is the perimeter and area for the first 2 stages of the island?

CUMULATIVE REVIEW

1. What is the mode for this set of numbers?

    19.7   19.3   20.9   19.7   18.6   18.8

    A 20.9   **B** 19.7

    C 19.5   **D** not given

2. What is the sum of percentages in a circle graph?

    A 90   **B** 100   **C** 180   **D** 360

3. Which is the correct method for finding 47×6?

    A $(50 \times 6) - 3$

    B $(47 \times 10) - 4$

    C $(40 \times 6) + (7 \times 6)$

    D $(40 + 6) \times (7 + 6)$

Use the diagram to answer questions 4 and 5.

4. What type of line is l?

    A perpendicular

    B transversal

    C parallel

    D plane

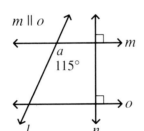

5. What is the measure of an angle that is supplementary to $\angle A$?

    A 65°   **B** 115°

    C 90°   **D** 180°

6. What is the measure of the fourth angle?

    A 115°

    B 65°

    C 295°

    D 148°

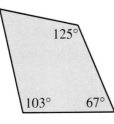

7. 3,801 is divisible by which number?

    A 8   **B** 6

    C 3   **D** 9

8. What is the prime factorization of 88?

    A $2 \cdot 2 \cdot 2 \cdot 11$ **B** $2 \cdot 2 \cdot 11$

    C $2 \cdot 4 \cdot 11$ **D** $2^4 \cdot 11$

9. What is the GCF of 24 and 180?

    A 24   **B** 6

    C 18   **D** 12

10. What is the LCM of 11 and 15?

    A 11   **B** 55

    C 165   **D** 330

11. Give the value for n.

    $$\frac{6}{7} = \frac{n}{28}$$

    A 12   **B** 24

    C 6   **D** 18

12. Matt has 5 shirts and 3 pairs of shorts. How many different outfits can he wear?

    A 8   **B** 15

    C 2   **D** not given

13. The coach of a field hockey team chose 15 of the 45 players who tried out for the team. What fraction of the players were chosen?

    A $\frac{1}{5}$ **B** $\frac{2}{5}$

    C $\frac{3}{8}$ **D** $\frac{1}{3}$

7

INTRODUCTION TO ALGEBRA

MATH AND SCIENCE

DATA BANK

Use the Science Data Bank on page 493 to answer the questions.

1 What is the difference between the atomic weights of calcium (Ca) and carbon (C)?

2 The atomic weight of oxygen (O) is how many times greater than that of helium (He)?

3 Compare the molecular weights of carbon monoxide and carbon dioxide. What is the reason for the difference in their molecular weights?

4 **Using Critical Thinking** Study the symbols for the compounds. When both hydrogen and oxygen are present, is there a relationship between them? Is this relationship always the same?

Algebraic Expressions
Addition and Subtraction

LEARN ABOUT IT

EXPLORE **Examine the Situation**

Did you ever stop at a booth like this one when the fair was in town? The booth operator claims he can guess your weight within 5 pounds and your age within 3 years.

TALK ABOUT IT

1. Give three weights close enough to 85 pounds for the operator to win.

2. What are two ages for a twelve-year-old—one higher, one lower—he could say and lose?

Diagrams can help you understand **algebraic expressions** such as $w + 5$.

Examples

A Describe the greatest weight the operator could guess and win.

word phrase	algebraic expression	diagram
weight plus five	$w + 5$	

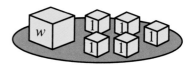

B Describe the least age the operator could guess and win.

word phrase	algebraic expression	diagram
age less three	$a - 3$	

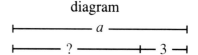

TRY IT OUT

Write an expression and draw a diagram for each word phrase.

1. weight plus seven
2. age plus eight
3. weight less two
4. age less five

Write algebraic expressions for these word phrases. Use *n* to stand for "a number."

1. 3 more than a number

2. A number decreased by 5

3. The sum of 97.1 and a number

4. 100 minus a number

Write word phrases for these expressions.

5. $x + 14$

6. $953 - n$

7. $w - 79.2$

8. $p + 13.8$

9. $13.27 + f$

10. $y - 0.14$

Draw diagrams and write algebraic expressions to show:

11. *m* miles more than 1.5 miles

12. 38 years less than *y* years

13. *d* degrees more than 98.7

14. *j* inches decreased by 3.54 inches

APPLY

MATH REASONING Write an algebraic expression for the perimeter of each figure.

15.

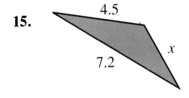

16.

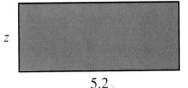

PROBLEM SOLVING

17. A ticket to the carnival is *d* dollars for children. The cost is $2 more for adults. Write an expression for the cost of one adult ticket.

18. The cost of the "guess my weight" game is *c* cents for adults. The cost for a child is 25¢ less. Write an expression for the cost of a child's game.

▶ **USING CRITICAL THINKING   Use a Counterexample**

Label each statement true or false. Give a counterexample for each false statement.

19. If *n* is a whole number, the next whole number is $n + 1$.

20. If *n* is an even number, the preceding even number is $n - 2$.

21. If *n* is a whole number, the preceding whole number is $n - 1$.

22. If *n* is a prime number, the next prime number is $n + 2$.

More Practice, page 532, set B

Algebraic Expressions
Multiplication and Division

LEARN ABOUT IT

EXPLORE **Imagine the Situation**

About how far can you jump? Can you estimate the difference within an inch or two? Imagine for a moment you are on the moon where the gravity is one-seventh what it is on earth, and that your jump distance would be seven times as long.

TALK ABOUT IT

1. How far would you go on earth in ten jumps? How far on the moon?

2. If a 700-pound moon creature could jump 210 inches on the moon, what would it weigh on earth? How far could it jump on earth?

Variables can be used with multiplication and division in algebraic expressions. For multiplication, "10 times j" can be written in three ways:

$$10 \times j \qquad 10 \cdot j \qquad 10j$$

Diagrams are helpful in showing relationships in such expressions.

- Let j stand for jump distance. Describe the length of 10 jumps.

word phrase	algebraic expression	diagram
ten jumps	$10 \cdot j$ or $10j$	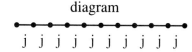

- Describe how to change jump distance from inches to feet.

word phrase	algebraic expression	diagram
inches divided by twelve	$j \div 12$ or $\dfrac{j}{12}$	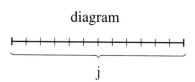

TRY IT OUT

Write expressions and draw diagrams for:

1. 6 strides of length t

2. five times weight k

3. length l divided by 4

4. the width of a rectangle: area a, length 37

PRACTICE

Write an algebraic expression and draw a diagram for each situation.

1. length *l* divided by 3

2. a jump 2 times as high as *j*

3. six times as much milk as *m* pints

4. a weight *w* divided into thirds

Write an algebraic expression that tells you how many:

5. feet are in *y* yards

6. minutes are in *h* hours

7. pennies are worth *d* dollars

8. meters are in *k* kilometers

Write an algebraic expression that tells how to change:

9. *p* pounds into tons

10. *i* inches into feet

11. *d* days into weeks

12. *q* quarts into gallons

APPLY

MATH REASONING

13. Write a multiplication or division expression that will give the value of the ?. The "value" inside the rectangle shows the area of the rectangle.

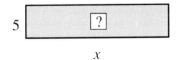 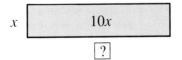 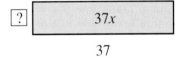

PROBLEM SOLVING

14. A child's stride is *k* inches. Her father's stride is 3 times as long. Write an expression for the father's stride.

15. A good standing broad jump might be *h* inches. Write an expression that gives the number of feet this would equal.

MIXED REVIEW

Find the answers. Express in lowest terms.

16. $\frac{7}{8} - \frac{1}{8}$

17. $\frac{3}{4} + \frac{4}{5}$

18. $\frac{5}{6} - \frac{2}{3}$

19. $\frac{1}{5} \times \frac{3}{7}$

Write in standard notation.

20. 1.724×10^3

21. 1.02×10^4

22. 1.473×10^2

Problem Solving
Translating Phrases into Algebraic Expressions

UNDERSTAND
ANALYZE DATA
PLAN
ESTIMATE
SOLVE
EXAMINE

LEARN ABOUT IT

Many problems we need to solve can be represented by algebraic expressions. Here are some examples.

A A new saw blade cost 40¢ more to make than an old, less efficient blade. Write an expression for the cost of making a new saw blade.

Let x be the cost of the older saw blade.

$x + 40$ The cost of the new saw blade is 40¢ more.

B A power planer smooths a number of rough boards each hour. Write an expression for the number of boards planed in a 24-hour day.

Let b be the number of boards planed each hour.

$24b$ The number of boards planed in a 24-hour day.

C A lumber yard is separated equally into a work area, a sales area, and a storage area. Write an expression that shows how much of the building is used for each purpose.

Let g be the size of the lumber yard.

$\frac{g}{3}$ The lumber yard is divided in three parts, so each part is a third of the total.

TRY IT OUT

Translate each situation into an algebraic expression.

1. Mrs. Wilson just had a birthday. Let n be Mrs. Wilson's age. Write an expression that tells what Mrs. Wilson's age was 12 years ago.

2. Maria started running d miles each week. After one month she doubled the distance. Write an expression for the weekly distance she ran the second month.

3. A software engineer earns three times as much as she did in her old job five years before. Let h be her salary five years ago. Write an expression for her current salary.

4. A factory replaced old motors with new motors that each used 100 watts less power. Let p be the power used by each old motor. Write an expression for the power each new motor uses.

Solve. Use any problem solving strategy.

1. Wye Oak tree in Maryland is the largest white oak in the United States. It is 102 ft tall and its crown is 1,598 ft wide. The average seventh grader is $5\frac{1}{4}$ ft tall. About how many seventh graders lying head to toe would it take to equal the Wye Oak's width?

2. Carol wants to plant a lemon tree, a walnut tree, an avocado tree, and an orange tree in a row at the back of her yard. How many different arrangements are possible?

3. Some species of bamboo can grow as much as 35 in. per day! At this rate how long would it take a plant 44 in. tall to reach 27 feet?

4. Foresters planted 42 trees in a park, including 15 oaks. The rest were Douglas firs. How many Douglas firs did they plant?

5. In 1984 a limb fell off the Wye Oak. It weighed more than 6 African elephants, which average $6\frac{1}{2}$ tons. How much did the limb weigh?

6. The General Sherman sequoia tree in Sequoia National Park is 274.9 ft tall. It now grows at about 0.04 in. per year. How long will it take for the tree to get a foot taller?

7. Norma has a piece of ironwood and a piece of cork, both the same size. The ironwood is six times as heavy as the cork. Together they weigh 84 pounds. How much does each piece weigh?

8. **Write Your Own Problem**
Write a problem that can be solved using this numerical expression.

$$10.00 - 5(1.75)$$

Then solve your problem.

Solving Equations Using Objects

LEARN ABOUT IT

An **equation** is a mathematical sentence stating that two expressions name the same number. You can use color chips to model equations and the process of solving equations.

EXPLORE Use Objects to Represent an Equation

Work in groups. Here is how to show the equation

$$x - 2 = 4$$

Use chips and paper squares $\boxed{x}$ for the unknown x to show these equations.

(a) $x + 3 = 7$ **(b)** $2x = 8$

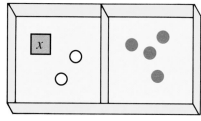

$x - 2 = 4$

TALK ABOUT IT

1. How many chips and of what color did you use for equation (a)?

2. How did you decide how many $\boxed{x}$ squares to use for equation (b)?

3. In (b), why should the $\boxed{x}$ squares be the same size?

You can use the color chips and squares to find the value of the unknown, or variable $\boxed{x}$. Follow these steps to find the value of the $\boxed{x}$.

             Add 1 red to each side.   **Remove the red and white**   **Separate into 2**
                                         that "cancel" each other.   **equal groups.**

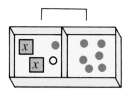 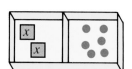 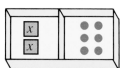

So $\boxed{x}$ is the same as ●●●

TRY IT OUT

Use objects to find what $\boxed{x}$ stands for in terms of color chips.

1. 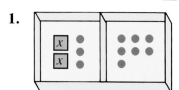   **2.** 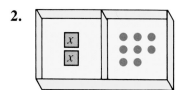   **3.**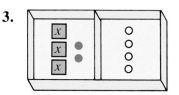

Use objects to find what x stands for in terms of color chips.

1.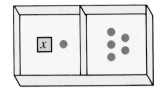

2.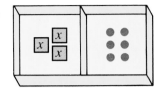

3.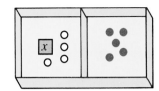

4.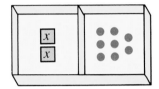

5.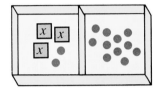

6.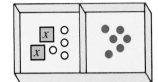

7.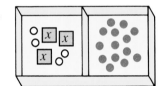

8.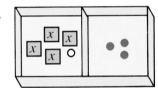

APPLY

MATH REASONING Use objects to find what x represents in terms of color chips. Start by getting all x on the same side of the line.

9.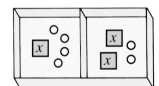

10.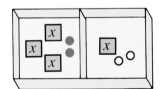

PROBLEM SOLVING

11. The equation $d = 2t$ gives the distance you can walk in t hours at a rate of 2 mph. Assume you can average 2 mph. How long would it take you to walk 12 miles?

▶ **USING CRITICAL THINKING   Analyze the Equation**

Write a problem that you might solve using each of the following equations.

1. $x + 5 = 9$ **2.** $a - 13 = 21$ **3.** $4t = 32$

4. $2s + 5 = 16$ **5.** $6y - 1 = 2$ **6.** $6x = 24$

More Practice, page 532, set D

Using Critical Thinking
Analyzing Data to Discover a Pattern

Three salespersons, Ms. Carter, Mr. Hoffman, and Ms. Biloxi, take a train to one of five different bus stops, depending on which customers they are calling on. Ms. Carter keeps records to compare the length of each train ride to the cost of the ride.

"I believe it will cost us $48 to get to bus stop 4," said Ms. Carter.

"No," said Mr. Hoffman. "I don't agree. According to this pattern, it should cost only $43."

"You're both wrong," Ms. Biloxi said. "The cost is only $33."

Bus Stop Number	Length of Ride	Cost of Ride
1	20 minutes	$13
2	30 minutes	$18
3	50 minutes	$28
4	60 minutes	?
5	90 minutes	?

TALK ABOUT IT

1. What are the three salespersons trying to do?

2. To check and extend the numbers in the cost column of the table, which salesperson might have—

   a) started with 13, and then added 5, then 10, then 15?
   b) first added 5, then doubled the amount added?
   c) added 5, then 10, then 5?

3. Which, if any, do you think was correct? Explain. Can you give an equation that shows how to find the numbers for the costs in this table?

TRY IT OUT

Look for a possible pattern. Copy and complete each table.

1.
miles	cost
5	$10
6	$11
9	$14
12	?
17	?

2.
months	number sold
2	5
3	?
4	9
5	11
6	?

3.
hours	number of pages
12	4
18	6
21	?
?	9
36	?

MIDCHAPTER REVIEW/QUIZ

Match each word expression with one of the algebraic expressions. If the variable a represents your present age, which expression represents

1. someone who is twice as old as you?

2. someone who is half as old as you?

3. someone who is 2 years older than you?

4. someone who is 2 years younger than you?

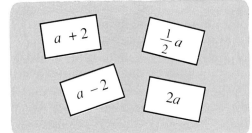

Write an algebraic expression for these phrases. Use n to stand for "a number."

5. a number increased by 5

6. 5 less than a number

7. 1 more than a number

8. 10 decreased by a number

9. 5 times as much as a number

10. one-fifth as much as a number

Multiple Choice. Choose the best answer.

11. Your next birthday is in d days. How many weeks is that?

    a. $d + 7$ **b.** $7d$ **c.** $\dfrac{d}{7}$ **d.** $d - 7$

12. You have q quarters. What is the value in dollars?

    a. $25q$ **b.** $100q$ **c.** $\dfrac{q}{4}$ **d.** $\dfrac{q}{100}$

Write a word phrase for these algebraic expressions.

13. $d + \$5.95$

14. $\$20 - d$

15. $10d$

16. $\dfrac{100}{d}$

17. $d - \$20$

18. $\dfrac{d}{100}$

PROBLEM SOLVING

Using the variable described, write the related algebraic expressions.

19. If l represents a leap year, what expression represents the following leap year? The previous leap year?

20. If you have n nickels, what is the value in pennies? In dollars?

21. If you are h inches tall, what is your height in feet? In yards?

22. Desmond's allowance is $5 more than his younger brother's. If Desmond receives d dollars, what does his brother receive?

Solving Equations Using Mental Math

LEARN ABOUT IT

EXPLORE **Evaluate the Expressions**

Make a true equation by supplying the missing number or numbers, and evaluating each side.

(a) $88 \div 4 = n \times 2$ **(b)** $24 \times y = z + 18$

Make two different true equations for each of these equations.

(c) $32 \times 3 = d + e$ **(d)** $h - 2 = k + 12$

TALK ABOUT IT

1. Is there only one value for n that makes equation **(a)** true? and one value for y and z that make a true equation in **(b)**?

A **solution** to an equation is a replacement for the variable that makes the equation true. To solve an equation means to find *all* solutions. Some equations can be solved with mental math.

Examples

A A student who wants to find the molecular weight of water, learns that half its molecular weight is 9. She wants to solve

$0.50 \times w = 9$

THINK: 0.50 times what number is 9? $0.50 \times 18 = 9$.

$w = 18$. The molecular weight of water is 18.

Check: $0.50 \times 18 = 9$, or $9 = 9$

B A chemist studying a sucrose molecule finds that the number of hydrogen atoms h can be found by solving $342 - h = 320$.

THINK: Ignore the 300 on each side. Subtract 20 from 42. $42 - 20 = 22$.

$h = 22$

There are 22 hydrogen atoms in a sucrose molecule.

Check: $342 - 320 = 22$, or $22 = 22$

TRY IT OUT

Use mental mathematics to solve each equation.

1. $5c = 100$ **2.** $3.7 - x = 2$ **3.** $\dfrac{42.6}{t} = 7.1$ **4.** $87.5 + z = 97.6$

Use mental math to solve each equation. Check.

1. $8x = 40$

2. $\frac{1}{10}r = 48$

3. $300 - t = 100$

4. $\frac{3}{19}w = 9$

5. $0.8g = 80$

6. $p + 25 = 1{,}000$

7. $50\% \times h = 250$

8. $43 + m = 44.7$

9. $n - 38 = 200$

10. $\frac{5}{10}l = 79.5$

11. $75\% \times k = 30$

12. $25b = 400$

13. $4y = 60$

14. $500 - a = 410$

15. $\frac{1}{5}e = 20$

16. $1\frac{1}{2}n = 15$

APPLY

MATH REASONING Decide which equations can be solved using mental math. Solve only those equations.

17. $4w = 100$

18. $z \div 60 = 10$

19. $\$97 + s = \$150$

20. $20.6 \times p = 600$

21. $300 - x = 230$

22. $b \times 7 = 14$

23. $q + 40 = 43.8$

24. $\frac{1}{3}y = 400$

PROBLEM SOLVING

Choose the equation needed to solve each. Use mental math to solve the equation.

25. 25 ml of acid drips into a test tube each minute. How long will it take to get 100 ml of acid?

    a. $25m = 100$ **b.** $\frac{m}{25} = 100$

26. Water makes up half of a certain solution. There are 12 grams of water. How much solution is there?

    a. $2s = 12$ **b.** $\frac{1}{2}s = 12$

27. Science Data Bank A chemical is known to contain methyl groups (CH_3). The methyl group portion of the chemical has a molecular weight of 30. How many methyl groups are present? Write an equation and solve it.

▶ **MENTAL MATH**

Use mental math to evaluate the algebraic expressions.

28. $8x + 2$ for $x = 4$

29. $20 - 6y$ for $y = 2$

30. $\frac{1}{3}z + 5$ for $z = 30$

31. $12 + \frac{1}{6}n$ for $n = 18$

32. $2(m + 9)$ for $m = 3$

33. $\frac{c + 15}{4}$ for $c = 5$

34. $7 - \frac{56}{t}$ for $t = 8$

35. $7(13 - b)$ for $b = 7$

36. $\frac{m - 9}{4}$ for $m = 17$

Problem Solving
Using Guess and Check to Solve Equations

UNDERSTAND
ANALYZE DATA
PLAN
ESTIMATE
SOLVE
EXAMINE

LEARN ABOUT IT

Many problems we need to solve can be modeled by equations with variables. The solution to the equation is the answer to the problem. A good strategy to solve equations is to **Guess and Check**.

Example

A complete bicycle service cost $15 more this year than last. This year it cost $43. What did it cost last year?

Let c be the cost last year.

Solve $c + 15 = 43$ to find the cost last year. Use guess and check.

First I'll try $c = 32$.

I'll try $c = 28$.

$32 + 15 = 47$ — too high
$28 + 15 = 43$ — correct

It cost $28 for a complete bicycle service last year.

TRY IT OUT

Solve. Use Guess and Check.

1. $x - 65 = 171$ **2.** $4n = 132$ **3.** $h + 123 = 306$

Solve the given equation using Guess and Check.

4. Tran's bike cost 5 times what his mother's cost 20 years ago. Tran paid $235 for his bike. What did his mother's bike cost?

Let c = the cost of his mother's bike. Solve $5c = 235$ to find the cost of his mother's bike.

5. A new mountain bike was on sale for $35 off the regular price. The sale price is $185. What was the original price?

Let b = the original price of the bike. Solve $b - 35 = 185$ to find the original price.

Solve. Use any problem solving strategy.

1. The 4 students in Anna's group are experimenting with pendulums. They cut a piece of string $5\frac{1}{3}$ ft long into 2 equal pieces. How long was each piece?

2. Al plans to renew his subscription to a science magazine. How much does he save each month over the newsstand price with a 1-year subscription?

N E W S S T A N D $2.95
Subscription Rates
1 Year $24.00
2 Years $45.00
3 Years $60.00

3. The Cowans have a large yard. Zach wanted his father to pay him 5¢ the first week to mow the yard, 10¢ the second week, 20¢ the third week, 40¢ the fourth week, and so on. What would Zach get the fifteenth week?

4. Emily's mother gave her money to buy lunches for 5 days. She spent $2.50 each day and has $1.50 left. How much money did her mother give her?

5. Felípe earns extra school money as a biology lab assistant 2 days a week. He earns $5.45 an hour. He worked 5 hours the first week, 7 hours the next, and 4 hours the third week. How much did Felípe earn?

6. Chen takes a long bike ride each weekend. This weekend he rode 47 miles, 19 miles more than last weekend. How far did he bike last weekend?

7. A bicycle race is held on a 0.5 km track. The bicyclists have to circle the track 35 times. How many kilometers long is the race?

8. Lew scored 36 points on a 10-question science test. The test had 3-point and 5-point questions. How many of each kind of question did Lew answer correctly?

Inverse Operations

Some equations can be solved using mental math and some by guessing and checking. This lesson introduces a key idea used in a third method.

EXPLORE Study the Diagram

The weight of the paper bag is unknown and labeled with the variable x. Each cube weighs 1 gram. Write an expression for the total weight resting on the scale.

TALK ABOUT IT

1. What could you do to read the weight of the bag directly from the scale?

2. What expression represents the weight on the scale, if 7 cubes are removed?

3. If the scale shows 94 grams with the bag and all 7 cubes, what would it show after the 7 cubes were removed?

In the expression $x + 7$, 7 has been added to x. To undo this action, you can subtract 7. "Adding 7" and "subtracting 7" are **inverse operations**.

Examples

A $x + 7$	adding 7 to x	**B** $n - 25$	subtracting 25 from n
$x + 7 - 7$	Subtracting 7 undoes adding 7.	$n - 25 + 25$	Adding 25 undoes subtracting 25.
x	The variable is alone.	n	The variable is alone.

Give the inverse operation.

1. adding 45.5   **2.** subtracting 3.5   **3.** subtracting 0.5   **4.** adding 152

Give the inverse operation that would get the variable alone.

5. $w + 15$ **6.** $f - 12$ **7.** $z + 2.4$ **8.** $p - 5\frac{2}{3}$

Write an algebraic expression for each picture below. Then give
the inverse operation that would get the variable alone.

1.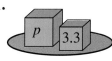

2.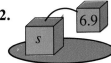

3. $\vdash 4.1 \dashv \!\!-\!\!-\!\! ? \!\!-\!\!-\!\!\dashv$

$\vdash \!\!-\!\!-\!\! z \!\!-\!\!-\!\!\dashv$

Write an algebraic expression for each phrase. Then give the inverse operation.

4. a less 40

5. t plus 16.5

6. 6 more than f

7. 4.7 less than d

8. q decreased by 1.4

9. $2\frac{3}{4}$ older than j

MATH REASONING Draw a diagram to show each expression. Give
the inverse operation that gets the variable alone.

10. $t - 4.5$

11. $x + 19$

12. $m + 8\frac{3}{8}$

13. $y - 4.19$

Simplify each expression. Give the inverse operation that gets the variable alone.

14. $(x - 14) + 8$

15. $(b + 27) - 3$

16. $(c + 1.56) + 4$

17. $(f - 8) - 32.5$

PROBLEM SOLVING

18. The weight w of an empty box can be
found from the expression $w + 10$.
What inverse operation isolates the
variable?

19. Shyra typesets books. How many digits
did she set for the page numbers of a
250-page book?

MIXED REVIEW

Find the answers. Express in lowest terms.

20. $9\frac{11}{12} - 7\frac{5}{6}$

21. $51\frac{7}{32} + 40\frac{7}{8}$

22. $88\frac{1}{10} - 8\frac{3}{5}$

23. $14 - 1\frac{4}{7}$

24. $4\frac{1}{8} \times 4\frac{4}{5}$

25. $1\frac{2}{7} \div 4\frac{3}{5}$

26. $12 \div \frac{1}{3}$

27. $3 \div \frac{3}{8}$

Give the measure of the angle described.

28. a right angle

29. the angle supplementary to $42°$

Solving Addition and Subtraction Equations

You have solved equations using mental math and by guessing and checking. Here you will use inverse operations.

EXPLORE **Compare the Diagram and Equation**
Scale A is balanced. The equation represented by the scale is given.

$x + 2 = 105$

100

A

TALK ABOUT IT

1. What would you have to do to have the bag alone on the left?

2. If you take away 2 blocks from the left, what would you have to do on the right side for the scale to keep it balanced?

3. What is the weight of the bag after taking away 2 blocks from each side of the scale?

The **addition and subtraction properties of equality** tell us that we can add or subtract the same number on both sides of an equation and the two sides will remain equal. We can use these properties together with the idea of inverse operations to solve equations.

$$\text{Solve } z + 48 = 962 \qquad \text{Since 48 is added to } z, \text{ we can isolate } z \text{ by subtracting 48.}$$
$$z + 48 - 48 = 962 - 48 \qquad \text{Subtract 48 from each side.}$$
$$z = 914$$
$$\textit{Check:} \quad 914 + 48 = 962 \qquad \text{Replace } z \text{ with 914}$$
$$962 = 962 \qquad \text{The solution checks.}$$

Other Examples

A
$$x - 17.9 = 483$$
$$x - 17.9 + 17.9 = 483 + 17.9$$
$$x = 500.9$$

B
$$51 = y + 18$$
$$51 - 18 = y + 18 - 18$$
$$33 = y$$

Solve and check.

1. $h - 465 = 3{,}087$ 2. $r + 78.3 = 200.5$ 3. $170 = t + 93$ 4. $13.4 = g - 28.5$

Solve and check.

1. $x - 47 = 781$ **2.** $y + 34.9 = 72.6$ **3.** $w - 14.3 = 7.1$ **4.** $48.2 = f - 6.8$

5. $z + 673 = 800$ **6.** $13.65 = r + 8.9$ **7.** $c - 67 = 435$ **8.** $b + 3.5 = 6.4$

9. $v + 93 = 281$ **10.** $391 = t + 78$ **11.** $n - 186 = 5$ **12.** $98 = m - 17$

13. $h + 4\frac{3}{5} = 12\frac{1}{5}$ **14.** $6\frac{1}{3} = j - \frac{1}{2}$ **15.** $m - 1.5 = 3$ **16.** $23\frac{4}{5} = k - 3\frac{1}{5}$

APPLY

MATH REASONING Solve and check. First decide whether you can use mental math.

17. $x + 19\frac{1}{2} = 281$ **18.** $t + 17.8 = 49$ **19.** $500 = v - 191$

20. $v - 8.2 = 19.4$ **21.** $121 = s + 68$ **22.** $n - 35\frac{3}{5} = 50$

Solve the equations represented below using mental math.

23.

24.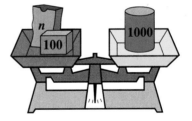

PROBLEM SOLVING

25. The deepest part of the Pacific Ocean is 35,820 ft. The highest mountain is 29,064 ft. How much difference is there between these points on earth?

26. The longest frog leap on record measures 17 feet 7 inches. How much longer is this than the human record for the standing long jump—12 ft 2.25 in.?

▶ **ESTIMATION**

Estimate the solution to each equation.

27. $n + 19.796 = 40.801$ **28.** $680.192 = v - 20.01$ **29.** $49\frac{5}{6} + t = 200$

30. $x + 1.009 = 2.081$ **31.** $t + 198.8 = 349.1$ **32.** $527.9 = v - 1,449.0$

More Practice, page 533, set B

213

More Inverse Operations

EXPLORE **Study the Situation** Chemists use thin glass tubes called pipettes to measure small amounts of liquid. Suppose 3 pipettes of pure water are used in a solution. The pipette holds p ml. Write an expression that gives the total amount of water used.

A chemist finds that v ml of the water evaporates from the solution in one hour. Write an expression that gives the amount of water that would evaporate in one quarter hour.

TALK ABOUT IT

1. What could you do to your expression for the total volume of water in the pipettes to find the volume of one pipette?

2. What could you do to your expression for the water evaporating in one quarter hour to find the amount evaporating in one hour?

In the expression $3p$, p is multiplied by 3. To undo this action, you can divide by 3. "Multiplying by 3" and "dividing by 3" are **inverse operations**.

Examples

A $3p$ multiplying p by 3

$\dfrac{3p}{3}$ Dividing by 3 undoes multiplying by 3.

p The variable is alone.

B $\dfrac{n}{12}$ dividing n by 12

$\dfrac{n}{12} \cdot 12$ Multiplying by 12 undoes dividing by 12.

n The variable is alone.

Give the inverse operation that would get the variable alone.

1. $16.7c$ **2.** $\dfrac{h}{48}$ **3.** $238v$ **4.** $\dfrac{k}{14.5}$

Give the inverse operation that would get the variable alone.

1. $\dfrac{t}{43}$ **2.** $18.35w$ **3.** $m \div 43$ **4.** $12.5n$

5. $x \div 918$ **6.** $7s$ **7.** $1.2k$ **8.** $g \div 24.5$

9. $8.73b$ **10.** $\dfrac{d}{4.37}$ **11.** $121x$ **12.** $\dfrac{r}{0.79}$

Write an algebraic expression for each. Then give the inverse operation that would get the variable alone.

13. five times d decibels **14.** Half of q dollars **15.** Twice as far as z miles

16. d dollars split four ways **17.** 3.5 times higher than p **18.** 4 times as old as Jan (j)

19. 29 times the width w **20.** area a divided by 14.5 **21.** six times h hours

MATH REASONING Give the inverse operation that would get the variable alone.

22. $14w$ **23.** $t \div 8.9$ **24.** $f - 48$ **25.** $z + 14.9$ **26.** $4r$

Multiply by a reciprocal to get the variable alone.

27. $\dfrac{1}{5}p$ **28.** $\dfrac{2}{3}r$ **29.** $\dfrac{5}{9}y$ **30.** $\dfrac{8}{3}k$ **31.** $\dfrac{17}{69}d$

PROBLEM SOLVING You may want to use your calculator.

32. Gold is 19.3 times as heavy as water. Write an expression that gives the weight of a cubic foot of gold, given the weight w of a cubic foot of water. Evaluate for $w = 62.4$ lb.

33. Science Data Bank Write an expression that shows how many times heavier an atom of lead is than an atom of carbon. Use the variable c for the atomic weight of carbon.

DATA BANK

▶ **CALCULATOR**

Use your calculator to evaluate the algebraic expressions.

34. $1.75z$ for $z = 2.7$ **35.** $\dfrac{k}{3.8}$ for $k = 26.98$ **36.** $18.85m$ for $m = 3.25$

37. $0.17p$ for $p = 8.1$ **38.** $23.7 + n$ for $n = 16.9$ **39.** $x - 2.34$ for $x = 11.42$

Solving Multiplication and Division Equations

You have solved equations using mental math and by guessing and checking. Here you will use inverse operations.

EXPLORE **Compare the Diagram and Equation**
Scale A is balanced. The equation represented by the scale is given.

TALK ABOUT IT

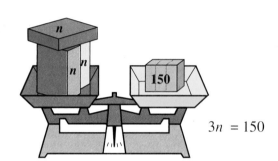

$3n = 150$

1. Three boxes of equal weight weigh 150 lb. How can you find the weight of one box?

2. What is the inverse operation that would get the variable alone in the expression $3n$?

The **multiplication and division properties of equality** tell us that we can multiply or divide by the same number on both sides of the equation and the two sides will remain equal. We can use these properties together with the idea of inverse operations to solve equations.

Solve $\dfrac{k}{45} = 36$ Since k is divided by 45, we can get k alone by multiplying.

$\dfrac{k}{45} \cdot 45 = 36 \cdot 45$ Multiply on both sides by 45.

$k = 1,620$

Check: $\dfrac{1,620}{45} = 36$ Replace k by 1,620.

$36 = 36$ The solution checks.

Other Examples

A $21y = 483$

$\dfrac{21y}{21} = \dfrac{483}{21}$

$y = 23$

B $52 = \dfrac{r}{7.5}$

$52 \cdot 75 = \dfrac{r}{7.5} \cdot 7.5$

$390 = r$

Solve and check.

1. $15s = 570$

2. $\dfrac{h}{14} = 17$

3. $2.4c = 408$

4. $\dfrac{p}{34} = 1.3$

216

Solve and check.

1. $7f = 147$ **2.** $v \div 73 = 13$ **3.** $34n = 79.9$ **4.** $\dfrac{t}{94} = 82$

5. $8h = 5.04$ **6.** $3.4k = 32.98$ **7.** $\dfrac{a}{96} = 24$ **8.** $\dfrac{w}{3} = 159$

9. $15b = 654$ **10.** $\dfrac{m}{24} = 5.6$ **11.** $18j = 918$ **12.** $\dfrac{q}{23} = 7.2$

APPLY

MATH REASONING Solve and check. Use mental math when you can.

13. $\dfrac{x}{5} = 20$ **14.** $11z = 66$ **15.** $5.7s = 74.1$ **16.** $\dfrac{r}{6} = 82$

17. $9x = 90.9$ **18.** $\dfrac{t}{15} = 46$ **19.** $\dfrac{n}{10} = 25$ **20.** $7m = 301$

21. $r - 75 = 300$ **22.** $\dfrac{r}{75} = 300$ **23.** $75r = 300$ **24.** $r + 75 = 300$

Find the area or the missing dimension.

25. 6, A = 486, ?

26. 14.5, A = ?, 20.7

27. 7, A = ?, 2, cut out, 3, 15

PROBLEM SOLVING

28. A gallon of water weighs 8.3 pounds. Milk weighs 1.03 times as much. How much does a gallon of milk weigh?

29. A dentist kept all the teeth he pulled from 1868 until 1904. They were later counted, and totaled 2,000,744. If the dentist worked every day of the year, about how many teeth did he pull per day?

▶ **USING CRITICAL THINKING** Use Visual Clues

Find out how much one egg weighs. Use mental math.

30.

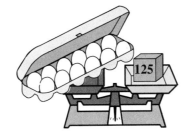

Applied Problem Solving
Group Decision Making

UNDERSTAND
ANALYZE DATA
PLAN
ESTIMATE
SOLVE
EXAMINE

Group Skill:
Listen to Others

Suppose your group owns the Bird Arcade. You buy birds at wholesale cost and sell them at a higher retail price. Decide how to determine the retail prices for birds so that you have a reasonable profit and can pay the expenses of running your shop.

Facts to Consider

1. Monthly expenses of running the shop are $675.

2. Your group needs enough profit to pay salaries of at least $1,200 per month.

3. Average wholesale prices and the average number of birds sold per month are given below.

Bird	Cost per bird	Average number sold per month
Parakeets	$8	22
Finches	$18	14
Canaries		
Male	$15	28
Female	$25	11
Cockateels	$36	8
Cockatoos	$250	2
Parrots	$160	2
Rare birds	$500	1

4. Other pet shop owners say they make a higher profit on less expensive birds than on more costly birds.

1. Complete the function table below to find the retail price if the wholesale price is multiplied by 1.5. W represents the wholesale price and R represents the retail price.

4. Use the average number of birds sold to estimate your group's profit if your retail prices are 1.5 times the wholesale price. Would the profit be enough to cover expenses and salaries?

	Parakeet	Finch	Canary (m)	Canary (f)	Cockateel	Cockatoo	Parrot	Rare
W	$8	$18	$15	$25	$36	$250	$160	$500
R	$12	$27						

2. Make a function to show the retail price if it is $20 more than the wholesale price.

What Is Your Decision

3. Does it make more sense to determine the retail price by multiplying or by adding? Why?

Make a function table to show how your group might determine the retail prices of your birds. You can use one function table for the lower priced birds and a different one for the higher priced birds. How much profit would your group make?

WRAP UP

Language Match

Match each English expression with the correct algebraic expression.

1. Mom is x years old. How old was she 7 years ago?

A $x + 7$

2. There are x shopping carts. How many rows are there with 7 carts in each row?

B $7x$

3. There are x boxes of perfume on the shelf. How much are they worth if each costs $7?

C $7 - x$

4. There were 7 people at the picnic. How many were there after x people went home?

D $x - 7$

5. Joe weighs x pounds. How much does Marvin weigh if he is 7 pounds heavier than Joe?

E $\frac{x}{7}$

6. There are x bags of seeds on the counter. How much does each cost if they cost $7 altogether?

F $\frac{7}{x}$

Sometimes, Always, Never

Which word should go in the blank, *sometimes*, *always*, or *never*? Explain your choice.

7. If $x = 12$, then $x - 3$ is __?__ equal to 15.

8. If $x = 3$ and $y = x + 2$, then y is __?__ equal to 5.

9. Adding 6 is __?__ the inverse of multiplying by 6.

10. Dividing by 4 is __?__ the inverse of multiplying by 4.

Project

Model a Function

You can model a function by pouring water from a cup into a larger container and noting how the height of the water in the container varies with the number of cups of water. Look for a pattern in your table to help you write a function of the form $h = f(n)$ that shows how the poured height of the water (h) is related to the number of cups.

n	1	2	3			
h						

CHAPTER REVIEW/TEST

Part 1   Understanding

1. Which expression stands for the word phrase "9 more than a number"?

   A $9 - n$ **B** $n \cdot 9$ **C** $n + 9$

2. Write an algebraic expression for 4 years more than a years.

3. Which operation will get the variable in the expression $S \div 23.4$ alone?

   A add 23.4   **B** multiply by 23.4

   C subtract 23.4   **D** divide by 23.4

4. Which operation will get the variable in the expression $S - 23.4$ alone?

   A add 23.4   **B** multiply by 23.4

   C subtract 23.4   **D** divide by 23.4

Part 2   Skills

Write an algebraic expression.

5. 18 less than a number y

6. the sum of a number n and 21

7. a weight w divided into fourths

8. the number of centimeters in m meters

9. 17 times a number c

10. the number of yards in f feet

Solve each equation.

11. $0.7n = 70$

12. $200 - b = 160$

13. $13 = r + 8$

14. $x - 90.5 = 200.5$

15. $\frac{r}{25} = 56$

16. $3.8c = 133$

Part 3   Applications

17. Complete the table.

hours(h)	3	4	5	?	7
earnings(e)	\$12	?	20	24	?

18. Reggie has 114 baseball cards. Lonny has three times as many cards. How many cards does Lonny have?

19. Write an expression that gives the value of the area. If the area is 135, find x.

20. Challenge Berry containers are packed 12 to a box. There are 6 more boxes of blueberries than strawberries and 28 boxes of berries in all. How many blueberry containers are there?

221

ENRICHMENT
Euclidean Algorithm

It is difficult to find the greatest common factor of large numbers using factoring. A method called the **Euclidean Algorithm** is simpler, especially when you use a calculator. The flowchart shows the steps to follow. The box at the right shows how to express remainders as whole numbers rather than decimals.

> **Remainders on the Calculator**
> $$49 \div 15 = 3.2\overline{6}$$
> 1) Multiply the divisor and the whole number part of the quotient.
> $$15 \times 3 = 45$$
> 2) Subtract this number from the dividend. The difference is the remainder.
> $$49 - 45 = 4 \leftarrow \text{remainder}$$

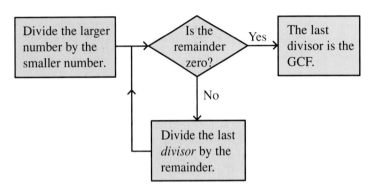

Here's how the flowchart works for 2,599 and 2,825.

$$\overset{1 \text{ R } 226}{2{,}599 \overline{)2{,}825}} \qquad \overset{11 \text{ R}113}{226 \overline{)2{,}599}} \qquad \overset{2 \text{ R } 0}{113 \overline{)226}}$$

$$\uparrow$$
$$\textbf{GCF}$$

Math Point: The Euclidean Algorithm works because the GCF of any two numbers also divides the difference of the two numbers. Since division is a quick way of doing repeated subtraction, the algorithm gives the GCF.

Find the greatest common factor of each pair of numbers.

1. 70 and 525   **2.** 475 and 1,501   **3.** 12,567 and 2,414

4. To qualify as Royal Surveyor of Mathematica you are given the job of dividing a rectangular field 100,001 m long and 1,001 m wide into equal-sized squares that are as large as possible. What is the largest size of the squares? What will be the total number of squares?

CUMULATIVE REVIEW

1. Which angle is bisected?

A

B

C

D

2. Which line segment cannot be used with 2 of the others to construct a triangle?

A •—•   B •————————•

C •———•   D •——————•

3. Which line is parallel to $\overleftrightarrow{RS}$?

R ← ————————→ S

A ←————————→

B ←————————→

C ←————————→

D ←————————→

4. Which fraction expresses $\frac{36}{48}$ in lowest terms?

A $\frac{2}{3}$ B $\frac{3}{4}$ C $\frac{1}{2}$ D $\frac{5}{6}$

5. What is the mixed number for $\frac{18}{4}$?

A $4\frac{1}{2}$ B 4 C $4\frac{1}{4}$ D $3\frac{3}{4}$

6. Which is a prime number?

A 39 B 41 C 57 D 51

7. Which balances if 1 quart $q = 2$ pints p, 1 thermos $t = 3$ quarts, and 4 cups $c = 1$ quart?

A $p = 3c$ B $5q = 4c + t$

C $8p = t$ D $t = 2c + 5p$

Solve.

8. $\frac{5}{6} - \frac{1}{6}$ A $\frac{1}{2}$ B $\frac{2}{3}$

C $\frac{1}{3}$ D 1

9. $\frac{7}{10} + \frac{1}{5}$ A $\frac{9}{10}$ B $\frac{4}{5}$

C $1\frac{2}{5}$ D $\frac{1}{2}$

10. $2\frac{7}{10} \times 3\frac{1}{3}$ A $\frac{81}{100}$ B 9

C $6\frac{7}{30}$ D $\frac{1}{9}$

11. $\frac{11}{12} \div \frac{5}{6}$ A $\frac{55}{72}$ B $4\frac{2}{5}$

C $\frac{10}{11}$ D $1\frac{1}{10}$

12. Select the numbers that make y a function of x.

x	1	8	3		
y	7	13	9	5	8

A 1, 8   B 3, 6
C 7, 9   D 1, 11

13. Elinor has a canister containing $15\frac{1}{3}$ cups of flour. If she uses $\frac{3}{4}$ of the flour, how many cups of flour will she use?

A $14\frac{7}{12}$ B $11\frac{1}{2}$

C $15\frac{1}{4}$ D $3\frac{5}{6}$

14. During one month Chaney spent $1\frac{5}{6}$ hours on the telephone talking to friends in Arkansas and $2\frac{2}{5}$ hours talking to friends in New Jersey. About how long did he talk to these friends?

A 4   B 3   C 5   D 6

8

RATIO
AND
PROPORTION

MATH AND
HEALTH AND FITNESS

DATA BANK

Use the Health and Fitness
Data Bank on page 500 to
answer the questions.

1 What was the engine
speed (in rpm) of the 1963
Ford-Lotus as it started to
accelerate through the south turn
of the Indy track?

2 Speeds of Indy 500 winners are given in both miles per hour and kilometers per hour. Use the data to estimate the number of kilometers in a mile.

3 Use the graphs to find the approximate time it took the Ford-Lotus to complete one lap around the track.

4 **Using Critical Thinking** Study winning speeds and prize money for the Indy 500 races for the years 1960, 1965, 1970, 1975, and 1980. Predict winning speed and prizes for 1990 and 1995.

Ratio

What Is the Biggest Danger to Our Environment?

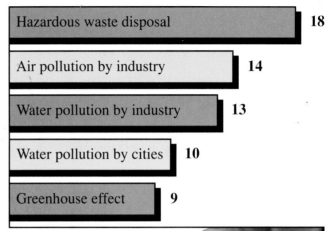

There is a special way to compare two numbers.

EXPLORE **Analyze the Graph**

100 people were surveyed about what they believe to be the greatest danger to our environment. The most significant responses are shown in the bar graph at the right.

Number of People

TALK ABOUT IT

1. Which was considered the most serious danger?

2. Which danger was picked by half as many people as "hazardous waste disposal"?

3. What do you think some other choices were that are not in the graph?

A **ratio** is a comparison of two numbers. It may be written in three different ways. The ratio of the number of people who picked "hazardous waste material" to the number of people who picked "greenhouse effect" can be written as:

18 to 9   18 : 9 $\frac{18}{9}$

A ratio is in **lowest terms** when the only common factor of the two numbers being compared is 1. The ratio 18 to 9 in lowest terms is 2 to 1. If you think of a ratio as a fraction, then $\frac{18}{9} = \frac{2}{1}$. They are **equal ratios.**

TRY IT OUT

Give each ratio in lowest terms. Use the graph above.

1. air pollution by industry to water pollution by cities

2. water pollution by cities to hazardous waste material

3. hazardous waste material to water pollution by cities

Write each ratio as a fraction in lowest terms.

1. 6 to 8   **2.** 16:36   **3.** 12 to 14   **4.** $\frac{30}{18}$

5. 17 to 17   **6.** $\frac{50}{15}$ **7.** 8:44   **8.** 150 to 25

9. $\frac{1,440}{48}$ **10.** 56 to 77   **11.** 12:48   **12.** $\frac{60}{32}$

APPLY

MATH REASONING   Draw a picture to show each ratio.

13. red sneakers to black sneakers   3:8   **14.** blondes to all students in the room   6:25

15. cans of juice to cans of water   3:1   **16.** boys to girls in a room   12:10

Copy and finish each picture to make equal ratios of white to black objects.

17. 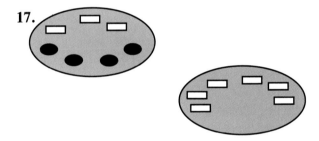   **18.**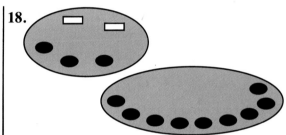

PROBLEM SOLVING

Round each number to the nearest thousand.
Then give the ratio of the areas in lowest terms.

19. Cape Cod to Assateague Island

20. Fire Island to Gulf Island

21. Cape Lookout to Cape Hatteras

22. Give two national seashores with areas
in a ratio of approximately 2:1.

National Seashores	Area (Acres)
Assateague	39,630
Canaveral	57,627
Cape Cod	43,526
Cape Hatteras	30,319
Cape Lookout	28,414
Cumberland Island	36,415
Fire Island	19,578
Gulf Islands	65,816
Padre Island	130,696
Point Reyes	71,045

▶ **USING CRITICAL THINKING**   **Organize an Argument**

23. Suppose a student said that both of the pictures at the right
show a ratio of 4 to 5. Write an argument that would
convince a classmate that this statement is correct or
incorrect.

More Practice, page 534, set A

Proportions

Indianapolis 500			
Year	Driver	Speed (avg.)	Fuel used in 4.5 min (avg.)
1949	Bill Holland	120 mph	6 gallons
1977	A.J. Foyt	160 mph	8 gallons

LEARN ABOUT IT

EXPLORE Analyze the Data

Speeds and fuel consumption for two winners of the Indianapolis 500 are shown in the chart.

TALK ABOUT IT

1. What is the ratio of winning speeds for 1949 to 1977?

2. What is the ratio of the fuel consumption for 1949 to 1977?

3. Are these ratios the same or different?

Two ratios are equal if the fractions formed are equivalent. An equation stating that two ratios are equal is a **proportion.**

Here are two methods you can use to determine if two ratios are equal or **proportional.**

Equivalent Fractions

$$\frac{3}{4} = \frac{120}{160}$$

Since the fractions are equivalent, the ratios 3:4 and 120:160 are equal.

Cross Products

$3 \cdot 160 = 480 \quad 4 \cdot 120 = 480$

$$\frac{3}{4} \diagup\!\!\!\diagdown \frac{120}{160}$$

Since the cross products are equal, the ratios are equal.

TRY IT OUT

Write $=$ or $\neq$ for each ⦀.

1. $\frac{8}{3}$ ⦀ $\frac{16}{6}$

2. $\frac{3}{8}$ ⦀ $\frac{4}{10}$

3. $\frac{14}{5}$ ⦀ $\frac{28}{10}$

4. $\frac{7}{8}$ ⦀ $\frac{12}{15}$

Write = or ≠ for each .

1. $\frac{2}{5}$ ⫸ $\frac{4}{106}$

2. $\frac{8}{12}$ ⫸ $\frac{2}{3}$

3. $\frac{4}{8}$ ⫸ $\frac{4}{16}$

4. $\frac{3}{8}$ ⫸ $\frac{8}{16}$

5. $\frac{3}{9}$ ⫸ $\frac{1}{3}$

6. $\frac{2}{7}$ ⫸ $\frac{6}{21}$

7. $\frac{3}{5}$ ⫸ $\frac{5}{9}$

8. $\frac{4}{10}$ ⫸ $\frac{8}{25}$

9. $\frac{5}{9}$ ⫸ $\frac{6}{10}$

10. $\frac{5}{2}$ ⫸ $\frac{40}{16}$

11. $\frac{20}{16}$ ⫸ $\frac{5}{4}$

12. $\frac{3}{7}$ ⫸ $\frac{4}{9}$

13. $\frac{1}{3}$ ⫸ $\frac{4}{11}$

14. $\frac{3}{21}$ ⫸ $\frac{1}{7}$

15. $\frac{2}{3}$ ⫸ $\frac{6}{12}$

16. $\frac{7}{8}$ ⫸ $\frac{6}{7}$

APPLY

MATH REASONING Use the clues to write a proportion.

17. Each ratio is equal to $\frac{2}{3}$. The numerator for one ratio is 8 and the denominator for the other ratio is 18.

18. Each ratio is equal to $\frac{4}{5}$. The numerator for one ratio is 40 and the denominator for the other ratio is 2.5.

PROBLEM SOLVING

19. One race car driver has a win-loss record of 16:4. A second has a record of 20:5. Are the win-loss ratios proportional?

20. Gear ratios compare the number of teeth in a pair of gears. In an auto transmission, first gear might have a ratio of 3:1, second gear 2:1, and first gear 1:1. Find a pair of gears in the chart that is **not** proportional to one of these ratios.

21. Health and Fitness Data Bank The ratio of first place Indy 500 wins from 1959 to 1980 for Roger Ward to Jim Clark is proportional to the ratio of wins of what driver to the wins of Bobby Unser?

Number of Gear Teeth
24 and 12
12 and 8
24 and 8
12 and 12
16 and 8

DATA BANK

▶ **USING CRITICAL THINKING**   **Apply Proportional Reasoning**

22. Suppose the ratio of veteran drivers to rookie drivers in a race is 5 to 1. From this information can you tell how many drivers are in the race? Explain your answer using examples.

More Practice, page 534, set B

Solving Proportions

You can use the fact that the cross products of a
proportion are equal to solve many problems.

EXPLORE Analyze the Process

The ratio of sneakers sold by a large
manufacturer in 1990 compared to 1980
is 2.5 to 1. In 1980, this company sold
210,000 pairs of sneakers. How many
sneakers were sold in 1990 by this
company?

Here is how to use a proportion to find the answer.

Write a proportion.	Solve. Use cross products.

$$\begin{array}{l} 1990 \to \\ 1980 \to \end{array} \quad \dfrac{2.5}{1} = \dfrac{n}{210,000} \quad \begin{array}{l} \leftarrow \text{sold in 1990} \\ \leftarrow \text{sold in 1980} \end{array}$$

$$2.5\,(210,000) = 1 \cdot n$$
$$n = 525,000$$

TALK ABOUT IT

1. Explain how you could have estimated the answer to this
   problem.

2. Give an answer to the problem above in a complete sentence.

Other Examples

A $\dfrac{16}{m} = \dfrac{24}{15}$

$$16 \cdot 15 = 24m$$
$$240 = 24m$$
$$\dfrac{240}{24} = \dfrac{24m}{24}$$
$$m = 10$$

B $\dfrac{28}{40} = \dfrac{35}{d}$

$$28d = 40 \cdot 35$$
$$28d = 1,400$$
$$\dfrac{28d}{28} = \dfrac{1400}{28}$$
$$d = 50$$

Solve. Use cross products.

1. $\dfrac{2}{x} = \dfrac{6}{9}$

2. $\dfrac{5}{6} = \dfrac{15}{x}$

3. $\dfrac{x}{10} = \dfrac{9}{30}$

4. $\dfrac{20}{6} = \dfrac{x}{15}$

230

Solve. Use cross products.

1. $\dfrac{x}{6} = \dfrac{6}{9}$

2. $\dfrac{8}{3} = \dfrac{x}{12}$

3. $\dfrac{10}{x} = \dfrac{18}{36}$

4. $\dfrac{4}{9} = \dfrac{20}{x}$

5. $\dfrac{1}{3} = \dfrac{x}{18}$

6. $\dfrac{5}{6} = \dfrac{x}{24}$

7. $\dfrac{2}{3} = \dfrac{8}{x}$

8. $\dfrac{15}{x} = \dfrac{10}{16}$

9. $\dfrac{15}{3} = \dfrac{x}{8}$

10. $\dfrac{10}{x} = \dfrac{4}{8}$

11. $\dfrac{2}{5} = \dfrac{x}{250}$

12. $\dfrac{15}{1} = \dfrac{x}{4}$

APPLY

MATH REASONING

13. Find two values for x and y so that $\dfrac{x}{20} = \dfrac{30}{y}$.

14. How many proportions can you make using only the numbers 1, 3, 4, 9, and 12?

PROBLEM SOLVING

15. A machine can package sneakers at a rate of 4 pairs every 12 seconds. How many pairs of sneakers can this machine package in 1 minute?

Let p = number of pairs of sneakers that can be packed in 1 minute.

$$\begin{array}{c}\text{pairs} \rightarrow \\ \text{seconds} \rightarrow \end{array} \dfrac{4}{12} = \dfrac{p}{60}$$

16. Black sneakers compared to red sneakers sold in a ratio of 4 to 2 one month. If this ratio is maintained, how many of each color sneaker were sold out of a total of 600?

17. The ratio of high-top sneakers sold to low-top sneakers sold at a particular store one day is 2 to 5. The store sold 150 low-top sneakers that day. How many sneakers did they sell all together?

 ALGEBRA

Solve each proportion. Check your solution.

18. $\dfrac{3}{4} = \dfrac{n}{20}$

19. $\dfrac{x}{10} = \dfrac{20}{50}$

20. $\dfrac{30}{m} = \dfrac{3}{10}$

21. $\dfrac{2m}{20} = \dfrac{64}{80}$

22. $\dfrac{8}{5} = \dfrac{32}{x}$

23. $\dfrac{2}{3n} = \dfrac{15}{45}$

More Practice, page 231, set C

Rate

LEARN ABOUT IT

Comparisons of numbers with different units of measure, such as distance and time, are often used to describe changing situations.

EXPLORE **Complete a Table**

Work in groups. Copy and complete the table below to find how long it would take to travel 270 miles on the freeway averaging 45 miles in 1 hour, including stops.

distance (mi)	45	90	135	180	225	270
time (hr)	1	2	?	?	?	?

TALK ABOUT IT

1. How did you decide what numbers to place in the table?

2. What would you have estimated the total time to be?

3. Give a reasonable answer in a complete sentence to the problem.

A **rate** is a ratio that involves two different units. A rate is usually given as a quantity per unit such as miles per hour. This is called a **unit rate.**

Examples A race car traveled 500 miles in 3.79 hrs. About what rate in miles per hour did this car average?

$$\text{miles} \rightarrow \frac{500}{3.79} = \frac{m}{1} \leftarrow \text{hours}$$

$m = 131.9$ (rounded to the nearest tenth)

The car traveled at an average rate of 131.9 miles per hour.

TRY IT OUT

Find the unit rate.

1. $\dfrac{\$48}{6 \text{ hr}}$

2. $\dfrac{65 \text{ km}}{10 \text{ L}}$

3. $\dfrac{1{,}100 \text{ words}}{5 \text{ minutes}}$

232

Find the unit rate.

1. $\dfrac{\$12}{3 \text{ tickets}}$

2. $\dfrac{88 \text{ ft}}{2 \text{ s}}$

3. $\dfrac{\$600}{12 \text{ yd}^3}$

4. $\dfrac{\$88,400}{4 \text{ years}}$

5. $\dfrac{120 \text{ cars}}{3 \text{ hr}}$

6. $\dfrac{100 \text{ books}}{40 \text{ students}}$

7. $\dfrac{3,200 \text{ Kbits}}{4 \text{ discs}}$

8. $\dfrac{60 \text{ TVs}}{20 \text{ homes}}$

9. $\dfrac{48 \text{ degrees}}{24 \text{ hr}}$

APPLY

MATH REASONING Describe a real situation in which each rate might be used.

10. dollars per hour

11. miles per gallon

12. beats per minute

13. revolutions per minute

14. miles per second

15. cars per minute

PROBLEM SOLVING

16. A race car used 333 gallons of gasoline in a 500 mile race. About how many gallons were used per mile?

17. A race car driver has a total earnings of $90,000 for 12 races. What are this driver's average earnings per race?

18. Suppose a new car was advertised to get 20 miles per gallon (mpg) in town and 26 mpg on the highway. How many more miles might you expect to get from 10 gallons of gasoline driving on the highway rather than in town?

19. It takes 12 minutes to paint lines dividing a race track into 3 sections. It takes the same amount of time to paint each dividing line. How long would it take to paint lines dividing a track into 5 sections?

20. **Health and Fitness Data Bank** Find how many seconds it took the Ford Lotus to go once around the 2.5 mile track.

MIXED REVIEW

Write an expression for each phrase.

21. 8 more than n

22. the number of seconds in m minutes

23. 7 less than p

24. half as long as r

Solve and check.

25. $x - 2.3 = 5$

26. $7y = 42$

27. $\dfrac{x}{7} = 4$

28. $\dfrac{x}{3} = \dfrac{2}{3}$

More Practice, page 534, set D

233

Problem Solving
Unit Pricing

UNDERSTAND
ANALYZE DATA
PLAN
ESTIMATE
SOLVE
EXAMINE

LEARN ABOUT IT

The cost of one unit of an item is called the **unit price.** You can find and compare unit prices of items to find which is the **better buy.** When you compare identical items, the item with the lowest price is usually considered the better buy.

Al's Musicland	Bob's Tops
cassette tapes: 5 for $1.05 CDs: $75 for 10 videotapes: 3 for $24.50 albums: 2 for $10	cassette tapes: 4 for $0.89 CDs: $62 for 8—Today Only videotapes: 5 for $35.95 albums: $5 each, 2 for the price of 1

Prices for items at two music stores are shown in the table. Which store offers a better buy on videotapes?

Ten CDs cost $75 at Al's Musicland. I can write and solve a proportion to find the unit price n.

Let n = cost of one CD at Al's
$\frac{75}{10} = \frac{n}{1}$ $10n = 75$ $n = \$7.50$

Let m = cost of one CD at Bob's
$\frac{62}{8} = \frac{m}{1}$ $8m = 62$ $m = \$7.75$

Eight CDs cost $62 at Bob's Tops. I can write and solve a proportion to find the unit price m.

Al's Musicland has the better buy.

TRY IT OUT

Find the better buy.

1. milk:
64 oz for $1.05, or 16 oz for $0.35

2. ground beef:
16 oz for $1.89, or 10 oz for $1.08

Solve. Use any problem solving strategy.

Some Strategies	
Act Out	Solve a Simpler Problem
Use Objects	Make an Organized List
Choose an Operation	Work Backward
Draw a Picture	Look for a Pattern
Guess and Check	Use Logical Reasoning
Make a Table	Write an Equation

1. A grocery store has fruit drinks on sale, 6 cans for $1.95. Separately each can costs $0.35. How much do you save buying the 6 cans on sale?

2. Mrs. McClure can buy 30 calculators for $142.50, including tax. How much is each calculator?

3. Farah's father said Farah could help in his wood shop for 6 hours a week. He agreed to pay her $25 a week. How much does she earn per hour?

4. The graph below shows the average prices of movie tickets at the same theater in 1980 and in 1990. How much less would a family of four (2 adults and 2 children) have paid in 1980?

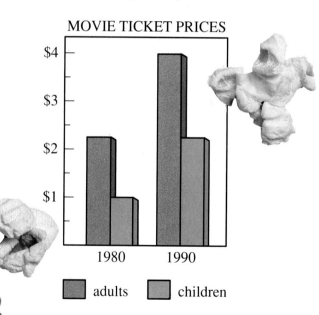

MOVIE TICKET PRICES

5. Lavonna bought two bottles of orange juice. One bottle cost $0.75 more than the other. In all, she paid $3.25. What was the price of each bottle?

6. Aki was allowed to get one drink and 1 treat at the basketball game. How many choices did she have for a drink-treat combination?

Drinks: orange juice; small, medium, large
carrot juice; small and large
apple juice; small, medium, large

Treats: dried fruit
popcorn, small and large
pretzels

7. A two-day pass to a fair is $37. If you bought two one-day passes, you would pay $23.95 a day. How much do you save buying the two-day pass?

8. A box of biscuits cost $0.89. On the box it says, "New larger size—75 biscuits!" About how much does each biscuit cost?

9. Tubes of oil paint can be bought in sets of 5 for $13.75 or bought separately for the unit price. What would it cost to buy 2 tubes of this oil paint?

Missing Data Each of the problems below is missing data that is needed to solve the problem. Tell what data is missing. Make up reasonable data. Solve the problem using your data.

10. A book of swim club passes cost $14.25. What was the cost of one pass?

11. A daily bus pass is $0.75. How much cheaper per day is a monthly pass?

235

Using Critical Thinking
Making Judgments

LEARN ABOUT IT

The art teacher, Ms. Jackson, asked her students to cut out rectangles of different sizes and shapes.

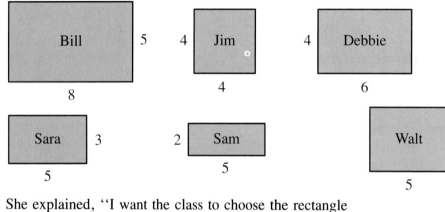

Bill 5 / 8
4 Jim 4 / 4
4 Debbie 6
1 Dot 7
Sara 3 / 5
2 Sam 5
Walt 4 / 5
6 Bo 2

She explained, "I want the class to choose the rectangle that has the most pleasing shape."

"That's easy," said Bruce. "It's the 4-by-4 square."

"You may be right," Ms. Jackson said, "but ancient Greeks believed the most pleasing shape to be the one whose sides forms a ratio of about 1.618 to 1. They named it the Golden Rectangle."

1. What does Ms. Jackson want the class to do?

2. Which rectangles do you think have pleasing shapes? Why?

3. Use a calculator. Which rectangle above is closest in proportion to the Golden Rectangle? Was it one of the rectangles you chose?

TRY IT OUT

1. Try to find other rectangles with whole-number dimensions that approximate the Golden Rectangle.

2. Find the ratio of total height to waist height for several persons. Calculate the mean of these ratios. Describe your results.

236

MIDCHAPTER REVIEW/QUIZ

This chart shows how some students spent their time from 4 p.m. to 5 p.m. yesterday. Write each ratio as a fraction and decide if the statement is true or false.

homework	~~IIII~~ ~~IIII~~
sports practice	~~IIII~~
music practice	IIII
chores (or job)	~~IIII~~ I
other	~~IIII~~

1. One out of every 3 students did homework.

2. One out of every 5 students did chores.

3. The ratio of students doing homework to students practicing music is 5 to 2.

4. The ratio of students doing chores to students practicing music or sports is 2 to 3.

Express each ratio as a fraction in simplest form. Write a statement telling which students from the chart are being compared.

5. 4:6

6. 10 to 5

7. 5 out of 30

8. 10:10

Write = or ≠ for each 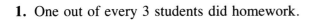 .

9. $\frac{3}{4}$ 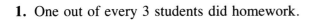 $\frac{9}{16}$

10. $\frac{4}{6}$ 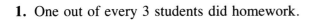 $\frac{6}{9}$

11. $\frac{8}{4}$ 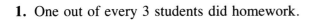 $\frac{10}{5}$

12. $\frac{20}{16}$ 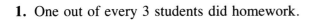 $\frac{15}{12}$

13. $\frac{6}{22}$ 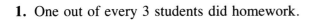 $\frac{2}{7}$

Write each rate as a fraction in simplest form.

14. 24 laps in 12 minutes

15. 180 miles with 15 gallons

16. $6 for 24 ounces

17. 25 heartbeats in 10 seconds

Solve these proportions.

18. $\frac{9}{4} = \frac{x}{28}$

19. $\frac{5}{x} = \frac{15}{24}$

20. $\frac{3}{20} = \frac{6}{x}$

21. $\frac{x}{8} = \frac{30}{12}$

22. $\frac{x}{15} = \frac{4}{6}$

23. $\frac{18}{6} = \frac{x}{5}$

24. $\frac{14}{x} = \frac{7}{1}$

25. $\frac{21}{35} = \frac{27}{x}$

PROBLEM SOLVING

26. Geraldo rode his bicycle 18 miles in 90 minutes. At this rate, how long would it take him to ride 30 miles?

27. The coach kept track of Rosina's time at the end of each lap. Her rate for the first lap was 90 seconds per lap. What was her rate at the end of each of the other laps? What happened to her speed as the number of laps increased?

lap	time
1	1 min 30 sec
2	3 min 10 sec
3	5 min
4	6 min 40 sec

Scale Drawings

LEARN ABOUT IT

EXPLORE **Make Some Measurements**

Work in groups. In a **scale drawing** of an object, all dimensions of the object are reduced by the same ratio or scale. In the drawing at the right, 1 in. = 12 ft.

Measure the walls of each bedroom to the nearest $\frac{1}{16}$ inch.

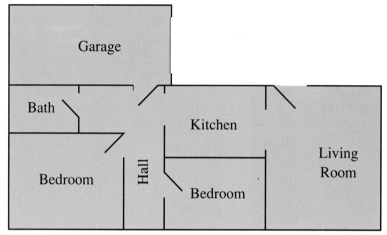

FLOOR PLAN: 2 Bedroom Home   Scale: 1 in = 12 ft

TALK ABOUT IT

1. Is the scale the same for each of the rooms?

2. Which bedroom seems smaller? Do your measurements show this?

You can use the scale of a scale drawing to set up a proportion and find actual dimensions.

Example Find the actual length of l of the outside wall of the garage.

Scale: 1 in. = 12 ft   Measurement in the drawing = $1\frac{3}{4}$ in.

$$\frac{1}{12} = \frac{1\frac{3}{4}}{l} \quad \text{so} \quad l = 12 \cdot 1\frac{3}{4} = 21 \text{ ft}$$

TRY IT OUT

Find the actual dimensions for each.

1. the dimensions of the living room

2. the dimensions of the large bedroom.

Find the actual dimensions given the scale drawing dimensions.
The scale is $\frac{1}{2}$ in. = 8 ft.

1. a living room $1\frac{1}{8}$ in. long

2. a garage $2\frac{3}{4}$ in. long

3. a yard $3\frac{1}{16}$ in. wide

4. a fence $12\frac{3}{8}$ in. long

Find the scale measurement. Use a scale of 1 in. = 8 ft.

5. 20 ft   **6.** 5 ft   **7.** 9 ft   **8.** 80 ft   **9.** 50 ft

APPLY

MATH REASONING

10. Suppose you need to make a scale drawing of a room
12 ft by 18 ft on an 8.5 in. by 11 in. piece of paper, and
you want a 1 to 2 in. border around the figure.
What scale should you use?

PROBLEM SOLVING

Use a ruler and the map. Its
scale is 800 miles = 1 in.
What is the approximate
distance from

11. Miami to New Orleans

12. Seattle to Denver

13. Denver to New York

14. Los Angeles to San
Francisco

15. Data hunt—Find a map or scale drawing.
On it find three actual distances by solving
a proportion.

ESTIMATION

The scale on the map below in 1 in. = 250
miles. Use this to estimate the following
distances. Do not measure.

16. Amarillo to Dallas   **17.** Austin to Fort Worth

18. Dallas to Houston   **19.** San Angelo to San Antonio

More Practice Page 533, Set C

Exploring Algebra
Using Variables

EXPLORE **Analyze the Data**

The activity of animals often varies with the weather. Crickets chirp a lot in warm weather, but not as much when it is cooler.

B.C.

DID YOU KNOW IF YOU COUNT THE CRICKET CHIRPS IN ONE MINUTE, DIVIDE BY FOUR THEN ADD FORTY IT GIVES YOU THE OUTSIDE TEMPERATURE?

FAHRENHEIT OR CELSIUS?

by johnny hart

IS THERE SUCH A THING AS METRIC CRICKETS?

CLUMSY'S BAIT SHOP

Source: B.C. by permission of Johnny Hart and Field Enterprises, Inc. 1975.

TALK ABOUT IT

1. For 60 chirps per minute, what would the temperature be?

2. For 4 chirps per minute, what would the temperature be?

3. Are you using the Fahrenheit or Celsius temperature scale?

Algebraic expressions can show relations between variables.

Examples You might write an algebraic expression to find the amount earned for different amounts of time worked.

A Let h = number of hours worked.

The rule in words: The amount earned is 4 times the number of hours.

The rule as an algebraic expression: $4h$

hours worked	1	2	3	4	5	h
amount earned	4	8	12	?	?	?

B Let h = number of hours worked.

The rule in words: The amount earned is 3 times the number of hours, plus 1.

The rule as an algebraic expression: $3h + 1$

hours worked	1	2	3	4	5	h
amount earned	4	7	10	?	?	?

Write the rule in words and as an algebraic expression.

1.

hours	1	2	3	4	5	h
rental fee	2.50	5.00	7.50	10.00	?	?

Copy and complete the tables below. Write the rule in words and as an algebraic expression for each table.

1.

input	0	1	2	3	4	?	a
output	0	2	4	?	8	10	?

2.

input	0	1	2	3	4	?	b
output	0.1	1.1	2.1	?	?	5.1	?

3.

input	5	10	15	?	25	?	c
output	24	49	74	99	?	199	?

4.

input	1	3	5	7	?	11	d
output	6	16	26	?	46	?	?

MATH REASONING

5. Construct a table of values for the algebraic expression $4n - 2$.

6. Construct a table of values for the algebraic expression $3(x + 5)$.

PROBLEM SOLVING

7. A car rental agency charges $65.00 per day. You get 100 free miles. For every mile over 100, the charge is an additional $0.22. What is the cost of a car rented for 2 days and driven 250 miles?

8. Data Hunt Find the cost of renting something on an hourly basis. Then try to find an algebraic expression that relates hours to cost.

▶ **USING CRITICAL THINKING   Use Careful Reasoning**

9. There was a young lady of Lee
Whose age had a last digit three.
　　If you total the two,
　　Which is easy to do,
One less than a square you will see.

How old is the lady?

Similar Figures

EXPLORE Make a Drawing

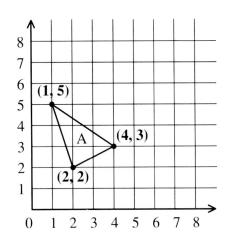

- Draw a grid with axes numbered to 25.
- Copy triangle *A*.
- Multiply the coordinates of each vertex of triangle *A* by the same number (from 2 to 5). Plot and connect these points on the same grid.
- Measure the angles and sides of each figure.

TALK ABOUT IT

1. What do you notice about corresponding angles in these figures? Corresponding sides?

2. What proportion can you write to show how the sides of triangle *A* compare to the sides of the new triangle?

The two triangles are **similar.** In similar figures, corresponding angles have the same measure and the ratios of corresponding sides are equal.

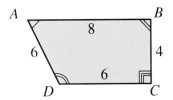
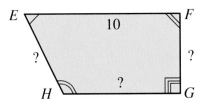

Corresponding Angles
∠*A* and ∠*E*
∠*B* and ∠*F*
∠*C* and ∠*G*
∠*D* and ∠*H*

$\overline{AB}$ and $\overline{EF}$ are corresponding sides: $\frac{AB}{EF} = \frac{8}{10}$, and $\frac{8}{10} = \frac{4}{5}$. So all other sides will be in a ratio of 4:5 (small figure to large figure). *BC* is 4, so *FG* is 5. $\overline{DC}$ and $\overline{HG}$ are corresponding sides, so $\frac{6}{HG} = \frac{4}{5}$. Solving this proportion gives *HG* = 7.5 cm. So, *EH* must also be 7.5 cm.

Δ*ABC* is similar to Δ*DEF*. Use a proportion to find:

1. length *x*   2. length *y*

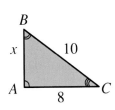
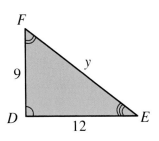

Use proportions to find the unknown lengths for these similar figures.

1.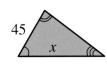

2.

3.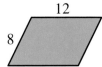

4.

MATH REASONING

5. Suppose two triangles are similar, with corresponding sides in a ratio of 3:4. One side of one triangle is 12 cm. What can you conclude about the corresponding side of the other triangle? Explain.

PROBLEM SOLVING

6. Find the height of the wall shown at the right.

7. Find the distance across the river. (Distances are in feet.)

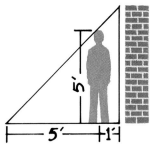 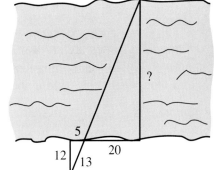

8. Understanding the Question Tell which question below asks the same thing as the one in this problem:

A surveyor made the measurements shown in the picture at the right. How long is the lake?

a) What is the length of the side that corresponds to 120 m?
b) What is the length of the side that corresponds to 30 m?
c) What is the total length of side $\overline{AD}$?

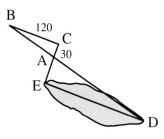

USING CRITICAL THINKING   Make a Generalization

11. Draw a rectangle. Draw another rectangle with sides twice as long as the first rectangle. How do the areas of the two figures compare? Repeat using rectangles whose sides are in a ratio of 1:3. Can you make a generalization about areas of similar rectangles?

More Practice, page 534, set E

The Special Ratio π

LEARN ABOUT IT

EXPLORE **Measure Some Circles** Work in Groups

- Measure the **diameters** of four circular objects to the nearest mm. Then use string and a ruler to find the **circumference** of each object to the nearest mm. Record your results.

- For each object, find $\frac{C}{d}$ to the nearest hundredth.

TALK ABOUT IT

1. How do C and d compare for each object?

For every circle, the ratio $\frac{C}{d}$ is the same. We use the Greek letter π (pi) for this ratio. The decimal for π is unending and does not repeat.

$$\pi = 3.14159265358979323846643 \ldots$$

We commonly use 3.14 and $\frac{22}{7}$ as approximations for π. Many kinds of calculators have a special key for π.

Because $\pi = \frac{C}{d}$, the circumference of a circle is $C = \pi d$.
Because the diameter is twice the radius ($d = 2r$), we can write $C = 2\pi r$.

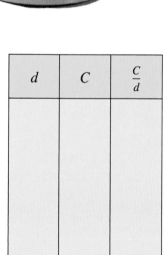

d	C	$\frac{C}{d}$

Examples

A Find the circumference of a circle with a radius of 8.5 cm.

$C = 2\pi r$
$\approx 2(3.14)(8.5)$ ≈ means "is approximately equal to"
$C \approx 53.38$ The circumference is 53.38 cm.

B Find the circumference of a circle with a diameter of 14 cm.

$C = \pi d \approx \frac{22}{7} \cdot 14 = 44$ The circumference is 44 cm.

TRY IT OUT

Find the circumference for each diameter or radius. Use 3.14 or $\frac{22}{7}$ for π.

1. $d = 3$ cm   **2.** $r = 0.75$ m   **3.** $d = 42$ cm   **4.** $d = 70$ m

Use a compass to construct 5 circles. Measure the diameter of each to the nearest mm. Copy and complete the table at the right. Use 3.14 for π. Find the circumference of each circle using $C = \pi d$.

	diameter	circumference
1.	–	–
2.	–	–
3.	–	–
4.	–	–
5.	–	–

Find the circumference of each circle. Use $\frac{22}{7}$ for π.

6. $d = 21$ in.

7. $r = 7$ yd

8. $d = 10\frac{1}{2}$ in.

9. $r = \frac{3}{4}$ yd

10. $d = 28$ ft

11. $r = 4\frac{1}{2}$ in.

APPLY

MATH REASONING Find the diameter of each circle. Use a calculator.

12. $C = 18.84$ cm

13. $C = 17.27$ m

14. $C = 3.768$ cm

15. Give a formula to find d when you know the value for c.

PROBLEM SOLVING

16. Which do you think is greater—the height of a juice can or its circumference? Make a conjecture. Then test your conjecture by measuring the height and diameter of a can. Use $C = \pi d$ to find the circumference. You may want to check your findings using a string.

17. What is the diameter of a tree that has a circumference of 11.46 m?

MIXED REVIEW

Evaluate each expression for $a = \frac{1}{2}$, $b = \frac{2}{5}$, $c = \frac{1}{6}$.

18. $b(a + c)$

19. $(a \cdot b) \cdot c$

20. $ba + bc$

21. $a(b \cdot c)$

Write each decimal as a lowest term fraction or mixed number.

22. 0.45

23. 1.02

24. 17.44

25. 0.0004

Write each using exponential notation.

26. $x \cdot x \cdot x$

27. $16 \cdot 16 \cdot 16 \cdot 16$

28. $7 \cdot 7 \cdot 7 \cdot 7 \cdot 7 \cdot 7$

More Practice, page 535, set A

Problem Solving
Using the Strategies

UNDERSTAND
ANALYZE DATA
PLAN
ESTIMATE
SOLVE
EXAMINE

LEARN ABOUT IT

Some problems can be solved in several ways. Chris tried **Guess and Check.** Mike used the strategy **Work Backwards.**

> Nate's class had a car wash to raise money for soccer camp. On Saturday, Loan washed half as many cars as Nate. Kate washed 3 more cars than Loan. Bill washed 5 cars less than Kate. Bill washed 6 cars. How many did Nate wash?

Chris's solution:

> Try 10 cars
> $10 \div 2 = 5$
> $5 + 3 = 8$
> $8 - 5 = 3$ too small
>
> Try 20 cars
> $20 \div 2 = 10$
> $10 + 3 = 13$
> $13 - 5 = 8$ too big
>
> Try 16 cars
> $16 \div 2 = 8$
> $8 + 3 = 11$
> $11 - 5 = 6$ correct

Mike's solution:

> Nate's cars $\xrightarrow{\times 2}$ Loan's cars $\xrightarrow{+3}$ Kate's cars $\xrightarrow{-5}$ Bill's cars $= 6$
> Working backwards
> $16 \xleftarrow{\times 2} 8 \xleftarrow{-3} 11 \xleftarrow{+5} 6 \leftarrow$

Nate washed 16 cars.

TRY IT OUT

1. On Sunday, 4 more students washed cars. Rico washed 2 more cars than Trish. LaQuisha washed twice as many cars as Rico. Brad washed 4 fewer than Rico. Brad washed 16 cars. How many did Trish wash?

2. Four classes raised money for camp. Miguel's class raised $15 more than Lois' class. Damone's class raised a third as much as Miguel's class. Tonya's class raised $32, twice as much as Damone's class. How much did Lois' class raise?

246

Solve. Use any problem solving strategy.

1. The Miracle Mile Super Car Wash washed 162 cars in 6 hours. At this rate, how many cars would be washed in 2 hours?

2. Nate's class kept a record of the number of cars they cleaned on Saturday and Sunday. They charged $1.75 for a wash and $2.50 for a wash and vacuum. Use the chart to find how much they made on Sunday.

	Wash	Vac
Sat.	42	19
Sun.	56	23

3. Use the chart to find how many fewer people want a wash and vacuum job than a wash only.

4. Reggie and Dan are planning to bike 9 mi to a lake. Reggie can bike 6 mph, and Dan can bike 4 mph. They want to arrive at the same time. How much of a head start should Dan have?

5. Lisa bought a pack of graph paper for her cooperative learning group. Tom needed 5 sheets. Becky took twice as many as Tom. Aaron needed 3 fewer sheets than Becky. Lisa has 18 sheets left. How many sheets were in the pack?

6. Nina, Beth, and Julie competed in a 6K race. In how many different orders could they finish?

7. Gilberto takes care of his sister after school. He opened a savings account with his first month's earnings. The next week he deposited $15 more. Then he withdrew $9 to buy a book. The following week he deposited another $7. At the end of the month he withdrew half of what was left. Now his account has $18. How much did he deposit when he opened the account?

8. LuAnn made a scale model of her room. The model is 16 in. wide, 20 in. long, and 12 in. high. The actual room is 15 ft long. How wide is it?

SUPPORT OUR SOCCER CAMP! ☺!

WASH $1.75

WASH & VAC $2.50

BEST WASH IN TOWN!

Data Collection and Analysis
Group Decision Making

UNDERSTAND
ANALYZE DATA
PLAN
ESTIMATE
SOLVE
EXAMINE

Doing an Investigation

Group Skill:
Explain and Summarize

Hold the eraser of a pencil about 50 centimeters from your eyes at eye level. Focus carefully on the eraser of the pencil. Slowly bring the pencil closer to your eyes until you suddenly see two erasers instead of one. This is your critical point of focus. How far is this point from the bridge of your nose? Does this distance change much from person to person? Investigate to find out.

Collecting Data

1. Try this experiment with each person in your group. Each time measure the distance of the critical point of focus to the bridge of the nose. Measure to the nearest tenth centimeter. Make a table to record the data you collect.

Name	Distance from critical focus point to the bridge of the nose
Ann	6.7 cm
Craig	7.9 cm
Jerzy	8.8 cm

2. Try this experiment with at least 20 more people. Although it is impossible to select a **random** sample that represents the population of the world, you can choose a sample that is fairly representative of the people in your area. One way to do this is to choose people to represent different age groups (children and adults) and different gender groups (males and females).

Organizing Data

1. Group the distances you recorded in your table so that you can make a bar graph. Tally the number of people that fall into each **interval** or group of measurements.

Distance in centimeters	Number of people
0.0 - 1.9	
2.0 - 3.9	
4.0 - 5.9	/
6.0 - 7.9	//// //
. . . .	
. . . .	
. . . .	

2. Make a bar graph using the grouped data from your table.

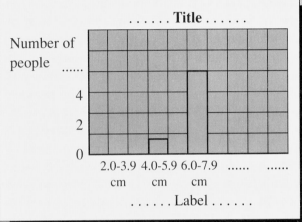

Presenting Your Analysis

3. Write a report of your results. Be sure to tell how you selected your sample, how you collected your data, and what your findings were. Include your tables and graphs.

WRAP UP

What's the Value of a Letter?

Use words from the vocabulary list to answer the following
questions. Write all ratios in lowest terms.

1. In the word *algebra,* what is the ratio of vowels to consonants?

2. In the term *cross product*, what is the ratio of the number of
vowels to the number of words in the term?

3. Write a true proportion for the number of letters in these
terms: *rate, equivalent, equal, thousand.*

4. If vowels cost $1.15 each, how much would you need in
order to buy all the vowels in the word *approximately*?

5. If consonants cost $.85 for 2, how much would all the
consonants in *proportion* cost?

6. Using the same rates as in questions 5 and 6, how much
would it cost to buy the entire word *rectangle*?

Sometimes, Always, Never

Which word should go in the blank, *sometimes*, *always*, or
never? Explain your choice.

7. If the ratio of boys to girls in a class is __?__ 3 to 2, there
are more boys than girls in the class.

8. If the ratio of a team's wins to losses is __?__ 5 to 3 and
they win 2 of the next 3 games, the new ratio of wins to
losses is 7 to 5.

Project

Sports statistics use ratios to describe how a player is
performing. Choose several players in a sport you enjoy. Find
statistics and write several ratios for each set of statistics. For
example, baseball ratios might include *hits* to *at bats* or *total
bases* to *hits*. Basketball ratios could include *goals made* to
goals attempted.

Compare the ratios for players you have chosen. Do the ratios
explain why one player is more valuable than another?

CHAPTER REVIEW/TEST

Part 1 Understanding

1. Which are equal ratios?

   A $\frac{15}{24} = \frac{3}{8}$ B $\frac{150}{6} = \frac{25}{1}$

   C $\frac{60}{32} = \frac{30}{8}$ D $\frac{150}{6} = \frac{25}{2}$

2. Complete the table. Write an algebraic expression for the rule.

Input (I)	1	2	3	4	5
Output (O)	3	6	?	?	?

Part 2 Skills

Write each ratio as a fraction in lowest terms.

3. $\frac{50}{14}$ 4. 28:40   5. 10 to 252

Write $=$ or $\neq$ for each ⫽.

6. $\frac{3}{2}$ ⫽ $\frac{12}{8}$ 7. $\frac{2}{15}$ ⫽ $\frac{6}{40}$ 8. $\frac{3}{15}$ ⫽ $\frac{15}{75}$ 9. $\frac{4}{3}$ ⫽ $\frac{2}{12}$

Solve each proportion.

10. $\frac{5}{9} = \frac{20}{x}$ 11. $\frac{12}{18} = \frac{x}{21}$ 12. $\frac{x}{12} = \frac{14}{6}$

Find the unit rate.

13. $\frac{\$348}{4\ \text{tires}}$ 14. $\frac{\$19.50}{3\ \text{tickets}}$ 15. $\frac{120\ \text{pages}}{60\ \text{min}}$

16. Find x for these similar figures.

Find the circumference of each circle.

17. Use $\frac{22}{7}$ for π. $d = 98$ cm

18. Use 3.14 for π. $r = 3\ m$

Part 3 Applications

19. Ms Matzner's class is building a scale model of the Parthenon. The dimensions of the face must have a ratio as close as possible to the Golden Rectangle (about 1.618 to 1). Which dimensions should be used?

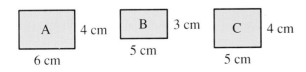

20. A movable belt for a can-labeling machine travels 115 cm in 5 seconds. How far does the belt move in 7 seconds?

21. **Challenge** Which is the best buy: 7 oz for $1.99, 11 oz for $2.79, or 16 oz for $3.29? If the 11 oz size goes on sale for $2.39, which is the better buy? What would the sale price have to be in order for it to be the best buy?

ENRICHMENT
Law of Levers

A lever is a simple machine that is used to move heavy objects with a small amount of effort. The diagram at the right shows the parts of a lever.

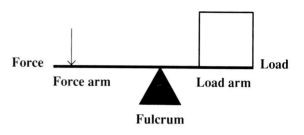

The pictures below can help you understand the law of simple levers.

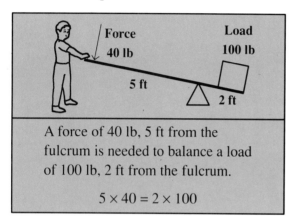

A force of 40 lb, 5 ft from the fulcrum is needed to balance a load of 100 lb, 2 ft from the fulcrum.

$$5 \times 40 = 2 \times 100$$

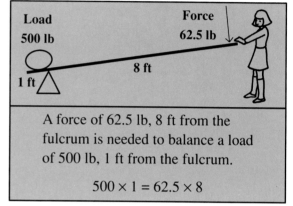

A force of 62.5 lb, 8 ft from the fulcrum is needed to balance a load of 500 lb, 1 ft from the fulcrum.

$$500 \times 1 = 62.5 \times 8$$

These examples illustrate the law of levers to balance a load.

Load × Load arm = Force × Force arm

This can also be expressed as a proportion: $\dfrac{\textbf{Load}}{\textbf{Force}} = \dfrac{\textbf{Force arm}}{\textbf{Load arm}}$

This is an example of an **inverse proportion.** What do you think this means?

Give the missing number for each part of this lever table.

	Load	Load arm	Force arm	Force
1.	600 lb	2 ft	6 ft	?
2.	1,000 lb	0.5 ft	10 ft	?
3.	?	3 ft	8 ft	60 lb
4.	250 lb	?	4 ft	25 lb
5.	84 lb	2.5 ft	?	20 lb

6. Milo weighs 75 lb and her father weighs 180 lb. If Milo's father sits on a seesaw 2.5 ft from the fulcrum, how far from the fulcrum must Milo sit to balance the seesaw?

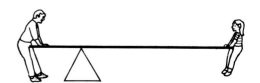

Cumulative Review

1. Which fraction is greater than $\frac{6}{7}$?

   A $\frac{8}{9}$ B $\frac{5}{6}$

   C $\frac{4}{5}$ D $\frac{9}{11}$

2. What is the mixed number for 3.28?

   A $3\frac{14}{25}$ B $3\frac{7}{50}$

   C $3\frac{7}{25}$ D $5\frac{4}{5}$

3. Which fraction is a repeating decimal?

   A $\frac{33}{50}$ B $\frac{7}{20}$

   C $\frac{4}{15}$ D $5\frac{4}{5}$

Add or subtract.

4. $3\frac{3}{5}$
   $+ 8\frac{3}{4}$

   A $11\frac{7}{20}$ B $11\frac{3}{4}$

   C $12\frac{7}{10}$ D $12\frac{7}{20}$

5. $20\frac{5}{8}$
   $- 5\frac{1}{6}$

   A $15\frac{11}{24}$ B $15\frac{19}{24}$

   C $14\frac{19}{24}$ D $15\frac{5}{12}$

6. $\left(\frac{4}{9} - \frac{1}{3}\right) + \frac{5}{6}$

   A $\frac{1}{9}$ B $\frac{17}{18}$ C $\frac{13}{18}$ D $\frac{5}{6}$

7. Find the fraction of the number.

   $\frac{2}{5} \times 35$

   A 14   B 87.5

   C 9   D 22.5

8. Which is the algebraic expression for the sum of a number w and 18?

   A $18 - w$ B $w + w + 18$

   C $w + 18$ D $w \cdot 18$

9. Which is the algebraic expression that tells how many centimeters are in m meters?

   A $1,000m$ B $100m$

   C $10m$ D $0.01m$

Use mental math to solve for n.

10. $n - 38.3 = 21.7$

    A 16.6   B 50

    C 60   D 59

11. $25 \times n = 300$

    A 8   B 12

    C 7.5   D 7

12. What is the expression for the width of this rectangle?

    36
    $A = 36x$?

    A w B x

    C 36   D $36 - x$

13. A pair of hiking boots is on sale for $25 off the regular price. The sale price is $140. What is the regular price?

    A 115   B 125

    C 165   C 120

9

PERCENTS

MATH AND
SOCIAL STUDIES

DATA BANK

Use the Social Studies Data Bank on page 499 to answer the questions.

1 According to the *Investm Survey* what would have been the best and the wo investments during the 15 years prior to 1988?

2 What kind of property caused people to lose nearly 8% of their investment in 1987?

3 Which company listed on the New York Stock Exchange had the lowest percent yield the week prior to January 1, 1989?

4 **Using Critical Thinking** Suppose you could buy 100 shares of any stock. What factors would you consider before deciding which stock to buy? What resources might you use to help you make your decision?

255

Percent

You can use what you know about proportions to understand percent.

EXPLORE **Discover a Pattern**

Have you ever bought something at a convenience store? A recent survey found that 1 out of every 5 convenience store customers is between ages 12 and 18. Complete the table at the right to find how many people out of 100 customers are between 12 and 18 years old.

1	2	3	4	5	6	?
5	10	?	?	?	?	100

TALK ABOUT IT

1. How did you decide what to write in each column of the table?

2. Did you find a shortcut for completing the table? Explain your method.

3. Give a ratio equal to 1:5 that has 100 as the second number.

A ratio of a number to 100 is called a **percent.** Percent means *per hundred* and is represented by the symbol %. You can express a percent as a fraction, as a decimal, or write it using the % symbol.

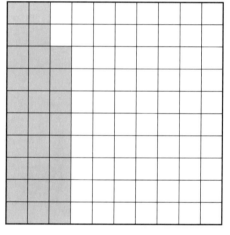

Fraction: $\dfrac{28}{100}$

Decimal: 0.28

Percent: 28%

Give a fraction, a decimal, and a percent for each shaded region.

1.

2.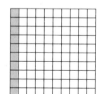

3.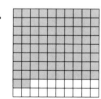

Give a fraction, a decimal, and a percent for each shaded region.

1.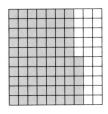

2.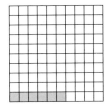

3.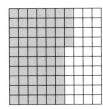

4.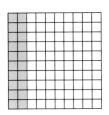

5.

6.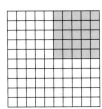

APPLY

MATH REASONING

Copy the number line. Mark and label each fraction, decimal, or percent on it.

0.%   100%

7. 25%

8. $\frac{50}{100}$

9. 99%

10. 0.05

11. 80%

12. 2%

13. 15%

14. 0.75

PROBLEM SOLVING

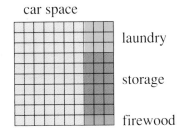

Lou made a scale drawing of his new garage. Each square represents one square foot. Give the percent of the total area for each of the following areas.

15. storage

16. laundry

17. car space

18. firewood

▶ ESTIMATION

Estimate the percent each letter represents.

19.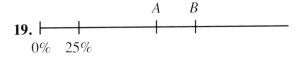

20.

21.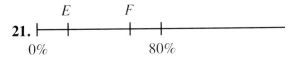

22.

Percents and Fractions

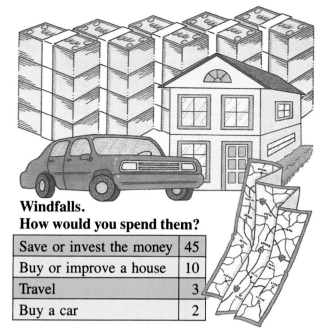

EXPLORE Analyze the Process

Suppose you won $30,000 with the restriction that you must use the entire amount in one way. What would you do? What percent of 60 people surveyed said they would either save or invest the money? To find the answer, express $\frac{45}{60}$ as a percent.

Windfalls.
How would you spend them?

Save or invest the money	45
Buy or improve a house	10
Travel	3
Buy a car	2

Set up a proportion.	Solve the proportion.	Express as a percent.
$\dfrac{45}{60} = \dfrac{n}{100}$	$60n = 45 \cdot 100$ $n = \dfrac{45 \cdot 100}{60} = 75$	$\dfrac{45}{60} = 75\%$

TALK ABOUT IT

1. Why was 100 used in setting up the proportion?

2. How could you have used estimation to tell that the answer to the problem above must be greater than 50%?

3. Use a complete sentence to answer the problem above.

You can use the meaning of percent to express a percent as a fraction.

Example Express 80% as a fraction in lowest terms.

$$80\% = \frac{80}{100} = \frac{80 \div 20}{100 \div 20} = \frac{4}{5}$$

Other Examples

A percent → fraction

$$45\% = \frac{45}{100} = \frac{9}{20}$$

B fraction → percent

$$\frac{2}{5} = \frac{n}{100}; n = 40, \text{ so } \frac{2}{5} = 40\%$$

Express each percent as a fraction.

1. 5%　　　　　　　**2.** 60%

Express each fraction as a percent.

3. $\dfrac{1}{10}$　　　　　　**4.** $\dfrac{3}{20}$

Express each percent as a fraction in lowest terms.

1. 75%   **2.** 40%   **3.** 24%   **4.** 42%   **5.** 70%

6. 55%   **7.** 2%   **8.** 29%   **9.** 92%   **10.** 85%

Express each fraction as a percent.

11. $\frac{4}{5}$ **12.** $\frac{13}{20}$ **13.** $\frac{3}{10}$ **14.** $\frac{3}{12}$ **15.** $\frac{1}{4}$

16. $\frac{63}{100}$ **17.** $\frac{10}{25}$ **18.** $\frac{180}{400}$ **19.** $\frac{19}{50}$ **20.** $\frac{24}{25}$

APPLY

MATH REASONING Estimate the value of the variable. Check your estimate by expressing your fraction as a percent.

21. Tammy had 25 out of n items correct for a score of about 62%.

22. Jerry had 25 out of m items correct for a score of about 31%

PROBLEM SOLVING

Suppose you won $30,000, but had to invest it for two years. Where would you put your money?

Windfalls: How would you save them?

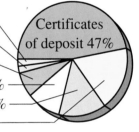

23. What fraction of the people surveyed said mutual funds?

24. What fraction said precious metals or collectibles?

Collectibles 2%
Precious metals 2%
Individual stocks 7%
Bond mutual funds 10%
Stock mutual funds 14%
Real estate 18%
Certificates of deposit 47%

25. Social Studies Data Bank Write the 1-year investment return for diamonds as a decimal. If you had invested $100 in diamonds for that year, what would your return have been?

DATA BANK

▶ **MENTAL MATH**

It is useful to know the fraction equivalents for certain percents. Use mental math to give a fraction for each percent.

26. 50%   **27.** 25%   **28.** 75%   **29.** 10%

Use mental math to give the percent for each fraction.

30. $\frac{1}{10}$ **31.** $\frac{1}{2}$ **32.** $\frac{3}{4}$ **33.** $\frac{1}{4}$

More Practice, page 535, set C

Percents and Decimals

Top USA cities for winter vacations

Honolulu 87.4%
Miami 52.1%
L.A. 36.5%
Denver 33.5%
San Francisco 31.7%

Source: American Express;
Nov. 1988 survey of 167 travel agents

EXPLORE Examine the Data

Work in groups. Need a vacation? Need to get away from the cold? The graph shows the results of a survey about favorite winter vacation spots.

TALK ABOUT IT

1. Which vacation spot is most popular?

2. Which is least popular?

3. Why do you think the sum of the percentages is greater than 100?

Percents can be expressed as decimals.

$$87.4\% = \frac{87.4}{100} \qquad \text{Percent means per hundred.}$$

$$= 0.874 \qquad \text{To divide by 100, move the decimal point two places to the left.}$$

Decimals can be expressed as percents.

$$0.521 = \frac{521}{1000}$$

$$= \frac{52.1}{100} \qquad \text{Find an equivalent fraction with a denominator of 100.}$$

$$= 52.1\%$$

Other Examples

A $0.242 = 24.2\%$ **B** $0.05 = 5\%$	Shortcut: move the decimal point two places to the **right**.

C $36.5\% = 0.365$ **D** $8\% = 0.08$	Shortcut: move the decimal point two places to the **left**.

TRY IT OUT

Express each percent as a decimal.

1. 16%   **2.** 25.5%

Express each decimal as a percent.

3. 0.2   **4.** 0.043

Express each percent as a decimal.

1. 35%   **2.** 2%   **3.** 80%   **4.** 14.5%   **5.** 9%

6. 23%   **7.** 5%   **8.** 17%   **9.** 32%   **10.** 0.01%

Express each decimal as a percent.

11. 0.4   **12.** 0.83   **13.** 0.105   **14.** 3.6   **15.** 0.41

16. 0.03   **17.** 1.01   **18.** 0.0007   **19.** 0.052   **20.** 0.2832

APPLY

MATH REASONING   Give two values that can replace the variable to make a true statement.

21. 0.045 is less than n which is less than 5%.

22. 99% is less than m which is less than 0.999.

23. 0.15% is less than t which is less than 0.16%.

PROBLEM SOLVING

24. In a survey of 50 high school seniors, 38 said they were saving at least a portion of their money earned at part time jobs. What percent of the students are saving some of their earnings? Express this percent as a decimal.

25. The same survey found that 90% of the students spent part of their earnings for personal expenses such as clothing. Express this percent as a decimal.

MIXED REVIEW

Solve.

26. $\dfrac{10}{40} = \dfrac{25}{x}$ **27.** $x - \dfrac{3}{5} = 2$ **28.** $3a = 18$ **29.** $24{:}x = 10{:}7$

Find the value of each expression.

30. $42 + 10 \times 12$ **31.** $4 \times (3.1 + 4.9)$ **32.** $24 \div 8 + 9 \times 4$ **33.** $8.7 \times 3.2 \div 8.7$

Fractions, Decimals, and Percents

LEARN ABOUT IT

EXPLORE Evaluate the Data

Work in groups. Discounts are often advertised using percents or fractions. Which discount in the ads at the right is greater?

SALE
⅖ OFF

PRICES SLASHED
45% OFF

TALK ABOUT IT

1. Explain what you did to compare the discounts.

2. Is there another way you could have compared the discounts? Explain.

3. Would you rather have a discount shown as a percent or as a fraction? Why?

You can compare fractions and percents easily using a calculator.

Example.

Compare $\frac{2}{5}$ and 45%.

$\frac{2}{5}$ means $2 \div 5$. Use a calculator to find the quotient.

$\frac{2}{5} = 0.40$ and 45% = 0.45. So, 45% off is the greater discount.

$$0.4$$

Other Examples

A Compare $\frac{5}{6}$ and 80%.

$\frac{5}{6} \approx 0.83$

80% = 0.80

$\frac{5}{6} > 80\%$

B Compare $\frac{5}{12}$ and 38%.

$\frac{5}{12} \approx 0.42$

38% = 0.38

$\frac{5}{12} > 38\%$

TRY IT OUT

Use a calculator to find which is greater.

1. 30% or $\frac{1}{3}$

2. 15 out of 18 or 90%

3. $\frac{35}{60}$ or 55%

Use a calculator to find which is greater.

1. $\frac{2}{3}$ or 67%

2. 35% or $\frac{2}{7}$

3. $\frac{5}{8}$ or 60%

4. $\frac{1}{6}$ or 16.7%

5. 45% or $\frac{11}{20}$

6. $\frac{3}{13}$ or 26%

7. $\frac{11}{10}$ or 97%

8. $\frac{7}{8}$ or 90%

9. $\frac{2}{9}$ or 25%

10. $\frac{1}{3}$ or 33.3%

11. 32% or $\frac{3}{2}$

12. $\frac{10}{12}$ or 77%

APPLY

MATH REASONING Arrange in order from least to greatest.

13. $\frac{1}{7}$, 91%, 1.9%, $\frac{2}{5}$, 0.77

14. $\frac{5}{8}$, 0.355, 41%, 66.6%, 0.624

.625   .41 .660

15. 49%, 0.94, $\frac{4}{9}$, 4.9, $\frac{9}{4}$

.4A , 9A .4A 2.35

16. 9.9%, $\frac{3}{8}$, 0.162, 40%, 0.3

.0.9   .375 .162 .40 6.3

PROBLEM SOLVING

17. A newspaper story said 38% of a certain city's population was concerned about water pollution. Another paper said about $\frac{2}{5}$ of the people were concerned. Could both reports be correct? Explain.

18. After a 30% markdown, small yard chairs were on sale for $10 and large chairs for $15. A local church group bought 12 chairs, some of each kind, and spent a total of $155. How many chairs of each size did they buy?

Water pollution concerns 38% of town's citizens

Two-fifths of town's-people want pollution stopped today!

▶ **CALCULATOR**

19. Explore the percent key on your calculator. Write a brief paragraph explaining what this key does. Give examples.

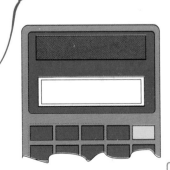

More Practice, page 536, set A

Exploring Algebra
Functions and Function Notation

LEARN ABOUT IT

EXPLORE **Complete the Table**

Many professionals charge a fee which is a function of the number of hours worked. For example, a plumber might charge a flat rate of $35 plus $40 an hour for labor. Copy and complete the table.

Hours (h)	1	2	3	4	5
Labor fee (dollars)	75	115	?	?	?

TALK ABOUT IT

1. How did you decide on the fee for 3 hours? 4 hours? 5 hours?

2. If this plumber works 5 hours at each of two different places, how will the total labor fee be calculated?

For each h, there is exactly one fee. It is a function of h. The **rule** is: multiply the hours (h) by 40 and add 35. We choose the letter f to denote a function and write:

$$f(h) = 40h + 35$$

This is read "f of h equals 40h plus 35."

To **evaluate a function,** substitute the given value for the variable in the function.

Example Find $f(2)$ for $f(h) = 40h + 35$

$f(2)$ means to find the value of $40h + 35$ when $h = 2$
$f(2) = 40 \cdot 2 + 35 = 115$
$f(2) = 115$

TRY IT OUT

Evaluate each function for the value given.

1. Find $f(12)$ for $f(x) = x + 25$

2. Find $f(8)$ for $f(x) = 5x - 14$

3. Find $f(0)$ for $f(x) = x^2 + 5$

4. Find $f(2)$ for $f(a) = 6a^2$

Evaluate each function for the value given.

1. Find $f(5)$ for $f(x) = 3x - 4$

2. Find $f(2)$ for $f(x) = \dfrac{x + 8}{5}$

3. Find $f(7)$ for $f(y) = 6(y + 4)$

4. Find $f(0)$ for $f(a) = (a + 6) \cdot (a + 7)$

5. Find $f(6)$ for $f(h) = \dfrac{1}{2}h^2$

6. Find $f\left(\dfrac{1}{2}\right)$ for $f(d) = 6 - 4d$

Copy and complete each table.

7. $f(x) = 5x + 10$

x	0	1	2	5	10
$f(x)$					

8. $f(x) = x^2 + 6$

x	0	2	4	10	20
$f(x)$					

MATH REASONING

9. Use the $f(x)$ notation to write a function so that $f(5) = 18$.

10. Use the $f(x)$ notation to write a function so that $f(2) = 0$.

PROBLEM SOLVING

11. The labor charge at a certain scooter repair shop is given by the function $f(h) = 45h$, where h is the number of hours worked. What would be the labor cost for 3 hours of work?

12. Data Hunt Find the hourly labor charge of repairing something in your town. Express the relation between the labor charge and the number of hours as a function using the $f(x)$ notation.

▶ **ALGEBRA**

Find the pattern. Copy and complete the tables below.

 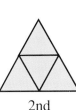 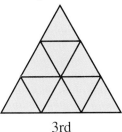

1st   2nd   3rd

Design	1	2	3	4	5	6
Perimeter	3	6	9	12	15	18
Number of small $\triangle$'s	1	4	9	16	25	36

13. Give the function rule for the relation between the design number and the perimeter of the large triangle.

14. Give the function rule for the relation between the design number and the number of small triangles.

Large and Small Percents

EXPLORE Analyze the Data

A **quota** is a goal such as the number of units a salesperson is expected to sell.

TALK ABOUT IT

> **IMF Employees' NewsLetter**
>
> June was a great month! Fast Computers's individual sales quota was 5 units, but Margo, our top salesperson, sold 8 units. And of the 150 units sold last fall, only one came back for repair! Keep up the good work!

1. Margo sold more than her quota. What is the ratio of her actual sales to her quota? Is the ratio more or less than 100%?

2. What is the ratio of repaired computers to total computers sold for the fall? Is that greater or less than the ratio of 1 to 100?

You can write a ratio as a percent using a proportion or by dividing.

Example Write the ratio of Margo's sales to her quota as a percent.

Using a proportion:

$$\frac{8}{5} = \frac{x}{100}$$

$$x = \frac{800}{5} = 160$$

By dividing:

$$\frac{8}{5} = 8 \div 5 = 1.6$$
$$= 160\%$$

Other Examples Write the ratio of computers repaired to computers sold as a percent.

Using a proportion:

$$\frac{1}{150} = \frac{x}{100}$$

$$x = \frac{100}{150} \approx 0.7$$

By dividing:

$$\frac{1}{150} = 1 \div 150 \approx 0.0066667$$
$$\approx 0.7\%$$

You can also express a percent as a fraction or as a decimal.

$$120\% = \frac{120}{100} = 1.2 \qquad \frac{1}{2}\% = 0.005 \text{ or } \frac{1}{200}$$

Express each fraction as a percent. Round to the nearest tenth of a percent.

1. $\frac{3}{2}$ **2.** $\frac{1}{200}$ **3.** $\frac{5}{1000}$ **4.** $\frac{8}{4}$

Express each percent as a fraction or as a decimal.

5. 110% **6.** 300% **7.** $\frac{1}{5}\%$ **8.** $\frac{3}{8}\%$

Express each fraction as a percent. Round to the nearest tenth of a percent.

1. $\frac{7}{4}$ 2. $\frac{9}{5}$ 3. $\frac{3}{1000}$ 4. $\frac{1}{125}$

5. $\frac{17}{10}$ 6. $\frac{4}{900}$ 7. $\frac{3}{700}$ 8. $\frac{27}{20}$

9. $\frac{24}{15}$ 10. $\frac{7}{1000}$ 11. $\frac{7}{800}$ 12. $\frac{10}{7}$

Express each percent as a fraction and as a decimal.

13. 130%   14. 250%   15. $\frac{2}{5}\%$ 16. $\frac{1}{8}\%$

17. $\frac{1}{10}\%$ 18. 125%   19. 140%   20. $\frac{3}{4}\%$

21. 408%   22. $\frac{3}{50}\%$ 23. $\frac{7}{8}\%$ 24. 295%

MATH REASONING Use estimation to choose the best answer.

25. 135% of 60 is   **A.** 8.1   **B.** 81   **C.** 810

26. 0.5% of 200 is   **A.** 1   **B.** 10   **C.** 100

27. 500% of 100 is   **A.** 50   **B.** 100   **C.** 500

PROBLEM SOLVING

28. A car salesperson's quota for one month was 12 cars. So far he has sold 8. How many more does he need to sell to reach 150% of his quota?

29. Another car salesperson sold 35 cars in the first 6 months of the year and 45 cars the second six months. He sold 125% of his quota for the year. What was his quota?

USING CRITICAL THINKING Make a Generalization

30. You can express a percent like 12.5% as a decimal number by moving the decimal point 2 places to the left and dropping the percent symbol. Does this rule apply to percents greater than 100 and less than 1? Use examples to justify your conclusion.

More Practice, page 536, set B

Using Critical Thinking
Finding Percent Patterns

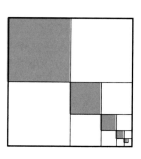

YIELD

Julie showed Bill these three shaded triangles. "This is a weird problem," she announced. "Without drawing all the triangles, I'm supposed to figure out what percent of a triangle that has each side divided into 10 segments is white and what percent is red. I don't think the problem can be solved without drawing the triangles."

"It does look tough," replied Bill. "But I see a pattern in the table that might help!"

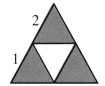 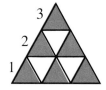 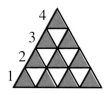

Number of Segments	White triangles	Red triangles	Total triangles	% red	% white
2	1	3	4	75	25
3	3	6	9	67	33
4	6	10	16	62	38

TALK ABOUT IT

1. What problem was Julie trying to solve? What were the special conditions of the problem?

2. How was the data in the table obtained?

3. What patterns do you see in the table that might help Julie solve the problem?

TRY IT OUT

1. What is the solution to the problem?

2. What do you estimate the percentages would be for a triangle with 1000 segments? 1,000,000 segments?

3. What percent of this square is shaded? (Assume the shading pattern continues.)

MIDCHAPTER REVIEW/QUIZ

Fill in the blanks with the number of tiles from the grid.

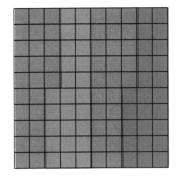

1. The ratio of red tiles to total tiles is _?_ to _?_.

2. _?_ out of the _?_ tiles are blue.

3. _?_ out of the _?_ tiles are not green.

Copy and complete each ratio table. Finish the equation to show the percent.

4.

9	?	?
25	50	100

$\dfrac{9}{25} = ?\%$

5.

54	?	?	?
72	8	4	100

$\dfrac{54}{72} = ?\%$

Express each fraction as a percent.

6. $\dfrac{21}{50}$

7. $\dfrac{2}{5}$

8. $\dfrac{12}{80}$

9. $\dfrac{45}{75}$

Express each percent as a fraction.

10. 28%

11. 15%

12. 64%

13. 72%

Express each percent as a decimal.

14. 7%

15. 0.75%

16. 250%

17. 5%

Express each decimal as a percent.

18. 0.75

19. 0.04

20. 1.5

21. 5

22. Copy and complete the chart.

Fraction	Decimal	Percent
$\dfrac{3}{5}$		
		32%
	0.04	

23. Copy and complete the charts.

x	0	1	6	7
$f(x) = x + 2$	?	?	?	?

x	0	1	6	7
$f(x) = \dfrac{x + 2}{3}$	?	?	?	?

PROBLEM SOLVING

24. Leslie needs 72% to pass the quiz. Will she pass with 18 out of 24 correct?

25. Use percent to decide which player is best at free throws.

player A:	108 out of 150
player B:	36 out of 45
player C:	99 out of 132

Fractional Percents

HOME MORTGAGE RATE...

9.6% APR

LEARN ABOUT IT

EXPLORE **Analyze the Process**

Suppose your parents were offered a home mortgage rate of $9\frac{5}{8}\%$. Another bank is advertising the rate shown at the right. Which is the lower interest rate?

To compare these rates, express each one as a decimal.

Express the fractional part of the percent as a decimal.	Rewrite the percent using the decimal in place of the fraction.

Divide 5 by 8 to change $\frac{5}{8}$ to a decimal.

$$\frac{5}{8} = 0.625$$

$9\frac{5}{8}\% = 9.625\%$

TALK ABOUT IT

1. How did you change $\frac{5}{8}$ to a decimal?

2. How could you have estimated that $9\frac{5}{8}\%$ is greater than 9.5%?

3. Use a complete sentence to answer the problem above.

To express a percent which has a decimal as one with a fraction, change the decimal part of the percent to a fraction.

$$10.75\% = 10\frac{75}{100}\% = 10\frac{3}{4}\%$$

Other Examples

A $12\frac{1}{2}\% = 12.5\% = 0.125$

B $0.052 = 5.2\% = 5\frac{2}{10}\% = 5\frac{1}{5}\%$

TRY IT OUT

Express each percent as a decimal.

1. $5\frac{1}{2}\%$

2. $11\frac{1}{8}\%$

3. $9\frac{1}{4}\%$

4. $8\frac{1}{10}\%$

Express each decimal as a percent with a fraction.

5. 0.105

6. 0.0725

7. 0.1224

8. 0.011

Express each percent as a decimal.

1. $5\frac{3}{5}\%$ **2.** $7\frac{1}{4}\%$ **3.** $46\frac{7}{8}\%$ **4.** $1\frac{13}{100}\%$

5. $4\frac{1}{8}\%$ **6.** $76\frac{1}{25}\%$ **7.** $14\frac{3}{20}\%$ **8.** $21\frac{13}{50}\%$

Express each decimal as a percent with a fraction.

9. 0.348   **10.** 0.061   **11.** 0.4975   **12.** 0.216

13. 0.0714   **14.** 1.255   **15.** 0.0125   **16.** 0.17625

APPLY

MATH REASONING Copy the underlined number. Insert a decimal point to make the decimal number equal to the given percent. Write extra zeros if necessary.

17. $5\frac{7}{8}\% = \underline{5875}$ **18.** $14\frac{1}{4}\% = \underline{1425}$ **19.** $102\frac{1}{5}\% = \underline{1022}$

PROBLEM SOLVING

20. Interest rates for certificates of deposits at 5 banks are shown in the table. Write these interest rates in order from smallest to largest.

21. **Social Studies Data Bank** Express the yields of stocks in Grace, Harris, and the Motel 6 corporations as decimals. Does the company with the highest yield also pay the highest dividend?

CD Rates ($10,000 minimum)
9.25%
9.05%
$9\frac{1}{3}\%$
$9\frac{2}{5}\%$
9%

MIXED REVIEW

Find the circumference of a circle with the given diameter. Use $\frac{22}{7}$ for π.

22. $d = 14$ mm   **23.** $d = 4\frac{1}{2}$ cm   **24.** $d = 10$ m   **25.** $d = 5\frac{2}{3}$ km

Write each fraction as a decimal. Use a bar to show repeating decimals.

26. $\frac{7}{8}$ **27.** $\frac{1}{6}$ **28.** $\frac{3}{11}$ **29.** $\frac{2}{10}$

More Practice, page 536, set C

Problem Solving
Estimating Percents

UNDERSTAND
ANALYZE DATA
PLAN
ESTIMATE
SOLVE
EXAMINE

LEARN ABOUT IT

Many real-world problems involving percent ask for an estimate rather than an exact answer.

> A reporter investigated the number of women working in the law enforcement profession in a certain state. The data collected is shown at the right. About what percent of women officers are state police?

Women Officers

Sheriff's Department-
153

Local Police -
64

State Police -
26

> To solve this problem I need to know the total number of people surveyed.

$$153 + 64 + 26 = 243$$

> I can divide the number in the state police by the total to get a decimal.

$$\frac{26}{243}$$

> I can substitute compatible numbers to estimate this percent.

$$\frac{26}{243} \text{ is about } \frac{25}{250} = \frac{1}{10} = 10\%$$

About 10% of the women officers are state police.

TRY IT OUT

Solve. Use estimation.

1. About what percent of the women in the survey work in sheriff's departments?

2. About what percent of women in the survey data above work for local police?

3. In one police department, there were 12 women officers in 1980. In 1990, there were 21. If there was a total of 65 officers in 1990, about what percent were women?

4. In a certain town 10 out of 30 officers are women. Over the next 5 years, 10 more officers will be hired. Estimate how many women must be hired to reach a 38% level for women officers?

Solve. Use any problem solving strategy.

1. Twenty-three students signed up to attend five panel discussions on careers in law enforcement. Two students were unable to attend. What percent of the students went to the discussions?

2. The Police Officers Association in a certain town recommended that 23 women officers be added to the police force over the next 10 years. Use the graph to estimate how many women officers the Association wants at the end of four years.

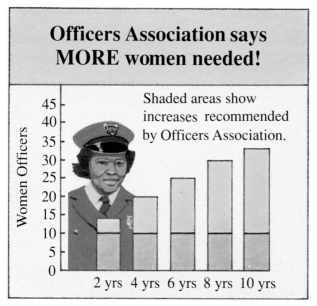

Officers Association says MORE women needed!

Shaded areas show increases recommended by Officers Association.

Women Officers

2 yrs 4 yrs 6 yrs 8 yrs 10 yrs

3. A survey of 118 students showed that 87 of them believed women could be effective law enforcement officers. About what percent was that?

4. Officer Ferrer bought a Spanish dictionary for $4.50 and 3 practice tapes for $23.85. How much did each practice tape cost?

5. Some of the police officers in a certain city are learning to speak Spanish. On March 23, one of them learned 7 new words. The next day she learned 7 more new words. At this rate, how many new words will she know by the end of the month?

6. In a survey, 148 students said they planned to go to college. Twelve of those students planned to pursue careers in law enforcement. What fraction of the students is that? What percent?

7. There are 8 female and 35 male officers in a certain police department. About what percent of the officers are female? male?

8. **Think About Your Solution**
   Solve. Mr. Brier has his students solve problems in groups. Today there are 26 students in 7 groups. Some of the groups have 4 students, others have 3 students. How many groups of each size are there?

   a. Write your answer in a complete sentence.
   b. Write a brief description of how you solved the problem.
   c. Name the strategy or strategies you used.

Problem Solving
Using the Strategies

UNDERSTAND
ANALYZE DATA
PLAN
ESTIMATE
SOLVE
EXAMINE

LEARN ABOUT IT

Some problems can be solved using the strategy **Write an Equation.**

Find the average price of a home 8 years ago for the city described in the newspaper article at the right.

Newspaper Reports House-Prices

Bloomington - A local real estate agent was quoted as saying that the average house price today in this growing midwestern city is 2.5 times greater than what it was just about 8 years ago. The average price of a house today is $105,000.

Answer these questions to help you represent a real-world situation by an equation.

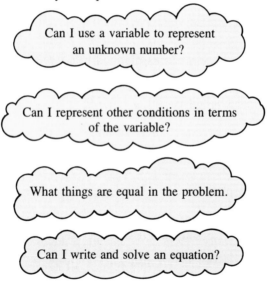

Can I use a variable to represent an unknown number?

Let p = average price 8 years ago

Can I represent other conditions in terms of the variable?

$2.5p$ is the price of a home today

What things are equal in the problem.

$2.5p$ must equal $105,000

Can I write and solve an equation?

$2.5p = 105,000 \qquad p = 42,000$

The average price of a home in this city 8 years ago was $42,000.

TRY IT OUT

Write and solve an equation for each problem.

1. Keisha saw a sign that said "Los Angeles—475 miles." Several hours later, she saw another sign giving the distance as 290 miles. How many miles had she traveled between these signs? (Let d be the distance between the signs.)

2. A run-for-life campaign made $35,784. The money was shared equally among 6 charities. How much did each charity receive? (Let m be the amount each charity received.)

Solve. Use any problem solving strategy.

Some Strategies	
Act Out	Solve a Simpler Problem
Use Objects	Make an Organized List
Choose an Operation	Work Backward
Draw a Picture	Look for a Pattern
Guess and Check	Use Logical Reasoning
Make a Table	Write an Equation

1. There were 19 different dishes on the buffet table. Eight were main dishes, 5 were salads, and the rest were desserts. How many of the dishes were desserts?

2. Mrs. Newby bought 8 packages of plates, 3 packages of plastic glasses, and a package of napkins for the buffet. Use the price list to find how much she spent.

3. Franklin had 2 twenty-dollar bills. He spent $27 on placemats. Use the price list to find how many packages of placemats Franklin bought.

4. Twenty-three students and 35 out of 48 parents came to the dinner. About what percent of the parents came to the dinner?

5. For Open House, Mia's school planned special activities in 3 different rooms. Each activity took 10 minutes. How long did it take 5 groups of people to see all 3 activities in order.

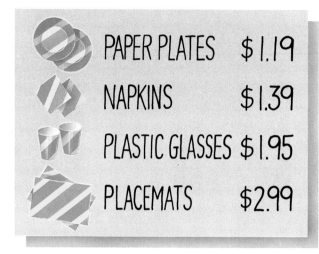

PAPER PLATES $1.19

NAPKINS $1.39

PLASTIC GLASSES $1.95

PLACEMATS $2.99

6. A carpenter cut a piece of moulding into 5 equal length sections. Each section was 15 in. What was the total length of the moulding?

7. Barry spent $45 from his savings for a bicycle helmet. He had $115 left in his savings. How much did he have before he bought the helmet?

8. Carla's school offers French, Spanish, and Japanese. There are 7 more students enrolled in Spanish than in French. Twice as many students are taking Spanish as Japanese. There are 19 students enrolled in Japanese. How many students are taking Spanish?

Applied Problem Solving
Group Decision Making

UNDERSTAND
ANALYZE DATA
PLAN
ESTIMATE
SOLVE
EXAMINE

Group Skill:
Check for Understanding

Your group is writing an article giving recommendations for fall travelers. The group will review five cities: Athens, Hong Kong, Paris, Rio de Janeiro, and Tokyo and rank them from most desirable to least desirable.

Facts to Consider

- Most people consider temperatures in the seventies and low eighties to be most desirable.

- Most people like lots of sunny days. Rain definitely spoils a vacation.

- High humidity is less desirable than low humidity, particularly when the temperature is high.

- Hotel and food costs are major considerations for most travelers.

- Your group's decision should be based on some, but not necessarily all of the data in the following table. Decide which data should have the greatest influence on your ranking.

	Hours of sunshine	Afternoon temp °F	Afternoon humidity %	Chances of a dry day %	Expenses per day (dollars)
Athens	9:26	84	42	92	94
Hong Kong	6:28	85	72	58	169
Paris	5:37	70	54	81	211
Rio de Janeiro	5:06	75	65	84	111
Tokyo	4:32	79	65	61	244

1. Suppose you assign points so that the city with the lowest daily expense receives 5 points, the next lowest receives 4 points, the next 3 points, and so on. What city would receive 3 points? 1 point?

2. Suppose you assign points to the cities according to the chances of a dry day. Which city would receive the highest number of points? the lowest number of points? Are the rankings for dry days the same as the rankings for daily expenses?

3. Add the number of points earned for daily expenses and for dry days. Which city has the most points?

4. You could decide to make the ranking for daily expenses worth twice as much as the ranking for dry days. Then how many points would each city receive?

Rank the cities from most to least desirable. Defend your group's decision by explaining how you scored the data for each city.

277

WRAP UP

Percent Match

Match each term on the left with the best example on the right.

1. percent
2. proportion
3. function
4. quota
5. discount

A $f(w) = w + 3$

B per hundred

C goal of a salesperson

D a percent off the regular price

E $\frac{2}{5} = \frac{n}{100}$

Sometimes, Always, Never

Which word should go in the blank, *sometimes*, *always*, or *never*? Explain your choice.

6. A percent is __?__ written as a whole number followed by the symbol, %.

7. In a function, each member of one set is __?__ matched with exactly one member of another set.

8. A decimal can __?__ be expressed as a percent by moving the decimal point 2 places to the left.

9. A mixed number can __?__ be expressed as a percent.

10. A discount can __?__ be expressed as a 3-digit whole number percent.

Project

Find five situations in your classroom that could be described by a fraction or a mixed number. Record each situation and the fraction or mixed number. Then find the decimal and percent that would also describe each. For example, there are $1\frac{1}{2}$ times as many students with brown eyes as there are with blue eyes.

CHAPTER REVIEW/TEST

Part 1   Understanding

1. Give a fraction, a decimal, and a percent for the shaded region.

Compare these fractions, decimals, and percents. Tell whether the statement is true or false.

2. $87.5\% > \frac{7}{8}$

3. $\frac{5}{12} < 45\%$

4. $120\% = 1.2$

5. $0.5316 = 53\frac{8}{25}\%$

Part 2   Skills

Express each fraction as a percent.

6. $\frac{9}{20}$

7. $\frac{4}{16}$

8. $\frac{9}{1,000}$

9. $\frac{7}{5}$

Express each percent as a fraction in lowest terms.

10. 74%

11. 28%

12. 350%

13. $\frac{3}{5}\%$

Express each percent as a decimal.

14. 35.5%

15. 6%

16. 130%

17. $12\frac{7}{8}\%$

Express each decimal as a percent.

18. 0.48

19. 0.1886

20. 0.0251

Part 3   Applications

21. What percent of this tangram puzzle is shaded?

22. In one police district, 8 out of 35 officers are over 56 years of age. Estimate the percent of officers who are older than 56?

23. The labor charge at Danville Bike Shop is given by the function $f(h) = 34h$, where h is the number of hours worked. What would be the labor cost for $2\frac{1}{2}$ hours of work?

24. **Challenge** A group of 57 people are to view 4 exhibits. All must start at A and finish at D. No more than 12 people are permitted in an exhibit at a time. It takes about 20 min to view one exhibit. How long will the group be at the museum? What percent of the total time will each person be viewing the exhibits?

ENRICHMENT
Squares and Square Roots

You can use colored tiles to learn more about squares and square roots. Select enough tiles to make a 10 × 10 square. Each tile is 1 square unit (1 unit^2). What is the area of the square?

$$10 \times 10 = 100$$

The area of the square is 100 units^2

Select some more tiles. This time make a square with an area of 400 units^2. How many tiles are on each side of the square?

The number of tiles on each side of the square is the **square root** of the area.

$$20 \times 20 = 400$$

The square root of 400 is 20. A **radical sign** $\left(\sqrt{} \right)$ is used to indicate a square root.

$$\sqrt{400} = 20$$

Give the length of one side of the square.

1.

Area
36 cm^2

2.

Area
81 m^2

3.

Area
225 ft^2

Give the area of the square.

4.

13 m

5.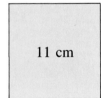

11 cm

6.

25 ft

Find the square root.

7. $\sqrt{25}$

8. $\sqrt{1}$

9. $\sqrt{169}$

10. $\sqrt{49}$

11. $\sqrt{289}$

12. $\sqrt{10{,}000}$

CUMULATIVE REVIEW

Find the products.

1. $\frac{4}{5} \times \frac{2}{3} \times \frac{3}{7}$

 A $\frac{8}{15}$ B $\frac{1}{4}$ C $\frac{8}{35}$ D $\frac{6}{35}$

2. $6\frac{3}{5} \times 4\frac{2}{3}$

 A $24\frac{2}{5}$ B $6\frac{13}{15}$ C $25\frac{4}{15}$ D $30\frac{4}{5}$

3. Find the quotient.

 $1\frac{5}{6} \div 3\frac{1}{2}$

 A $\frac{11}{21}$ B $\frac{11}{12}$ C $\frac{5}{21}$ D $\frac{1}{2}$

4. Which expression gives the inverse operation for "2.75 less than m"?

 A add m

 B add 2.75

 C subtract 2.75

 D subtract 275

5. Which is the algebraic expression and the inverse operation for the phrase "6 times as old as Dee (d)"?

 A $6 + d$, subtract 6

 B $\frac{6}{d}$, multiply by 6

 C $6 \cdot d$, divide by 6

 D $6 - d$, add d

6. Solve for r.
 $18.65 = r + 7.9$

 A 26.55   B 10.75

 C 2.36   D 11.56

7. Solve for h.
 $\frac{h}{96} = 32$

 A 3,072   B 3

 C 0.33   D 64

8. Which fraction names the ratio 144 to 16?

 A $\frac{12}{1}$ B $\frac{9}{1}$ C $\frac{1}{9}$ D $\frac{11}{100}$

9. Which is a true proportion?

 A $\frac{7}{10} = \frac{14}{22}$ B $\frac{2}{3} = \frac{1}{6}$

 C $\frac{3}{8} = \frac{6}{16}$ D $\frac{4}{5} = \frac{32}{42}$

10. Which is the best buy for tortilla chips?

 A 14 oz for $1.59   B 18 oz for $2.19

 C 10 oz for $1.39   D 4 oz for 59¢

11. If the scale is $\frac{1}{2}$ in. = 4 ft, what is the actual length of a family room that is $3\frac{3}{4}$ in. long on a scale drawing?

 A 15 ft   B $7\frac{1}{2}$ ft

 C 60 ft   D 30 ft

12. What is the circumference of a circle with $r = 0.85$ cm? Use 3.14 for π.

 A 5.338 cm   B 2.669 cm

 C 2.27 cm   D 1.33 cm

13. A machine can fill 3 bottles in 8 s. At this rate, how long will it take to fill 48 bottles?

 A 16 s   B 18 s

 C 128 s   D 144 s

14. A porpoise swam 114 km in 3 h. About how many kilometers did it swim per hour?

 A 48 km   B 342 km

 C $1\frac{9}{10}$ km   D 38 km

10

APPLICATIONS
OF PERCENT

MATH AND
HEALTH AND FITNESS

DATA BANK

Use the Health and Fitness
Data Bank on page 502 to
answer the questions.

1. Which group of twelve-
year-olds, boys or girls, has
a smaller average weight
range for most given heights?

2 Which has the most calories, a serving of soup, a serving of applesauce, or a granola bar?

3 How many granola bars would a person have to eat in a day to get 100% of the recommended daily allowance of protein?

4 **Using Critical Thinking** Describe any trends you can find in comparing weights of boys and girls as height increases. What factors may explain these trends?

Finding a Percent of a Number

LEARN ABOUT IT

You can use proportions and equations to find a percent of a number.

EXPLORE **Analyze the Process**

Of the first 40 United States Presidents, 20% were former teachers. How many of the Presidents were teachers? To find the answer, copy and complete the ratio table.

20	?	?
100	10	40

TALK ABOUT IT

1. How you can predict whether the answer will be greater or less than $\frac{1}{4}$ the number of Presidents.

2. How did you decide what numbers to write in the ratio table?

3. Give the answer to the problem in a complete sentence.

Of the first 40 U.S. Presidents, 15% had six or more children. How many Presidents had six or more children?

Use A Proportion

$$\frac{15}{100} = \frac{n}{40}$$
$$00n = 600$$
$$n = 6$$

Write 15% as a ratio.

Write the ratio of n to the total.

Method 2 Write an Equation

15% of 40 is what number?

Write 15% as a decimal.

$$0.15 \times 40 = n$$
$$6 = n$$

Use the question to write an equation.

Of the first 40 Presidents, 6 had six or more children.

Other Examples

A What is 75% of 24?

$$n = \frac{3}{4} \times 24$$
$$n = 18$$

Sometimes you can use the fraction for the percent.

B Find 125% of 60.

$$1.25 \times 60 = n$$
$$75 = n$$

C Find 3.6% of 45.

$$0.036 \times 45 = n$$
$$1.62 = n$$

TRY IT OUT

Give the percent of each number.

1. 35% of 44 = __?__

2. $33\frac{1}{3}$% of 96 = __?__

3. 150% of 98 = __?__

Give the percent of each number.

1. 24% of 84   **2.** 25% of 80   **3.** 95% of 700   **4.** 10.3% of 78

5. 50% of 62   **6.** 150% of 48   **7.** 80% of 75   **8.** 21% of 54

9. 10% of 250   **10.** 30% of 30   **11.** 110% of 60   **12.** 18% of 325

13. 75% of 36   **14.** 200% of 800   **15.** 8% of 94   **16.** 6.5% of 200

17. 40% of 45   **18.** 13% of 620   **19.** 165% of 90   **20.** 8.5% of 400

Use mental math to find 10% of each number.

21. 870   **22.** 25   **23.** 8,000   **24.** 1,000,000

Use mental math to find 1% of each number.

25. 1,000   **26.** 80   **27.** 260   **28.** 50,000

29. What is 12.5% of 124?   **30.** 3% of 66 is what number?

MATH REASONING Evaluate each statement for the values given.

31. 24% of y
  $y = 36$

32. 32% of y
  $y = 45$

33. 110% of y
  $y = 95$

PROBLEM SOLVING

34. Each statement refers to the first 40 presidents. How many presidents does each statement tell about?
12.5% wore beards.
15% were born in log cabins.
42.5% were reelected while in office.

35. Data Hunt Use an almanac to decide whether each statement is true or false about the first 40 presidents.
20% were from Virginia.
17.5% were in their 40's when inaugurated.

36. President Washington's salary was 12.5% of President Reagan's salary. President Reagan's salary was $200,000 per year. How much was President Washington's salary?

▶ **USING CRITICAL THINKING Discover a Pattern**

37. Suppose you pick a number and take 50% of it. Then you take 50% of the new number. If you continue taking 50% of each new number, will your answers get larger or smaller? Will your answer ever be 0? Explain.

More Practice, page 536, set D

Estimating a Percent of a Number

LEARN ABOUT IT

You can use what you know about compatible numbers to estimate a percent of a number.

EXPLORE **Study the Information**

Herb helps out at his brother Bo's music studio. Bo puts in 75 hours a week and has very odd working hours. Table 1 shows how he spends his time.

TALK ABOUT IT

1. What percents in Table 2 are closest to the first percent in Table 1?

2. What fractions are equal to these percents?

3. What is $\frac{1}{5}$ of 75? About how many hours a week does Bo spend recording albums?

Table 1: How Bo Spends His Time

Recording albums	23%
Recording music for TV ads	12%
Recording for radio ads	11%
Recording for training programs	22%
Recording demos	32%

To estimate a percent of a number, substitute compatible numbers that simplify the computation.

Estimate 67% of 121.

Think   67 is about $66\frac{2}{3}\%$ or $\frac{2}{3}$.

121 is about 120.

120 is compatible with $\frac{2}{3}$.

$\frac{2}{3} \times 120 = 80$

67% of 121 is about 80.

Table 2: Fractions ⟷ Percents

$\frac{1}{2} = 50\%$	$\frac{1}{8} = 12\frac{1}{2}\%$
$\frac{1}{3} = 33\frac{1}{3}\%$	$\frac{1}{10} = 10\%$
$\frac{1}{4} = 25\%$	$\frac{2}{3} = 66\frac{2}{3}\%$
$\frac{1}{5} = 20\%$	$\frac{3}{4} = 75\%$

TRY IT OUT

Use compatible numbers to estimate.

1. 48% of 83   **2.** 65% of 92   **3.** 19% of 24   **4.** 35% of 311

Estimate.

1. 76% of 39

2. 48% of 120

3. 12.8% of 77

4. 26% of 850

5. 21% of 51

6. $9\frac{1}{2}$% of 2,000

7. 12% of 65

8. 34% of 34

9. 74% of 50

10. 19% of 112

11. 35% of 82

12. 67% of 89

13. 18% of 78

14. 51% of 617

15. 48.5% of 77

16. 23% of 95

17. 13% of 73

18. 32% of 67

19. 65% of 298

20. 10.7% of 5,902

21. About how much is 26% of 35?

22. Estimate 12% of 56.

APPLY

MATH REASONING

23. To estimate 24% of 43, José substituted compatible numbers and found 25% of 44. His answer was 11. Using his calculator, he found that the exact answer is 10.32. José concluded that using compatible numbers causes you to over estimate. Do you agree? If not, give a counter-example.

PROBLEM SOLVING

24. Use Table 1 on page 286 to estimate how many hours a week Bo spends recording music for training programs.

25. A band gets 13% of the sales of a cassette it recorded. The cassette sells for $7.95. About how much does the band get for 1 cassette? for 10,000 cassettes?

MIXED REVIEW

Write each percent as a decimal.

26. 40%

27. 75%

28. 82%

29. 2%

30. 510%

31. 8.5%

32. $40\frac{1}{2}$%

33. $\frac{1}{4}$%

Evaluate the expression $a \cdot b \div a + c$ for the values given.

34. $a = 10$, $b = 15$, $c = 20$

35. $a = 4\frac{1}{2}$, $b = 5\frac{7}{8}$, $c = 1\frac{1}{4}$

More Practice, page 536, set E

Finding Simple Interest

LEARN ABOUT IT

EXPLORE **Study the Information**

Pete and Harry borrowed $1,026 from their Aunt Lucy to buy a used Wave Skimmer. They agreed to pay her back in 18 months at an interest rate of 3% per year.

TALK ABOUT IT

1. What amount is the principal that Pete and Harry owe?

2. What is the interest rate, and what is the time in years?

3. Explain whether Pete and Harry will pay more or less than the principal and why.

To find out how much interest is owed, use this formula.

$$I = P \cdot R \cdot T$$

Principal (P)	the amount of money loaned or saved
Interest Rate (R)	a percent of the principal
Time (T)	the length of time the principal is loaned or saved
Interest (I)	a special fee that is paid to the lender or saver
Amount (A)	the principal plus the interest

You can use a calculator to find the interest that Pete and Harry owe.

$P = \$1,026$ $R = 0.03\ (3\%)$ $T = 1.5$ years (18 months)

1,026 ⊠ 3 ▦ ⊠ 1.5 ▭ [46.17] They owe $46.17 in interest.

To find the total amount to be paid back, add the principal and the interest.

$$A = P + I$$

1,026 ⊞ 46.17 ▭ [1,072.17]

Pete and Harry will pay Aunt Lucy a total of $1,072.17.

TRY IT OUT

Use a calculator to find the interest (I) and the total amount (A).

1. $P = \$3,000$
   $R = 12\%$ per year
   $T = 2$ years

2. $P = \$2,500$
   $R = 16\%$ per year
   $T = 8$ months

3. $P = \$9,000$
   $R = 7.5\%$ per year
   $T = 2\frac{1}{2}$ years

288

Use your calculator to find the interest (I).

1. $P = \$6,600$
$R = 19\%$
$T = 3$ months

2. $P = \$750$
$R = 13\%$
$T = 2$ years

3. $P = \$500$
$R = 8\%$
$T = 1$ year

4. $P = \$20,000$
$R = 16\%$
$T = 6$ months

5. $P = \$5,000$
$R = 12\%$
$T = 6$ years

6. $P = \$32,000$
$R = 18\%$
$T = 1\frac{1}{2}$ years

7. $P = \$3,600$
$R = 14\%$
$T = 9$ months

8. $P = \$850$
$R = 6\%$
$T = 2\frac{1}{2}$ years

Use your calculator to find the total amount (A).

9. $P = \$600$
$R = 6\%$
$T = 4$ years

10. $P = \$1,800$
$R = 10\%$
$T = 5$ years

11. $P = \$3,500$
$R = 17\%$
$T = 6$ months

12. $P = \$9,200$
$R = 13\%$
$T = 3\frac{1}{2}$ years

MATH REASONING Use mental math. Decide which loan in each pair earns more interest.

13. $500 at 20% interest for 1 year **or** $2,000 at 10% interest for 1 year

14. $1,500 at 20% for 6 months **or** $4,000 at 10% for 1 year

15. $1,500 at 20% for 18 months **or** $2,000 at 10% for 1 year

PROBLEM SOLVING

16. Manny borrowed $175 from his sister to buy a wet suit. She charged him 12% interest. If Manny paid his sister back four months later, what was the total amount he had to pay?

17. Marie's family is saving for a fiberglass boat. The banks they called pay interest rates of 5.5%, 5.8%, 6.1%, 6.4%, and 6.5%. How much can they earn if they invest $800 for 1 year?

▶ **ALGEBRA**

Solve. Use the interest formula $I = P \cdot R \cdot T$.

18. Find T if $I = \$600$
$P = \$2,000$
$R = 15\%$ use 0.15.

19. Find P if $I = \$200$
$R = 16\%$
$T = 1$ year

Applying Percent
Finding the Percent One Number is of Another

LEARN ABOUT IT

EXPLORE Examine the Data

Each month, the Health Club members weigh themselves and measure their body fat. Alan's body fat is 15% of his weight, and Meg's is 20%. What percent of Zoe's weight is fat?

TALK ABOUT IT

1. How can you represent Zoe's body fat as a ratio?

2. Does this problem suggest setting up a proportion? Explain why or why not.

Exactly what percent of Zoe's weight is body fat?

Student	Weight	Body Fat
Alan	100 lbs.	15 lbs.
Meg	80 lbs.	16 lbs.
Zoe	90 lbs.	18 lbs.

Here are two methods for finding the percent one number is of another.

Use A Proportion

Write the ratio of body fat to weight.

$$\frac{18}{90} = \frac{n}{100}$$

Write the unknown percent as a ratio.

$$90n = 1,800$$

$$n = 20$$

Zoe's body is 20% of her total weight.

Write an Equation

18 is what percent of 90?

Write the question as an equation.

$$18 = n \times 90$$

$$\frac{18}{90} = n$$

$$0.2 = n = 20\%$$

Rewrite the decimal as a percent.

Other Examples

A What percent of 8 is 12?

$$n \times 8 = 12$$

$$n = \frac{12}{8}$$

$$n = 1.5 = 150\%$$

12 is 150% of 8.

B What percent is 14 out of 21?

$$n = \frac{14}{21}$$

$$n = 0.666\ldots = 66\frac{2}{3}\%$$

14 is $66\frac{2}{3}\%$ of 21.

TRY IT OUT

1. 18 is what percent of 24?

2. What percent of 15 is 45?

Solve.

1. 12 is what percent of 60?

2. What percent of 2 is 8?

3. What percent of 800 is 4?

4. 14 is what percent of 42?

5. What percent of 55 is 33?

6. 121 is what percent of 968?

7. 36 is what percent of 16?

8. What percent of 72 is 27?

9. What percent of 40 is 9?

10. 52 is what percent of 78?

11. 1 is what percent of 250?

12. What percent of 64 is 288?

13. What percent of 240 is 80?

14. 98 is what percent of 140?

APPLY

MATH REASONING Estimate and write $<$, $>$, or $=$ for each ▥.

15. 15 out of 45 is ▥ 50%.

16. 20 out of 25 is ▥ 50%.

17. 8 out of 27 is ▥ $33\frac{1}{3}$.

18. 24 out of 32 is ▥ $66\frac{2}{3}$.

PROBLEM SOLVING

19. Sam consumes a total of 3,500 calories per day. If 1,000 of these calories are in the form of fats, what percent of Sam's daily food intake is fat? Does he consume more or less fat than the recommended 30% maximum?

DATA BANK

20. **Health and Fitness Data Bank**
Suppose that your average daily intake is 3,000 calories. What percent of your daily calorie total would you get from one granola bar? If you ate 4 oz of applesauce and 4 oz of soup, what percent of your daily calorie total would you get from each?

▶ **CALCULATOR**

The diameter of a small round trampoline is about 40 inches. Using the formula $C = \pi d$, you can find that the circumference of the trampoline is about 125.6 inches.

21. What percent of the trampoline's circumference is the diameter?

22. Draw another circle and measure the diameter. Use the formula to find the circumference. What percent of the circumference is the diameter?

More Practice, page 536, set G

Percent of Increase or Decrease

EXPLORE **Study the Situation**

Danny's pet python, Kohima, was 4 ft long
when he bought her. She grew 1 ft in a year.

TALK ABOUT IT

1. What fraction of the python's original length is 1 foot?

2. Is it reasonable to say that Kohima's length increased by
   25% of her original length? Explain.

Danny's pet boa grew from 20 in to 33 in in a year. What is
the percent of increase?

First, use a calculator to find the **amount of increase.**

new amount − original amount = amount of increase

$$33 \quad \boxed{-} \quad 20 \quad \boxed{=} \quad \boxed{13}$$

Leave 13 on display.

The amount of increase is 13 in.

Next, use a calculator to find the **percent of increase.**

$$\frac{\text{amount of increase}}{\text{original amount}} = \text{percent of increase}$$

$$13 \; \boxed{\div} \; 20 \quad \boxed{\%} \quad \boxed{65}$$

The percent of increase from 20 to 33 in is 65%.

To find the percent of decrease, first find the amount of
decrease. Then divide the amount of decrease by the original
amount.

Example Find the percent of decrease from 40 to 15.

$$40 \; \boxed{-} \; 15 \; \boxed{=} \; \boxed{25} \; \boxed{\div} \; 40 \; \boxed{\%} \; \boxed{62.5}$$

The percent of decrease is 62.5%.

Use a calculator to find the percent of increase or decrease.

1. 60 to 80   **2.** 200 to 120   **3.** 64 to 72   **4.** 72 to 64

Find the percent of increase or decrease.

1. 75 to 93

2. 56 to 70

3. 80 to 44

4. 78 to 104

5. 120 to 84

6. 46 to 23

7. 105 to 126

8. 20 to 39

9. 275 to 242

10. 70 to 63

11. 45 to 99

12. 80 to 92

13. 128 to 112

14. 175 to 91

15. 96 to 108

16. 57 to 95

17. 112 to 42

18. 225 to 189

19. What is the percent of increase from $35 to $42?

20. If the price drops from $32 to $20, what is the percent of decrease?

APPLY

MATH REASONING Use mental math to find the percent of increase and decrease. What conclusions can you draw?

21. $6 \rightarrow 12$ and $12 \rightarrow 6$

22. $4 \rightarrow 5$ and $5 \rightarrow 4$

23. $3 \rightarrow 9$ and $9 \rightarrow 3$

PROBLEM SOLVING

24. When Judy's boa got a wheezing cough, she gave him 60 mg of medication. Later, she increased the dosage to 100 mg. What was the percent of increase?

25. The heat lamp in a snake cage burned out, causing the cage temperature to drop from 100° to 78°. What was the percent of decrease?

26. A female boa constrictor averages about 1 ft 8 in. at birth. It grows to an average length of 8 ft 10 in. at maturity. What is the percent of increase?

27. If a snake is 72 in. long, the sum of the width, length, and height of its cage should be at least 72 in. If each of the dimensions of the cage is a multiple of four, identify one set of possible dimensions.

▶ **USING CRITICAL THINKING** **Support Your Conclusion**

28. If a snake is 18 in. long at birth and grows 12 in. a year, will the percent of increase in its length from year to year remain the same, keep increasing, or keep decreasing? Support your conclusion with examples.

More Practice, page 537, set A

Using Critical Thinking

"This cereal is on sale," said Mrs. Evans, as she took a close look at the ad near the boxes. "I wonder which size is the better buy."

"What do you mean?" Mr. Evans said. "One box costs 25% less, and you get 25% more cereal in the other box. Obviously, you're getting cereal for the same price per ounce in either box."

Mrs. Evans thought for a few moments. "Something is strange here," she said. "I think the small box is the better buy!"

TALK ABOUT IT

1. What is the decision to be made in this situation? What facts can be used?

2. Do you think Mrs. Evans is correct? Explain why or why not.

3. How much does the smaller box cost on sale? How much does the cereal cost per ounce?

4. How many ounces of cereal are in the larger box? What is the cost per ounce?

5. What conclusion can you draw in this case? Do you think this will be true in every case?

1. Box A contains 24 oz of crackers. It is on sale for 50% off the regular price of $4.80. Box B, which contains 50% more crackers than Box A, costs $4.80. Which box has a lower cost per ounce? To the nearest cent, how much less is the cost per ounce for this box?

2. A bag of corn chips that weighs 12 oz usually sells for $1.80. This week it is on sale for $33\frac{1}{3}$% off the regular price. Another bag holds $33\frac{1}{3}$% more corn chips than the first bag. Set a price for the second bag so that neither bag of corn chips is a better buy.

MIDCHAPTER REVIEW QUIZ

Find the percent of a number.

1. 75% of 80

2. 10% of 45

3. 50% of 250

4. 7% of 92

5. 6.5% of 184

6. 143% of 800

Estimate the percent of a number.

7. 52% of 159

8. 35% of 362

9. 19% of 74

10. 24% of 825

11. 38% of 308

12. 65% of 21

Find the interest (I) and the total amount (A).

13. Principal: $4,800
Rate: 12.5%
Time: 3 years

14. Principal: $2,500
Rate: 3.5%
Time: $1\frac{1}{2}$ years

Find the percent one number is of another.

15. 54 is what percent of 72?

16. What percent of 24 is 15?

17. What percent of 24 is 36?

18. 24 is what percent of 8?

Find the percent of increase or decrease.

19. Distance: from 8 km to 10 km

20. Team: from 45 players to 18 players

21. Practice: from 12 hours to 4 hours

22. Work: from 15 hours to 20 hours

PROBLEM SOLVING

23. Kathy spent about 9 hours sleeping, 8 hours doing schoolwork, and 2 hours playing ball. About what percent of the day was taken up by these activities combined?

24. Bay City has sunny days about 68% of the year. About how many cloudy days does Bay City have each year?

25. Because of vacations, newspaper deliveries drop off in the summer. Find the percent of increase or decrease in customers from April to May and from May to June.

Month	Customers
April	125
May	150
June	120

Applying Percent
Finding a Number From a Percent

Spectra Video

45 American Classics } 10%

total movies

LEARN ABOUT IT

EXPLORE **Analyze the Situation**

At Spectra Video, 10% of the movies are American Classics. There are 45 American Classic videos. How many videos does the store have in all?

TALK ABOUT IT

1. If 10% of the total equals 45 movies, what does 20% of the total equal?

2. If 10% of the total equals 45 movies, what does 30% of the total equal?

3. Explain how to solve this problem by continuing this pattern?

Suppose a store has 430 comedy movies. This is 20% of the movies in the store. How many movies are there altogether?

Use a Proportion

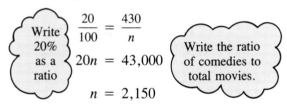

Write 20% as a ratio
$$\frac{20}{100} = \frac{430}{n}$$
$$20n = 43,000$$
Write the ratio of comedies to total movies.
$$n = 2,150$$

There are 2,150 movies in the store.

Write an Equation

20% of what number is 430?

Write the percent as a decimal.
$$.20 \times n = 430$$
$$n = \frac{430}{.20}$$
$$n = 2,150$$
Use the question to write an equation.

Other Examples

A 40% of what number is 1.8?

Write the percent as a decimal
$$0.40 \times n = 1.8$$
$$n = \frac{1.8}{.40}$$
$$n = 4.5$$

40% of 4.5 is 1.8.

B 84 is 200% of what number?

$$84 = 2 \times n$$
$$\frac{84}{2} = n$$
$$42 = n$$

84 is 200% of 42.

TRY IT OUT

Find the missing number.

1. 8% of what number is 4?

2. 3.6 is 12% of what number?

Solve.

1. 20% of what number is 18?

2. 52 is 13% of what number?

3. 83 is 100% of what number?

4. 5% of what number is 20?

5. 80% of what number is 15?

6. 40 is 160% of what number?

7. 52 is 50% of what number?

8. 6% of what number is 21?

9. 60% of what number is 333?

10. 84 is 7% of what number?

11. 15 is 75% of what number?

12. 15% of what number is 48?

APPLY

MATH REASONING Use mental math to find the mystery numbers.

13. 1% of the number is 6. (Hint: If 1% of the number is 6, how much is 100%?)

14. 1% of the number is 8.

15. 1% of the number is 24.

PROBLEM SOLVING

16. At Dalby Video, 38 movies were not returned on time over the weekend. If 25% of the movies rented over the weekend were not returned on time, how many movies were rented in all?

17. A member of Spectra Video pays $26.40 to buy a videotape. This price is 88% of the price that a nonmember pays. What would a nonmember pay for the same videotape?

18. At The Movie Store, 5% of the movies are science fiction. Of the science fiction movies, 44 are rated PG. If 55% of the science fiction movies are rated PG, how many movies of all kinds does the store have?

 ## MIXED REVIEW

Copy and complete the table.

19.

x	1	2	3	10	20	40
f(x) = 5x − 2						

20.

x	1	2	3	4	5	10
$f(x) = \frac{1}{2}x + 4$						

Find the answers using mental math.

21. 2000 − 4

22. 4 × 405

23. 3.2 + 8.5 + 7.8

Discounts and Sale Prices

EXPLORE Study the Information

A **discount** is an amount of money that is subtracted from the regular price when an item is on sale. The **discount percent** is the percent of the regular price that is subtracted. The sale price is the price of the item after the discount has been subtracted. The diagram below shows how these terms are related.

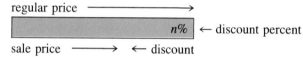

regular price
$n\%$ ← discount percent
sale price ———→   ← discount

TALK ABOUT IT

1. Use terms from the diagram to describe the numbers 15% and $42 on the sign. What two amounts on the diagram are not on the sign?

2. A sale of 15% off means that you save 15 cents on every regular price dollar. How much would you save on $10? on $42?

Jody bought kneepads at 25% off the regular price of $32.96.

You can use your calculator to find the discount.

regular price × discount percent = discount
32.96   ⊠   25 %   8.24   The discount is $8.24.

Then you can find the sale price on your calculator.

regular price − discount = sale price
32.96   ⊟   8.24 ⊟   24.72   The sale price is $24.72.

TRY IT OUT

Use a calculator to find the discount and the sale price.

1. Regular price: $60.50
   Discount percent: 30%

2. Regular price: $75.25
   Discount percent: 40%

3. Regular price: $65.80
   Discount percent: 15%

298

Use a calculator to find the discount and the sale price.

1. Regular price $358.88
   Discount percent 25%

2. Regular price $813.25
   Discount percent 20%

3. Regular price $119.50
   Discount percent 10%

4. Regular price $18.90
   Discount percent 30%

5. Regular price $16.40
   Discount percent 15%

6. Regular price $150.80
   Discount percent 35%

7. Regular price $99.95
   Discount percent 40%

8. Regular price $12.50
   Discount percent 18%

9. The regular price of $32.60 is discounted 25%. What is the sale price?

10. What is the discount on $240.75 at 8% off?

APPLY

MATH REASONING

11. Find a and b
    a is 50% of b. $a + b = 90$

12. Find c and d.
    25% of c is d. $c + d = 100$

PROBLEM SOLVING

13. Jolene needed a helmet to skate on the half-pipe at Skateboard Plaza. She bought a helmet for 60% off the regular price of $31.50. How much did she save? How much did she pay?

14. Rafael had $35 saved. After his skateboard was damaged, Rafael had to spend $20 on repairs. What percent of his savings did he spend on the repairs?

15. **Extra Data** Solve the problem. Identify the data that was not needed. Every 6 months Jake needs new skateboard wheels, which range in price from $42 to $52 per set. Yesterday he bought a $42 set of wheels for 20% off. How much did he pay?

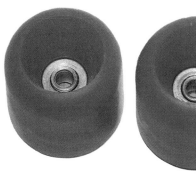

MENTAL MATH

Use mental math to find the discounts.

16. Regular price of $60 at 15% off

17. Regular price of $90 at 20% off

18. Regular price of $80 at 25% off

19. Regular price of $40 at 30% off

Making Circle Graphs

A circle graph is one way of comparing percents.

EXPLORE Study the Graph

Work in groups. The graph at the right shows the results of a survey of women's eating habits. The circle is divided into sectors of different sizes to show what percent of the women's daily diets were made up of different kinds of foods.

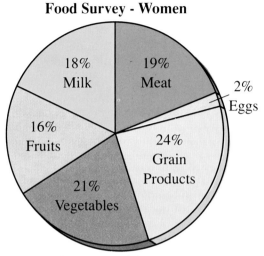

Food Survey - Women

Daily Total = 845 grams

TALK ABOUT IT

1. What percent of the women's daily food intake was vegetables?

2. How many degrees are in a circle? What percent of the total degrees in the circle do you think are included in the sector labeled Vegetables?

3. How can you estimate the number of degrees in the sector labeled Vegetables?

Here are the steps for making a circle graph.

- Draw a circle and mark the center point.
- An angle with a vertex at the center of a circle is called a **central angle**. Use a calculator to find the number of degrees for each central angle. Round to the nearest whole degree.
- Use a protractor to draw each central angle.
- Label each sector and title the graph.

Finding the Number of Degrees in Each Central Angle					
360	⊠	18	%	64.8	⟶ 65°
360	⊠	19	%	68.4	⟶ 68°
360	⊠	2	%	7.2	⟶ 7°
360	⊠	24	%	86.4	⟶ 86°
360	⊠	21	%	75.6	⟶ 76°
360	⊠	16	%	57.6	⟶ 58°

TRY IT OUT

Carl's doctor told him that his daily diet should consist of the following: 25% Fats, 15% Protein, 60% Carbohydrates.

Make a circle graph to show the information that Carl's doctor gave him. Remember to label each sector and title your graph.

Use the data from each survey to make a circle graph. Use a calculator to find the number of degrees in each central angle.

1. Survey question: Do you check labels to find out what is in the food you eat?

Always	22%
Usually	29%
Sometimes	41%
Never	8%

2. Survey question: How often do you exercise or work out?

Every day	35%
Every 2–3 days	25%
Once a week	32%
Occasionally	5%
Never	3%

MATH REASONING

3. Can you make a circle graph showing the data from the survey?

Survey question: What kinds of exercise do you enjoy? Check as many as you like.)

Sports	67%	Swimming	35%
Running/jogging	42%	Walking	24%
Biking	52%	Push-ups	11%

PROBLEM SOLVING

4. Gail took a survey of students in her health class. She found that 10 students drank whole milk, 12 drank low fat milk, and 8 drank nonfat milk. If she shows her results on a circle graph, how many degrees will there be in each central angle?

5. Health and Fitness Data Bank Lewis ate 4 oz of soup, 4 oz of applesauce, and a granola bar. How many grams of carbohydrates did he eat? What percent of the total carbohydrates did each item provide? To show this data on a circle graph, how many degrees will Lewis need in each central angle?

▶ **ESTIMATION**

6. Estimate the number of degrees in each central angle if this data were shown on a circle graph. Choose the angle in the box that is closest to the exact angle.

Survey question: How many servings of fruits and vegetables do you eat daily?

Three or more servings	65%
Two servings	23%
One serving or less	12%

10°	120°
45°	240°
90°	300°

More Practice, page 537, set D

Exploring Algebra
Solving Percent Problems

LEARN ABOUT IT

EXPLORE Solve to Understand

You can use equations with percents to calculate your grades and even to determine how many test items you must answer correctly to get a good grade. If there are 40 items on a test, how many must you answer correctly to get an A?

94%–100%	A
85%– 93%	B
75%– 84%	C
65%– 74%	D
0%– 64%	F

TALK ABOUT IT

1. What is the smallest percent of correct answers that will earn a grade of A?

2. Explain how you can write an equation to find the lowest number of correct answers that will give you an A on a 40-point test. What equation can you use to determine what you need for a grade of B?

Translating words into equations can help you solve percent problems.

What score is 94% of 40 points?

$$n \stackrel{\downarrow}{=} 94\% \times 40$$
$$n = .94 \times 40$$
$$n = 37.50 \quad \text{Round to 38.}$$

Check: Does a score of 38 out of 40 make sense as an A?

What percent is 27 correct out of 33?

$$n \stackrel{\downarrow}{=} \frac{27}{33}$$
$$n = 0.818181. . . \text{ Round to .82.}$$
$$n = 82\%$$

Check: Is $\frac{27}{33}$ close to $\frac{8}{10}$ or 80%?

79% of what number is 38?

$$79\% \times n \stackrel{\downarrow}{=} 38 \quad \text{Isolate } n.$$
$$0.79n \div 0.79 = 38 \div 0.79$$
$$n = 48.10 \quad \text{Round to 48.}$$
$$n = 48$$

Check: Is 38 points about 80% of 48?

TRY IT OUT

Translate to an equation and solve.

1. What number is 75% of 60?

2. What percent of 60 is 48?

3. 35 is 70% of what number?

4. 20 out of 25 is what percent?

Translate to an equation and solve.

1. 35% of 200 is what number?

2. 38 is 50% of what number?

3. 70 out of 95 is what percent?

4. 60% of 40 is what number?

5. 45 is 60% of what number?

6. 53 out of 80 is what percent?

Use mental math to solve for *n*.

7. 10% of *n* = $80

8. 30 out of 200 = *n*%

9. 1% of $90 = *n*

10. 75% of *n* = 300 lb

11. 25 out of 75 = *n*%

12. 25% of 4 cm = *n*

APPLY

MATH REASONING

13. Find 20% of 65 and 65% of 20.

14. Find 70% of 49 and 49% of 70.

15. Why is *a*% of *b* equal to *b*% of *a*?

PROBLEM SOLVING

Write and solve an equation for each problem.

16. The human body is about 70% water by weight. How many pounds of your own body is water?

17. An adult has about 5 quarts of blood. When an adult donates a pint of blood, what percent of the body's blood is donated?

18. **Unfinished Problem** Write an interesting problem that can be solved using some or all of the following data.

> An apple is 85% water.
> A 5 lb bag of apples costs $1.59.

▶ **CALCULATOR**

19. Suppose you are a teacher and want to convert an entire class's test scores into percents. If the test was worth 30 points, you can divide each score individually by 30. How can you make this task easier using the "repeating function" on your calculator? Make a flowchart to change scores of 27, 25, 23, and 22 into percents by pressing ÷ 30 just one time.

Problem Solving
Problems Without Solutions

| UNDERSTAND |
| ANALYZE DATA |
| PLAN |
| ESTIMATE |
| SOLVE |
| EXAMINE |

LEARN ABOUT IT

You have solved problems that have one or more possible solutions. Some problems do not have solutions.

Ticket Prices	
Adults	$3.25
Senior Citizens	$2.75
Children	$2.50

Drew and 2 friends went to the Wild Animal Park. Drew used a $10 bill to buy 3 tickets. The cashier gave him $1.55 change. What kinds of tickets did Drew buy?

I can make an organized list to help me find the possibilities.

My list shows that Drew could not buy 3 tickets and get $1.55 change. The cashier gave the wrong amount of change.

Adult	Senior	Child	Total	Change
3	0	0	9.75	.25
2	1	0	9.25	.75
2	0	1	9.00	1.00
1	2	0	8.75	1.25
1	1	1	8.50	1.50
1	0	2	8.25	1.75
0	3	0	8.25	1.75
0	2	1	8.00	2.00
0	1	2	7.75	2.25
0	0	3	7.50	2.50

TRY IT OUT

Solve. If there is no solution, explain why.

1. Margaret bought 2 tickets to the Wild Animal Park. She gave the cashier a $10 bill and got $4.75 change. What kinds of tickets did Margaret buy?

2. At the Park, Ari saw some giraffes and some ostriches. He counted 7 heads and 25 feet. How many giraffes did Ari see?

3. Keiko gave a vendor 5 coins totalling $.90 to buy a frozen yogurt bar. What coins did she use?

4. Before going to the Park, Lee read an article about giraffes. The article was on 4 consecutive pages. Lee noticed that the page numbers added up to 55. On what page did the article begin?

Solve. Use any problem solving strategy.

1. An ostrich egg is 8 in long and weighs 3.9 lb. The diameter of the egg is 75% of its length. Find the diameter of the ostrich egg.

2. The table gives some facts about giraffes. Use the table to find what percent of a male giraffe's height is in its neck.

Giraffe Facts	
Height: Male - 17 ft	Female - 14 ft
Weight: Male - 3000 lb	Female - 2500 lb
Neck: $6\frac{1}{2}$ ft	
Tail: 6 ft 8 in	

3. A walking giraffe takes strides that are 15 ft long. If you take strides that are 3 ft long, how many more strides will you have to take than a giraffe takes to cover 1 mile?

4. A newborn giraffe may stand over 6 ft tall and weigh 150 lb. By the time it is 1 year old, it will be almost 10 ft tall. By what percent does a giraffe's height increase during the first year?

5. A group of 32 people visited the Wild Animal Park. The group included $\frac{1}{3}$ as many teachers as students and 2 more parents than teachers. How many students were in the group?

6. A male ostrich weighs about 11% as much as a male giraffe. Use the table to find out about how much a male ostrich weighs.

7. When a giraffe raises its head, it has to lift the weight of about $5\frac{1}{2}$ seventh graders. The average seventh grader weighs 100 lb. How many pounds does the giraffe have to lift?

8. **Talking About Your Solution**
Doug wants to buy some picture postcards of the animals at the Wild Animal Park. Small postcards are sold in packages of 5, and large postcards are sold in packages of 3. If Doug bought a total of 8 packages containing 35 postcards in all, how many packages of each size did he buy? Explain what you have found to a classmate.

Data Collection and Analysis
Group Decision Making

UNDERSTAND
ANALYZE DATA
PLAN
ESTIMATE
SOLVE
EXAMINE

Doing A Survey

Group Skill:
Disagree in an Agreeable Way

How informed are the students at your school about news events? Do they know about what is happening locally? What about internationally? Work with your group to conduct a survey to find out.

Collecting Data

1. Talk with your group about events that happened in the news this week. Look through newspapers or news magazines to help you remember. Pick one important local event, state event, national event, and international event.

2. Write one question about each event that you think someone who reads or watches the news should be able to answer.

3. Conduct your survey with at least 30 students at your school. Make a table to keep a record of your results.

Organizing Data

4. Count the people from your survey who got one question correct, two questions correct, three questions correct, and so on. Then calculate the percent of the total number of people for each category.

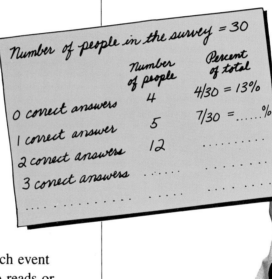

Number of people in the survey = 30

	Number of people	Percent of total
0 correct answers	4	4/30 = 13%
1 correct answer	5	7/30 = ...%
2 correct answers	12	....
3 correct answers	......	....
......	......	

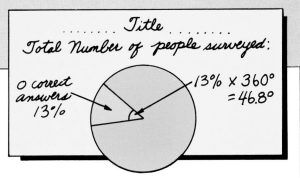

.... Title ....
Total Number of people surveyed:

0 correct answers 13%

13% × 360° = 46.8°

5. Make a circle graph using the data in your chart. How many parts will your circle graph have? What measuring instruments will you need?

6. Tell how you selected your sample. Was it selected randomly? Did your sample include a fair representation of all students in your school? Why or why not?

7. Do you think your results would be similar if you surveyed students your age in schools nationwide? Give two or three reasons for your answer.

8. Write a paragraph about your results that could be placed in a school newspaper.

WRAP UP

Percent Application Match

Match each term on the left with the best example(s) on the right.

1. regular price
2. interest rate
3. discount
4. sale price
5. principal
6. discount percent
7. interest

a. $\frac{1}{3}$ off—now only $9.95!

b. save 50%

c. $27.20 paid in addition to loan of $500

d. a car loan for $8,000

e. $50 earned on a savings account

f. save $10!

g. 25% off

h. $150 deposit in savings

i. originally $25.00

j. $7\frac{1}{2}\%$ paid on savings

Sometimes, Always, Never

Which word should go in the blank, *sometimes*, *always*, or *never*? Explain your choice.

8. The number of degrees in a central angle of a circle graph __?__ equals the percent represented by that sector.

9. *a*% of *b* is __?__ the same amount as *b*% of *a*.

10. A discount is __?__ less than the regular price.

11. Using compatible numbers to estimate percents __?__ results in underestimation.

Project

This price list was given to a salesperson so she could mark down items for a sale. However, some of the numbers did not print. Your job is to complete the list.

Original Price	Discount Percent	Sale Price
$50.00	25%	
$42.00	$33\frac{1}{3}\%$	
$35.00		$14.00
	20%	$22.40
$22.00		$14.30
	10%	$13.50

308

CHAPTER REVIEW/TEST

Part 1   Understanding

1. Match.
   - A 1% of 400   X 40
   - B 10% of 400   Y 40,000
   - C 1% of ? is 400   Z 4

2. Complete. In a circle graph, the sum of the degrees in all the central angles is __?__, and the sum of all the percents is __?__.

3. What compatible numbers can be used to estimate 73% of 395?

4. Estimate and write $<$, $>$, or $=$ for the ▓. 5 out of 16 is ▓ 25%.

Part 2   Skills

Give the percent of each number.

5. 5.5% of 300

6. 140% of 45

7. 75% of 88

Use a calculator to find the interest (I) and the total amount (A).

8. $P = \$400, R = 6.5\%, T = 1$ year

9. $P = \$5,000, R = 8\%, T = 2\frac{1}{2}$ years

10. 15 is what percent of 40?

11. What percent of 32 is 168?

Find the percent of increase or decrease.

12. 56 to 126

13. 120 to 75

14. 48 to 64

Translate to an equation and solve.

15. What percent is 38 out of 95?

16. What number is 16% of 125?

Part 3   Applications

17. In a recent survey of adults, 45% said their favorite recreational activity was sports, 20% said reading, 20% said travel, and 10% said watching TV. Can you make a circle graph showing the data from the survey? Explain.

18. A 64-oz box of Brand A detergent is on sale for 25% off the regular price of $3.20. A box of Brand B detergent contains 25% more than the other and costs $3.20. Which brand has a lower cost per ounce? How much less?

19. A certain bicycle is on sale for 20% off the regular price of $189.50. Find the discount and the sale price of this bicycle.

20. **Challenge** During a recent survey of teenagers, 72 said they preferred action movies. This was 48% of those who answered the survey. How many teenagers did not prefer action movies?

ENRICHMENT
The Four-Color Problem

What is the greatest number of colors needed to color a map if no two regions sharing a border may be the same color? Mapmakers had long believed the answer was 4. It took mathematicians more than 100 years to prove that four colors is the solution to the problem. The proof, found in 1976, by two mathematicians from the University of Illinois, Kenneth Appel and Wolfgang Haken, required more than 1,000 hours of computer time.

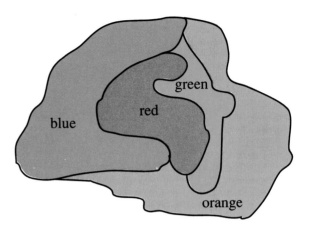

Trace or draw regions like these. Color the regions in 4 or fewer colors.

1. 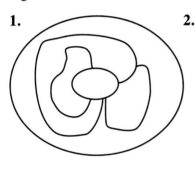 **2.** 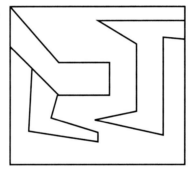 **3.**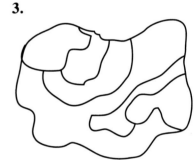

4. Draw your own map that requires at least four colors. Can you draw one that requires more than four colors?

5. Use an outline map of the continental United States. Choose a region containing at least 10 states. Show that the states can be colored in four or fewer colors.

CUMULATIVE REVIEW

1. Which is the inverse operation for "decreased by $1\frac{3}{4}$"?

   A subtract $1\frac{3}{4}$ B add $1\frac{3}{4}$

   C multiply by $1\frac{3}{4}$ D divide by $1\frac{3}{4}$

2. Solve.
   $16P = 432$

   A $p = 6{,}912$ B $p = 27$
   C $p = 0.037$ D $p = 416$

3. Which fraction in lowest terms names the ratio 78:108?

   A $\frac{13}{18}$ B $\frac{2}{3}$ C $\frac{7}{9}$ D $\frac{13}{17}$

4. Which algebraic expression expresses the rule for this table?

b	0	1	2	3	4	5
?	2	5	8	11	14	17

   A $4b - 1$ B $4b - 7$
   C $2b + 3$ D $3b + 2$

5. Find the length of x for this pair of similar figures.

   A 3   B 72
   C 8   D 12

   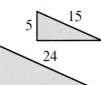

6. Which expresses the percent for the shaded region?

   A 42%

   B 58%

   C 0.42

   D $\frac{68}{100}$

7. Which percent expresses the fraction $\frac{7}{20}$?

   A 14%   B 2.86%
   C 65%   D 35%

8. Which fraction expresses 18%?

   A $\frac{3}{25}$ B $\frac{9}{25}$ C $\frac{6}{50}$ D $\frac{9}{50}$

9. Which is the percent for 0.076?

   A 76%   B 760%
   C 7.6%   D 0.76%

10. Which is the decimal for 12.9%?

    A 1.29   B 12.9
    C 0.129   D 129.0

11. Find $f(7)$ for $f(y) = 5y + 2$.

    A 37   B 35
    C 14   D 45

12. The highest point in South Dakota is Harney Peak. If 69 m is subtracted from its height and the difference is divided by 2, the quotient is 1,069 m, which is the height of the highest point in North Dakota. Work backward to find the height of Harney Peak.

    A 36,880.5 m   B 2,207 m
    C 500 m   D 2,069 m

13. A book salesperson's quota for one month was 340 copies of a particular book. So far she has sold 200 copies. How many more does she need to sell to reach 125% of her quota?

    A 85 books   B 140 books
    C 225 books   D 425 books

11

INTEGERS

MATH AND
SOCIAL STUDIES

DATA BANK

Use the Social Studies Data Bank on page 497 to answer the questions.

1 If a person leaves Miami a 1:00 pm and flies to Housto and arrives at 2:30 pm loc time, how long was the flight?

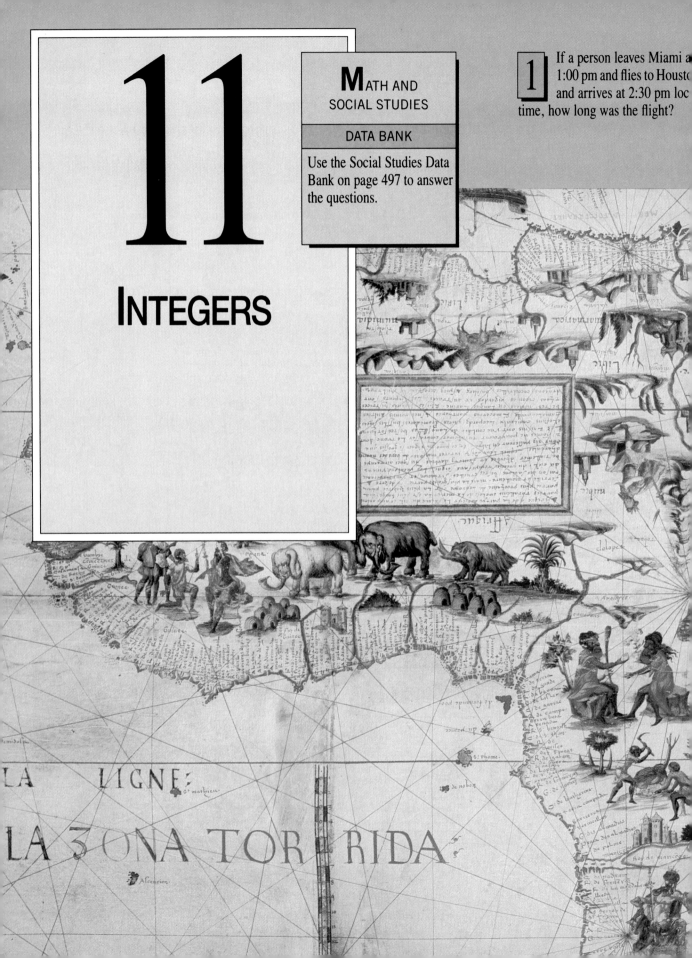

LA LIGNE

LA ZONA TORRIDA

2 Suppose you start at 5°N latitude, travel south 20°, then head north 18°. At what latitude are you?

3 What are the latitude and longitude of the point at which the Equator crosses the Prime Meridian?

4 **Using Critical Thinking** Make a time chart using your own time zone as the basis. List at least six cities in six time zones different from yours. Decide what a person in each city might be doing when you are eating lunch.

Understanding Integers

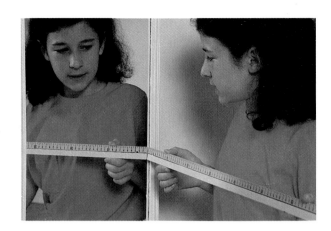

EXPLORE **Discover a Pattern**
Work in groups. Give a word that means the opposite. For example, for the word "up," you could write "down."

fast   raise   east   above   full

large   hot   win   inside   positive

TALK ABOUT IT

1. What action is the opposite of running a ball 5 yards upfield?

2. What is the opposite of a 10 degree drop in temperature?

Every number has an **opposite.** You can see that a number and its opposite are the same distance from 0. This distance is called the **absolute value** of the number. The whole numbers together with their opposites form the set of **integers.**

Integers

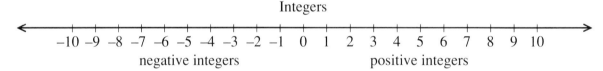

negative integers   positive integers

We write $^+2$ for the integer **positive 2.**

We write $^-2$ for the integer **negative 2.**

The opposite of $^+2$ is $^-2$.   The opposite of $^-2$ is $^+2$.

The opposite of 0 is 0.

As with whole numbers, the integer farther to the right on the number line is the greater integer. $^-2$ is greater than $^-10$.

TRY IT OUT

Give the integer suggested by the situation and its opposite.

1. a loss of $5   **2.** a gain of 12 yards

3. spent $5.00   **4.** 10 seconds before liftoff

Give the integer suggested by the situation and its opposite.

1. 7 degrees below zero

2. 900 feet below sea level

3. 2 strokes over par

4. $20 mark down

Write the integer or integers described.

5. the integers 3 units from zero

6. the integers 3 units from $^+2$

7. the smallest positive integer

8. the integers between $^+5$ and $^-5$

Write $<$, $>$, or $=$ for each ⫸.

9. $^+5$ ⫸ $^-5$

10. $^+1$ ⫸ $^-4$

11. $^-5$ ⫸ $^-4$

12. $^-1$ ⫸ $^-1$

13. $^-100$ ⫸ $^-400$

14. $^+6$ ⫸ $^+6$

MATH REASONING Complete the statement.

15. The opposite of a positive integer is a __?__ .

16. The opposite of a negative integer is a __?__ .

17. Zero is neither __?__ nor __?__ .

PROBLEM SOLVING

18. Emergency phones were placed on a highway. Locate each phone on a number line labeled from $^-10$ to $^+10$.

a. Phone A is 6 units left of $^-2$.

b. Phone B is 4 units right of $^-2$.

c. Phone C is at the opposite of $^-9$.

d. Phones E and F are 4 units from $^+1$.

▶ **EXPLORING ALGEBRA**

The absolute value of a number gives its distance from zero on the number line.

$|^+5| = 5$ The absolute value of $^+5$ equals 5.
$|^-5| = 5$ The absolute value of $^-5$ equals 5.

Show the following integers on a number line.

19. the integers with absolute value 3.

20. the integers with absolute value less than 2.

21. the negative integers with absolute value less than 5.

More Practice, page 537, set E

315

Properties of Integers

LEARN ABOUT IT

EXPLORE Study the Chart

Work in groups. Write a numerical example for each property by substituting $x = 2$, $y = 5$, and $z = 10$ in the algebraic examples.

Properties and Descriptions	Algebraic Example
Opposites Property: The sum of any number and its opposite is zero.	$x + (^-x) = 0$
Zero Property for Addition: The sum of any number and zero is equal to the number.	$x + 0 = x$
One Property: The product of any number and one is equal to the number.	$x \cdot {}^+1 = x$
Commutative Property: Changing the order of addends (factors), does not change the sum (product).	$x + y = y + x$ $x \cdot y = y \cdot x$
Associative Property: Changing the grouping of addends (factors), does not change the sum (product).	$(x + y) + z = x + (y + z)$ $(x \cdot y)z = x(y \cdot z)$
Distributive Property: Multiplying a sum by a number is the same as multiplying each addend by the number and then adding.	$x(y + z) = xy + xz$

TALK ABOUT IT

1. The commutative property applies to which operations?

2. Consider $(4 + 5)3$. Does the distributive property apply?

The properties let you rearrange addends or factors.

A $(^-4 + {}^+2) + {}^+4 = (^-4 + {}^+4) + {}^+2$ **B** $^-25(^-19 \cdot {}^+4) = (^-25 \cdot {}^+4) \cdot {}^-19$

TRY IT OUT

Name the property or properties you would use to find n.

1. $^+1 \cdot {}^-3 = n$

2. $^-2 + {}^+2 = n$

3. $^-2 + n = {}^-2$

4. $n + {}^+1 = 0$

5. $n + {}^+1 + {}^+2 = {}^+2 + {}^+1$

6. $^+2 \cdot (^-5n) = (^+2 \cdot {}^-5) \cdot {}^+1$

Use the opposites property to solve the equation.

1. $^-4 + {}^+4 = n$ **2.** $^-16 + n = 0$ **3.** $(^-3 + {}^+3) + {}^-5 = n$

Use the zero property or the one property to solve the equation.

4. $^-12 + 0 = n$ **5.** $n + {}^+3 = {}^+3$ **6.** $n \cdot {}^+1 = {}^-25$

Rewrite each expression using the commutative property.

7. $^-27 \cdot {}^+13$ **8.** $^+125 + {}^-25$ **9.** $(^-2 + {}^+5) + {}^-5$

Rewrite each expression using the associative property.

10. $(^-27 \cdot {}^+5)^-2$ **11.** $^+25 + (^-25 + {}^+153)$ **12.** $(0 \cdot {}^-331) \cdot {}^+127$

Rewrite each expression using the distributive property.

13. $^-2 \cdot (^+5 + {}^-5)$ **14.** $^+4 \cdot (^-25 + {}^+1)$ **15.** $(^-24 + {}^+31) \cdot {}^-20$

APPLY

MATH REASONING Use the properties to solve each equation.

16. $^+8 + (^+5 + n) = {}^+8$ **17.** $^+10 + (m + {}^+2) = {}^+2$ **18.** $^+2(h + {}^+8) = 0$

PROBLEM SOLVING

19. Find the cost for 6 boys and 4 girls to go to an outdoor concert where tickets cost $5 each.

20. Kerri has 4 books and 3 magazines which are 5 days overdue at the library. The cost is 25¢ per day for each item overdue. How much does Kerri owe?

MIXED REVIEW

21. 32% of 100 is what number?   **22.** 18 is what percent of 72?

23. 10% of what number is 16?   **24.** 85% of 60 is what number?

25. $3{:}x = 18{:}75$ **26.** $x{:}14 = 30{:}50$ **27.** $10{:}15 = x{:}9$

Estimate.

28. $321 \cdot 478$ **29.** $11\frac{3}{4} \cdot 8\frac{5}{7}$ **30.** $12 + 9 + 11 + 10 + 8$

More Practice, page 538, set A

Adding Integers

EXPLORE **Use Counting Chips**

Each white chip represents $^+1$. Each red chip represents $^-1$. Since they are opposites, they have a sum of 0 and are said to "cancel each other." It's easy to see that the chips in box A represent $^+2$ if you first "cancel" the pairs of opposites.

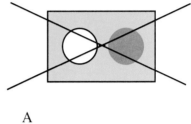

Work with a partner. One of you selects some white chips and records the integer the chips represent. The other selects some red chips and records the integer those chips represent. Combine both sets of chips and record the integer they represent. Repeat the activity several times using different numbers of red and white chips.

A

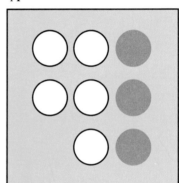

TALK ABOUT IT

1. When you and your partner combined chips, how did you decide what integer they represented?

2. What happens if you choose the same number of red and white counters?

You can use counting chips to model addition with integers.

$^+3 + {}^+4$ means $\underset{\text{OO}}{\text{OO}}$ $\underset{\text{OO}}{\text{OO}} \longrightarrow \underset{\text{OOOO}}{\text{OOO}}$ so $^+3 + {}^+4 = {}^+7$.

$^-2 + {}^-3$ means ●● ●●● $\longrightarrow$ ●●●●● so $^-2 + {}^-3 = {}^-5$.

$^+4 + {}^-1$ means $\underset{\text{OO}}{\text{OO}}$ ● $\longrightarrow \underset{\text{OO}}{\text{OO}}$ so $^+4 + {}^-1 = {}^+3$.

$^+7 + ({}^+3 + {}^-3)$ means $\underset{\text{OOOO}}{\text{OOO}}$ $\underset{\text{●●●}}{\text{OOO}} \longrightarrow \underset{\text{OOOO}}{\text{OOO}}$ so $^+7 + ({}^+3 + {}^-3) = {}^+7$.

Use chips to model each sum. Write a complete equation.

1. $^-2 + {}^-2$ **2.** $^+6 + {}^+5$ **3.** $^+5 + {}^-3$ **4.** $^-2 + {}^+6$

5. $^+3 + {}^-3$ **6.** $^-8 + 0$ **7.** $^+3 + ({}^-7 + {}^-7)$ **8.** $^-6 + ({}^+5 + {}^+6)$

Write an integer addition equation for each picture. Give the sum.

1. 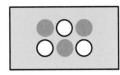 **2.** 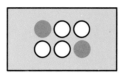 **3.**

Find the sums.

4. $^+4 + {}^-3$ 　　**5.** $^-3 + {}^-5$ 　　**6.** $^+7 + {}^+2 + {}^-2$ 　**7.** $^-5 + {}^+3$

8. $^+6 + {}^-6$ 　　**9.** $^-2 + {}^-3$ 　　**10.** $^-4 + {}^+8 + {}^+4$ 　**11.** $^-6 + {}^-3$

12. $^+3 + {}^+4$ 　　**13.** $^-6 + {}^-8 + {}^+8$ 　**14.** $^+5 + {}^-7 + {}^-5$ 　**15.** $^-8 + {}^+2$

16. $^+4 + {}^-7$ 　　**17.** $^+5 + {}^+9$ 　　**18.** $^-8 + {}^-8$ 　　　**19.** $^+10 + {}^-1$

NUMBER SENSE Complete the statement. Use sometimes, always, or never.

24. The sum of two negative numbers is __?__ positive.

25. The sum of a negative number and a positive number is __?__ negative.

26. The sum of a positive number and its opposite is __?__ zero.

27. The sum of a negative number and zero is __?__ positive.

PROBLEM SOLVING

28. The morning temperature was 6° below 0. By noon it had risen 5°. Later it dropped 8°. What was the temperature then?

DATA BANK

29. **Social Studies Data Bank** A plane leaves London at 5 pm and arrives in Seattle 9 hours later. What time is it in Seattle?

▶ **ESTIMATION**

The number line shows one addend. Choose another addend from the chart so that the sum of the addends will have the required sign. Then, estimate the sums.

$^+27$	$^-18$	$^+32$
$^-10$	$^+50$	$^-60$
$^+9$	$^-21$	$^+30$

Example

positive sum
-31 　　　0

Second addends can be 32 or 50.
Estimated sums: about 0, about 20.

30. 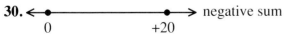 negative sum
0 　　$+20$

31. positive sum
-27 　　0

32. positive sum
0 　　$+25$

33.  negative sum
-15 　　0

More Practice, page 538, set B

Subtracting Integers

This shows $^+3$

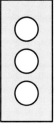

LEARN ABOUT IT

EXPLORE **Use Counting Chips**

Work in groups. Suppose you use counting chips to represent an integer. You can add pairs of positive and negative chips and not change the value of the integer. Use counting chips to model the subtraction problems below. Write an equation to express what you did with the chips.

a) $^+3 - {}^+2$ Start with $^+3$. Take away $^+2$.

b) $^-3 - {}^-2$ Start with $^-3$. Take away $^-2$.

c) $^+2 - {}^-5$ Start with $^+2$. Take away $^-5$.

d) $^-2 - {}^-5$ Start with $^-2$. Take away $^-5$.

This also shows $^+3$

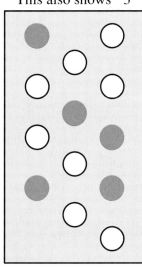

TALK ABOUT IT

1. For which of the problems did you have to add some positive-negative pairs?

2. Which problem above has the same answer as $^-2 + {}^+5$?

3. Which problem above has the same answer as $^+3 + {}^-2$?

The following relationships can be shown using counting chips.

$^+3 - {}^+2 = {}^+1$ and $^+3 + {}^-2 = {}^+1$ $^-3 - {}^-2 = {}^-1$ and $^-3 + {}^+2 = {}^-1$

$^+2 - {}^-5 = {}^+7$ and $^+2 + {}^+5 = {}^+7$ $^-2 - {}^-5 = {}^+3$ and $^-2 + {}^+5 = {}^+3$

To **subtract** one integer from another, **add its opposite.**

$^+8 - {}^+3 = {}^+8 + {}^-3 = {}^+5$ (To subtract $^+3$, add $^-3$.)

$^-12 - {}^-18 = {}^-12 + {}^+18 = {}^+6$ (To subtract $^-18$, add $^+18$.)

From now on, numbers other than zero, without $(-)$ or $(+)$ signs, are assumed to be positive.

TRY IT OUT

Subtract.

1. $5 - {}^-2$ **2.** $^-2 - 5$ **3.** $0 - {}^-3$ **4.** $^-15 - {}^-2$

Subtract.

1. $4 - {}^-3$ **2.** $1 - 5$ **3.** ${}^-6 - {}^-5$ **4.** ${}^-6 - 5$

5. ${}^-13 - {}^-14$ **6.** ${}^-9 - 1$ **7.** $8 - 7$ **8.** $3 - 12$

9. ${}^-11 - {}^-11$ **10.** $0 - 15$ **11.** ${}^-99 - 1$ **12.** $0 - {}^-7$

13. $14 - {}^-8$ **14.** ${}^-13 - {}^-6$ **15.** $23 - 10$ **16.** ${}^-12 - 5$

17. ${}^-4$ subtracted from 14 is what number?

Evaluate each expression. Compute inside parentheses first.

18. $({}^-10 - {}^-15) + 7$ **19.** $14 + ({}^-19 - 15)$ **20.** ${}^-8 - (9 - 1)$

MATH REASONING Evaluate each algebraic expression for the values given.

21. $x - {}^-7$ for $x = 15$ and $x = {}^-6$ **22.** $m + {}^-24$ for $m = {}^-8$ and $m = 24$

23. $34 + t$ for $t = 28$ and $t = {}^-16$ **24.** $17 - h$ for $h = {}^-21$ and $h = 0$

PROBLEM SOLVING

25. One day the temperature in Chicago was 5°C. The next it was 3°C. How many degrees had the temperature dropped?

26. Social Studies Data Bank How many hours ahead is the time in Berlin compared to the time in Denver?

▶ **CALCULATOR**

If your calculator has a ⌈ +⟳− ⌉ (change sign) key, it can find opposites and use negative integers in calculations.

Example: Find ${}^-63 - {}^-116$

Find the differences using a calculator.

Enter	Press	Display
63	+⟳−	− 63
	−	
116	+⟳− =	− 116
		53

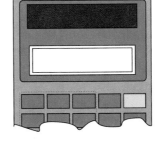

27. $235 - 129$ **28.** $329 - 535$

29. ${}^-56 - 79$ **30.** ${}^-78 - 23$

31. ${}^-23 - {}^-213$ **32.** ${}^-46 - {}^-35$

33. $181 - {}^-118$ **34.** $91 - {}^-88$

More Practice, page 538, set C

Using Critical Thinking
Integer Multiplication Patterns

$$3 \times 4 = 12 \qquad 3 \times {}^-4 = ?$$
$$3 \times 3 = 9 \qquad 2 \times {}^-4 = ?$$
$$3 \times 2 = 6 \qquad 1 \times {}^-4 = ?$$
$$3 \times 1 = 3 \qquad 0 \times {}^-4 = ?$$
$$3 \times 0 = 0 \qquad {}^-1 \times {}^-4 = ?$$
$$3 \times {}^-1 = ? \qquad {}^-2 \times {}^-4 = ?$$
$$3 \times {}^-2 = ? \qquad {}^-3 \times {}^-4 = ?$$
$$3 \times {}^-3 = ?$$
$$3 \times {}^-4 = ? \qquad Mike$$

LEARN ABOUT IT

Susan's group was trying to figure out some rules for multiplying integers. "I would guess it works like addition," said Susan. "Since $3 + {}^-1$ is a positive number, maybe $3 \times {}^-1$ would be a positive number."

"You're probably right," said Jeff.

"Hold it!" said Mike. "I've got some patterns here that show something different!"

TALK ABOUT IT

1. What is the group trying to do?

2. Do you think Susan's idea is correct? Explain.

3. Copy and complete Mike's integer multiplications. What patterns do you see?

4. What rules for multiplying integers do Mike's patterns suggest?

TRY IT OUT

Copy and complete the tables. Look for patterns.

1. $6 \times 3 = $ ▓
   $6 \times {}^-1 = $ ▓

   $6 \times 2 = $ ▓
   $6 \times {}^-2 = $ ▓

   $6 \times 1 = $ ▓
   $6 \times {}^-3 = $ ▓

   $6 \times 0 = $ ▓
   $6 \times {}^-4 = $ ▓

2. $5 \times {}^-2 = $ ▓
   $1 \times {}^-2 = $ ▓

   $4 \times {}^-2 = $ ▓
   $0 \times {}^-2 = $ ▓

   $3 \times {}^-2 = $ ▓
   ${}^-1 \times {}^-2 = $ ▓

   $2 \times {}^-2 = $ ▓
   ${}^-2 \times {}^-2 = $ ▓

3. $0 \times {}^-4 = $ ▓

   ${}^-1 \times {}^-4 = $ ▓

   ${}^-2 \times {}^-4 = $ ▓

   ${}^-3 \times {}^-4 = $ ▓

Use the patterns you have found to find these products.

4. $7 \times {}^-4$

5. $9 \times {}^-2$

6. ${}^-3 \times 5$

7. ${}^-4 \times {}^-2$

8. ${}^-8 \times {}^-4$

9. 6×9

10. ${}^-6 \times {}^-9$

11. ${}^-6 \times 9$

MIDCHAPTER REVIEW/QUIZ

Name the integers described.

1. the opposite of ⁻3

2. the integers from ⁻3 to 0

3. the integers 3 units from ⁻2

4. the negative integers greater than ⁻4

Write < or > for each 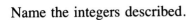.

5. ⁻1 ▥ ⁻4   **6.** ⁻20 ▥ ⁺10   **7.** 0 ▥ ⁻13   **8.** ⁻32 ▥ ⁻20

Use the properties to find the missing integers.

9. $n + 6 = 0$

10. ⁻5 + 5 = n

11. (⁻3 + n) + 2 = 2

12. $n \cdot 1 = $ ⁻4

13. (⁻3 · n) · ⁻1 = ⁻3 · ⁻1

14. ⁻3 + (n + ⁻1) = ⁻3 + ⁻1

15. In these sets of chips, a red chip has value ⁻1 and a white chip has value 1. What is the value of each set of chips?

A    B    C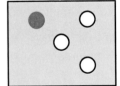

16. What chips could you add to set A to get a value of 2?

17. What chips could you remove from set B to get a value of 1?

Find the sums or differences.

18. ⁻12 + ⁻9

19. 3 + ⁻3 + ⁻6

20. 4 − 8

21. 25 + ⁻5

22. ⁻3 − ⁻4

23. 92 + ⁻92

24. ⁻3 − 5

25. 0 − 6

26. 13 − 72

PROBLEM SOLVING

27. In a set of chips, a red chip has value ⁻1 and a white chip has value ⁺1. Begin with 4 chips and add 2 chips. How many different sums are possible?

Multiplying Integers

EXPLORE Study the Diagram

Suppose you are walking along Grove Street near Oakdale school. Use the drawing to tell whether you would be to the LEFT or to the RIGHT of the school in each situation.

a) Walking east, →, you have passed the school.

b) Walking west, ←, you have passed the school.

TALK ABOUT IT

1. What information do you need to tell which side of the school you would be on?

2. If LEFT is negative and RIGHT is positive, in which situation would you be on the positive side of the school? on the negative side?

You can model integer multiplication on a number line.

←— Going west (–)   —→ Going east (–)
Before passing 0 (–)   After passing 0 (+)

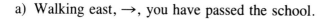

Going → at 5 mph, 2 hrs before passing zero you would be at ⁻10.
$$5 \cdot {}^-2 = {}^-10$$

Going ← at 3 mph, 2 hrs after passing zero you would be at ⁻6.
$${}^-3 \cdot 2 = {}^-6$$

Rule: The product of a positive integer and a negative integer is negative.

Going → at 2 mph, 3 hrs after passing zero you would be at 6.
$$2 \cdot 3 = 6$$

Going ← at 4 mph, 2 hrs before passing zero you would be at 8.
$${}^-4 \cdot {}^-2 = 8$$

Rule: The product of two positive integers or two negative integers is positive.

TRY IT OUT

Multiply. Use a number line to show the multiplication.

1. $3 \cdot 2$ 2. $^-2 \cdot {}^-2$ 3. $^-4 \cdot 1$ 4. $5 \cdot {}^-1$

Multiply.

1. $4 \times {}^-3$ 2. ${}^-3 \times {}^-7$ 3. ${}^-2 \times {}^-7$ 4. 5×9

5. ${}^-6 \times {}^-5$ 6. $12 \times {}^-5$ 7. 9×6 8. ${}^-13 \times {}^-3$

9. ${}^-20 \times 8$ 10. $15 \times {}^-8$ 11. ${}^-1 \times {}^-1$ 12. $0 \times {}^-21$

13. ${}^-14 \times {}^-10$ 14. ${}^-25 \times 4$ 15. $3 \times {}^-35$ 16. ${}^-4 \times {}^-22$

Evaluate each expression.

17. $({}^-2 \times 3) \times {}^-2$ 18. $(5 \times {}^-2) \times {}^-3$ 19. $({}^-4 \times {}^-7) \times {}^-4$

20. $5 \times ({}^-4 \times {}^-6)$ 21. ${}^-6 \times (13 \times {}^-2)$ 22. $({}^-8 \times 5) \times 10$

MATH REASONING Find the pattern. Give the next three integers.

23. $1, {}^-1, 3, {}^-3, 5, {}^-5, \underline{\ ?\ }, \underline{\ ?\ } \underline{\ ?\ }$ 24. $10, 7, 4, 1, {}^-2, \underline{\ ?\ } \underline{\ ?\ } \underline{\ ?\ }$

25. $2, {}^-4, 8, {}^-16, 32, \underline{\ ?\ } \underline{\ ?\ } \underline{\ ?\ }$ 26. ${}^-2, {}^-3, {}^-5, {}^-9, {}^-17, \underline{\ ?\ } \underline{\ ?\ } \underline{\ ?\ }$

PROBLEM SOLVING

27. Fines for overdue videotapes are $1 per day for an ''old release'' and $2 per day for a ''new release''. How much change would you get from $20 if you returned 2 old and 2 new releases 3 days late?

28. Eight TVs in a video store are connected by wires. Each set is connected to each other set with one wire. How many wires are needed to connect all the sets?

Use your calculator to find the interest and the total amount.

29. $P = \$2578$
$R = 7\%$ per year
$T = 3$ years

30. $P = \$100$
$R = 6.5\%$ per year
$T = 1.5$ years

31. $P = \$10,500$
$R = 10.5\%$ per year
$T = 15$ years

Find the answers.

32. $\frac{1}{6} + 5\frac{5}{9}$ 33. $18\frac{1}{2} - 3\frac{3}{4}$ 34. $1\frac{1}{3} \times 4\frac{3}{7}$ 35. $6\frac{3}{8} \div 5$

More Practice, page 538, set D

Dividing Integers

LEARN ABOUT IT

EXPLORE **Examine the Relationship**

Consider the equation $12 \times 5 = 60$. There are two related division equations:

$$60 \div 12 = 5 \quad \text{and} \quad 60 \div 5 = 12.$$

Write two related division equations for each multiplication equation.

a) $^-8 \cdot 6 = ^-48$
b) $7 \cdot ^-5 = ^-35$
c) $^-9 \cdot ^-5 = 45$

TALK ABOUT IT

1. When a positive integer is divided by a negative integer, is the quotient positive or negative?

2. When a negative integer is divided by a positive integer, is the quotient positive or negative?

The quotient of a **positive** and a **negative** integer is **negative.**

The quotient of **two positive** or **two negative** integers is **positive.**

Examples

A $^-72 \div 24 = ^-3$ Check: $^-3 \cdot 24 = ^-72$

B $\dfrac{^-96}{^-12} = 8$ Check: $8 \cdot ^-12 = ^-96$

C $0 \div ^-18 = 0$ Check: $0 \cdot ^-18 = 0$

Remember, you cannot divide by 0!

TRY IT OUT

Find the quotient.

1. $^-24 \div ^-3$
2. $\dfrac{36}{^-12}$
3. $^-56 \div 7$
4. $\dfrac{0}{2}$

5. $\dfrac{35}{^-7}$
6. $^-100 \div ^-25$
7. $\dfrac{88}{^-12}$
8. $^-135 \div 15$

Use the given multiplication fact to find the missing quotients.

1. $-20 \cdot 4 = -80$
$-80 \div -20 = $ ▦
$-80 \div 4 = $ ▦

2. $-6 \cdot 4 = -24$
$-24 \div -6 = $ ▦
$-24 \div 4 = $ ▦

3. $-3 \cdot -12 = 36$
$36 \div -3 = $ ▦
$36 \div -12 = $ ▦

Use multiplication to decide if each equation is correct.

4. $-15 \div 3 = -5$ **5.** $-27 \div 9 = 3$ **6.** $32 \div -8 = -4$ **7.** $-18 \cdot -3 = -6$

8. $-12 \div -4 = 3$ **9.** $15 \div -15 = 0$ **10.** $\dfrac{16}{-4} = -4$ **11.** $\dfrac{-48}{8} = -6$

Find the quotients.

12. $-22 \div 11$ **13.** $-27 \div -9$ **14.** $12 \div -1$ **15.** $-1 \div -1$

16. $-45 \div -3$ **17.** $72 \div -6$ **18.** $32 \div 8$ **19.** $-13 \div -13$

20. $-51 \div 3$ **21.** $72 \div 9$ **22.** $42 \div -7$ **23.** $-13 \div -1$

24. $\dfrac{-144}{-12}$ **25.** $\dfrac{250}{-25}$ **26.** $\dfrac{-196}{-49}$ **27.** $\dfrac{-420}{-70}$

28. Divide 54 by the opposite of 9.   **29.** Divide -27 by -3.

MATH REASONING Use the clues to find the mystery numbers.

30. Our product is 24 and our sum is -10.   **31.** Our product is -16 and our sum is 0.

32. Our product is -60 and our sum is 4.   **33.** Our product is 104 and our sum is -21.

PROBLEM SOLVING

34. A hot air balloon ascended 100 ft in 20 seconds, descended 12 ft in 3 seconds, and then descended 16 ft in 8 seconds. What was the change in altitude?

35. A hot air balloon ascends at the rate of 50 ft per second. If it continues to climb at the same rate, how long will it take to reach an altitude of 1250 ft?

▶ **MENTAL MATH**

Find the value of each expression. Do operations inside parentheses and above or below fraction bars first.

36. $(36 \div -6) \div -3$ **37.** $36 \div (-6 \div -3)$ **38.** $\dfrac{-15 \cdot 2}{-3}$ **39.** $\dfrac{25 \cdot 0}{-25}$

40. $\dfrac{-1 + 3}{2}$ **41.** $\dfrac{-2 + -6}{-4}$ **42.** $\dfrac{-80}{-15 + 5}$ **43.** $\dfrac{-8 + -7}{-3 + -2}$

More Practice, page 538, set E

Graphing Integer Coordinates

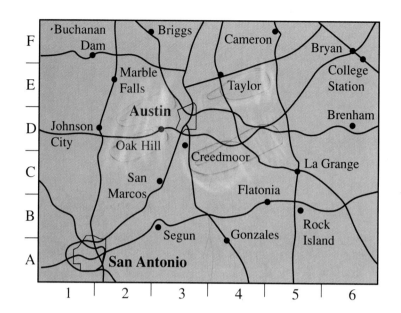

LEARN ABOUT IT

EXPLORE Study the Map

Maps often use a system of letters and numbers to help you locate a particular place. Give the letter and then the number that describes the location of each of the following cities.

a) Austin   b) Oak Hill
c) Taylor   d) Creedmoor

TALK ABOUT IT

1. Could you have named the section using the number first and then the letter?

2. Can you think of a way to describe a section of the map using only numbers instead of a number and a letter? Explain.

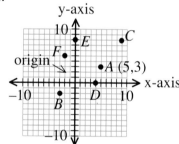

In a **rectangular coordinate system,** two perpendicular lines, called **axes,** intersect at a point called the **origin.** The horizontal axis is called the **x-axis** and the vertical axis is called the **y-axis.** Each point on the plane can be named using an **ordered pair** of numbers. An ordered pair gives the **coordinates** of the point.

The coordinates of the point A are the ordered pair (5, 3).

The first coordinate, 5, is the distance from 0 on the x-axis.

The second coordinate, 3, is the distance from 0 on the y-axis.

TRY IT OUT

Name the coordinates of the points. Use the coordinate system above.

1. B **2.** C **3.** D **4.** E **5.** F

Draw a set of coordinate axes and graph the following points.

6. (2, 3)   **7.** (4, 0)   **8.** ($^-$1, 2)   **9.** ($^-$3, $^-$5)   **10.** (0, $^-$1)

Give the coordinates of the vertices of each polygon.

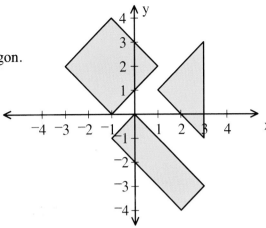

1. triangle

2. square

3. rectangle (not the square)

Graph each set of points. Connect them in the order given to form a polygon. Name the polygon.

4. (⁻4, 4), (2, 4), (2, ⁻2)

5. (⁻2, ⁻3), (2, ⁻3), (4, 0), (0, 0), (⁻2, 3), (⁻4, 0)

6. (0, 0), (⁻2, ⁻1), (⁻3, ⁻4), (3, ⁻1)

7. (4, 0), (0, 3), (⁻4, 0), (⁻2, ⁻3), (2, ⁻3)

8. (1, 2), (⁻3, 3), (⁻4, ⁻1), (0, ⁻2)

9. (3, 4), (⁻3, 3), (⁻4, ⁻3), (2, ⁻2)

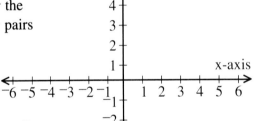

MATH REASONING For each exercise, draw and number the coordinate axes as shown. Graph the ordered integer pairs indicated.

10. The coordinates are opposites.

11. The sum of the coordinates is 3.

12. The second coordinate is 1 more than the first coordinate.

PROBLEM SOLVING

13. Social Studies Data Bank The Wilsons are planning a trip to Austin to see the State Capitol, the Bee Creek Preserve, and the Longhorn Dam. Give the letter and number that tell where each of these are found on the map.

▶ **USING CRITICAL THINKING Make a Generalization**

14. List five ordered pairs which lie on the same horizontal line. What generalization can you make about the y-coordinates of points that lie on the same horizontal line? Repeat this exercise for a vertical line.

15. Can you make a generalization about all points that have an x-coordinate of 0? a y-coordinate of 0?

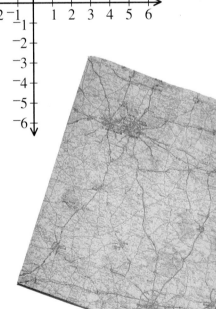

Exploring Algebra
Graphing Equations

EXPLORE **Study the Situation**

A solution of an equation like $y = 5x + 2$ is an ordered pair (x, y) that makes the equation true.

$(^-1, ^-3)$ is a solution of $y = 5x + 2$
$$^-3 = 5\,(^-1) + 2.$$

Graph the ordered pairs in each list and connect the points with a line. Then find two other ordered pairs that could be in the list.

(x, y)	(x, y)	(x, y)
$(0,\ ^-2)$	$(0, 0)$	$(0, 1)$
$(1,\ ^-1)$	$(-1, 1)$	$(1, 3)$
$(2, 0)$	$(1,\ ^-1)$	$(2, 5)$
$(^-1,\ ^-3)$	$(2,\ ^-2)$	$(^-1,\ ^-1)$
$(^-2,\ ^-4)$	$(^-3, 3)$	$(^-2,\ ^-3)$
$(4, 2)$	$(5,\ ^-5)$	$(^-3,\ ^-5)$
$(3, ?)$	$(3, ?)$	$(3, ?)$
$(^-4, ?)$	$(^-4, ?)$	$(^-4, ?)$
$\vdots$	$\vdots$	$\vdots$

TALK ABOUT IT

1. How did you find additional ordered pairs?

2. For each list, describe the relationship between the x-values and the y-values.

3. Which list of ordered pairs is described by each of the equations below?

$$y = 2x + 1 \qquad y = {}^-x \qquad y = x - 2$$

x	y
0	2
1	1
2	0

Equations of the form $y = ax + b$ are called **linear equations.** The graph of the solutions forms a straight line.

Example Graph the quation $y = 2 - x$. First, find at least three ordered pairs that are solutions to $y = 2 - x$.

Let $x = 0$	Let $x = 1$	Let $x = 2$
$y = 2 - 0$	$y = 2 - 1$	$y = 2 - 2$
$y = 2$	$y = 1$	$y = 0$
$(0, 2)$ is a solution.	$(1, 1)$ is a solution.	$(2,0)$ is a solution.

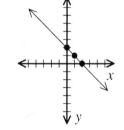

Now graph the ordered pairs and draw a line through the points.

Make a table of ordered pairs and graph each equation.

1. $y = {}^-2x$

2. $y = \dfrac{x}{2}$

3. $y = {}^-x - 4$

Make a table of ordered pairs and graph each equation.

1. $y = 2x + 1$ **2.** $y = \,^-x + 2$ **3.** $y = 3 - x$ **4.** $y = \dfrac{x}{2} - 1$

5. $y = 2x - 1$ **6.** $y = 5x$ **7.** $y = \,^-x$ **8.** $y = 1 - 2x$

9. $y = 3x + 1$ **10.** $y = 4 - x$ **11.** $y = 2x - 5$ **12.** $y = 3x - 3$

13. $y = \dfrac{x}{2} - 2$ **14.** $y = \,^-2x + 4$ **15.** $y = 2 - 3x$ **16.** $y = 3 + x$

APPLY

MATH REASONING

17. Graph these equations on the same axes: $y = x + 3$ and $y = 2x + 3$. At what point do the two graphs intersect?

18. Graph these equations on the same axes: $y = \,^-2x + 3$ and $y = \,^-2x + 1$. What do you notice about the graphs?

PROBLEM SOLVING

19. Mark makes $5 washing a car and $10 mowing a yard. How many of each job could he have done to make $200 for summer camp?

20. In basketball, a long field goal is worth 3 points, and a short one 2 points. If a player scored 30 points on field goals, how many of each could she have made?

21. Talk About Your Solution If you had 40 feet of fence to build a rectangular dog pen, you could use the formula $P = 2L + 2W$ to find lengths and widths that would work. Which pair (L, W) would give your dog the biggest pen.

USING CRITICAL THINKING   Analyze the data

22. Complete the table to find ordered pairs of integers for which the product of the two integers is $^-12$. Then graph the ordered pairs and connect them. What do you discover? Is this a linear relationship?

x	1	2	3	4	6	12	$^-1$	$^-2$	$^-3$	$^-4$	$^-6$	$^-12$
y	$^-12$	$^-6$										

23. Make a table of five ordered pairs that are solutions to the equation $y = x^2$. Graph the ordered pairs and connect them. What do you discover? Is this a linear relationship?

Problem Solving
Problems with More than One Solution

UNDERSTAND
ANALYZE DATA
PLAN
ESTIMATE
SOLVE
EXAMINE

LEARN ABOUT IT

Some problems have more than one answer.
When you find an answer to a problem,
before stopping, ask yourself if there may
be other solutions.

Todd plays drums in a band. His
sister Molly is on the swim team. The
band practices every 4th day and the swim
team practices every 3rd day. Both have
practice on March 1. On what other days
in March do they both practice?

I'll use **Guess and
Check** to get an answer.

Now, I need to check for
other answers. I'll use
the strategies **Make an
Organized List** and **Draw
a Picture** to help me.

Try March 10.
Todd 1 $\xrightarrow{+4}$ 5 $\xrightarrow{+4}$ 9 $\xrightarrow{+4}$ 13
Molly 1 $\xrightarrow{+3}$ 4 $\xrightarrow{+3}$ 7 $\xrightarrow{+3}$ 10
*Todd doesn't practice
March 10 but Molly does
and her next practice is
March 13.*

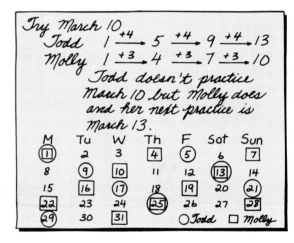

Todd and Molly both have practice again on
March 13 and March 25.

TRY IT OUT

Solve. Be sure to check for more than one solution.

1. Kyle and Lori are both on a swim team.
   Kyle's team practices every other day
   and Lori's team practices every third
   day. They both have practice on
   March 8. On what other days in March
   do they both practice?

2. Rob swims laps with a kick board
   everyday. Some days he swims 6 laps
   and some days he swims 10 laps. In
   9 days Rob swam 70 laps with the kick
   board. On how many days did he swim
   10 laps?

Solve. Use any problem solving strategy.

1. The Orthlieb Pool in Casablanca is 1574 ft long, 246 ft wide, and has an area of about 8.9 acres. A football field has an area of about 1.1 acres. How many football fields would it take to cover the area of the Orthlieb Pool?

2. Tyrone swims laps 5 days a week. Last week he swam 38 laps on Monday, 41 on Tuesday, 50 on Wednesday, 49 on Thursday, and 52 on Friday. Find the average number of laps Tyrone swam each day?

3. Coach Taylor bought some juice for after the swim meet. He bought 36 cans, some in 4-packs and some in 6-packs. How many 6-packs of juice did he buy?

4. The diving pool is 10 ft deep. When Eric's hands touch bottom, his feet are 4 ft below the surface of the pool. How far are Eric's feet from the bottom of the pool?

5. Five swimmers competed in a 200-meter race. Jan finished 6 sec behind Bev. Nicole beat Jan by 2 sec and Tina beat Nicole by 4 times that many seconds. NaSun finished in 3 min 8 sec and was 12 sec behind Tina. What was Bev's time?

6. The first 52 swimmers to arrive at the swim meet came in groups of 4 or 5. How many groups of each size were there?

7. Berta found 4 coins in the locker room. The coins added up to $.65. What coins did Berta find?

8. **Understanding the Operations**
   What operation would you use to solve this problem? Why? Replace the variables with reasonable numbers and solve the problem.

   Coach Sanchez has x towels. She gave y to each member of the diving team. How many divers are on the team?

Group Decision Making
Applied Problem Solving

UNDERSTAND
ANALYZE DATA
PLAN
ESTIMATE
SOLVE
EXAMINE

Group Skill:
Listen to Others

Learn About It

While hiking near Obstacle Pass, Juanita and
Teresa have been surrounded by dense fog
and cannot find their way back. Your group's
mission is to contact them by radio and lead
them safely back to camp. What directions
could you give them?

Facts to Consider

- The only thing Juanita and Teresa can see
  is their fluorescent compass.

- They know they are at (⁻7, 4) on the
  map. The campground is at (3, ⁻5).

- You can use the map below.

- The distance from Pinnacle Point to Hippo
  Rock is 0.5 kilometers.

Some Questions to Answer

1. What is your group being asked to do?

2. Why would knowing the number of strides per kilometer help you give directions?

3. How could you figure out strides per kilometer? Could Teresa and Juanita help you figure it out? Could you do it without their help?

4. How could acting out the situation help your group solve the problem?

What Is Your Decision?

Present your group's plan for leading Teresa and Juanita to safety. Describe how you worked it out. Trade your directions with another group. Do the directions work?

WRAP UP

Integer Match

Match each term with the best explanation or example.

1. linear equation   **A** the distance from 0 to a number on the number line

2. absolute value   **B** opposite of a positive integer

3. negative integer   **C** numbers found in an ordered pair

4. coordinates   **D** y = 4x + 5

Sometimes, Always, Never

Which word should go in the blank, *sometimes*, *always*, or *never*? Explain your choice.

5. An integer __?__ has an opposite different from itself.

6. When a negative integer is divided by another negative integer, the quotient is __?__ negative.

7. When a computation is done with two positive integers, the result will __?__ be positive.

8. If one integer is greater than another, its absolute value will __?__ be greater than the absolute value of the other.

Project

Draw a picture on a rectangular coordinate system. Each corner of your drawing should be at a point that can be described by an ordered pair of integers. Make a list of these ordered pairs in the order they should be connected to make your drawing. Give your list to a classmate to try to duplicate your shape or picture.

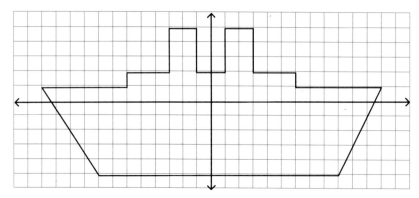

CHAPTER REVIEW/TEST

Part 1 Understanding

Match.

1. opposites property
2. one property
3. commutative property
4. zero property

A $^-4 + 0 = ^-4$

B $^-2 + 2 = 0$

C $^-3 \cdot 1 = -3$

D $^-3 \cdot 4 = 4 \cdot ^-3$

5. Complete. The ordered pair for the point where the x-axis and y-axis intersect is __?__.

6. Which of the ordered pairs is a solution for $y = x - 3$?

   A $(8, 5)$ B $(0, 3)$

   C $(3, -1)$ D $(5, 8)$

7. Name two integers with an absolute value of 7.

8. What is the largest negative integer?

Part 2 Skills

Compute

9. $^-7 + ^+10$

10. $^-15 + ^-3 + ^+3$

11. $^-10 - 4$

12. $^-8 - (4 - 7)$

13. $^-12 \div ^-2$

14. $^-4 (^-2 \cdot ^-3)$

15. Evaluate $3p(7 - ^-2)$ for $p = ^-2$.

16. Name the coordinates of point G.

17. What point is named by $(^-4, 0)$?

18. Make a table of 5 ordered pairs and graph the equation: $y = ^-2x + 1$

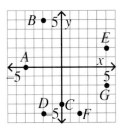

Part 3 Applications

19. Ginny has swim team practice every other day. She has band practice every fifth day. On April 2, she had both swim and band practice. On what other days in April did she have both types of practice?

20. **Challenge** A hot-air balloon ascended at 4 ft per sec for 5 seconds, and then descended at 2 ft per sec for 3 seconds. Use an integer to describe the change in altitude.

337

ENRICHMENT
Scientific Notation

Study the patterns in the table.

Number	Power of 10	Number	Power of 10
10	10^1	$0.1 = \frac{1}{10}$	10^{-1}
100	10^2	$0.01 = \frac{1}{100}$	10^{-2}
1,000	10^3	$0.001 = \frac{1}{1000}$	10^{-3}
10,000	10^4	$0.0001 = \frac{1}{10000}$	10^{-4}

Very large numbers or very small numbers are often written in
a style called **scientific notation.**

A number is written in scientific notation if
it is written as the product of a number
greater than or equal to 1, but less than 10,
and a power of ten.

The radius of the universe is about
30,000,000,000,000,000,000,000
kilometers.

$$3 \times 10^{22} = 3 \times 10,000,000,000,000,000,000,000.$$
$$= 30,000,000,000,000,000,000,000$$

3.0×10^{22}
Scientific Notation

Numbers less than one use negative
exponents for the powers of 10.

Wavelength of red light:
6.4×10^{-4}
Scientific Notation

$$6.4 \times 10^{-4} = 6.4 \times \frac{1}{10^4}$$

$$= \frac{6.4}{10000} = 0.00064$$

Write each number as a whole number or decimal.

1. 3.7×10^4 **2.** 8.7×10^{-3} **3.** 6×10^6 **4.** 1.4×10^{-5}

5. The diameter of the earth is about
4×10^4 km. The diameter of the sun is
about 4.4×10^6 km. How much greater
than the earth's diameter is the sun's
diameter?

6. A virus is about 2×10^{-7} cm in length.
Bacteria are about 3.5×10^{-1} cm in
length. Which is the longer of the two?
How much longer?

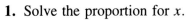

CUMULATIVE REVIEW

1. Solve the proportion for x.

$$\frac{10}{16} = \frac{15}{x}$$

   A 150   **B** 240   **C** 24   **D** 2.38

2. The rectangles are similar. What is x?

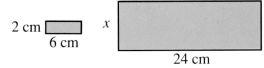

   A 144 cm   **B** 8 cm

   C 72 cm   **D** 6 cm

3. What is the circumference?
Use 3.14 for π.

   A 26.376 m

   B 52.752 m

   C 13.188 m

   D 55.39 m

4. Which is the greatest?

$$\frac{9}{20}, \quad 8\%, \quad 0.39, \quad \frac{12}{25}, \quad 18.45\%$$

   A 18.45%   **B** $\frac{9}{20}$

   C 0.39   **D** $\frac{12}{25}$

5. Which decimal expresses $32\frac{7}{8}\%$?

   A 32.875   **B** 0.32875

   C 32.7   **D** 0.327

6. What is the estimated percent?
22 out of 51 people

   A 20%   **B** 25%   **C** 40%   **D** 50%

7. What is 25% of 9?

   A 0.36   **B** 3.2   **C** 4   **D** 2.25

8. What is the best estimate?
38.6% of 197

   A 80   **B** 70   **C** 60   **D** 40

9. Find the amount of interest on a $7,000 loan for 3 years at 12%.

   A $840   **B** $1,680

   C $2,520   **D** $9,520

10. What percent of 16 is 5?

   A 3.2%   **B** 31.25%

   C 1.2%   **D** 0.8%

11. Which expresses the percent of increase from 275 to 480?

   A 57.3%   **B** 21.9%

   C 42.7%   **D** 74.5%

12. 20% of what number is 17?

   A 85   **B** 340   **C** 54   **D** 34

13. Norman and Galen packed bags of fruit. Norman put the fruit in the bag and Galen sealed it. Each step took 6 seconds. How long did it take to pack and seal 45 bags?

   A 4 min 30 sec   **B** 4 min 36 sec

   C 9 min   **D** 9 min 6 sec

14. A group of 60 people visiting the Wild Animal Park included 35% students and $\frac{1}{3}$ as many senior citizens. Ticket prices for adults are $4.00 each. The total cost of tickets was $166.50. What portion of that amount was for student tickets?

   A $38.50   **B** $128.00

   C $28.98   **D** not enough information

12

PROBABILITY

MATH AND SCIENCE

DATA BANK

Use the Science Data Bank on page 491 to answer each question.

1 In the second generation of pea plants, what is the ratio of plants with red blossoms to white ones?

2 If you had 100 such second-generation pea plants, about how many of them would you expect to have white blossoms?

3 In Pascal's Triangle, what is the sum of the numbers in row 1? row 2? row 3? row 4?

4 **Using Critical Thinking** Study Pascal's Triangle carefully to see how many things you can list that are true for it. For instance, can you find a pattern in your answers to question 3? Can you figure out what numbers would be listed in row 8?

Chance Events

Impossible ├─┼─┼─┼─┼─┼─┼─┤ Certain
A B C D E F G H

LEARN ABOUT IT

EXPLORE Estimate the Chance

- Copy this line.

- Study event **1** below. Decide how likely it is to occur. Write the number 1 above the A if you think it is impossible. If you think it's certain, write the 1 above H. If you think it is somewhat likely, write the 1 in between A and H. Then do the same with the other events.

1. A friend secretly picks the number 1, 2, 3, or 4. You guess the number in one try.

2. The earth will make one complete revolution in the next 24 hours.

3. The names of all students in your room are put in a box. A girl's name is drawn.

4. The names of all students in your room are put in a box. Your name is drawn.

5. It will rain on July 4th this year in your area.

6. Your schoolhouse will be struck by lightning this week.

TALK ABOUT IT

1. What events did you place at or near H? Why did you give them this high rating?

2. What events did you place at or near A? Explain.

Impossible events are assigned a value of 0 and events that are certain are assigned a value of 1. But most events are assigned values between 0 and 1. In this chapter we will study two important ways to find such values for events, and ways to apply these values to solve problems.

TRY IT OUT

1. Describe an impossible event and a certain event.

2. Describe an event that is about as likely to occur as not.

3. A bag holds 10 red marbles and 1 black marble. Where on the line above would you place the event *selecting the black marble*? *selecting a red marble*?

- Copy this line.

Impossible ├─┼─┼─┼─┼─┼─┤ Certain
A B C D E F G H

Place each of the following events on your line.

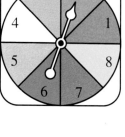

1. Spinning a number less than 10.

2. Spinning a number greater than 10.

3. Spinning an 8.

4. Spinning an even number.

The faces of the cube at the right are numbered 1 to 6.

5. Throwing a 3 on the cube.

6. Throwing a number divisible by 2.

7. Throwing a number less than 4.

8. Throwing an odd number.

APPLY

MATH REASONING

9. Suppose you toss a fair coin twice. Where on the line would you place the event *getting 2 "heads" in a row*? *2 "tails" in a row*? Explain.

10. Suppose you toss a fair coin ten times. Where on the line would you place the event *getting all "heads"*? Explain.

PROBLEM SOLVING

11. Wendy Tallman has hit 75% of her free throws in basketball games this year. Now she is at the free throw line for 2 free throws. Where on the line would you place the event *making both free throws*?

ESTIMATION

12. Suppose you spin this spinner. Where on the line would you put the events *landing on red? landing on yellow? landing on blue? landing on white? landing on green?*

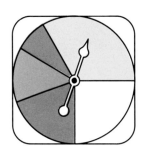

More Practice, page 539, set A

Sample Spaces

EXPLORE **Conduct an Experiment**
Work in groups. Start a table like the one
at the right. Then toss a coin and a number
cube at the same time. Write the outcomes
you get in the table. Repeat the experiment
about twenty times.

Coin Outcome	Cube outcome
H	3
T	1
T	6
H	5

TALK ABOUT IT

1. How many outcomes are possible on the coin toss?

2. How many outcomes are possible for the cube toss?

3. How many different combined outcomes did you get?

The list of all possible outcomes for an experiment is called its
sample space. The sample space of the coin-cube experiment
has 12 possible outcomes.

(H, 1)   (H, 2)   (H, 3)   (H, 4)   (H, 5)   (H, 6)
(T, 1)   (T, 2)   (T, 3)   (T, 4)   (T, 5)   (T, 6)

Each outcome in the coin-cube sample space is **equally likely**
to happen, if the coin and the number cube are fair.

An **event** is any outcome or combination of outcomes from the
sample space of an experiment.

Example A

Event: Heads and an even number
Outcomes: (H, 2), (H, 4), (H, 6)
Three outcomes make up this event.

Example B

Event: Tails and a number less than 3
Outcomes: (T, 1), (T, 2)
Two outcomes make up this event.

TRY IT OUT

Use the coin-cube experiment. Give the outcomes that make up
each of the following events.

1. Tails and a 5

2. Heads and a number greater than 4

3. Tails and an odd number

4. Heads and any number

1. List the sample space of all outcomes for drawing one of these cards.

Use the sample space from number 1 above. List all the outcomes for each of these events.

2. Drawing an ace.

3. Drawing a heart card.

4. Drawing an even number.

5. Drawing a card > 4

6. List all possible outcomes in the sample space for spinning this spinner once.

List all the outcomes for each of these events.

7. Spinning an odd number

8. Spinning an even number

9. Spinning a square number

10. Spinning a multiple of 4

APPLY

MATH REASONING

11. Using 10 cards from a regular deck, devise an event with 2 outcomes. Devise an event with 5 outcomes.

PROBLEM SOLVING

12. The Card-Spinner experiment: draw 1 of the 4 cards above and spin the spinner shown once. How many outcomes are in the sample space?

13. In the Card-Spinner experiment, what outcomes make up the event of getting the same number on the card as on the spinner?

14. What outcomes are in the event of getting a sum of 8 for the numbers on the card and spinner?

15. Be a Problem Finder Make up an event for the Card-Spinner experiment. List the outcomes in your event.

▶ **ALGEBRA**

16. Use the Card-Spinner experiment from above. Give the outcomes in each of the events A through D.

Let c = number on the card.

A. $c + s = 7$ **B.** $c + s > 7$

Let s = number on the spinner.

C. $s - c = 2$ **D.** $cs = 12$

Probability of an Event

EXPLORE Conduct an Experiment

Work in groups. Put 10 counters in a bag. Use 4 red, 3 green, 2 blue, and 1 white. Pull 1 counter from the bag at a time and record the color in a table. Return the counter to the bag. Repeat this 50 times. Combine your results with those of another group.

TALK ABOUT IT

1. Before doing this experiment, which color would you have predicted to occur the most times? the least times? Why?

2. How do the actual results compare with your prediction?

3. If you repeated this experiment 1,000 times, do you think the results would change?

When each outcome of a sample space is equally likely, the probability of any event is this ratio:

$$\textbf{Probability of an event} = \frac{\textbf{Number of outcomes in an event}}{\textbf{Total number of outcomes}}$$

If **E** is an event made up of **N** outcomes out of a total of T outcomes, then we may write:

$$P(\textbf{E}) = \frac{\textbf{N}}{\textbf{T}} \quad \textbf{P(blue counter)} = \frac{\textbf{blue outcomes}}{\textbf{total outcomes}} = \frac{2}{10}$$

The probability of an event is always a number greater than or equal to 0 (impossible) and less than or equal to 1 (certain).

TRY IT OUT

Give the probability of each event for the counter game.

1. $P(\text{red})$ **2.** $P(\text{red or blue})$ **3.** $P(\text{gold})$ **4.** $P(\text{not gold})$

5. $P(\text{green})$ **6.** $P(\text{green or blue})$ **7.** $P(\text{not red})$ **8.** $P(\text{red or gold or blue})$

Give the probability of each event using this spinner.

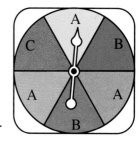

1. $P(A)$ **2.** $P(B)$ **3.** $P(C)$

4. $P(A \text{ or } B)$ **5.** $P(D)$ **6.** $P(A \text{ or } B \text{ or } C)$

Give the probability of each event of drawing one marble from the box.

7. $P(\text{red marble})$

8. $P(\text{blue marble})$

9. $P(\text{white marble})$

10. $P(\text{red or white})$

11. $P(\text{not red})$

12. $P(\text{not white})$

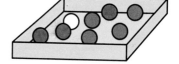

13. On a coin, what is $P(\text{heads})$?

APPLY

MATH REASONING

14. If you toss two number cubes, are you as likely to get a sum of 5 or 6 as you are to get a sum of 7 or 8? Explain. (Make an addition table for the numbers from 1 to 6.)

PROBLEM SOLVING

15. Two number cubes are tossed. What are the outcomes in the event of getting a sum of 10? What is $P(\text{sum} = 10)$?

16. Which sum has the highest probability of happening when two number cubes are tossed? What is the probability? Show why.

17. Data Hunt Toss two number cubes fifty times. Record the sum of the numbers for each toss. Which sum happened most often? Compute the probability of getting this sum.

MIXED REVIEW

Solve.

18. What number is 35% of 200?

19. 62 is what percent of 100?

20. 325% of 15 is what number?

21. What percent of 20 is 15?

Find the answers.

22. $^-32 \div 8$ **23.** $^-20 + {}^-30$ **24.** $50 - {}^-18$ **25.** $^-8 \cdot {}^-9$

More Practice, page 539, set C

Probability Experiments

EXPLORE **Study the Situation**

Patty and Carlos were planning to toss a coin 100 times and record the number of heads.

Patty said, "We should get 50 heads."

Carlos disagreed. He said, "I expect we'll get something close to that, but all 100 tosses could come up heads."

Who do you think is right? Toss a coin 100 times and record the outcomes.

TALK ABOUT IT

1. Why would Patty think they should get 50 heads?

2. Do you think it is possible to get 100 heads in 100 tosses?

3. How many heads did you get? Is this what you expected?

The **experimental probability** of an event is the ratio of the number of times the event occurs to the number of trials.

$$\text{Exp } P(E) = \frac{\text{Number of times E occurs}}{\text{Number of trials}}$$

When the number of trials is large, the experimental probability of an event is usually close to the mathematical probability of the event.

Example A

Toss a coin 100 times. Get heads 53 times.

$\text{Exp } P(H) = \frac{53}{100}$ $P(H) = \frac{1}{2}$

$\text{Exp } P(H)$ is close to $P(H)$.

Example B

Toss a number cube 36 times. Get a five 2 times.

$\text{Exp } P(5) = \frac{2}{36} = \frac{1}{18}$ $P(5) = \frac{1}{6}$

$\text{Exp } P(5)$ is not too close to $P(5)$.

TRY IT OUT

Find the experimental probability of each event.

1. Toss a coin 40 times. Get Heads 23 times.

2. Toss a number cube 50 times. Get a four 7 times.

Find the experimental probability of each event.

1. Toss a coin: result is 34 heads, 26 tails.
   Exp P(H) = ? Exp P(T) = ?

2. Toss two number cubes 75 times and get a sum of seven 15 times. Exp P(seven) = ?

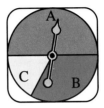

3. A spinner experiment with outcomes A, B, and C: result is A, 24 times, B, 20 times, C, 4 times. Exp P(A) = ?
   Exp P(B) = ? Exp P(C) = ?

MATH REASONING

4. Lionel tossed two fair coins together 100 times. He got heads on both 65 times. Does this seem reasonable? Explain.

PROBLEM SOLVING

5. Bend the "long end" of a paper clip up. When the paper clip is tossed on the floor it will land with the long end up or down. Estimate how many times it will be up in 100 tosses. Do the experiment. What is the experimental probability of "up"? Can you find the exact probability of "up"?

6. A traffic engineer observed that in one hour 26 cars, 12 buses, and 15 trucks drove down a street. What is the probability that the next vehicle to use the street is a car? That it is not a car?

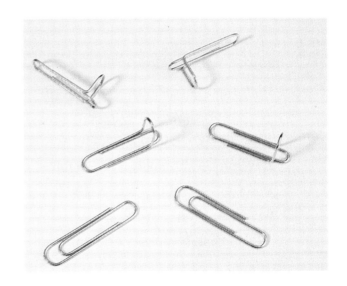

▶ **CALCULATOR**

7. Who had an experimental probability closest to the mathematical probability? What is their combined experimental probability? Use decimals and give answers to the nearest thousandth.

Juan : 237 heads in 459 tosses
Jessica : 293 heads in 560 tosses
Paulo : 171 heads in 354 tosses

Using Critical Thinking
Analyzing and Testing Formulas

Mr. Muddle, a disorganized experimenter, had written 3 formulas on a card.

"I can't remember which of the formulas I used to find an approximate value for π."

Digging through his desk, he pulled out a piece of paper. "Aha! Here is how to do the experiment. I drop a needle several times and record how many times it hits or misses the parallel lines. Then I enter this data into the correct formula, and out comes a number close to π. But I still don't know which formula! I'll just have to try to figure it out."

Mr. Muddle began dropping his needle on the lines and recorded the results.

Formulas
1. $\pi \approx$ Hits $\div$ Misses (?)
2. $\pi \approx$ Misses $\times$ Hits $\div 2 \times$ Drops (?)
3. $\pi \approx$ Drops $\times 2 \div$ Hits (?)

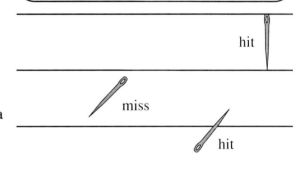

Hits	Misses
IIII IIII	IIII III

TALK ABOUT IT

1. What is Mr. Muddle trying to do?

2. What is meant by "hit", "miss" and "drop"?

3. Using the results shown in the table, which formula do you think is the correct one? Can you be sure? Explain.

Get a toothpick and try Mr. Muddle's experiment.

1. Draw six parallel lines as far apart as your toothpick.

2. Drop the toothpick at least 30 times; record hits and misses.

3. Use the correct formula. Is the result close to π?

4. Combine your total hits and misses with some classmates and see if you get a more accurate answer.

MIDCHAPTER REVIEW/QUIZ

Think about one spin of the spinner shown.
What are the chances of spinning each of the following.

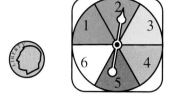

1. 2

2. a number less than 5

3. 7

4. a prime number

Complete the table of all outcomes of spinning the spinner and tossing a dime. Which outcomes show the events described?

5. an even number and heads

6. a number less than 10 and tails

7. a factor of 6 and tails

Spinner	Dime
1	H
1	T
2	H

Give the probability for each event if one marble is drawn from the box.

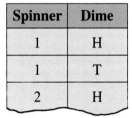

8. P (red)

9. P (white or green)

10. P (not blue)

11. P (yellow)

The table shows the results of 50 spins.

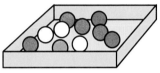

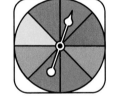

red	blue	yellow	green
‖‖‖ ‖‖‖ ‖‖‖ ‖‖‖	‖‖‖ ‖‖‖	‖‖‖ ‖	‖‖‖ ‖‖‖ ‖‖‖‖

12. What are the mathematical probabilities of spinning each color?

13. What are the experimental probabilities of spinning each color?

14. What is the experimental probability of spinning blue or yellow?

PROBLEM SOLVING

15. If two number cubes are tossed, how many outcomes are in the sample space?

16. If two number cubes are tossed, what outcomes are in the event of getting a sum of 5? A sum of 15?

17. Two number cubes were tossed 25 times. Ten of those times the sum was 7. What is Exp P (sum = 7)?

18. One number cube was tossed 25 times. Five of those tosses came up 4. How does Exp P (4) compare to P (4)?

Exploring Algebra
Inequalities

EXPLORE Study the Statements

People often make statements that compare numbers. We can use variables and inequality symbols to express these ideas.

A. Most 12-year-old boys weigh at least 55 lb.

B. Most 12-year-old girls are under 6 ft tall.

TALK ABOUT IT

1. Nelson is 12 years old. Do you think he weighs 55 pounds? 30 pounds? 65 pounds?

2. Marla is 12 years old. Is it likely that she is 5 ft tall? 6 ft tall?

Mathematical statements that compare or order numbers can be written with inequality symbols.

$<$ less than $>$ greater than
$\leq$ less than or equal to $\geq$ greater than or equal to

Some statements can be written as inequalities.

Let w be weight of a 12-year-old boy.
Statement **A** can be written: $w \geq 55$.

Inequalities can be drawn as graphs on a number line.

The filled-in dot means that
55 is a solution to $w \geq 55$.

Let h be the height of a 12-year-old girl.
Statement **B** can be written: $h < 6$.

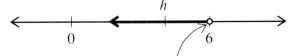

The empty dot means that
6 is not a solution to $h < 6$.

Write an inequality for each statement and graph it on a number line.

1. Children must be less than 2 years old to ride free on buses.

2. You can be fined for driving faster than 55 miles per hour.

Write an inequality for each statement.

1. Age A is greater than 14.

2. Weight w is less than 100 lb.

3. Height h is at least 5 ft.

4. Probability P is at most $\frac{1}{3}$.

5. Cost c will be at least $100.

6. Time t is less than 30 yr.

Write inequalities for these graphs.

7.

        0   21   x

8.

        0   79   y

9.

        0   t   21

10.

        0   R   3.5

11.

        0   k   781

12.

        0 1   L

Draw graphs for these inequalities.

13. $c \le 50$ **14.** $Z > 11$ **15.** $Q < 400$ **16.** $m \ge 100$ **17.** $F > \frac{4}{5}$

MATH REASONING Answer each question with **always, sometimes,** or **never.**

18. If $x < 10$, is $x < 8$?

19. If $x > 39$, is $x > 38$?

20. If $x \le 400$, is $x + 5 \le 400$?

21. If $x \ge 75$, is $x = 75$?

22. If $x < 50$, is $x \le 50$?

23. If $x > 900$, is $x > 900.56$?

PROBLEM SOLVING

24. In a group of more than 45 persons, the probability is more than $\frac{9}{10}$ that two of them have the same birth date. Write and graph two inequalities, one for the group size and one for the probability.

25. Science Data Bank Suppose someone gave you a random group of first and second generation pea plants. What fraction of them could you expect to have red blossoms?

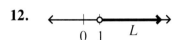

DATA BANK

► **USING CRITICAL THINKING   Support Your Conclusion**

26. Mrs. Willis traveled 200 miles and used a little less than 5 gallons of gasoline. What can you conclude about her gas mileage?

Tree Diagrams and Compound Events

LEARN ABOUT IT

Tree diagrams can help you solve some
probability problems.

EXPLORE Study the Situation

If a couple has an equal chance of having a
brown-eyed or a blue-eyed child, what are
the chances that all 3 of their children will
have brown eyes?

TALK ABOUT IT

1. If their first child has brown eyes, is
   their second child more likely to have
   blue eyes?

2. Are they as likely to have 3 children
   with blue eyes as 3 with brown eyes?

3. Estimate how often all 3 children in such
   a family will have brown eyes.

A **tree diagram** can show **compound
events**. A child will have either brown
(B) or blue (b) eyes, each with a
probability of $\frac{1}{2}$ or 0.5. The tree
shows there are 8 equally likely
outcomes, including BBB for 3
brown-eyed children.

$P(\text{BBB}) = 0.5 \times 0.5 \times 0.5$
$= 0.125$

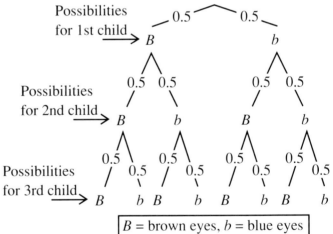

B = brown eyes, b = blue eyes

TRY IT OUT

Use the tree diagram above. Give the probability of each event.

1. $P(\text{BBb})$ 2. $P(\text{bBb})$ 3. $P(\text{BbB})$

4. $P(\text{one child is blue-eyed})$ 5. $P(\text{two are blue-eyed})$

354

In Exercises 1–7 use the tree diagram for 2 spins of the spinner.
Give the probability of each event. Treat Y as a consonant.

1. $P(X,X)$ 2. $P(Z,Y)$

3. P(both letters the same)

4. P(both letters different)

5. P(both letters consonants)

6. P(both letters vowels)

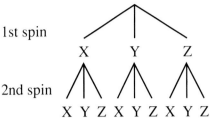

$P(X) = \frac{1}{3}$

$P(Y) = \frac{1}{3}$

$P(Z) = \frac{1}{3}$

In Exercises 7–10 use the tree diagram and spinner at right.

7. What is $P(A)$?   8. What is $P(B)$?

9. In 2 spins, what event is most likely?
   What is its probability?

10. In 2 spins, what event is least likely?
    What is its probability?

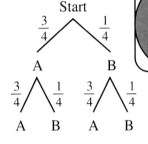

MATH REASONING

11. Draw a spinner with sections x and y. Assign probabilities to
    each so the probability of getting two x's on two spins is $\frac{16}{25}$.

PROBLEM SOLVING

12. Make a tree diagram for a family with 3
    children, showing boys (**X**) and girls (**O**).
    What is the probability of having 3 boys?

14. **Science Data Bank** Draw a tree
    diagram to show the different
    combinations of boys and girls that
    could occur in a family of 4 children.
    Relate this to row 4 of Pascal's Triangle.

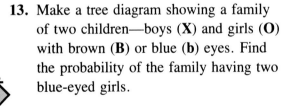

13. Make a tree diagram showing a family
    of two children—boys (**X**) and girls (**O**)
    with brown (**B**) or blue (**b**) eyes. Find
    the probability of the family having two
    blue-eyed girls.

▶ **USING CRITICAL THINKING**   Generalize

15. If you drew 4 cards from a deck of 52,
    which set of cards do you think you
    would be most likely to draw? Explain.

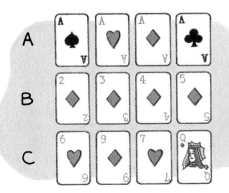

More Practice, page 539, set E

Problem Solving
Using the Strategies

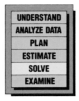

UNDERSTAND
ANALYZE DATA
PLAN
ESTIMATE
SOLVE
EXAMINE

Some problems can be solved using the strategy **Solve a Simpler Problem.**

Counting line segments when there are 10 dots is too difficult. Try solving simpler problems. **Make a Table** and **Look for patterns** to help you find a solution to the original problem.

How many different line segments can be made on a segment with 10 distinct points? (Note: Line segments of the same length but with a different position are considered different.)

First, I'll try 2 dots, then 3 dots, and so on.

dots	2	3	4	5	6	7	8	9	10
segments	1	3	6	10	15	21	28	36	45
pattern	—	2+1	3+3	4+6	5+10	6+15	7+21	8+28	9+36

I'll organize the data in a table and look for a pattern.

There are 45 distinct line segments on a segment with 10 distinct points.

TRY IT OUT

Solve. Think about a simpler problem to help.

1. There were 64 teams in a national college basketball tournament this year. When a team lost, it was eliminated from the tournament. How many games were needed to determine a national champion?

2. What is the greatest number of pieces a round pizza can be cut with 10 straight cuts? [Note: All cuts do not have to pass through the center of the pizza, and all pieces do not have to be the same size.]

3. A radio call-in show gives cash to the first caller to answer a question correctly. The amount depends on how many calls it takes to get a correct answer. If the first caller is correct, the prize is $3, the second is $6, the third is $12, and so on. How much would the twelfth caller win?

4. ROCK radio has 5 traffic reporters and 8 newscasters who work in traffic reporter-newscaster pairs. How many different pairs are possible for this station?

Solve. Use any strategy.

1. Americans buy 120,000 new radios each day. How many are bought in a year?

2. Brenda has 10 sweaters—3 cardigan and the rest pullovers. If she grabs one in a hurry, what is the probability that she will get a pullover?

3. Mrs. Kai bought a new clock radio. Use the ad to find the sale price before taxes.

Electronics Super Sales Bargains

20% off

	Regular Price
Clock Radios	69.95
VCRs	225.50
CD Players	279.50
Receivers	398.00

4. Rick bought 2 items at the electronics sale. Use the ad to find how many combinations of 2 items he could have bought.

5. ZYXW radio goes off the air from 1:00 a.m. to 5:30 a.m. every day. The rest of the time is shared equally among three disk jockeys. How long is each DJ on the air each day?

6. Jared wanted to mail a letter to a DJ. He knew the last three digits of the DJ's ZIP code were 3, 0, and 8, but he couldn't remember the order. So he guessed. What is the probability of Jared being right?

7. In Dallas there are 49 radio stations. There are 11 fewer AM stations than FM stations. How many stations of each kind are there.

8. **Developing a Plan** Carla had 16 cans of juice to share with the members of the electronics club. They sat around a table and passed the box of cans. Each person took 1 until none was left. Carla took the first and last can. How many members were seated around the table?

   a. List two or more strategies you think might help you solve this problem.

   b. Solve the problem.

   c. Look back at your solutions. What strategies did you use?

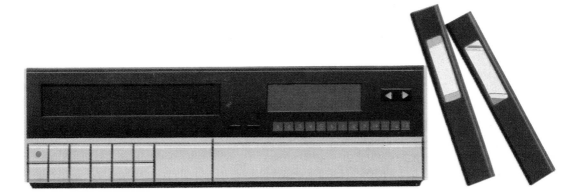

Expected Value

Outcomes of an experiment can have different numerical values, so we may want to know the *average numerical value* of the outcomes.

EXPLORE Do an Experiment

Work in groups. A school fair has a Wheel of Fortune which you get to spin 10 times. If you get a total of 40 or more, you win a prize. What are your chances of winning a prize? Make a spinner like the Wheel and see what happens in 10 spins.

WHEEL OF FORTUNE

GET 40 OR MORE POINTS IN 10 SPINS TO WIN A PRIZE

TALK ABOUT IT

1. Do you have an equal chance of winning and losing? Explain.

2. About how many times would you expect a 1 to come up in ten spins of the wheel? a 7 to come up?

We want to know the average number of points we can expect to get for each spin. This is called the **expected value**.

The expected value can be found by dividing the total points we expect to get in a number of spins by that number of spins.

$$\text{Expected value} = \frac{\text{Total points}}{\text{Number of spins}}$$

In **10** spins we expect:

4 ones	$\rightarrow$	**4 points**
3 fours	$\rightarrow$	**12 points**
2 sevens	$\rightarrow$	**14 points**
1 ten	$\rightarrow$	**10 points**
Total		**40 points**

$$\text{Expected value} = \frac{40}{10} = 4.0$$

The expected value for one spin is 4.0 points. So players can expect to get 4.0 × 10, or 40 points, and win more often than not.

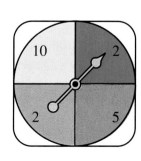

1. Suppose this spinner is spun 40 times. What is the expected value of each spin?

2. Does the expected value change if the spinner is spun 100 times?

Copy and complete the table for the spinner experiment.

	Outcome	Number expected in 60 spins	Total points
1.	1	30	
2.	5	20	
3.	10	10	
4.	Total of all spins		
5.	Expected Value		

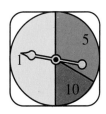

Spin the spinner 60 spins

$P(1) = \frac{1}{2}, P(5) = \frac{1}{3}, P(10) = \frac{1}{6}$

Find the expected value for each spinner experiment. Make a table like the one shown for Exercises 1–5.

6.

Spin 100 times

7.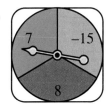

Spin 30 times

8.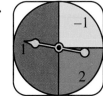

Spin 40 times

MATH REASONING

9. Make a spinner with outcomes 1, 2 and 3 so that the expected value in 100 spins is 1.7. (Hint: The expected number of each outcome is a multiple of 10.)

PROBLEM SOLVING

10. Hillary said that when a die is tossed, the expected value for each toss is 3. Explain why Hillary is either right or wrong.

MIXED REVIEW

11. $^-14 - {}^-20$

12. $^-14 + {}^-20$

13. $^-14 \cdot {}^-20$

14. $0 \cdot {}^-32$

15. $^-32 \div {}^-4$

16. $8 - \frac{3}{4}$

17. $4 \cdot \frac{1}{2}$

18. $4 \div \frac{1}{2}$

Data Collection and Analysis
Group Decision Making

UNDERSTAND
ANALYZE DATA
PLAN
ESTIMATE
SOLVE
EXAMINE

Doing a Questionnaire

Group Skill:
Explain and Summarize

How well do you think your taste in music matches your friends' taste? Do you have a tendency to like or dislike the same songs? You can make a questionnaire to help you see how well you agree.

Collecting Data

1. Work as a group to make a list of about 20 songs. They may be old or new, but they should be familiar to everyone. Suggest songs that you like and songs that you don't like very well, but don't let anyone know how you feel about the songs.

2. Cut your list apart so that each song is on a separate slip of paper. Put the slips into a bag or box and draw 10 to make your questionnaire. On the questionnaire ask for a rating from 1 to 20 for each song.

> *Questionnaire*
> Rate each song using a number from 1 to 20, where 1 means "strongly dislike" and 20 means "like very much."
>
> | | Rating |
> |---|---|
> | 1. Be Bop Tonight | _____ |
> | 2. Sweet Baby | _____ |
> | 3. Time | _____ |
> | 4. .... | _____ |
> | 5. | |

3. Test the questionnaire to see if it needs revision. Make a copy for each person in your group and anyone else with whom you want to compare song likes and dislikes.

4. Have each person in your group fill out the questionnaire privately.

5. With a partner from your group, make a scattergram using the data from your questionnaires. Write your names along the scales of the scattergram. Plot a point for each question on the questionnaire. Each point represents an ordered pair showing how the two of you rated the song.

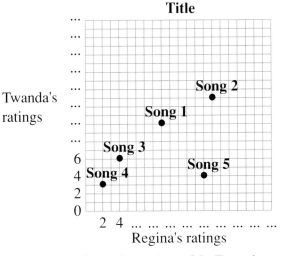

Title

Twanda's ratings

Song 2

Song 1

Song 3

Song 4   Song 5

6
4
2
0

2 4 ... ...

Regina's ratings

Regina gave Song 1 a rating of 9; Twanda gave it a rating of 10.

6. Choose a different partner and make another scattergram.

7. Examine the scattergrams made in your group. Discuss how they are similar and how they are different.

8. How would the scattergram look if you and your partner agreed exactly on every question? Explain.

9. Which graphs in your group seem to show a lot of agreement between partners? very little agreement between partners? Be prepared to tell the rest of the class how you drew these conclusions.

WRAP UP

Probability Word Hunt

What word or term used in this chapter matches the description below.

1. mathematical statements that compare numbers that are not equal

2. the ratio of the number of outcomes in an event to the total number of outcomes

3. describes each outcome of an experiment done with a fair coin

4. the list of all possible outcomes for an experiment

5. the average numerical value of the outcome of an experiment

6. a series of outcomes of an experiment

7. the ratio of the number of times an event occurs to the number of trials

8. any outcome or combination of outcomes of an experiment

9. a special type of drawing or picture that can show a series of outcomes to an experiment

Sometimes, Always, Never

Which word should go in the blank, *sometimes, always,* or *never*? Explain your choice.

10. The probability of an event that *may* occur is __?__ expressed as a whole number.

11. In an experiment, all possible outcomes are __?__ equally likely.

12. The experimental probability of an event is __?__ the same as the mathematical probability of an event.

13. The probability of a compound event __?__ equals the sum of the probabilities of each part of the event.

Project

Sometimes statistics are presented in ways that are misleading.

Find an example of misleading statistics in a newspaper or magazine. How can you tell the statistics are misleading? Present the same data in a way that is NOT misleading.

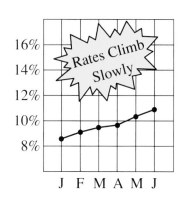

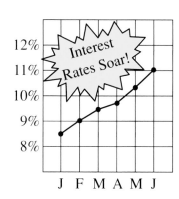

CHAPTER REVIEW/TEST

Part 1   Understanding

True or false?

1. Outcomes of an experiment are always equally likely.

2. The probability of an event is always less than 1.

3. The value of π is closest to

    A $23 \div 7$ **B** $7 \times 23 \div 2 \times 30$

4. The expected value for one spin of spinner A is

    A 10   **B** $\frac{1}{4}$ **C** $2\frac{1}{2}$

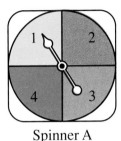
Spinner A

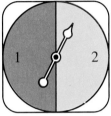
Spinner B

Part 2   Skills

5. List the sample space of all outcomes if spinners A and B are spun.

6. List all the outcomes for spinning a single 2.

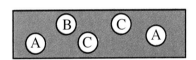

Use the experiment of drawing one chip from this box.

7. P(B) = ___?___   **8.** P(D) = ___?___   **9.** P(not A) = ___?___   **10.** P(A or C) = ___?___

11. Out of 50 draws, A is drawn 35 times. What does Exp P(A) equal?

12. Write and graph an inequality for the statement "Price p is more than $5."

Part 3   Applications

13. One day, Todd sold 12 records, 47 tapes, and 28 CDs. Find the probability that the first item he will sell the next day is a CD, that it is not a CD.

14. Students may select pizza, yogurt, or a sandwich, plus milk or juice. Draw a tree diagram of the lunches available. Find the probability of selecting pizza with milk or juice.

15. There are 12 men, 14 women, and 9 children on a bus. To find the probability that the next person to get on would be a woman, you could use the same strategy as what other problem on this page? Find the probability.

16. Challenge Maria has homework at least 3 out of 5 days. Draw a graph indicating the probability of Maria's having homework today.

ENRICHMENT
Simulating a Probability Problem

Robin Hood is returning from Nottingham to Sherwood Forest. The map shows the different routes he can take. The Sheriff of Nottingham is trying to catch Robin at one of the 4 bridges. The probability that Robin will find an open bridge is $\frac{1}{2}$. What is the probability that Robin will find an open route to Sherwood?

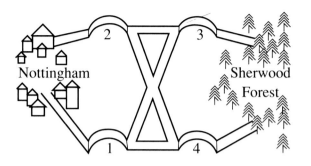

You can **simulate** or **model** the problem this way.

- Use a **random digit generator** to get a list of digits 0 to 9. Let even digits = open bridge and odd digits = closed bridge.
- Keep a record of open and closed bridges. Then after each trial use the map to decide if there is an open route for Robin Hood.

Trial 1: 2, 5, 1, 3
Trial 2: 7, 4, 4, 6

Trial	Bridge 1	Bridge 2	Bridge 3	Bridge 4	Open Route?
1	Open	Blocked	Blocked	Blocked	No
2	Blocked	Open	Open	Open	Yes

1. Try the simulation of the problem for 20 trials. How many times was there an open route?

2. What is the experimental probability of an open route?

    $\text{Exp. } P(\text{Open}) = \dfrac{\text{No. of open routes}}{\text{No. of trials}}$

3. Combine your results for 20 trials with those of your classmates. What is the probability of an open route using the combined trials?

4. Is Robin Hood more likely to find an open route to Sherwood Forest or is he more likely to find a blocked route?

CUMULATIVE REVIEW

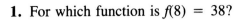

1. For which function is $f(8) = 38$?

   A $f(x) = 3x + 12$ **B** $f(x) = 50 - 5x$

   C $f(x) = 3(x + 4)$ **D** $f(x) = 7x - 18$

2. Which fraction expresses $\frac{3}{8}\%$?

   A $\frac{3}{800}$ **B** $\frac{3}{80}$ **C** $\frac{3}{8,000}$ **D** $\frac{300}{8}$

3. Which percent expresses 0.456?

   A $0.45\frac{3}{5}\%$ **B** $4.5\frac{3}{5}\%$

   C $45\frac{3}{5}\%$ **D** $0.045\frac{3}{5}\%$

4. What is the total amount to be paid back on a loan of $3,200 for 18 months at 17% simple interest?

   A $3,744   **B** $12,992

   C $4,016   **D** $544

5. What percent of 5 is 9?

   A 55%   **B** 180%

   C 18%   **D** 1.8%

6. Which is the sale price?
Regular Price: $58.50
Discount percent: 25%

   A $43.87   **B** $73.13

   C $14.63   **D** $33.50

7. What is the number of degrees in a central angle for a sector of 25%?

   A 100°   **B** 90°

   C 28°   **D** not given

8. Which integer is suggested by this situation: a discount of $55?

   A 55   **B** 0   **C** $^-$55   **D** $^-$45

9. Name the property used.
$$10 \cdot (5 + {}^-1) = (10 \cdot 5) + (10 \cdot {}^-1)$$

   A associative   **B** commutative

   C one   **D** distributive

10. Find the sum.
$^-8 + {}^-25$

   A $^-17$ **B** $^-33$

   C 17   **D** 33

11. Subtract.
$^-20 - {}^-7$

   A $^-27$ **B** 27

   C $^-13$ **D** 13

12. Multiply.
$^-12 \cdot {}^-4$

   A $^-48$ **B** 16

   C $^-16$ **D** 48

13. The low temperature for one day in January was $^-12$°F. The high temperature for that day was 22°F. What was the mean or average temperature that day?

   A 10°F   **B** 34°F

   C 17°F   **D** 5°F

14. The first 50 students to arrive at the game came in groups of 3 and 4. How many groups of each size were there? Which is *not* a possible answer?

   A 2 groups of 3; 11 groups of 4

   B 6 groups of 3; 8 groups of 4

   C 13 groups of 3; 4 groups of 4

   D 14 groups of 3; 2 groups of 4

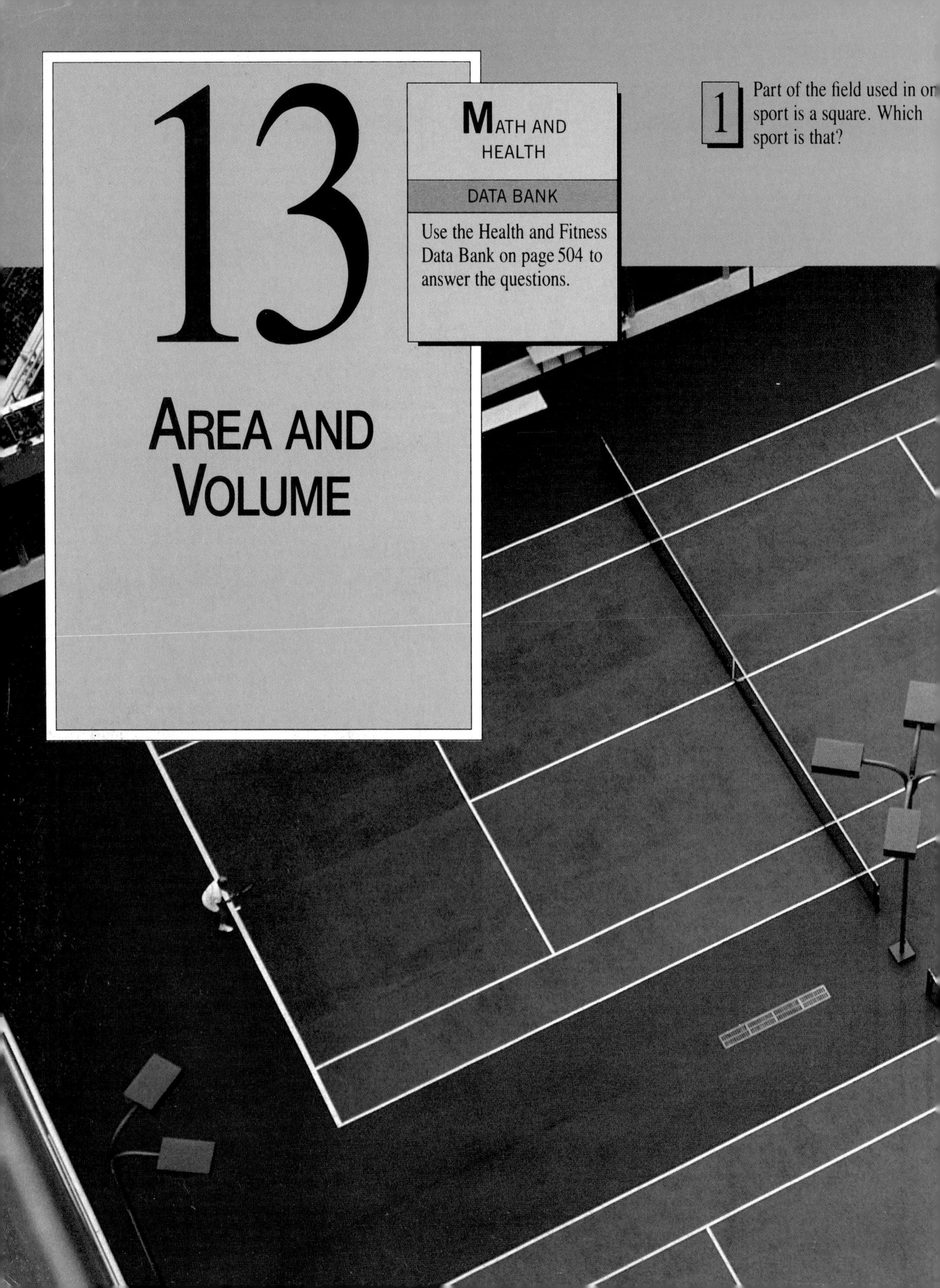

13

AREA AND VOLUME

MATH AND HEALTH

DATA BANK

Use the Health and Fitness Data Bank on page 504 to answer the questions.

1 Part of the field used in one sport is a square. Which sport is that?

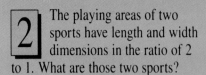
2 The playing areas of two sports have length and width dimensions in the ratio of 2 to 1. What are those two sports?

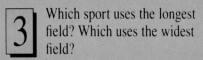
3 Which sport uses the longest field? Which uses the widest field?

4 Using Critical Thinking
Many sports require the use of a ball. Determine the ratio of each ball's circumference to its diameter as a decimal. What do you notice about these ratios? Why are they so close to each other? Why aren't they equal?

Exploring the Concept of Area

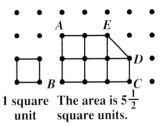

1 square unit

The area is $5\frac{1}{2}$ square units.

LEARN ABOUT IT

The **area** of a figure is the number of square units needed to cover the figure. Polygon *ABCDE* has an area of $5\frac{1}{2}$ square units.

EXPLORE Study the Information

Figure F at the right has been divided into regions that are rectangles or triangles. Trace Figure F on dot paper. Divide Figure F into the least possible number of rectangular and triangular regions. How many regions did you make?

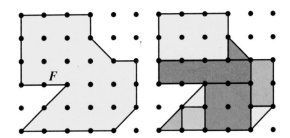

TALK ABOUT IT

1. Find the area of each rectangle that you indicated for Figure F.

2. Find the area of each triangle that you indicated for Figure F.

3. What is the total area of Figure F?

Here are two principles you can use to find the areas of some figures.

HALF-RECTANGLE PRINCIPLE The area of a triangle is half the area of a rectangle. Look at the area of the shaded triangles.

ADDITION PRINCIPLE If you divide an irregular figure into rectangles and triangles, you can find the area of the figure by adding the areas of the rectangles and triangles.

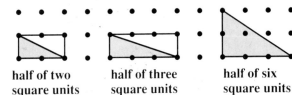

half of two square units

half of three square units

half of six square units

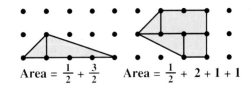

Area $= \frac{1}{2} + \frac{3}{2}$

Area $= \frac{1}{2} + 2 + 1 + 1$

TRY IT OUT

Find the areas of these figures.

1.
2.
3.
4.
5.

Find the area of each figure and tell which principle or
principles you used.

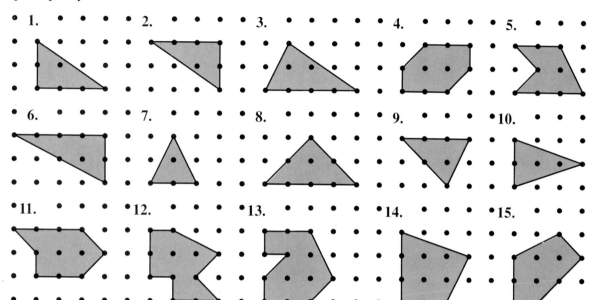

1. 2. 3. 4. 5.

6. 7. 8. 9. 10.

11. 12. 13. 14. 15.

MATH REASONING

16. Estimate. The area of this figure is slightly more than how
    many square units?

17. Estimate. The area of this figure is slightly more than how
    many square units?

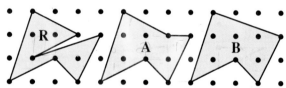

PROBLEM SOLVING

18. Which simpler region, A or B, would
    give a better estimate for the area of
    Figure R? Estimate the area of R.

▶ **ALGEBRA**

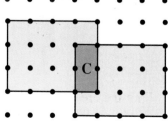

19. The area of the purple region on the right is 22 units^2. x is
    the area of each of the large rectangles, and y is the area of
    the rectangle C common to the two large rectangles. Which
    of these equations is true?

    A $2x + y = 22$ **B** $2x - y = 22$ **C** $x + y = 22$

More Practice, page 540, set B

Area of Rectangles and Parallelograms

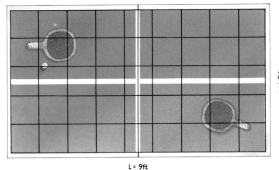

L = 9ft

w = 5ft

LEARN ABOUT IT

EXPLORE Study the Diagram

The Pep Club wants to buy a game table for the school, but the table must have an area less than 50 square feet.

TALK ABOUT IT

1. What is the length of the table? What is the width?

2. Find the product, **length × width**. Then find the area of the table by counting the squares. How do the two numbers compare?

3. Is this table within the school's size restrictions?

Area of rectangle = length × width

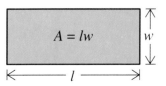

$A = lw$

w

l

A parallelogram has a **base** and a **height**.

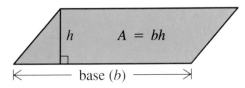

h $A = bh$

base (b)

Areas are equal

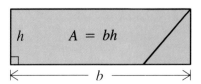

h $A = bh$

b

Area of a parallelogram = base × height

Find the area of this parallelogram.

$A = bh$
$A = 5 \times 4 = 20$

The area of the parallelogram is 20 cm².

4 cm

5 cm

TRY IT OUT

Find the area of each rectangle or parallelogram.

1. 4 cm

8 cm

2. 5 cm

6 cm

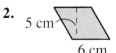

3. 4 cm

4 cm

4. 5 cm

6.5 cm

Find the area of each rectangle.

1. $l = 12$ cm
   $w = 8$ cm

2. $l = 25$ m
   $w = 10$ m

3. $l = 3.8$ m
   $w = 2.0$ m

4. $l = 22$ mm
   $w = 9$ mm

5. $l = 6.5$
   $w = 2.8$ cm

6. $l = 30$ cm
   $w = 30$ cm

7. $l = 7.4$ m
   $w = 0.5$ m

8. $l = 2.8$ km
   $w = 1.6$ km

Find the area of each parallelogram.

9. $b = 15$ cm
   $h = 8$ cm

10. $b = 24$
    $h = 12$ cm

11. $b = 3.1$ m
    $h = 2.0$ m

12. $b = 32$
    $h = 9$ m

13. $b = 4.9$ cm
    $h = 3.0$ cm

14. $b = 16.8$ m
    $h = 5.2$ m

15. $b = 18$ cm
    $h = 12$ cm

16. $b = 32.5$ m
    $h = 11.7$ m

17. Find the area of a rectangle 42 feet long and 28 feet wide.

18. Find the area of a parallelogram with a base of 1.3 in. and a height of 0.4 in.

APPLY

MATH REASONING

19. Draw a rectangle equal in area to a 6×15 rectangle, but not equal in perimeter to a 6×15 rectangle.

20. Draw a rectangle equal in perimeter to a 10×16 rectangle, but not equal in area to a 10×16 rectangle.

PROBLEM SOLVING

21. Plastic sheeting to cover a swimming pool costs $1.50 per square yard. How much will it cost the YMCA to cover its pool which is 25 by 12 yards?

DATA BANK

22. **Health and Fitness Data Bank** The triangular part of home plate has an area of $72\frac{1}{4}$ in^2. Compare the total area of home plate with the area of one of the other bases. Which is larger?

▶ MENTAL MATH

Use the method shown at the right to calculate mentally the area of each parallelogram.

 48 in.   6 in.

23. $b = 72$ in.
    $h = 12$ in.

24. $b = 48$ in.
    $h = 3$ in.

25. $b = 12$ ft
    $h = 2$ yd

Think: 6 in. × 48 in.
= $\frac{1}{2}$ ft × 4
= 2 ft^2

More Practice, page 540, set C

Area of Triangles and Trapezoids

EXPLORE **Discover a Relationship**

Make two exact copies of the triangle and
two exact copies of the trapezoid shown at
the right. Label them as shown. Then place
the two triangles together to form a
parallelogram. Place the two trapezoids
together to form a parallelogram.

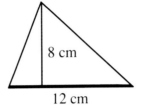

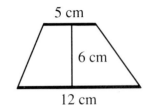

5 cm

8 cm

6 cm

12 cm

12 cm

TALK ABOUT IT

1. Using the two triangles, how many
   different parallelograms can you form?
   How many of these have a side
   12 cm long?

2. Use the two trapezoids to form a
   parallelogram. How long is the side of
   the parallelogram?

The area of the triangle is $\frac{1}{2}$ the area of
the parallelogram.

The area of the trapezoid is $\frac{1}{2}$ the area of
the parallelogram.

$h = 8$ cm

$b = 12$ cm

$A = \frac{1}{2}bh$

$A = \frac{1}{2} \times 8 \times 12 = 48$

The area of the triangle is 48 cm^2.

$h = 6$ cm

$b_1 = 5$cm

$b_2 = 12$ cm

$A = \frac{1}{2} h(b_1 + b_2)$

$A = \frac{1}{2} \times 6(5 + 12) = 51$

The area of the trapezoid is 51 cm^2.

Find the area of each triangle or trapezoid.

1. 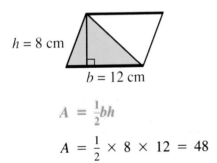 $h = 9$ cm

   $b = 16$ cm

2. $h = 8$ cm
   $b = 16$ cm

3. 12.7 cm
   8 cm
   16.1 cm

4. $b = 7$ cm
   $h = 9$ cm

5. $b = 2.7$ cm
   $h = 0.08$ cm

6. $b_1 = 7.2$ dm
   $b_2 = 5$ dm $\quad h = 4$ dm

Find the area of each triangle or trapezoid.

1.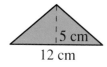
5 cm
12 cm

2.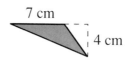
7 cm
4 cm

3.
15 m
12 m

4. $b = 25$ m $h = 10$ m

5. $b = 23$ cm $h = 9$ cm

6. $b = 48$ cm $h = 73$ cm

7.
4.0 cm
5 cm
6.4 cm

8.
10 m
6 m
9 m

9.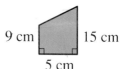
9 cm   15 cm
5 cm

10. $b_1 = 24$ m $b_2 = 5$ m
$h = 7$ m

11. $b_1 = 24$ cm $b_2 = 48$ cm
$h = 12$ cm

12. $b_1 = 9.6$ cm $b_2 = 5$ cm
$h = 3.2$ cm

MATH REASONING Find the areas. If needed data are missing, write "missing data."

13.
15 cm
8 cm

14.
6 cm
5 cm 4 cm
9 cm

15.
5.5 cm   5 cm
11 cm

PROBLEM SOLVING

16. Two irregularly shaped building lots are for sale. Lot A costs $22,000. Lot B costs $19,800. Which lot costs less per square foot?

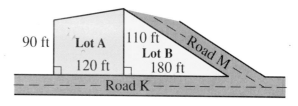

90 ft Lot A 110 ft Lot B Road M
120 ft 180 ft
Road K

Find the answers.

17. $^-18 + {^-21}$

18. $100 - {^-15}$

19. $25 \cdot {^-5}$

20. $^-32 - 14$

21. $^-21 \cdot {^-10}$

22. $40 \div {^-20}$

23. $^-24 - {^-16}$

24. $^-21 \cdot 0 \div 16$

Give the probability for each event of drawing a sock from a drawer containing 4 blue socks, 2 white socks, and 5 red socks.

25. 1 blue sock

26. 1 red sock

27. a red or blue sock

More Practice, page 540, set D

Area of Circles

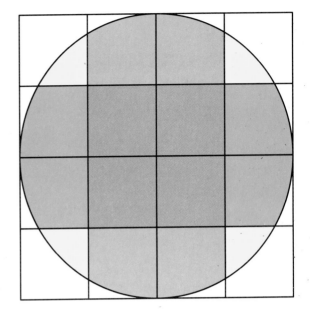

LEARN ABOUT IT

A **circle** is a set of points in the plane that are an equal distance from a given point called the **center**.

EXPLORE Study the Diagram The circular table shown at the right is covered by a grid, with each square representing one square foot of area. Estimate the area of the table.

TALK ABOUT IT

1. How many complete squares colored ▨ are there?

2. About how many square are ☐ ? ▨ ?

3. Explain why an estimate of 16 ft^2 is not reasonable.

If the grid covering the table is cut apart, the squares can be rearranged to form slightly more than three 2 × 2 square grids.

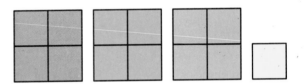

The squares covering a circle with radius r can be rearranged to form slightly more than three grids, each measuring $r \times r$. This suggests the formula used to find the area of a circle.

   Area of a circle = π × square of radius

$A = \pi r^2$ ⟨Use 3.14 for π.⟩ $A = 3.14 \times 2^2$ $A = 3.14 \times 4$ $A = 12.56$

The area of the circle is about 12.56 ft^2.

TRY IT OUT

Find the approximate area of each circle. Use 3.14 for π.

1. $r = 8$ cm   **2.** $r = 0.75$ cm   **3.** $r = 0.5$ cm   **4.** $r = 12$ cm

Find the approximate area of each circle. Use 3.14 for π. You may want to use your calculator.

1. $r = 6$ cm

2. $d = 20$ mm

3. $r = 0.9$ cm

4. $r = 12$ cm

5. $d = 100$ m

6. $r = 0.1$ cm

7. $r = 2$ cm

8. $d = 8$ cm

9. $r = 11$ cm

10. $r = 1$ m

11. $r = 1.5$ m

12. $d = 4.4$ m

13. $d = 0.6$ cm

14. $r = 75$ cm

15. $d = 9$ cm

16. Find the approximate area of a circle whose diameter is 25 cm.

17. Find the approximate area of a semicircle whose radius is 3.2 cm.

APPLY

<u>MATH REASONING</u> Round your answer to the nearest hundredth.

18. Find the area of a circle with diameter 35.2 cm.

19. A circle has a circumference of 100 m. Find its area.

PROBLEM SOLVING

20. Five people are seated at a round table that is 42 in. in diameter. How much area is there at the table for each person?

42 in.

21. Six people are seated at a 36-in. by 52-in. rectangular table. Five people are seated at the table from problem 20. Which table is more crowded? Explain.

▶ **CALCULATOR**

22. The compass center is at 0. At how many units should the compass opening be set to draw a circle with an area of approximately 80 square units?

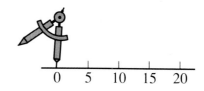

More Practice, page 540, set E

Area of Irregular Shaped Figures

You may be able to find the area of an irregular shaped figure by combining several methods that you know.

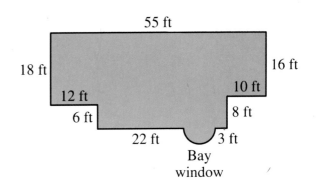

EXPLORE **Study the Diagram**

Suppose that you want to build a house with this shape and you need to know how many square feet of floor space there will be.

TALK ABOUT IT

1. What is the diameter of the bay window?

2. Why is 16 × 55 not a reasonable estimate of the area of the house?

3. Which product is the best estimate of the area?
   a) 18 × 55   b) 24 × 55   c) 28 × 55

Here is how to find the exact area of the figure above.

Area of rectangle A $18 \times 12 = 216 \text{ ft}^2$

Area of rectangle B $24 \times 33 = 792 \text{ ft}^2$

Area of semicircle D $\frac{1}{2} \times 3.14 \times 4^2$

$\qquad\qquad\qquad\quad = 25.12 \text{ ft}^2$

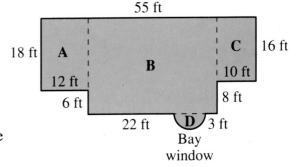

Add the areas of A, B, C, and D.
$216 + 792 + 160 + 25.12 = 1193.12$ The area of the figure is 1193.12 ft^2.

Find the area of these figures. All lengths are in centimeters.

1.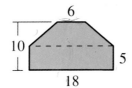

2.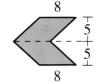

3.

Find the areas of these figures. All lengths are in meters.

1.

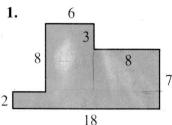

2.

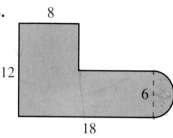

3.

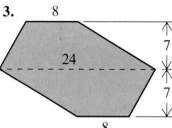

4.

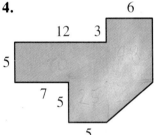

5.

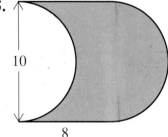

6.

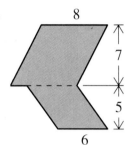

APPLY

MATH REASONING

7. Estimate the area of Figure **A** by thinking of it as a rectangle. Is your estimate high or low?

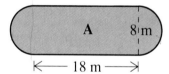

PROBLEM SOLVING

8. The diagram at the right shows the stage for a theater in the round. The stage is going to be resurfaced with a material that costs $3.75 per square foot. How much will the resurfacing cost?

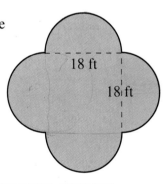

9. **Health and Fitness Data Bank** Grass seed costs $1.45 per pound. One pound is needed to seed 500 square feet. How much does it cost to plant grass on a football field?

DATA BANK

▶ **ESTIMATION**

10. These four lakes are among the world's top ten in area. Use estimation to rank these lakes in order from largest to smallest.

Lake Superior

Lake Huron

Lake Malawi

Lake Great Bear

Problem Solving
Using the Strategies

| UNDERSTAND |
| ANALYZE DATA |
| PLAN |
| ESTIMATE |
| SOLVE |
| EXAMINE |

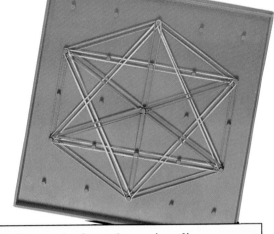

LEARN ABOUT IT

To solve some problems, you may find it helpful to use more than one strategy. To solve this problem you can **Draw a Picture**, **Solve a Simpler Problem**, **Make a Table**, and **Look for a Pattern**.

> A **diagonal** of a polygon is a line segment that joins any 2 non-adjacent verticles. How many diagonals does a 10-sided polygon have?

> You can begin with simpler problems and draw a picture.

3 sides
0 diagonals

4 sides
2 diagonals

> Then you can make a table of the number of sides and the number of diagonals and look for a pattern.

Number of Sides	Number of Diagonals
3	0
4	2
5	5
6	9
7	14
8	20
9	27
10	35

+2, +3, +4

5 sides
5 diagonals

6 sides
9 diagonals

A 10-sided polygon has 35 diagonals.

TRY IT OUT

1. Oblong numbers are numbers that can be modeled by a rectangular array with the length one unit more than the width. The first oblong number is 2. Find the 8th oblong number.

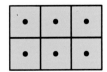

2. How many different squares are there in the figure below?

378

Solve. Use any problem solving strategy.

<table>
<tr><th colspan="2">Some Strategies</th></tr>
</table>

Some Strategies	
Act Out	Solve a Simpler Problem
Use Objects	Make an Organized List
Choose an Operation	Work Backward
Draw a Picture	Look for a Pattern
Guess and Check	Use Logical Reasoning
Make a Table	Write an Equation

1. A basketball hoop has an inside diameter of 18 inches. The hoop itself is $\frac{5}{8}$ inches in diameter. Find the area inside the hoop.

2. Barraca spent $14.50 to have a print framed for his room. Use the diagram below to find the area of the framed print.

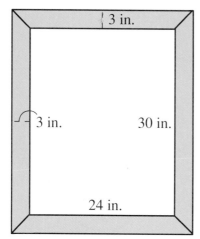

3 in.

3 in.   30 in.

24 in.

3. There are two different rectangles whose sides are integers and whose area and perimeter are the same. Find the dimensions.

4. Mai was the first person to arrive at a basketball game. Each group that arrived after Mai had 2 more people than the group before. After the 15th group went in, how many people were at the game?

5. Sean and Leslie were playing a game with marbles. They played two rounds and each of them won one round. The winner of each round had to double the loser's marbles. At the end of 2 rounds they each had 12 marbles. How many marbles did each have in the beginning?

6. The members of the rock climbing club always climb in pairs. There are 36 different pairs possible. How many members are in the club?

7. Framing material is sold by the inch. Use the diagram at the left to find out how many inches of framing material were needed.

8. A doubles tennis court is 78 feet long and 36 feet wide. A singles court is the same length but 9 feet narrower. How much more area does a doubles court have than a singles court?

Using Critical Thinking

Jon and Marion were arranging tables for a party. They had small square tables that would seat one person on a side. If they used four tables, they found there were two possibilities for the number of people that could be seated, 10 people or 8 people.

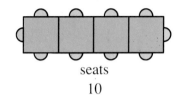

seats
10

They had 16 same-size square tables. They wanted to know the different numbers of people that could be seated by arranging these 16 tables. [Note: Each table must be side by side with at least one other table. Arrangements with openings in the middle with no way to get there do not count.]

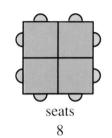

seats
8

TALK ABOUT IT

1. What are Jon and Marion trying to do?

2. Can you give another arrangement of 4 tables that also seats 10 people?

3. What are the different numbers of people that can be seated with 16 tables.

4. What arrangement will always give the largest number of people? Why?

5. Do you notice any patterns in the number of people that can be seated?

TRY IT OUT

Use what you learned above to answer these questions.

1. If a figure has a given area, is the perimeter of that figure always the same? Explain.

2. Suppose a figure has a perimeter of 10 in. Is the area of the figure fixed or can it vary? Use examples to convince a classmate your answer is correct.

3. Suppose you have a 2 ft by 8 ft rectangle. What is the effect of doubling the dimensions of each side on the area of the figure? Do you think this is true for all plane figures? Explain.

Find the area of each figure. Use $\pi = 3.14$ when needed.

1.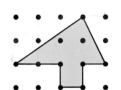

2.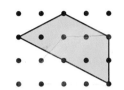

3. rectangle
$l = 15; w = 12$ cm

4. parallelogram
$l = 8.4$ m; $w = 3.5$ m

5.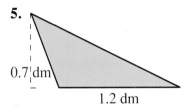
0.7 dm
1.2 dm

6.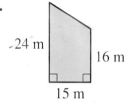
24 m
16 m
15 m

7. circle
radius $= 2.5$ m

8. circle
diameter $= 100$ cm

9.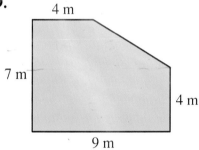
4 m
7 m
4 m
9 m

10.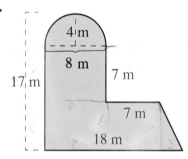
4 m
8 m
17 m
7 m
7 m
18 m

PROBLEM SOLVING

Use the data from the diagrams to answer the following.

11. Is the area of $\triangle ABC$ 5 units^2 or 6 units^2? Explain

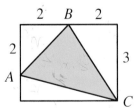
2   B   2
2   3
A
C

12. Find more than one way to calculate the area of $\triangle XYZ$.

y
6   8
4.8
x   3.6   6.4   z

13. What will it cost to tile the square patio if tiles for the area of the circle costs $30 per square meter and the tiles for the surrounding area cost $20 per square meter?

10 m

Exploring Algebra
Solving a Formula for a Given Variable

LEARN ABOUT IT

EXPLORE **Study the Information**

Shirley wanted to show her class the way to tell how far away a lightning flash is by counting the seconds from the flash until the sound of thunder. The only formula she could find is shown on her paper at the right.

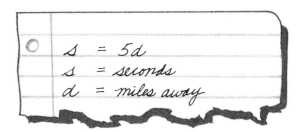

$$s = 5d$$
$$s = seconds$$
$$d = miles\ away$$

TALK ABOUT IT

1. How many seconds does it take for a lightning flash that is 2 miles away to be heard 3 miles away?

2. Why is the formula that Shirley is using not exactly what she needs to accomplish her purpose?

A formula may need to be rewritten to be useful in a certain situation. You can rewrite a formula to get a particular variable alone. Use the same techniques that you use for solving an equation. Here is an example:

A rectangle with an area of 200 and a length of 62.5 has what width?

Strategy: Rewrite $A = lw$ so w is isolated. (area = length × width)

$$\frac{A}{l} = \frac{lw}{l} \quad \text{so} \quad \frac{A}{l} = w$$

Evaluate the new formula for $A = 200$, $l = 62.5$.

$$w = \frac{200}{62.5}$$
$$w = 32.5$$

TRY IT OUT

Solve the formula for the area of a triangle $A = \frac{1}{2}bh$ for h. Find the height of a triangle with area 36 and base 9.

Solve each area formula for the missing dimension. Then find the missing dimension.

1.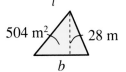
1,936 m² — 44 m
l

2.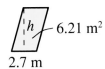
0.63 mm² — *w*
0.9 mm

3.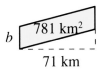
30.15 km² — 6.0 km
b

4.
504 m² — 28 m
b

5.
h — 297.5 cm²
17 cm

6.
1.125 km² — 1.5 km
b

7.
360 cm² — 24 cm
b

8.
h — 6.21 m²
2.7 m

9.
b — 781 km²
71 km

MATH REASONING

C = 28.27 in.
C = 37.7 in.
C = 50.27 in.

10. Rewrite the formula for circumference of a circle to get *r* alone. Use your calculator to find the radius of each pizza.

PROBLEM SOLVING

11. Students in seventh grade need at least 650 cm² of space at a school desk. What is the length of a rectangular desk with this area if the width is 26 cm?

12. What are the dimensions (length and width) necessary for the "take home boxes" for the pizzas in problem 10?

13. Data Hunt Find the dimensions of the largest pizza ever cooked. Write a paragraph that relates the size of the pizza to a familiar object about the same size.

▶ **ESTIMATION**

14. Estimate the square feet of material needed to make the sail of a windsurfer. Use the picture at the right to help you make an estimate.

Surface Area of Prisms and Cylinders

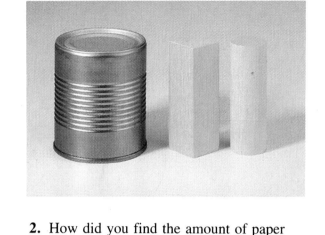

LEARN ABOUT IT

EXPLORE **Measure Some Objects**

Work with a partner. Find a cylinder and a prism. Suppose you had to cover each of these with contact paper. What is the least amount of paper you would need for each?

TALK ABOUT IT

1. How did you find the amount of paper needed for the prism?

2. How did you find the amount of paper needed for the cylinder?

3. Can you describe how you might find the amount of paper needed to cover any prism or cylinder?

Imagine cutting a prism and cylinder apart and laying them flat. The **surface area** of a figure is the sum of the areas of all these plane regions.

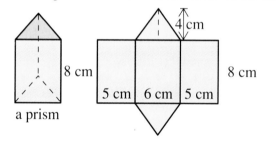

a prism

Area of each $\triangle$ = $\frac{1}{2} \times 6 \times 4 = 12$ cm^2

Area of one $\square$ = $8 \times 6 = 48$ cm^2

Area of two $\square$ = $8 \times 5 = 40$ cm^2

Surface area =
$(2 \times 12) + 48 + (2 \times 40) = 152$ cm^2

a cylinder

Area of each circle =
$\pi \times 2^2 \approx 12.56$

Area of the rectangle =
$2\pi \times 2 \times 8 \approx 100.48$

Surface area =
$2 \times 12.56 + 100.48 = 125.6$ cm^2

TRY IT OUT

Find the surface area of each space figure.

1.
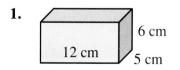
6 cm
12 cm
5 cm

2.
5 cm
6 cm

3.
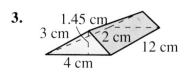
1.45 cm
3 cm
2 cm
12 cm
4 cm

Find the total surface area of each solid figure. Use a calculator.

1.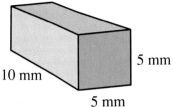

5 mm
10 mm
5 mm

2.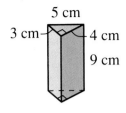

5 cm
3 cm 4 cm
9 cm

3.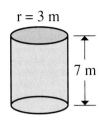

r = 3 m
7 m

4.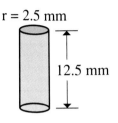

r = 2.5 mm
12.5 mm

5.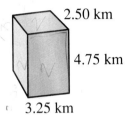

2.50 km
4.75 km
3.25 km

6.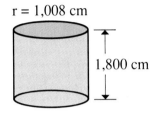

r = 1,008 cm
1,800 cm

APPLY

MATH REASONING The surface area of a box with length (*l*),
width (*w*), and height (*h*) is given by the formula
Surface Area = 2 (*lw* + *lh* + *wh*).

Use this formula to find the surface area of boxes with
these dimensions.

7. $l = 9$ cm
$w = 2.5$ cm
$h = 7$ cm

8. $l = 2$ cm
$w = 1.5$ cm
$h = 3$ cm

9. $l = 3.5$ cm
$w = 2$ cm
$h = 6$ cm

PROBLEM SOLVING

10. What is the surface area of a mailing
carton that is 18 cm long, 12 cm high,
and 5 cm wide?

11. A cylindrical can has a radius of 3 in.
and a height of 12 in. How many square
inches of paper are needed for the
label?

▶ **USING CRITICAL THINKING Discover a Rule**

12. A cube is a prism whose faces are all squares. Complete
the table below and devise a rule that tells the surface area
of a cube with an edge length of *k* units.

length of edge	1	2	3	4	5	. . .	k
surface area	6 × 1	6 × 4	6 × 9	?	?	. . .	?

1 cm

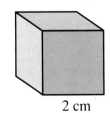
2 cm

More Practice, page 541, set B

Exploring the Concept of Volume

EXPLORE Study the Diagram

Building **A** has been built with 9 cubes and building **B** has been built with 6 cubes. Build a building using 12 cubes. Then build a building using 5 cubes.

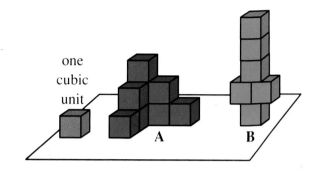

one cubic unit

A   B

TALK ABOUT IT

1. How many different buildings can you build using 12 cubes? Do you think you can build one building, five buildings, or more than five?

2. Which building uses the largest amount of space, building **A** or **B**?

3. Of building **A**, building **B**, and the two buildings you built, which one uses the most space? Which uses the least space? Explain.

4. If you move one cube in your 12 cube building so that it becomes taller, have you increased the amount of space used? Explain.

A unit of volume is a cube with one unit on each edge. It is called a **cubic unit** (unit^3). The **volume** of a space figure is the number of cubic units contained in the figure. To find the volume of a space figure, count the number of cubic units.

cubic unit

TRY IT OUT

Find the volume of each figure. The hidden back view looks like the corner of a box.

1.

2.
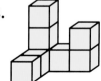

3.
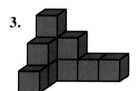

4.

Find the volume of each of these space figures. The hidden
back view looks like the corner of a box.

1.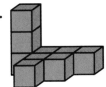

2.

3.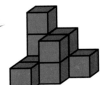

4.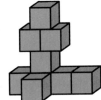

5.

6.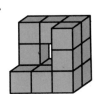

7.

8.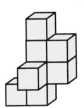

APPLY

MATH REASONING

9. Use estimation to order these four space
figures from smallest volume to largest volume.

a)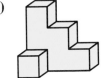

b)

c)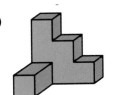

d)

PROBLEM SOLVING

10. Estimate the number of blocks needed
to build a staircase like the one at the
right but with 10 steps. Then find the
exact answer.

▶ **USING CRITICAL THINKING Support Your Conclusion**

11. Find the volume and the surface area of
this space figure.

12. Jane claims that all space figures with a volume of 6 units^3
have the same surface area. Do you agree? Why or
why not?

More Practice, page 541, set C

Volume of Prisms

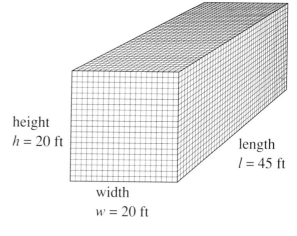

EXPLORE Study the Information

Knowing the volume of a handball court helps determine what size heating and air conditioning systems to use. Suppose this handball court is filled with boxes that are each 1 cubic foot in size. How can you find the volume of the handball court without counting the cubes?

height
$h = 20$ ft

length
$l = 45$ ft

width
$w = 20$ ft

A handball court is the shape of a rectangular prism.

TALK ABOUT IT

1. How many cubes are along the length of the court? How many cubes are along the width?

2. Do you think it is reasonable to say that the number of cubes in the bottom layer is equal to **length × width**?

3. How many such layers of cubes are there in the handball court?

4. Find **length × width × height**. How does your product compare to the volume of the court?

Volume = length × width × height

$V = lwh$

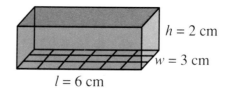

$h = 2$ cm
$w = 3$ cm
$l = 6$ cm

The formula can be restated this way.

Volume = Area of Base × height

$V = Bh$

Use the formula $V = Bh$ to find the volume of any prism.

$h = 5$ cm
$B = 23$ cm^2

$h = 6$ cm
$B = 15$ cm^2

Find the volume of each prism.

1.
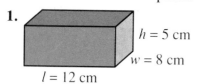
$h = 5$ cm
$w = 8$ cm
$l = 12$ cm

$B = 18$ cm^2
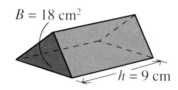
$h = 9$ cm

3.
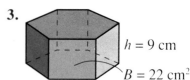
$h = 9$ cm
$B = 22$ cm^2

388

Find the volume of each rectangular prism.

1. $l = 12.5$ cm
$w = 4$ cm
$h = 6$ cm

2. $l = 0.8$ m
$w = 0.5$ m
$h = 0.6$ m

3. $l = 25$ dm
$w = 8$ dm
$h = 5$ dm

4. $l = 25$ mm
$w = 9$ mm
$h = 12$ mm

Find the volume of each prism.

5.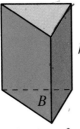

$B = 5$ cm^2
$h = 9$ cm

6.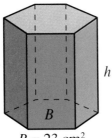

$B = 23$ cm^2
$h = 12$ cm

7.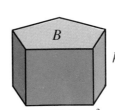

$B = 35.5$ cm^2
$h = 7$ cm

8.

$B = 8.5$ cm^2
$h = 12$ cm

APPLY

MATH REASONING

9. A prism that has a volume of 192 cm^3 has a height of 24 cm. Find the area of its base.

10. A rectangular prism with a volume of 500 cm^3 has a height of 20 cm. One side of the base is 5 cm long. How do you know that the base is a square?

PROBLEM SOLVING

11. The electric company says that it costs an average of 6 cents per year to heat or air condition one cubic foot of room space. At this rate, about how much should a health club expect to spend on its 18,000 ft^3 handball court in a month?

DATA BANK

12. Health and Fitness Data Bank How much does it cost to fill a water polo pool to a depth of 3.3 meters if water costs charges $1.50 per 100 cubic feet? (HINT: 1 cubic meter = 35.29 cubic feet.)

▶ USING CRITICAL THINKING   Support Your Conclusion

13. Suppose that your school class is picking strawberries for a local farmer as a class moneymaking project. Your personal quota toward the class goal is to pick either ten 18 cm × 28 cm × 1 cm boxes or two 36 cm × 56 cm × 24 cm boxes. Which will you pick and why?

Volume of Cylinders

A cylinder is like a prism, except that it has a circular base. Finding the volume of a cylinder is like finding the volume of a prism.

EXPLORE Solve to Understand

Jane wants to estimate the volume of this mug in order to see how many milliliters it will hold.

TALK ABOUT IT

1. What is the diameter of the base of the mug?

2. Imagine that the mug is surrounded by a prism. What is the volume of the prism?

3. If the mug has 75% the volume of the surrounding prism, what is the approximate volume of the mug?

4. How many milliliters does the mug hold?

To find the volume of a cylinder use this formula.

$$\text{Volume} = \text{Area of Base} \times \text{height}$$
$$V = Bh \quad \text{or} \quad V = \pi r^2 h$$

$r = 3$ cm and $h = 9$ cm
$V \approx 3.14 \times 3^2 + 9$
$V \approx 254.34$ cm^3

Use 3.14 for π.

The volume of the mug is about 254 cm^3, and it has a capacity of about 254 ml.

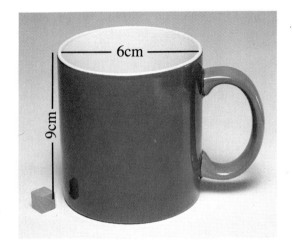

6cm

9cm

A mug is shaped like a cylinder. One cubic centimeter has the capacity of one milliliter.

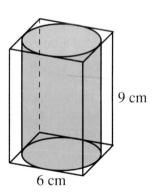

9 cm

6 cm

TRY IT OUT

Find the volume of each cylinder. Use 3.14 for π.

1. $r = 8$ cm
   $h = 13$ cm

2. $r = 2.5$ cm
   $h = 7.5$ cm

3. $r = 5$ cm
   $h = 4.5$

4. $r = 12$ cm
   $h = 7$ cm

Find the volume of each cylinder. Use 3.14 for π.

1.

$r = 5$ cm
$h = 12$ cm

2.

$r = 7$ dm
$h = 10$ dm

3.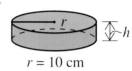

$r = 10$ cm
$h = 4$ cm

4.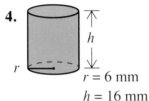

$r = 6$ mm
$h = 16$ mm

5.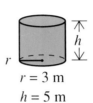

$r = 3$ m
$h = 5$ m

6.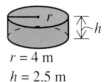

$r = 4$ m
$h = 2.5$ m

7. The cylindrical tank has a diameter of 8 m and a height of 7 m. Find the volume of the tank.

APPLY

MATH REASONING

8. A cylinder 7 cm in diameter is surrounded by a cube. Estimate the volume of the cylinder as 75% of the volume of the cube.

9. Estimate how many milliliters of milk there are in a mug that is 9 cm in diameter and 12 cm high.

PROBLEM SOLVING

10. A can of tennis balls is approximately 8 cm in diameter and 20 cm high. Find its volume.

11. About how many cans of tennis balls will it take to fill a 3 liter bottle?

MIXED REVIEW

Write an inequality for each sentence.

12. Height H is greater than 6

13. Age A is less than 12

Find the percent of increase or decrease to the nearest tenth of a percent.

14. $12 to $10

15. $10.50 to $11.00

16. $15.99 to $12.10

More Practice, page 542, set A

Volume of Pyramids and Cones

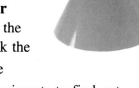

LEARN ABOUT IT

A **cone** has a circular base. A **pyramid** has a polygonal base.

EXPLORE **Use a Cone and a Cylinder**

Compare a cone and a cylinder with the same radius and height. Do you think the cone has $\frac{1}{3}$, $\frac{1}{2}$, or $\frac{3}{4}$ the volume of the cylinder? Complete one of these experiments to find out.

- Count the number of cones full of sand or water needed to fill the cylinder.
- Submerge the cone and the cylinder, one at a time, in a container of water. Compare the rise in water level.

TALK ABOUT IT

1. Which fraction did you discover to be the correct one for comparing the two volumes? Did you match your prediction?

A cone and a pyramid have the same volume formula.

Pyramid: $V = \frac{1}{3}Bh$

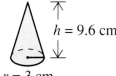

$V = \frac{1}{3}Bh$

$V = \frac{1}{3} \times 15.6 \times 4$

$V = 20.8$

$B = 15.6$ cm^2

$h = 4$ cm

The volume of the pyramid is 20.8 cm^3.

Cone: $V = \frac{1}{3}Bh$.

$V = \frac{1}{3}\pi r^2 h$

$h = 9.6$ cm

$r = 3$ cm

$V = \frac{1}{3} B h$

$V = \frac{1}{3} \times 3.14 \times 3^2 \times 9.6$

$V \approx 90.48$

The volume of the cone is 90.48 cm^3.

TRY IT OUT

Find the volume of each figure.

1.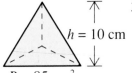
$h = 10$ cm
$B = 85$ cm^2

2.
$h = 10$ cm
$r = 4$ cm

3.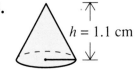
$h = 1.1$ cm
$r = 0.6$ cm

4.
$h = 6$ m
$B = 25$ m^2

Find the volume of each figure.

1.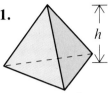

$B = 30 \text{ cm}^2$
$h = 9 \text{ cm}$

2.

$r = 2 \text{ cm}$
$h = 3 \text{ cm}$

3.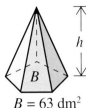

$B = 63 \text{ dm}^2$
$h = 12 \text{ dm}$

4.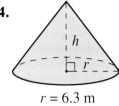

$r = 6.3 \text{ m}$
$h = 8 \text{ m}$

5. cone
$r = 10 \text{ cm}$
$h = 12 \text{ cm}$

6. pyramid
$B = 1,200 \text{ m}^2$
$h = 60 \text{ m}$

7. pyramid
$B = 2.4 \text{ m}^2$
$h = 0.6 \text{ m}$

8. cone
$r = 1.8 \text{ m}$
$h = 2.4 \text{ m}$

9. cone
$r = 33 \text{ mm}$
$h = 40 \text{ mm}$

10. pyramid
$B = 2.25 \text{ m}^2$
$h = 1.2$

11. cone
$r = 0.4 \text{ cm}$
$h = 2.7 \text{ cm}$

12. pyramid
$B = 4,224 \text{ mm}^2$
$h = 7.2 \text{ mm}$

13. Find the volume of a pyramid with a height of 5 cm and a square base whose edge lengths are 4 cm.

14. Find the volume of a cone whose height is 9.2 cm and whose base has a radius of 7 cm.

MATH REASONING

15. A pyramid and a cone are inscribed in cubes whose edges are 4 cm long. How many cm³ larger is the pyramid than the cone?

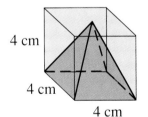
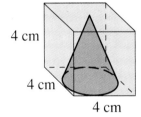

PROBLEM SOLVING

16. Which is heavier, a cube of gold 1 cm on each edge, or a pyramid of gold with a square base 2 cm on each edge and 1 cm high? Explain.

▶ **USING CRITICAL THINKING** Analyze the Situation

17. These two space figures are inscribed in identical cubes. Do you think the volume of figure A is less than, equal to, or greater than figure B? Explain.

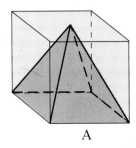
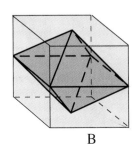

A   B

More Practice, page 542, set B

Problem Solving
Data from a Blueprint

| UNDERSTAND |
| ANALYZE DATA |
| PLAN |
| ESTIMATE |
| SOLVE |
| EXAMINE |

LEARN ABOUT IT

To solve some problems you need data from an outside source. Here, you need data from a blueprint.

The blueprint at the right shows the floor plan for a 2-bedroom apartment. Mr. Wilson wants to put new carpet in the living room and dining room. How many square yards of carpet does he need?

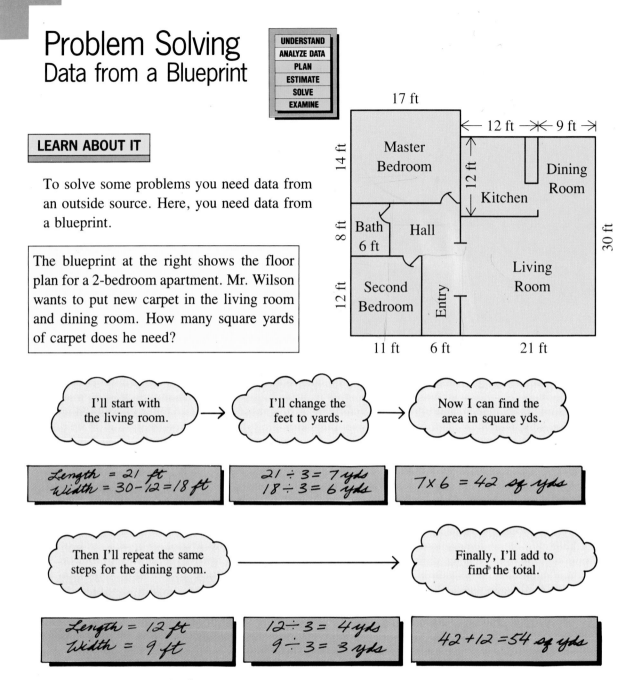

I'll start with the living room. → I'll change the feet to yards. → Now I can find the area in square yds.

Length = 21 ft
Width = 30 - 12 = 18 ft

21 ÷ 3 = 7 yds
18 ÷ 3 = 6 yds

7 × 6 = 42 sq yds

Then I'll repeat the same steps for the dining room. → Finally, I'll add to find the total.

Length = 12 ft
Width = 9 ft

12 ÷ 3 = 4 yds
9 ÷ 3 = 3 yds

42 + 12 = 54 sq yds

Mr. Wilson needs 54 yd^2 of carpet for the living room and dining room.

TRY IT OUT

1. Find the total area of the 2 bedrooms.

2. How many square feet of tile does Mr. Wilson need for the floor in the entry and hall.

3. How many square yards of carpet are needed for the master bedroom?

394

Solve. Use any problem solving strategy.

1. Mrs. Wilson is putting a flowered border on the walls in the master bedroom. Use the blueprint on the left page to find how many feet of 4-inch-wide wallpaper border she needs for the top edge of the walls.

2. Mr. Wilson bought a new refrigerator. The freezer compartment is 1 ft wide, 4.8 ft high, and 1.5 ft deep. How many cubic feet of freezer space does the refrigerator have?

3. Mrs. Wilson wants to paint the walls of the second bedroom sage green. The walls are 8 ft high. Use the blueprint on the left page to find how much area she needs to paint.

4. Kitchen cabinets are available in 4 different finishes—white enamel, oak, beech, and walnut. The hardware comes in white, black, chrome, and brass. If Mr. Wilson does not want to use white hardware, how many combinations does he have to choose from?

5. Mr. Wilson paid $687.92, including tax, for the refrigerator. He paid $200 down and the balance in 6 equal monthly payments. How much was each monthly payment?

6. Mrs. Wilson bought a cylindrical planter that is 2 ft high. The diameter of the base is 3 ft. How many cubic feet of potting soil will she need to fill the planter.

7. **Suppose . . .** Solve.
A double roll of wallpaper covers 36 sq ft. If the front wall of the living room in the blueprint is 8 ft high, how many double rolls of wallpaper will you need to buy to cover the wall?

Tell which of the following pieces of information would change the solution to the problem above.

a. There is a window 9 ft long and 5 ft high in the wall.
b. Wallpaper is on sale for 15% off.
c. A roll of wallpaper is 27 inches wide.

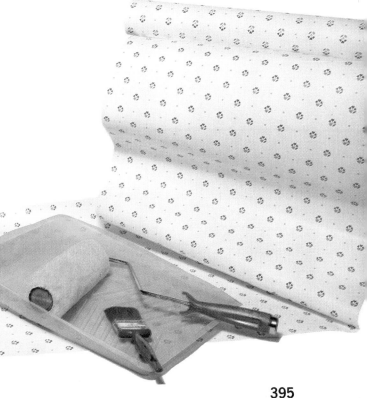

Applied Problem Solving
Group Decision Making

UNDERSTAND
ANALYZE DATA
PLAN
ESTIMATE
SOLVE
EXAMINE

Group Skill:
Listen to Others

Your class decided to manufacture leather wristbands for students in the school. Your group needs to figure out how much it will cost to make the wristbands, how much to charge per wristband, and what sizes to offer.

Facts to Consider

- The wristbands will look something like the one in the picture.
- The leather comes in strips 6 in. wide and 50 in. long for $10.95 or 8 ft^2 for $50.00.
- The wristbands will snap together. Snaps cost 20¢ each.
- You can use leather tools from the art room for cutting, punching holes, and creating designs.

- A sample of the measurements of student's wrists produced these results:

Circumference of Wrist	Number of Students
5"	3
$5\frac{1}{4}$"	3
$5\frac{1}{2}$"	5
$5\frac{3}{4}$"	6
6"	7
$6\frac{1}{4}$"	7
$6\frac{1}{2}$"	8
$6\frac{3}{4}$"	4
7"	3

- You expect about 15% of the 1,280 students in the school to buy wristbands.

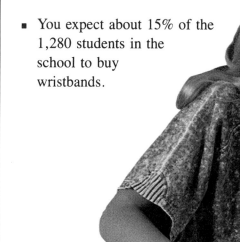

1. If you graph the results of the survey, what conclusions can you draw? How many sizes should you offer?

2. How could you use a paper model of the wristband to decide how long each size wristband will be with the snaps in place? How wide should it be?

3. How many wristbands can be made from one piece of leather?

4. How much profit will you make on each wristband?

What Is Your Decision?

Your group should make a flyer advertising the wristbands. Indicate the design of the wristbands, available sizes, and cost.

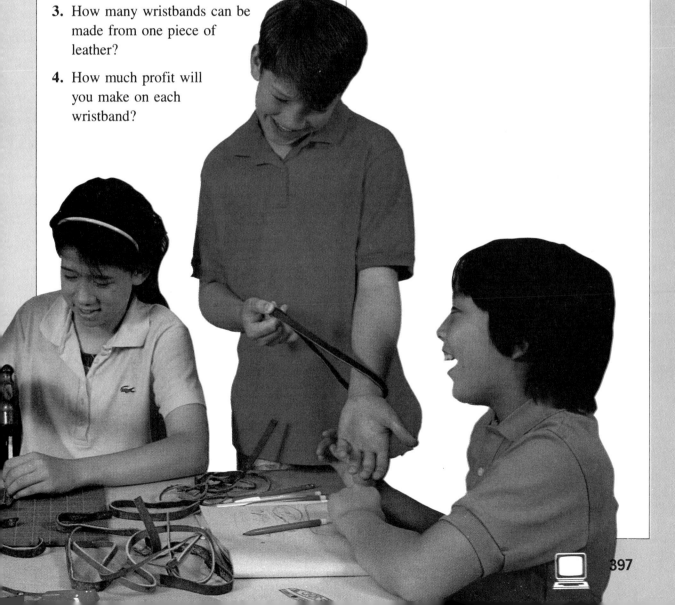

WRAP UP

Geometric Figures

Use a word or term from this chapter to label the indicated parts of each figure. Then name the figure.

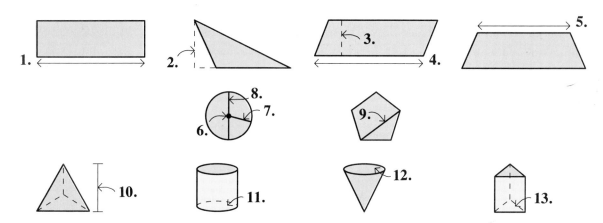

Sometimes, Always, Never

Which word should go in the blank, *sometimes*, *always*, or *never*? Explain your choice.

14. The area of a triangle is __?__ half the area of a rectangle whose length equals the triangle's base.

15. The area of a quadrilateral with at least one pair of parallel sides __?__ equals the base times the height.

16. Doubling the diameter of a circle will __?__ more than double its area.

17. The sum of the areas of the flat surfaces of a solid figure __?__ equals the figure's surface area.

18. A cone with the same height and base as a cylinder __?__ has $\frac{1}{2}$ the volume of that cylinder.

19. Two figures with the same volume __?__ have the same surface area.

Project

Regina stacked 27 small cubes to form a large cube. She painted the outside of the large cube. How many small cubes are painted on 4 sides? On 3 sides? On 2 sides? On 1 side? On 0 sides?

Build a large cube from 64 small cubes.

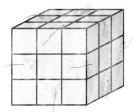

CHAPTER REVIEW/TEST

Part 1   Understanding

True or false?

1. Halving the diameter of a circle will halve its area.

2. All figures made of 6 unit cubes will not have the same surface area.

3. Use mental math to find the area of a parallelogram with a base of 36 in. and a height of 48 in.

4. The formula for the area of a triangle solved for b is

   A $b = \frac{A}{2h}$ **B** $b = \frac{h}{2A}$ (**C** $b = \frac{2A}{h}$

Part 2   Skills

Find the area of each figure.

5.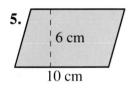

6.

7.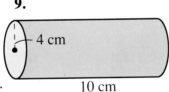

Find the surface area of each prism or cylinder.

8.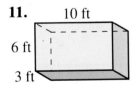

9.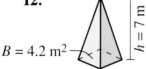

10.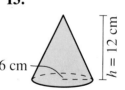

Find the volume of each figure.

11.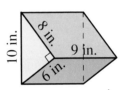

12. $B = 4.2 \text{ m}^2$, $h = 7$ m

13. 6 cm, $h = 12$ cm

Part 3   Applications

14. Find the area of this deck.
20 ft, 12 ft, 2 ft, 4 ft

15. Find the volume of clay needed to make this planter.

8 in., 6 in., 7 in., 1 in., 8 in., 8 in.

16. Challenge How many square yards of carpet are needed for the living room, dining room, and bedroom of this apartment?

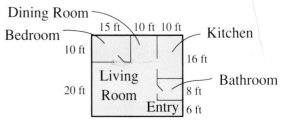

ENRICHMENT
Volume of Composite Space Figures

This store display stand is a kind of **composite space figure.** It is formed by combining two simpler space figures.

To find the volume of the display stand, find the volume of each simpler figure and then add to find the total volume.

Volume A = 12 × 8 × 12
        = 1,152

Volume B = 12 × 12 × 16
        = 2,304

Total volume = 1,152 + 2,304 = 3,456

The total volume is 3,456 in.^{3}

Find the volume of each of these composite space figures. All dimensions are in inches.

1.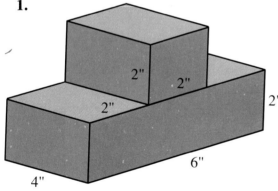

2.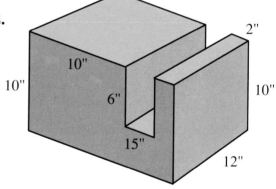

3. Find the volume of this barn.

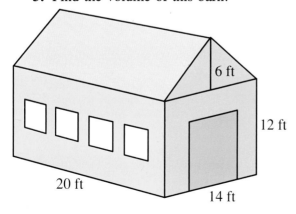

4. Find the volume of this swimming pool.

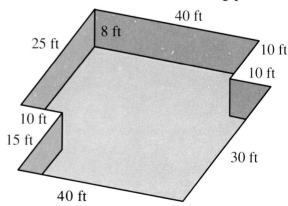

Cumulative Review

1. Which is the percent of decrease from 500 to 200?

   A 70%   **B** 40%

   C 90%   **D** 60%

2. 90 is 150% of what number?

   A 135   **B** 0.6

   C 60   **D** 1.66

3. Which is the correct equation to solve: 70% of 50 is what number?

   A $0.70 = 50 \times n$ **B** $0.70 \div 50 = n$

   C $50 \div 0.70 = n$ **D** $0.70 \times 50 = n$

4. Which is correct?

   A $^-12 > {}^-5$ **B** $^-2 > {}^-5$

   C $7 < {}^-4$ **D** $9 < {}^-10$

5. Which equation shows the associative property?

   A $3 \cdot (5 + {}^-5) = 3 \cdot 5 + 3 \cdot {}^-5$

   B $^-7 + {}^-1 = {}^-1 + {}^-7$

   C $(^-7 + 0) + 7 = {}^-7 + (0 + 7)$

   D $(^-7 + 0) + 7 = (^-7 + 0) + 7$

6. Multiply.

   $^-5 \cdot (^-4 \cdot 5)$

   A 100   **B** 80   **C** $^-100$ **D** $^-4$

7. Which coordinate is missing from the set of points for the vertices of the polygon?

   $(6, 3)$ $(1,6)$ $(^-3, {}^-1)$

   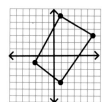

   A $(4, {}^-1)$

   B $(1, {}^-4)$

   C $(6, 2)$

   D $(^-3, 0)$

8. Which word describes any outcome or combination of outcomes from the sample space of an experiment?

   A certain   **B** even

   C impossible   **D** event

9. What is Exp P(B) of this spinner experiment?

   Outcomes: A 24 times

   B 15 times

   C 11 times

   A $\dfrac{12}{25}$ **B** $\dfrac{11}{50}$ **C** $\dfrac{3}{10}$ **D** $\dfrac{1}{4}$

10. Which inequality is expressed on the graph?

    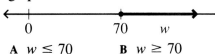

    A $w \le 70$ **B** $w \ge 70$

    C $w > 0$ **D** $w > 70$

11. What does a tree diagram show?

    A compound events   **B** patterns

    C frequencies   **D** range

12. Steve has 4 pencils—red, green, yellow, and black—in his desk drawer. If he reaches into the drawer without looking, what is the probability of getting the green pencil?

    A $\dfrac{1}{4}$ **B** $\dfrac{1}{3}$ **C** $\dfrac{1}{2}$ **D** $\dfrac{3}{4}$

13. If Darla tosses a penny and a nickel 20 times, what is the probability that both coins come up heads?

    A $\dfrac{1}{2}$ **B** $\dfrac{1}{10}$ **C** $\dfrac{1}{4}$ **D** $\dfrac{1}{5}$

14

MATH AND
SCIENCE

DATA BANK

Use the Science Data Bank
on page 492 to answer the
questions.

1 On graph paper, draw the
figure described in Examp
of Logo programs.

MOTION
GEOMETRY

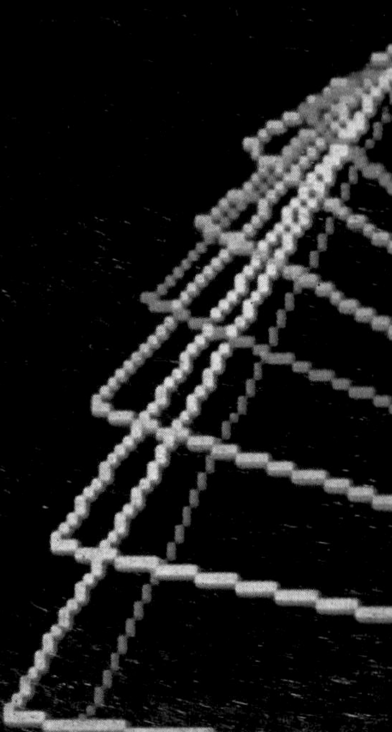

2 What figure should the turtle draw following instructions in Example 2? Example 3?

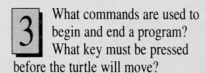 **3** What commands are used to begin and end a program? What key must be pressed before the turtle will move?

4 Using Critical Thinking
Visualize the drawings you would get from running Examples 1 through 4. Compare the programs. How are they related? How are the drawings related?

403

Lines of Symmetry

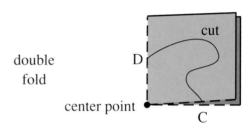

single fold

cut

B   fold line   A

EXPLORE **Discover a Pattern**

- Make a single fold in a piece of paper and cut from point *A* to *B*. The fold line in the resulting figure is a **line of symmetry.**
- Make a double fold in a piece of paper and cut around the center point from *C* to *D*.
- Experiment with a triple fold. Make sure the third fold goes through the center point. What kind of pattern results?

double fold

cut

D

center point

C

TALK ABOUT IT

1. How many lines of symmetry does the figure with a double fold have?

2. How many lines of symmetry does the figure with a triple fold have?

Some geometric figures have lines of symmetry.

one line of symmetry

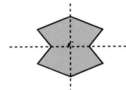

two lines of symmetry

no lines of symmetry

A **regular polygon**—a polygon with vertex angles the same measure and sides the same length—has several lines of symmetry.

four lines of symmetry

six lines of symmetry

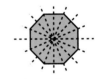

eight lines of symmetry

TRY IT OUT

Is the dotted line a line of symmetry?

1.
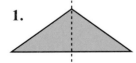

2.
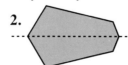

3.
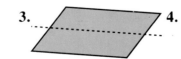

4.
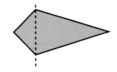

Is the dotted line a line of symmetry?

1.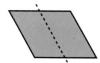

2.

3.

4.

5.

6.

Draw each figure on graph paper. Draw all lines of symmetry.

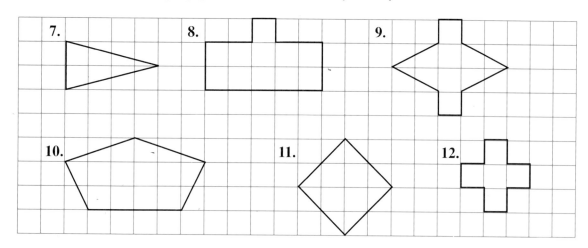

MATH REASONING

13. Trace and complete the figure so the dotted line is a line of symmetry.

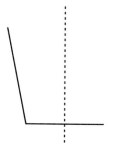

PROBLEM SOLVING

14. **Data Hunt** Find a photograph which has a line of symmetry.

15. What are the coordinates of points B, C, and D if both the x and y axes are lines of symmetry for polygon $ABCD$?

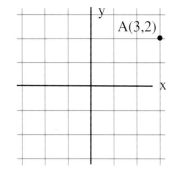

▶ **USING CRITICAL THINKING   Draw a Counterexample**

16. Is it true that any quadrilateral with exactly one line of symmetry is a trapezoid? If not, draw a counterexample.

More Practice, page 542, set C

Reflection in a Line

EXPLORE **Complete the Activity**

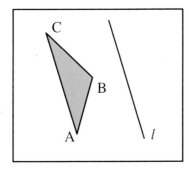 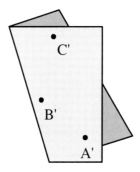 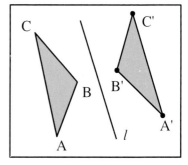

Draw △ABC and line l. Fold along l keeping △ABC on the outside of the paper.

Mark points A', B', and C' that coincide with the vertices of △ABC.

Unfold the paper and draw △A'B'C'.

TALK ABOUT IT

1. Set a mirror on line l perpendicular to the paper. What do you see?

2. How is the fold line l related to $\overline{BB'}$?

When you look at △ABC, in the mirror on the reflection line l, △ABC appears to be △A'B'C'. So, △A'B'C' is called the mirror or **reflection image** of △ABC in line l.

The reflection image of ABCD in l is EFGH.

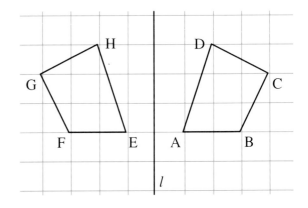

Draw each figure and its reflection image in the line l. Use graph paper.

1.    **2.** 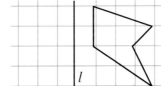   **3.**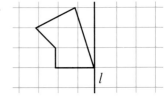

Draw each figure and its reflection image on graph paper.

1.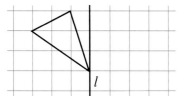

2.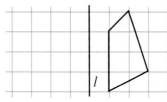

3.

Draw the figures and the reflection line for each pair on graph paper.

4.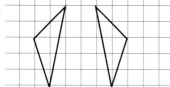

5.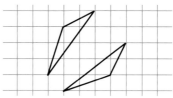

6.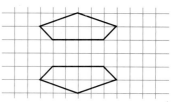

APPLY

MATH REASONING

7. Draw this figure on graph paper. Point *D* is the reflection image in line *l* of a point *C*. Draw △*ABC* and its reflection image in line *l*.

8. Does △*ABC* have a line of symmetry? How do you decide? If it does draw it.

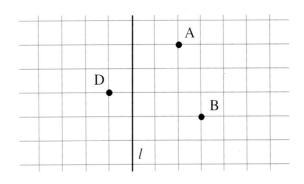

PROBLEM SOLVING

9. Decode this message.

os skool sidt nosɐǝɹ ǝɥT
sɐw ti tɐɥt si ǝƃuɐɹts
.ɹoɹɹim ɐ ɥtiw nǝttiɹw

10. Find three words with reflection images in a horizontal line that are also words.

MOM
ꟽOꟽ

▶ **MENTAL MATH**

Use mental math to find the answers.

11. $(8 \times 5) \times 9$

12. 10×57

13. $143 \div 10$

14. 0.1×56

15. $300 - 99$

16. $25 + 37 + 75$

17. $16,000 \div 4$

18. $1,300 - 299$

19. $50 \times 29 \times 20$

More Practice, page 542, set D

Turn Symmetry

LEARN ABOUT IT

EXPLORE **Use Dot Paper**

A computer language called Logo was used to draw this figure. If the figure is turned a quarter turn it looks identical to the original figure. We say it has $\frac{1}{4}$ **turn symmetry.** On Logo paper or 5 × 5 dot paper, draw 3 figures with these characteristics:

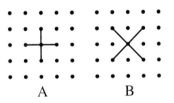

- All figures begin at a center point.
- All figures end at the outer rows of dots.
- All figures have $\frac{1}{4}$ turn symmetry.

TALK ABOUT IT

1. How many of your figures have pattern A at the center?

2. How many of your figures have pattern B at the center?

3. How many of your figures have a line of symmetry?

A   B

To test for **turn symmetry,** first trace the figure. Then hold the center point fixed and turn the tracing. If the tracing can be turned a **full turn** (360°) before it coincides with the original figure, the figure does **not** have turn symmetry.

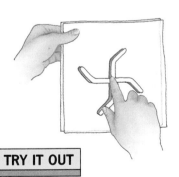
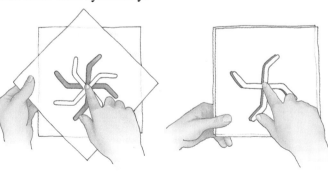

TRY IT OUT

The turn symmetry of each figure is what fraction of a full turn?

1.   **2.**   **3.**   **4.**

Does the figure have turn symmetry?

1.   **2.** 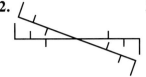   **3.**   **4.**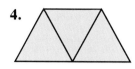

The turn symmetry of each figure is what fraction of a full turn?

5.   **6.**   **7.** 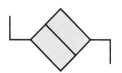   **8.**

Complete each figure so that is has the specified turn symmetry.

9. 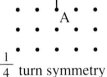   **10.** 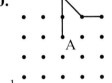   **11.** 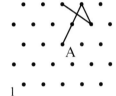   **12.**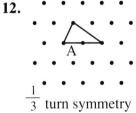

$\frac{1}{4}$ turn symmetry $\frac{1}{4}$ turn symmetry $\frac{1}{6}$ turn symmetry $\frac{1}{3}$ turn symmetry

MATH REASONING

13. Describe the turn symmetries of a regular octagon and a regular pentagon.

PROBLEM SOLVING

14. Science Data Bank Which of the Logo designs have turn symmetry? Give the fraction of turn for each.

MIXED REVIEW

Find the area.

15. 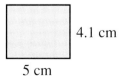   **16.** 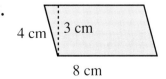   **17.**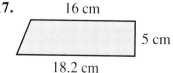

4.1 cm   5 cm

4 cm   3 cm   8 cm

16 cm   5 cm   18.2 cm

Rotations

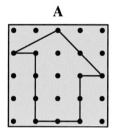

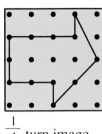

$\frac{1}{4}$ turn image

LEARN ABOUT IT

EXPLORE **Examine the Diagram**

If arrow A is turned $\frac{1}{4}$ turn in a clockwise direction, the resulting figure is a $\frac{1}{4}$ **turn image** or **rotation image** of A.

TALK ABOUT IT

B   C

1. How would you draw a $\frac{1}{2}$ turn image of A on dot paper?

2. Does a turn reverse the figure's sense of direction?

3. Are arrows B and C $\frac{1}{2}$ turn images of each other?

Trace flag A on tracing paper and turn the tracing paper keeping the **turn center,** point O, fixed. You can see:

- Flag B is a $\frac{1}{6}$ turn image of flag A.

- Flag C is a $\frac{1}{3}$ turn image of flag A.

- Flag E is a $\frac{1}{2}$ turn image of flag B.

- Flag F is not the turn image of any flag since it has a different sense of direction.

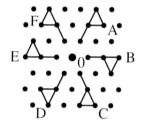

TRY IT OUT

1. Is flag D a $\frac{1}{6}$, a $\frac{1}{2}$, or a $\frac{1}{3}$ turn image of flag C?

2. Is flag B a $\frac{1}{6}$, a $\frac{1}{2}$, or a $\frac{1}{3}$ turn image of flag E?

Draw the indicated turn images on dot paper.

3.
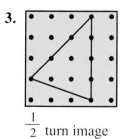
$\frac{1}{2}$ turn image

4.
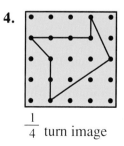
$\frac{1}{4}$ turn image

5.
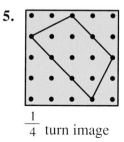
$\frac{1}{4}$ turn image

6.
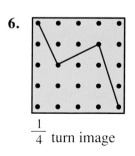
$\frac{1}{4}$ turn image

Draw the $\frac{1}{2}$ turn image of each figure on dot paper.

1. 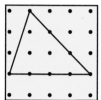 **2.** 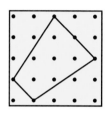 **3.** 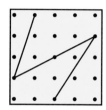 **4.**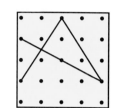

Draw the $\frac{1}{4}$ turn image of each figure on dot paper.

5.   **6.** 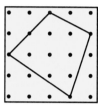 **7.** 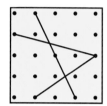 **8.**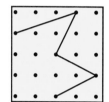

APPLY

MATH REASONING

9. Draw the figure and its $\frac{1}{2}$ turn image about turn center O.

10. Complete the figure so it has $\frac{1}{4}$ turn symmetry.

PROBLEM SOLVING

11. The $\frac{1}{2}$ turn image about turn center O of letter A is not a letter of the alphabet. For which capital letters is the $\frac{1}{2}$ turn image a letter of the alphabet? (Hint: Use tracing paper.)

12. A health bar manufacturer wants to design a name for the bar so that its package reads the same from top to bottom. One suggestion was to call it the *Now Mon* bar. Find two other names that meet these conditions.

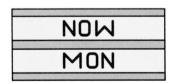

▶ **USING A CALCULATOR**

13. Enter $(4 - 3.8711) \times 6$ on your calculator. Why might this be called a "polite greeting" problem? Write your own polite greeting problem.

Exploring Algebra
More Patterns and Functions

LEARN ABOUT IT

EXPLORE Solve to Understand

How far does a sky diver fall before opening a parachute? If the diver is high enough that air resistance does not matter, the formula

$$d = 16t^2$$

gives the distance in feet for seconds of time.

TALK ABOUT IT

1. How far would a diver fall if his chute opens 2 seconds after he jumps?

2. A free fall of 5 seconds would be how far? a free fall of 10 seconds?

Algebraic equations often have variables raised to a power. In the equation above, the variable t is raised to the second power or "squared."

Example Complete the table for $y = 2x^2 + 5$.

x	0	1	2	3	10
$y = 2x^2 + 5$	5	7	13	23	205

TRY IT OUT

Copy and complete the tables.

1.

H	0	1	5	10	50
$H^2 + 10$	10	?	?	?	?

2.

Z	0	1	3	8	10	50
$Z^2 - 5$	-5	?	?	?	?	?

3.

N	0	1	5	10	25
$(H^2 \div 2) + 1$	?	?	?	?	?

4.

M	0	1	5	11	20	33
$3M^2 - 1$	?	?	?	?	?	?

Make a table showing 5 solutions for each equation.

5. $y = 3x^2 - 2$

6. $y = 2x^2 + x + 3$

7. $y = |x| + 5$

MIDCHAPTER REVIEW/QUIZ

Draw each figure on graph paper. Draw all lines of symmetry.

1.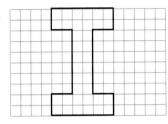

2.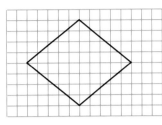

3.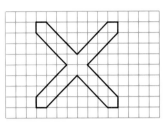

Draw each figure and its reflection image on graph paper.

4.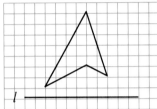

5.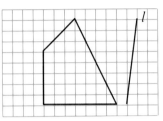

6.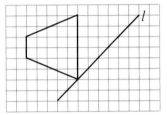

Does the figure have turn symmetry? What fraction of a turn?

7.

8.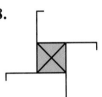

9.

10.

11. Draw this figure so that it has center at
A and $\frac{1}{4}$ turn symmetry.

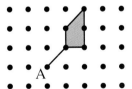

12. Draw this figure and its $\frac{1}{2}$ turn image.

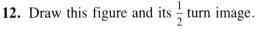

PROBLEM SOLVING

When an equilateral triangle is reflected around each of its
sides, the new figure is an equilateral triangle.

Draw the image you get when you reflect these figures around
each of their sides. Describe what you notice about the new
shapes and the lines of symmetry.

13. scalene triangle

14. isosceles right triangle

15. square

Problem Solving
Using the Strategies

UNDERSTAND
ANALYZE DATA
PLAN
ESTIMATE
SOLVE
EXAMINE

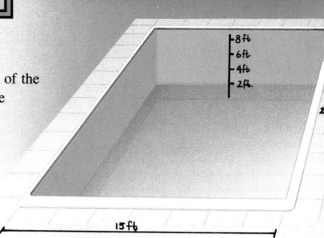

LEARN ABOUT IT

Sometimes a problem asks you to change some of the data and then observe the effect the data change has on the solution. **This problem explores the effect that changing one dimension of a solid causes on the volume of the solid.**

The picture shows a rectangular pool with 2 ft of water in it. Find the volume of water in the pool. Now change the water's depth to 4 ft and find the volume. Then change the depth to 8 ft and find the volume. What effect does changing the depth have on the volume?

Width	Length	Depth	Volume
15	20	2	600
15	20	4	1,200
15	20	8	2,400

×2 ×2

First, I'll find the volume with 2 ft of water and record my data in a table.

Then I'll find the volume for 4 ft of water and record it in the table.

Now I'll do the same for 8 ft of water.

I see a pattern. Each time the depth is doubled, the volume is also doubled.

TRY IT OUT

Solve. Find how changing one dimension of the solid causes changes in volume.

1. A circular swimming pool has 3 ft of water in it. The diameter of the pool is 20 ft. Find the volume of water in the pool. If the depth of the water is increased to 6 ft, what happens to the volume?

2. A cylindrical tank is 10 ft high and 6 ft in diameter. If the diameter of the tank is changed to 12 ft, what happens to the volume?

Solve. Use any problem solving strategy.

Some Strategies	
Act Out	Solve a Simpler Problem
Use Objects	Make an Organized List
Choose an Operation	Work Backward
Draw a Picture	Look for a Pattern
Guess and Check	Use Logical Reasoning
Make a Table	Write an Equation

1. A rectangular container is 8 in. wide, 10 in. long, and 4 in. high. What happens to the volume of the container if you halve both the width and the length?

2. The width of a rectangular pool is one third of its length. The depth is 8 ft less than the width. If the depth is 6 ft, find the width of the pool.

3. Jackson invited 18 friends to a swimming party. He bought 4 6-packs of juice, a 2-lb can of peanuts, and 3 boxes of frozen yogurt bars. Use the advertised prices to find how much Jackson spent.

4. Ellen has a $20 bill. She spent $13.50 on cheese snacks. Find how many packages of cheese snacks Ellen bought.

5. Jose, Ben, Carrie, and Reja took turns diving off the diving board. In how many different orders could they have dived?

6. Tamara is making cylinders 5 in. high from a piece of paper. She started by making a cylinder with a base of radius 2 in. and then increased the radius by 1 in. until she had 8 cylinders. What was the volume of the 8th cylinder?

7. If you double all three dimensions of the container shown below what happens to the volume?

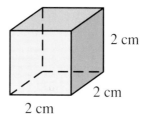

8. A rectangular fish tank holds 180 gallons of water. The volume of one gallon of water is 0.134 cu ft. What is the volume of the fish tank?

Translations

EXPLORE Examine the Diagram

The unshaded triangle is a **slide** or **translation image** of the
shaded triangle. Imagine tracing the shaded triangle and sliding
the tracing paper until the traced triangle coincides with the
unshaded triangle.

TALK ABOUT IT

1. Which of the arrow patterns describes the slide that moves
   the shaded triangle onto the unshaded triangle?

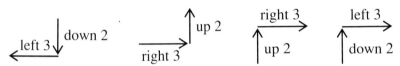

2. When a figure slides, do angle size, segment length, or area
   change?

A slide is described by an arrow which shows *horizontal*
(right or left) and *vertical* (up or down) changes. Arrow *AB*
describes a (right 3 and up 1) slide.

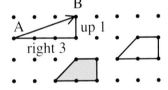

A double arrow describes two slides in opposite directions. If
you slide a figure repeatedly in opposite directions the resulting
pattern has **slide symmetry.**

A   B

... ℃ ℃ ℃ ℃ ℃ ℃ ...

figure

This pattern has slide symmetry

TRY IT OUT

1. Which slide moves the shaded triangle onto the unshaded one?
   a. (right 3, up 2)   **b.** (right 3, up 1)   **c.** (right 3, up 3)

2. Draw the shaded triangle on dot paper and draw its
   (left 2, down 2) slide image.

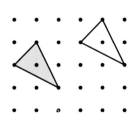

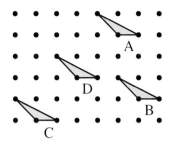

1. Which slide moves A to D?
 a. (right 2, up 2)
 b. (left 2, down 2)
 c. (right 1, up 2)

2. Which slide moves C to A?
 a. (right 2, up 2)
 b. (right 4, up 4)
 c. (right 2, up 4)

3. Which slide moves B to A?
 a. (left 1, up 3) b. (right 1, down 1) c. (right 2, down 4)

For each problem draw the quadrilateral on dot paper. Then draw its slide image as directed.

4. (3 right, 2 up)   **5.** (1 left, 3 down)

6. (1 right, 2 up)   **7.** (2 right, 1 down)

8. Which pattern does not have slide symmetry? Why not?

a)

b)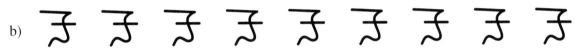

APPLY

MATH REASONING

 9. Draw a pattern with slide symmetry.

 10. Draw a pattern with slide symmetry and $\frac{1}{2}$ turn symmetry.

PROBLEM SOLVING

 11. A slide can describe change in an aircraft's position. How many degrees right (longitude) and degrees up (latitude) describe the arrow between these two positions?

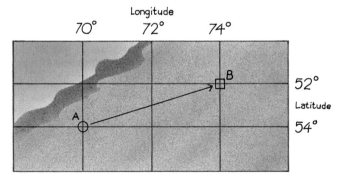

 12. Science Data Bank Which Logo Example has slide symmetry?

EXPLORING ALGEBRA

 13. Use the figure to find the slide from point A to point B if (x, y) is $(2, 1)$.

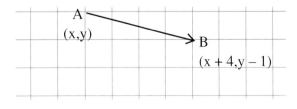

417

Motions and Congruence

EXPLORE **Examine the Diagrams**

The triangles in each pair are identical in size and shape.

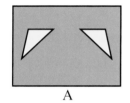 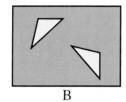 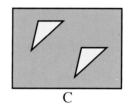 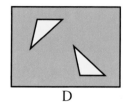

A   B   C   D

TALK ABOUT IT

1. In A and B are the triangles related by a reflection or a turn? Use tracing paper to find the reflection line or turn center.

2. What type of motion relates the triangles in C?

3. What types of motion relate the triangles in D?

Congruent figures are the same size and shape. If two figures are congruent, one can be moved onto the other by a reflection, a turn, a slide, or a combination of these motions.

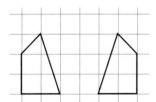 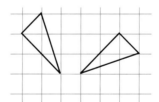 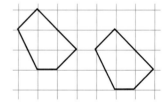

A figure and its reflection image are congruent.

A figure and its turn image are congruent.

A figure and its slide image are congruent.

TRY IT OUT

Are the figures congruent? If so, what motion or combination of motions moves one figure onto another?

1. 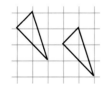   2. 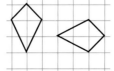   3. 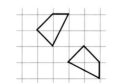   4.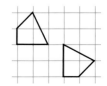

418

Decide if the figures are congruent.

1. 　　2. 　　3. 　　4.

Are the figures congruent? If so, what motion or combination of motions moves one figure onto another?

5. 　　6. 　　7.

8. 　　9. 　　10.

APPLY

MATH REASONING

11. Use dot paper. Draw 2 congruent pentagons related by a slide followed by a reflection.

12. Use dot paper. Draw 2 congruent hexagons related by a reflection followed by a turn.

PROBLEM SOLVING

13. Congruent right triangles were used to make a pattern in an 8 m by 10 m courtyard. Use graph paper to find at least one of the patterns that could have been made. Are there others?

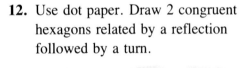 MIXED REVIEW

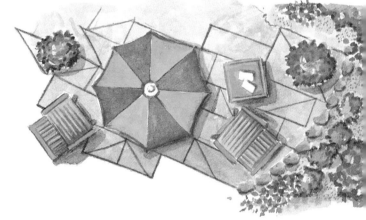

Solve.

14. 40% of 150 is what number?

15. What number is 38% of 100?

16. 15 is what percent of 60?

17. 110% of 50 is what number?

Using Critical Thinking
Analyzing a Figure

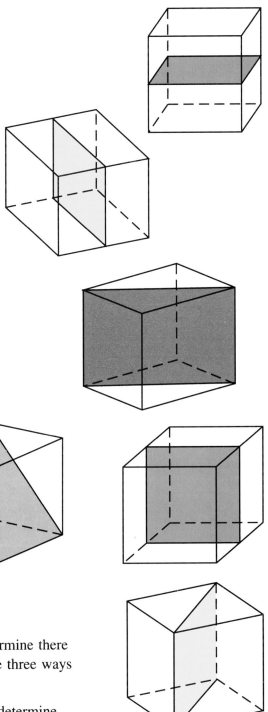

LEARN ABOUT IT

Jan, Tyrone, and Miguel constructed a cube out of pipe cleaners for a geometry project.

Their teacher said, "Suppose you have a piece of cardboard that you could use to cut straight through your cube. How many ways could you cut the cube into two equal sections?"

Jan, Tyrone, and Miguel worked on the question separately and reported their results to the teacher.

Jan said, "There are only 3 ways."

"No, there are 6 ways," said Tyrone.

"You're both wrong," said Miguel. "There are an unlimited number of ways."

"You could all be correct," said the teacher, "depending on your assumptions."

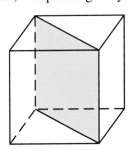
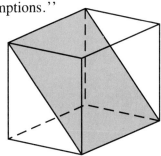

TALK ABOUT IT

1. What are these students trying to do?

2. What assumptions might Jan have made to determine there were only three ways to cut the cube? Show the three ways she found.

3. What assumptions might Tyrone have made to determine there were six ways? Show the ways he found.

4. How could there be an unlimited number of ways?

420

Find how many ways each figure can be divided into two equal parts. List the assumptions you make.

1.

2. Suppose you have a rectangular solid that you will cut using the following guidelines.

- A cut must pass through an edge of the solid, OR a cut must be perpendicular to a face of the solid.
- Cuts which result in the same shaped sections are the same.

How many ways can you cut the rectangular solid into two equal sections?

3. Suppose you use only the first condition above. How many ways can you cut the rectangular solid into two equal pieces?

4. Suppose you could place a pencil through a cube as shown at the right. Notice the cube can rotate around the pencil and return to what looks like its original position without actually completing a full revolution. Can you find other ways to insert the pencil in the cube so the same thing happens?

Problem Solving
Estimating the Answer

UNDERSTAND
ANALYZE DATA
PLAN
ESTIMATE
SOLVE
EXAMINE

LEARN ABOUT IT

Before you solve a problem it is important to decide what would be a reasonable answer.

To do this, you can estimate the answer.

A survey of 7,825 households found that 28% have home computers. How many of the surveyed households have home computers?

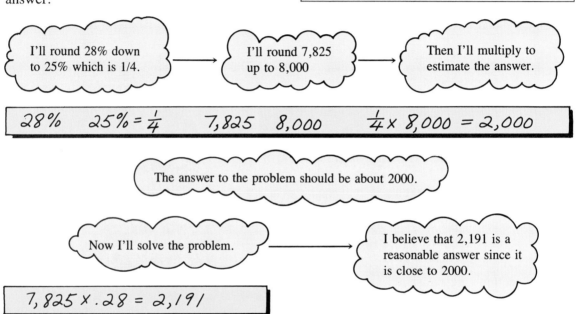

I'll round 28% down to 25% which is 1/4.

I'll round 7,825 up to 8,000

Then I'll multiply to estimate the answer.

$$28\% \qquad 25\% = \frac{1}{4} \qquad 7,825 \qquad 8,000 \qquad \frac{1}{4} \times 8,000 = 2,000$$

The answer to the problem should be about 2000.

Now I'll solve the problem.

I believe that 2,191 is a reasonable answer since it is close to 2000.

$$7,825 \times .28 = 2,191$$

TRY IT OUT

Before solving the problem, estimate the answer. Then solve the problem and decide if your answer is reasonable.

1. A survey of 361 households found that 18% have compact disc players. How many of the households surveyed have compact disc players?

2. When Marta and Desmond opened their business they bought a cordless telephone for $189.95 and a telephone answering machine for $112.50. The tax was $18.15. How much did they spend?

3. In a group of 6,150 households, 12% have camcorders and 74% have videocassette recorders. How many more households have videocassette recorders than camcorders?

4. A survey found that 2,737 out of 4,025 households have compact audio systems. What percent is that?

Solve. Estimate your answer first.

1. In one year, sales of color TV sets were $9,879 million. The next year sales increased by $436 million. What were the sales the second year?

2. Brenda spent $3.19 for a message tape for her telephone answering machine. The tape will record for 45 min. If the average message is 30 sec, how many messages will fit on the tape?

3. Mr. Diexler has 4 different computer activities for his students. Each activity takes 3 min longer than the one before. It takes 46 min to complete all the activities. How long does the third activity take?

4. There are more than 91,500,000 United States households with an average 2.6 people per household. Color TV sets are in 95% of these households. How many households have color TV sets?

5. The table shows estimates of factory sales of home information equipment for two different years. Use the table to find by what percent the sales of home computers increased from one year to the next.

■ **Factory Sales**
Estimates in millions of dollars

Home Information Equipment		
Home computers	3,150	3,500
Corded and cordless telephones	1,040	1,080
Cellular telephones	300	380
Telephone answering devices	545	610

6. Use the table to find how much greater the factory sales of home information equipment were the second year.

7. Madison Junior High has eight new computers for three classrooms. Each classroom needs at least one computer. In how many ways can the computers be divided among the classrooms?

8. Write Your Own Problem
Write a problem that the table could help solve.

5	10	15	20	25	30	35
2	4	6	8	10	12	14

Data Collection and Analysis
Group Decision Making

UNDERSTAND
ANALYZE DATA
PLAN
ESTIMATE
SOLVE
EXAMINE

Doing an Investigation

Group Skill:
Check for Understanding

Think about a pendulum. Does it swing faster with a longer or a shorter string, or does it swing at the same speed no matter what the length of the string? Work in groups to investigate your hypothesis.

Collecting Data

1. To make a pendulum, tie a weight to a length of string. Your group will need four pendulums: 25 cm, 50 cm, 75 cm, and 100 cm long.

2. Hold or tape the pendulum so that it swings freely—a complete swing is across and back again. Time 10 swings of the pendulum and keep a record of the times.

3. For each pendulum, compute the average time of one swing. Record the data in your chart.

Length of string	Number of seconds for 10 swings	Average time for one swing
25 cm	_____	_____
50 cm	_____	_____
75 cm	_____	_____
.	.	.
.	.	.
.	.	.

Organizing Data

4. Make a line graph to show what happens to the average time of one swing when the length of the pendulum is increased. Adjust the scales to fit your group's data.

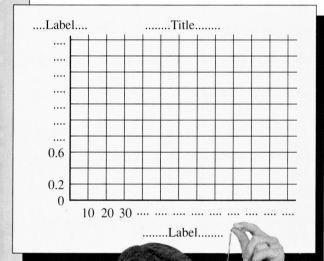

....Label.... ....Title........

....
....
....
....
....
....
....
0.6
0.2
0

10 20 30 ....

........Label........

Presenting Your Analysis

5. Write a brief report to tell how your group did the investigation and what your findings were. Was your hypothesis correct?

6. Predict the average time of a swing if the pendulum were 60 cm long or 150 cm long. Explain how you made your predictions.

WRAP UP

Calculator Message

For each item, use your calculator to follow the directions for the correct choice. Do not clear your calculator between items. If you make all correct choices, you will discover the type of mark you deserve for your work.

1. If congruent, figures must have
   A the same shape and size, *enter 1,234*.
   B a line of symmetry, *enter 4,321*.

2. If a line of symmetry is a line
   A on which a figure can be folded so that the two parts fit exactly, *multiply by 3*.
   B across which a figure has been translated, *divide by 3*.

3. If the translation image of a figure is its appearance after a
   A reflection, *subtract 912, press* $\boxed{=}$ *and turn your calculator around*.
   B slide, *add 912, press* $\boxed{=}$ *, and turn your calculator around*.

Sometimes, Always, Never

Which word should go in the blank, *sometimes*, *always*, or *never*? Explain your choice.

4. A polygon __?__ has more than one line of symmetry.

5. If two figures are __?__ congruent, one may be moved onto the other by a reflection, turn, slide, or combination of these.

6. A reflection image and a translation image __?__ appear the same.

7. If a figure must be turned a full turn before it coincides with the original figure, it __?__ has turn symmetry.

8. The turn center for the turn image of a figure is __?__ a point on the figure.

Project

This large equilateral triangle was made by taking a smaller equilateral triangle and drawing its image after a rotation, a slide, and a reflection. Using dot paper, make other large polygons by drawing the polygon's image after a rotation, a slide, and a reflection.

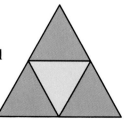

CHAPTER REVIEW/TEST

Part 1 Understanding

1. True or false? All figures have at least one line of symmetry.

2. If the height of a solid is tripled then its volume __?__.

3. Does a regular hexagon have turn symmetry?

4. What changes when a figure slides?
   A angle size   B position
   C size   D direction

Part 2 Skills

Copy Figure C on graph paper for each problem.

5. Draw all lines of symmetry.

6. Draw Figure C's reflection in the y-axis.

7. Draw Figure C's $\frac{1}{4}$ turn image about turn center (0,0).

8. Draw Figure C's (right 3, down 2) slide image.

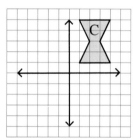

9. Draw a pair of figures that are reflections of each other and indicate the line of reflection.

10. Make a table showing 5 solutions for $y = 3x^2 + 4$.

11. Draw a pattern with slide symmetry.

12. Draw two congruent right triangles on graph paper.

Part 3 Applications

13. How many ways can a rectangular prism be divided into two equal parts? List the assumptions you make.

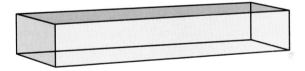

14. A survey found that 62% of the 478 students at Central School ride the bus to school. Estimate the number of students who ride the bus.

15. **Challenge** The formula for finding the volume of a 4-ft-high cylinder is $V = 4\pi r^2$. Make a table showing solutions of this formula to determine what radius is needed for this cylinder to have a volume of about 100 ft^3.

ENRICHMENT
Making Tesselations

The Dutch artist, M. C. Escher (1898–1972) used the idea of translations to create some unusual works of art.

You can create your own Escher-like pictures, called **tesselations,** by following the instructions below.

A. Draw a square and cut it out. Cut out a simple curve from one side.

B. Slide the cutout to the opposite side of the square and tape it to the edge, keeping the cutout the same distance from the corners.

C. Trace around the new figure translating it horizontally, and vertically again and again to form a tesselation that would eventually cover your paper. Add some other touches of your own to make the picture more interesting.

You can also change both pairs of opposite sides of the square to get even more interesting figures.

Try making some other tesselation designs of your own.

CUMULATIVE REVIEW

1. Divide.

$25 \div {}^-5$

A 20   **B** $^-5$ **C** 5   **D** $^-125$

2. Which numbers complete the table of values for $y = \frac{x}{4} + 1$?

x	8	4	2	0	$^-4$	$^-8$
y	3	2		1		$^-1$

A 1.5 and $^-0.5$ **B** 1.5 and $^-0.1$
C 1.2 and $^-0.05$ **D** 1.5 and 0

3. Which is not a possible outcome for drawing two of these cards at a time?

4. What is the probability of drawing an even-numbered card from the hat?

A $\frac{3}{5}$

C $\frac{2}{5}$ **D** $\frac{1}{2}$

5. Which inequality expresses the statement: length l is less than 35 ft?

A $l < 35$ **B** $35 > l$
C $35 < l$ **D** $l \leq 35$

6. What is the expected value for this spinner experiment in 10 spins?

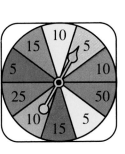

A 14   **B** 15
C 17.5   **D** 18

Find each area in exercises 7–9.

7.

A 3 units^2
B $3\frac{1}{2}$ units^2
C 4 units^2
D $4\frac{1}{2}$ units^2

8. $h = 17$ cm, $b = 56$ cm

A 952 cm^2
B 9,520 cm^2
C 146 cm^2
D 1,904 cm^2

9. $b_2 = 75$ cm, $h = 62$ cm, $b_1 = 120$ cm

A 319 cm^2
B 159.5 cm^2
C 257 cm^2
D 6,045 cm^2

10. The dimensions of a garden are 13.8 m by 4.5m. A narrow wooden walk 20 cm wide and 15.8 m long will be built through it. What planting area remains?

A 253.9 m^2 **B** 33.44 m^2
C 58.94 m^2 **D** 46.3 m^2

11. A rectangular room has a length of 7 m and a width of 4 m. The height of the wall is 2.5 m. A door and two windows take up about 8 m^2. What is the remaining area of the four walls?

A 70 m^2 **B** 47 m^2
C 19.5 m^2 **D** 55 m^2

15

EXTENDING ALGEBRA

MATH AND
LANGUAGE ARTS

DATA BANK

Use the Language Arts Data Bank on page 495 to answer the questions.

 What was the area of the floor of Thoreau's house?

2 How much, per square foot, did Thoreau's house cost to build?

 3 Today the cost of building a house is about $50 per square foot. How many times more than the cost per square foot of Thoreau's house is this?

 4 **Using Critical Thinking** What does Carl Sandburg's poem tell you about how he viewed arithmetic? How would you answer Sandburg's last question—"Who is better at arithmetic, you or your mother?" Explain.

431

Extending Order of Operations

EXPLORE **Solve to Understand**

In his book, *Walden,* Thoreau talks about buying a ticket to Fitchburg, Massachusetts. For each example, write an expression to show how you could calculate Thoreau's cost.

TALK ABOUT IT

1. Do both problems have the same answer?

2. Write an algebraic expression using parentheses to show how to compute each problem.

We can extend the rules for the order of operations to include exponents.

- Compute within grouping symbols first.
- Do computations with exponents.
- Multiply and divide in order from left to right.
- Add and subtract in order from left to right.

TICKETS TO FITCHBURG
70¢ FARE INCREASE = 90¢

A. Find the cost of riding twice at the low fare and once at the high fare.

B. Find the cost of riding twice at both the low and high fare.

Examples

A Evaluate $4 + (5 - k) \cdot 7$ for $k = 3$.

Solution:	$4 + (5 - 3) \cdot 7$	Substitute 3 for k.
	$= 4 + 2 \cdot 7$	Compute inside parentheses first.
	$= 4 + 14$	Multiply before adding.
	$= 18$	Add.

B Evaluate $(3 + 4) \cdot (7 - f)^2$ for $f = 9$.

Solution:	$(3 + 4) \cdot (7 - 9)^2$	Substitute 9 for f.
	$= 7 \cdot (^-2)^2$	Compute inside parentheses first.
	$= 7 \cdot 4$	Do computations with exponents.
	$= 28$	Multiply.

Evaluate the expression.

1. $6 + 10 \div 5$ **2.** $4 \cdot 3 + 8 \div 2$ **3.** $5(3 - 12)$ **4.** $x^2 + 2x$ for $x = 3$

Evaluate each numerical expression.

1. $2 \cdot 6 + 4 \cdot 2$

2. $30 - 5 \cdot 4 \div 2$

3. $6 + 4 (2 - 3)^2$

4. $(27 + 5) \div 4 + 4$

5. $24 \div 4 \div 2$

6. $20 - 12 \div 2 + 7$

7. $44.5 - 3.4 \cdot 2$

8. $12 \cdot 6 (15.2 + 9)$

9. $21\frac{5}{6} - 8\frac{1}{3} \cdot 2$

Evaluate each algebraic expression.

10. $2(4 + b)$
for $b = 8$

11. $b + 8 \cdot 6 \div 2$
for $b = {}^-7$

12. $28 - 6k^2 \div 10$
for $k = {}^-5$

13. $h^2 - 8 \cdot 5 + 7$
for $h = 5$

MATH REASONING Write and evaluate an expression for each statement.

16. Multiply 3 and 12; subtract the product from 50.

17. Subtract 2 from 23, and then divide by 7.

18. Add 10 to the product of $^-5$ and 7.

Rewrite each expression. Use parentheses to give the answer shown.

19. $45 - 15 \div 5 - 2 = 40$ **20.** $45 - 15 \div 5 - 2 = 4$ **21.** $45 - 15 \div 5 - 2 = 10$

PROBLEM SOLVING

22. Language Arts Data Bank Write an expression to illustrate Carl Sandburg's description of doubling a number. (Let 3 = "a few.") Then substitute a number in the expression and evaluate.

23. Thoreau said it cost $30 a year to rent one of Cambridge College's 32 dorms. With all rooms filled, but giving 5 students a $10 discount, how much did the college earn in yearly room rentals?

24. In the 1850s a day laborer earned about $.90 per day. If he worked 26 days in one month, and spent $\frac{9}{10}$ of his income on living expenses, how much would he have left at the end of the month?

CALCULATOR

Use your calculator's memory keys to evaluate these expressions without writing down any intermediate steps.

25. $24 \cdot 57 + 1424 \div 89$

26. $57.8 - 9.3 \cdot 4.1 - (7.43 - 3.5)$

Problem Solving
Using Guess and Check to Solve Equations

UNDERSTAND
ANALYZE DATA
PLAN
ESTIMATE
SOLVE
EXAMINE

LEARN ABOUT IT

The strategy **Guess and Check** is useful for solving equations.

> Tanya's class ordered 10 pizzas for a class party. The cost for the basic pizzas was $54. There was a charge of $2 for each topping. The total bill, excluding tax, was $68. How many toppings did the class choose?

Let t be the number of toppings. $2t$ is the cost of the toppings. $2t + 54$ is the cost of the basic pizzas plus the toppings. Solve $2t + 54 = 68$ to find the number of toppings.

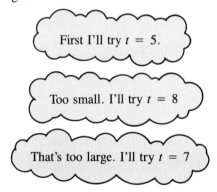

> First I'll try $t = 5$.

> Too small. I'll try $t = 8$

> That's too large. I'll try $t = 7$

$$2 \cdot 5 + 54 = 10 + 54$$
$$= 64 \quad too\ low$$

$$2 \cdot 8 + 54 = 16 + 54$$
$$= 70 \quad too\ high$$

$$2 \cdot 7 + 54 = 14 + 54$$
$$= 68 \quad correct$$

The class ordered 7 toppings for the pizzas!

TRY IT OUT

Solve. Use Guess and Check.

1. Mr. Adams took his children to a movie. Tickets were $6 for adults and $4 for children. The total cost was $30. How many children did Mr. Adams take?

   Let n = the number of children.
   Solve $4n + 6 = 30$.

2. Costs for bowling at a certain bowling alley are $2 for shoes and $4 for each game. Alea spent $18. How many games did she bowl?

   Let n = the number of games.
   Solve $4n + 2 = 18$.

434

1. Certain long distance phone calls cost $0.75 for the first 3 minutes and $0.10 for each additional minute. What is the cost of a 15 minute phone call at these rates?

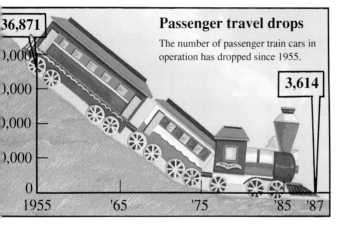

Passenger travel drops

The number of passenger train cars in operation has dropped since 1955.

36,871

3,614

1955   '65   '75   '85 '87

2. Estimate the percent of decrease in train travel from 1955 to 1987.

3. About how many times more passenger cars were in use in 1955 than in 1987?

4. According to the survey below, about how many households chose apples?

5. According to the survey about how many more households chose bananas than seedless grapes?

6. A certain car rental costs $45 a day plus $10 for each additional hour past 24 hours. How many hours past one day was a person who owed $75, excluding tax?

7. A family rented a car for 2 days at $34.95 a day (24 hrs) plus 30¢ a mile for each mile over 100 miles. There was also an $8 per hour late charge. What was the rental fee for this car, if it was returned 1 hour late with 145 miles on it?

8. A rectangular patio is made up of 1-foot square blocks and has an area of 120 square ft. What are the maximum and minimum perimeters possible?

Most popular snack fruits

1,317 households surveyed

74%
66%
55%
26%
14%

Apples   Bananas   Seedless grapes   Oranges   Strawberries

Using Inverse Operations

EXPLORE **Analyze the Situation**

Charlie bought a 6-pack of apple juice and an orange. The orange cost 45¢.

Let j stand for the cost of a single can of juice.

TALK ABOUT IT

1. What algebraic expression involving j represents the total cost of the 6-pack of juice and the orange?

2. If you know the total cost of the 6-pack and orange, how can you find the cost of the 6-pack alone?

3. If you know the cost of the 6-pack, how can you find the cost of 1 can of juice?

You can build an algebraic expression starting with a variable and combining it with numbers using arithmetic operations.

Start with j
Multiply by 6 $6j$
Add 45 $6j + 45$

To get back to the variable you can "undo" the expression by using **inverse operations** in the reverse order.

Start with $6j + 45$
Subtract 45 $6j$
Divide by 6 j

Example

Start	n	Start	$5n - 3$	
Multiply by 5	$5n$	Add 3	$5n$	$(5n - 3 + 3)$
Subtract 3	$5n - 3$	Divide by 5	n	$(5n \div 5)$

Show how to build and undo each expression.

1. $4n + 5$ **2.** $\frac{g}{2} - 6$ **3.** $\frac{h}{8} + 7$ **4.** $5d - 18$

436

Show how to build and undo each expression.

1. $4x + 2$ **2.** $10y - 8$ **3.** $\dfrac{x}{3} - 4$ **4.** $\dfrac{a}{5} - 2.5$

5. $7.2r + 1$ **6.** $^{-}4t - 2$ **7.** $\dfrac{s}{5} - \dfrac{1}{2}$ **8.** $\dfrac{x}{3} - 14.8$

APPLY

MATH REASONING Write an algebraic expression that represents each situation.

9. Cable TV costs: $25 installation fee, plus $20 per month for m months.

10. Pizza cost: $7.50, plus $0.75 for each extra topping (t).

11. Summer earnings: $15 per yard ($y$), less $125 for the cost of the mower.

12. Checking account cost: $4 service charge, plus $0.10 per check ($c$).

Write an algebraic expression for the area of the shaded figure.

13.

w | Area = ? | 11 | 3 | 3

14.

5 | Area = ? | 2 | l | 3

PROBLEM SOLVING

15. Let h be the cost of 1 granola bar. Write an expression for an 8-pack of granola bars and a carton of milk that costs $.96.

16. Let w be the weight of dry cereal in ounces. Write an expression that shows the weight of a 10 pack of cereal and a pound of bananas.

MIXED REVIEW

Solve.

17. $x + 7 = 15$ **18.** $2.4 + a = 7.6$ **19.** $4a = 8.4$ **20.** $3b = 72$

21. $N - 10 = 22$ **22.** $\dfrac{x}{9} = 10$ **23.** $\dfrac{x}{3} = 2.8$ **24.** $a - 1\dfrac{1}{2} = 3\dfrac{1}{4}$

Find the answers using mental math.

25. $2000 - 4 = x$ **26.** $4 \times 405 = b$ **27.** $3.2 + 8.5 + 7.8 = x$

28. $8 \times 203 = n$ **29.** $420 + 280 + 170 = c$ **30.** $3004 - 1999 = y$

More Practice, page 543, set C

Solving Two-Step Equations

EXPLORE **Solve Using Counting Chips**

Work in groups. The diagram shows a model of the equation $4x + 2 = 14$. Use chips to find the value of the variable.

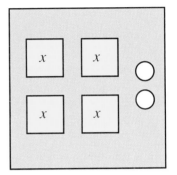

TALK ABOUT IT

1. What did you do first with the counters?

2. What algebraic expression results when 2 objects are removed from both sides?

3. If $4x = 12$, how did you decide on the value of x?

Follow these steps to solve two-step equations.

- Identify the order in which the operations have been applied to the variable.
- Undo the operations in reverse order by applying the inverse operations on both sides of the equation.

Examples Solve.

A
$$3n - 4 = 11$$
$$3n - 4 + 4 = 11 + 4$$
$$3n = 15$$
$$3n \div 3 = 15 \div 3$$
$$n = 5$$

First n was multiplied by 3. Then 4 was subtracted.
Undo subtracting 4 by adding 4 to both sides.

Divide by 3 to undo multiplying by 3.
Check: $3 \cdot 5 - 4 = 11$ ✓

B
$$\frac{x}{8} + 5 = 7$$
$$\frac{x}{8} + 5 - 5 = 7 - 5$$
$$\frac{x}{8} = 2$$
$$\frac{x}{8} \cdot 8 = 2 \cdot 8$$
$$x = 16$$

Undo adding 5 by subtracting 5 from both sides.

Multiply by 8 to undo dividing by 8.
Check: $\frac{16}{8} + 5 = 7$ ✓

Solve and check.

1. $5y - 7 = 33$

2. $2.07 = 6n - 0.15$

3. $90 = \frac{g}{5} - 45$

Solve and check.

1. $4x - 5 = 19$

2. $\dfrac{n}{2} + 3 = 13$

3. $\dfrac{c}{3} + 3 = {}^{-}3$

4. $15z + 5 = 230$

5. $6.2 = 3.2b - 0.2$

6. $5\dfrac{1}{2} = 4 + 3z$

7. $\dfrac{t}{3} - 12 = 7$

8. $^{-}5v - 7 = 28$

9. $4s + 6 = 4$

10. $\dfrac{1}{2} + \dfrac{d}{4} = 108$

11. $^{-}8 = {}^{-}3x + 58$

12. $25x - 135 = {}^{-}135$

13. $17 + \dfrac{u}{7} = 108$

14. $\dfrac{u}{2} + 4 = 31$

15. $19 - 4w = 91$

APPLY

MATH REASONING Use the distributive property to help solve these equations.

16. $4(x - 8) = 52$

17. $90 = \dfrac{1}{2}(n + 6)$

18. $2(4t + 3) = 24$

Write an equation for each diagram. Solve and check the equation.

19.
$$\mathrel{\mid\!\longleftarrow} 101 \longrightarrow\!\mid$$
$$\mid\text{-- V --}\mathbin{\ast}\text{-- V --}\mathbin{\ast}\text{-- V --}\mathbin{\ast}\text{-7-}\mid$$

20.
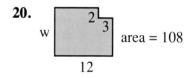
area = 108

PROBLEM SOLVING

21. Fingernails grow about 1.5 inches per year. The world record for a fingernail is 37 inches. The solution to the equation $1.5\,y + 0.5 = 37$ tells how many years it might take to grow a 37-inch fingernail. Solve the equation to find out.

22. Suppose you have $10 and you save x dollars of your allowance each week. The solution to the equation $52x + 10 = 200$ tells how much you need to save each week to buy a new bicycle one year from now. Find the amount you need to save.

▶ USING CRITICAL THINKING

Write a word problem which can be solved using each equation. Solve and check the equation.

23. $x + 5 = 3.5$

24. $3x - 1 = 7$

Using Critical Thinking
Inventing Activities for a Function Machine

LEARN ABOUT IT

As a class project, Beth's group built a function machine.

"You put in a card with an **input** number," said Beth. "The machine applies a rule to the number and prints an **output.**"

"What will we do with it?" asked La Quint."

"We can give an input number and a rule and ask someone to act as the brains of the machine and give the output number."

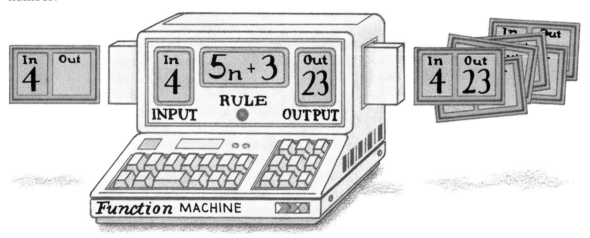

TALK ABOUT IT

1. How could a student be the "brains" of the machine?

2. Can different rules produce the same output given the same input?

TRY IT OUT

1. Give a rule and several output numbers. Have your partner give the input numbers.

2. Give several input, output number pairs and have your partner give the rule.

3. Suppose you hooked two function machines with different rules together so that the output of the first machine is the input to the second? Does the order of hookup make a difference in the output number? Give an example.

4. Can you think of two different rules that produce a final output which equals the original input?

MIDCHAPTER REVIEW/QUIZ

Evaluate each expression. Use $x = 6$, $y = {}^-2$ and $z = 12$ as needed.

1. $4 \times 3 + 4 \times 2$

2. $18 - 2 \times 3 + 4$

3. $81 \div 6 - 3 \times 2$

4. $8 - 2 \times 5.5$

5. $12.4 \div 0.2 + 6$

6. $9 \times (5 - x) \div (7 + 2)$

7. $120 \div y \times 15$

8. $6y - 28 \div {}^-7$

9. ${}^-18 \div (z - 18) + 10$

Make a reasonable guess and show the check.

10. Johnny is 9 years older than Sue. Together their ages are 25. Guess Sue's age.

11. The temperature of a solution was 30°. During an experiment, the temperature dropped $\frac{1}{2}$° each minute until it reached 12°. Guess the number of minutes.

Match each situation with one of the expressions from the list.

12. 2 pounds of butter (b) and a $2-bag of oranges

13. a pound of butter (b) and a $2-bag of oranges shared by two

14. $\frac{1}{2}$ pound of butter (b) and a $2-bag of oranges

A. $(b + 2) \div 2$

B. $2b + 2$

C. $\frac{1}{2}b + 2$

Write an expression for each situation.

15. work for h hours at $5 per hour less $10 for taxes

16. cab fare $3.50 plus $1.10 per mile for m miles

17. cost of a half pound of apples a and a $1-container of juice

18. cost of $\frac{1}{4}$ pound of butter (b) less a $0.25 refund

Tell the two steps to undo each expression.

19. $3t - 7$

20. $2r + 5$

21. $\frac{1}{4}k - 10$

22. $\frac{1}{3}w + 2.4$

Solve these equations.

23. $2x - 4 = 8$

24. $\frac{1}{3}x + 2 = 5$

25. $3x + 2.7 = 18$

26. $4x - 6 + 2x = 24$

PROBLEM SOLVING

27. Each month Melanie donates one-tenth of her earnings to charity and puts $5 into savings. This month those costs totaled $25. What were her earnings? How much was left for other expenses?

28. Bob bought 2 sandwiches and a 75¢ drink for $4.25. How much did each sandwich cost?

441

Graphing Inequalities

LEARN ABOUT IT

EXPLORE **Analyze the Data**

ABOUT HENRY DAVID THOREAU
Born in 1817; Died in 1862 Published *Walden* in 1854 Yearly income from farm—at least \$23 Yearly cost to run farm—less than \$15 Farm land worth more than \$8 per acre Earned over \$13 in a year for day labor Concord, Mass. lowest temperature $^-26°$ Concord, Mass. highest temperature $103°$

TALK ABOUT IT

1. What is the smallest yearly income that Thoreau's farm could have brought in?

2. What is the most it cost him to run his farm for a year?

3. What inequality shows the temperature range in Concord?

Inequality symbols ($>$, $<$, $\geq$, and $\leq$) can be used individually or in pairs to describe sets of numbers.

Examples

A Write an inequality to express the years (y) prior to the publication of *Walden* and graph the solution.

Walden was published in 1854.
$y < 1854$ is the inequality.

B Write an inequality to express the range of temperatures (t) in Concord and graph the solution.

Temperatures range from $^-26$ to 103
$^-26 \leq t \leq 103$ is the inequality.

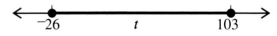

TRY IT OUT

Graph each inequality.

1. $x < 4$

2. $a > 6$

3. $-3 < h < 7$

442

Write an inequality for each sentence.

Write a sentence for each inequality.

1. Savings (*s*) are more than $1,000.

6. $n < 300$

2. The distance (*d*) is at least 5000 mi.

7. $d \leq {}^-20$

3. The speed (*s*) is less than 55 mph.

8. $t < {}^-300$

4. The temperature (*t*) is colder than $^-20$ C.

9. $t > {}^-30$

5. Savings (*s*) are between $50 and $500.

10. ${}^-35 < t < 50$

Graph each inequality.

11. ${}^-13 < y$

12. $a \geq 45$

13. $x \leq {}^-39$

14. $x < 15$

15. $x > 45.6$

16. $k < {}^-14\frac{2}{3}$

17. $h \geq {}^-98$

18. $d \leq 5.3$

19. ${}^-14 < y < 38$

20. $15 \geq t > 5$

21. ${}^-23 < l \leq {}^-15$

22. ${}^-200 < f < {}^-35$

MATH REASONING Write an inequality for each graph.

23.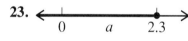

24.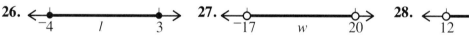

25.

26. $\begin{array}{ccc} \bullet & & \bullet \\ {}^-4 & l & 3 \end{array}$

27. $\begin{array}{ccc} \circ & & \circ \\ {}^-17 & w & 20 \end{array}$

28. $\begin{array}{ccc} \circ & & \circ \\ 12 & b & 47 \end{array}$

PROBLEM SOLVING

29. Language Arts Data Bank Write and graph an inequality to show how many animal crackers you might be offered in Sandburg's poem.

30. Write and graph an inequality expressing the value of Thoreau's 11-acre farm, if one acre were worth more than $8.

DATA BANK

Write each decimal as a lowest-term fraction or mixed number.

31. 0.18

32. 5.02

33. 3.5

34. 3.50

Evaluate each expression for $x = 0.3$, $y = 4.7$, $z = 7.2$

35. $zx + y$

36. $z(x + y)$

37. $zx + zy$

38. $(y + x)z$

More Practice, page 543, set D

Solving Inequalities

LEARN ABOUT IT

EXPLORE   Analyze the Situation

Scale A is unbalanced. It represents the inequality $x + 2 > 14$. The scale will remain as it is if the same amount is added to or taken away from each side.

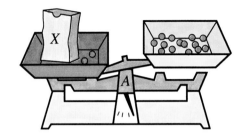

TALK ABOUT IT

1. What can you do to get the paper bag by itself on the left-hand pan?

2. If this action is repeated on the right-hand side, how many marbles will be left?

3. What inequality does the scale now suggest?

Use the same procedure for solving addition and subtraction inequalities as you did for solving equations. **Identify** the operation applied to the variable. **Undo** the operation by using the inverse operation on both sides of the inequality.

Examples

A Solve. $x - 4 < 18$ 4 is subtracted from x.

$x - 4 + 4 < 18 + 4$ Undo subtracting 4 by adding 4 to both sides.

$x < 22$

Check the computation.	Check the inequality symbol.
Rewrite $x - 4 = 18$	Choose a value from $x < 22$
Substitute $22 - 4 = 18$ $4 = 4 \checkmark$	Substitute $20 - 4 < 18$ $16 < 18 \checkmark$

B Solve. $^-5 < t - 12$ Check $^-5 = t - 12$ Choose a value for t.

$^-5 + 12 < t - 12 + 12$ $^-5 = 7 - 12$ $^-5 < 8 - 12$

$7 < t$ or $t > 7$ $^-5 = {}^-5 \checkmark$ $^-5 < {}^-4 \checkmark$

TRY IT OUT

Solve and check.

1. $^-14 < x + 5$

2. $n - 25 \leq 63$

3. $^-34 \geq m + 23$

444

Solve and check.

1. $t - 14 < 38$ **2.** $^-24 < c + 10$ **3.** $y + 100 \geq 125$ **4.** $g - 50 \geq {}^-30$

5. $l + 22 < 49$ **6.** $150 > h - 200$ **7.** $p + 8 \leq {}^-14$ **8.** $x - 70 > 0$

9. $^-30 \geq z + 26$ **10.** $^-42 + k < 21$ **11.** $100 \leq x - 100$ **12.** $v - 81 > {}^-17$

13. $19 + t \leq 0$ **14.** $w + 22 > 22$ **15.** $121 < 20 + q$ **16.** $y - 31 \geq {}^-29$

APPLY

MATH REASONING Solve the inequalities represented by the diagrams.
Like objects have the same weight. Each marble weighs one unit.

17.    **18.**

Use **mental math** to solve these inequalities.

19. $110 < y + 10$ **20.** $30.75 \geq n + 0.75$ **21.** $x - 25 > 50$

PROBLEM SOLVING

22. Eric had a 3.5-second head start, but was beaten in the 440-yard dash. How long had he run when the winner crossed the finish line in 62.9 seconds?

23. Sheila owed her mom $24.39 when she got a paper route. Within 2 months she paid back her mother and saved $113. How much had Sheila earned?

24. Unfinished Problem Write a problem that could be solved using this information.

The United States owes other countries over $2 trillion. There are approximately 225 million people in this country.

ESTIMATION

Estimate each solution to the nearest whole number.

25. $x + 14.978 < 285.004$ **26.** $^-23.894 \geq x - 24.011$ **27.** $37\frac{8}{9} > x + 18$

More Practice, page 543, set E

Equivalent Expressions

represents the variable x

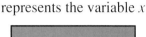

EXPLORE   Analyze a Model

You can use algebra tiles to model operations with variables.
The tiles below show the expression $x + 4$.

represents 1 unit

 $x + 4$

Write an algebraic expression for each set of tiles.

(a)    (b)

TALK ABOUT IT

1. How did you find algebraic expressions
for (a) and (b)?

2. Use the distributive property to give two
algebraic expressions for (b).

Examples

A Write an equivalent expression for $(3x + 4) + (2x + 5)$.
Use algebra tiles to show your expressions are equivalent.
$$(3x + 4) + (2x + 5) = 5x + 9$$

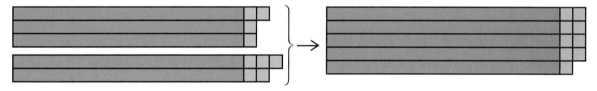

B Use the distributive property to give an equivalent expression
for $3(2x + 1)$. Show the expression with algebra tiles.
$$3(2x + 1) = 6x + 3$$

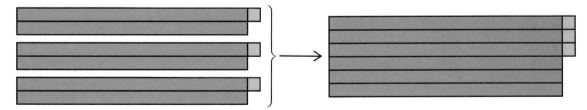

Use tiles to find an equivalent expression.

1. $(5x + 1) + (x + 2)$ **2.** $4(x + 2)$ **3.** $(2x + 1) + (x + 3)$

446

Give an equivalent expression. Use algebra tiles.

1. $(2x + 4) + (x + 2)$

2. $(2x + 7) + (2x + 1)$

3. $3x + 4 + 3x$

4. $2(x + 1)$

5. $3(2x + 4)$

6. $5 + 2x + 2 + 4x$

Try these without algebra tiles.

7. $4x + 3 + 6x + 1$ 8. $2x + 4x + 5x$ 9. $7x + 2x + 4x + 6$

APPLY

<u>MATH REASONING</u> Simplify each expression.

10. $3(x + 2) + 4x$ 11. $5(2x + 1) + 6$ 12. $2(2x + 2) + 3(2x + 3)$

13. Draw a diagram to show how might you use the algebra tiles to simplify $5x + 5 + (^-2) + (^-3x)$.

<u>PROBLEM SOLVING</u>

14. A company designed a cement patio as shown at the right. The length of the large square section is represented by x. Write an algebraic expression for the area of the patio.

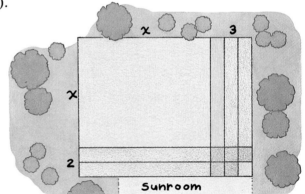

▶ <u>USING CRITICAL THINKING</u> **Analyze a Model**

15. Use the distributive property and the algebra tiles to write an expression equivalent to $3x + 6$.

16. Use the distributive property to write an expression equivalent to $4x + 12$. Can you find more than one way to do this?

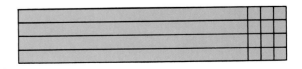

Group Decision Making
Applied Problem Solving

UNDERSTAND
ANALYZE DATA
PLAN
ESTIMATE
SOLVE
EXAMINE

Group Skill
Disagree in an Agreeable Way

Learn About It

Your group has been selected to be on a national student committee to reenact a Pony Express ride. You need to devise a plan to show how students will ride from St. Joseph, Missouri to Sacramento, California. You will need to decide how many students will participate, how far each rider will go, and how many horses are necessary. You must also estimate what day the last rider will arrive in Sacramento.

Facts to Consider

- The distance formula is $d = rt$, where d = distance, r = rate, t = time.
- Riders can ride at a rate of approximately:
    20 miles per hour over flat land
    10 miles per hour over desert
     5 miles per hour over mountains
- The longest distance one rider can go is 75 miles.
- Riders will ride day and night.
- Horses need to be changed every 10 to 15 miles.
- The trip will start at 6 am on May 1.

Questions to Answer

1. How can you use the map to find the length of the entire trip?

2. Will each rider go the same distance? Why or why not?

3. How can you use the distance formula to find how long the ride will take?

What Is Your Decision?

Present your group's riding assignments and the plan for changing horses. Give your arrival date and explain how you got it. Use a reference book to find out about the original Pony Express. How does your plan compare?

WRAP UP

Terminology Square

Write the number of the statement that best matches each term.

1. Inverse operations

2. exponent

3. order of operations rule

4. inequality

5. equivalent expressions

6. distributive property

A $3 + s \geq 6$

B compute within grouping symbols first

C connects addition and multiplication when both operations are involved

D Indicates power to which a base is raised

E addition and subtraction

F $3(x + 4) + 2x$ and $5x + 12$

Sometimes, Always, Never

Which word should go in the blank, *sometimes*, *always*, or *never*? Explain your choice.

7. In an expression containing several operations, addition should __?__ be done first.

8. The inverse of subtraction is __?__ division.

9. To undo an expression, you follow the reverse order as in building the expression, and __?__ use inverse operations.

10. Inequalities __?__ contain the symbols $>$ and $<$.

11. The least possible solution of an inequality is __?__ shown on a graph by a small open circle.

Project

Make a Model

Use color tiles or paper squares (one unit square) to model rectangles with the given dimensions.

Write an expression which could be used to find the area of each rectangle. Can an area model show multiplication of any two variables? Explain. Use examples.

450

CHAPTER REVIEW/TEST

Part 1   Understanding

1. List the rules for the order of operations.

2. ___?___ operations are used to "undo" expressions.

3. Describe how the expression $3p - 7$ was built.

4. Describe how to "undo" the expression $\frac{b}{3} + 4$.

5. Start with an input of 23. Give two different rules that will produce the same output.

6. $2(7x + 4) = 14x + 8$ is an example of what property?

Part 2   Skills

Evaluate each expression.

7. $3(4 + 7) - 2$

8. $35 - 2x^2 \div 3$ for $x = 2$

Solve and check each equation or inequality.

9. $5s - 3 = 4.5$

10. $6(h + 4) = 96$

11. $15 + t > 20$

12. $z - 50 \leq 74$

Graph each inequality.

13. $^-7 < q$

14. $^-2 \leq s < 5$

Give an equivalent expression for each.

15. $(3x + 4) + (2x + 5)$

16. $4(2x + 3) + 3x$

Part 3   Applications

Write an algebraic expression for each.

17. Dessert: $1.25 for yogurt, plus $.50 for each topping (t)

18. Games won (w) were more than 5.

19. **Challenge.** A parking lot charges $2 for the first hour and $.75 for each additional hour. The total charge for a car was $5. How many hours past the first hour was the car parked there?

ENRICHMENT
Combinations and Probability

The seventh grade class must elect two persons to the Student Council. Five students, Alyssa, Barry, Charles, Dean, and Edwina are running for election. How many different **combinations** of 2 students are possible to be selected from the 5 students?

If Alyssa and Barry (A, B) are one choice, the combination of Barry and Alyssa (B, A) is not a new choice.

1. Make a list of all the possible combinations of 2 people from the 5 people. Use the letters of the first names to make the list easier to make.

2. Suppose the 5 names were put in a hat and 2 names were drawn out without looking. What is the probability that Dean and Edwina would be the two names drawn?

3. What is the probability that a boy's name and a girl's name would be drawn from the hat?

4. What is the probability that both names will be girl's names?

5. Suppose Frank decided to run for Student Council making a total of 6 students. How many combinations of 2 students out of the 6 students are possible?

6. What is the probability that two boy's names will be drawn from the list of 4 boys and 2 girls?

7. Is it more likely that 2 boy's names will be drawn from a list of 4 boys and two girls, or a boy's name and a girl's name? Guess, then check your guess by making a list of the combinations.

CUMULATIVE REVIEW

1. What is $P(\text{odd number})$?

  A $\frac{1}{2}$ **B** $\frac{1}{4}$

  C $\frac{1}{3}$ **D** $\frac{2}{3}$

2. Which inequality is expressed by the graph?

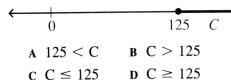

  A $125 < C$ **B** $C > 125$

  C $C \leq 125$ **D** $C \geq 125$

3. What is the width?

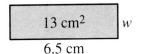

  A 2 cm
  B 7 cm
  C 3 cm
  D 1 cm

4. What is the surface area of the prism?

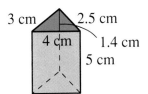

  A 50.3 cm^2
  B 47.5 cm^2
  C 50.1 cm^2
  D 53.1 cm^2

5. What is the volume of a cylinder with $r = 4$ cm and $h = 6$ cm? Use 3.14 for π.

  A 602.86 cm^3 **B** 150.72 cm^3

  C 753.6 cm^3 **D** 301.44 cm^3

6. What is the volume of a cone with $r = 4$ cm and $h = 6$ cm? Use 3.14 for π.

  A 602.86 cm^3 **B** 100.48 cm^3

  C 753.6 cm^3 **D** 301.44 cm^3

7. How many lines of symmetry does this polygon have?

  A 4
  B 5
  C 8
  D 10

8. Figure A is what turn image of figure B?

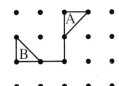

  A $\frac{1}{4}$ **B** $\frac{1}{2}$

  C $\frac{1}{3}$ **D** $\frac{1}{6}$

9. Which pair of numbers completes the table?

P	1	3	4
$(3 P^2 \div 2) - 1$	0.5	?	?

  A 12.5, 23   **B** 6, 8

  C 7.5, 8.5   **D** 10, 20

10. A water storage tank has the shape of a cylinder. The diameter of the tank is 4 m and the height is 5 m. If the diameter is changed to 8 m, the volume is

  A doubled   **B** tripled

  C quadrupled   **D** multiplied by 20

11. A survey of 1,627 auto owners found that 18% have cellular telephones. Which is the best estimate of how many of the surveyed auto owners have telephones in their cars?

  A 40   **B** 160

  C 400   **D** 320

16

EXTENDING LOGICAL REASONING

MATH AND LANGUAGE ARTS

DATA BANK

Use the Language Arts Data Bank on page 502 to answer the questions.

1. Use the American Sign guage alphabet to compl this analogy: N is to M is to ___?___.

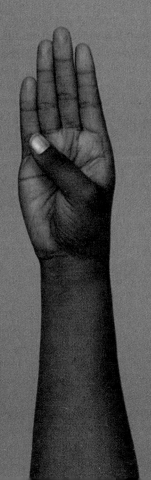

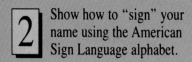

2 Show how to "sign" your name using the American Sign Language alphabet.

3 In A. C. Doyle's story, *Adventure of the Dancing Men*, Sherlock Holmes deciphers a code made of stick figures that stand for letters of the alphabet. Make up your own "dancing men" code for the letters A through Z.

4 **Using Critical Thinking** Poe's and Doyle's characters deciphered codes using probability and deduction. They knew which letters of the alphabet are most commonly used. Devise a way to find the most frequently used letters in English.

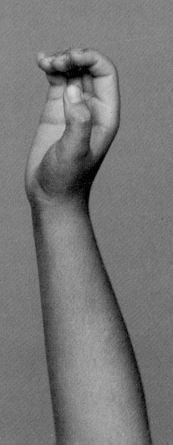

Inductive Reasoning
Discovering Number Patterns

LEARN ABOUT IT

EXPLORE **Analyze the Situation**

The picture to the right shows how you might find the number of games to be played in a round-robin checkers tournament.

people	games
2	1
3	3
4	6

TALK ABOUT IT

1. Do you see a pattern that shows how the number of games depends on the number of players? What does your pattern indicate for 5 people? 6 people? 20 people? *n* people?

When you discover a pattern that you think works, try it in several cases. If the pattern works for those cases, then you might conclude that it will work for all cases. This is called **inductive reasoning.**

Example At birth Kristy got $100. Each birthday thereafter she got $100 more than the last. How much will she have in all at age 20?

Solution A table can help. Try different patterns.

age	amount ($100s)	total ($100s)	pattern 1	pattern 2
0	1	1	0 + 1	(1 · 2) ÷ 2
1	2	3	1 + 2	(2 · 3) ÷ 2
2	3	6	2 + 3	(3 · 4) ÷ 2
. . .	. . .	. . .	. . .	. . .
n	*n* + 1	?	*n* + (*n* + 1)	(*n* + 1)(*n* + 2) ÷ 2

Both patterns work for ages 0 and 1, but pattern 1 fails for age 2. It seems that $(n + 1)(n + 2) \div 2$ gives the total saved by age *n*. For $n = 20$, the total would be $21 \cdot 22 \div 2 = 231$. So, Kristy would have 231 hundred dollars or $23,100.

TRY IT OUT

1. How many dots would be in the 50th picture?

What is the sum of

1. the first 30 counting numbers?

counting numbers	1 2 3 4 5 6 ... 30
sum	1 3 6

2. the first 25 even numbers?

position of number	1st 2nd 3rd 4th ... 25th
even number	2 4 6 8
sum	2 6 12

3. the first 50 odd numbers?

position of number	1st 2nd 3rd 4th ... 50th
odd number	1 3 5 7
sum	1 4 9

4. the cubes of the first 40 counting numbers?

numbers	1 2 3 4 5 ... 40
cubes of numbers	1 8 27 64 125
sum	1 9

APPLY

MATH REASONING

5. Use a calculator to start writing the decimal for $\frac{9}{11}$. Use inductive reasoning to tell what digit occupies the 100th place to the right of the decimal point.

PROBLEM SOLVING Use inductive reasoning to solve.

6. Henry's rich uncle gave him $100 the day Henry was born, and promised to increase the gift by $200 each birthday. How much should Henry have on his 21st birthday if he saves it all?

7. A wheel with 36 spokes has how many spaces between the spokes?

8. Data Hunt In the 18th century an astronomer named Bode used inductive reasoning to decide where unseen planets should be, if they existed. His decision partially turned out to be correct. Look up Bode's law and describe in your own words the pattern he devised.

▶ **USING CRITICAL THINKING Visualize**

9. The gear on the right end is turning clockwise. As it does, it turns the next gear, and this action continues down the line. In which direction, clockwise or counterclockwise, does the 100th gear from the right turn?

Inductive Reasoning
Discovering Geometric Patterns

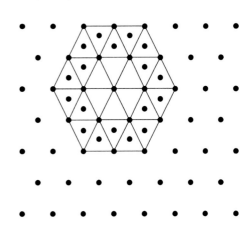

EXPLORE **Make a Model**

Use isometric dot paper to make layers of triangles. Shade the inner 6—they make up the first layer. Put a dot in each triangle in the second layer—it has 18 triangles. Put a check in each triangle in the 3rd layer. Be sure you have 30 checks.

TALK ABOUT IT

1. How many triangles are in the 4th layer? in the 5th layer?

2. How could you find the number of triangles in the 25th layer—it's too hard to draw!

Inductive reasoning is often used to discover geometric relationships. You consider simple cases like the problem given, organize your work, and look for a pattern. When you discover a pattern, you test it on a few more simple cases. If the pattern holds true, you can give the answer to the original problem.

Example How many different-sized squares are there on an 8 × 8 checkerboard?

Solution: Use simple cases as shown to the right. The pattern for the first 3 cases says the number of squares in the 4 × 4 should be $1^2 + 2^2 + 3^2 + 4^2$. We count and find it.

1^2 or 1

$1^2 + 2^2$ or 5

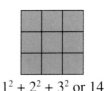
$1^2 + 2^2 + 3^2$ or 14

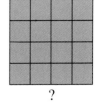
?

A checkerboard has $1^2 + 2^2 + 3^2 + 4^2 + 5^2 + 6^2 + 7^2 + 8^2$, or 204 squares!

TRY IT OUT

1. Find the number of vertices (corner points) on an 8 × 8 checkboard without drawing it.

Draw pictures to help you solve these. Use inductive reasoning.

1. How many vertices would there be on a 3-dimensional polyhedron like the one shown, but 50 "blocks high"?

2. How many vertices would there be on a square polyhedron like the one shown below, but made from 64 "blocks"?

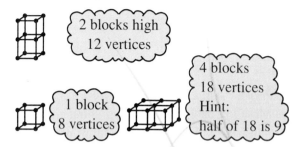

2 blocks high
12 vertices

1 block
8 vertices

4 blocks
18 vertices
Hint:
half of 18 is 9

MATH REASONING

3. Two students found different answers to this problem. Their teacher said both were right. Can you find both answers?

An architect used 100 blocks to build a pyramid like the one started at the right. There is 1 block on the top, 4 blocks on the second layer, and so on. What are the dimensions of the bottom layer in order to use as many of the 100 blocks as possible?

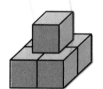

PROBLEM SOLVING

4. Jeremiah built geometric figures like those to the right. How many triangles would be along the bottom, for a model with 100 small triangles altogether?

5. Unfinished Problem Make up a problem which can be answered using the following data. Answer the problem.

Toothpicks come 250 to a box, and a box costs 45¢.

Use a tree diagram to find the probability for two spins on the spinner.

6. $P(R,R)$ **7.** $P(B,B)$ **8.** $P(Y,Y)$

Solve.

9. What is 35% of 300?

10. 82 is what percent of 90?

11. $\frac{1}{2}$% of 40 is what number?

12. 20 is 40% of what number?

Discovering Relationships

EXPLORE Analyze the Situation

Mr. Goldbach was thinking about prime
numbers and noticed something interesting.

TALK ABOUT IT

1. What type of numbers are circled on the
   chalkboard?

2. What type of numbers are the addends?

3. Can you find an even number greater than 2 that cannot be
   written as the sum of primes?

Mathematical relationships, like Goldbach's conjecture are
sometimes well known. Frequently they are made by students
like yourself, and come from simply noticing the mathematics
around you.

Example Jenny Goldinger found a way to divide one fraction
by another. It worked if the fractions were just right.

Jenny's Solution: Jenny found that, when
$a \div c$ and $b \div d$ are whole numbers,
fractions can be divided by using:

$$\frac{a}{b} \div \frac{c}{d} = \frac{a \div c}{b \div d}$$

Her shortcut was to divide numerator by
numerator, and denominator by denominator,
if possible.

On the chalkboard:

$$\textcircled{4} \quad \textcircled{6} \quad \textcircled{8} \quad \textcircled{10} \quad \textcircled{12}$$
$$2+2 \quad 3+3 \quad 5+3 \quad 3+7 \quad 7+5$$

$$\textcircled{30} \quad \textcircled{32} \quad \textcircled{34} \quad \textcircled{36}$$
$$17+13 \quad 3+29 \quad 3+31 \quad 17+19$$

$$\frac{15}{28} \div \frac{3}{4} = \frac{15 \div 3}{28 \div 4} = \frac{5}{7}$$

CHECK $\dfrac{15}{28} \div \dfrac{3}{4} = \dfrac{15}{28} \times \dfrac{4}{3} = \dfrac{5}{7}$

1. Write down any 6 odd numbers. Find the
   sum. Is it even or odd?

2. Write down any 7 odd numbers. Find the
   sum. Is it even or odd?

3. If all your classmates got an even
   number for 1 above, what would you
   conclude?

4. If all of your classmates got an odd
   number for 2 above, what would you
   conclude?

Do these problems Jenny's way.

1. $\dfrac{12}{35} \div \dfrac{3}{5}$ **2.** $\dfrac{10}{21} \div \dfrac{5}{7}$ **3.** $\dfrac{24}{25} \div \dfrac{8}{5}$ **4.** $\dfrac{8}{9} \div \dfrac{4}{3}$

Use only prime numbers as addends below.

5. $14 = $ |||| $+$ |||| **6.** $16 = $ |||| $+$ |||| **7.** $18 = $ |||| $+$ |||| **8.** $20 = $ |||| $+$ ||||

9. $22 = $ |||| $+$ |||| **10.** $24 = $ |||| $+$ |||| **11.** $26 = $ |||| $+$ |||| **12.** $28 = $ |||| $+$ ||||

Jenny Goldinger didn't quit where we left off in the example. She found a way to rename the dividend (first) fraction so she could continue dividing her way.

Use Jenny's method on these problems:

Here's what to do when the numerators divide ok, but the denominators don't!

$$\frac{4}{21} \div \frac{2}{9} = \frac{9}{9} \times \frac{4}{21} \div \frac{2}{9}$$
$$= \frac{9 \times 4}{9 \times 21} \div \frac{2}{9}$$
$$= \frac{9 \times 4 \div 2}{9 \times 21 \div 9}$$
$$= \frac{18}{21}$$

13. $\dfrac{12}{7} \div \dfrac{3}{5}$ **14.** $\dfrac{8}{5} \div \dfrac{4}{3}$ **15.** $\dfrac{6}{7} \div \dfrac{2}{3}$

MATH REASONING

16. Is the sum of an *even number of odd numbers* an even number, or an odd number?

17. Is the sum of an *odd number of odd numbers* an even number, or an odd number?

PROBLEM SOLVING

18. A student named Karl Gauss came up with this method of adding the first 100 counting numbers.

He could do any such computation mentally, astounding his teachers. Use this method to find the sum of the first 20 counting numbers. Then the first 40.

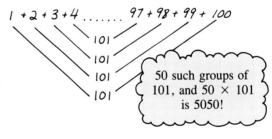

$1 + 2 + 3 + 4 \ldots\ldots 97 + 98 + 99 + 100$

101
101
101
101

50 such groups of 101, and 50×101 is 5050!

▶ **USING CRITICAL THINKING**   **Justify Your Answer**

19. Think how Jenny might rename the dividend $\dfrac{2}{9}$ in the problem $\dfrac{2}{9} \div \dfrac{5}{3}$, so that she could use her method of dividing numerators and dividing denominators. Write the problem and solve it the way Jenny would.

Informal Proof in Algebra

EXPLORE Analyze a Situation

You used a pattern to find the number of games played if there are 20 players in a round-robin tournament. If you asked, "How do I *know* my answer is correct?" you are asking the right question. Imagine you are one of the 20 players.

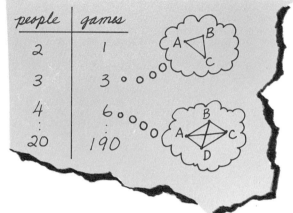

TALK ABOUT IT

1. How many games do **you** have to play? How many other players must play that many games?

2. Why are games counted twice in saying 20×19 is the number? How can the double count be corrected?

The examples below show **informal proof** in algebra.

Example A Show that, if there are n players, then there must be $n(n - 1) \div 2$ games in the tournament.

Informal Proof: Each of the n people plays every other player, and there are $n - 1$ other players. So, $n(n - 1)$ gives the total number of games, except that they have been counted twice. Therefore $n(n - 1) \div 2$ is the final number of games.

Example B How does this number trick work?

> Pick *any* number. Add 7.
> Multiply by 2. Subtract 4.
> Divide by 2.
> Subtract your original number.
> You get the answer 5.

Solution: Let n be your number (any number).
Step 1: $n + 7$
Step 2: $2(n + 7)$ or $2n + 14$
Step 3: $2n + 14 - 4$, or $2n + 10$
Step 4: $(2n + 10) \div 2$, or $n + 5$
Step 5: $n + 5 - n$, or 5.

1. In a 64-team tournament, a team is eliminated if it loses one game. How many games will determine a champion?

2. Find a rule that determines the number of games needed for any number of teams. Give an informal proof for your rule.

Try each number trick below. Then write the steps that show
why each works.

1. Pick any number. Add 5 to your number. Multiply the result
   by 3. Add 12. Divide by 3. Subtract your number. Is your
   answer 9?

2. Pick any number. Add 3. Multiply result by 4. Subtract 12.
   Subtract your number twice. Divide by 2. Is your answer the
   number?

3. Pick any number. Subtract 6. Multiply by 2. Add 15.
   Subtract 1. Divide by 2. Subtract your number. Is your
   answer 1?

4. Martha was a fifth grader who liked to puzzle her teacher by
   doing multiplication problems that had the correct answer,
   but the partial products did not look like anyone else's. Use
   her method to find 26 × 53.

```
   32              60
  x45             x28
  ───             ───
   90              00
  135             168
  ─────           ─────
 1,440           1,680
```

PROBLEM SOLVING

5. If ten people are playing musical chairs,
   how many times does the music have to
   stop to find a winner if one chair is
   removed each time?

6. **Talk about your solution** Develop an
   informal proof that the music must stop
   $k - 1$ times to find a winner, if k people
   are playing and one chair is removed
   each time.

▶ **USING CRITICAL THINKING   Support Your Conclusion**

Some logical thinking is not based on algebra or even
mathematics. Briefly justify your answers below.

7. Place the last 16 letters of the alphabet above or below the
   line, using the pattern for the first 10:

```
 A       E F   H I
───────────────────────
   B C D     G     J
```

8. What is the next letter of the alphabet that follows these?
   M V E M J S U N ?

Informal Proof in Geometry

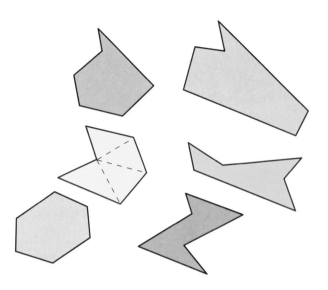

LEARN ABOUT IT

In the last lesson you considered how
situations from algebra could be proved with
logical thinking. Here you will see similar
reasoning, but in geometry.

EXLORE **Make a Model**

Trace the hexagons. Can you divide each
hexagon into triangles by connecting the
vertices of the hexagons with line segments?

TALK ABOUT IT

1. Into how many triangles did you divide each hexagon?

2. What is the measure of the angles of a triangle?

3. How can you find the sum of the measures of the angles of
a hexagon?

The activity above shows how to demonstrate informally that
the angles of any hexagon total $4 \cdot 180°$. These steps can be
summarized into an informal proof.

Example Give a reasoned argument that the sum of the
interior angles of a hexagon is given by $4 \cdot 180°$.

A hexagon can be divided into 4 triangles so that the angles of
the hexagon are also the angles of the triangles. Since the
angles of a triangle measure $180°$, the measures of the angles of
four triangles is $4 \cdot 180°$. Therefore the angles of the hexagon
also measure $4 \cdot 180°$.

TRY IT OUT

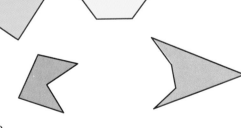

Trace the pentagons.

1. Can each pentagon be divided into
triangles similar to the way the hexagons
were divided? How many triangles?

2. What is the measure of the angles of a pentagon?

464

Consider this pattern of dot figures.

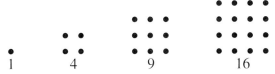

1   4   9   16

Consider this pattern of rectangles.

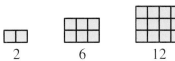

2   6   12   20

1. How many dots are in the next figure?

2. What is the area of the next rectangle?

3. How many dots are in the 100th figure?

4. What is the area of the 100th rectangle?

Consider this pattern of cubes.

5. List the surface areas of the first five cubes.

6. What is the surface area of the 100th cube?

6 • 1   6 • 4   6 • 9

Write each number as the sum of two primes.

7. $48 = \text{▨} + \text{▨}$

8. $84 = \text{▨} + \text{▨}$

9. $56 = \text{▨} + \text{▨}$

10. Show why this trick works. Pick any number and double it. Add 18. Add your original number. Divide by 3. Subtract 6. The answer is your original number.

11. Each time the number of sides in a polygon increases by 1, the sum of the angles _____ by _____.

PROBLEM SOLVING

Franz and Maddy solved different problems. Both used the fact that $1 + 2 + 3 + \ldots + n = n(n + 1) \div 2$. Solve the problems.

12. Franz's problem: Find the number of toothpicks needed to build the 100th model.

13. Maddy's problem: Find the sum of the first 50 multiples of 3.
$(3 + 6 + 9 + \ldots + 150 = ?)$

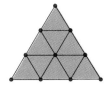

14. Suppose you wanted to know if any odd number can be written as the sum of primes. How would you begin? Show examples and make a conjecture.

15. A dodecagon is a polygon with 12 sides. Use mental math to calculate the sum of the interior angles. Draw a dodecagon and the triangles needed to prove your calculation is correct.

Logical Inference

LEARN ABOUT IT

If . . . then statements can be chained together to make new logical inferences.

EXPLORE Analyze the Situation

In Edgar Allen Poe's story, *The Gold Bug,* Legrand deciphers a message that leads to these conclusions. Each conclusion has been written as an **If . . . then** statement.

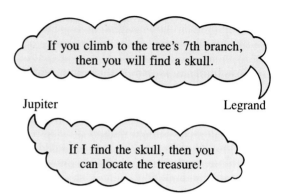

If you climb to the tree's 7th branch, then you will find a skull.

Jupiter   Legrand

If I find the skull, then you can locate the treasure!

TALK ABOUT IT

1. If Jupiter climbs to the 7th branch, what does Legrand expect him to find?

2. What will assure Legrand of locating the treasure?

3. If Legrand tells Jupiter, "If I find the treasure, I'll give you half," what is implied for Jupiter if he climbs to the 7th tree branch?

Statements of the form **If A then B** can be thought of as **A *implies* B,** and written **A $\Rightarrow$ B.**

When we know **(A $\Rightarrow$ B)** *and* **(B $\Rightarrow$ C),** we can write **A $\Rightarrow$ C.** This allows us to chain logical statements.

Examples

Statement P: **If** you can read sign language, **then** you can read this message.
Statement Q: **If** you can read this message, **then** you know my secret.
Conclusion: **If** you read sign language, **then** you know my secret.

Statement S: **If** x is odd, **then** $x + 1$ is even.
Statement T: **If** $x + 1$ is even, **then** $x + 2$ is odd.
Conclusion: **If x** *is odd,* **then** $x + 2$ is odd.

TRY IT OUT

1. Write the conclusion by chaining the statements. Is it true?

   Statement L: If $5x$ is odd, then x is odd.
   Statement K: If x is odd, then $x + 1$ is even.

PRACTICE

Write conclusions from chaining these statements.

1. If the gym is locked, then we will return.
If we return, then we can do more math.

2. If Jim is taller than Sue, then Jim is over 6 feet tall.
If Jim is over 6 feet tall, then he will play ball.

3. If n is prime, then 2 doesn't divide n.
If 2 doesn't divide n, then n is an odd number.

4. If $y < 0$, then $y^2 < 0$. If $y^2 < 0$, then $y^2 - 1 < 0$.

Write your own **B** $\Rightarrow$ **C** statement, and chain it with each
A $\Rightarrow$ **B** statement.

5. If it rains today, then I'll stay inside.　　**6.** If we win today, then we'll win the league.

7. If I join scouts, then I'll go to camp.　　**8.** If we get a pet, then I'll feed it.

APPLY

MATH REASONING　Use reasoning to write **B** statements to make
A $\Rightarrow$ **B** true. Check with your calculator.

9. If $\boxed{3}$ $\boxed{-}$ $\boxed{2}$ $\boxed{=}$ $\boxed{=}$ $\boxed{=}$ $\boxed{=}$ is pressed, then the display shows ___?___.

10. If $\boxed{3}$ $\boxed{\times}$ $\boxed{2}$ $\boxed{=}$ $\boxed{=}$ $\boxed{=}$ $\boxed{=}$ is pressed, then the display shows ___?___.

PROBLEM SOLVING

11. "If a dime floats on water, then pigs have wings." Is that
statement true? Why?

12. Language Arts Data Bank　What does
this message say?

MIXED REVIEW

Find the answers.

13. 25% of 82 $= x$　　**14.** $^-15 + 40 = c$　　**15.** $1.617 \div 0.07 = s$

16. $^-18 \cdot {}^-11 = a$　　**17.** $4.7 \cdot (0.03) = x$　　**18.** $^-28 \div 7 = t$

19. $3\frac{2}{7} + 4\frac{1}{8} = n$　　**20.** $20 - 4\frac{3}{11} = d$　　**21.** $^-17 - {}^-15 = u$

Reasoning from Graphs

EXPLORE **Analyze the Situation**

As part of a research project, Keisha's bicycle was equipped with a small computer that recorded her speed continuously. After a trip to school, the computer printed out this graph.

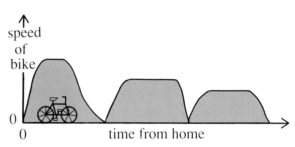

TALK ABOUT IT

1. What is Keisha doing when the graph line slopes up, like this: ╱ ?

2. What is happening on the trip when the graph line is flat, like this: ── ?

3. What is Keisha doing when the graph line slopes down, like this: ╲ ?

4. How many stops did Keisha make? Which stop was the most abrupt? How can you tell?

5. On which part of the trip did Keisha go the fastest?

Graphs like the one above have uses in science and medicine. Such graphs tell a story.

Example Write a story about Keisha's trip that would interpret the graph above.

Solution: Keisha started at home and picked up speed until she reached a steady rate. She stopped first for a traffic light. She started again and travelled at a constant rate for awhile, but had to stop suddenly for a dog. Keisha started for a third time, reaching another constant rate. She gradually slowed down as she arrived at school.

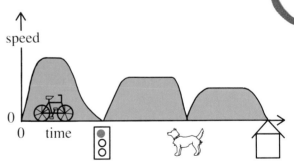

TRY IT OUT

Trace Keisha's graph on your paper.

1. Change the graph to show that Keisha slowed down but did not completely stop at the light.

2. Change the graph so that Keisha's fastest speed was the constant part of the 2nd leg.

3. Rewrite and modify the story above to match these changes.

Read the story and answer the questions.

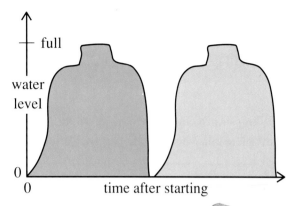

Mia used a tub to wash her dog Sam. She put water in the tub, then put Sam in and washed him. She removed Sam and emptied the water. Mia added more water and made Sam return for a rinse. Sam jumped out, so she let him go and emptied the tub.

1. What is happening when the graph of the water level slopes up?

2. What is happening when the graph slopes down?

3. Trace the graph. Mark it to show when Sam is in the tub.

4. Change the graph. Show that Mia made Sam return to continue being rinsed before emptying the water.

5. This story of a skydiver has been jumbled up. Trace the graph and place a letter on the graph to show each event.

   A *He opened the parachute.*
   B *He landed on the ground.*
   C *He leaped from the plane.*
   D *He floated gently down.*
   E *He was in "free fall" after jumping.*

APPLY

PROBLEM SOLVING

6. Jamie planned to practice typing 15 minutes a day. Trace the axes, and graph the story of Jamie's progress.

   Jamie made steady progress during the fall, and had doubled his speed by December. He didn't practice over Christmas and his January score was almost as bad as his September score. He made steady progress during the spring and finally got back to his December score, but lost a little ground in May and June.

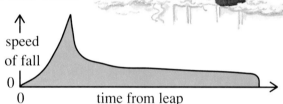

ESTIMATION

Look at the original graph of Keisha's trip to school.

7. Her fastest speed was 12 miles per hour. About what were her other 2 constant speeds?

8. Keisha left home at 8:00. If the trip took 20 minutes, about when were her first two stops?

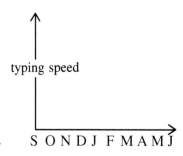

Problem Solving
Finding Related Problems

| UNDERSTAND |
| ANALYZE DATA |
| PLAN |
| ESTIMATE |
| SOLVE |
| EXAMINE |

When you have a problem to solve, thinking of a related problem may help. Here are two related problems.

Al and his two sons went on a wilderness trip. They had an inflatable raft that could hold either the two boys or Al. How many trips would they have to make to cross a river?

Ray went 5 miles up the river in a raft. He could paddle 2 mi in 30 min, but then he would rest for 10 min and drift one half mile downstream. How long did it take Ray to go the 5 miles?

I can solve both problems by using objects or drawing a picture.

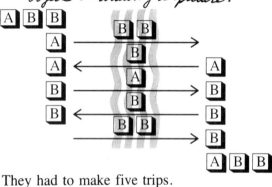

They had to make five trips.

I'll try using objects.

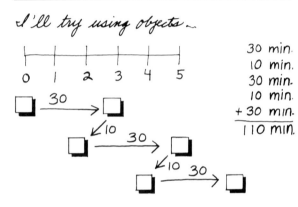

	30 min.
	10 min.
	30 min.
	10 min.
+	30 min.
	110 min.

It took Ray 110 minutes to go 5 miles.

TRY IT OUT

Decide which problems are related. Then solve each one.

1. There are 93 students in after-school clubs. 18 belong to the wilderness club and 26 belong to the bike club. 5 belong to both clubs. How many students are in one club only?

2. Bob, Ian, and Adam got food for a hiking trip. Bob put a third in his pack. Later, Ian put a third of the remaining food in his pack. 4 pounds were left. How much food did they buy?

3. June and Carmen were playing a game with stones. They played 3 rounds. June won the first 2 rounds and Carmen won the third. After each round the loser had to double the winner's stones by giving away some of her own. They each had 16 stones at the end. How many stones did each girl start with?

4. Nicole, Sue, Carlos, and Ben all play different sports: soccer, track, volleyball, and baseball. Ben has batting practice once a week. Nicole does not like to run, but she is good at hitting the ball over the net. Carlos had a soccer game on Saturday. Which sport does each play?

Solve. Use any strategy.

Some Strategies

Act Out	Solve a Simpler Problem
Use Objects	Make an Organized List
Choose an Operation	Work Backward
Draw a Picture	Look for a Pattern
Guess and Check	Use Logical Reasoning
Make a Table	Write an Equation

1. A small raft is 5 ft 4 in. long and weighs about 9 lb. When inflated it weighs about 12 lb. By what percent does its weight increase when it is inflated?

River Raft Sales!

Rafts	Pump
1-person $24.99	$13.50
2-person 45.99	

Life Vests $6.88 to $10.88
Oars $14.95

2. Orin bought a 1-person raft, a pump, and oars. The sales tax is 6%. Use the list prices to find what Orin spent.

3. Wendy has a coupon for 15% off on a raft. She bought a 2-person raft. Use the list price to find how much she saved with the coupon.

4. In 1854, the ship *Flying Cloud* sailed from New York to San Francisco around the horn in 89 days and 8 hours. 135 years later, *Thursday's Child* made the same trip in 80 days and 20 hours. How much faster was *Thursday's Child*?

5. A group of hikers plans to take a 3-day trip. There are 3 different trails to their first stop at Hidden Meadow, 5 different trails to Alpine Lake, and 2 different trails back to their starting point. How many different routes can they take?

6. A climbing rope 75 ft long is formed into a coil 18 in. in diameter. About how many loops will be in the coil?

7. *Thursday's Child* sailed 14,500 mi in 89 days and 20 hours. About how many miles did it average in a day?

8. Determining Reasonable Answers
The crew of *Thursday's Child* carried 180 cans of tuna on their trip. A case of tuna holds 12 cans, and costs $10.68. Decide if the number shown on the calculator is a reasonable answer to the question, "How much did the 180 cans of tuna cost?" If it is not reasonable, explain why.

Data Collection and Analysis
Group Decision Making

UNDERSTAND
ANALYZE DATA
PLAN
ESTIMATE
SOLVE
EXAMINE

Doing a Simulation

Group Skill:
Encourage and Respect Others

Suppose you are taking a true-false quiz with 5 items. You didn't study at all the night before, so you decide to choose your answers by flipping a coin. What are the chances that you will get at least 4 answers correct? You and your group conduct a simulation to find out.

Collecting Data

1. Work with your group to make up a "pretend" true and false quiz with 5 questions. Make an answer key to show the correct answers.

Science Quiz
Mark each answer true or false
1. _F_ Rising air causes thunderstorms
2. _T_ Cold air is heavier than warm air
3. _F_ Winter is caused by ducks flying south
4. ___
5. ___

2. Toss the five coins and record "true" for each head and "false" for each tail. This will complete one trial. Your group will conduct at least 200 trials.

Organizing Data

3. "Correct" each quiz to find out how many you got correct. Make a table to record your results.

Number of Correct Answers	Number of Quizzes
1	⊞⊞
2	⊞⊞ ⊞⊞ II
3	⊞⊞ ⊞⊞ II
4	⊞⊞
5	III

4. Make another table to show how many quizzes had *at least* 1 correct answer, *at least* 2 correct answers, *at least* 3 correct answers, and so on. Then compute the percent of the total quizzes that fall into each category.

Number of Quizzes	Percent of the Total Quizzes
At least 1 correct answer 172	$\frac{172}{200} = 86\%$
At least 2 correct answers 147	$\frac{147}{200} = 73.5\%$
At least 3 correct answers	
At least 4 correct answers	
At least 5 correct answers	

5. Talk with your group to decide what kind of graph to use to display the percentages for each category in the second table. Could you use a bar graph or a circle graph? Make the graph.

6. According to your simulation results, about what percent of the time would you get at least 4 answers correct on your quiz by flipping a coin?

7. Write a letter to your principal explaining your results. Do you think true-false quizzes are fair to those who study for the quizzes?

WRAP UP

Logical Vocabulary

Select the correct term or name from this chapter to complete each sentence.

1. Making a generalization based on a pattern seen in several cases is called ____.

2. Mathematical patterns include number patterns and ____ patterns.

3. The statement that an even number greater than 2 can be written as the sum of primes is known as ____.

4. A method of mentally adding large amounts of consecutive counting numbers was discovered by ____.

5. The logical thinking steps that explain a mathematical pattern make up an ____.

6. *And, or,* and *If . . . then* are used to make ____ statements.

7. Writing A $\Rightarrow$ C from A $\Rightarrow$ B and B $\Rightarrow$ C is known as ____.

8. The symbol $\Rightarrow$ that is used in chaining logical statements means ____.

Sometimes, Always, Never

Which word should go in the blank, *sometimes*, *always*, or *never*? Explain your choice.

9. An odd number greater than 3 can __?__ be written as the sum of two primes.

10. If a pattern works for ten cases, it will __?__ work for all cases.

11. If you know the number of sides a polygon has, you can __?__ find the sum of the measures of its angles.

12. The sum of an odd number of odd numbers plus an even number is __?__ an even number.

13. If only one part of a compound statement is true, the statement is __?__ false.

Project

The numbers 3, 5, 4, 7, 5, 9, 6 are written in a sequence. Their order follows the pattern:
+ 2, − 1, + 3, − 2, + 4, − 3, . . .
Make up a sequence and write the first 5 to 7 numbers.
Exchange sequences with a classmate and determine the pattern.

CHAPTER REVIEW/TEST

Part 1 Understanding

Use the terms "inductive reasoning" or "informal proof" to complete the statements.

1. __?__ is a reasoning method which uses patterns to reach a conclusion.

2. An __?__ answers the question, "How do I know my answer is correct?"

3. __?__ can be used to discover geometric relationships by analyzing patterns.

4. A list of statements that provide a reasoned argument is an __?__ .

Part 2 Skills

5. Find the sum of the first 30 even numbers. What pattern did you use?

6. Find the sum of the measures of the angles of a dodecagon (12 sides).

7. Write the steps to show why this trick works. *Pick any number and double it. Add 20. Divide by 2. Subtract 10. You get your original number.*

Label each statement true or false.

8. $3 + 7 = 10$ or $3 < 2$.

9. $2 \cdot 25 = 50$ and 7 is even.

Write conclusions from chaining these statements. Label each true or false.

10. If n is any even number, then $n + 2$ is even. If $n + 2$ is even, then n cannot be 25;

11. If $n + 3 = 5$, then $n = 2$. If $n = 2$, then $n \times 3 = 6$.

Part 3 Applications

12. Sue deposited $1 in her savings on January 2. Each week she increased her deposit by $1. Find how much she will have saved in 52 weeks.

13. To make a design, a piece of string is used for each diagonal. How many pieces of string are needed for the diagonals of a polygon with 15 sides?

14. Jason had to read 3 assignments for a total of 44 or 45 pages. Two assignments contained an odd number of pages and the other an even number. How many pages did he have to read?

15. **Challenge** The number of diagonals of a hexagon can be found by drawing a diagram. Use a similar strategy to solve the following: Each of seven people shakes hands with each of the others. How many handshakes were made?.

Barry likes word anagrams. An anagram is a scrambled word. By arranging the letters in the correct order the original word can be spelled. Each different arrangement of the letters in a word is a **permutation** of the letters. Using the four letters T, P, S, and O how many permutations of the four letters can you find?

| T | P | S | O |

You can use the strategy of making a list to find all the permutations.

The completed list at the right shows there are 24 permutations of the 4 letters. The underlined permutations form 6 sensible words.

TPSO	POST	OSTP	STPO
TPOS	POTS	OSPT	STOP
TSOP	PTOS	OTSP	SOPT
TSPO	PTSO	OTPS	SOTP
TOPS	PSOT	OPTS	SPTO
TOSP	PSTO	OPST	SPOT

If you shuffled the four cards and then turned them over in order, the **probability** of getting a sensible word would be $\frac{6}{24}$ or $\frac{1}{4}$.

Notice that there are 4 choices for the first letter, then 3 choices for the 2nd letter, 2 choices for the 3rd letter, and 1 choice for the last letter. To find the total number of permutations we need to multiply the choices.

Number of permutations = 4 × 3 × 2 × 1 = 24.

For each set of lettered cards give:
a) the number of permutations of the letters
b) the probability of forming a sensible word.

1. | T | A | C |

2. | A | C | S | R |

3. | N | O |

4. How many permutations of the letters MAPRIDY are there? One of the permutations spells a familiar geometric word. What is it?

5. What is the probability that you can shuffle these cards and then turn up a well-known math word spelled correctly?

| P | R | I | Z | E | T | O | A | D |

CUMULATIVE REVIEW

1. What is the volume?

   A 96 mm^3

   B 28 mm^3

   C 192 mm^3

   D 288 mm^3

   4mm 8mm 3mm

2. What is the volume of a cone whose height is 4 cm and whose base has a radius of 3 cm? Use 3.14 for π.

   A 113.0 cm^3 **B** 37.68 cm^3

   C 75.36 cm^3 **D** 56.52 cm^3

3. Which slide moves the shaded figure onto the unshaded one?

   A (left 1, down 1)

   B (left 2, up 1)

   C (left 1, up 1)

   D (left 2, down 2)

4. Evaluate the algebraic expression.
   $(138 - 4k^2) \div 10$ for $k = 5$

   A 128   **B** $^-$26.2

   C 3.8   **D** 9.8

5. Solve for h
   $16.9 = 4 + 3h$

   A 4.3   **B** 6.97

   C 9.63   **D** 5.63

6. Which is the inequality for this sentence? The depth (d) is at least 70 feet below sea level.

   A $d \geq {}^-70$ **B** $d \leq {}^-70$

   C $^-70 \leq d$ **D** $70 \leq d$

7. Solve for V.
   $V - 56 > {}^-13$

   A $V > 43$ **B** $V > 69$

   C $V > 85$ **D** $V > 70$

8. Which is the expression equivalent to $4(3x + 7)$?

   A $4x = 7$ **B** $12x + 28$

   C $4x = 11$ **D** $12x + 21$

9. Which are the next 3 numbers in this pattern 1, 8, 27, 64, . . .

   A 81, 100, 121   **B** 125, 243, 729

   C 157, 380, 919   **D** 125, 216, 343

10. Which is the correct equation for the sum of two primes?

    A $88 = 47 + 21$ **B** $80 = 41 + 39$

    C $80 = 37 + 43$ **D** $130 = 57 + 73$

11. In a campaign button collection there are 15 more modern than old buttons. There are 121 buttons altogether. How many old buttons are there?

    A 53   **B** 54

    C 67   **D** 68

12. Which algebraic expression represents this situation? Lawn service: $75 for clean up, plus $15 per week for w weeks.

    A $(75 + 15)w$

    B $75w + 15$

    C $75 + 15w$

    D $75 + 15 + w$

RESOURCE BANK AND APPENDIX

APPENDIX

Subtracting Whole Numbers

Mt. Kangchenjhan, part of the Himalayan mountains in India, is 22,700 feet high. Mt. Whitney, located in California, is 14,494 feet high. How much higher is Mt. Kangchenjhan than Mt. Whitney?

Since we want to know how much higher Mt. Kangchenjhan is than Mt. Whitney, we subtract.

$$22,700 - 14,494$$

Subtract the ones. Trade if necessary.	Subtract the tens. Trade if necessary	Subtract the hundreds. Trade if necessary.	Subtract the thousands. Trade if necessary.

$$
\begin{array}{r}
{\scriptstyle 6\,9\,10} \\
22,\cancel{700} \\
-14,494 \\
\hline
6
\end{array}
\qquad
\begin{array}{r}
{\scriptstyle 6\,9\,10} \\
22,\cancel{700} \\
-14,494 \\
\hline
06
\end{array}
\qquad
\begin{array}{r}
{\scriptstyle 6\,9\,10} \\
22,\cancel{700} \\
-14,494 \\
\hline
206
\end{array}
\qquad
\begin{array}{r}
{\scriptstyle 11\,26\,9\,10} \\
\cancel{22},\cancel{700} \\
-14,494 \\
\hline
8,206
\end{array}
$$

Mt. Kangchenjhan is 8,206 feet higher than Mt. Whitney.

> Estimate to determine if your answer is reasonable.
>
> $$
\begin{array}{r}
22,700 \approx 22,000 \\
14,494 \approx -14,000 \\
\hline
8,000
\end{array}
$$

Other Examples

$$
\begin{array}{r}
{\scriptstyle 19\,9\,9\,11} \\
\cancel{20,\cancel{001}} \\
-18,922 \\
\hline
1,079
\end{array}
$$

> $2000 - 1 = 1999$

$$
\begin{array}{r}
{\scriptstyle 10} \\
{\scriptstyle 0\,\,9\,9\,14} \\
\cancel{41,004} \\
-17,106 \\
\hline
23,898
\end{array}
$$

> $100 - 1 = 99$

$$
\begin{array}{r}
{\scriptstyle 2\,9\,9\,10} \\
\cancel{3,000} \\
-\quad 78 \\
\hline
2,922
\end{array}
$$

TRY IT OUT

1.
$$
\begin{array}{r}
4,000 \\
-1,458 \\
\hline
\end{array}
$$

2.
$$
\begin{array}{r}
7,021 \\
-\quad 682 \\
\hline
\end{array}
$$

3.
$$
\begin{array}{r}
3,004 \\
-1,027 \\
\hline
\end{array}
$$

4.
$$
\begin{array}{r}
32,001 \\
-17,127 \\
\hline
\end{array}
$$

5.
$$
\begin{array}{r}
50,070 \\
-49,125 \\
\hline
\end{array}
$$

Multiplying Whole Numbers

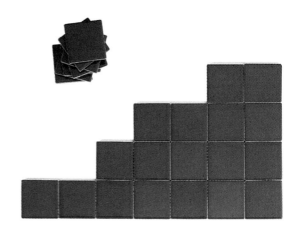

Kevin is covering a rectangular counter top with small square tiles, which are 1 inch on each side. The counter is 106 inches long, and 24 inches wide. How many tiles will Kevin need to cover the counter?

Since each of the 106 rows will have 24 tiles, we multiply.

106 × 24

106 rows

2,544 tiles

**24 tiles
per row**

```
   106
×   24
   424   ← Multiply by the ones. Trade if necessary.
 2,120   ← Multiply by the tens. Trade if necessary.
 2,544   ← Add the products
```

Estimate to determine if
your answer is reasonable.
106 ≈ 100
24 ≈ 20
100 × 20 = 2,000

Kevin needs 2,544 tiles.
This is reasonable, since the estimated answer is 2,000.

Other Examples

```
    426            329           1,007
×   217         ×  310         ×   208
  2 982            000           8 056
  4 260          3 290          00 000
 85 200         98 700         201 400
 92,442        101,990         209,456
```

These zeros are
place holders.

TRY IT OUT

1.   871   2.   803   3.   2,008   4.   782   5.   8,019
    × 59   × 251   ×   507   × 620   × 108

483

Dividing Whole Numbers: 1-Digit Divisors

Tamara has found a box full of old family photographs and she wants to organize them in a photo album. Each page holds 8 photographs. She finds that there are 217 photos. How many pages does she need?

Since each album page holds 8 photos, she divides the number of photos by 8.

$$217 \div 8$$

Decide where to start.

↓

$$\begin{array}{r} 2 \\ 8\overline{)217} \\ \underline{16} \\ 5 \end{array}$$ ← Divide.

← Multiply.

← Subtract and compare.

Estimate: $21 + 8 \approx 2$

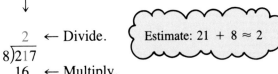

5 < 8?

$$217 \div 8 = 27 \text{ R } 1$$

$$\begin{array}{r} 27 \\ 8\overline{)217} \\ \underline{16} \\ 57 \\ \underline{56} \\ 1 \end{array}$$ ← Divide.

← Multiply

← Subtract and compare.

Estimate: $57 \div 8 \approx 7$

1 < 8?

Estimate to determine if the answer is reasonable.

$$217 \approx 200$$
$$8 \approx 10$$

$$200 \div 10 = 20$$

If Tamara uses 27 pages for her photos she will still have 1 photo left over, so she needs 28 pages if she wants to mount all her photos.

Other Examples

$$\begin{array}{r} 240 \text{ R } 2 \\ 9\overline{)2162} \\ \underline{18} \\ 36 \\ \underline{36} \\ 02 \end{array}$$

When you bring a number down, you must put a number in the quotient

$$\begin{array}{r} 608 \text{ R } 3 \\ 4\overline{)2435} \\ \underline{24} \\ 035 \\ \underline{32} \\ 3 \end{array}$$

TRY IT OUT

1. $6\overline{)3,206}$ **2.** $8\overline{)2,163}$ **3.** $7\overline{)4,915}$ **4.** $9\overline{)18,072}$

Dividing Whole Numbers:
2 and 3-Digit Divisors

Richard's family wants to drive from Los Angeles to Dallas, a distance of 2,251 kilometers. On previous trips, they have averaged 325 kilometers per day. At this rate, how many days will it take Richard's family to make this trip?

We can divide the total distance by the average distance per day to determine the number of days to make this trip.

$2{,}251 \div 325$

| Decide where to start. | Round the divisor and quotient, and estimate. | Divide. Multiply. Subtract and compare. |

```
        6    ← Divide.
325)2,251
    1 950    ← Multiply.
      301    ← Subtract and compare.
```

Estimate: $\dfrac{2{,}000}{300} = \dfrac{20}{3} \approx 6$

$2{,}251 \div 325 = 6 \text{ R } 301.$

After 6 days, Richard's family will have 301 kilometers left to travel. It will take them almost 7 days to drive to Dallas.

Other Examples

```
     97  R 34
42)4,108
   3 78
    328
    294
     34
```

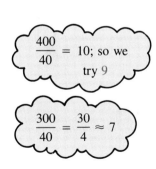

$\dfrac{400}{40} = 10$; so we try 9

$\dfrac{300}{40} = \dfrac{30}{4} \approx 7$

```
       70  R 13
682)47,753
    47 74
       13
```

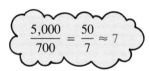

$\dfrac{5{,}000}{700} = \dfrac{50}{7} \approx 7$

TRY IT OUT

1. 41)2,043

2. 28)9,102

3. 314)32,037

4. 789)23,682

Adding and Subtracting Decimals

Laurel keeps a record of the number of gallons of gasoline needed to fill the gas tank each time she refills her car. At the end of each month she calculates the total, which tells her how much gasoline she has used that month.

17.2 + 20.1 + 18.82 + 19.03

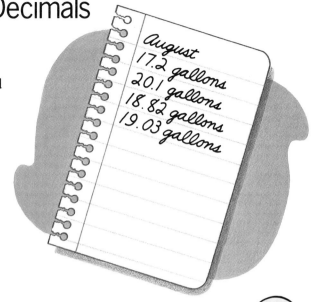

august
17.2 gallons
20.1 gallons
18.82 gallons
19.03 gallons

Write the problem with the decimal points in line.	Add (or subtract) as with whole numbers.	Place the decimal point in line with the others.
17.2	17.2	17.2
20.1	20.1	20.1
18.82	18.82	18.82
19.03	19.03	19.03
	75 15	75.15

Estimate to determine if your answer is reasonable.

17.2 ≈ 20
20.1 ≈ 20
18.82 ≈ 20
19.03 ≈ 20
_____
80

The total is 75.15 gallons.
This is reasonable as the estimated total is 80 gallons.

Other Examples

8.1 − 4.02

    8.10   Annex
  −4.02   zeros.
  _____
    4.08

$16 + $8.95

  $16.00   Remember,
  + 8.95 $16 = $16.00.
  _____
  $24.95

TRY IT OUT

1. $2.42 + $8.10 + $6

2. 17.01 − 16.9

3. 14.7 + 8 + 1.21

4. $8 − $6.17

5. 12 + 0.04 + 7.91

6. 27.014 − 0.819

Rounding Numbers

The 1980 census showed Florida had a population of 9,739,992. This is approximately 10,000,000 people.

Since population changes daily, we often round off the numbers. 10,000,000 is 9,739,992 rounded to the nearest million. Rounded numbers are also easier to remember.

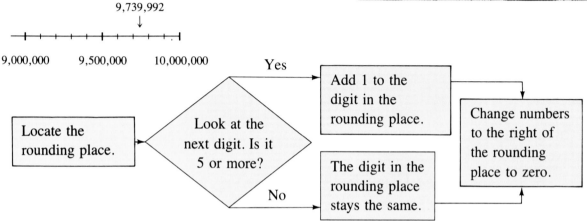

Round 9,739,992 to the nearest ten-thousand

9,739,992   9,739,992   {9 > 5} ⟶ {3 + 1 = 4} ⟶ 9,740,000

Round 3.143 to the nearest hundredth.

3.143   3.143   {3 < 5}   3.140 = 3.14

Round 148.127 to the place indicated.

Nearest whole number   Nearest hundred   Nearest hundredth

148.127 → 148   148.127 → 100   148.127 → 148.13

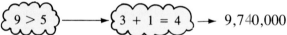

Since 7 > 5, we add 1 + 2

TRY IT OUT

Round each to the a) nearest whole number, and b) nearest tenth.

1. 42.145   **2.** 1.261   **3.** 15.17   **4.** 177.807   **5.** 19.672   **6.** 83.152

Multiplying and Dividing by Powers of Ten

While using his calculator, Roger noticed the following patterns.

123.456 × 10	= 1,234.56		123.456 ÷ 10	= 12.3456
123.456 × 100	= 12,345.6		123.456 ÷ 100	= 1.23456
123.456 × 1000	= 123,456		123.456 ÷ 1,000	= 0.123456
123.456 × 10,000	= 1,234,560		123.456 ÷ 10,000	= 0.0123456

Roger thought of a way to find these products and quotients mentally.

To **multiply** by a power of ten:

Count the number of zeros.

Move the decimal point 1 place to the **right** for each zero.

31.42 × 10 =   3 1 4. 2
1.293 × 100 =   1 2 9. 3
6.15 × 1,000 =   6 1 5 0.   Add a zero to get 3 places.
84 × 100 =   8 4 0 0.

To **divide** by a power of ten:

Count the number of zeros.

Move the decimal point 1 place to the **left** for each zero.

14.87 ÷ 10 =   1 .4 8 7
213.07 ÷ 1,000 =   0 .2 1 3 0 7
5.71 ÷ 100 =   0 .0 5 7 1   Add a zero to get 2 places.
814 ÷ 10 =   8 1 .4
1,300 ÷ 100 =   1 3 .0 0 = 13

TRY IT OUT

1. 321.47 × 10

2. 321.47 ÷ 10

3. 14.128 × 100

4. 23.04 × 100

5. 13.5 × 100

6. 4.145 ÷ 1,000

7. 46 ÷ 100

8. 1300 ÷ 10

Multiplying Decimals

Sarah wants to be an astronaut. She is reading books about space travel, and notes that gravity on the moon's surface is 0.17 of the gravity on the earth's surface. Therefore Sarah's weight on the moon is 0.17 of her weight on Earth. Sarah weighs 92.5 pounds, and she wants to determine what she weighs on the moon.

To find her weight on the moon, Sarah can multiply her weight on Earth by 0.17.

$$92.5 \times 0.17$$

Multiply as with whole numbers.	Write the product so it has the same number of decimal places as the sum of the decimal places in the factors.	Estimate to determine if your answer is reasonable.

$$
\begin{array}{r}
92.5 \\
\times\ 0.17 \\
\hline
6475 \\
9250 \\
\hline
15725
\end{array}
$$

$$
\begin{array}{r}
92.5 \leftarrow \text{1 decimal place} \\
\times\ \ 0.17 \leftarrow \text{2 decimal places} \\
\hline
6\ 475 \\
9\ 250 \\
\hline
15.725 \leftarrow \text{3 decimal places}
\end{array}
$$

Sarah's weight on the moon is 15.725 pounds. This is reasonable as the estimate is 18 pounds.

Other Examples

$$
\begin{array}{r}
4.02 \leftarrow \text{2 decimal places} \\
\times\ \ 0.56 \leftarrow \text{2 decimal places} \\
\hline
24\ 12 \\
2\ 01\ 00 \\
\hline
2.35\ 12
\end{array}
$$

$$
\begin{array}{r}
2416 \leftarrow \text{0 decimal places} \\
\times\ 1.05 \leftarrow \text{2 decimal places} \\
\hline
12080 \\
0000 \\
241600 \\
\hline
2{,}536.80 = 2{,}536.8
\end{array}
$$

TRY IT OUT

1.	2.	3.	4.	5.
52.4 × 8.6	2.06 ×1.75	18.2 ×0.08	1,004 × 3.25	0.715 × 4.08

Math and Science Data Bank

World Population of Primates

Region	Number of Species
Rain Forests	
Africa	47
Madagascar	7
Asia	15
Neotropics	44
Woodlands	
Africa	7
Madagascar	12
Asia	4
Savannas	
Africa	11
Neotropics	2

Life Stages of Primates (in years)

	Infant Phase	Juvenile Phase	Adult Phase	Average Life Span
Lemur	0.5	2	11	14
Macague	1.5	6	20	27
Gibbon	2	6	20	28
Orangutan	3.5	7	30	41
Chimpanzee	5	10	30	45
Gorilla	3	9	27	39

Math and Science Data Bank

Pascal's Triangle

Blaise Pascal discovered this triangle which is used to determine combinations.

To find the probabilities of boy/girl combinations in a family of **4** children, look at **Row 4**.

The sum of the numbers in that row is 16, so there are 16 possible combinations.

The numbers at the ends of the rows show the least likely combinations. There is a 1 in 16 chance of all girls or all boys.

The most likely combination is shown by the middle circle. The chance for 2 boys and 2 girls is 6 in 16.

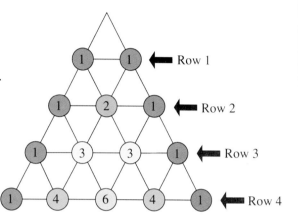

Probability and Heredity
Blossom Colors of Pea Plants

Parent Generation

A pure red (RR) is crossed with a pure white (WW).

First Generation

These plants are all red hybrids – RW – a cross between red and white. Since red is the dominate gene, all these plants have red blossoms.

Second Generation

When plants with both red and white genes are crossed there are four possible outcomes.

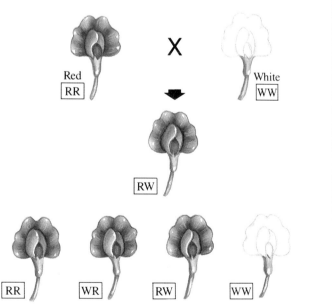

More than 100 years ago Gregor Mendel, an Austrian monk, studied the properties of ordinary garden pea plants. His experiments opened up a new field called genetics – the science of heredity.

Math and Science Data Bank

The programming language, Logo, can produce some interesting computer graphics. Pressing the RETURN (or ENTER) key after a command, causes a "turtle" to move about the screen, drawing a line as it goes.

COMMAND		EFFECT
FORWARD N	(FD N)	Moves turtle forward N steps.
BACK N	(BK N)	Moves turtle backward N steps.
LEFT D	(LT D)	Turns turtle left D degrees.
RIGHT D	(RT D)	Turns turtle right D degrees.
HOME		Returns turtle to home (starting) position.
PENUP	(PU)	Puts turtle into non-drawing mode.
PENDOWN	(PD)	Puts turtle back into drawing mode.
CLEARSCREEN	(CS)	This command varies with Logo programs.
CLEARGRAPHICS	(CS)	It is used to erase the entire screen.
REPEAT X		Tells turtle to repeat (X number of times) the commands found inside the brackets.

You can put sets of commands together, give them a name, and the turtle will remember it.

Example 1

TO SQUARE   Each procedure begins with TO and a name.
REPEAT 4 [FD 10 RT 90]   The program can be one line (like this) or more.
END   This shows the END of the program.

Now the turtle will draw the square whenever you type the word SQUARE and press RETURN or ENTER.

Example 2

TO TRIANGLE
REPEAT 3 [FD 10 RT 120]
END

Example 3

TO HOUSE
SQUARE
FD 10 RT 30
TRIANGLE
END

Example 4

TO TOWN
REPEAT 4 [HOUSE PU 120 FD 20 RT 90 PD]
END

Math and Science Data Bank

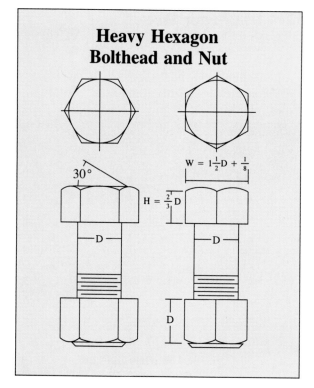

Heavy Hexagon Bolthead and Nut

$30°$

$W = 1\frac{1}{2}D + \frac{1}{8}$

$H = \frac{2}{3}D$

D

D

D

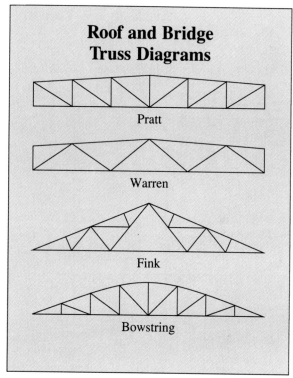

Roof and Bridge Truss Diagrams

Pratt

Warren

Fink

Bowstring

Atomic Weights

Element	Symbol*	Approx. Atomic Wt.**
Hydrogen	H	1
Helium	He	4
Carbon	C	12
Nitrogen	N	14
Oxygen	O	16
Calcium	Ca	40
Gold	Au	197
Lead	Pb	207

*The symbol stands for one atom of the element.

**The atomic weight shows how much one atom of an element weighs when compared with atoms of other elements. The basis of these numbers is carbon, which is assigned the atomic weight of 12.

Molecules and Molecular Weights

Compound Name	Symbol*	Approx. Molecular Weight**
Oxygen gas	O_2	32
Carbon monoxide	CO	28
Carbon dioxide	CO_2	44
Water	H_2O	18
Methane	CH_4	16
Sucrose	$C_{12}H_{22}O_{11}$	342
Caffeine	$C_8H_{10}N_4O_2$	194

*The subscript tells how many atoms of an element are present. No subscript means just one atom is present.

**These are determined by adding the atomic weights of all the elements involved. For example, carbon dioxide contains one carbon atom (at. wt. = 12) plus two oxygen atoms (at. wt. = 16 each). So the molecular weight of $CO_2 = 12 + 2(16) = 12 + 32 = 44$.

Math and Science Data Bank

Average TV Viewing Time – Hours per Week

(Based On Nielsen Estimates, Nov., 1986. Rounded To Nearest Half Hour.)

	Daytime (Mon-Fri 10am-4:30pm)	Afternoon (Mon-Fri 4:30-7:30pm)	Evening (Mon-Sun 8-11pm)	Sat. Morning (7am-1pm)	Weekly Total
Women (Age 18 & over)	6½	5	10½	1	35
Men (Age 18 & over)	3	4	9	½	29½
Teens (Age 12-17) Female	2½	4	6½	1	20½
Teens (Age 12-17) Male	2	4	6½	1	22½
Preschoolers (Age 2-5)	6½	5	4½	2	28
Children (Age 6-11)	2½	5	6	2	23½
All Persons	4½	4½	9	1	30½

US Households with Communication Devices

(Rounded to Nearest Percent)

	1950	1960	1970	1980	1985	1987
Phones	NA	79	87	93	92	93
Radios	93	96	99	99	99	99
TVs	4	87	95	98	98	98
VCRs	NA	NA	NA	1	21	49

(NA = Number Not Available)

Math and Language Arts Data Bank

Excerpt from Walden

I have thus a tight shingled and plastered house, ten feet wide by fifteen long, and eight-feet posts, with a garret and a closet, a large window on each side, two trap doors, one door at the end, and a brick fireplace opposite. The exact cost of my house, paying the usual price for such materials as I used, but not counting the work, all of which was done by myself, was as follows:

Boards	$8.03	mostly shanty boards.
Refuse shingles for roof and sides	4.00	
Laths	1.25	
Two second-hand windows with glass	2.43	
One thousand old brick	4.00	
Two casks of lime	2.40	That was high.
Hair	0.31	More than I needed.
Mantle-tree iron	0.15	
Nails	3.90	
Hinges and screws	0.14	
Latch	0.10	
Chalk	0.01	
Transportation	1.40	I carried a good part on my back.
In all	$28.12	

These are all the materials excepting the timber, stones and sand, which I claimed by squatter's right.

Arithmetic

Arithmetic is where numbers fly like pigeons in and out of your head.

Arithmetic tells you how many you lose or win if you know how many you had before you lost or won.

Arithmetic is seven eleven all good children go to heaven – or five six bundle of sticks.

Arithmetic is numbers you squeeze from your head to your hand to your pencil to your paper till you get the answer.

Arithmetic is where the answer is right and everything is nice and you can look out of the window and see the blue sky – or the answer is wrong and you have to start all over and try again and see how it comes out this time.

If you take a number and double it and double it again and then double it a few more times, the number gets bigger and bigger and goes higher and higher and only arithmetic can tell you what the number is when you decide to quit doubling.

Arithmetic is where you have to multiply – and you carry the multiplication table in your head and hope you won't lose it.

If you have two animal crackers, one good and one bad, and you eat one and a striped zebra with streaks all over him eats the other, how many animal crackers will you have if somebody offers you five six seven and you say No no no and you say Nay nay nay and you say Nix nix nix?

If you ask your mother for one fried egg for breakfast and she gives you two fried eggs and you eat both of them, who is better in arithmetic, you or your mother?

Carl Sandburg

495

Math and Social Studies Data Bank

Latitude and Longitude

The position of each point on the globe can be represented by a unique pair of numbers. The **longitude** gives the east-west location (from 0 to 180 degrees), while **latitude** indicates distances north or south of the equator (from 0 to 90 degrees.

Bird's Eye View of Longitude

180° E

110° W

Prime Meridian

N

Prime Meridian

90° 80° 70° 60° 50° 40° 30° 20° 10°   10° 20° 30° 40° 50° 60° 70° 80° 90°

Western Longitude

Eastern Longitude

N
90°
80°
70°
60°
50°
40°
30°
20°
10°
Northern Latitude
Equator
0°
10°
20°
Southern Latitude
30°
40°
50°
60°
70°
80°
90°
S

Math and Language Arts Data Bank

American Sign Language Alphabet

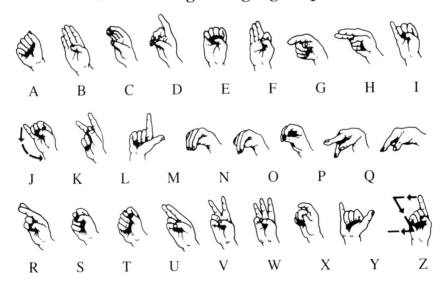

A   B   C   D   E   F   G   H   I

J   K   L   M   N   O   P   Q

R   S   T   U   V   W   X   Y   Z

Math and Social Studies Data Bank

World Time Zones

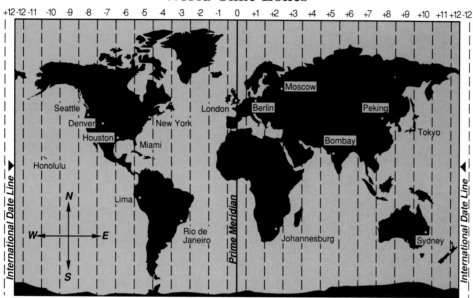

The world's time zones start at the prime meridian (0) and divide the world into 24 sections. The 12th zone east (+ 12) and the 12th zone west (− 12) are separated by an imaginary line called the International Date Line (IDL).

When going west, set your watch back one hour for each time zone you cross. Going east, set your watch forward one hour for each time zone you cross.

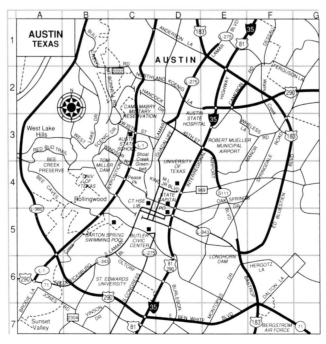

Math and Social Studies Data Bank

Foreign Money

Great Britain

Currency Unit: Pound Sterling (£)
   Denominations: 1, 5, 10, 20, and 50 pound notes
Coins: 100 pence (p) = 1 pound
   Denominations: 1, 2, 5, 10, 20, and 50 pence, 1 pound

Exchange rate	Pounds per U.S. Dollar	
(Yearly Average)	1970	.4174
	1975	.4501
	1980	.4302
	1985	.7708

Canada

Currency Unit: Dollar ($)
   Denominations: 1, 2, 5, 10, 20, 50, 100, 1000
Coins: 100 cents (¢) = 1 Canadian dollar
   Denominations: 1, 5, 10, 25, 1 dollar

Exchange rate	Canadian Dollars per U.S. Dollar	
(Yearly Average)	1970	1.0103
	1975	1.0175
	1980	1.1693
	1985	1.3658

Japan

Currency Unit: Yen (¥)
   Denominations: 1,000, 5,000, 10,000
Coins: Yen
   Denominations: 1, 5, 10, 50, 100, 500

Exchange rate	Yen per U.S. Dollar	
(Yearly Average)	1970	357.60
	1975	296.78
	1980	226.63
	1985	238.47

Mexico

Currency Unit: Peso ($)
   Denominations: 1,000, 5,000, 10,000, 20,000, 50,000
Coins: Peso
   Denominations: 1, 5, 10, 20, 50, 100, 500

Exchange rate	Pesos per U.S. Dollar	
(Yearly Average)	1970	12.5
	1975	12.5
	1980	70
	1985	1600

New York Stock Exchange Weekly Report
January 1, 1989

Stock	Dividend	Yield %	P/E Ratio	Sales (100s)	High	Low	Last	Chg
Alcoa	1.40	2.5	6	6153	56	54⅜	56	+ 1½
Boeing	1.60	2.6	16	14783	61⅞	58⅝	60⅝	+ ⅞
Grace	1.40	5.4	11	6111	26¼	25⅛	26	+ ¾
Harris	.88	3.3	16	3460	27⅛	26	27	+ ⅜
Motel 6	1.22	10.1	....	266	12⅛	11⅜	12⅛	+ ⅜
OutbdM	.80	2.6	8	3115	32⅛	30½	31	+ ¼
Skyline	.48	3.1	12	909	15¾	15	15½	+ ¼
ToysRU	....	....	21	8589	38	36⅝	37⅛	+ ⅝
Winnbg	.40	4.3	27	1319	9¼	8⅞	9¼	+ ¼

NOTES:

- **Stock** name is an abbreviation of the corporation's name.
- **Dividend** is a part of the profits paid to stockholders for each share of stock. Some companies do not pay dividends.
- **Yield** (expressed as a percent) is the dividend divided by the price of one share of stock.
- **P/E (Price to Earnings) Ratio** is found by dividing the price of one share of stock by the earnings (company's profits) per share.
- **Sales** tell show many hundreds of shares of stock were sold during the week.

- **High** and **Low** are the highest and lowest price one share of the stock sold for during the week of December 27 to December 30, 1988. (Numbers are in dollars and fractions of dollars. For instance, 30½ means $30.50.)
- **Last** is the closing price on Friday afternoon, December 30, 1988.
- **Chg** gives the change (in dollars and fractions of dollars) between the closing price of this week and that of last week.
- *New High for the Year

Math and Social Studies Data Bank

Survey of Investment Earnings

	1 Year	5 Years	10 Years	15 Years
U.S. Coins	10.7%	11.4%	16.3%	18.8%
Oil	27.4%	−11.8%	3.0%	13.9%
U.S. Stamps	0.5%	−1.3%	11.8%	13.6%
Gold	29.1%	6.8%	9.2%	11.9%
Silver	39.8%	4.0%	9.7%	10.3%
Treasury Bills	5.7%	8.5%	10.2%	9.2%
Old Master Paintings	8.6%	9.5%	9.7%	9.2%
Bonds	5.7%	19.7%	9.7%	8.7%
Stocks	20.6%	24.1%	13.9%	8.6%
Chinese Ceramics	6.7%	3.4%	11.3%	8.3%
Housing	6.8%	4.8%	7.4%	8.2%
U.S. Farmland	−7.9%	−7.8%	1.5%	6.3%
Diamonds	7.0%	10.2%	8.9%	4.1%

NOTES: Figures are for periods ending June 1, 1988. Figures for more than one year are compounded annual rates of return (earnings).

Math and Health and Fitness Data Bank

Standard Conversions

Cooking Measurements

3 teaspoons = 1 tablespoon
4 tablespoons = ¼ cup
5⅓ tablespoons = ⅓ cup
1 ounce = 28.35 grams
1 pound = 16 ounces
1 cup = 8 fluid ounces
2 cups = 1 pint
2 pints = 1 quart
4 quarts = 1 gallon
2 gallons = 1 peck
4 pecks = 1 bushel
1 quart = 946.4 milliliters
1 liter = 1.06 quarts

Ingredient Equivalents

5 eggs = about 1 cup
1 stick butter (or margarine) = ½ cup = ¼ pound
4 cups sifted all-purpose flour = 1 pound
4 to 5 cups grated cheese = 1 pound
1 orange = 6 to 8 tablespoons juice
1 lemon = 3 tablespoons juice
1 gallon water = about 8.3 pounds

Math and Health and Fitness Data Bank

Pizza Snackers

Spread:

Heat until melted and mixed together:

- ¼ pound processed cheese spread
- ¼ cup margarine (½ stick)

Then add the rest of the ingredients:

- 3 green onions, finely chopped
- ½ cup tomato paste (4 ounces)
- 1 tablespoon chopped parsley
- ½ teaspoon oregano
- dash of pepper

(This spread keeps well in the refrigerator or indefinitely in the freezer.)

Snackers:

Spread on English muffins, bagels, or crackers. Heat under broiler, in toaster oven, or microwave until topping begins to bubble. Serve warm.

Indianapolis 500 Winners

Year	Driver	Speed (mph)	Speed (kph)	Purse
1959	Rodger Ward	135.86	218.65	$338,100
1960	Jim Rathmann	138.77	223.33	$369,150
1961	A. J. Foyt	139.13	223.91	$400,000
1962	Rodger Ward	140.29	225.77	$462,152
1963	Parnelli Jones	143.14	230.36	$494,031
1964	A. J. Foyt	147.35	237.14	$506,625
1965	Jim Clark	150.69	242.51	$628,399
1966	Graham Hill	144.32	232.26	$691,809
1967	A. J. Foyt	151.21	243.35	$737,109
1968	Bobby Unser	152.88	246.04	$809,627
1969	Mario Andretti	156.87	252.46	$805,127
1970	Al Unser	155.75	250.66	$1,000,002
1971	Al Unser	157.74	253.86	$1,001,604
1972	Mark Donohue	162.96	262.26	$1,011,846
1973	Gordon Johncock	159.04	255.95	$1,001,846
1974	Johnny Rutherford	158.59	255.22	$1,015,686
1975	Bobby Unser	149.21	240.13	$1,101,322
1976	Johnny Rutherford	148.73	239.36	$1,037,775
1977	A. J. Foyt	161.33	259.64	$1,116,807
1978	Al Unser	161.36	259.68	$1,145,225
1979	Rick Mears	158.90	255.72	$1,271,954
1980	Johnny Rutherford	142.86	229.87	$1,502,425

Ford Lotus Vehicle – Indianapolis Track

March 27, 1963
Average Speed 150.501 mph

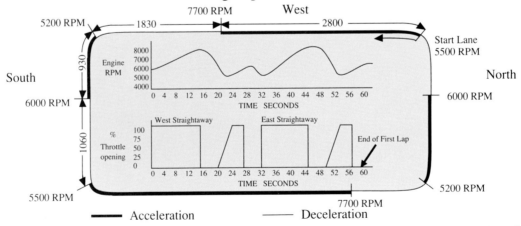

In 1963 a prototype Ford-Lotus was designed to check throttle angles and rpm limits on a 150 mph lap at the Indianapolis track.

Math and Health and Fitness Data Bank

SERVING SIZE	1 bar (1 oz)
CALORIES	130
PROTEIN (g)	2
TOTAL CARBOHYDRATES (g)	17
FAT (g)	6
CHOLESTEROL (mg)	–
SODIUM (mg)	95

% U.S. RECOMMENDED DAILY ALLOWANCES

PROTEIN	2%
VITAMIN A	*
VITAMIN C	*
THIAMINE	2%
RIBOFLAVIN	2%
NIACIN	2%
CALCIUM	2%
IRON	2%

SERVING SIZE	½ cup (4 oz)
CALORIES	90
PROTEIN (g)	0
TOTAL CARBOHYDRATES (g)	22
FAT (g)	0
CHOLESTEROL (mg)	–
SODIUM (mg)	20

% U.S. RECOMMENDED DAILY ALLOWANCES

PROTEIN	*
VITAMIN A	*
VITAMIN C	100
THIAMINE	*
RIBOFLAVIN	*
NIACIN	*
CALCIUM	*
IRON	2%

– information not available
* < 2% of the U.S. RDA of this nutrient

SERVING SIZE	½ cup (4 oz)
CALORIES	90
PROTEIN (g)	0
TOTAL CARBOHYDRATES (g)	22
FAT (g)	0
CHOLESTEROL (mg)	–
SODIUM (mg)	20

% U.S. RECOMMENDED DAILY ALLOWANCES

PROTEIN	*
VITAMIN A	*
VITAMIN C	100
THIAMINE	*
RIBOFLAVIN	*
NIACIN	*
CALCIUM	*
IRON	2%

– information not available
* < 2% of the U.S. RDA of this nutrient

Math and Language Arts Data Bank

"The Adventure of the Dancing Men" from the *Complete Sherlock Holmes* by Sir Arthur Conan Doyle

In this adventure of murder and secret codes, Sherlock Holmes uses logical reasoning to solve Mr. Cubitt's mystery. Cubitt shows Holmes some strange drawings which appear around his house. Later Holmes deciphers the code and realizes Cubitt and his wife, Elsie, are in grave danger.

Dancing Men Messages	Messages as Deciphered by Holmes
	AM HERE ABE SLANEY
	AT ELRIGES
	COME ELSIE
	NEVER

Below Holmes explains to Watson how he begins to decipher the messages.

"Having once recognized, however, that the symbols stood for letters, and having applied the rules which guide us in all forms of secret writings, the solution was easy enough. The first message submitted to me was so short that it was impossible for me to do more than to say, with some confidence, that the symbol stood for E. As you are aware, E is the most common letter in the English alphabet, and it predominates to so marked an extent that even in a short sentence one would expect to find it most often. Out of fifteen symbols in the first message, four were the same, so it was reasonable to set this down as E. It is true that in some cases the figure was bearing a flag, and in some cases not, but it was probable, from the way in which the flags were distributed, that they were used to break the sentence up into words. I accepted this as a hypothesis, and noted that E was represented by .

"But now came the real difficulty of the inquiry. The order of the English letters after E is by no means well marked, and any preponderance which may be shown in an average of a printed sheet may be reversed in a single short sentence. Speaking roughly, T, A, O, I, N, S, H, R, D, and L are the numerical order in which letters occur;

502

Math and Health and Fitness Data Bank

Average Weights for 12-Year-Olds

Height	Girls Weight Range (pounds)	Boys Weight Range (pounds)		Height	Girls Weight Range (pounds)	Boys Weight Range (pounds)
4'2"	55–71	56–62		5'	82–98	92–96
4'3"	57–73	60–64		5'1"	86–101	96–100
4'4"	60–76	62–67		5'2"	89–104	100–104
4'5"	63–79	65–70		5'3"	92–106	104–108
4'6"	66–81	67–73		5'4"	97–109	108–112
4'7"	69–84	72–77		5'5"	102–111	112–116
4'8"	72–87	77–83		5'6"	106–116	116–120
4'9"	75–90	81–86		5'7"	110–120	119–124
4'10"	77–93	84–88		5'8"	114–124	122–128
4'11"	80–96	88–92		5'9"	118–127	125–132

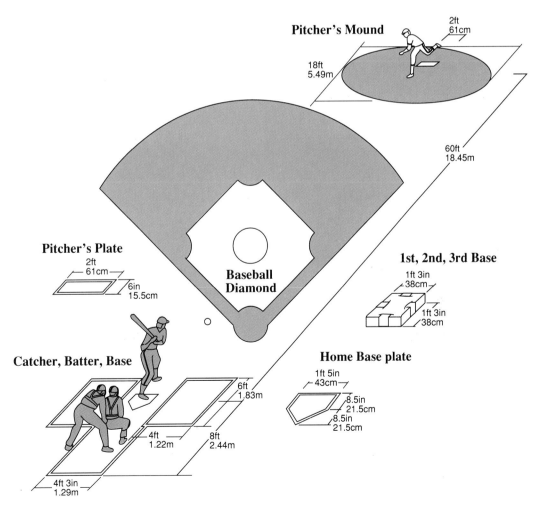

Pitcher's Mound
2ft
61cm

18ft
5.49m

60ft
18.45m

Pitcher's Plate
2ft
61cm
6in
15.5cm

Baseball Diamond

1st, 2nd, 3rd Base
1ft 3in
38cm
1ft 3in
38cm

Catcher, Batter, Base

Home Base plate
1ft 5in
43cm
8.5in
21.5cm
8.5in
21.5cm

6ft
1.83m

4ft
1.22m

8ft
2.44m

4ft 3in
1.29m

503

Math and Health and Fitness Data Bank

Sports Playing Areas and Ball Dimensions

Sport	Playing Area or Field Dimensions	Approx. Ball Circumference	Ball Diameter
Baseball	90 × 90 feet (diamond)	9 inches	2.9 inches
Basketball	26 × 15 meters	76 cm	24.2 cm
Curling	138 × 14 feet	stone: 36 inches	11.5 inches
Football	360 × 160 feet	oval	11 inches long
		circle: 22 inches	7 inches
Olympic Swimming	50 × 21 meters	none	—
Pool (Billiards)	10 × 5 feet	7 inches	2¼ inches
Soccer	100 × 73 meters	70 cm	22.3 cm
Squash	32 × 21 feet	5 inches	1.6 inches
Table Tennis	9 × 5 feet	4.71 inches	1.5 inches
Tennis	78 × 36 feet (doubles)	7.85 inches	2.5 inches
Volleyball	18 × 9 meters	66 cm	21 cm
Water Polo	30 × 20 meters (maximum)	70 cm	22.3 cm

Size of playing area is an important part of a game. Areas that are too large or too small can make games too difficult, or perhaps too easy. That is why official sports rules usually call for specific playing area dimensions.

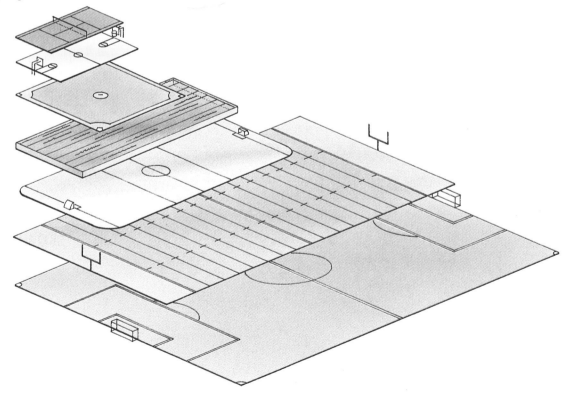

Math and Fine Arts Data Bank

Frequencies in Hertz* for Two Octaves in the Diatonic Scale

The pitch of a musical note may be high or low. For each pitch there is a number called the **frequency**, the number of vibrations per second. When the note C1 (middle C) is played on a piano, a string of the piano vibrates 264 times per second.* Higher notes have higher frequencies and lower notes have lower frequencies.

*If the piano is tuned to a diatonic scale. There are other scales, and the chromatic scale is most common.

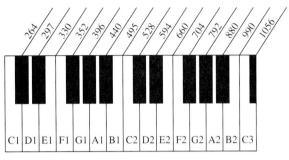

*1 Hertz = 1 cycle per second

Note Values and Divisions

A note's value tells how many counts the note is to be played or sung.
A half note is played half as long as a whole note.
A quarter note is played one quarter as long as a whole note or half as long as a half note, and so forth.

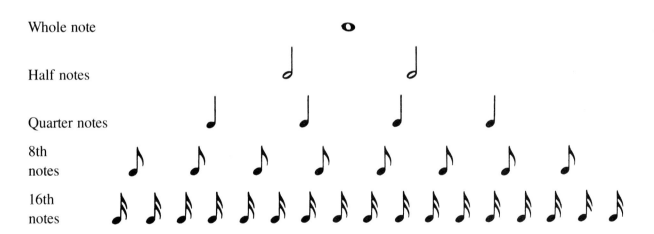

Other notes include the 32nd note 𝅘𝅥𝅰 the 64th note 𝅘𝅥𝅱 etc.

A *dot* after any note indicates that the length of the note be increased by half. For instance, 𝅗𝅥. equals 𝅗𝅥𝅘𝅥 and 𝅘𝅥𝅮. equals 𝅘𝅥𝅮𝅘𝅥𝅯

505

Solving Equations

Enter the largest number you can on your calculator. The largest number most calculators can display is 99999999. Now clear your calculator. Pressing $\boxed{\text{CE/C}}$ clears the last entry and error conditions. Pressing $\boxed{\text{CE/C}}$ $\boxed{\text{CE/C}}$ clears the display and operation. Pressing $\boxed{\text{ON/AC}}$ clears the memory, display, and operation.

To instruct your calculator to solve problems involving the basic operations ($+$, $-$, $\times$, and $\div$), enter the key code just the way you say the problem.

Problem	Key Code	Display
1024 + 54 =	1024 $\boxed{+}$ 54 $\boxed{=}$	1078
112.34 − 10.2 =	112.34 $\boxed{-}$ 10.2 $\boxed{=}$	102.14
2.115 × 1.33 =	2.115 $\boxed{\times}$ 1.33 $\boxed{=}$	2.81295
60 ÷ 1.5 =	60 $\boxed{\div}$ 1.5 $\boxed{=}$	40
99999999 + 1 =	99999999 $\boxed{+}$ 1 $\boxed{=}$	Error
0.0003 ÷ 30000 =	.0003 $\boxed{\div}$ 30000 $\boxed{=}$	Error
67 ÷ 0	67 $\boxed{\div}$ 0 $\boxed{=}$	Error

The last three problems create Error conditions. When a number is too large, many calculators display an Overflow Error. When a number is too small for the calculator, there is an Underflow Error. Attempting to divide by zero creates a Logic or Arithmetic Error.

With most calculators, if you divide 68 by 8 your result is 8.5. The $\boxed{\text{Int} \div}$ key on the Math Explorer allows you to find the quotient and remainder.

$$68 \ \boxed{\text{INT} \div} \ 8 \ \boxed{=} \qquad 8 \qquad 4$$
$$\text{-Q-} \quad \text{-R-}$$

Activity

This is a game for two or three players. Each one needs a calculator and a game marker. Players each enter 10000 on their calculators. Take turns. Draw 1 card from a deck and move clockwise the number of spaces it shows. Move one space for face cards and aces. Operate as shown in the center of the track, using the number in your display and the number on the track. The first person to get an error message is the winner.

Order of Operations

To solve a multiple-step problem, do operations inside parentheses first. Next multiply and divide from left to right. Then add and subtract from left to right.

Enter the problem $7 + 8 \times 5$ on your calculator. If your calculator displays the correct total, 47, it follows order of operations. If your calculator displays 75, it performs operations as they are entered. You can find the correct total by entering the problem as $8 \times 5 + 7$.

Enter $(8 + 5) \times 13$. Your display should show 169.

You can use the memory keys on your calculator to remember the result of one calculation while you do another calculation.

M+	Adds the display to the calculator's memory
M−	Subtracts the display from the calculator's memory
MR	Recalls the total in memory

Example: Find $7 \times 8 - 32 \div 8$.

	Enter	Display
ON/AC	7 ✕ 8 ＝ M+	56
	32 ÷ 8 ＝ M−	4
	MR	52

Example: Find y if $y = 18 - (17 - 8)$. Then evaluate $(3 + y) \times (y - 3)$.

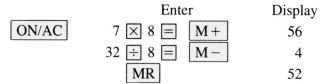

ON/AC 18 − (17 − 8) ＝ M+	9
(⎯ 3 + MR)⎯ ✕ (⎯ MR − 3)⎯ ＝	72

Activity

Place parentheses where necessary to make each equation true.

1. $6 \times 5 + 5 \times 3 = 180$

2. $120 \div c - 18 = 10$ where $18 + 7 + 3 + 2 = c$

3. $124 - 15 \times 26 - 19 = 19$

4. $25 + 17 \div 56 \div 8 = 6$

Fractions and Decimals

To find the decimal equivalent of a fraction, divide the numerator by the denominator. Find the decimal for 17/42.

Enter $\boxed{\text{ON/AC}}$ 17 $\boxed{\div}$ 42 $\boxed{=}$. The display shows 0.4047619.

Find decimals for 7/8, 17/5, 22/23, and 7/6. Your display should show 0.875, 3.4, 0.9565217, and 1.1666667.

To add, subtract, multiply, or divide fractions, use their decimal equivalents. First change mixed numbers to improper fractions.

Subtract 3 3/7 − 1/2. First change the problem to 24/7 − 1/2.

$\boxed{\text{ON/AC}}$ 24 $\boxed{\div}$ 7 $\boxed{-}$ 1 $\boxed{\div}$ 2 $\boxed{=}$ 2.9285714

Multiply 7/8 × 3/4.

$\boxed{\text{ON/AC}}$ 7 $\boxed{\div}$ 8 $\boxed{\times}$ 3 $\boxed{\div}$ 4 $\boxed{=}$ 0.65625

or $\boxed{\text{ON/AC}}$ 7 $\boxed{\div}$ 8 $\boxed{=}$ $\boxed{\text{M}+}$ 3 $\boxed{\div}$ 4 $\boxed{\times}$ $\boxed{\text{MR}}$ $\boxed{=}$ 0.65625

To divide by a fraction, you can multiply by its reciprocal. Use the reciprocal key $\boxed{1/x}$ to find the reciprocal of 2/3.

Enter 2 $\boxed{\div}$ 3 $\boxed{=}$ $\boxed{1/x}$. The display will show 1.5.

Below are three ways to find 9/10 ÷ 2/3. Try them.

$\boxed{\text{ON/AC}}$ 9 $\boxed{\div}$ 10 $\boxed{=}$ $\boxed{\text{M}+}$ 2 $\boxed{\div}$ 3 $\boxed{=}$ $\boxed{1/\times}$ $\boxed{\times}$ $\boxed{\text{MR}}$ $\boxed{=}$ 1.35

$\boxed{\text{ON/AC}}$ 9 $\boxed{\div}$ 10 $\boxed{\times}$ 3 $\boxed{\div}$ 2 $\boxed{=}$ 1.35

$\boxed{\text{ON/AC}}$ 9 $\boxed{\div}$ 10 $\boxed{\div}$ $\boxed{(}$ $\boxed{(}$ 2 $\boxed{\div}$ 3 $\boxed{)}$ $\boxed{)}$ $\boxed{=}$ 1.35

Activity

Write any number from 1 through 10 in each box. Make true equations.

1. $\dfrac{\square}{\square} + \dfrac{\square}{\square} = 1.75$

2. $\dfrac{\square}{\square} \div \dfrac{\square}{\square} = 0.525$

3. $\dfrac{\square}{\square} - \dfrac{\square}{\square} = 1.95$

4. $\dfrac{\square}{\square} \times \dfrac{\square}{\square} = 0.8333333$

Computing with Fractions

The $\boxed{\text{F}\rightleftarrows\text{D}}$ key on your Math Explorer calculator changes a fraction to a decimal or a decimal to a fraction (if the decimal has 3 or fewer places.) Find the decimal for 3/4. Use the $\boxed{/}$ key to enter the fraction.

	Enter	Display
	$\boxed{\text{ON/AC}}$ 3 $\boxed{/}$ 4 $\boxed{\text{F}\rightleftarrows\text{D}}$	0.75
	$\boxed{\text{F}\rightleftarrows\text{D}}$	75/100

N/D → n/d in the display means that the fraction is not in simplest form. To simplify the fraction, press $\boxed{\text{Simp}}$ $\boxed{=}$ until N/D → n/d disappears from the display. You may also simplify the fraction by a factor you choose.

$\boxed{\text{ON/AC}}$ 0.75 $\boxed{\text{F}\rightleftarrows\text{D}}$ $\boxed{\text{Simp}}$ 25 $\boxed{=}$ 3/4

Use the Math Explorer's $\boxed{\text{Unit}}$ key to enter the whole number part of a mixed number. Find the decimal for 2 5/8.

$\boxed{\text{ON/AC}}$ 2 $\boxed{\text{Unit}}$ 5 $\boxed{/}$ 8 $\boxed{\text{F}\rightleftarrows\text{D}}$ 2.625

The $\boxed{\text{Ab/c}}$ key on the Math Explorer changes improper fractions to mixed numbers. For example, 16 $\boxed{/}$ 9 $\boxed{\text{Ab/c}}$ gives a display of 1 u 7/9.

To solve problems involving fractions on the Math Explorer, enter the key code just the way you write the problem.

Problem	Key Code	Display
2/3 + 4/5 + 1/9	2 $\boxed{/}$ 3 $\boxed{+}$ 4 $\boxed{/}$ 5 $\boxed{+}$ 1 $\boxed{/}$ 9 $\boxed{=}$ $\boxed{\text{Ab/c}}$	1 u 26/45
1 27/40 − 3/8	1 $\boxed{\text{Unit}}$ 27 $\boxed{/}$ 40 $\boxed{-}$ 3 $\boxed{/}$ 8 $\boxed{=}$ $\boxed{\text{Simp}}$ 4 $\boxed{=}$	1 u 3/10
1/4 × (1/3 + 5/6)	1 $\boxed{/}$ 4 $\boxed{\times}$ $\boxed{(}$ 1 $\boxed{/}$ 3 $\boxed{+}$ 5 $\boxed{/}$ 6 $\boxed{)}$ $\boxed{=}$	7/24
5/8 + 1/4 ÷ 1/2	5 $\boxed{/}$ 8 $\boxed{+}$ 1 $\boxed{/}$ 4 $\boxed{\div}$ 1 $\boxed{/}$ 2 $\boxed{=}$ $\boxed{\text{Ab/c}}$	1 u 1/8

Activity

Insert +, −, ×, and ÷ signs and parentheses to make true equations.

1. 7/8 ⫴ 3/4 ⫴ 1/2 = 2 1/8

2. 9/10 ⫴ 4/5 ⫴ 3/4 = 17/20

3. 5/6 − 1/2 ⫴ 2/3 = 1/2

4. 5/8 ⫴ 1/2 ⫴ 5/6 = 5/6

Using Constants to Evaluate Expressions

Here is a fast way to do the same calculation on a group of numbers. Use the constant key $\boxed{\text{Cons}}$ to store an operation and a number. From then on, when you press the constant key the calculation will be performed on the number in the display.

Evaluate $a \times 3$ for $a = 5, 9, 14,$ and 42.

$\boxed{\text{ON/AC}}$ $\boxed{\times}$ 3 $\boxed{\text{Cons}}$ 5 $\boxed{\text{Cons}}$ 9 $\boxed{\text{Cons}}$ 14 $\boxed{\text{Cons}}$ 42 $\boxed{\text{Cons}}$.

The display should show 15, 27, 42, and 126.

With some calculators, the $\boxed{=}$ key acts as a constant key. Entering $\boxed{\times}$ 3 $\boxed{=}$ sets 3 as the constant. Try the key code above, but enter $\boxed{=}$ in place of $\boxed{\text{Cons}}$.

Now evaluate the expressions $a \times 3$, $a \div 3$, $a + 3$, and $a - 3$ for $a = 3, 12, 18,$ and 21. Check your answers mentally.

Calculations involving circles often require the number π, the ratio of the circumference of a circle to its diameter. Entering $\boxed{\times}$ $\boxed{\pi}$ $\boxed{\text{Cons}}$ sets the constant key to multiply by 3.1415927. Evaluate $\pi \times b$ for $b = 2, 6,$ and 5.

$\boxed{\text{ON/AC}}$ $\boxed{\times}$ $\boxed{\pi}$ $\boxed{\text{Cons}}$ 2 $\boxed{\text{Cons}}$ 6 $\boxed{\text{Cons}}$ 5 $\boxed{\text{Cons}}$

Estimate to decide if your calculator is multiplying by π.

Most calculators have a floating decimal point, allowing the number of decimal places in the display to vary. The $\boxed{\text{Fix}}$ key on the Math Explorer lets you choose from 0 to 7 decimal places. $\boxed{\text{ON/AC}}$ $\boxed{\text{Fix}}$ 2 $\boxed{\pi}$ gives a display of 3.14 and $\boxed{\text{ON/AC}}$ $\boxed{\text{Fix}}$ 6 $\boxed{\pi}$ gives a display of 3.141593.

Use the $\boxed{\text{Fix}}$ key to find values for π with 3, 4, and 5 decimal places.

Activity

Use the formula $C = 2\pi r$. Find the circumference of each circle. Use the $\boxed{\text{Fix}}$ key to round each answer to the nearest tenth.

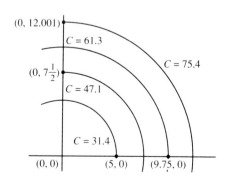

510

Integers

The $\boxed{+\!/\!-}$ key changes the sign of the number in the display. Enter $\boxed{\text{ON/AC}}$ 8 $\boxed{+\!/\!-}$. Then press $\boxed{+\!/\!-}$ again. The display will first show -8 and then 8.

Use the $\boxed{+\!/\!-}$ key to do problems involving integers.

Problem	Key Code	Display
$9 + {}^-9$	9 $\boxed{+}$ 9 $\boxed{+\!/\!-}$ $\boxed{=}$	0
${}^-9 + {}^-9$	9 $\boxed{+\!/\!-}$ $\boxed{+}$ 9 $\boxed{+\!/\!-}$ $\boxed{=}$	${}^-18$
${}^-15 - 8$	15 $\boxed{+\!/\!-}$ $\boxed{-}$ 8 $\boxed{=}$	${}^-23$
${}^-15 - {}^-8$	15 $\boxed{+\!/\!-}$ $\boxed{-}$ 8 $\boxed{+\!/\!-}$ $\boxed{=}$	${}^-7$
$7 \times {}^-8$	7 $\boxed{\times}$ 8 $\boxed{+\!/\!-}$ $\boxed{=}$	${}^-56$
${}^-7 \times {}^-8$	7 $\boxed{+\!/\!-}$ $\boxed{\times}$ 8 $\boxed{+\!/\!-}$ $\boxed{=}$	56
$35 \div {}^-5$	35 $\boxed{\div}$ 5 $\boxed{+\!/\!-}$ $\boxed{=}$	${}^-7$
${}^-35 \div 5$	35 $\boxed{+\!/\!-}$ $\boxed{\div}$ 5 $\boxed{=}$	${}^-7$
${}^-35 \div {}^-5 - 3$	35 $\boxed{+\!/\!-}$ $\boxed{\div}$ 5 $\boxed{+\!/\!-}$ $\boxed{-}$ 3 $\boxed{=}$	4
${}^-(6 + 4) \div 2$	$\boxed{(}$ 6 $\boxed{+}$ 4 $\boxed{)}$ $\boxed{+\!/\!-}$ $\boxed{\div}$ 2 $\boxed{=}$	${}^-5$
${}^-7 + 8 \times {}^-4$	7 $\boxed{+\!/\!-}$ $\boxed{+}$ 8 $\boxed{\times}$ 4 $\boxed{+\!/\!-}$ $\boxed{=}$	${}^-39$
$36 \div {}^-2 \div {}^-3$	36 $\boxed{\div}$ 2 $\boxed{+\!/\!-}$ $\boxed{\div}$ 3 $\boxed{+\!/\!-}$ $\boxed{=}$	6

Activity

Connect these points *in order* to figure out which X marks the spot where the treasure is buried.

	x-coordinate	**y-coordinate**
1.	${}^-35 \div 7$	$23 + {}^-26$
2.	$({}^-5 + {}^-6) + 13$	${}^-7 \times {}^-10 \div 14$
3.	$(75 \div {}^-5) + 17$	${}^-4 \times {}^-10 \div {}^-8$
4.	${}^-9 + 5$	${}^-11 - {}^-15$
5.	${}^-42 \div ({}^-10 + 3)$	$18 \times {}^-2 \div 36$

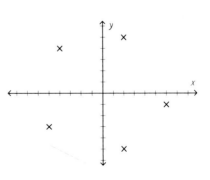

Exponents, Powers, and Roots

The $\boxed{x^2}$ key multiplies a number by itself, or **squares** a number.

To find 15^2, use this key code: Display
$\boxed{\text{ON/AC}}$ 15 $\boxed{x^2}$ 225

The $\boxed{\sqrt{}}$ key finds the **square root** of the number in the display. It finds a number that can be multiplied by itself to equal the display number.

$\boxed{\text{ON/AC}}$ 225 $\boxed{\sqrt{}}$ 15

$\boxed{\text{ON/AC}}$ 225 $\boxed{+\overset{\curvearrowright}{}-}$ $\boxed{\sqrt{}}$ Error

You cannot take the square root of a negative number. The calculator will display a **Sign Error**. To calculate powers of 10 use the $\boxed{10^n}$ key.

10^4 $\boxed{\text{ON/AC}}$ $\boxed{10^n}$ 4   10000

3.2×10^{-4} $\boxed{\text{ON/AC}}$ 3.2 $\boxed{x}$ $\boxed{10^n}$ $\boxed{+\overset{\curvearrowright}{}-}$ 4 $\boxed{=}$ 0.00032

To find 15^5 you can use several different key codes. Using the $\boxed{y^x}$ key is the most efficient way to raise a number to a power.

$\boxed{\text{ON/AC}}$ 15 $\boxed{\times}$ 15 $\boxed{\times}$ 15 $\boxed{\times}$ 15 $\boxed{\times}$ 15 $\boxed{=}$ 759375

$\boxed{\text{ON/AC}}$ 15 $\boxed{y^x}$ 5 $\boxed{=}$ 759375

Finding the 5th root of 759375, or $\sqrt[5]{759375}$, is the inverse of finding 15 raised to the 5th power.

$\boxed{\text{ON/AC}}$ 759375 $\boxed{y^x}$ 5 $\boxed{1/x}$ $\boxed{=}$ 15

Use the $\boxed{+\overset{\curvearrowright}{}-}$ key to raise a number to a negative power.
To find 5^{-2} enter $\boxed{\text{ON/AC}}$ 5 $\boxed{y^x}$ 2 $\boxed{+\overset{\curvearrowright}{}-}$ $\boxed{=}$.
The display will show 0.04.

Activity

Find a digit, 1-9, for each letter. Make a true equation.

1. $a^2 + b^2 + c^2 = d^2$ **2.** $a^3 + b^3 + c^3 = d^3$

3. $\sqrt{a} + \sqrt{b} = \sqrt{c}$ **4.** $a^2 = b^4$

Percent

The percent key $\boxed{\%}$ converts the number in the display to a decimal by dividing it by 100 (or multiplying it by .01). Try this.

Enter $\boxed{\text{ON/AC}}$ 55 $\boxed{\%}$. The display will show 0.55.

Here is how to use the calculator to solve some common percent problems.

Percent of a Number. If sales tax rate is 6%, what is the tax on $79.80?

Enter $\boxed{\text{ON/AC}}$ 79.80 $\boxed{\times}$ 6 $\boxed{\%}$ $\boxed{=}$. The display will be 4.788.
Pressing $\boxed{\text{Fix}}$ 2 sets 2 decimal places, and rounds the display to 4.79.

Mike put headlights on 25% of the bikes in his shop. He put headlights on 16 bikes. How many bikes are in the shop?

$\boxed{\text{ON/AC}}$ 16 $\boxed{\div}$ 25 $\boxed{\%}$ $\boxed{=}$ 64

Percent of Increase. There is 20% more rain this year than last year. Last year's rainfall was 35 inches. How many inches are there this year?

$\boxed{\text{ON/AC}}$ 35 $\boxed{+}$ 20 $\boxed{\%}$ $\boxed{=}$ 42
or   35 $\boxed{\times}$ 1.20 $\boxed{\%}$ $\boxed{=}$ 42

Percent Discount. At 25% off, what is the sale price of a shirt that originally sells for $28.60?

$\boxed{\text{ON/AC}}$ 28.60 $\boxed{-}$ 25 $\boxed{\%}$ $\boxed{=}$ 21.45
or   28.60 $\boxed{\times}$ 75 $\boxed{\%}$ $\boxed{=}$ 21.45

Activity

Petros makes jewelry. His wholesale prices are shown on the chart.

1. Petros gives his friends a 10% discount. What is the discount price for each item?

2. Sal at Sal's Jewelry Store buys Petros' jewelry at wholesale prices and marks it up 45% to sell in her store. That is the retail price. What is the retail price of each item?

Wholesale Prices		Disc	Retail
Men's ring	$240	216.00	348.00
Woman's Ring	275	247.50	398.75
Pins	60	54.00	87.00
Gold Earrings	120	108.00	174.00
Silver Earrings	95	85.50	137.75
Tie Tack	90	81.00	130.50

3. What percent of the discount price is Sal's retail price?

Averages

The winning average for a baseball team is the number of games won divided by the number of games played. Which of these teams had the best winning average? Try to decide by making estimates.

Team	Won	Lost	Average
Astros	67	45	?
Braves	68	49	?
Dodgers	64	44	?
Giants	69	50	?
Padres	62	48	?
Reds	65	51	?

The computer program below can be used to find averages when the win-loss record of a team is known. Try the program and arrange the teams in order of highest to lowest winning averages.

```
10    GOSUB 200
20    INPUT"HOW MANY GAMES WERE WON?";W
30    INPUT"HOW MANY GAMES WERE LOST?";L
40    PRINT
50    PRINT"WINNING AVERAGE  = ";W/(W + L)
60    PRINT
70    PRINT"DO YOU WANT TO FIND ANOTHER TEAM'S":INPUT
      "WINNING PERCENTAGE(Y/N)?";Y$
80    IF LEFT$(Y$,1( = "Y"THEN:PRINT:PRINT:GOSUB 220:
      GOTO 20
90    END
200   PRINT:PRINT:PRINT"PERCENTAGES":PRINT"ESTIMATE
      WHICH TEAM HAS THE BEST":PRINT"WINNING
      PERCENTAGE.CHECK THE ESTIMATE":PRINT"WITH THE
      COMPUTER.MAKE A CHART TO"
210   PRINT"SHOW EACH TEAM'S STANDING IN ORDER.":PRINT:
      PRINT
220   PRINT "TEAM";TAB(10)"WON";TAB(20)"LOST"
230   PRINT"ASTROS";TAB(10)67;TAB(20)45
240   PRINT"BRAVES";TAB(10)68;TAB(20)49
250   PRINT"DODGERS";TAB(10)64;TAB(20)44
260   PRINT"GIANTS";TAB(10)69;TAB(20)50
270   PRINT"PADRES";TAB(10)62;TAB(20)48
280   PRINT"REDS";TAB(10)65;TAB(20)51
290   PRINT:PRINT:RETURN
```

Prime Factorization

The Woolie Winka Widget factory produces 123,123 widgets each day. The widgets are packed in boxes that will hold only a prime number of widgets. What prime numbers are factors of 123,123? What strategies might you use to find the prime factors?

It may be difficult to find the prime factorization of some large numbers using a calculator or pencil and paper. The following computer program will find the prime factors for any number you may choose. Check to see if 1,000,001 is prime.

```
10    GOSUB 200
20    INPUT "FIND PRIME FACTORS OF WHAT NUMBER?";X:X1
      =X
30    PRINT:PRINT "DIVIDE "X" BY WHAT PRIME NUMBER?"
40    INPUT D: IF D = 1 THEN 160
50    IF D = 2 THEN 70
60    GOSUB 120
70    Q = X/D
80    IF Q <> INT (Q) THEN PRINT D" DOES NOT DIVIDE "X:
      GOTO 30
90    N = N + 1:F(N) = D
100   PRINT X"/"D" = "Q: IF Q = 1 THEN 160
110   X = Q: GOTO 30
120   FOR C = 2 TO D − 1
130   IF D/C = INT (D/C) THEN 150
140   NEXT C: RETURN
150   PRINT "D" IS NOT A PRIME NUMBER.":GOTO 30
160   PRINT:PRINT"THE PRIME FACTORS OF "X1" ARE:":
      FOR J = 1 TO N − 1:PRINT F(J)", ",:NEXT J: PRINT F(N):
      PRINT: INPUT "DO YOU WANT TO TRY AGAIN?";Y$
170   IF LEFT$(Y$,1) = "Y" THEN PRINT:GOTO 10
180   END
190   PRINT:PRINT:PRINT"PRIME FACTORIZATION"
200   PRINT "THIS PROGRAM CAN HELP YOU FIND THE"
210   PRINT "PRIME FACTORS OF A NUMBER. USE THE"
220   PRINT "RULES OF DIVISIBILITY TO CHOOSE PRIME"
230   PRINT "DIVISORS.GOOD FIRST CHOICES ARE 2 OR 3."
240   RETURN
```

Mean and Median

The 12 longest rivers in the world, listed in alphabetical order are given in the table.

What is the median length of the rivers?
What is the mean length of the rivers?

To solve the problem you must sort the numbers according to size. You must find the sum of the numbers and divide. The computer program below will do all of these tasks quickly and accurately.

River	Length (mi)
Amazon	3,912
Amur	2,704
Congo	2,716
Irtish	2,758
Lena	2,652
Mississippi	3,741
Nile	4,180
Ob	3,459
Parana	2,795
Yangtze	3,602
Yellow	2,900
Yenisei	2,800

```
10    PRINT:PRINT:PRINT"FINDING MEAN AND MEDIAN":PRINT
      "ENTER HOW MANY NUMBERS YOU WANT AND":PRINT
      "TYPE THEM IN ANY ORDER. THE COMPUTER":PRINT"WILL
      SORT THE NUMBERS AND GIVE THE MEAN":PRINT"AND
      MEDIAN."
20    PRINT:INPUT"HOW MANY NUMBERS DO YOU WANT?";N:
      DIMX(N)
30    PRINT"TYPE EACH NUMBER AND PRESS <RETURN>."
40    FOR I = 1 TO N:PRINT I;:INPUT X(I):C = C + X(I):NEXTI:PRINT
50    FOR I = 1 TO N − 1
60    FOR J = 1 TO N − 1
70    IFX(J)< = X(J + 1)THEN GOTO 90
80    T = X(J):X(J) = X(J + 1):X(J + 1) = T
90    NEXT J
100   NEXT I
110   PRINT"THE "N" NUMBERS IN ORDER ARE:"
120   FOR I = 1 TO N:PRINTI,:PRINTX(I):NEXT I
130   PRINT:IF INT(N/2)<>N/2 THEN PRINT "THE MEDIAN IS
      ";X(INT(N/2) + 1):GOTO 150
140   PRINT"THE MEDIAN IS"(X(N/2) + X((N/2) + 1))/2
160   PRINT:INPUT"DO YOU WANT TO TRY AGAIN?";Y$
170   IF LEFT$(Y$,1) = "Y" THEN PRINT:GOTO 10
180   END
```

Lowest-Terms Fractions

A television poll showed that 36,960 people out of 42,240 people watched a event on TV.

Can you estimate a simple fraction for the part of the people that watched the program? Then try finding the lowest-terms fraction.

To find the lowest-terms fraction, you can divide numerator and denominator by their greatest common factor (GCF). For large numbers the GCF may be hard to find so you may have to divide repeatedly by smaller factors. The computer program below will do this for you, quickly and accurately.

```
10    GOSUB 140:PRINT:PRINT
20    INPUT"ENTER THE NUMBERATOR";A
30    INPUT"ENTER THE DENOMINATOR";B
40    A1 = A:B1 = B
50    Q = INT(B1/A1)
60    R = B1 - (Q*A1)
70    IF R = 0 THEN GOTO 100
80    LET B1 = A1:LET A1 = R
90    GOTO 50
100   PRINT:PRINT"THE GCF OF";A;"AND";B;" = ";A1
110   LET A2 = A/A1:LET B2 = B/A1
120   PRINT:PRINT A;"/";B;"IN LOWEST TERMS IS";A2;"/";B2
130   END
140   PRINT"LOWEST TERMS FRACTIONS"
150   PRINT"ENTER THE NUMERATOR AND THE DENOMINATOR";PRINT"OF ANY
      FRACTION. THE COMPUTER WILL GIVE":PRINT"THE GREATEST COMMON
      FACTOR AND THE":PRINT"LOWEST TERMS FRACTION."
160   RETURN
```

Tables of Values

Jessica wanted to complete a table of values for the equation $y = 6x + 14$ in order to make a graph of the equation. She chose 8 values for x and needed to compute the corresponding values for y.

What are the numbers for y in the table of values?

When many values of an expression must be computed, a computer can make the task easier and quicker. Use the computer program below to find tables of values for any equation of the form $y = Ax + B$, where A and B are constants and x and y are variables.

Equation: $y = 6x + 14$	
x	y
-6	?
-4	?
-2	?
0	?
2	?
4	?
6	?
8	?

```
10    PRINT:PRINT:PRINT"TABLE OF VALUES"
20    PRINT"ENTER THE VALUES FOR A AND B IN THE"
30    PRINT"EQUATION Y = AX + B."
40    PRINT:INPUT"A = ";A:INPUT"B = ";B
50    PRINT:PRINT"EQUATION: Y = ";A;"X + ";B
60    PRINT:INPUT"HOW MANY VALUES FOR X?";N
70    FOR K = 1 TO N
80    INPUT"ENTER A VALUE FOR X";X(K)
90    Y(K) = A*X(K) + B:NEXT K
100   PRINT:PRINT"X","Y"
110   FOR K = 1 TO N
120   PRINT X(K),Y(K)
130   NEXT K
140   PRINT:INPUT"DO YOU WANT TO TRY AGAIN?";Y$
150   IF LEFT$(Y$,1) = "Y" THEN PRINT:GOTO 10
160   END
```

Interest

Once a year Karen's parents put $1,200 in a savings account for her college expenses. The account earns 8.5% interest per year. The interest is added to the account once a year. Karen will start college 8 years from now. How much do you estimate will be in the account at that time?

To solve the problem many calculations are needed. A calculator would be useful, but a computer program such as the one below will quickly compute the interest and the total amount for each year.

```
10    GOSUB 130:PRINT
20    INPUT"HOW MUCH SAVINGS PER YEAR?";P
30    P1 = P
40    INPUT"ENTER THE INTEREST RATE(9 FOR 9%).";R
50    PRINT"HOW YEARS WILL THE SAVINGS ACCOUNT BE":INPUT"BE OEN?";T
60    PRINT"YEAR"; TAB(17)"INTEREST" ;TAB(33)"AMOUNT"
70    FOR N = 1 TO T
80    I = INT(P*R)/100:I2 = I2 + I
90    A = P + I
95    PRINT N,12,A
100   P = A + P1
110   NEXT N
120   END
130   PRINT:PRINT:PRINT"INTEREST"
140   PRINT"ENTER THE AMOUNT OF SAVINGS PER YEAR,":PRINT"THE INTEREST
      RATE, AND THE NUMBER":PRINT "OF YEARS TO SAVE AND THE COMPUTER
      WILL"
150   PRINT "CALCULATE THE TOTAL INTEREST EARNED AND":PRINT THE
      PRINCIPLE FOR EACH YEAR."
160   RETURN
```

Circle Graphs

A survey of the students at Monroe School showed these facts about the way students got to school each day.

Walk	280
Bus	412
Car	88
Bicycle	106

Suppose you want to show these statistics on a circle graph in the school newspaper. What is the angle needed for each sector of the graph? What is the percent of all students that each sector repesents?

The computer program below will find the measure of the angle for each sector of the circle graph and the percent of the total that each sector represents. More powerful computer programs such as a spreadsheet would also draw the circle graph. Use the program to help you make a circle graph.

```
10    PRINT:PRINT:PRINT"MEASURES OF CIRCLE GRAPH
      ANGLES":PRINT"ENTER THE NUMBER OF SECTORS AND
      LIST":PRINT"THE AMOUNT OF EACH SECTOR. THE
      COMPUTER":PRINT"WILL FIND THE MEASURE FOR EACH
      SECTOR":PRINT"OF THE GRAPH AND THE PERCENT OF
      THE"
20    PRINT"TOTAL THAT EACH SECTOR REPRESENTS.":PRINT:
      PRINT"HOW MANY SECTORS WILL THE CIRCLE GRAPH":
      INPUT"SHOW?";N
30    PRINT"ENTER THE NUMBER FOR EACH SECTOR AND":
      PRINT"PRESS RETURN."
40    T=0: FOR K=1 TO N
50    INPUT A(K):T=T+A(K)
60    NEXT K
65    PRINT:PRINT
70    PRINT"NUMBER";"ANGLE","PERCENT"
80    FOR K=1 TO N
90    PRINT A(K),INT(100*A(K)*360/T)/100,INT(10000*A(K)/
      T)/100
100   NEXT K
110   PRINT:INPUT"DO WANT TO TRY ANOTHER?";Y$
120   IF LEFT$(Y$,1)="Y" THEN PRINT:GOTO 10
130   END
```

Probability Spinner

Jan wanted to solve a probability problem with a spinner divided into 12 sectors of equal size. She needed to spin the spinner 100 times and record the number of times each of the 12 numbers appeared. She did not have a spinner and thought this experiment would take a long time to complete.

Will each number come up the same number of times? How many times do you predict each number will occur?

Computers can be programmed to simulate probability problems. The program below can be used to simulate a spinner with any number of equal sectors. It could be used to simulate a coin toss by choosing a spinner with 2 sectors. It could simulate a die by choosing a spinner with 6 sectors. You can choose any number of trials for the spinner.

```
10    PRINT"PROBABILITY SPINNER":PRINT"THIS IS AN
      EXPERIMENT IN PROBABILITY.":PRINT"CHOOSE A SPINNER
      WITH ANY NUMBER OF":PRINT"EQUAL PARTS. CHOOSE
      ANY NUMBER OF":PRINT"SPINS. THE COMPUTER WILL
      QUICKLY GIVE":PRINT"THE OUTCOME."
20    PRINT:INPUT"HOW MANY SECTORS OF EQUAL SIZE?";X
30    DIM D(X)
40    FOR N = 1 TO X:D(N) = 9: NEXT N
50    INPUT"HOW MANY SPINS DO YOU WANT?";Y
60    FOR I = 1 T Y:R = INT(X*AND(1)) + 1
70    LET D(R) = D(R) + 1:NEXT I
80    PRINT"NUMBER","FREQUENCY"
90    FOR N = 1 TO X:PRINT N,D(N):NEXT N
100   PRINT:INPUT"DO YOU WANT TO TRY ANOTHER?";Y$
110   IF LEFT$(Y$,1) = "Y" THEN PRINT:GOTO 10
120   END
```

MORE PRACTICE BANK

Set A   For use after page 5
Give the value of the red digit in each numeral.

1. 17,609   **2.** 589,403   **3.** 200,041,892   **4.** 35,719,260

Set B   For use after page 7
Write the following problems.

1. an addition problem to help solve $27 - 16 = $ _____

2. a multiplication problem related to $49 \div 9 = $ _____

3. a subtraction problem related to $325 + 612 = $ _____

4. a division problem related to 18×3 _____

Set C   For use after page 9
Evaluate each expression. Follow the order of operations.

1. $27 + 12 \times 3$ **2.** $9 \times 4 - 6 \div 3$ **3.** $(33 + 7) \times 15$

Set D   For use after page 15
Find the missing numbers.

1. $27 \times 26 = n \times 27$ **2.** $9 \times (8 \times 2) = $ **3.** $n \times 6 = 6 \times 23$
$9 \times (n \times 8)$

4. $5 \times (9 + 3) = (n \times 9) + (5 \times 3)$ **5.** $20 \times (n + 5) = (20 \times 30) + (20 \times 5)$

Set E   For use after page 17
Solve using mental math.

1. $16 + 8 + 14 + 7$ **2.** $3 \times 37 \times 10$ **3.** $25 - 8 - 13$ **4.** $17 + 23 + 14$

Set A **For use after page 19**

Estimate each sum or difference by rounding to the nearest hundred.

1. 278 + 415   **2.** 930 − 666   **3.** 2,311 + 892   **4.** 1,747 − 1,288

Estimate each product or quotient. Use rounding.

5. 87 × 6   **6.** 237 × 9   **7.** 2,774 ÷ 58   **8.** 788 ÷ 38

Set B **For use after page 33**

Write >, =, or < for each ▓.

1. 0.83 ▓ 0.87   **2.** 0.4 ▓ 0.2   **3.** 0.715 ▓ 0.725   **4.** 0.35 ▓ 0.350

Set C **For use after page 35**

Add, subtract, or multiply.

1. 3.04 + 1.99   **2.** 18.057 + 3.96   **3.** 0.1040 + 0.7794   **4.** 108.04 − 67.16

5. 0.406 − 0.198   **6.** 2 × 0.7   **7.** 3 × 0.4   **8.** 4 × 0.04

Set D **For use after page 37**

Estimate the sum or difference using front-end estimation.

1.	**2.**	**3.**	**4.**
276	6,128	10,079	$83.95
818	3,192	− 8,843	− 53.77
+ 430	+ 5,831		

Estimate the sum. Use clustering.

6. 84 + 83 + 81 + 77   **7.** 145 + 153 + 151 + 147   **8.** 2,799 + 3,142 + 3,193

Set E **For use after page 39**

Find each quotient to the nearest hundredth.

1. $9.1\overline{)46.21}$ **2.** $0.42\overline{)1.08}$ **3.** $6.2\overline{)3.74}$ **4.** $0.32\overline{)0.851}$

Set A   For use after page 43

Write each number using scientific notation.

1. 347,612,000   **2.** 36,982,151   **3.** 13.972006

Set B   For use after page 49

Express each length in meters.

1. 163 cm   **2.** 38.4 dm   **3.** 5 km   **4.** 6,388 mm   **5.** 238 cm

Express each length in kilometers.

6. 2,000 m   **7.** 2,135 m   **8.** 23,000 cm   **9.** 807 m   **10.** 45,000 cm

Set C   For use after page 51

Which measurement is more precise?

1. 72.32 m to the nearest cm or 72 m to the nearest m?

2. 1600 m to the nearest m or 15.7 km to the nearest dam?

3. 8 m to the nearest m or 46 cm to the nearest mm?

Set D   For use after page 53

Give the missing numbers.

1. 2,000 g = __?__ kg   **2.** 500 mg = __?__ g   **3.** 0.454 kg = __?__ g

MORE PRACTICE BANK

Set A   For use after page 65

Use the line graph to answer the questions.

1. How many adults attended on Sunday?

2. Did more children or adults attend on Saturday? About how many more?

3. On what day was the difference between numbers of children and adults the greatest?

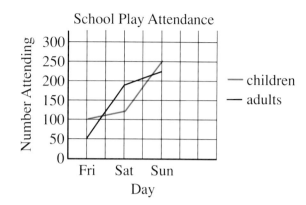

School Play Attendance

Set B   For use after page 67

Use the circle graph to answer the questions.

1. Are more or less than half of the members in the soprano section?

2. Which two sections combined make up exactly half of the choir?

3. The alto and soprano sections are all girls. The tenor and bass sections are all boys. By how much do the girls outnumber the boys?

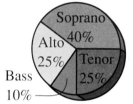

7th Grade 40-Member Choir

Study and TV Viewing
in Mr. Valez' Class
(1 week)

Set C   For use after page 69

Use the scattergram to answer the questions

1. About how many hours of television were watched by the student who studied the most hours?

2. About how many hours of studying were put in by the student who watched the most hours of television?

3. Does the scattergram show positive, negative, or no correlation?

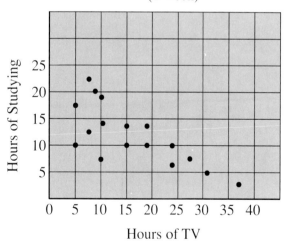

Set D   For use after page 71

Solve using mental math. Use compensation or break apart.

1. 327 + 75   **2.** 88 × 2   **3.** 430 × 6   **4.** 99 × 25   **5.** 515 + 59

Set A   For use after page 79

Make a stem and leaf table for the following data.

Orienteering club member ages: 13, 25, 18, 56, 37, 28, 66, 15, 34, 54, 63, 22, 27, 31, 45, 43, 21, 48, 50, 30, 67, 69

Set B   For use after page 81

Make a frequency table and a histogram using the data shown in the table below on number of hours people surveyed exercise in a week.

Survey Response	Tally
0–1 hours	⊞⊞
2–3 hours	⊞⊞ ⊞⊞ l
4–5 hours	⊞⊞ ll
6 or more hours	ll

Set C   For use after page 95

Give the number of vertices (*V*), faces (*F*), and edges (*E*) of each figure.

1. 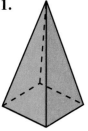　**2.** 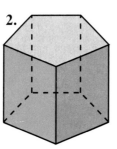　**3.** 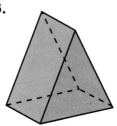　**4.**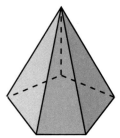

Set D   For use after page 97

Draw a picture of each cross-section.

1. 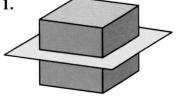　**2.** 　**3.**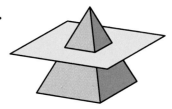

Set E   For use after page 99.

Use a protractor. Draw and label triangles with the following angles.

1. 105°, 23°, 52°　　　**2.** 45°, 75°, 60°　　　**3.** 28°, 37°, 115°

Set A   For use after page 103

Find the measure of the third angle in each triangle.

1.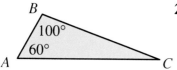

2.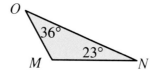

3.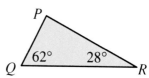

Set B   For use after page 109

1. Name a pair of parallel lines.

2. Name two right angles.

3. Name a pair of perpendicular lines.

4. Name a transversal.

5. Which angles have a measure of 130°?

6. What is the measure of ∠7?

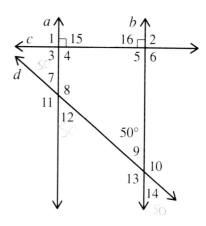

Set C   For use after page 111

1. Use a ruler and a compass to construct a square *ABCD*.

2. Construct a trapezoid *WXYZ* that has two right angles.

MORE PRACTICE BANK

Set A   For use after page 113

1. Draw $\overline{XY}$. Bisect $\overline{XY}$ using a ruler and a compass.

2. Draw $\overline{MN}$. Construct the perpendicular bisector of $\overline{MN}$.

3. Draw acute $\angle G$. Bisect $\angle G$ with a ruler and a compass.

4. Draw obtuse $\angle H$. Then bisect $\angle H$ with a ruler and a compass.

Set B   For use after page 127

Decide if each number is divisible by 2, 3, 5, 9, 10, or none of these numbers.

1. 714   **2.** 420   **3.** 9,125   **4.** 123   **5.** 3,150

Set C   For use after page 129

Write P (prime), C (composite), or N (neither) for each number.

1. 29   **2.** 48   **3.** 37   **4.** 43   **5.** 49   **6.** 1

Find the composite number in each list and give its prime factors.

7. 19, 29, 39, 59   **8.** 3, 7, 9, 11   **9.** 17, 27, 37, 47   **10.** 19, 91, 17, 71

Set D   For use after page 131

Give the prime factorization of each number.

1. 98   **2.** 56   **3.** 68   **4.** 150   **5.** 7,350

Set A   For use after page 133

Find the GCF of each pair of numbers.

1. 30, 135　　　**2.** 28, 20　　　**3.** 25, 36　　　**4.** 200, 75　　　**5.** 200, 64

Set B   For use after page 135

Find the LCM of each pair of numbers.

1. 4, 10　　　**2.** 6, 9　　　**3.** 18, 45　　　**4.** 11, 6　　　**5.** 36, 45

Set C   For use after page 139

Write the missing numerator or denominator.

1. $\dfrac{1}{4} = \dfrac{}{8}$　　　**2.** $\dfrac{2}{3} = \dfrac{}{6}$　　　**3.** $\dfrac{4}{9} = \dfrac{12}{}$　　　**4.** $\dfrac{3}{5} = \dfrac{15}{}$　　　**5.** $\dfrac{3}{11} = \dfrac{}{33}$

Set D   For use after page 141

Write each fraction in lowest terms.

1. $\dfrac{6}{10}$　　　**2.** $\dfrac{9}{27}$　　　**3.** $\dfrac{80}{100}$　　　**4.** $\dfrac{22}{44}$　　　**5.** $\dfrac{14}{30}$

MORE PRACTICE BANK

Set A   **For use after page 143**

Write each mixed number as an improper fraction.

1. $1\frac{5}{8}$ **2.** $3\frac{3}{4}$ **3.** $1\frac{1}{9}$ **4.** $3\frac{3}{7}$ **5.** $8\frac{2}{3}$ **6.** $6\frac{2}{5}$

Set B   **For use after page 147**

Write each decimal as a lowest-terms fraction or as a mixed number.

1. 0.8   **2.** 0.3   **3.** 0.09   **4.** 0.12   **5.** 3.04   **6.** 2.125

Write each fraction as a decimal.

7. $\frac{3}{5}$ **8.** $\frac{27}{4}$ **9.** $\frac{15}{16}$ **10.** $\frac{7}{25}$ **11.** $\frac{1}{5}$ **12.** $\frac{80}{100}$

Set C   **For use after page 149**

Write the decimal for each fraction. Use a bar to show repeating decimals. Use a calculator.

1. $\frac{3}{5}$ **2.** $\frac{7}{9}$ **3.** $\frac{5}{30}$ **4.** $\frac{4}{5}$ **5.** $\frac{6}{9}$ **6.** $\frac{3}{9}$

Set D   **For use after page 151**

Compare the fractions. Write > or < for each .

1. $\frac{7}{12}$ $\frac{5}{5}$ **2.** $\frac{2}{3}$ $\frac{5}{9}$ **3.** $\frac{3}{8}$ $\frac{1}{3}$ **4.** $\frac{1}{6}$ $\frac{2}{9}$

Set E   **For use after page 163**

Add or subtract.

1. $\begin{array}{r} \frac{3}{8} \\ + \frac{3}{4} \\ \hline \end{array}$

2. $\begin{array}{r} \frac{3}{7} \\ + \frac{5}{14} \\ \hline \end{array}$

3. $\begin{array}{r} \frac{5}{9} \\ + \frac{5}{6} \\ \hline \end{array}$

4. $\begin{array}{r} \frac{5}{12} \\ - \frac{3}{8} \\ \hline \end{array}$

5. $\begin{array}{r} \frac{5}{6} \\ - \frac{3}{5} \\ \hline \end{array}$

6. $\begin{array}{r} \frac{7}{10} \\ - \frac{1}{4} \\ \hline \end{array}$

MORE PRACTICE BANK

Set A For use after page 167

Add.

1. $3\frac{5}{9}$
   $+ 4\frac{1}{6}$

2. $4\frac{3}{5}$
   $+ 5\frac{11}{15}$

3. $6\frac{1}{7}$
   $+ 6\frac{2}{3}$

4. $2\frac{2}{3}$
   $+ 6\frac{5}{6}$

5. $14\frac{7}{8}$
   $+ 3\frac{1}{8}$

Set B For use after page 169

Subtract.

1. $8\frac{1}{2}$
   $- 4\frac{2}{3}$

2. $4\frac{2}{8}$
   $- 3\frac{1}{2}$

3. $7\frac{1}{10}$
   $- 4\frac{3}{5}$

4. $5\frac{3}{9}$
   $- 1\frac{10}{12}$

5. $6\frac{3}{4}$
   $- 2\frac{12}{16}$

Set C For use after page 177

Find the fraction of the number.

1. $\frac{2}{3}$ of 9

2. $\frac{4}{5}$ of 10

3. $\frac{1}{6}$ of 12

4. $\frac{5}{6}$ of 12

5. $\frac{1}{2} \times 6$

Set D For use after page 179

Find the products.

1. $\frac{3}{5} \times \frac{1}{9}$

2. $\frac{1}{2} \times \frac{4}{5}$

3. $\frac{3}{4} \times \frac{2}{3}$

4. $\frac{5}{12} \times \frac{3}{10}$

5. $\frac{3}{7} \times \frac{14}{27}$

Set E For use after page 181

Find the products.

1. $3\frac{1}{3} \times \frac{1}{2}$

2. $2\frac{1}{2} \times 1\frac{1}{3}$

3. $3\frac{1}{5} \times 1\frac{1}{4}$

4. $1\frac{7}{8} \times 2\frac{2}{5}$

5. $2\frac{1}{4} \times 5\frac{1}{3}$

Set F For use after page 183

Find the quotients.

1. $\frac{2}{3} \div \frac{1}{8}$

2. $\frac{3}{5} \div \frac{2}{3}$

3. $\frac{7}{8} \div \frac{1}{4}$

4. $\frac{3}{10} \div \frac{2}{5}$

5. $\frac{1}{4} \div \frac{3}{4}$

Set A   For use after page 185

Find the quotients.

1. $3\frac{1}{3} \div 2\frac{2}{3}$ **2.** $4\frac{2}{3} \div 2\frac{1}{3}$ **3.** $3\frac{3}{4} \div 3$ **4.** $\frac{5}{6} \div 1\frac{2}{3}$ **5.** $4\frac{1}{2} \div 1\frac{5}{8}$

Set B   For use after page 197

Write an algebraic expression for each phrase.

1. 5 more than a number

2. the sum of a number and 15

3. a number decreased by 23.7

4. 0.33 less than a number

Set C   For use after page 199

Write an algebraic expression for each phrase.

1. 4 times a number t

2. a number z divided by 5

3. 8 times a number d

4. a number k divided by 7

Set D   For use after page 203

The scale shown is balanced.

1. Use the same symbols to draw another balanced scale.

2. Use the same symbols to draw an unbalanced scale.

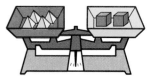

Set E   For use after page 207

Solve. Use mental math.

1. $6x = 54$ **2.** $10y = 80$ **3.** $7p = 49$ **4.** $2n = 32$ **5.** $\frac{m}{5} = 100$

Set A For use after page 211

Give the inverse operation that would get the variable alone.

1. $x - 18$ **2.** $y + 32$ **3.** $z + 8.4$ **4.** $a - 7\frac{6}{7}$

Set B For use after page 213

Solve.

1. $x + 9 = 25$ **2.** $s + 12 = 40$ **3.** $t + 14 = 24$ **4.** $m + 3 = 15$

Set C For use after page 215

Give the inverse operation that would get the variable alone.

1. $m \div 34$ **2.** $25.4n$ **3.** $\frac{t}{48}$ **4.** $16s$ **5.** $32r$

Set D For use after page 217

Solve.

1. $\frac{n}{18} = 1$ **2.** $18z = 180$ **3.** $8r = 88$ **4.** $\frac{x}{4} = 13$ **5.** $7n = 231$

Set A   For use after page 227

Write each ratio as a fraction.

1. 8 to 9   **2.** 5:11   **3.** 3 out of 4   **4.** 9 to 7

Set B   For use after page 229

Write $=$ or $\neq$ for each ▥.

1. $\dfrac{2}{6}$ ▥ $\dfrac{5}{15}$ **2.** $\dfrac{3}{4}$ ▥ $\dfrac{9}{10}$ **3.** $\dfrac{6}{12}$ ▥ $\dfrac{5}{10}$ **4.** $\dfrac{3}{5}$ ▥ $\dfrac{4}{7}$ **5.** $\dfrac{1}{8}$ ▥ $\dfrac{4}{32}$

Write each ratio as a fraction in lowest terms.

6. 3 out of 18   **7.** 8:12   **8.** 10 to 35   **9.** 9 out of 24   **10.** $\dfrac{45}{60}$

Set C   For use after page 231

Solve each proportion.

1. $\dfrac{2}{5} = \dfrac{4}{x}$ **2.** $\dfrac{70}{100} = \dfrac{x}{10}$ **3.** $\dfrac{9}{3} = \dfrac{12}{x}$ **4.** $\dfrac{7}{14} = \dfrac{2}{x}$ **5.** $\dfrac{3}{25} = \dfrac{9}{x}$

Set D   For use after page 233

Write the rate for each statement.

1. $130 for 2 tires   **2.** 43 km in $\dfrac{1}{2}$ h   **3.** $100 for 50 kg

4. 81 words per min.   **5.** $200 for 30 days   **6.** 50 m in 20 s

Set E   For use after page 243

Find the length x for each pair of similar figures.

1. x ▭
          5 mm

4 mm ▭
          10 mm

2.

12 cm   21 cm
     x
          14 cm

Set A   **For use after page 245**

Find the missing value. Use 3.14 for π.

1. $C = ?$
   $d = 3.4$ cm

2. $C = 55$ cm
   $d = ?$

3. $C = ?$
   $d = 3$ km

4. $C = 15$ m
   $d = ?$

Set B   **For use after page 257**

Write a fraction and a percent for each ratio.

1. 8 to 100

2. 17 to 100

3. 6 per hundred

4. 37 out of 100

5. 39 to 100

6. 95 to 100

7. 100 to 100

8. 1 per hundred

Set C   **For use after page 259**

Write each fraction in lowest terms. Then write the percent for the fraction.

1. $\frac{3}{6}$

2. $\frac{6}{15}$

3. $\frac{12}{48}$

4. $\frac{18}{30}$

5. $\frac{14}{20}$

Set D   **For use after page 261**

Write each percent as a decimal.

1. 67%

2. 6%

3. 74%

4. 3%

5. 18%

Write each decimal as a percent.

6. 0.33

7. 0.12

8. 0.37

9. 0.6

10. 0.18

Set A   For use after page 263

Complete the table.

Fraction	$\frac{1}{4}$			$\frac{2}{5}$	
Decimal		0.80			
Percent			15%		5%

Set B   For use after page 267

Write each percent as a decimal.

1. 235%   **2.** 163%   **3.** $17\frac{2}{3}\%$ **4.** $6\frac{1}{3}\%$ **5.** $1\frac{1}{4}\%$

Set C   For use after page 271

Write each decimal as a percent.

1. 0.0033   **2.** 1.333   **3.** 0.755   **4.** 0.150   **5.** 3.280

Set D   For use after page 285

Find the percent of each number.

1. 15% of 60   **2.** 12% of 30   **3.** 12% of 25   **4.** 90% of 50   **5.** 70% of 8

Set E   For use after page 287

Estimate.

1. 21% of 40   **2.** 48% of 120   **3.** 32% of 60

4. 75% of 39   **5.** $9\frac{1}{2}\%$ of 2,000   **6.** 18% of 78

Set F   For use after page 289

Find the interest.

1. P = \$3,000
R = 12% per year
T = 2 years

2. P = \$20,000
R = 16% per year
T = 6 months (Use 0.5 year.)

3. P = \$2,500
R = 1.5% per month
T = 5 months

Set G   For use after page 291

Find the percent.

1. 18 is what percent of 30?   **2.** 45 is what percent of 36?   **3.** What percent of 6 is 15?

4. What percent is 11 out of 44?   **5.** What percent is 14 out of 20?   **6.** What percent is 6 out of 150?

Set A   For use after page 293

Find the percent of increase or decrease. Round to the nearest tenth.

1. 55 to 130   **2.** 32 to 90   **3.** 75 to 50   **4.** 23 to 110   **5.** 300 to 250

Set B   For use after page 297

Solve.

1. $75\% \cdot n = 12$ **2.** $36\% \cdot n = 27$ **3.** $16\% \cdot n = 8$ **4.** $30\% \cdot n = 18$ **5.** $72\% \cdot n = 36$

Set C   For use after page 299

Find the discount and the sale price.

1. Regular Price: $60   **2.** Regular Price: $75   **3.** Regular Price: $240
   Discount Percent: 15%   Discount Percent: 50%   Discount Percent: 20%

Set D   For use after page 301

Draw a circle graph using the following data to show how
Andrew uses his leisure time.

Sports: 45%; Club activities: 20%; Reading: 10%; Personal computer: 15%

Set E   For use after page 315

Write $<$ or $>$ for each ▦.

1. $^{+}8$ ▦ $^{-}2$ **2.** $^{-}4$ ▦ $^{+}4$ **3.** $^{-}1$ ▦ 0 **4.** $^{-}3$ ▦ $^{-}7$ **5.** $^{+}10$ ▦ $^{-}10$

Set A   **For use after page 317**

Find the missing integers.

1. $^+5 + {}^-5 = $ ▓   **2.** $^+10 + 0 = $ ▓   **3.** $^+4 + $ ▓ $ = 0$ **4.** ▓ $ + {}^-6 = {}^-6$

Set B   **For use after page 319**

Find the sums.

1. $^-3 + {}^-1$ **2.** $^-7 + {}^-2$ **3.** $^+1 + {}^+6$ **4.** $^-3 + {}^-8$ **5.** $^+9 + {}^+5$

Set C   **For use after page 321**

Subtract.

1. $^-5 - {}^-1$ **2.** $^+6 - {}^-3$ **3.** $^-8 - {}^+5$ **4.** $^+6 - {}^-4$ **5.** $^-3 - {}^-3$

Set D   **For use after page 325**

Multiply.

1. $7 \cdot {}^-3$ **2.** $^-6 \cdot {}^-1$ **3.** $5 \cdot {}^-3$ **4.** $^-9 \cdot {}^-5$ **5.** $3 \cdot 9$

Set E   **For use after page 327**

Find the quotients.

1. $14 \div {}^-2$ **2.** $^-30 \div {}^-6$ **3.** $45 \div {}^-9$ **4.** $64 \div {}^-8$ **5.** $^-35 \div 7$

Set A   For use after page 343

Copy this line. Place each of the following events on your line.

Impossible ├──┼──┼──┼──┼──┼──┼──┤ Certain
        A B C D E F G H

1. Spinning a number less than 8

2. Spinning a number greater than 8

3. Spinning an odd number

Set B   For use after page 345

List all the outcomes for each event using a 1-6 number cube.

1. Tossing an even number

2. Tossing a multiple of 3

3. Tossing an odd number

Set C   For use after page 347

Give the probability of each event.

1. $P(A)$ **2.** $P(B)$ **3.** $P(C)$

4. $P(D)$ **5.** $P(A \text{ or } C)$ **6.** $P(B \text{ or } D)$

Set D   For use after page 349

Find the experimental probability of each event.

1. Toss a coin: result is 43 heads, 37 tails.

    Exp $P(H) =$ __?__   Exp $P(T) =$ __?__

2. Toss two number cubes six times: result is a sum of 4 five times.

    Exp $P(4) =$ __?__

Set E   For use after page 355

Use the tree diagram for 2 spins of the spinner. Give the probability of each event.

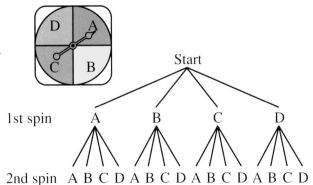

1. $P(A,A)$

2. $P(B,C)$

3. $P(\text{both letters the same})$

4. $P(\text{both letters different})$

MORE PRACTICE BANK

Set A   For use after page 359

Find the expected value for each spinner experiment.

1. Spin 40 times

2. Spin 80 times

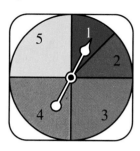

Set B   For use after page 369

Find the area of each figure and state principle used.

1.

2.

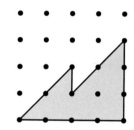

Set C   For use after page 371

Find the area of each rectangle or parallelogram.

1. $l = 12$ cm   **2.** $l = 25$ m   **3.** $l = 3.8$ m   **4.** $b = 15$ cm   **5.** $b = 24$ cm
  $w = 8$ cm $w = 10$ m $w = 2.0$ m $h = 8$ cm $h = 12$ cm

Set D   For use after page 373

Find the area of each triangle.

1. $b = 47$ km   **2.** $b = 25$ cm   **3.** $b = 43$ m   **4.** $b = 57$ mm   **5.** $b = 68$ dm
  $h = 5$ km $h = 7$ cm $h = 6$ m $h = 41$ mm $h = 53$ dm

Set E   For use after page 375

Give the area of each circle. Use 3.14 for π.

1. $r = 10$ ft   **2.** $d = 8$ in.   **3.** $r = 2.5$ in.   **4.** $r = 0.5$ mi   **5.** $d = 7$ ft

540

Set A   For use after page 377

Find the area of each figure.

1.

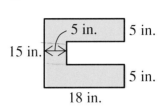

2.

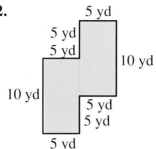

3.

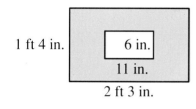

Set B   For use after page 385

Find the surface area of the following figures.

1.

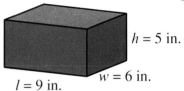

2.

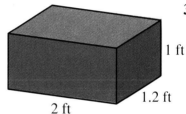

3.

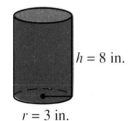

Set C   For use after page 387

Find the volume of each space figure.

1.

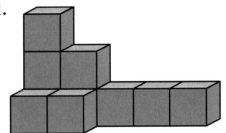

2.

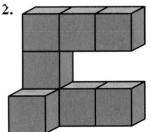

Set D   For use after page 389

Find the volume of each rectangular prism. Use $V = lwh$.

1. $l = 5$ in.
$w = 4$ in.
$h = 10$ in.

2. $l = 3.5$ ft
$w = 2$ ft
$h = 4.5$ ft

3. $l = 6$ in.
$w = 3$ in.
$h = 6$ in.

4. $l = 2$ ft 3 in.
$w = 2$ ft 1 in.
$h = 6$ in.

Set A   For use after page 391

Find the volume of each cylinder. Use $V = \pi r^2 h$. Use 3.14 for π.

1. $r = 10$ in.
$h = 5$ in.

2. $r = 4$ ft
$h = 13$ ft

3. $r = 6$ in.
$h = 1$ ft 3 in.

4. $r = 7$ ft
$h = 2$ ft

Set B   For use after page 393

Find the volume of each figure.

1.

$h = 12$ cm

10 cm   10 cm

2.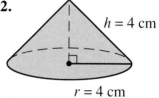

$h = 4$ cm

$r = 4$ cm

3.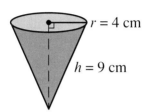

$r = 4$ cm

$h = 9$ cm

Set C   For use after page 405

Draw each figure on graph paper. Draw all lines of symmetry.

1.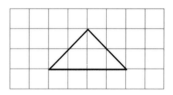

2.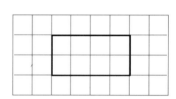

3.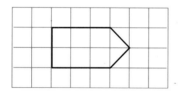

Set D   For use after page 407

Draw each figure on graph paper. Then draw the reflection image in the line l.

1.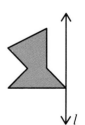

2.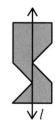

Set A   For use after page 409

The turn symmetry of each figure is what fraction of a full turn?

1. 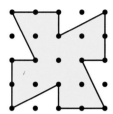   2. 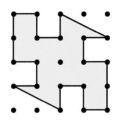   3. 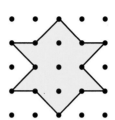   4.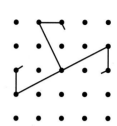

Set B   For use after page 433

Evaluate each expression.

1. $3 \cdot 5 + 7 \cdot 2$ **2.** $18 - 11 \cdot 3 - 3$ **3.** $(6 - 10) \cdot 8 - 3$ **4.** $32 - 8 \cdot 20 - 91$

Set C   For use after page 437

Give the two steps to undo each expression.

1. $3.6t - 25$ **2.** $\frac{1}{8}r + 5.2$ **3.** $20x \div 12$ **4.** $16h + 30$

Set D   For use after page 443

Graph each inequality.

1. $x > {}^-2$ **2.** $x \le 0$ **3.** $x < 1$

4. $3 > x > {}^-1$ **5.** ${}^-1 < x < 0$ **6.** $2 < x \le 5$

Set E   For use after page 445

Solve the inequalities.

1. $c - 32 < 59$ **2.** $g + 125 \ge 140$ **3.** $x + 15 > 30$

4. $y + 12 \le {}^-8$ **5.** $h - 8 < 30$ **6.** $t - 6 < {}^-21$

Set F   For use after page 457

Find the sum of

1. the first twelve nonzero even numbers   **2.** the first twelve odd numbers

Set A   For use after page 11

Solve. Use the 6-Point Checklist.

1. The estimate for repairing Jamie's car was $896.00. The actual cost was $1,107.19. How much more was the actual cost than the estimate?

2. Lorenzo has 87¢. He spends 69¢ for a ball point pen for school. Later he earns 50¢ more. How much money does he have then?

Set B   For use after page 21

Solve. Decide if you need an exact answer or an estimate.

1. Ashley traveled 783 km during April. She traveled 627 km during May. What was the total for the two months?

2. Lamont got 27 people to sign for his walk in a charity "Walk-a-thon." Louise got 32 people to sign for her. Each person pledged $0.60 per km for the 10-km walk. Will the pledges raise more or less than $200.00?

Set C   For use after page 41

Write a question to complete each problem.

1. A souvenir shop ordered 1,350 sweatshirts and 4,800 t-shirts. They had 19 sweatshirts and 562 T-shirts left by the end of the tourist season.

2. A souvenir mug is priced at $10.95 in ceramic and $6.50 in plastic. A cup and saucer set is $27.99.

Set D   For use after page 55

Solve. Use any problem-solving strategy. Name the strategy you used.

1. Manuel is 2 years older than Anya. Anya is 1 year older than Drew. The sum of their ages is 49. How old is each?

2. Trash cans were placed every 100 ft along a 1,000 ft parade route. A can was at the start and the finish. How many cans were used?

Set E   For use after page 75

Solve. Use any problem-solving strategy.

1. Brian taped music for a school dance. Each song was 4 minutes long. He used 3 double-sided tapes with 30 minutes on each side. How many songs did he tape?

2. A total of 248 students attended last year's dance. There were 22 more girls than boys. How many girls and how many boys attended last year's dance?

MORE PRACTICE BANK

Set A   For use after page 85
Solve.

1. A zoo membership is $10.50 per adult, $8.25 per student, and $5.00 per child, under 6 years of age. How much will a family of 2 adults and 3 teenagers save by buying a $35 family membership?

2. The zoo sold 184 child and student memberships over a 24-day period. This was 4 times the number of adult memberships sold. How many memberships were sold in all?

Set B   For use after page 107
Solve.

1. Tara made a dinosaur skeleton model. Its body was 3 times as long its head. It's head was $\frac{1}{2}$ as long as its tail. If the total length of the model was 24 cm, how long was each part?

2. The Wizards asked not to be the last to give their science presentation. The Einsteins asked to be first. How many different ways could the Wizards, Einsteins, Newtons, and Mad Scientists be ordered if their requests are honored?

Set C   For use after page 117
Use the chart to solve.

1. How much more wattage is used by 2 model 521 units than by 1 model 522 unit?

2. How much wattage is consumed by 3 model 522 units?

Electric Heating Units		
Model No.	Wattage	Voltage
520	650	208
521	1,300	240
522	1,500	240

Set D   For use after page 153
Solve.

1. When Hillside marching band is arranged in rows of 2, 3, or 4, there is always 1 left over. The band can march in rows of 5 with no members left over. What is the lowest number of members the band might have?

2. The band instructor had each of 9 trumpet players play a duet with every other trumpet player one time during the year. How many duets were played?

Set E   For use after page 171
Solve.

1. A checkerboard has 8 rows of 8 squares. How many different squares are there on a checkerboard?

2. A computer lab teacher wants to set up 10 computers so that each computer is connected by a separate cable to every other computer. How many separate cables will she need?

MORE PRACTICE BANK

Set A   For use after page 172

Solve. Estimate by rounding to the nearest whole number. Then find the exact answer.

1. The school record for the standing broad jump was $20\frac{1}{2}$ ft. Bonnie made a jump of $18\frac{5}{6}$ ft. How much shorter than the school record was her jump?

2. Franklin ran in a 2-mile race. He ran the first mile in $5\frac{1}{2}$ min. He ran the second mile in $6\frac{1}{10}$ min. What was his total time for the race?

Set B   For use after page 187

Solve.

1. A $6\frac{1}{2}$ oz can of water-packed tuna provides 45 grams of protein. If a family of 4 shares equally a hot dish made from 13 oz of tuna, how much protein will each family member consume?

2. The average American consumes 5 grams of sodium a day. This is ten times the daily amount the average person needs. What is the daily requirement for the average person?

Set C   For use after page 201

Write each phrase as an algebraic expression.

1. the sum of x and 9

2. 5 less than 12

3. 3 more than n

4. a number divided by 4

5. the product of t and 8

6. a number increased by 7

Set D   For use after page 235

Solve.

1. A season's pass for 5 Act Two theatre productions is $69.95. Tickets for a single production are $15.99 each. How much would you save with a season pass?

2. Grandma's Attic costumes rent for $21.50 a day or $120 a week. If you need the costumes for 12 days, is it cheaper to rent by the day or by the week?

Set E   For use after page 247

Solve.

1. Jed mixed 2 partly used cans of paint. He poured as much red paint into the blue as was left in the blue can, then poured into the red can as much of this mixture as the red paint left in the can. This left 8 pints in each can. How much of each color did he use?

2. An interior decorator mixed 4 parts of white paint to 1 part of yellow paint to make the shade she wanted. How much of each color paint will she need to mix to paint a 500 sq ft area if 1 quart covers 100 sq ft?

MORE PRACTICE BANK

Set A   For use after page 273

Solve.

1. Applicants for law enforcement positions in one city must miss no more than 50 questions on a written exam of 200 questions to qualify. What percent of the questions must be answered correctly?

2. One question on the law enforcement exam was missed by 38 out of 51 applicants. Estimate the percentage of applicants who missed the question.

Set B   For use after page 273

Estimate a percent for each problem.

1. At Oakridge School, 25 out of 300 students joined the chess club. Estimate what percent his was.

2. At another school, 37 out of 150 students said they wanted to join the army after their schooling had ended. Estimate this percent.

Set C   For use after page 275

Solve.

1. At an awards dinner two school coaches went around to greet guests. One coach spent 2 minutes at each table she visited. The other spent 4 minutes per table. How long did it take for all 30 tables to be greeted if no table was greeted by both coaches?

2. The awards dinner was attended by 208 people in all. There were 4 more female students than male students and twice as many adults as male students. How many students and how many adults attended the dinner?

Set D   For use after page 305

Solve. If there is no solution, tell why.

1. Raisa used $1 to buy a $0.60 bag of peanuts. She received 4 coins in change. None of the coins was a dime. What coins did she receive?

2. Loren gave 5 coins to pay for a $0.78 drink. He received a nickel in change. What coins did Loren use to buy the drink?

Set E   For use after page 333

Solve.

1. Althea sold $2, $4, and $8 raffle tickets. She sold 5 tickets for a total of $24. How many tickets of each price did she sell?

2. Juan said he had 17 coins totaling $1.15. How many coins of each type did he have?

MORE PRACTICE BANK

Set A   For use after page 357   Solve.

1. Kara has a salad with avocado, melon, pineapple, and a strawberry. She won't eat pineapple right after a strawberry. In how many different orders can she eat each fruit?

2. Leif made a list to see how many different ways the letters in his name could be arranged. How many of the arrangements of the letters of his name form words?

Set B   For use after page 379   Solve.

1. The first four triangular numbers are given. Find the tenth triangular number.

    • 　ᐰ　ᐰ　ᐰ
    1　 3　 6　 10

2. How many different equilateral triangles are there in the figure below?

Set C   For use after page 415   Solve.

1. A large size cube-shaped gift box has a volume that is 8 times the volume of a medium size box in the same shape. The medium size box is 6 in. high. What is the height of the large size box?

2. A frozen yogurt cone and a cylindrical dish have the same base. The cone's height is 6 times the cylinder's height. How much greater than the volume of the cylinder is the volume of the cone?

Set D   For use after page 423   Solve. Estimate your answer first.

1. A compact disc holds 70 min of music. A record album holds 50 min of music. How many more minutes of music does the compact disc give?

2. A compact disc sale advertised 35% off the regular price of $12.99 per disc. A competing store advertised 2 discs for $18.99. Which sale offers the better price per disc?

Set E   For use after page 469   Write conclusions from chaining these statements.

1. If I read the novel, then I will be entertained. If I am entertained, then I will be happy.

2. If Tom is taller than Bill, then he is taller than 6 feet. If Bill is taller than Fred, then Bill is taller than 6 feet 3 inches.

Set F   For use after page 473   Solve.

1. A factory inspector found defects in 3 out of every 25 rafts she inspected. At this rate, how many defective rafts might she expect to find in 375 rafts?

2. A boat would cover 35 miles a day, then drift back 10 miles each night. At this rate, how many days will it take to go 150 miles?

GLOSSARY

absolute value (|a|) The distance of a number from zero on the number line. |3| = 3; |−3| = 3

acute angle An angle that has a measure less than 90°.

acute triangle A triangle in which each angle has a measure less than 90°.

addend A number that is added.

algebraic expression An expression that contains at least one variable; for example, $x + 7$.

angle Two rays with a single endpoint, called the vertex of the angle.

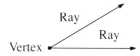

arc A part of a circle.

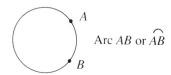

Arc AB or $\overset{\frown}{AB}$

area The measure of a plane region in terms of square units.

associative property The sum (or product) of three or more numbers is the same regardless of grouping:
$(a + b) + c = a + (b + c)$ or
$(a \cdot b) \cdot c = a \cdot (b \cdot c)$

average See *mean*.

base (in exponential notation) In the expression a^n, a is the base.

base (in numeration) The type of grouping involved in a system of numeration. In base eight, 346 means 3 sixty-fours, 4 eights, and 6 units.

base (of a polygon) Any side of a polygon may be referred to as a base.

Base (of a space figure) See examples below.

Bases of a cylinder   Base of a cone   Base of a pyramid

BASIC A simple programming language.

basic counting principle If one thing can be done in m ways, and a second thing can be done in n ways, then the two things can be done in $m \cdot n$ ways.

bias Systematic error in gathering data.

binary A base-two system of numeration.

bisect To divide into two congruent parts.

box and whiskers graph A graph which shows how a collection of data are grouped or spread.

capacity The volume of a space figure given in terms of liquid measure.

cardinal number A number used for counting; for example, 6 people.

central angle An angle that has its vertex at the center of a circle.

chord A segment with both endpoints on a circle.

circle A set of points which are all the same distance from a given point called the center of the circle.

circumference The distance around a circle.

commutative property The sum (or product) of any two numbers is the same regardless of the order in which they are added (or multiplied):
$a + b = b + a$ or $a \cdot b = b \cdot a$

complementary angles Two angles whose measures have a sum of 90°.

composite number A number greater than 0 with more than two different factors.

cone A space figure, a circular base and one vertex.

551

congruent Geometric figures are congruent if they have the same size and shape.

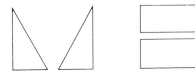

coordinate axes Two intersecting perpendicular number lines used for graphing ordered number pairs.

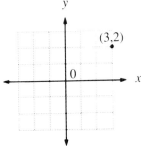

coordinates An ordered number pair matched with a point in the coordinate plane.

cross products In the equation $\frac{a}{b}$ $\frac{c}{d}$, the products ad and bc are called cross products. Two ratios $\frac{a}{b} = \frac{c}{d}$ are equal if and only if $ad = bc$.

cross section The intersection of a space figure and a plane.

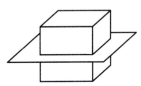

cube (numeration) A number raised to the third power. 8 is the cube of 2 because $2^3 = 8$. Also, to raise a number to the third power.

cube (space figure) A 6-sided prism whose faces are all congruent squares.

customary units Units of the system of measurement often used in the United States: pounds, ounces, tons, cups, pints, quarts, gallons, inches, feet, yards, miles. See *Table of Measures*.

cylinder A space figure with two congruent circular bases in parallel planes.

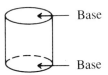

data A collection of facts that have not yet been processed into information.

decagon A polygon that has ten sides.

decimal system The place-value numeration system that uses the digits 0 through 9, and groups by tens.

degree (°) A unit of measure for angles, $\frac{1}{90}$ of a right angle.

degree Celsius (°C) Unit for measuring temperature. On the Celsius scale, water freezes at 0°C and boils at 100°C.

degree Fahrenheit (°F) Unit for measuring temperature. On the Fahrenheit scale, water freezes at 32°F and boils at 212°F.

denominator For each fraction $\frac{a}{b}$, b is the denominator.

diagonal A segment connecting two non-consecutive vertices of a polygon.

diameter A segment that passes through the center of a circle and has endpoints on the circle.

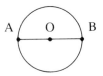

difference The number resulting from subtraction.

digits The basic symbols used in a place-value system of numeration. In base ten, the symbols are *0, 1, 2, 3, 4, 5, 6, 7, 8*, and *9*.

distributive property Connects addition and multiplication when both operations are involved. $a(b + c) = a \cdot b + a \cdot c$

dividend The number to be divided in a division problem.

$$\begin{array}{r} 3 \leftarrow \text{Quotient} \\ \text{Divisor} \rightarrow 5\overline{)17} \leftarrow \text{Dividend} \\ \underline{15} \\ 2 \leftarrow \text{Remainder} \end{array}$$

divisible A given number is divisible by a second number if the remainder is zero.

divisor See *dividend*.

dodecahedron A space figure with twelve faces.

Regular dodecahedron

edge One of the segments making up any of the faces of a space figure.

equally likely outcomes Outcomes that have the same chance of occurring.

equal ratios Ratios that give the same comparison. $\frac{9}{27}$ and $\frac{1}{3}$ are equal ratios.

equation A mathematical sentence using the equality symbol ($=$). $x - 27 = 102$ is an equation.

equilateral triangle A triangle with all three sides the same length.

equivalent fractions Fractions that represent the same number, such as $\frac{1}{3}$, $\frac{2}{6}$, and $\frac{3}{9}$.

estimate An approximation for a given number. Often used in the sense of a rough calculation.

expanded numeral A representation of a number as a sum of multiples of 10 such as:

$4,325 = 4,000 + 300 + 20 + 5$ or
$4 \times 10^3 + 3 \times 10^2 + 2 \times 10 + 5$

exponent A number that tells how many times another number is to be used as a factor.

$$5 \cdot 5 \cdot 5 = 5^3 \begin{array}{l} \leftarrow \text{Exponent} \\ \leftarrow \text{Base} \end{array}$$

exponential notation A system of representing numbers using an exponent.

face A polygonal region that is part of the surface of a space figure.

factor A number that is multiplied by another to yield a product.

factor tree A diagram suggestive of a tree showing the prime factorization of a number.

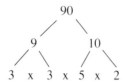

flowchart A diagram that gives ⌐ons in a logical order.

formula A general fac⸋ ⸜pressed by using symbols. For exa⸗ ⸍ A of any parallelogram ⸍ . height h is given by the formula

fraction A number in the form $\frac{a}{b}$ when $b \neq 0$.

frequency The number of times a given item occurs in a set of data.

function A rule that relates or matches each element of one set to exactly one element of another set.

greatest common factor (GCF) The greatest number that is a factor of each of two or more numbers.

greatest possible error (GPE) Half the measurement unit used. GPE indicates the degree of precision at a measurement.

heptagon A seven-sided polygon.

hexagon A six-sided polygon.

histogram A bar graph showing frequencies.

improper fraction A fraction numerator is greater than or equal to its denominator.

inductive reasoning A conclusion based on observing patterns; generalizing from examples.

inequality A mathematical sentence that compares or orders; for example, $x < 3$.

integer Any whole number or its opposite.

inverse operation Operations that undo each other. Adding 5 is the inverse of subtracting 5.

isosceles triangle A triangle with at least two congruent sides.

least common denominator (LCD) The least common multiple of the denominators of two or more fractions. The LCD of $\frac{5}{6}$ and $\frac{3}{4}$ is 12.

least common multiple (LCM) The smallest non-zero number that is a multiple of each of two or more whole numbers. The LCM of 4 and 6 is 12.

line of symmetry A line on which a figure can be folded so that the two parts fit exactly.

logo A programming language used to create simple graphics.

lowest-terms fraction A fraction for which the (GCF) of the numerator and denominator is 1.

mean An average; the sum of a set of numbers divided by the number of members of the set.

median The middle number of a set of numbers that are arranged in order. If there is no single middle number, it is the mean of the two middle numbers.

metric system A measurement system in which the meter is the basic unit of measure. See *Table of Measures*.

microsecond One millionth of a second.

midpoint A point that divides a segment into two-congruent segments.

mixed number A number such as $4\frac{2}{3}$ that has a whole number part and a fractional part.

mode In a list of data the mode is the number or item that occurs most often. There may be more than one mode.

multiple A number that is the product of a given number and a whole number.

$3 \cdot 8 = 24$ 24 is a multiple of 3.

negative integer A number less than zero and the opposite of a whole number.

$\{-1, -2, -3, \ldots\}$

nonagon A nine-sided polygon.

numeral A symbol for a number.

numerator For each fraction $\frac{a}{b}$, a is the numerator.

obtuse angle An angle with a measure greater than 90° and less than 180°.

obtuse triangle A triangle with one angle measuring more than 90°.

octagon An eight-sided polygon.

one property See *property of one*.

opposites property The sum of any number and its opposite is zero. $n + {}^-n = 0$

ordered pair A number pair arranged in order so there is a first number and a second number; the coordinates of a point in a plane such as (2, 7).

ordinal A number used to designate place or rank; for example, the *first* place winner.

outcome A possible result in a probability experiment.

parallel lines Lines in the same plane that do not intersect.

parallelogram A quadrilateral whose opposite sides are parallel.

pentagon A five-sided polygon.

percent (%) Literally, "per hundred." A way to compare a number with 100.

perimeter The sum of the length of the sides of a polygon.

period Each group of three digits starting with the ones digit is a period.

permutation A selection of a number of objects from a set, and in a particular order.

perpendicular lines Two intersecting lines that form right angles.

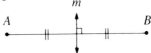

perpendicular bisector A line that bisects a segment and is perpendicular to it.

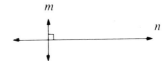

$m \perp bis \overline{AB}$

pi (π) The ratio of the circumference of a circle to its diameter. The decimal for π is unending and does not repeat.
$\pi = 3.141592 \ldots$

pint (pt) A customary unit of liquid measure equal to 2 cups.

place value The value given to the place a digit may occupy in a numeral. In the decimal system, each place of a numeral has ten times the value of the place to its right.

polygon A closed plane figure formed by segments.

polyhedron A closed space figure whose faces are polygonal regions.

positive integer An integer greater than zero $\{1, 2, 3, \ldots\}$.

pound (lb) A customary unit of weight measurement.

power A product in which each factor is the same; for example, 8 is the third power of 2.
$2 \times 2 \times 2 = 2^3 = 8$.

precision One measurement is more precise than another if it has a smaller GPE.

prime factorization The expression of a composite number as the product of prime factors.
$36 = 2^2 \cdot 3^2$

prime number A whole number, greater than 1, that has exactly two factors, itself and 1.

principal Money loaned, usually at a given interest rate and for a specified time.

prism A space figure whose bases are congruent parallel polygons and whose faces are parallelograms.

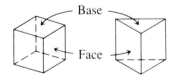

Base

Face

probability (of an event) The ratio of the number of certain outcome can occur to the number of total possible outcomes.

product The number that results when two numbers are multiplied.

property of one Any number multiplied by 1 will equal the number:
$a \times 1 = a$

property of zero For every number a, $a + 0 = a$.

proportion An equation stating that two ratios are equal:
$\frac{3}{18} = \frac{1}{6}$

protractor An instrument for measuring the number of degrees (°) in an angle.

pyramid A space figure with a polygonal base and triangular faces with a common vertex.

Pythagorean theorem In a right triangle, $a^2 + b^2 = c^2$.

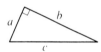

quadrilateral A four-sided polygon.

quotient See *dividend*.

radius A segment or length of a segment from the center of a circle to a point on the circle. Half the diameter.

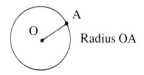

Radius OA

range The difference between the greatest number and the least number in a set of data.

rate A ratio that compares different kinds of units; for example, miles per hour.

ratio A comparison of two numbers expressed as a fraction, for example $\frac{3}{4}$.

ray A part of a line that has one endpoint and extends endlessly in one direction.

A B Ray AB or AB

reciprocals Two numbers are reciprocals if their product is 1. 7 and $\frac{1}{7}$ are reciprocals.

rectangle A parallelogram with four right angles.

region All the points in the part of a plane bounded by a simple closed curve.

regular polygon A polygon with all sides the same length and all angles the same measure.

relatively prime Two numbers with a GCF of 1 are relatively prime. 8 and 27 are relatively prime.

repeating decimal A decimal whose digits from some point on, repeat endlessly. 6.2835835 . . . and 0.3333333 . . . are repeating decimals. They may also be written as 6.2$\overline{835}$ and 0.$\overline{3}$ respectively.

rhombus A parallelogram whose sides all have the same length.

right angle An angle that measures 90°.

right triangle A triangle with a right angle.

sample space The set of all possible outcomes of an experiment. The sample space of a coin toss has two outcomes: *heads, tails.*

scale drawing A drawing made so that distances in the drawing are proportional to actual distances.

scalene triangle A triangle with all three sides having different measures.

scientific notation A system of writing numbers as the product of a power of 10 and a number greater than or equal to 1, but less than 10. 2,300,000 = 2.3 × 10^6

segment Two points and all points between them.

A ——————— B Segment AB or $\overrightarrow{AB}$

simulation (probability) A representation of a probability experiment.

similar figures Two or more figures with the same shape but not necessarily the same size.

space figure A (three-dimensional) geometric figure whose points do not all lie in the same plane.

sphere The set of all points in space at a fixed distance from a given point.

square (geometry) A quadrilateral with four right angles and all sides the same length.

square (numeration) A number raised to the second power. 9 is the square of 3. Also, to raise a number to the second power. 3^2 = 9.

square root The square root $\sqrt{x}$ of a number x is a number y such that $y \cdot y = x$.

statistics Facts or data of a numerical kind.

stem and leaf plot a system for organizing and presenting data so that frequencies can easily be compared.

Stem	Leaf
1	0, 1, 3
2	2, 1, 5, 7
3	1, 2, 4, 3, 6
4	2, 1

straight angle An angle that has a measure of 180°.

sum The result of the addition operation.

supplementary angles Two angles whose measures have a sum of 180°

surface area The sum of the areas of all the faces of a space figure.

terminating decimal A decimal that represents the quotient of a whole number and a power of 10.

$0.5 = \frac{5}{10}$ $1.28 = \frac{128}{10^2}$ $0.0307 = \frac{307}{10^2}$

tesselation An infinite set of congruent figures that can be fitted together to fill a plane completely.

tetrahedron A polyhedron with four triangular faces.

trapezoid A quadrilateral with one pair of parallel sides.

Parallel sides

transversal A line that intersects two given lines.

triangle A three-sided polygon.

unit An amount of a quantity used as a standard of measurement.

unit price Cost per unit.

variable A symbol, usually a letter, used to represent a number in an expression or an equation.

vertex (vertices) A point that two rays of an angle have in common. Also, the common point of any two sides of a polygon or the common point of intersection of three or more faces of a polyhedron.

Vertex

volume The measure of a space figure in terms of a unit cube.

Venn diagram A special diagram using overlapping circles showing how data are related.

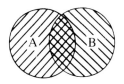

whole number Any number in the set {0, 1, 2, 3, . . .}.

zero property See *property of zero*.

1 Operations, Properties, and Problem Solving

Page 5
1. two thousand three hundred fifty-one
6. $(2 \times 1,000) + (1 \times 100) + (5 \times 10) + (9 \times 1)$
10. 11,011   **19.** 702 R1   **23.** 555

Page 7
1. 7 + ? = 16   **4.** 5, 5   **7.** 69

Page 9
2. 20   **7.** 0   **16.** 27   **21.** $20

Page 11
1. A   **4** A   **7.** $14.00

Page 15
2. distributive   **5.** commutative   **8.** 2   **11.** 19
14. $9.00

Page 17
2. 526   **7.** 280   **13.** 235   **16.** 7,700
18. $36 less   **22.** 107   **32.** 8

Page 19
1. 3,000   **6.** 100   **9.** 6   **16.** 16,000
19. 300   **21.** 660   **24.** 10   **27.** 9,000
31. 20,000 lb

Page 21
6. 827   **9.** 273,988   **15.** 31   **20.** 199.9

Page 23
2. 47   **9.** 10   **12.** 4
15. $(4 \times 8) - 2 = 30$
17. $(10 \times 5) + 10 = 60$ **22.** $13

2 Decimals and Measurement

Page 33
1. $\frac{7}{1,000}$ **4.** 30   **8.** 0 or $\frac{0}{1,000}$ **11.** 0.0121
14. >   **17.** <   **20.** 0.043, 0.24, 0.34
25. $355.00

Page 35
1. 4.66   **4.** 52.69   **7.** 38.54   **10.** 3.5880
13. 282.1   **15.** 0.72   **18.** 2.16
23. 319.2 km

Page 37
2. 60   **6.** 160   **9.** 25   **12.** 160
15. 180 km

Page 39
1. 10   **4.** 1,000   **9.** 5.3   **12.** 17.9
14. 0.6   **17.** 4   **21.** 3   **27.** $1.22

Page 41
2. $1.80   **6.** 7,000,000 ft^3 **7.** 1,000,000 acres

Page 43
2. 87^3 **6.** 100 × 100, 10,000   **9.** 4
12. 4.87   **15.** 19,000   **18.** 1,57893 × 10^8
21. 2.35 × 10^{10} **26.** 1.5 × 10^8 km

Page 45
1. 12, 22   **4.** 4, 5, 10   **8.** 15, 75
10. $7.50, $10.50, $13.50, $16.50, $19.50
13. 560

Page 49
1. 0.62   **3.** 0.000017   **8.** 0.176
11. 3,509,000   **14.** 3,590   **17.** A
20. C   **27.** 20 laps   **30.** 793
35. 648

Page 51
14. addition   **17.** 10   **20.** 19

Page 53
3. 0.108   **6.** 0.016   **8.** 6,700   **11.** 4 kL
17. C   **20.** C

Page 55
2. 9 cuts   **5.** 1,125 L   **8.** $11.55

3 Data Analysis and Statistics

Page 67
1. 18%   **4.** More than a third   **10.** Africa
(65), Neotropics (46), Asia (19), Madagascar (19)

Page 69
8. >   **11.** >   **12.** 13.88   **15.** 50.2

Page 71
1. 147   **4.** 255   **8.** $49.90   **13.** 168
17. 1,050   **20.** 208   **22.** 115   **25.** 98

28. $17.94   **33.** 36 picked ''more clothes'';
18 picked ''more records''   **35.** 398   **38.** 978

Page 75
1. $44.45   **4.** 42 7th grade boys   **5.** 12 outfits
8. 23 balloons

Page 77
3. 66.9; 65.25; 64.5

Page 79
1. $4, $5   **3.** $6.25, $3.25   **7.** 11.40, 11.50,
11.50   **8.** $2.50

Page 81
5. 499.5 and 599.5   **7.** 18   **10.** 1.068
12. ≈180

Page 83
1. 16, 20, 60; number of students times 4 equals the
cost   **4.** 49, 249; take half the number of people
then subtract one to find the number of prizes
8. $35.00

Page 85
1. 1,400 large animals   **4.** Thurs. ≈ 160,
Fri ≈ 190, Sat ≈ 330, Sun ≈ 250   **5.** 117 lb

4 Geometry

Page 95
1. prism: 6 vertices, 5 faces, 9 edges   **4.** pyramid:
7 vertices, 7 faces, 12 edges   **5.** prism: 10 vertices,
7 faces, 15 edges   **8.** neither: 10 vertices, 7 faces,
15 edges   **16.** 7 total faces, 4 hidden faces

Page 97
1. y **4.** x **6.** z **15.** associative   **17.** 80
19. 69.8   **22.** 0.2

Page 99
1. 25°; acute   **4.** 135°; obtuse   **7.** 45°; acute
8. 25°; acute   **12.** 50°   **15.** 4°   **17.** 73°
18. 45°   **26.** 55°   **29.** 110°   **31.** 130°

Page 103
8. 69°   **12.** Plan b

Page 107
1. Einsteins, Wizards, Newtons, Mad Scientists,
Superstars   **4.** 4 adult tickets   **7.** 44°, 88°, 48°

Page 109
1. ∠1, ∠2, ∠5, ∠6   **4.** ∠3, ∠8,
11, ∠13   **8.** m∠3 = 145°   **11.** 38°
13. m∠2 = 180 − x

Page 111
9. 13.56 m

Page 115
8. 24 triangles   **11.** 160   **14.** s^3
16. 1.89477×10^5

Page 117
1. 1,662 mi   **4.** 5 people ordered shrimp, 3
people ordered enchiladas   **7.** 6 trips

5 Number Theory and Fractions

Page 127
2. no   **5.** no   **8.** no   **11.** yes   **14.** no
17. 3, 9   **20.** 3, 4, 6, 9   **23.** 3, 9
28. Disagree; 114 is divisible by 6 since it is
divisible by both 2 and 3 (114 is even and the sum
of its digits is divisible by 3)

Page 129
1. prime   **3.** composite   **6.** no   **12.** yes
15. 1, 2, 3, 6, 9, 18, 27, 54   **20.** Subtraction

Page 131
7. $2^3 \cdot 11^2$ **11.** 5^3 **16.** 7   **20.** 3
21. 100 cubes

Page 133
1. 1, 3; GCF = 3   **4.** 1, 2, 4, 8; GCF = 8
7. GCF = $3 \cdot 5$ = 15   **10.** 9   **13.** 11
16. 63   **19.** 16   **22.** 16   **27.** 2, 3, or 6
students per team   **31.** 1.2196×10 **34.** 161.2

Page 135
1. 30: 30, 60, 90, 120, . . .
12. 12, 24, 36, 48, 60, . . . LCM = 60
4. 10: 10, 20, 30, 40, . . . 6: 6, 12, 18, 24, 30,
. . . LCM = 30   **9.** 70   **13.** 45   **18.** 75
23. 374   **26.** 42   **30.** 3.98 in.

Page 139
2. 21   **5.** 21   **8.** 4   **11.** 66   **14.** $\frac{8}{20}, \frac{10}{25},$
$\frac{12}{30}$ **17.** yes   **19.** $\frac{16}{25}$

Page 141

2. 5   **5.** $\frac{2}{3}$ **8.** $\frac{12}{25}$ **11.** $\frac{5}{6}$ **16.** $\frac{6}{7}$

19. 91 copies   **22.** $\approx \frac{30}{70} = \frac{3}{7}$

Page 143

1. $1\frac{1}{8}$ **6.** $3\frac{2}{5}$ **10.** $\frac{54}{7}$ **15.** $\frac{187}{20}$ **19.** $3\frac{2}{3}$

Page 145

1. yes   **6.** yes   **9.** no

Page 147

1. $\frac{7}{50}$ **8.** $7\frac{9}{10}$ **10.** 1.6   **15.** 6.007

18. 0.25   **21.** 60°   **24.** 543

27. 12.81

Page 149

1. $0.\overline{43}$ **6.** $0.4\overline{6}$ **12.** $0.\overline{3}$

17. $\frac{95}{99} = 0.\overline{95}$

Page 151

2. <   **8.** <   **11.** >   **16.** <

19. $\frac{2}{7}, \frac{1}{3}, \frac{3}{5}, \frac{9}{11}$ **22.** >   **28.** Flores

Page 153

1. 418 students   **7.** 5 students

6 Fraction Operations

Page 163

1. $\frac{4}{6} = \frac{2}{3}$ **6.** $\frac{1}{8}$ **11.** $\frac{11}{35}$ **14.** $\frac{17}{20}$

17. $\frac{8}{2} + \frac{6}{4} = 5\frac{1}{2}$ **20.** $\frac{21}{50}$

Page 165

2. 11   **7.** 5   **14.** 15   **18.** $3\frac{1}{2}$mi

22. $3 \cdot 5 \cdot 7$ **26.** $3\frac{7}{50}$ **31.** 19

Page 167

1. $6\frac{1}{3}$ **8.** $22\frac{7}{15}$ **15.** $11\frac{11}{24}$ **20.** 57

23. $53\frac{3}{4}$ in.   **26.** $9\frac{4}{5}$ **29.** $9\frac{2}{3}$

Page 169

1. $2\frac{3}{5}$ **6.** $\frac{5}{8}$ **11.** 10   **14.** 33   **18.** $1\frac{3}{4}$ cup

21. $76\frac{2}{3}$ **24.** $10\frac{1}{8}$

Page 171

2. 6 days   **8.** $2^9 = 512$ pieces

Page 175

1. yes   **5.** no   **8.** yes

Page 177

1. 4   **6.** 17   **10.** $m = 7$ **13.** $b = 5$

16. 35   **20.** 12   **25.** 140

Page 179

2. $\frac{1}{12}$ **7.** 1   **12.** $\frac{1}{9}$ **17.** $\frac{3}{8}$ **18.** $\frac{1}{8}$

Page 181

3. $13\frac{3}{4}$ **6.** 33   **11.** 33   **15.** 72   **18.** 60

24. 90°   **28.** 0.35   **33.** 9

Page 183

2. $1\frac{1}{2}$ **5.** $\frac{1}{14}$ **8.** $1\frac{1}{9}$ **11.** $1\frac{3}{4}$ **16.** $1\frac{1}{4}$ min

Page 185

2. $3\frac{1}{4}$ **7.** $\frac{8}{17}$ **10.** $20\frac{2}{3}$ **13.** 3   **16.** 4.

19. 4   **22.** $2\frac{1}{24}$ **24.** $8\frac{8}{9}$ or about 9 days

Page 187

2. 3 times   **6.** 34 granola bars

7 Introduction to Algebra

Page 197

2. $n - 5$ **5.** A number increased by 14

10. A number 0.14 less than y **13.** $98.7 + d$

18. $c - 25$ **21.** True

Page 199

4. $\frac{w}{3}$ **7.** $100d$ or $100 \cdot d$ **10.** $\frac{i}{12}$ **14.** $3k$

17. $1\frac{11}{20}$

Page 201
1. About 300 7th-graders   **6.** 300 yr

Page 203
2. $x = 2$ red chips   **5.** $x = 3$ red chips   **11.** $6h$

Page 207
1. $x = 5$ **6.** $p = 975$ **10.** $l = 159$
15. $e = 200$ **18.** $z = 600$ **23.** $q = 3.8$
26. a; $s = 24g$

Page 209
1. $2\frac{2}{3}$ ft   **4.** \$14   **7.** 17.5 km

Page 211
2. $s - 6.9$; add 6.9   **6.** $f + 6$; subtract 6
9. $j + 2\frac{3}{4}$; subtract $2\frac{3}{4}$ **15.** $b + 24$; subtract 24
19. 642 digits   **22.** $79\frac{1}{2}$ **27.** 8   **28.** 90°

Page 213
2. $y = 37.7$ **5.** $z = 127$ **10.** $t = 313$
14. $j = 6\frac{5}{6}$ **19.** $v = 691$ **22.** $n = 85\frac{3}{5}$
25. 64,884 ft   **29.** $t = 150$

Page 215
1. multiply by 43   **6.** divide by 7
10. multiply by 4.37   **15.** $2z$; divide by 2
19. $29w$; divide by 29   **25.** subtract 14.9
30. $\frac{3}{8} \cdot \frac{8}{3} k = k$ **32.** $19.3w$; 1,204.32 lb.

Page 217
1. $f = 21$ **4.** $t = 7708$ **9.** $b = 43.6$
12. $q = 165.6$ **15.** $s = 13$ **20.** $m = 43$
26. 300.15   **28.** 8.549 lb

8 Ratio and Proportion

Page 227
1. $\frac{3}{4}$ **7.** $\frac{2}{11}$ **12.** $\frac{15}{8}$ **20.** $\frac{10}{33}$

Page 229
2. $=$ **7.** $\neq$ **10.** $=$ **16.** $\neq$
18. $\frac{40}{50} = \frac{2.0}{2.5}$ **19.** yes

Page 231
2. $x = 32$ **5.** $x = 6$ **10.** $x = 20$
16. 400 black; 200 red   **19.** $x = 4$
22. $x = 20$

Page 233
1. \$4 per ticket   **4.** \$22,100 per year
9. 2 degrees per hour   **18.** 60 mi   **21.** $n + 8$
26. $y = 6$

Page 235
1. 15¢   **6.** 32 combinations   **9.** \$5.50

Page 241
2. 3.1, 4.1, $b + 0.1$ **7.** \$163

Page 243
1. $x = 75$ **6.** 6 ft

Page 245
6. $C = 66$ in.   **11.** $C = 28\frac{2}{7}$ in.
14. $d = 1.2$ cm   **17.** about 3.65 m   **21.** $\frac{1}{30}$
24. $17\frac{11}{25}$ **27.** 16^4

Page 247
1. 54 cars   **4.** $\frac{3}{4}$ h   **7.** \$23

9 Percents

Page 257
2. $\frac{6}{100}$, 0.06, 6%   **5.** $\frac{98}{100}$, 0.98, 98%
15. 18%   **18.** 3%

Page 259
1. $\frac{3}{4}$ **8.** $\frac{29.}{100}$ **11.** 80%   **14.** 25%
19. 38%   **24.** $\frac{1}{25}$ **27.** $\frac{1}{4}$ **30.** 10%

Page 261
2. 0.02   **5.** 0.09   **8.** 0.17   **11.** 40%
16. 3%   **19.** 5.2%   **24.** 76%; 0.76
27. $2\frac{3}{5}$ **33.** 3.2

SELECTED ANSWERS

Page 263

2. 35%   **5.** $\frac{11}{20}$ **10.** $\frac{1}{3}$ **14.** 0.355, 41%,

0.624, $\frac{5}{8}$, 66.6   **17.** Yes. 0.38 rounds to 0.4;

$\frac{2}{5}$ = 0.4

Page 265

1. $f(5) = 11$ **4.** $f(0) = 42$ **8.** 6, 10, 22,
106, 406   **11.** $f(3) = 135$; cost = $135

Page 267

1. 175%   **4.** 0.8%   **7.** 0.4%   **12.** 142.9%

15. $\frac{1}{250}$, 0.004   **18.** $1\frac{1}{4}$, 1.25   **23.** $\frac{7}{800}$, 0.00875

28. 10 cars

Page 271

1. 0.056   **6.** 0.7604   **11.** $49\frac{3}{4}$%

14. $125\frac{1}{2}$%   **20.** 9%, 9.05%, 9.25%, $9\frac{1}{3}$%, $9\frac{2}{5}$%

23. $14\frac{1}{7}$ cm   **26.** 0.875

Page 273

1. 91%   **6.** $\frac{3}{37}$; 8%

Page 275

2. $16.76   **7.** $160

10 Applications of Percent

Page 285

1. 20.16   **7.** 60   **12.** 58.5   **16.** 13
19. 148.5   **22.** 2.5   **27.** 2.6   **36.** $25,000

Page 287

4. 210   **7.** 8   **12.** 60   **17.** 9   **21.** 9
26. 0.4   **29.** 0.02   **34.** 35

Page 289

1. $313.50   **6.** $8,640   **9.** $744
14. $4,000 at 10% interest for 1 year
16. $182   **19.** P = $1,250

Page 291

1. 20%   **6.** 12.5%   **9.** 22.5%   **14.** 70%
17. <   **19.** 29%; less

Page 293

1. 24% increase   **6.** 50% decrease   **10.** 10%
decrease   **13.** 12.5% decrease   **18.** 16%
decrease   **23.** 200% increase; $66\frac{2}{3}$% decrease

26. 430%

Page 297

1. 90   **6.** 25   **9.** 555   **12.** 320   **14.** 800
17. $30.00   **21.** 1996

Page 299

2. $162.65, $650.60   **5.** $2.46, $13.94
9. $24.45   **14.** 57%   **17.** $18.00

Page 301

2. 126°, 90°, 115°, 18°, 11°   **4.** Whole milk,
120°; lowfat milk, 144°; nonfat milk, 96°

Page 303

1. 35 × 200 = n, n = 70   **6.** $\frac{53}{80}$ = n,

n = 66.25%   **9.** $0.90   **11.** n = $33\frac{1}{3}$ **17.** 10%

Page 305
2. 38%   **6.** 330 lb

11 Integers

Page 315
1. $^-7$, $^+7$ **6.** $^-1$, $^+5$ **9.** >   **14.** =
16. positive integer

Page 317
2. n = 16   **5.** n = 0   **7.** $^+13 \cdot {}^-27$
10. $^-27({}^+5 \cdot {}^-2)$ **13.** $({}^-2 \cdot {}^+5) + ({}^-2 \cdot {}^-5)$
16. n = $^-5$ **19.** $50   **22.** 25%   **25.** 12.5
30. ≈ 50

Page 319
2. $^-2 + {}^+4 = {}^+2$ **5.** $^-8$ **10.** $^+8$
13. $^-6$ **18.** $^-16$ **25.** sometimes
28. 9° below 0

Page 321
1. 7   **4.** $^-11$ **8.** $^-9$ **11.** $^-100$
19. $^-20$ **22.** $^-32$, 0   **25.** 2°C

Page 325
1. $^-12$ **5.** 30   **8.** 39   **11.** 1   **15.** $^-105$
18. 30   **21.** 156   **27.** $2.00   **30.** $9.75;

$109.75   **33.** $14\frac{3}{4}$

Page 327
2. 4, ⁻6   **5.** Incorrect   **8.** Correct   **13.** 3
17. ⁻12   **20.** ⁻17   **25.** ⁻10   **31.** 4, ⁻4
34. ⁺72   **37.** 18   **40.** 1   **43.** 3

Page 329
2. (⁻1, 0), (1, 2), (⁻1, 4), (⁻3, 2)

Page 333
2. 46 laps   **7.** 2 quarters, 1 nickel, 1 dime or 3 nickels, 1 50-cent piece

12 Probability

Page 343
1. At H   **6.** Near the middle   **11.** In the right half

Page 345
1. AH, 2D, 3S, 4H   **5.** AH   **8.** 2, 4, 6, 8
13. (AH, 1) (2D, 2) (3S, 3) (4H, 4)

Page 347
2. $\frac{2}{6}$ or $\frac{1}{3}$ **5.** $\frac{0}{6}$ **8.** $\frac{3}{8}$ **11.** $\frac{4}{8}$ or $\frac{1}{2}$

15. (4, 6); (5, 5); (6, 4); $\frac{3}{36}$ or $\frac{1}{12}$ **18.** 70

23. ⁻50

Page 349
2. $\frac{15}{75}$ or $\frac{1}{5}$

6. Exp P(car) $= \frac{26}{53}$; Exp P(not a car) $= \frac{12 + 15}{53} = \frac{27}{53}$

Page 353
1. $A > 14$ **4.** $P \leq \frac{1}{3}$ **8.** $y \geq 79$

11. $k \leq 781$ **19.** always   **23.** sometimes

Page 355
1. $\frac{1}{9}$ **4.** $\frac{2}{3}$ **9.** $P(AA) = \frac{9}{16}$

Page 357
2. $\frac{7}{10}$ **5.** 6.5 h

Page 359
2. 100   **5.** $3\frac{5}{6}$ **7.** 0   **10.** wrong; EV $= 3.5$
12. ⁻34   **15.** 8   **18.** 8

13 Area and Volume

Page 369
16. $1\frac{1}{2}$ units²   **18.** A; 6 units²

Page 371
1. 96 cm²   **5.** 18.2 cm²   **8.** 4.48 km²
11. 6.2 m²   **14.** 87.36 m²   **17.** 1,176 ft²
21. $450   **24.** 1 ft²

Page 373
2. 14 cm²   **5.** 103.5 m²   **9.** 60 cm²
14. 30 cm²   **17.** ⁻39   **20.** ⁻46   **25.** $\frac{4}{11}$

Page 375
1. 113.04 cm²   **5.** 7,850 m²
8. 50.24 cm²   **11.** 7.065 m²
16. 490.6 cm²   **20.** 276.9 in²

Page 377
2. 170.13 m²   **5.** 80 m²   **8.** $3,122.55

Page 379
4. 225 people   **7.** 132 in.

Page 383
11. 25 cm

Page 385
1. 250 mm²   **5.** 70.875 km²   **8.** 27 cm²
10. 732 cm²

Page 387
2. 7 units³   **5.** 10 units³   **8.** 8 units³

Page 389
1. 300 cm³   **4.** 2,700 mm³   **7.** 248.5 cm³
11. $90

Page 391
2. 1,538.6 dm³   **5.** 141.3 m³   **10.** 1,004.8 cm³
12. $H > 6$

Page 393
1. 90 cm³   **4.** 332.34 cm³   **6.** 24,000 m³
11. 0.45 cm³   **14.** 471.84 cm³

Page 395
1. 62 ft   **5.** $81.32

14 Motion Geometry

Page 405
1. Yes   **6.** No   **15.** ($^-$3, 2), ($^-$3, $^-$2), (3, $^-$2)

Page 407
11. 360   **14.** 5.6   **18.** 1,001

Page 409
1. Yes   **4.** No   **6.** $\frac{1}{6}$ **15.** 20.5 cm^2

Page 411
11. H, I, M, N, O, S, W, X, Z

Page 415
1. Volume is divided by 4.   **4.** 9 packages
7. Volume is multiplied by 8.

Page 417
2. b   **11.** 4° right, 2° up

Page 419
2. Yes   **5.** congruent, reflection
10. congruent, slide, turn, reflection
16. 25%

Page 423
1. $10,315 million   **4.** 86,925,000 households
7. 21 ways

15 Extending Algebra

Page 433
2. 20   **5.** 3   **8.** 1,742.4   **11.** 17
24. $2.34   **25.** 1384

Page 435
1. $1.95   **4.** About 900 households
8. maximum: 242 ft; minimum: 44 ft

Page 437
9. 25 + 20m **12.** 4 + 0.10c **15.** 8h + 0.96   **17.** 8
20. 24   **23.** 8.4   **25.** 1,996   **28.** 1,624   **30.** 1,005

Page 439
1. $x = 6$ **4.** $z = 15$ **8.** $v = {}^-7$

11. $x = 22$ **14.** $u = 54$ **17.** $n = 174$
21. $y \approx 24.33$ yr

Page 443
1. $s > 1,000$ **4.** $t < {}^-20$ **7.** $d \le {}^-20$
9. $t > {}^-30$ **31.** $\frac{9}{50}$ **34.** $3\frac{1}{2}$ **37.** 36

Page 445
1. $t < 52$ **4.** $g \ge 20$ **7.** $p \le {}^-22$ **10.** $k < 63$
13. $t \le {}^-19$ **16.** $y \ge 2$ **20.** $30 \ge n$ **23.** $137.39

Page 447
1. $3x + 6$ **4.** $2x + 2$ **7.** $10x + 4$
10. $7x + 6$ **14.** $(x + 2)(x + 3)$

16 Extending Logical Reasoning

Page Page 457
1. 465   **4.** 672,400   **6.** $48,400

Page 459
1. 204 vertices   **6.** $\frac{1}{16}$
9. 105   **12.** 50

Page 461
1. $\frac{4}{7}$ **4.** $\frac{2}{3}$ **7.** 7, 11   **10.** 5, 19 or 7, 17   **14.** $\frac{6}{5}$
17. odd number

Page 463
1. Let n be your number.
    Step 1: $n + 5$
    Step 2: $3(n + 5)$ or $3n + 15$
    Step 3: $3n + 15 + 12$ or $3n + 27$
    Step 4: $(3n + 27) \div 3$ or $n + 9$
    Step 5: $n + 9 - n$ or 9

Page 465
9. $(1,002 - 2) \cdot 180°$, or $180,000°$

Page 469
3. If n is prime, then n is an odd number.   **9.** $^-5$
11. Yes. If A is false, the statement is true.
14. 25   **17.** 0.141   **20.** $15\frac{8}{11}$

Page 471
7. about 9 mph and about 7 mph

Page 473
1. $33\frac{1}{3}\%$ **4.** 8 days; 12 h   **7.** about 160 mi

INDEX

ACKNOWLEDGMENTS

Illustration Acknowledgments

Doron Ben-Ami p. 140, 141, 150, 151, 284, 519
Alex Bloch p. 127, 143, 148, 275, 432, 442
Tom Bowker p. 172, 316
Fred Carlson p. 116, 168, 182
John Carlyle p. 10, 16, 19, 153, 176, 209
Linda Cook p. 490, 492, 497, 501
Kenneth P. Crippen p. 32, 38, 39, 105, 115, 154, 164, 181, 183, 200, 260, 315
Tony Crnkovich p. 90, 352
David Cunningham p. 78, 243, 273, 292
Andrea J. Fong p. 469, 504
Simon Galkin p. 45, 167, 171, 179, 209, 218, 305
Bill Gerhold p. 428
Jeff Hukill p. 502
Rich Lo p. 40, 41, 54, 56, 57, 74, 78, 80, 82, 84, 106, 116, 118, 119, 136, 152, 156, 170, 174, 180, 186, 188, 189, 192, 208, 234, 246, 304, 306, 307, 332, 344, 349, 350, 351, 352, 356, 360, 382, 394, 414, 422, 423, 434, 452, 456, 461, 462, 463, 472, 474, 475
Tim McWilliams p. 120, 222, 275, 515, 521
Debra Morse p. 503
Randy Nelsen p. 357
Tim O'Toole p. 84, 113, 201, 338
Alison Perreault p. 40, 41, 66, 262, 303, 383, 421, 435, 457, 471, 506
Linda Reilly p. 36, 196, 208, 247, 264, 414, 435, 461, 517
Eileen Rosen p. 375, 419
Nancy Spier p. 491
Carol Stutz p. 252
Dave Taylor p. 228, 354, 448
Sam Thiewes p. 50, 55, 132, 134, 139, 146, 204, 229
Nancy Lee Walters p. 18, 74, 75, 82, 85, 100, 104, 106, 117, 166, 187, 205, 258, 270, 324, 355, 396, 415, 429, 436, 440, 447, 460, 486
Jim Williams p. 170, 294, 304, 322, 344, 345, 358, 370, 408, 417, 445

Photograph Acknowledgments

Chapter 1: 2-3 Hank Morgan/Rainbow; 4 Steve Leonard/ TIME Magazine; 5 © Brent Jones; 7 Kathleen Culbert-Aguilar*; 11 John Hollis*; 21 © Brent Jones; 24-25 Diane Graham-Henry*; 26 © David R. Frazier Photolibrary

Chapter 2: 30-31 Ben Mitchell/The Image Bank; 37 © Mitchell B. Riebel—Sportschrome East/West; 41 Runk/ Schoenberger/Grant Heilman Photography, Inc.; 55 © Four Footed Fotos; 56-57 Kathleen Culbert-Aguilar, Equipment: Grand Sporting Goods*; 60 Kathleen Culbert-Aguilar*

Chapter 3: 62-63 James Sugar/Black Star; 64 Kathleen Culbert-Aguilar*; 65 Kathleen Culbert-Aguilar*; 71 Kathleen Culbert-Aguilar*; 72 The Bettmann Archive; 74-75 Kathleen Culbert-Aguilar*; 76 © George Holton/National Audubon Society Collection/Photo Researchers; 80 © Bill Reavers/Viesti Associates; 85 © Wendy Bass/Viesti Associates; 86-87 Diane Graham-Henry*

Chapter 4: 92-93 Edith G. Haun/Stock, Boston; 94 Kathleen Culbert-Aguilar*; 97 Kathleen Culbert-Aguilar*; 98 Kathleen Culbert-Aguilar*; 99 Kathleen Culbert-Aguilar*; 103 Kathleen Culbert-Aguilar*; 104 Kathleen Culbert-Aguilar*; 107 © Mary E. Messenger 1989; 108 Diane Graham-Henry*; 112-113 Kathleen Culbert-Aguilar*; 114 Kathleen Culbert-Aguilar*; 117 © Robert Frerck/Odyssey Productions; 118-119 Diane Graham-Henry*

Chapter 5: 124-25 Ed Bock/The Stock Market; 126 Diane Graham-Henry*; 129 Courtesy of Don and Pat Valenti; 135 William Boehm/West Stock; 138 Diane Graham-Henry*; 147 Kathleen Culbert-Aguilar*; 152 © Bob Daemmrich; 153 © 1987 Lawrence Migdale; 154-55 Kathleen Culbert-Aguilar*

Chapter 6: 160-61 Luis Villota/The Stock Market; 168 © Don & Pat Valenti 1989; 174 Kathleen Culbert-Aguilar*; 176 © Ron Wyatt—Sportschrome East/West; 184 Camerique/H. Armstrong Roberts; 186 Kathleen Culbert-Aguilar*; 188-89 Diane Graham-Henry*

Chapter 7: 194-95 Stuart L. Craig/Bruce Coleman Inc.; 198 NASA; 206 © Custom Medical Stock Photo; 214B Kathleen Culbert-Aguilar*; 214T © The Stock Market/Peter Beck 1987; 218 Kathleen Culbert-Aguilar*; 219 Camerique/H. Armstrong Roberts

Chapter 8: 224-25 Focus On Sports; 226 © Randy Brandon/ SIPA-PRESS; 230 © David R. Frazier Photolibrary; 231 Kathleen Culbert-Aguilar*; 232 © Ed Kashi 1988; 234T Kathleen Culbert-Aguilar*; 234B Kathleen Culbert-Aguilar*; 236 Kathleen Culbert-Aguilar*; 240 By permission of Johnny Hart and Creators Syndicate, Inc.; 244 Diane Graham-Henry*; 245 Kathleen Culbert-Aguilar*; 246 Mary E. Messenger © 1989; 248-49 Diane Graham-Henry*

Chapter 9: 254-55 Larry Barnes/Black Star; 261 Diane Graham-Henry*; 265 Kathleen Culbert-Aguilar*; 268 Kathleen Culbert-Aguilar. Sign courtesy of the City of Waukegan, IL*; 273 John Hollis*; 276-77 Kathleen Culbert-Aguilar*

Chapter 10: 282-83 Tony Duffy/(Allsport) / West Light; 285 Kathleen Culbert-Aguilar*; 286 Diane Graham-Henry*; 288 © 1986 Rick Doyle/Focus On Sports; 290 © Don & Pat Valenti 1989; 291 Kathleen Culbert-Aguilar*; 298 © Brent Jones; 299 Kathleen Culbert-Aguilar*; 301 Kathleen Culbert-Aguilar*; 302 © Don & Pat Valenti 1989; 306-07 © Don & Pat Valenti 1989

Chapter 11: 312-13 The British Museum/Robert Harding Picture Library; 314 Diane Graham-Henry*; 326 © 1987 Lawrence Migdale; 329 Kathleen Culbert-Aguilar*; 331 Kathleen Culbert-Aguilar*; 332 © Brian Drake—Sportschrome East/West; 333 Focus On Sports; 334-35 © 1989 Rob Outlaw

Chapter 12: 340-41 R. Carr/Bruce Coleman Inc.; 342 Kathleen Culbert-Aguilar*; 346 Diane Graham-Henry*; 348 Kathleen Culbert-Aguilar*; 349 John Hollis*; 360-61 Kathleen Culbert-Aguilar*

Chapter 13: 366-67 Chuck O'Rear/West Light; 371 Kathleen Culbert-Aguilar*; 378 Kathleen Culbert-Aguilar*; 379 Kathleen Culbert-Aguilar*; 382 © David R. Frazier Photolibrary; 383 © Sharon Green—Sportschrome East/West; 384 John Hollis*; 389 John Hollis*; 390 Kathleen Culbert-Aguilar*; 392 Kathleen Culbert-Aguilar*; 395 Kathleen Culbert-Aguilar*; 396-97 Diane Graham-Henry*

Chapter 14: 402-03 McKinley Williams; 409 Leonard Lee Rue III/H. Armstrong Roberts; 412 © Pat Rogers—Sportschrome East/West; 415 © Brent Jones; 421 Kathleen Culbert-Aguilar*; 422 © David R. Frazier Photolibrary; 423 © Don & Pat Valenti 1989; 424 John Hollis*; 424-25 Diane Graham-Henry*

Chapter 15: 430-31 Dan McCoy/Rainbow; 434 Diane Graham-Henry*; 444 John Hollis*; 448-49 © Craig Aurness/ West Light

ACKNOWLEDGMENTS

Chapter 16: 454-55 Janice Sheldon*; 456-57 John Hollis*; 466 John Hollis*; 468 John Hollis*; 470-71 John Hollis*; 472 S. Taylor/H. Armstrong Roberts; 473 © Joe Viesti/Viesti Associates; 474-75 Kathleen Culbert-Aguilar*

Skills Review Bank: 482 © William Thompson; 483 John Hollis*; 484 Ferret Research, Inc.; 485 © Craig Aurness/West Light; 487 © 1987 Edward Slater/Southern Stock; 488 Kathleen Culbert-Aguilar*; 489 NASA

Data Bank: 498 Tom Stack/Tom Stack & Associates

*Photographs taken expressly for Addison-Wesley